SHAKESPEARE AND VIRTUE

This volume maps Shakespearean virtue in all its plasticity and variety, providing thirty-eight succinct, wide-ranging chapters that reveal a breadth and diversity exceeding any given morality or code of behavior. Clearly explaining key concepts in the history of ethics and in classical, theological, and global virtue traditions, the collection reveals their presence in the works of Shakespeare in interpersonal, civic, and ecological scenes of action. Paying close attention to individual identity and social environment, the chapters also consider how the virtuous horizons broached in Shakespearean drama have been tested anew by the plays' global travels and fresh encounters with different traditions. Including sections on global wisdom, performance, and pedagogy, this handbook affirms virtue as a resource for humanistic education and the building of human capacity.

JULIA REINHARD LUPTON is Distinguished Professor of English at the University of California (UC), Irvine. She is the author or co-author of five books on Shakespeare, including *Shakespeare Dwelling: Designs for the Theater of Life* (2018), *Thinking with Shakespeare: Essays on Politics and Life* (2013), and *Citizen-Saints: Shakespeare and Political Theology* (2006). She is the co-director of the New Swan Shakespeare Center at UC, Irvine.

DONOVAN SHERMAN is Associate Professor of English at Seton Hall University, South Orange, New Jersey. His most recent book is *The Philosopher's Toothache: Embodied Stoicism in Early Modern English Drama* (2021). He is also the author of *Second Death: Theatricalities of the Soul in Shakespeare's Drama* (2016) and co-author of the last two editions of the textbook *Theatre Brief* (2020 and 2023).

SHAKESPEARE AND VIRTUE

A Handbook

EDITED BY

JULIA REINHARD LUPTON

University of California, Irvine

DONOVAN SHERMAN

Seton Hall University

CAMBRIDGE
UNIVERSITY PRESS

CAMBRIDGE
UNIVERSITY PRESS

University Printing House, Cambridge CB2 8BS, United Kingdom

One Liberty Plaza, 20th Floor, New York, NY 10006, USA

477 Williamstown Road, Port Melbourne, VIC 3207, Australia

314–321, 3rd Floor, Plot 3, Splendor Forum, Jasola District Centre, New Delhi – 110025, India

103 Penang Road, #05–06/07, Visioncrest Commercial, Singapore 238467

Cambridge University Press is part of the University of Cambridge.

It furthers the University's mission by disseminating knowledge in the pursuit of education, learning, and research at the highest international levels of excellence.

www.cambridge.org
Information on this title: www.cambridge.org/9781108843409
DOI: 10.1017/9781108918589

First published 2023

A catalogue record for this publication is available from the British Library.

Library of Congress Cataloging-in-Publication Data
NAMES: Lupton, Julia Reinhard, 1963– editor. | Sherman, Donovan, editor.
TITLE: Shakespeare and virtue / edited by Julia Reinhard Lupton, University of California, Irvine; Donovan Sherman, Seton Hall University, New Jersey.
DESCRIPTION: Cambridge, United Kingdom ; New York, NY : Cambridge University Press, 2023. | Includes bibliographical references and index.
IDENTIFIERS: LCCN 2022022786 | ISBN 9781108843409 (hardback) | ISBN 9781108918589 (ebook)
SUBJECTS: LCSH: Shakespeare, William, 1564–1616 – Ethics. | Shakespeare, William, 1564–1616 – Philosophy. | Virtue in literature. | Virtues in literature | Shakespeare, William, 1564–1616 – Characters. | Shakespeare, William, 1564–1616 – Dramatic production. | BISAC: LITERARY CRITICISM / European / English, Irish, Scottish, Welsh | LCGFT: Literary criticism. | Essays.
CLASSIFICATION: LCC PR3007 .S395 2023 | DDC 822.3/3–dc23/eng/20220712
LC record available at https://lccn.loc.gov/2022022786

ISBN 978-1-108-84340-9 Hardback

Contents

v

Contributors

YASIN BASARAN is Assistant Professor of Philosophical and Religious Sciences at Marmara University.

SARAH BECKWITH is Katherine Everett Gilbert Professor of English at Duke University.

DANIEL BLOOM is Associate Professor of Philosophy at West Texas A&M University.

MICHAEL BRISTOL is Greenshields Professor Emeritus at McGill University.

SANFORD BUDICK is Professor Emeritus at Hebrew University.

MARIACRISTINA CAVECCHI is Associate Professor of English Literature at the University of Milan.

KATHARINE A. CRAIK is Research Lead and Professor in Early Modern Literature at Oxford Brookes University.

CHRISTOPHER CROSBIE is Associate Professor of English at North Carolina State University.

KEVIN CURRAN is Professor of English Literature at the University of Lausanne.

JANE HWANG DEGENHARDT is Professor of English at the University of Massachusetts, Amherst.

JEFFREY S. DOTY is Associate Professor at the University of North Texas.

EWAN FERNIE is Chair of Shakespeare Studies and Fellow at the Shakespeare Institute, University of Birmingham.

JENNIFER FLAHERTY is Professor of English at Georgia College.

INDIRA GHOSE is Professor Emeritus of English Literature at the University of Fribourg.

JEFFREY GORE is Senior Lecturer of English at the University of Illinois Chicago.

SHEIBA KIAN KAUFMAN is Lecturer of English at the University of California, Irvine.

SEAN KEILEN is Professor of Literature at the University of California, Santa Cruz.

JAMES KUZNER is Associate Professor of English at Brown University.

UNHAE PARK LANGIS is an independent scholar at the New Swan Shakespeare Center, University of California, Irvine.

KATARZYNA LECKY is Surtz Associate Professor of English at Loyola University Chicago.

KELLY LEHTONEN is Assistant Professor of English at the King's College, New York.

JOAN PONG LINTON is Associate Professor of English at Indiana University.

VINCENT LLOYD is Professor of Theology and Religious Studies at Villanova University.

JULIA REINHARD LUPTON is Distinguished Professor of English at the University of California, Irvine.

NICK MOSCHOVAKIS is an unaffiliated scholar.

KATE NARVESON is Professor of English at Luther College.

BENJAMIN PARRIS is Visiting Assistant Professor of English at the University of Pittsburgh.

NEEMA PARVINI is Director at the Academic Agency in London.

FREDDIE ROKEM is Professor Emeritus of Theatre Arts at Tel Aviv University.

JESSICA ROSENBERG is Assistant Professor of English at the University of Miami.

JENNIFER R. RUST is Associate Professor of English at Saint Louis University.

DAVID SCHALKWYK is Professor of Shakespeare Studies at Queen Mary University of London.

DONOVAN SHERMAN is Associate Professor of English at Seton Hall University.

STEPHANIE SHIRILAN is Associate Professor of English at Syracuse University.

DAVID CARROLL SIMON is Associate Professor of English at the University of Maryland, College Park.

JOSEPH STERRETT is Associate Professor of English at Aarhus University.

RICHARD STRIER is Frank L. Sulzberger Distinguished Service Professor Emeritus of English at the University of Chicago.

JOSEPH TURNER is Associate Professor of English at the University of Louisville.

DONALD WEHRS is Hargis Professor of English Literature at Auburn University.

RICHARD WILSON is Sir Peter Hall Professor of Shakespeare Studies at Kingston University.

PAUL YACHNIN is Tomlinson Professor of Shakespeare Studies at McGill University.

Acknowledgements

This volume was born in a seminar at the Folger Research Institute on Shakespeare and virtue, led by Julia Lupton in November 2017. Many members of that gathering became contributors to this book; Donovan Sherman agreed not only to contribute, but also to co-edit. We would like to thank the Folger Research Institute for their ongoing interest and support. Cambridge University Press encouraged us to broaden the scope beyond the United States, and we were happy to invite scholars from Canada, Denmark, Israel, Switzerland, Turkey, and the United Kingdom to contribute. Thanks to funding from the New Swan Shakespeare Center at the University of California, Irvine, we were able to secure excellent research assistance from Peter Cibula and Olivia Rall. We would also like to thank Emily Hockley and the editorial team at Cambridge University Press for their support, professionalism, and attention to detail. Working on this volume with so many learned and lively scholars has affirmed our initial insight: since virtue involves skilled, ends-oriented action in the service of shared worlds, it is best explored in concert with others.

Introduction

Julia Reinhard Lupton and Donovan Sherman

Virtue Infinite and Virtue Patched: The Matter of This Handbook

Towards the end of *Antony and Cleopatra*'s Act Four, the Egyptian queen greets her Roman lover after his unexpectedly successful battle with Octavius:

> O infinite virtue, coms't thou smiling from
> The world's great snare uncaught? (4.8.17–18)[1]

"Infinite virtue" evokes virtue's primal meanings as force, capacity, and dynamic potential. Throughout the Renaissance, virtue fostered many definitions that would be familiar to us today, from a code of moral behavior to a winsome quality of mind. But Cleopatra's usage recalls its long history as a potency cultivated through practice. For Aristotle, *aretē*, the excellence or goodness of a thing, meant the capacity that allows a particular organ, faculty, craft, or even plant to achieve its end. Remnants of Aristotle's model live on today when we speak of "virtue" simply to mean "quality," whether realized or unrealized. In this sense, nearly everything has virtue insofar as it has potential to reveal its inherent aspects. We see this same inclusivity in Shakespeare, where jests have virtues (1HIV 1.2.143), and so do conjunctions: "Your 'if' is the only peacemaker; much virtue in 'if'" (AYLI 5.4.85). The extramoral meanings of virtue, ranging from the particular property or power of a mineral to the liveliness and ensoulment of the universe itself, existed in concert with moral renderings of virtue as the excellence achieved by human beings as marks of their good character and worldly effectiveness.[2] Sometimes Shakespeare gestured to several

---

[1] All Shakespeare citations from *New Oxford Shakespeare Online*, ed. Gary Taylor et al., unless otherwise noted.
[2] Holly Crocker, *The Matter of Virtue: Women's Ethical Action from Chaucer to Shakespeare* (University of Pennsylvania Press, 2019), 1–3.

I

senses of virtue at once, as when Portia appeals to the tormented Brutus: "You have some sick offence within your mind, / Which, by the right and virtue of my place, / I ought to know of" (JC 2.1.267–269). Portia bolsters her inquiry with a claim of propriety born of her rank, but also, by counterpoising her "virtue" to his "sick offense," gestures to virtue as quality, as inherent worth deserving of a spouse's confession. Portia also conjures virtue's gendered associations. It can signify virginity and thus suggest a paternalistic equivalence of spiritual health with sexual agency; so too can it recall the Latin *virtus,* with its root *vir* (man). When Cleopatra praises Antony's infinite virtue, she brings to mind both embedded virility and a broader sense of boundless energy in order to distinguish the magnanimous exuberance of her lover's heroism from the more disciplined Roman morality represented by Octavius and Octavia. She celebrates virtue's cosmic reach, capable of "find[ing] out new heaven, new earth" (1.1.17).

Shakespeare's virtue overflows attempts to measure its cultural bounds. Shortly before Cleopatra's greeting, Antony has hailed her as a veritable sun goddess ("thou day o'th'world"), and he tells his companion, "To this great fairy I'll commend thy acts, / Make her thanks bless thee" (12–13). He addresses her as an Isis-like divinity, a Black Madonna who embodies ancient wisdom, fertility, and the sovereign power of blessing, a cult that she herself organizes with consummate skill (3.6.16).[3] The queen of "infinite variety" (2.2.234), Cleopatra knows all about infinite virtue, including its multiple roots in Mediterranean philosophies, sciences, and mystery religions. This vigorous, enlivening virtue ropes Roman valor and the Hellenistic pantheon of allegorical deities to Egyptian gods and indigenous animisms, mapping a cosmic and cosmopolitan scope for virtue as human and more than human capacity. A related vocabulary surfaces when Cordelia speaks with the Doctor about the care of her father:

> All blest secrets,
> All you unpublished virtues of the earth,
> Spring with my tears, be aidant and remediate
> In the good man's distress!   (4.4.15–18)

Shakespeare fashions Cordelia into a semi-divine icon of virtue, who blends human excellence with virtue as sheer relational power and healing efficacy. What is pagan in Cleopatra is Christianized in Cordelia, whose

---

[3] Ruben Espinosa, "Marian Mobility, Black Madonnas, and the Cleopatra Complex," in *Travel and Travail: Early Modern Women, English Drama, and the Wider World*, eds. Patricia Akhimie and Bernadette Andrea (University of Nebraska Press, 2019), 250–272.

echoing of Mary and Jesus has been well-documented. Yet she also recalls Woman Wisdom, who was present with God at creation (Proverbs 3, 8) and entered the Israelite religion from pagan sources.[4]

Shakespeare orchestrates virtue as a force that weaves among persons, genders, animals, cosmologies, and cultures. His drama practices a catholicity that recalls the wise fool Feste's earthy gloss, in *Twelfth Night,* of St. Paul: "Anything that's mended is but patched. Virtue that transgresses is but patched with sin, and sin that amends is but patched with virtue" (1.5.38–40). In Romans, Paul rhetorically asks, "What shall we say, then? Shall we continue in sin, that grace may abound?"[5] Paul's answer is a swift "God forbid," but Feste marinates in the complexity of the question; he labels virtue as a form of grace in a maneuver similar to Cordelia's overlaying of Christian benediction with ancient wisdom. Virtue as a "patch" does not restore the soul's fabric to lost perfection but leaves its stitches legible, rendering one's spiritual domain a motley of experiences and histories requiring further work. This sense of virtue as both divine grace and profane materiality surfaces in Friar Lawrence's paean to his garden in *Romeo and Juliet,* explored in this volume by Jessica Rosenberg's chapter on stewardship. Praising the "womb" of the earth, the Friar imagines its inhabitants as newborns seeking nourishment: "We sucking on her natural bosom find, / Many for many virtues excellent, / None but for some and yet all different." He ends with a homiletic couplet that gestures to virtue's moral valences: "Virtue itself turns vice, being misapplied; / And vice sometimes by action dignified" (2.3.8–10, 17–18). Here we see the seams of Shakespeare's patched virtue, as different understandings of the word – as elemental potential, Christian piety, and allegorical device – jostle alongside one another.

This handbook aims to map and tap the patched, infinite virtue of Shakespearean drama: its inheritance of diverse classical virtue discourses, including Aristotelian, Stoic, and skeptic philosophies of the good life; the imperfect passage of ancient virtue ethics into Christian theology; the confluences among diverse wisdom traditions; virtue's environmental, embodied, and performative dimensions; and the plays' own capacities to move, transform, bless, and inspire. Virtue, rooted in ancient Greek and Roman philosophy and in global wisdom literatures and vernacular knowledges, illuminates the affective lives of Shakespeare's characters along with their participation in shared worlds, the powers they

---

[4] Leo G. Perdue, *Wisdom Literature: A Theological History* (Westminster Knox Press, 2007), 44–59.
[5] Romans 6:1 KJV.

exercise for the creation and destruction of community, and the responsibilities they confer on their audiences and readers. While we reaffirm
virtue as a powerful tool for civic and social good, we also acknowledge
its ambivalent inheritance. Around the world, both Shakespeare and virtue have been used to colonize and discipline populations and to police
nonnormative identities. The right has appropriated the traditional virtues as a weapon against political correctness, while the left has developed
alternative forms of virtuous engagement around social justice projects.[6]
In this volume, contributor Mariacristina Cavecchi treats the reparative
power of Shakespeare in prison education with a salutary skepticism, and
contributor Vincent Lloyd approaches the racist legacy of *The Tempest*
through the lens of Black theology. Neema Parvini, on the other hand,
draws on Jonathan Haidt and Moral Foundation Theory to further a perspective on human moral capacity that is more tragic than utopian, more
Burke than Rousseau. Virtue is owned by neither right, left, nor center.
Although our own politics are progressive, we would like this book to resonate in many contexts, ranging from public universities and community
education settings to faith-based colleges and programs retooling virtue
for student learning and empowerment. Our starting assumption is that
peoples around the world have cultivated ways of thinking about human
flourishing and that the virtuous possibilities explored in Shakespearean
drama have been expanded and revitalized by the plays' global travels;
surely this is a sentiment many can share regardless of background, ideology, or circumstance.

In upholding Shakespeare and virtue as resources for humanistic education, we take our lead from Martha Nussbaum's foundational work on
virtue, liberal education, and capacity building.[7] We also look to virtue
anthropologist Cheryl Mattingly (*Moral Laboratories*) and feminist philosopher Lisa Tessman (*Burdened Virtues*), who actively recover virtue as
a resource for diverse social actors.[8] We understand virtue as an aspirational engine of actualization for all persons; as an urge towards social
connection within and across distinct communities of belonging; and

[6] See *The Arden Research Handbook of Shakespeare and Social Justice*, ed. David Ruiter (Arden/
Bloomsbury, 2020); and *Teaching Social Justice Through Shakespeare: Why Renaissance Literature
Matters Now*, eds. Hillary Eklund and Wendy Beth Hyman (Edinburgh University Press, 2019).

[7] Martha Nussbaum, *Creating Capabilities: The Human Development Approach* (Harvard University
Press, 2011); *Poetic Justice: The Literary Imagination and Public Life* (Beacon Press, 1997); and
Frontiers of Justice: Disability, Nationality, Species Membership (Harvard University Press, 2006).

[8] Lisa Tessman, *Burdened Virtues: Virtue Ethics for Liberatory Struggles* (Oxford University Press,
2005); Cheryl Mattingly, *Moral Laboratories: Family Peril and the Struggle for a Good Life* (University
of California Press, 2014).

as the intentional channeling of strength and yearning into the courage to be seen and heard. Shakespeare's work, with its boundless theatrical energy, centuries of commentary and adaptation, and inquiries into human achievement and disaster, does more than just represent virtue and vice. Rather, Shakespearean drama, a collaborative, self-renewing practice that trains judgment, attention, and empathy while staging the aims and sources of human capacity, has the power to reinvigorate the role of virtue in our lives. In this sense our aim is decidedly old-fashioned in the belief that Shakespeare can *help* readers, students, and audiences realize their potential, even as we celebrate his glorious ambivalence and refusal to be captured in any one prescriptive model.[9]

Shakespeare's patched virtues contribute to a thick liberalism in which overlapping sets of shared ends and goals (*teloi*) are fostered through co-created stories about where a society has come from and where it wants to go. Virtues such as kindness, hospitality, care, humility, and trust make room for a robust pluralism with respect to both politics and wisdom. Respect, with one foot in the zone of modern tolerance and another in the history of awe and reverence, pivots between ancient and modern virtues and models the possibility of bridging them.[10] The age of Shakespeare inherited classical and monotheistic virtues but also stood on the cusp of the modern ethics of Rousseau, Kant, and Hume. Shakespeare's plays remix ancient and modern ethics along with secular and religious world views and thus expand the scope of virtue in early modernity and the contemporary world.

This weave of multiple legacies provokes an important point about how we consider history in this book. Some of the virtue traditions explored here have lineages that extend to Shakespeare's life; see, for instance, the revival and renovation of Stoicism in the Renaissance, which found purchase with continental writers such as Justus Lipsius, English moralists like the bishop Joseph Hall, and towering intellectual figures like Michel de Montaigne – to say nothing of the translations of Seneca's drama and essays that perched in libraries throughout Europe. Other engagements are

[9] For a similar call to follow Shakespeare as pedagogical example well-suited to our times, see Scott Newstok, *How to Think Like Shakespeare: Lessons from a Renaissance Education* (Princeton University Press, 2020).

[10] Michel Foucault analyzes the development of these virtues from the Hellenistic to modern ages, with particular attention to their potential to solidify into discourses of discipline that inhere to state formation; see volume three of his series *The History of Sexuality*, entitled *The Care of the Self*, trans. Robert Hurley (Random House, 1986), as well as his lectures at the Collège de France, notably *The Hermeneutics of the Subject*, ed. Frédéric Gros, trans. Graham Burchell (Picador, 2005).

less historically straightforward. For example, Shakespeare may not have directly encountered the work of Aristotle, whose *Nicomachean Ethics* provides many crucial support beams in the architecture of our volume. But Aristotelian virtues were everywhere. Thomas Wright's *Passions of the Mind* (1601), for instance, takes up an Aristotelian grammar in mounting its defense of the passions against the Stoics: "if the passions of the mind are not moderated according to reason (and that temperature virtues requires) immediately the soul is molested with some malady."[11] When we feel passions correctly, he stresses, we embrace a kinship with Jesus and Job, whose rich catalogue of psychic sufferings – fear and trembling, anger, sadness – temper themselves through an orientation, via reason, with the divine.[12] Aristotle was also taken up by Jewish and Islamic philosophers, detailing parallel tracks to ruminations such as Wright's. In true Shakespearean fashion, we hope to maintain an awareness of the wisdom literatures that supplied the cultural texture and room-tone of Shakespeare's life, but also to celebrate his play's capacities, as profound works of art, to converse with thinkers across time and space.

This volume is a handbook, a form that would not be out of place in Shakespeare or Seneca's time, and which has deep roots in virtue ethics. Late classical philosophers such as Epictetus (c. 50–135 CE) wrote handbooks (*enchridia*) that presented philosophy as a broadly teachable practice relevant to daily life. In the Renaissance, Erasmus (1469–1536) followed suit by writing his *Enchiridion milites Christiania,* or "Handbook for the Christian Soldier" (1503), which aimed to bracket divisive and inscrutable theological disputes in favor of a "philosophy of Christ" that would combine the essence of the Gospels with the teachings of classical humanism.[13] In Shakespeare's age, householders, housewives, and physicians also composed and read handbooks (they called them manuals) to help them manage the complex ecologies of their enterprises. In our century, handbooks have become popular in academic publishing as a way of collecting major statements on a topic in a digestible and definitive form; this

---

[11] Thomas Wright, *The Passions of the Mind* (London, 1601). The text has been lightly modernized for clarity. Neema Parvini comments on Shakespeare's direct and indirect access to Aristotle and Aquinas in texts such as Wright's in *Shakespeare's Moral Compass* (Edinburgh University Press, 2018), 84–89.

[12] The Stoics acknowledged feelings as well. See Margaret Graver, *Stoicism and Emotion* (University of Chicago Press, 2009). For more on the Stoic view of the passions as madness, especially as taken up in the Renaissance, see Gordon Braden, *Anger's Privilege: Renaissance Tragedy and the Senecan Tradition* (Yale University Press, 1985).

[13] *Discourses and Selected Writings of Epictetus,* ed. Robert Dobbin (Penguin Classics, 2008); *The Erasmus Reader,* 2nd edn., ed. Erika Rummel (University of Toronto Press, 1990).

volume contributes to that model but also aims to return the handbook as a genre to its origins in the ancient *enchiridion*. The writings of Epictetus, collected by his pupil Arrian, were labeled as a handbook for practical reasons: the aim was to have his sayings "on hand," readily available as an instrument for navigating life. Although this handbook is academic and historical, we hope that it retains this pragmatic aspect, and that readers will feel invited to consider the transformative potentialities of their own classrooms, households, and communities. We posit that humanistic pedagogy already cultivates virtues such as prudence, respect, courage, trust, service, and care, and we contend that a more intentional approach to virtue will amplify the capacity-building outcomes of liberal education, with implications for the employability, citizenship, and life-long learning of our graduates.

A Strong Mast and a Mingled Yarn: Shakespeare's Virtue Ecologies

Shakespeare does not mobilize his drama to endorse any particular virtue or virtue ethics so much as he creates entire worlds, which we call *virtue ecologies,* that comprise the cognitive, affective, social, and physical environment in which human agents develop their person-affirming capacities. In ancient philosophy and Shakespearean drama, the open sea frequently pictures the risky environments in which human beings exercise virtues that consist of their attunement to the needs and outlooks of other people, the shifting dangers and affordances of the situation, and their own skills and strengths. The sea is an emblem of what philosophers call "moral luck": The idea that happiness and the good life, though requiring virtuous activity, are also contingent on external affairs, from the circumstances of one's own birth and social condition (slave or free? Black or white? rich or poor? male or female?) to the privations of disease, loss of livelihood, bereavement, captivity, and war. The scandal of such contingency would lead the Stoics to fashion an ideal of happiness largely divorced from material circumstances, with profound implications first for Christianity and later for Kant.[14] This divestment from the outer world would lead Lipsius, the Renaissance Neo-Stoic, to define his prized virtue of constancy as "a right and immoveable strength of the mind, neither lifted up, nor pressed

---

[14] For an overview of the Stoic view of the good life, see John Sellars, *The Art of Living: The Stoics on Nature and the Function of Philosophy* (Ashgate, 2003).

down, with external or casual accidents."[15] Aristotle's virtues are more worldly, however; realized *in* the world through practices that act *upon* the world, virtue also exposes the actor *to* the world. At the end of the *Nicomachean Ethics*, he asserts that the virtues "result from the body," are "closely bound up with the passions," and depend on our interactions with other people to be realized: the virtues are "concerned with what is composite in us, and the virtues of this composite thing are characteristically human" (1178a). In *The Fragility of Goodness*, Nussbaum is attuned to those moments in Aristotle in which the flow of virtue becomes a patchwork of inhibitions and impediments. This patchwork, with its shifting intensities of vulnerabilities and assertions, evokes an organic sense of virtue's cultivation. The metaphor of flourishing, often used to translate *eudaimonia* or happiness as the goal and outcome of virtuous activity, implies a natural ecosystem of mutual dependencies that require communal tending.

In *Twelfth Night*, the Captain describes Sebastian's recourse to several virtues, including courage, prudence, and hope, as he struggles to survive a shipwreck:

> I saw your brother,
> Most provident in peril, bind himself—
> Courage and hope both teaching him the practice —
> To a strong mast that lived upon the sea.
> Where, like Arion on the dolphin's back,
> I saw him hold acquaintance with the waves
> So long as I could see.   (1.2.11–16).

Closely allied with the involuntary surge of passion in concert with bodily readiness, courage, the defining virtue of warrior-heroes, stems from the *thymós*, the spirited part of the Platonic *psyche* or soul that lies between its intellectual and sensual elements.[16] Sebastian surges out of the sea just as his own courage wells up and infuses him with the strength to fight the waves. "Most provident in peril," he uses his prudence in order to lash himself to a broken mast, placing him in a line of shipwrecked, wave-tossed heroes reaching back to Aeneas and Odysseus.[17] Courage and prudence count among the four cardinal virtues of ancient philosophy, along with justice and temperance; of the four, courage exists at the furthest remove

---

[15] Justus Lipsius, *Two Bookes of Constancie*, trans. John Stradling (London, 1595), 9. Language has been lightly modernized for clarity.

[16] Paul Tillich, *The Courage to Be*, 3rd edn. (Yale University Press, 2014), 3.

[17] Unhae Park Langis, *Passion, Prudence, and Virtue in Shakespearean Drama* (Continuum/Bloomsbury, 2011); Kevin Curran, ed., *Shakespeare and Judgment* (University of Edinburgh Press, 2017).

from reason, while prudence, classified by Aristotle as an intellectual virtue, consists in largely cognitive activity.[18] Balancing these two cardinal virtues, Sebastian is also armed with hope, an affect of loving anticipation kindled by the thought of his sister Viola, who may need his care and who belongs to their capsized world. Hope is one of three theological virtues enumerated by St. Paul, along with faith and love. Courage and prudence, cardinal virtues, respond to danger, pain, hardship, and opportunity in the present under the guidance of reason, while hope, a theological virtue, expresses love in and for the future as embodied by another person or being, beyond rational calculation. "Provident" invokes providence as well as prudence, implying a view of the cosmos as amenable to human projects and hence capable of becoming a partner in the effort of survival.

In *Twelfth Night*, the sea figures an environment beset by risk and chance, but also a scene of multiple affordances that, when properly approached with the comportments and skills of several virtues, can be used as tools for survival. Sebastian is destitute, without family and friends, and in search of better fortunes with his sister Viola. They may be impoverished, but they do have the educational benefits of a noble upbringing; Viola "can sing / And speak … in many sorts of music," talents she will use to gain employment with Duke Orsino (1.2.53–54). The sea visualizes their unmoored situation as orphans and economic refugees, their exposure to moral luck. Is that broken mast still another danger that threatens Sebastian on the open sea, or can it be harnessed into a life-preserver that will help guide him to the shore? Will the waves beat him down or does their rhythm offer a means of survival, as he learns to "hold acquaintance" with their dips and crests, becoming their friends? Finally, Sebastian, despite all his virtuous skills and abilities, will not actually survive the sea on his own; rather, the love and friendship of Antonio, a pirate and outlaw in the land in which they find themselves, will hazard all to assist Sebastian. An ensemble of cardinal and theological virtues, acquired skills and capacities, and the gracious help of another will help Sebastian make his way to shore, giving that repurposed mast both its immediate usefulness and its indexical, forward-pointing character.

In *All's Well that End Well*, Shakespeare shares a sentiment that recalls Feste's patches of virtue and sin: "The web of our life is of a mingled yarn, good and ill together: our virtues would be proud, if our faults whipped

---

[18] Michael S. Brady, "Moral and Intellectual Virtues," in *Oxford Handbook of Virtue*, ed. Nancy E. Snow (Oxford University Press, 2018), 783–799.

them not; and our crimes would despair, if they were not cherished by our virtues" (4.3.54–56). In both passages, Shakespeare tempers a humanist confidence in virtuous self-fashioning with a darker, more Augustinian vision of human sinfulness, touching upon the Reformation's deep uneasiness with virtue ethics, as discussed by Kate Narveson in this volume.[19] Yet in this instance, as with Feste, virtue retains its power to patch and darn, to mend and repair, which, in a damaged world of thoughtlessness, greed, and cruelty, describes so much of what it means to be moral. Within a tangle of conflicting tendencies and failed projects, the mingled yarn traces a provisional order, a way through the labyrinth of life. Furthermore, it locates the potential for virtue's infusion in the everyday, in humble and domestic objects familiar to a servant or housewife; Marina, in *Pericles*, labels household work as a form of virtue as she staves off Boult, her pimp and captor: "I can sing, weave, sew, and dance, / With other virtues, which I'll keep from boast: / And I will undertake all these to teach" (4.6.182–185). Singing, weaving, sewing, dancing, and teaching are virtues insofar as they are personal qualities, skills, or aptitudes that also offer occasions for providential release. They manifest virtue in Aristotle's material sense and in a Jewish and Christian sense as well, insofar as they participate in creation, whose ordering wisdom infuses blades of grass, falls of sparrows, nutshells, and needles just as it does miracles. Marina's virtue ecology encompasses her bodily capacities, her relational abilities, and the whims of luck – or perhaps grace – as turbulent and as rhythmic as the sea where she was born.

The mingled yarn of virtue traces the effort at narrative sense-making that winds through landscapes of brutalizing self-interest and shattered trust in search of restored connections. Shakespeare's plays stage the fragility of goodness, whether virtue is cynically weaponized in a tragedy like *Othello,* where Iago weaves the virtues of Othello, Desdemona, and Cassio into a net to snare them all, or the heroes are exposed to chance and deprived of basic resources, like the political exiles, climate refugees, and gender outliers of *King Lear, Pericles, As You Like It,* and *Twelfth Night.* Depicting the vicissitudes of moral luck in emblematic environments such as city, sea, and forest, Shakespeare enjoins us to evaluate the patched character of human action within settings composed of the

[19] For a study of this problem, see Paul Cefalu, *Moral Identity in Early Modern English Literature* (Cambridge University Press, 2004). On Aristotle versus Augustine, see Alisdair MacIntyre, *Three Rival Versions of Moral Inquiry: Encyclopaedia, Genealogy, and Tradition* (University of Notre Dame Press, 1990), 105–126.

energies, skills, powers, and privileges that unevenly shape the pursuit of happiness for a plurality of actors.[20] Swerving from endorsements to critiques of human constancy, the plays view with skepticism the potential for virtue to appear as mere performative pursuit – "Assume a virtue, if you have it not," Hamlet tells his mother (3.4.162) – while genuinely inquiring as to virtue's mutability. "So our virtues / Lie in the interpretation of our time," muses Aufidius in *Coriolanus* (4.7.49), though he is answered, as if across a gulf, by Imogen, who wonders at the simple cavern of her exiled brothers, imagining "Great men, / That had a court no bigger than this cave, / That did attend themselves and had the virtue / Which their own conscience seal'd them – laying by / That nothing gift of differing multitudes" (*Cymbeline* 3.7.54–58). Is virtue subjected to the sociabilities of the crowd, or rooted inside our consciences? Shakespeare patches these views into shifting and profoundly unsettled meditations on human ability. When his characters are faced with complementary visions of moral and philosophical world-making, they must stake out their lives in acts of courageous self-realization.

Shakespeare's characters navigate their lives through a mingled yarn composed of classical, theological, and modern virtues that together help fashion a provisional and only intermittently realized post-secular space that belongs to no single religion and to no race, class, or gender. *Aretē,* the Greek word for virtue, is derived from the superlative of *agathos* (good), and thus indicates the best that an action can achieve. *Aretē* is related to the *aristeia* of the heroes, the battles in which noble men proved their excellence. This heroic-aristocratic background feeds the hierarchical and masculine underpinnings of much virtue discourse. Yet proponent of Black classicism Patrice Rankine argues that ancient Mediterranean societies understood human beings as having "a fundamental worth or status" shared by aristocrats with women, slaves, children, strangers, and even animals.[21] Especially when epic becomes romance, these other vessels of natural nobility could become heroes of virtue in their own right. Shakespeare draws many of his narratives from this romance milieu of manifold nobilities and unexpected excellences in order to discover virtue across the vast and varied landscape of creaturely capacity.

---

[20] See Julia Annas, *Intelligent Virtue* (Oxford University Press, 2011) for more on the interconnectedness of different virtues and values.

[21] Patrice Rankine, "Dignity in Homer and Classical Greece," in *Dignity: A History,* ed. Remy Debes (Oxford University Press, 2017), 19–46. On Black classicism, see Patrice Rankine, *Ulysses in Black: Ralph Ellison, Classicism, and African American Literature* (University of Wisconsin Press, 2008) and *Aristotle and Black Drama: A Theater of Civil Disobedience* (Baylor University Press, 2013).

"A Mirror Up to Nature": Shakespeare's Theater of Virtue

Echoing Hamlet, the theologian Paul Tillich identified virtue with the "courage to be," the will to choose being over nonbeing by exiting the dormancies of routine, embracing the risks of attachment, and confronting the terrors of guilt and uncertainty.[22] Tillich's friend, the great twentieth-century political thinker Hannah Arendt, defined courage as the act of "leaving one's private hiding place and showing who one is, disclosing and exposing one's self."[23] These definitions of courage as existential self-disclosure already indicate virtue's deep connection with drama and dramaturgy. When Hamlet describes theater as a mirror that shows "virtue her feature, scorn her own image," he is asking drama to enact moral situations on stage in a manner that clarifies values and prompts self-reflection (3.2.18). But he is going deeper than that: to mirror is to manifest, to make what is latent or unremarked tangible and visible. Such manifestation occurs every time theater makers reach into the text to find "the very age and body of the time" (3.2.18–19): Shakespeare's time, but also their own. In this volume, Freddie Rokem identifies the historical unfolding of virtue in performance with the art of dramaturgy, in which modern productions renew classic drama by actualizing latent capacities in response to current urgencies and present judgment.

In *Twelfth Night*, Sir Toby associates virtue with the arts of performance when he urges Sir Andrew Aguecheek to dance his way through life, from going to church to urinating:

> Wherefore are these things hid? Wherefore have these gifts a curtain before 'em? … Why dost thou not go to church in a galliard and come home in a coranto? My very walk should be a jig. I would not so much as make water but in a cinquepace. What dost thou mean? Is it a world to hide virtues in? (*Twelfth Night* 1.3.102–107).

Shining through Toby's comic query is the Biblical injunction about the candle and the bushel basket, which counsels that virtues be practiced and shared, not hidden away: "Neither do men light a candle, and put it under a bushel, but on a candlestick; and it giveth light unto all that are in the house."[24] The proverb elucidates the primal showing of virtue in performance that Hamlet notes in his advice to the players. Although Toby and Shakespeare are mocking the bad education of Sir Andrew, dancing *was*

---

[22] Tillich, *The Courage to Be*, 38.
[23] Hannah Arendt, *The Human Condition* (University of Chicago Press, 1957), 186.
[24] Matthew 5:15, KJV.

defended as a virtuous practice in humanist pedagogy: Sir Thomas Elyot (c. 1490–1546) recommends such sports as wrestling, running, swimming, and hunting and then, like Marina, turns to dancing, which "may be an introduction unto the first moral virtue, called prudence."[25] Drawing on wisdom's global frames, he defends dancing using Greek, Hebrew, Indian, and Ethiopian examples.[26] Like dance and theater, virtues are physical, incorporating timing and coordination; cognitive, requiring judgment and foresight; and social and situational, involving roles, partners, privileges, occasions, and audiences.

Not only is the theater a method of realizing virtue; virtue itself is often conceived of as theatrical. Pierre Hadot, in *Philosophy as a Way of Life*, reminds us that ancient philosophy revealed itself through experience, not through the absorption of doctrine or purely intellectual pursuits. Instead, as Jennifer Rust explains in her contribution, philosophy was a form of *askesis*, or exercise, and often contained theatrical overtones; consider, for instance, the *praemeditatio malorum* ("premeditation on misfortunes"), in which, as Hadot describes, "we are to represent to ourselves poverty, suffering, and death. We must confront life's difficulties face to face, remembering that they are not evils, since they do not depend on us."[27] This ancient practice winds its way through Stoicism and transmutes into the mortification of the flesh encouraged by St. Ignatius and other beacons of Christian virtue. Performed virtue took place in internal image-making, but also in presenting our character outwardly to the world. Epictetus famously exhorted his students to imagine that "thou art an actor in a play of such a kind as the teacher may choose; if short, of a short one, if long, of a long one."[28] At all times, one is exposed and expressive, connected to others. Seneca praises dialogue, rather than one-sided lectures, as the premium mode of philosophical practice because "it works its way into the mind bit by bit. Speeches prepared in advance and delivered before a crowd make for more noise, but less intimacy" (38.1). Even reading, the most seemingly solitary philosophical labor, Hadot claims, "is always implicitly a dialogue."[29] The theatrical intimacy of virtue thus entails responsibility: Our scene partners watch, listen, and converse with us as we conduct our virtue work, and in doing so they ensure that we hone this work like a craft.

[25] Sir Thomas Elyot, *The Book named The Governor*, ed. S. E. Lehmberg (Everyman's Library, 1962), 78.
[26] Ibid., 71–77.
[27] Pierre Hadot, *Philosophy as a Way of Life*, ed. Arnold Davidson, trans. Michael Chase (Blackwell, 1995), 85.
[28] Epictetus, *The Handbook (The Enchiridion)*, trans. Nicholas P. White (Hackett, 1983), 16.
[29] Hadot, 109.

Modern virtue ethicists call this overlap between acquiring a virtue and learning an art or craft the "skill analogy."[30] Aristotle compared *aretē* to playing a musical instrument; he cautioned that it must be practiced by one who is "serious" (*spoudaios*), in the classical sense of "correctly devoted"; the philosopher will also use this word when describing tragedy in his *Poetics* as "the imitation of an action (*praxis*) that is serious and complete and has a proper magnitude."[31] Alisdair MacIntyre identifies "practice" as one of virtue's three sustaining components (along with traditions and narrative) in his account of how virtues take shape in lived social experience. He defines practice as

> any coherent and complex form of socially established cooperative human activity through which goods internal to that form of activity are realized in the course of trying to achieve those standards of excellence which are appropriate to, and partially definitive of, that form of activity, with the result that the human powers to achieve excellence, and human conceptions of the ends and goods involved, are systematically extended.[32]

The examples he offers include friendship, teaching, and chess. Theater, we argue, is also a practice: it is "coherent and complex," it is a "socially established cooperative human activity," and it develops goods and criteria internal to its own operations. When theater creates a space of encounter, it "systematically extends ... the human powers to achieve excellence" by building out a given community's capacities for worldly imagination, affective response, and cooperative and organizational intelligence. In his chapter on moral agency, Michael Bristol shows how both Shakespearean drama and literary pedagogy are virtuous practices, skilled enterprises that engage virtue as the primal act of self-disclosure attendant upon all speech and action, practiced in an inherently relational space or environment with its own specialized affordances.

The ecology of the theatrical zone, with its improvisations, flourishes, failures, connections, missed cues, thunderous applauses, collaborative labors, and shared breath, is a scene of interdependence, of constant attunement to the shifts of energy, patterns of speech, and ineffable qualities that compel our attention. In his chapter on respect, Sandford Budick

---

[30] Linda Zagzebski, *Virtues of the Mind* (Cambridge University Press, 1996), 106–116. For a survey of major positions, see Matt Stichter, "Virtue as a Skill," in *Oxford Handbook of Virtue*, ed. Nancy E. Snow, (Oxford University Press, 2018), 57–81.

[31] *NE* 1098a; *Poetics*, trans. Hippocrates G. Apostle, Elizabeth A. Dobbs, and Morris A. Parslow (Peripatetic Press, 1990), 1449b.

[32] Alisdair MacIntyre, *After Virtue*, 187.

notes that the Stoics "saw the basis of all virtue in what they called an 'attention' or mindfulness (*prosochē*)." In her chapter on Rabbinic virtues, Stephanie Shirilan singles out *shmiat ha'ozen,* "a listening ear," as a quality of attention cultivated in Jewish liturgy and learning. Shakespearean drama repeatedly manifests the collaborative conjuring of drama out of the trained attention of actors and audiences. At the opening of *Much Ado About Nothing,* Beatrice and Benedick toss their nimble insults surrounded by the expectant and appreciative presence of their friends; without listeners, their retorts would fall very differently. In *A Midsummer Night's Dream,* Bottom's transformation is rendered credible by the flight and return of his terrified and fascinated friends as they circle on and off stage. Together the actors and the audience build what Hippolyta calls "something of great constancy" (5.1.26). Constancy means consistency (their story holds together), but constancy is also a virtue, the ability and will to remain true to an idea or a person within a changing situation requiring adjustment and adaptation.[33] Constancy is always a horizon (Shakespeare's plays teach us, time and again, that the pursuit of constancy often renders us inconstant), but its anchoring possibility provides a through-line for even the most chaotic of performances, as stumbling and makeshift as that of the rude mechanicals.

As a playwright, dramatic poet, and person of the theater, Shakespeare tests virtue as creative and capacity-realizing, rather than dry, prohibitive, and recitational. Shakespeare's generous enlistment of a broad range of ethical actors – girls, boys, and girl-boys; Moors, monsters, and Jews; English Puritans and Italian libertines; Viennese jurists and Veronese lovers; Roman citizens and Catholic saints – renders the Shakespearean stage into what Charles Taylor calls a moral space, a zone energized by compelling teloi and hidden story lines.[34] Since their original staging, the plays have been taken up and recomposed by global performance traditions, which are also wisdom traditions. Shakespeare's continued presence in contemporary teaching settings grants him unique status as a vehicle for cross-disciplinary and pedagogical work that can handle the virtues as tools for personal, social, and intellectual renewal. And Shakespeare has long provided a mirror in which virtue and scorn can be shown their own

---

[33] Jesse Lander, "Shakespearean Constancy in *Cymbeline,*" Shakespeare Association of America Seminar, 2020, in *Shakespeare's Theater of Virtue: Power, Capacity and the Good,* eds. Kent Lehnhof, Julia Reinhard Lupton, and Carolyn Sale (Edinburgh University Press, forthcoming, 2022).

[34] Charles Taylor, *The Sources of the Self: The Making of Modern Identity* (Harvard University Press, 1989).

images – recall, for instance, the much-debated Shakespeare in the Park production of *Julius Caesar* in 2017, which found uncanny echoes of the play's nuanced debates on political virtue in our own current day, or the many pandemic Shakespeare productions that have tested the powers of attachment and attention on remote platforms. His work remains, stubbornly and ingeniously, an ensemble of virtue exercises for us to test and train our own moral and dynamic skills.

This handbook builds on the work of many generations of previous scholars as well as on recent collections, including *Shakespeare and Renaissance Ethics*, edited by Patrick Gray and John D. Cox, and *Shakespeare and Moral Agency*, edited by Michael D. Bristol.[35] Other books that have inspired this project include Holly Crocker's *The Matter of Virtue*, Ewan Fernie's *Shakespeare for Freedom*, James Kuzner's *Shakespeare as a Way of Life*, Paul Kottman's *Love and Human Freedom*, Regina Schwartz's *Loving Justice, Living Shakespeare*, Neema Parvini's *Shakespeare's Moral Compass*, and Unhae Park Langis's *Passion, Prudence, and Virtue in Shakespearean Drama*.[36] We are pleased that several of these scholars are contributors to this project.

Part I, "Shakespeare and Virtue Ethics," explores the meanings and uses of virtue in classical philosophy that most resonate with Shakespearean drama, beginning with Aristotle and moving into Stoicism, skepticism, and asceticism. This section shows how virtue energizes Shakespeare's work with the mobile vectors of intentionality and desire shaped by habit, practice, and technique.

Part II, "Shakespeare's Virtues," zooms in on particular virtues. Each entry takes up scenes from Shakespeare to demonstrate the resilience and range of the virtue at hand as it takes shape in Shakespeare's dramatic poetry. These virtues both belong to Shakespeare's world and touch on areas of contemporary concern: stewardship and the environment; care and the medical humanities; hospitality and migration; trust and crises in communication; chastity and the politics of sex and gender; kindness, respect, and the conditions of community. The virtues included in this section have been selected on the basis of their formative role, explanatory force, and creative potential in Shakespearean drama.

---

[35] *Shakespeare and Renaissance Ethics*, eds. Patrick Gray and John D. Cox (Cambridge University Press, 2014); *Shakespeare and Moral Agency*, ed. Michael D. Bristol (Continuum, 2010).

[36] Ewan Fernie, *Shakespeare for Freedom: Why the Plays Matter* (Cambridge University Press, 2017); James Kuzner, *Shakespeare as a Way of Life* (Fordham University Press, 2016); Paul Kottman, *Love and Human Freedom* (Stanford University Press, 2018); Neema Parvini, *Shakespeare's Moral Compass* (Edinburgh University Press, 2018); Regina Schwartz, *Loving Justice, Living Shakespeare* (Oxford University Press, 2016).

Part III, "Shakespeare and Global Virtue Traditions," opens the virtues up beyond the classical and Christian humanisms most familiar to Shakespeare studies. The first two entries address the virtues in Judaism and Islam. Entries on Buddhism and ancient Persia invite readers to consider what wisdom literatures beyond the three monotheisms reveal about the good life in Shakespeare. Entries on Shakespeare at Robben Island and Black theology place virtue ethics in dialogue with social justice inquiry. The section ends with reflections on "globability."

Part IV, "Virtuous Performances," features four chapters that explore Shakespeare's virtues in practice. Virtue's affinities with theater inspire these pieces to study different facets of performance that range from the dramaturgical preparation of a production of *Hamlet*, to a contemporary adaptation of *Pericles* that centers on the global refugee crisis, to the reformative intentions of Shakespeare in prison, to the theatrical space of the university classroom. This section takes seriously the claim, rooted in ancient ethics and resurgent in contemporary theories of "practice as research," that virtue is always active.

We would like to offer a traveler's blessing as we embark on the journey of this book. For some readers, the virtues may inspire political activism and social justice projects, and for others the virtues may issue in a renewed pedagogy and more conscientious mentoring. For some, the virtues may foster community teaching and public humanities, and for others, the virtues may initiate the search for recovery, reconciliation and healing. Humility and humanity, Richard Wilson argues in his piece, are, or should be, connected commitments, and it is with a sense of humility in the face of the sheer vastness of the virtue discourses broached in this handbook that we submit this volume to you. May considering Shakespeare and virtue help us refocus our work as humanists by making what we do and why we do it become more visible, tangible, and transportable, to ourselves and to our publics. *Amen(d)*.

PART I

Shakespeare and Virtue Ethics

CHAPTER I

Aretē *(Excellence, Virtue)*

Jeffrey S. Doty and Daniel Bloom

Aristotle's notion of *aretē* provides a way of reading Shakespeare's plays that unifies the characters' actions in a manner parallel to how ethics unifies humanity. For Aristotle, *aretē*, meaning virtue or excellence, is the completion of a thing's nature. The virtuous pruning knife is the one that prunes vines excellently. Likewise, moral virtue, the part of *aretē* dealing with human action in the world, is determined by how completely a person embodies human nature (*Nicomachean Ethics* 1103a11–26).[1] By nature Aristotle means that which makes a thing be what it is, which is inherently tied to that thing's function (*NE* 1097b24). Thus, embodying human nature most fully is akin to acting as human as possible, which is being happy (*eudaimonia*). To determine what it means to be human is to identify that which differentiates human beings from that which they are most similar to (i.e., other animals). Aristotle thinks this difference is our rationality (*NE* 1097b34–1098a7). Hence, being as human as possible is being as rational as possible. There are two senses of being rational – intellectually and in action. The first corresponds to intellectual virtue, the second to moral virtue (*NE* 1103a1–10). Both senses of *aretē* are virtuous precisely because they fulfill human nature. As a result there is a sense in which Aristotelian virtue is a selfish endeavor; *I* strive to fulfill human nature in *myself*, and in doing so *I* achieve happiness along with its corresponding pleasures. And yet Aristotle also holds that moral virtue is a fundamentally political exercise: It is action that ties a person to other people.[2] An individual's role in the political community, their acting for the good of the whole, is necessary for the full cultivation of virtue, and hence a requirement for achieving their own selfish end.[3]

---

[1] Aristotle, *Nicomachean Ethics*, trans. Joe Sachs (Focus Publishing, 2002). Hereafter referred to as *NE*.

[2] Aristotle frequently discusses the relation between virtue and politics; see, for instance, *NE* 1.2 and 10.9 – the very beginning and the very end of the *Nicomachean Ethics*.

[3] *NE* 9.8 is dedicated to parsing the distinction between the good kind of selfishness discussed earlier, and the negative selfishness that is typically in opposition to the good of the whole. The key distinction is that the first is motivated by reason while the latter is motivated by desire.

The primary connection between the individual's virtue and political action is found in practical judgment (*phronēsis*), which has a dual character. Moral virtue requires both the exercise of practical judgment and one's obedience to that judgment (*NE* 1098a2–6). It is not enough to judge correctly; my judgment must also rule over my desires. Simply put, moral virtue is developed through training one's desire to be obedient to practical judgment, an obedience which, in turn, allows for the best exercise of practical judgment. The initial capacity for obedience is formed in the parent–child relation. As Aristotle says, "It makes no small difference, then, to be habituated in this way or in that straight from childhood, but an enormous difference, or rather all the difference" (*NE* 1103b25–26). The habituation of obedience is then further cultivated in the citizen–law relation. The cultivation of this obedience habituates a person to being rational. As a result of the obedience required for following the law, Aristotle says that there is a virtue of the citizen that is not identical with genuine virtue, but rather is a kind of imitation of it (*NE* 1179b29–34; *Politics* 1276b16–1278b5).[4] The good citizen is obedient to the good laws in a similar way to the virtuous person's obedience to practical judgment. The difference is that the virtuous person is obedient to reason that is their own, while the good citizen, taken merely as a citizen, is obedient to the reason of the ruler as revealed by the law. Civic virtue, however, is not limited to obedience to law. The full cultivation of virtue requires the wider political community because it is precisely through the *polis* that we are confronted with both more challenging judgments to make and more enticing objects of desire. Thus, being a member of the *polis* allows for both an imitation of genuine virtue (for those that do not have their desires in accordance with their own reason) and the fullest cultivation of genuine virtue (for rulers who must exercise their virtue in a more complete and challenging setting).

For Aristotle, then, virtuous action is both an act of self-love and good for the whole since what is truly good for the virtuous person benefits society at large. Acting at the expense of society through injustice harms the political community, and by harming the political community one undermines the very system that allows for the cultivation of virtue. In other words, it is in the best interest of the virtuous person to keep the state as healthy and successful as possible. This means that the selfishness of genuine virtue is not lost in my acting for the good of the political association;

---

[4] Aristotle, *Politics*, trans. C. D. C. Reeve (Hackett Publishing Company, 1998).

quite the contrary, this is precisely where it is most fully found. This is partly why Aristotle calls the human a political animal, and more so than any other animal because of our use of rational speech (*logos*), an ability intimately tied to practical judgment (*Pol.* 1253a1–18).

Reading Shakespeare with Aristotle focuses our attention on how characters negotiate questions of self-interest and common good as they aim for happiness. Our approach resembles character criticism. But whereas "character criticism" emphasizes the unique aspects of characters' individualities, explores why we identify with them, and explains their actions through their distinct personalities, an Aristotelian ethical criticism prioritizes action as that which discloses character. In the *Poetics*, Aristotle describes tragedy as the imitation of a morally serious *action* with personal and political consequences undertaken by a person exercising practical judgment (*Poetics* 1449b24–25).[5] Shakespeare's tragedies are not unified by a *single* action in the manner suggested by Aristotle. As Hegel explains, Shakespearean drama features multiple characters undertaking *actions* that have "specific ends drawn from the concrete spheres of family, state, and church."[6] Character criticism lauds Shakespeare for the particularity and depth of his representation of human subjectivity, but it is through actions – and the "specific ends" and webbed social relations that give these actions context – that his characters become intelligible. Each action itself is understood through its most complete form, ethical action. Thus, Aristotle's dynamic account of *aretē* provides a frame through which to read all action, and thereby offers a lens for understanding characters.

King Lear foregrounds the parent–child and citizen–ruler relations in the context of political succession. Lear's abdication plunges Britain into a kind of moral anarchy where a brutal form of "nature" as power, appetite, and dominance takes the place of "natural" ties that bind these people to one another in familial and political association. Those who unbridle their desires (Edmund, Regan, Goneril, and Cornwall) rise in power, while those bound to others through love and duty (Edgar, Kent, the Fool, Gloucester) are pressed outside of law and shelter into bare necessity. Edmund offers an apt starting point. In his first soliloquy, he makes explicit what he takes to be the tension between striving for individual virtue and collective good:

---

[5] Aristotle, *Poetics*, trans. Joe Sachs (Focus Publishing, 2006).
[6] Georg Wilhelm Friedrich Hegel, "Dramatic Poetry," from *Aesthetics: Lectures on Fine Art*, in *Philosophers on Shakespeare*, ed. Paul Kottman (Stanford University Press, 2009), 57–86, 73.

> Thou, Nature, art my goddess; to thy law
> My services are bound. Wherefore should I
> Stand in the plague of custom and permit
> The curiosity of nations to deprive me,
> For that I am some twelve or fourteen moonshines
> Lag of a brother? Why 'bastard'? Wherefore 'base'?[7]   (1.2.1–6)

Edmund's creative act of self-fashioning is to serve "nature" and challenge the customs and man-made law that deny him equal legal status (of inheritance and title) and impute to him lower or perverse moral capacities. Edmund may well be right that certain customs are unjust. The problem, however, is that this causes him to dismiss all custom and man-made law. This is exactly what he says in the letter he forges under Edgar's name:

> This policy and reverence of age makes the world bitter to the best of our times, keeps our fortunes from us till our oldness cannot relish them. I begin to find an idle and fond bondage in the oppression of aged tyranny, who sways not as it hath power but as it is suffered. (1.2.45–49)

Custom, he writes, keeps us from being all that we can be. Yet in the Aristotelian account, "policy and reverence of age" does not stifle "the best of our times" but rather serves as the period in which the young habituate themselves to the obedience (to parental authority and law) through which they develop civic virtue. Edmund's purely selfish desire to so readily and violently cast off the social ties that are responsible for the cultivation of a soul in proper order displays a person that never reaped the benefits of an obedient youth. Although his first soliloquy highlights an injustice in this polity done to those born outside of wedlock, his aim is not distributive justice or the reformation of those customs, but rather tearing violently through them so that he may indulge his resentment and follow his ambition. His rejection of custom and law leaves him with only the most basic natural distinction between strong and weak, which he then identifies with the distinction between those who "hath power" to satisfy their purely selfish desire and those who "suffer" custom. The irony is that, in the Aristotelian picture, it is the virtuous, those that are not determined by their purely selfish desire, that are able to satisfy their desire in the most complete way.

Because the motivating force behind Edmund's actions is desire alone rather than reason, he falls into vice, rendering him incapable of the loyalty to others that makes friendship and political association rewarding.

---

[7] Quotations from *King Lear* derive from the combined text in *The Norton Shakespeare*, eds. Stephen Greenblatt, Walter Cohen, Suzanne Gossett, Jean E. Howard, Katharine Eisaman Maus, and Gordon McMullan, 3rd ed. (Norton, 2016), 1.2.1–6.

Once pure desiderative self-interest (separated from reason and the good of the whole) is the sole motivating force, loyalty becomes possible only to oneself, and even this self-loyalty is unfaithful.[8] This is apparent in his betrayals of his father and brother as well as his giddy double-dealing with Regan and Goneril. Kent's understanding of self-interest is the opposite of Edmund's. His loyalty to Lear is absolute and his self-fulfillment is bound up with his master's. Kent opposes Lear only "when majesty falls to folly" precisely because such "opposition" is for the sake of Lear and the kingdom (1.1.147). He returns to serve him later out of the very same loyalty. The activity of service is its own reward: "To be acknowledged," he says to Cordelia, "is o'erpaid" (4.7.4). Kent's sense of how one's own moral virtue entwines with duty toward others is revealed in his anger at Oswald, more "serviceable villain" than true servant. Kent sees Oswald as an untrue servant because he nurtures his mistress's desires instead of drawing her toward practical reason and justice. When Kent says "Such smiling rogues / As these like rats oft bite the holy cords a-twain / Which are t[oo] intrince t'unloose," he imagines the political community as ropes of duty, obligation, and love that bind together the interests of disparate individuals (2.2.66–68). But these "holy cords" can be gnawed through by those who advance what they take to be their self-interests at the expense of the relationships on which the political community is sustained.

Kent cannot comprehend those who cast aside service for personal gain. Confined in the stocks, Kent asks "How chance the King comes with so small a train" (2.4.58–59). The Fool replies "An thou hadst been set i'th' stocks for that question, thou'dst well deserved it" (60–61). His song elaborates the tension between self-interest and loyalty:

FOOL: That sir which serves and seeks for gain,
       And follows but for form,
       Will pack when it begins to rain,
       And leave thee in the storm,
       But I will tarry; the Fool will stay,
       And let the wise man fly.
       The knave turns fool that runs away;
       The Fool no knave, pardie.
KENT: Where learned you this, Fool?
FOOL: Not i' th' stocks, Fool. (2.4.72–81)

---

[8] This self-loyalty is unfaithful because it entails a severing of one's desire from its proper ruling reason. In other words, vice itself is a kind of self-opposition (*NE* 9.8).

The Fool stayed with Lear because what is truly foolish is to be the one who "serves and seeks for gain," following "but for form." He and Kent each believe that for the virtuous there can be no gain at the expense of loyalty to one's superior. If the Fool understands the situation more clearly than Kent, it is because Kent's obedience to Lear is not genuine virtue, wherein (like the Fool) one understands all the options and chooses the beautiful one. Rather, like the guardians chosen for their spiritedness in Plato's *Republic,* Kent exemplifies civic virtue. Civic virtue is a kind of imitation of genuine *aretē*. In purely civic virtue, the subject is obedient to a practical judgment that is not his own, aligning his desires with the best interest of whomever he serves. (Which is not to say there is no room for disagreement about what is best for the king and kingdom, as Kent himself aptly demonstrates). In genuine *aretē*, one graduates to the obedience to one's own practical judgment. As Aristotle explains, "Practical wisdom [*phronēsis*] is the only virtue peculiar to a ruler (a truly virtuous person) ... practical wisdom is not the virtue of one who is ruled, but true opinion is" (*NE* 1140a–1145a). True opinion here is obedience to the proper thing. This is why law and upbringing are essential to our account: Being raised with discipline, and obedience to the law, habituates a person in a manner that imitates virtue, without being truly virtuous, in the same way that true opinion imitates knowledge without being genuine knowledge. This imitation in youth then, ideally, allows for a person's obedience to their own *phronēsis*. That Kent's individual virtue is incomplete is evident in his intimation of suicide at the play's end. Once the king is gone, so too is Kent's reason for being. If one is unable to be the king – that is, the person whose own selfish well-being is identified with the state – then one's own self-interest is inextricably tied to the fate of the one he serves.

Although Kent figures Oswald as a rat gnawing through "holy cords," it is Lear who severs the ties that bind the community. He divides the nation into parts and confers rule on Goneril and Regan, both of whom lack ethical capacities for rule and whose husbands appear locked in long-standing rivalry. Lear puts Cordelia in the impossible position of degrading her love for him into transactional courtly flattery, demanding that she prioritize his desire for praise and the prospect of fortune over her virtue. Pressed on her refusal to play along, she responds with terms of moderation and reciprocity: She loves him, as he should her, "according to my bond, no more nor less"; "I return those duties back as are right fit: / Obey you, love you, and most honor you" (1.1.91, 95–96). Cordelia refuses to cooperate with behavior she sees as beneath her father. Her opposition to her father is in both her father's best interest and the interest of the state. Cordelia's selfish pursuit of virtue – her obedience to the authority of her own reason – is inextricable from her sense of the common good and the good of her father. This remains true upon her return to Britain, where the attempt to save her father is the same thing as saving Britain. The fracturing of the state turns Lear into "Lear's shadow" (1.4.200). To return to the ancient image, the ruler is the soul and the kingdom is the body: The fate of one is tied to the fate of the other. This dual fracturing points to the problem that Cordelia, Kent, and Gloucester face. How can one act in ways that benefit the whole when the whole has been separated into rival parts? How virtuous can Lear's supporters be to restore a monarch whose last decree seems to have been for his own benefit and at the expense of his country? This question, we can now see, is the same as the question as to how the virtuous citizens can maintain loyalty to a king who has cast aside reason. Learning of "the division betwixt the dukes" and Cordelia's return, Gloucester tells Edmund "These injuries the king now bears will be revenged home. There's part of a power already footed. We must incline to the king" (3.3.10–12). They rally to the king because they judge the king's rule, whether nominal or actual, as the best of the available options. Albany offers to "resign / During the life of this old majesty / To him our absolute power" because he recognizes that the state requires a unifying principle (5.3.274–276). It has nothing to do with Lear's capacities to govern. For Kent, Gloucester, Cordelia, and Albany, Lear, even in his incapacitated state, organizes the ends of their political duties and binds them to one another more effectively than any of their other options.

Our focus on action through the lens of *aretē* provides a reading of *King Lear* that sets the characters in the context of a larger unity. *Aretē* is the expression of human nature. Thus, all characters, like all people, express *aretē* to a greater or lesser degree. *Aretē* unifies the characters and actions in precisely the way that a shared nature unifies us as people. While character criticism reveals the individuality of dramatic persons, our approach sees their differences within the greater likeness of human aims. The question of which interpretive lens to use – the one that focuses on our identity through a shared nature, or the one that distinguishes us based on our particularity – mirrors the most basic ethical question: Are we fundamentally the same or different? Are we defined by our humanity or individuality? In this way *King Lear* holds up the tension between the individual and the whole both in how the content is approached, through one's choice of lens, and in the content itself, through the struggle to maintain the unity of Britain.

CHAPTER 2

Dynamis *(Dynamism, Capacity)* and Energeia *(Actuality)*

Christopher Crosbie

For Shakespeare and his contemporaries, *dynamis* and *energeia* signified, respectively, potentiality (or capability) and actuality. The terms have their roots in Aristotelian metaphysics and mark various states of being as well as, by extension, the transition across such states: a block of wood, for instance, may have the potential (*dynamis*) to become a spoon or a chess piece; its form after being carved into the latter indicates its *energeia*.[1] Receiving extensive explication in Aristotle's *Metaphysics*, principally in Book *Theta* as part of the philosopher's theory of matter and form, the concepts find further articulation, in a distinctly moral vein, within the *Nicomachean Ethics* and *Eudemian Ethics*.[2] While the exact relation of Aristotle's metaphysical application of the terms to their ethical expressions remains of some debate, the distinction between potentiality and actuality serves a crucial role in the Aristotelian moral philosophy that would so deeply inform the early modern era. Parsing the fine meanings of Aristotelian *dynamis* and *energeia* can initially seem an exercise in studying mere scholastic niceties. As quickly becomes apparent, however, a comprehensive theory of potentiality and actuality carries profound implications for those who remain subject to such a framework in their daily, lived experience. The early-modern stage not only explores these implications with great subtlety but also draws a considerable degree of its emotive force from them. What does it mean, for instance, to claim – as, say, Miranda does of Caliban – that someone is "capable of all ill?"[3] Or incapable of doing any good? What are the ramifications of thinking of someone

---

[1] On Aristotle's ultimate preference for "*energeia*" over "*entelecheia*," which also means "actuality," see Stephen Makin, "*Energeia* and *Dunamis*," *The Oxford Handbook of Aristotle*, ed. Christopher Shields (Oxford University Press, 2012), 404–405.

[2] On Aristotle's metaphysical and ethical deployment of *dynamis*, see Eugene Garver, "Aristotle's Metaphysics of Morals," *Journal of the History of Philosophy* 27. 1 (1989), 7–28.

[3] All quotations come from William Shakespeare, *The Complete Pelican Shakespeare* (Penguin, 2002); *The Tempest*, 1.2.353.

(such as Henry Bolingbroke, for example) as having the potential to be a king, especially if still yet another (like Richard II) currently occupies the throne? How should one respond to an ambitious man – such as we find with Julius Caesar – displaying signs that he may, in the future, turn tyrannical? The language used to conceptualize potentiality carries with it very real material consequence – for not only individuals but also various forms of communities as well. In this brief space, I will chart Aristotelian notions of capability and potentiality – two resonances of Aristotle's term *dynamis* – as set against his understanding of actuality, or *energeia*, and, by recourse to *Julius Caesar* and *Richard II*, examine the Shakespearean stage as a signal space for exploring the social ramifications such ambiguous concepts can hold for individual and communal ethics.

To speak of "potentiality" or "capability" is to immediately locate a kind of crossroads, marking as these terms do pathways to various contingent futures. But for all the ethical – and, for our purposes, theatrical – intrigue thereby intrinsic to these concepts, Aristotle notably takes pains to foreground in his *Metaphysics* the importance of actuality instead. Indeed, although it might instinctively seem that potential precedes actualization, that the *ability or capacity to be* precedes the realization of that ability or capacity, Aristotle emphasizes that "actuality is prior to potency ... both in formula and in substantiality" and, in many aspects, even in time as well.[4] Aristotle's knotty metaphysical argument that follows can seem counter-intuitive but it works to preserve his ultimate adherence to a belief in a prime mover and accords with his broader teleological assumptions. Not only must a person or thing exist in order for potentiality to be present, argues Aristotle,[5] but also "everything that comes to be moves towards a principle, i.e. an end ... and the actuality is the end, and it is for the sake of this that the potency is acquired" (1050a). The argument for a prime mover may appear a conventional enough way to secure the primacy of actuality, but what of this latter claim? How can actuality be *prior* to potential in this way? Aristotle goes on to argue that (a) "eternal things are prior *in substance* to perishable things," (b) potencies "may either be or not be" and are thus, by nature, perishable, and (c) actuality, therefore, must be substantially prior to potentiality (1050b, emphasis added). This more complex formulation follows Aristotle's simpler summation when he observes, by way of illustration, that "animals do not see in order that they may

---

[4] Aristotle, *The Basic Works of Aristotle*, ed. Richard McKeon (Random House, 1941), 1049a.
[5] See *Basic Works*, 1049b, where Aristotle avers, "there is always a first mover, and the mover already exists actually."

have sight, but they have sight that they may see," an attempt to clarify how the *telos*, or end, in fact gives rise (however paradoxical it may sound) to what we understand as a potentiality or capability (1050b). Aristotle's securing of the primacy of actuality does heavy metaphysical lifting, but, in perhaps a more pragmatic register, it also serves to ground his analysis in the observable and established, something that well suits his application elsewhere of these metaphysical terms to his ethical theories. Actualized persons, things, actions, and states of being – whatever particular epistemological challenges they pose to the observer – present legible material from which one may work backward to underlying causes. Having established the importance of actuality, Aristotelianism opens for productive inquiry the complexities of tracing various forms of potentialities, including those that find actualization in Aristotelian *hexis* (disposition), *aretē* (excellence), and the *eudaimonia* (happiness; flourishing) characteristic of the ethical life.

But how should we understand Aristotle's notion of *dynamis*? Aristotle defines "potency" as "an originative source of change in another thing or in the thing itself *qua* other" (1046a). Though the main focus of his ensuing explanation depends upon this core idea of "an originative source of change," the distinction between whether a change occurs within the thing itself or within something else matters considerably, for Aristotle here initiates a useful investigation into the difference between "acting and of being acted on." On one level, these two forms of potency are the same, "for a thing may be 'capable' either because it can itself be acted on or because something else can be acted on by it" (1046a). Yet, concomitantly, they are subtly different. For the thing acted upon contains within it "a certain originative source" that *enables it* to be altered, such as we see in how the "oily can be burnt, and that which yields in a particular way can be crushed." The "other potency," by contrast, "is in the agent" and enables one to affect change outside oneself, such as when "the art of building [is] present" and construction emerges from that capability (ibid). To these fine distinctions, Aristotle further differentiates between *rational* and *nonrational* potentialities, the former taking pride of place in his ethical deliberations elsewhere. Nonrational potentiality "produces one effect" such as we see in the case of "the hot" which is "capable only of heating." Rational potentiality, by contrast, is "capable of contrary effects" such as we see, for example, in "the medical art[s]," which "can produce both disease and health" (ibid). This point is crucial for Aristotelian ethics because it means that, when referring to rational potentiality, something else is required to produce a particular effect rather than its antithesis.

Since it is impossible to produce contrary effects at the same time, Aristotle argues, something must intervene to direct the potency, as it were, and this thing is "desire or will" (1048a). Here we see not only the interconnectedness of multiple Aristotelian concepts as they pertain to ethical valuations but also the foundational components that inform Aristotle's notion of *eudaimonia*. For, finally, Aristotle also differentiates between innate potencies, "like the senses," or those which "come by practice, like the power of playing the flute, or by learning, like artistic power" (1047b). *Eudaimonia* for Aristotle develops partly by habituation, a process whereby agents exercise their desire or will to bring into realization the ethical potentialities available to them. Conceptualizing potentiality – and bringing the most preferable potentialities into actualization – becomes crucial for the development of right action, the habituation of good character, and the realization of a *eudaimonic* life.

A particularly intriguing ambiguity of Aristotle's *dynamis* lies in whether he means by this term (what we might call by way of differentiation) "potentiality" or "capability." In the *Metaphysics*, Aristotle avers that "[A] thing is capable of doing something if there will be nothing impossible in its having the actuality of that of which it is said to have the capacity" (1047a). Received variously as tautological or, at best, perplexingly opaque, the formulation is designed to explicate, in part, how we should think of *dynamis* in the case where one has the underlying ability to perform an action and yet, for one reason or another, does not. As Terence Irwin explains by way of analogy: "If I am a builder, but I lose all my tools and cannot replace them for a week, then for a week it is impossible for me to build; but since I do not change, I do not lose my potentiality to build."[6] Kevin Attell clarifies further, noting that Aristotle seems to mean that "while external conditions of possibility may determine whether I can exercise certain capacities, they do not determine the *existence* of these capacities." "[P]otentialities persist," it would appear, "even in the absence of the conditions in which they may be realized."[7] This distinction between the potential one might possess and the (in)capability one might momentarily experience under a set of particular conditions emerges from Aristotle's robust but at times ambiguous account of unrealized *dynamis*. With its volatile pitting of innate potentiality against material circumstances that could either facilitate or impede the realization of that potentiality, this distinction, moreover, brings Aristotelian metaphysics directly

---

[6] Terence Irwin, *Aristotle's First Principles* (Clarendon, 1988), 229.
[7] Kevin Attell, "Potentiality, Actuality, Constituent Power," *Diacritics* 39. 3 (2009), 35–53; esp. 40.

to bear on the social and ethical adjudications that would preoccupy much of Renaissance culture and drama.

Shakespearean drama – like all manner of early-modern writing ranging from metaphysics, natural philosophy, ethics, and beyond – repeatedly turns to this wellspring of Aristotelian assumptions regarding the move from potentiality into actualization in its many guises. One of the more pronounced ways we can see this is in Shakespeare's examination of the complex ethical dilemmas that emerge as individuals' potential for attaining political power come into conflict with the already-realized power of another – as well as the potentiality latent within communities themselves to take shape in peaceable or disastrously fractious ways as a result. Consider, for example, the case of *Julius Caesar*. When Cassius appeals to Brutus by observing how his own potential for greatness matches that of Caesar's and how the only impediment to realizing this potential lies in their own will or choice ("The fault, dear Brutus, is not in our stars, / But in ourselves that we are underlings"), he connects to a sensibility of potentiality and actuality that will register as readily apparent even to modern audiences (1.2.141–142). Significantly, the conspirators will further cast their violent intervention in a familiar language of communal potential, a quest to realize in Rome its ability to return to a more noble state. By its very nature, civil strife carries ramifications for large swaths of people, but here we see more than just an inability – as language from *Henry IV,* Part I has it – to "brook a double reign," or, indeed, any reign at all (*1 Henry IV* 5.4.65). Likewise, Cassius' appeal to Brutus extends beyond the kind of localized appeal to individual ambition such as we see in Lady Macbeth's assertion to her husband that others "have made themselves, and that their fitness now / Does unmake you" (*Macbeth* 1.7.53–54). Instead, the question of what the community *will be*, of what it will take shape as, becomes explicitly and provocatively fused with these correlative evocations of individual potentiality. As much as the play pits the individual potentials of aspiring rivals against each other, *Julius Caesar* also asks its audience to consider how such particular concerns never remain fully isolated, how – following the logic that every actualization carries with it new potentialities – the crises among individuals can ramify into new possible contraries, both positive and negative, for the larger polity as well.

While such moments that pivot on the question of potentiality and that intertwine individual and communal concerns may seem familiar to us, still others within *Julius Caesar* would likely have carried different, perhaps deeper, meaning for Shakespeare's contemporaries more attuned to a particular way of understanding *dynamis*. Brutus, for instance, justifies his planned assassination of Caesar by fashioning him as a potential tyrant on the verge of actualizing his power – "And therefore, think him as a serpent's egg, / Which, hatched, would as his kind grow mischievous, / And kill him in the shell" – and the formulation may well immediately strike us as dubious (2.1.32–34). For Brutus openly stipulates that he has no personal reason to spurn Caesar and is explicit that he must "fashion it thus" in order to arrive at his conclusion (2.1.30). But Brutus does more here than simply assert Caesar has the potential for tyranny: he subtly shifts the ground of his reasoning, moving as he does Caesar's impending moral choices out of the realm of *rational* potential and into that of the *non-rational*. By figuring Caesar as a serpent's egg, Brutus comfortably avoids the more challenging fact that, while Caesar *may* choose to turn tyrant, he equally may not: rational *dynamis*, recall, allows for either contrary. Instead, Brutus figures Caesar's potential within a framework that quietly recasts its *telos* along a single trajectory, so that, akin to Aristotle's "hot" which must inevitably heat, Caesar, the serpent's egg, will, perforce, grow mischievous. Notably, Brutus arrives at these already questionable claims about Caesar's serpent-nature by trading on the kind of fine distinction between capability and potentiality outlined earlier, noting how it will be the accoutrements of power – the incidental, momentary apparatus of political might – that will make him *capable* of affecting his designs, thereby (and here we witness another of Brutus' subtle shifts into categorical error) sealing Caesar's *nature*. Brutus' reasoning, questionable even to modern audiences, thus reveals considerably more problematic equivocations and slips in logic within the prevailing Aristotelian ethical framework of Shakespeare's own day.

Shakespeare likewise draws extensively on the era's underlying notions of *dynamis* and *energeia* in his portrayal of the rival claimants to the throne and the ensuing factional dispute in *Richard II*. The play famously cultivates ambiguity surrounding Henry Bolingbroke's intentions – does he actively pursue the throne or simply his confiscated holdings? – but his latent potential for kingship remains an accepted subtext of the play. With a bloodline that traces to Edward III, he is, in Northumberland's words, the "thrice-noble" Henry, a powerful figure whose potential (marked in the play by both heritage and aptitude) is perhaps most compellingly testified to by Richard's own anxious dealings with him even before Gaunt's death (3.3.103). The will-to-power and the material means to enact that will – the features of choice and a kind of material capability – also feature centrally in the play, accessible to early-modern and modern audiences alike. Indeed, when the gardener observes to Isabella how Richard holds "nothing but himself" while "in the balance of great Bolingbroke, / Besides himself, are all the English peers," he simply acknowledges the *realpolitik* behind pressing one's own advantage when bolstered by the temporary material circumstances which render one capable of attaining power, bare political realities that "every one doth know" (3.4.85, 87–88, 91). In this regard like *Julius Caesar*, the play studies the subtle distinctions between potentiality and capability, the ways the latter can facilitate the realization of one rational contrary over its opposite, and the ramifications such movements can hold for communities which are, themselves, attempting to collectively bring a vision of order into realization.

Richard II, however, also quietly trades on yet another prominent register of the era's discourses of potentiality – one perhaps less immediately obvious to modern audiences – in its repeated invocations of Bolingbroke's and Richard's individual capacity for, surprisingly enough, *yielding*. Before the walls of Flint Castle, Bolingbroke depicts Richard and himself as raging elements, the meeting of which must cause something to give way, and concludes "Be he the fire, I'll be the yielding water" (3.3.58). Tellingly, Shakespeare recalls this very imagery in the deposition scene when Richard imagines himself "a mockery king of snow, / Standing before the sun of Bolingbroke / To melt myself away in water drops!" (5.1.260–262). Aristotle, recall, figures potentiality as not only the ability to effect change in others but also the capacity to be acted *upon*, an instance where "a certain originative source" enables a thing to be crushed, or, in our present case, melted. Whether meant sincerely or as a shrewd political move, Bolingbroke describes his potential to yield by markedly foregrounding his desire, or will, to acquiesce, a figuration of potential brought into actualization by means of choice that remains astutely calibrated to a communal disposition – most explicitly voiced in the play by York and the gardener – eager for domestic stability. Richard, by contrast, betrays a streak of resistance in his employment of an otherwise similar image of yielding. For Richard, under coercion and with little choice but to submit, significantly frames his speech entirely as an imaginative hypothetical – "*O that I were a mockery king of snow,*" he begins – making no mention of an initiating choice that shifts potentiality into actuality, as he, instead, depicts himself as merely a nonrational entity capable of being acted upon without his intervening consent or responsibility. In this, *Richard II* directs attention to more than just the social ramifications of rival potential claims to the throne or of the incidental capabilities afforded by military advantage amid a civil war. The play also generates its tragic force by exploring Richard's capacity to be crushed – by forces both internal and external – while also revealing how here, even in his seemingly most direct expression of yielding, his will remains unbending, an expression of an ethical disposition, at once regrettable yet sympathetic, that remains prone to solipsism and disregard for a wider community.

In so far as drama, by its nature, trades in the matter of unfolding action, nuanced moral dispositions, conflicted motivations, and ethical dilemmas, the stage proves a natural home for exploring potentiality and actuality in unique ways. As the examples briefly sketched here indicate, Shakespearean drama exhibits a recurring interest in not only the complex interplay between *dynamis* and *energeia* but also the intriguing possibilities wrought by different resonances of *dynamis* itself. For the distinctions latent within *dynamis* – between acting and being acted upon; between having potential and having (or not having) momentary, material capability – frequently generate individual ethical dilemmas with wide social implications. Indeed, perhaps one of the most compelling aspects of Shakespeare's treatment of such matters can be found in the reverberating questions these conflicts pose for the various communal groups depicted on stage. For *dynamis* never remains localized to the individual person or particular moment; the actualization of one of the two contraries latent within rational *dynamis* carries with it consequences for the broader community, and, in turn, shapes the nature and character of that community. Whether Rome will be an empire or a republic, whether England will hold with Richard or turn Lancastrian, and – to return to a more pointed question adumbrated earlier and closer to the legacy of more recent history – whether Caliban will be treated as capable or incapable depends considerably upon underlying assumptions about potentiality, capability, and the process of bringing these to actualization. In all of this, the long Aristotelian tradition, upon such closer inspection, feels less distant, less rarefied, and less drily scholastic and, instead, very much a matter germane, indeed urgent, for the ethical quandaries and political determinations even to our own current moment.

CHAPTER 3

Technē *(Technical Expertise, Skill)*

Jeffrey Gore

As the base for our modern word *technology*, *technē* might seem an unlikely fit for a collection on virtue. But *technē* is a Greek word meaning "technical expertise" or "skill" as we associate with diverse practitioners, from musicians to cooks to medical doctors. *Technē* was translated into Latin as *ars*, or art, to describe the techniques that make a practice teachable – *ars rhetorica* or *ars poetica* – and it played a special role in the classical understanding of virtue.[1] In what is sometimes called the "craft analogy," Aristotle explains that we acquire virtues in a way similar to how we learn to perform professional activities or to play a musical instrument, such as the harp-like cithara: "the way we learn … how to do [things] is by doing them … people become builders by building, and cithara-players by playing the cithara; so too, we become just by doing just things, moderate by doing moderate things, and courageous by doing courageous things."[2] By this analogy, the habituating experiences that form the enduring disposition of the morally virtuous are comparable to the years of practice that form the virtuoso's skillful abilities. And on the basis of this analogy between the craft worker's attainment of skills and the citizen's moral development, one can trace a pathway through the *Nicomachean Ethics*, from *technē* through *hexis* (the durable disposition) to *aretē* (excellence or virtue) and *proairesis* (commitment or choice).[3]

Artisan characters practicing *technē* frequently appear in Shakespeare's plays, and the specialized knowledge of their trades often provides comic relief and social commentary. The gravedigger in *Hamlet* explains that

---

[1] For titles using *ars*, art, and *technē*, see *Aristotelous Technēs rhētorikēs biblia tria / Aristotelis de rhetorica seu arte dicendi libri tres* (London, 1619) and Ben Jonson, trans., *Q. Horatius Flaccus: His Art of Poetry* (London, 1640).

[2] Aristotle, *Nicomachean Ethics*, ed. Susan Broadie, trans. Christopher Rowe (Oxford University Press, 2002), 2.1 1103a30–1103b5.

[3] For the "craft analogy," see Tom Angier, *Technē in Aristotle's Ethics: Crafting the Moral Life* (Continuum, 2010), especially chapter 2.

corpses "pocky" from venereal diseases decay more quickly than others
(5.2.152–159), the shepherd Corin from *As You Like It* explains that shepherds don't normally kiss hands because theirs are "tarred over" from
covering sheep wounds (3.2.54–56), and the Nurse in *Romeo and Juliet*
explains that she weaned Juliet from breastfeeding by applying the bitter plant extract wormwood to her breast (1.3.28).[4] Of these three, the
Nurse is the most central character to her story, and in her tender care
for Juliet (which we little see from the girl's mother), she practices prudence, loyalty, and friendship and asserts courage in her defense of Juliet
against Lord Capulet's threatening outburst (1.3, 3.5). While virtuous
excellence depends upon the balance between extremes (i.e., the "golden
mean"), artisans often act in Shakespeare's work as a counter-balance to
the excesses of the powerful (*NE* 2.6.1106a15–1107a25). *The Tempest* opens
with a knowledgeable Shipmaster and Boatswain attempting to save their
ship from a storm ("Down with the topmast!"), while the royals on deck,
whom we soon learn to be villainous, argue with them over their manners
(1.1). The tailor in *The Taming of the Shrew* produces Katherine a stylish
dress of intricate pattern – "With a small compassed cape ... [and] a trunk
sleeve ... curiously cut" – but Petruchio showers him with abuse as one
of his schemes to intimidate his new wife (4.3.86–162). And Francis, the
apprentice tapster (bartender) in *1 Henry IV*, suffers the pranks of Prince
Harry and Poins, while Falstaff puts at risk the very lives of such abused
service workers in his mismanaged military efforts ("They'll fill a pit as well
as better").[5]

Readers will frequently find characters practicing *technē* on the margins
of Shakespeare's plays, which reflects both the virtue's intellectual heritage
and early-modern views on work and citizenship. Although Aristotle recognizes technical knowledge among other intellectual virtues (such as theoretical knowledge and practical wisdom), he sometimes casts *technē* in roles
that illustrate the margins of his ethical and political system as a whole.[6]
For instance, he sharply differentiates practical wisdom (*phronēsis*) from
technical expertise (*technē*), in that the capacity to deliberate over politics
and "the good life in general" requires a different mental faculty from

---

[4] All passages from Shakespeare are drawn from *The Norton Shakespeare*, eds. Stephen Greenblatt,
Walter Cohen, Suzanne Gossett, Jean E. Howard, Katharine Eisaman Maus, and Gordon McMullan
(W. W. Norton, 1997).
[5] *1 Henry IV*, 2.5 and 4.2.59.
[6] The five intellectual virtues for Aristotle include technical expertise (*technē*), systematic knowledge
(*epistēmē*), practical wisdom (*phronēsis*), intellectual accomplishment (*sophia*), and intelligence
(*nous*), *Nicomachean Ethics*, 6.3 1139b15–1139b20.

that needed to internalize the standardized techniques often at the heart
of specific artisan professions (6.5 1140a25–1140b5; 6.6 1140b30–1140b35).
While there is nothing inherently problematic in differentiating mental
faculties, this particular epistemological distinction maps all too coher-
ently onto Aristotle's more exclusionary views on citizenship: "the citizens
must not lead the life of mechanics [craftspeople] or tradesmen, for such
a life is ignoble and inimical to virtue. Neither must they be husbandmen
[farmers], since leisure is necessary both for the development of virtue and
the performance of political duties" (7.9 1328b35–1329a5).[7]

The artisan rebels in *2 Henry VI* acknowledge the uphill battle they
face to participate in government: "Virtue is not regarded in handicrafts-
men ... The nobility think scorn to go in leather aprons" (4.2.8–10). The
"leather apron" is a common synecdoche for artisans, supposedly incapable of participating in politics. In *Coriolanus*, the patrician Menenius
scorns the tribunes and their "apron-men" for giving voice to workers
and "garlic-eaters" (4.6.99–102). Similarly, in *Julius Caesar* Flavius and
Murellus accost workers making a holiday of Caesar's recent triumph:
"Where is thy leather apron and thy rule? / What dost thou with thy best
apparel on? ... You blocks, you stones, you worse than senseless things!"
(1.1.7–34).[8] Early-modern English politics was still often under the sway
of aristocrats and gentles – recognized by their inherited titles and their
wealth sufficient to "live without manual labour" – and Shakespeare
mobilizes these nongentle artisans to represent the dangers of populism
and arbitrary group (or "mob") violence.[9] The plebian laborers in *Caesar*,
for instance, are easily swayed by both Caesar's triumph (1.1.) and Mark
Antony's compelling sense of emotional appeal (3.2), and the rebellious
craftsmen in *Henry VI* – who famously vow to "kill all the lawyers" –
execute a poor village clerk for simply being literate (4.2.68–97).

Readers interested in classical virtues within a modern liberal polity can
find themselves tasked with untangling a philosophical heritage from the
moorings of premodern societies. Hannah Arendt argues that Aristotle's
bias against craft workers has less to do with a simple class prejudice and
more to do with his recognition of the property-owning citizen's freedom
(and time) to pursue politics and public life, "to transcend [their] own

---

[7] *Politics of Aristotle*, trans. Benjamin Jowett (Oxford University Press: 1885), 7.9 1328b35–1329a5.
[8] Theodore F. Kaouk, "Homo Faber, Action Hero Manque: Crafting the State in *Coriolanus*," *Shakespeare Quarterly* 66. 4 (2015), 409–439.
[9] William Harrison, *Description of England* (1577), 113–114, quoted in Peter Laslett, *The World We Have Lost* (Charles Scribner, 1984), 35.

[lives] and enter the world all have in common."[10] Whether we are considering the skills of the craftsperson or the standard procedures of the physician, the successful practice of *techné* depends, at least in part, upon the internalization of routines that, for the seasoned performer, require little deliberation. For Aristotle, however, deliberation – essentially, "stopping to think" – is key to practical wisdom (*phronēsis*), a necessary component in many of the other virtues, and at the heart of his politics. So when we consider that Elizabethan law (and often economic necessity) required nongentle laborers to work 14 hours a day in the summer and 10 in the winter, it is less surprising that Shakespeare would have regularly turned his creative attention to the aspirational few practicing any of the virtues other than *techné*.[11]

All that more miraculous, then, is the performance of virtue by the "rude mechanicals" in *A Midsummer Night's Dream* (3.2.9). Hardly a textbook case of aspirational *techné*, the play's artisan characters gather not to share skills to which they have dedicated their lives – as a carpenter, a weaver, a bellows-mender, a tinker, a tailor, and a joiner (or woodworker) – but to put on a play in the "interlude before the Duke and the Duchess" on their wedding night (1.2.5–6).[12] Although Egeus warns the Duke that the artisan players are "Hard-handed men ... Which never labored in their minds till now," the Duke encourages the court to express generosity as audience members: "The kinder we, to give them thanks" (5.1.72–105). Fertile virtue trajectories emerge for readers interested in the craft of theater and social class through other plays featuring "plays within the play," such as *Hamlet*, where the Prince offers a long and eloquent (but likely unnecessary) lesson on acting techniques to a group of professional players (3.2.1–40), or *Love's Labour's Lost*, where the nobles so mock the amateur performers of "The Nine Worthies" that they can hardly speak their lines (5.2.484–698). Similarly, the artisan actors in *Dream* suffer the interruptions of the nobles, they forget their lines and break character, and Bottom predictably overacts: "Thus die I: thus, thus, thus ... Now die, die, die, die, die" (5.1.288–295). But Flute as Thisbe – is it *techné* or a fluke? – speaks some of

---

[10] Hannah Arendt, *The Human Condition* (1958; University of Chicago Press, 2018), 65. See Arendt's chapter 2, "The Public and the Private Realm" and her notes on Fustel de Coulanges on how "time-consuming political activity was" in ancient Greece, 14, n. 10 and 65, n. 68. The point becomes even clearer if we imagine making well-informed political decisions without the advantage of printed or electronic media.

[11] *The Statute of Artificers* (1563), cited in Laslett, *The World We Have Lost*, 30.

[12] Aristotle devotes special attention to the dedication of the qualified or serious (*spoudaios*) practitioner, *Nicomachean Ethics*, 1.7 1098a5–15.

the play's most well-crafted lines in his final soliloquy: "O sisters three, / Come, come to me / With hands as pale as milk. / Lay them in gore, / since you have shore / With shears his thread of silk" (5.2.323–328).

A second virtue trajectory emerges in the social relationships *Dream*'s artisan actors form by sharing a practice. For Alasdair MacIntyre, a communal activity such as theater exercises virtues "internal to practices ... justice, courage and honesty." By "subordinating [themselves]" to the "purposes and standards which inform the practices" of theater – Flute accepts the role of playing a woman and Bottom accepts playing "no part but Pyramus" – the actors find opportunity to practice these internal virtues and achieve the external goods of a successful performance and a royal pension for life.[13] They exercise loyalty – Flute seems to care more about Bottom's lost pension than his own – and this transcendent quality bears comparison to the solidarity found among the "good lads of Eastcheap" in *1 Henry IV* whom one imagines fighting together one day on the battlefields of France in the play's sequel, *Henry V*.[14]

Although the social boundaries associated with *technē* may resemble modern divisions of labor between "white collar" and "blue collar" workers, these divisions do not tell the whole story. Aristotle's focus on *technē* allows him to recognize the common ground in all professions, in that they satisfy human needs: "health is the end of medicine, a ship of shipbuilding, victory of generalship, wealth of household management" (1.1 1094a5–10). On the other hand, not all professions are the same: Aristotle distinguishes the "architectonic," or "master-arts," where expertise takes on the responsibility of addressing the "greater good" of all of society (as we hope for with politicians) or when professional fields, such as medicine, require a balance between improvisational thinking and wisdom, when "no exact technique applies."[15] Readers of Shakespeare may find a concentrated practice of virtue in those characters who pursue medicine or the law. Lord Cerimon, the medical doctor from *Pericles*, acknowledges, "Virtue and

---

[13] Alasdair MacIntyre, *After Virtue: A Study in Moral Theory*, 3rd edn. (University of Notre Dame Press, 2007), 191.

[14] *Midsummer Night's Dream*, 4.2.18–22; *1 Henry IV*, 2.5.6–90; *Henry V*, 4.3.18–67. Although discussions of virtue often focus on the individual, for a focus on solidarity in a "cause beyond your private self," see Josiah Royce, *The Philosophy of Loyalty* (Macmillan, 1908), 55. I thank philosopher Paul Matthews for bringing this collective *ethos* to my attention.

[15] *Nicomachean Ethics*, 1.1 1094a25-b15; 2.2 1104a1–10; 6.5 1140a30–35. See Angier, *Technē in Aristotle's Ethics*, 102–103; Scott Newstok's anecdote about a master craftsman tuning a piano with a cigarette lighter in his chapter "Of Craft," *How to Think like Shakespeare: Lessons from a Renaissance Education* (Princeton University Press, 2020), 25–35; and Richard Sennett's argument that "there is nothing mindlessly mechanical about technique itself," *The Craftsman* (Yale University Press, 2008), 9.

cunning were endowments greater / Than nobleness and riches" in his life, and he is a paragon of devoted study and generosity (12.24–25). Those readers interested in medical ethics may take note of the medical caregivers' observance of confidentiality and disciplinary limits in *Macbeth* (5.1, 5.3) or the Doctor's violation of the Jailer's Daughter's consent in *The Two Noble Kinsmen* (5.4).

In her pursuit of the art of medicine, Helen in *All's Well That Ends Well* risks her life to persuade the ailing King to take a treatment she has derived from her late father's medical materials and challenges readers to recognize a fuller breadth to courage (2.1.98–209). While our default image of the virtue might be the masculine warrior, MacIntyre reminds us, "Courage, the capacity to risk harm or danger to oneself, has its role in human life because of [its] connection with care and concern [for individuals, communities, and causes]."[16] In *The Merchant of Venice*, Portia shows courage in donning the guise of a "young and learned" (and male) doctor of law in the court case to save Antonio. She follows courtroom procedures without hesitation – a miraculous mastery of *techne*, unaccounted for in the text – but it is her cunning sense of wisdom that turns the tables on Shylock's previously airtight legal claim (4.1). Whether Portia's successful final argument actually results in justice or excessive punishment is debatable; for a clearer example of consistent, just practice by a doctor of law – who also exercises discretion – readers can turn to the "well-practiced wise directions" of the Lord Chief Justice in *2 Henry IV* (5.2.63–141).

The most relevant part that *techne* plays in Shakespeare's work might not be in the representation of craft in his plays, but in the enduring role craft plays in making this work possible, which begins with education. While we moderns regularly think of art as "self-expression" or as the finished work of art one finds in a museum, *techne* is better understood as the teachable "art of" a practice, such as music, fencing, or writing an essay. The paragon for understanding Renaissance educational *techne*-as-virtue is arguably Roger Ascham, tutor for the young Queen Elizabeth, whose *The Schoolmaster* (1570) presents his innovative "double translation" method as a means to improve Latin instruction and, thus, to decrease the violent corporal punishment that was rampant in schools.[17] Ascham initially sought royal patronage through his book on archery, *Toxophilus* (1545), where he argues that the sport develops a person's aptitudes by

<hr />

[16] MacIntyre, *After Virtue*, 192.
[17] Roger Ascham, *The Schoolmaster* (1570), ed. Lawrence V. Ryan (Cornell University Press, 1967).

exercising, not just their skills at shooting, but their very capacity to receive instruction and to take pleasure in the pursuit of excellence.[18] Aristotle's "craft analogy," noted above, receives its fullest expression in Ascham, who writes that such an approach to "Euerye hand craft" can transform learners, as "Cicero sayeth ... to a newe nature."[19] Thomas Greene argues that Ascham understands the arts as exercises in moral judgment: "Ascham thought ... that the activity of choosing words sharpened the judgment to enable it better to choose actions. The series of manifold tiny decisions required to write a paragraph resembles, he thought, the larger decisions required to act judiciously in society."[20]

It is possible to speculate that Ascham served as Shakespeare's model for the pedantic schoolmaster-archer Holofernes in *Love's Labour's Lost*, and Shakespeare regularly pokes fun at excesses of learning in the liberal arts ("More matter with less art").[21] At the same time, it would be difficult to imagine his *oeuvre* without the education he often sharply ridicules, from the material he draws from Latin authors such as Ovid and Plutarch to his rich, often challenging syntax, which suggests the "pressures past" of parsing Latin verse. It is not hard as readers to recognize Shakespeare's value as an elite artist, who holds a "mirror up to nature."[22] But the challenge for us as teachers is usually in making this work accessible, and a more comprehensive understanding of *technē* lends us a hand in this endeavor. As Ben Jonson notes of Shakespeare, "a good poet's made as well as born," and the same can be said about a reader of literature. Ironically, the way Shakespeare may have begun this journey – as a "whining schoolboy ... creeping like snail / Unwillingly to school" – is the way that we ourselves regularly first encounter him, through a *technē*-rich engagement with the language arts curriculum.[23] When we truly succeed as teachers of Shakespeare, it is often because we have helped students recognize the joys

---

[18] Roger Ascham, *Toxophilus* (1545), ed. Peter Medine (Arizona Center for Medieval and Renaissance Studies, 2002), 91–97. Ascham's title is a coinage of the Greek words *toxon* (bow) and *philos* (lover).

[19] Ascham, *Toxophilus*, 125. Similarly, Ascham stresses that moral character can be similarly fashioned through both humanist language studies and other deliberate activities: "all pastimes, generally, which be joyned with labor," *The Schoolmaster*, 53.

[20] Thomas M. Greene, "Roger Ascham: The Perfect End of Shooting," *English Literary History* 36 (1969), 615.

[21] *Hamlet*, 2.2.97. Patricia Winson, "'A Double Spirit of Teaching': What Shakespeare's Teachers Teach Us," *Early Modern Literary Studies* Special Issue 1 (1997), 8.1–31, http://purl.oclc.org/emls/si-01/si-01winson.html.

[22] *Hamlet*, 1.5.100 and 3.2.20.

[23] Ben Jonson, "To the Memory of My Beloved, The Author, Mr. William Shakespeare, and What He Hath Left Us," *The Norton Anthology of English Literature*, ed. Stephen Greenblatt and M. H. Abrams, 8th edn., vol. B (W. W. Norton, 2006), 1445–1446, line 64; *As You Like It*, 2.7.144–146.

of learning and practicing *technē* – as Henry Staten writes, the "inherited, socially inscribed know-how that becomes woven into our neuromuscular substance by culture" – as tools to crack open aspects of language and culture that were just below the frozen sea within ourselves.[24] Rather than a boring collection of footnotes, the various tools we use to learn to read Shakespeare can help make us aware of the enabling tools that have helped us learn to live.[25]

[24] Henry Staten, *Techne Theory: A New Language for Art* (Bloomsbury, 2019), 11. For the "frozen sea" metaphor see Franz Kafka, letter to Oskar Pollak (1904), *Letters to Friends, Family, and Editors* (Schocken Books, 1977), 16.

[25] Examples of projects making *technē* problems in Shakespeare into virtue solutions include *The Hobart Shakespeareans* (2005), dir. Mel Stuart, featuring Rafe Esquith, Ian McKellen, and Michael York; the public-facing pedagogy of University of California Irvine Professor Julia Reinhard Lupton (see her *Citizen-Saints: Shakespeare and Political Theology* [University of Chicago Press, 2005], 251, n. 4 and "Cyber Shakespeare" at www.humanities.uci.edu/news/cyber-shakespeare); the Chicago-based Viola Project theater program for girls, www.violaproject.org; and the exquisite syllabi of educator and journalist Colleen Kennedy, particularly "How to Tell if You Are in a Renaissance Revenge Tragedy" and "Creating a Commonplace Book," https://204.academia.edu/ColleenKennedy.

CHAPTER 4

Eudaimonia *(Happiness)*

Katarzyna Lecky

Eudaimonia – usually translated as blessedness, flourishing, happiness, or wellbeing – is the affective dimension of an ethical life, the felt experience of the everyday practice of virtue. This chapter concentrates on a passage from Shakespeare's *Henry V* to explore how some early-modern English texts manifested this virtuous delight in the strawberry: a common plant exemplifying how an earthy, grounded mode of wellbeing can thrive in wild, weedy landscapes fraught with vice. For Shakespeare and his contemporaries, the strawberry embodied a goodness that flourished in the morally ambiguous vibrancy of the physical world. In literature and natural philosophy alike this plant spotlighted the pragmatic aim of Aristotelian ethics, which defined *eudaimonia* as the result of an individual life oriented around the flourishing of its community. The entanglements valorized by the practical virtue of the strawberry eroded perceived boundaries separating self from society, goodness from corruption, and the great from the lowly.

Henry V displays this understanding of *eudaimonia* when it invokes the strawberry to describe kingly growth.[1] The Archbishop of Canterbury expresses surprise that Henry's youthful "addiction … to courses vain, … companies unletter'd, rude and shallow, … riots, banquets, [and] sports" did not preclude his later success as a king. Ely replies,

> The strawberry grows underneath the nettle
> And wholesome berries thrive and ripen best
> Neighbour'd by fruit of baser quality.

---

[1] Scholarship has generally explored references to flora in Shakespeare's tetralogy through the plays' allusions to grafting. See Jean Feerick, "The Imperial Graft: Horticulture, Hybridity, and the Art of Mingling Races in *Henry V* and *Cymbeline*," *The Oxford Handbook of Shakespeare and Embodiment: Gender, Sexuality, and Race,* ed. Valerie Traub (Oxford University Press, 2016), 211–227; Vin Nardizzi, "Grafted to Falstaff and Compounded with Catherine: Mingling Hal in the Second Tetralogy," *Queer Renaissance Historiography: Backward Gaze,* eds. Vin Nardizzi, Stephen Guy-Bray, and Will Stockton (Ashgate, 2009), 149–169.

44

And so the prince obscured his contemplation
Under the veil of wildness; which, no doubt,
Grew like the summer grass, fastest by night,
Unseen, yet crescive in his faculty.   (1.1.63–69)[2]

Ely references the trope of the strawberry among weeds to describe Hal's maturation. The "wildness" of both plant and prince – their natural capacity to thrive effortlessly in England's common landscape – is the source of their virtues, as Canterbury affirms:

It must be so; for miracles are ceased;
And therefore we must needs admit the means
How things are perfected.   (1.1.70–73)

For the ecclesiast as well as the aristocrat, the prince's fruition among England's commonalty challenges definitions of *eudaimonia* that orient it to the divine or elite.[3] Henry is "perfected" through his embeddedness in a lowly society whose vices are its greatest virtues: he has learned the lessons appropriate to his sovereign state by entangling himself with the common lot. The archbishop rejects miracles as the cause of this growth to instead lend credence to a strain of early-modern natural philosophy and history that viewed vegetable life as the material evidence of practical virtue and framed botanical study as ethical experimentation.

The strawberry was enjoyed widely for its gustatory and medicinal qualities, or (in the words of contemporary herbalists) "vertues." Its ubiquity in gardens and untamed landscapes alike was augmented by its perceived ability to retain its native character while growing among noxious weeds and poisonous serpents. Literary, religious, and scientific writers marveled at the strawberry's capacity to succeed in such conditions. The art and literature of the Middle Ages and Renaissance portrayed the strawberry as at once virtuous and vicious, colored by a venereal chastity that made it a symbol of concupiscence simultaneously associated with the Virgin Mary.[4] This low-growing spreader (classified as a rhizome by modern botanists) thrived where good is indistinguishable from evil. In *Areopagitica* (1644), John Milton invokes this muddy material virtue when he offers his

---

[2] *Henry V* from The Folger Shakespeare, eds. Barbara Mowat, Paul Werstine, Michael Poston, and Rebecca Niles. Folger Shakespeare Library, 23 August 2020. https://shakespeare.folger.edu/shakespeares-works/henry-v/

[3] Feerick notes that Canterbury and Ely frame Henry as a "composite identity" (219).

[4] Walter S. Gibson, "The Strawberries of Hieronymus Bosch," *Cleveland Studies in the History of Art* 8 (2003), 24–33, 28–29; see also Lawrence J. Ross, "The Meaning of Strawberries in Shakespeare," *Studies in the Renaissance* 7 (1960), 225–240.

seminal argument against censorship: "how much we thus expell of sin, so much we expell of vertue: for the matter of them both is the same; remove that, and ye remove them both alike."[5] As an emblem of real-world virtue, the strawberry infused blessedness with sensuality to make this earthy joy the felt sense of an idealized "Vegetable Common-Wealth."[6]

Eudaimonic delight colors the language describing this commonwealth. The 1598 English translation *Aristotles Politiques* explains why "all liuing creatures" experience this material happiness:

> when Nature perceiued that the substance whereof she had created them, receiued not perfect wisedome, shee gaue them in steed thereof delight, and as it were a certaine kind of bait, which they might receiue for the welfare, preseruation, and keeping of their kind, ioining a vehement delight to the vse and exercise of those parts.[7]

Delight is the basic, bodied drive ensuring propagation – an essential type of flourishing – as well as the stand-in for a "perfect wisdom" not bound by human reason but instead open to all forms of life. Enjoyment equates creaturely with divine creation: it operates within a spectrum where pro-creation differs from the production of knowledge in degree rather than kind, and where human and nonhuman agents find common ground.[8] This translation defines vegetable delight as political:

> a Commonweale [of] all sorts of people... seemeth ... to bee the best and goodliest Commonweale of all: For as a garment decked with choice of floures, makes a very faire shewe, so dooth such a State, hauing in it variety of all kinds of manners and dispositions ... as children and women take delight to see such peeces of worke as are full of diuersitie, so many men will deeme this an excellent Common-weale, sith it is fraught with such varietie. (196)

This is an inclusive mode of appreciation, which views the aesthetics of human communities through the lens of flora. As mirrors of people, plants' innate virtues showcase the beauty inhering in organic ideals of communities,

[5] John Milton, *Areopagitica; A Speech of Mr. John Milton, For the Liberty of Unlicensed Printing, to the Parliament of England* (London, 1644), 18. Noel Sugimura highlights Milton's indebtedness to Aristotelian virtue ethics in "Matter of Glorious Trial": Spiritual and Material Substance in Paradise Lost (Yale University Press, 2009).

[6] Noah Biggs, *Mataeotechnia medicinae praxeōs* (Edward Blackmore, 1651).

[7] Aristotle, *Aristotles Politiques, or Discourses of Gouernment* (Adam Islip, 1598), 6.

[8] Marjorie Swann writes, "Throughout the sixteenth and seventeenth centuries, ensoulment and physiology linked men with plants"; in "Vegetable Love: Botany and Sexuality in Seventeenth-Century England," in *The Indistinct Human in Renaissance Literature*, eds. Jean E. Feerick and Vin Nardizzi (Palgrave Macmillan, 2012), 139–158, 141.

whose "diuersitie" and "varietie" spur an enjoyment that is also an ethical judgment about the virtues enlivening "an excellent Common-weale."

This botanical politics stands in subtle but significant contrast to the commonwealth of bees promoted by Canterbury in the next scene of Shakespeare's play. In response to Exeter's musings that "government, though high and low and lower, / Put into parts, doth keep in one consent," the archbishop speculates,

> Therefore doth heaven divide
> The state of man in divers functions,
> Setting endeavour in continual motion;
> To which is fixed, as an aim or butt,
> Obedience: for so work the honey-bees,
> Creatures that by a rule in nature teach
> The act of order to a peopled kingdom.
> ....
> So may a thousand actions, once afoot.
> End in one purpose. (1.2.187–220)

The fruition of Canterbury's model of distributive governance replaces Exeter's "consent" with "purpose," while truncating the duke's expansive topography of who and what counts in this governing system to "the state of man" alone. Exeter's inclusion of the "low and lower" gestures at the "baser quality" of those crucial to Henry's political flourishing, but Canterbury counters this with the Renaissance commonplace of a polity resembling the social life of bees. This purposeful body politic, which locates virtue in doing rather than being, stands opposed to the "crescive" model offered by the strawberry flourishing in a landscape that includes disobedience among its composite virtues. An industrious commonwealth is driven by a utilitarianism that hierarchically divides and even devalues its constituents; one that grows spontaneously trusts in the innate goodness of all already extant within it. Apian orderliness generates edification, but the tangled profusion of plants activates a receptive form of virtuous enjoyment that flourishes widely and needs no cultivation.

This botanical politics made the strawberry exemplary, and Shakespeare joined others in drawing from contemporary herbals (reference manuals on the innate beneficial qualities or "vertues" of flora), which extoled the study of plants as the path to wellbeing for both individuals and societies. This praxis-based system praised the goodness of untended landscapes; for example, John Gerard's entry on the strawberry in his 1597 *Herball* catalogues the plant's numerous "vertues" alongside a description of the places where they may be found: they "grow vpon hills and vallies, likewise in woods and other such places that bee something shadowie: they [also] prosper well in gardens" (845).[9] Gerard lists the places where the plant grows wild before its sites of cultivation, emphasizing how it thrives in ostensibly inauspicious ("shadowy") conditions as well as in domestication. Thomas Hill's 1577 *Gardeners Labyrinth* – the first practical gardening book in England, which saw seven editions through the mid-seventeenth century – also embraces England's native wildness. In his recipes for curative strawberry water, Hill advises, "The Beries which growe in woodes standing on hilles, are better commended to vse" (81).[10] Here, the cultivated version loses some of the natural potency that derives from the intertwined life of untended ecologies.

Herbal thinking thus contributed to the robust and searching explorations of virtue at the heart of Renaissance humanism. Jennifer Herdt points out that in this era considerations of virtue dominated a wide range of cultural, ecclesiastical, political, and soteriological theories of human excellence, and that these concerns were embedded in the material circumstances of a rapidly shifting society.[11] Markku Peltonen has shown that the development of virtue was an essential aspect of humanist pedagogy.[12] But as herbalists imported the language of humanism into plant study, they jettisoned celebrations of cultivated *virtus* in favor of a panoply of innate "vertues," reversing the thrust of the means and ends of virtue ethics. Moreover, herbalists inverted the typical emphasis on edification to instead emphasize the primacy of eudaimonic delight to the learning process – an inversion that shifted the aims of pedagogy from the cultivation of the individual to collective growth. In early-modern herbal thought a virtuous life emanates out of the vegetative soul: the ontological ground of a common nature shared by all living things. As herbalists explored the practical implications of the Aristotelian tripartite soul, they posited a form of life linking people to each other and their environment in vegetative symbiosis.

The experience of enjoyment signals the lived experience of this vegetable sociality. Lauren Berlant has argued that "affect [is] the very material of historical embeddedness."[13] In herbals, delight is eudaimonic: it signals

---

[9] John Gerard, *The Herbal: or, Generall Historie of Plantes* (London, 1597).

[10] Thomas Hill, *The Gardeners Labyrinth* (London, 1577).

[11] Jennifer Herdt, "Virtue, Identity, and Agency," *Journal of Medieval and Early Modern Studies* 42. 1 (2012), 3.

[12] Markku Peltonen, "Virtues in Elizabethan and Early Stuart Grammar Schools," *Journal of Medieval and Early Modern Studies* 42. 1 (2012), 157–179. See also Claire Preston's investigation of the humanism coloring naturalism in *The Poetics of Scientific Investigation in Seventeenth-Century England* (Oxford University Press, 2015), 20–23.

[13] Lauren Berlant, *Cruel Optimism* (Duke University Press, 2011), 66.

the felt immediacy of human matter flourishing together with plant matter. The herbalist's labor is shaped by this feeling; for instance, William Bullein's 1579 *Bulwarke of Defence* promises to help its users read "the vertues of euery Creature heere in Earth," including "Trees, Plantes, Fruictes, Flower, Hearbe, [and] Grasse" (C2r).[14] Bullein augments descriptions of flora with stories of "noble Men & Womē, which delited in the Flowers, & Fruictes of the groūd whose names for ye most part you shall fynde in the Simples" (C3r–v). He explains that their "chiefe delightes … were not in Bacchus Bankets, or Venus Games: but spent theyr tyme pleasauntly, in the sweete Fieldes among Fruictes, Flowers, & Spices of delight" (C3v). The study of plants is best in fields rather than gardens: it is a virtue-driven pedagogy that grounds itself in the organic profusion of the natural world.

In these texts and others, herbal wisdom begins and ends with surrendering to the enjoyment of flora, which inspires and guides deployments of the intellective will. Botanical knowledge stems from the vulnerability attending the experience of delight, which ravishes the senses through a radical openness to the world. This form of experiential learning lessens the tension between singularity – the basis of discrete classification on which scientific inquiry depends – and plurality; the herbalist has only to yield to the wild landscapes that testify to the interrelated nature of all life. James Kuzner notes that scholarship assumes an antipathy to vulnerability that overlooks its early-modern benefits: "for many Renaissance figures, shared vulnerability is central to community's existence."[15] The topography of the herbal paints a version of worldly virtue habituated in the practice of exploration and observation. It participates in "'the politics of the everyday' as the crucible in which the nature and terms of the public transcript have to be worked out and renewed. It is in the quotidian processes of renegotiation and adjustment that the codes of mutual obligation are tested and reinforced."[16] The political nature of the herbal emerges in its promotion of an aesthetic that finds beauty in interconnectedness, in strawberries growing among nettles.

---

[14] William Bullein, *Bulleins Bulwarke of Defence* (Thomas Marshe, 1579).
[15] James Kuzner, *Open Subjects: English Renaissance Republicans, Modern Selfhoods, and the Virtue of Vulnerability* (Edinburgh University Press, 2011), 3.
[16] J. C. Davis, "'A Standard which can never fail us': the Golden Rule and the construction of a public transcript in early modern England," in *Popular Culture and Political Agency in Early Modern England and Ireland: Essays in Honour of John Walter*, eds. Michael J. Braddick and Phil Withington (Boydell & Brewer, 2017), 166.

Not all botanical practitioners shared this rosy view of wildness: even as herbals proliferated in the early-modern English print market, the field of husbandry also garnered broad readerships. Gervase Markham's influential 1613 guide *The English Husbandman* argued that cultivation was the antidote to an innately tumultuous world. Strawberries do not appear in Markham's manual denouncing untilled land as prone to "all manner of offensiue wéedes."[17] In his epistle to the reader, the writer asserts, "it is most necessary for kéeping the earth in order, which else would grow wilde, and like a wildernesse, brambles and wéeds choaking vp better Plants, and nothing remayning but a Chaos of confusednesse."[18] He explicitly frames husbandry as a virtuous practice that will restore goodness to the errant English body politic:

> the nature of this worst part of this last age hath conuerted all things to such vildnesse that whatsoeuer is truely good is now esteemed most vitious … yet notwithstanding in this apostate age I haue aduentured to thrust into the world this booke, which nothing at all belongeth to the silken scorner, but to the plaine russet Husbandman.[19]

Markham offers an inclusive vision of moral agency that celebrates the ordinary practitioner over the elite subject, but his perspective makes unchecked growth an immoral danger, and virtue the product of inculcation. Even in Markham there is room for a "garden-plot for pleasure," but the trajectory of that delight has diverged from receptive enjoyment to valorize the work of instilling human virtue on a naturally vicious world.[20]

Markham's perspective is a deliberate counterpoint to Francis Bacon's essay on gardens, which emphasizes the world's sacred goodness by beginning, "God Almighty first planted a garden. And indeed it is the purest of human pleasures."[21] A sizable portion of Bacon's ideal garden mimics uncultivated land: "the heath, which is the third part of our plot, I wish it to be framed, as much as may be, to a natural wildness."[22] In keeping with the thought that cultivation deprives the vegetative of some of its native richness, he continues, "Trees I would have none in it, but some thickets,

---

[17] Gervase Markham, *The English Husbandman* (Henry Taunton, 1613), C3r.
[18] Ibid., A3v.
[19] Ibid., A1r.
[20] Ibid., 108.
[21] Francis Bacon, *The Essays*, ed. John Pitcher (Penguin, 1985), 197.
[22] Bacon, *The Essays*, 201. David Simon notes, "when human ambitions do not control the scene of investigation, Bacon explains, Nature takes the opportunity to speak unprompted." *Light Without Heat: The Observational Mood from Bacon to Milton* (Cornell University Press, 2018), 2.

made only of sweet-briar and honeysuckle, and some wild vine amongst; and the ground set with violets, strawberries, and primroses … And these to be in the heath, here and there, not in any order" (201). Whereas Markham counsels against "such store of naughtie weeds," Bacon's inclusion of humble indigenous species at the expense of more majestic examples makes the strawberry a key constituent of a divine English garden celebrating the low-growing, the vining, and the creeping.[23]

Over the course of *Henry V* Shakespeare's king sheds these lowly weeds as he moves to consolidate the British and French realms. By the end of the play Henry has transformed from an offshoot of rhizomatic flourishing to a representative of arboreal singularity – not a weed but a tree.[24] This metamorphosis changes the topography of his vegetable sovereignty from the untouched meadow to the engineered orchard, and makes pan-British identity grow out of a strong monarchical base. Nonetheless, the vegetative nature of the conversation between Hal and Falstaff in *1 Henry IV* underscores Bacon's contrast between the exceptionalism of the arboreal and the connective force of rhizomatic growth. Falstaff impersonates the king, referring to chamomile and blackberries – two common English plants often growing alongside strawberries – to complain about the prince's wildness. "The king" then qualifies, "and yet there is a virtuous man whom I have often noted in thy company" (2.4.431–433). This virtue is a type of flourishing that knits together what Bacon has separated: "If then the tree may be known by the fruit, as the fruit by the tree, then, peremptorily I speak it: there is virtue in that Falstaff" (2.4.441–444). Falstaff orients his fruition along the same axis as Hal's, and places them both within a form of vegetable life defined by continuum rather than division.

When Hal takes on his father's voice to accuse Falstaff of being a "trunk of humours" and "reverend vice," Falstaff protests that his seeming vices are human and thus innately virtuous:

> sweet Jack Falstaff, kind Jack Falstaff, true Jack
> Falstaff, valiant Jack Falstaff, and therefore more
> valiant being as he is old Jack Falstaff, banish not
> him thy Harry's company, banish not him thy
> Harry's company. Banish plump Jack, and banish
> all the world. (2.4.493–498)

---

[23] Markham, *The English Husbandman*, 21.
[24] Feerick discusses how at the conclusion of the play the "wild stock" of the king fails to graft with the French princess's "delicate scion" (*The Imperial Graft*, 221).

The virtues that Falstaff celebrates in himself are grounded in the over-
whelming fleshliness – the ability to embrace and enjoy the matter of
everyday life and its pleasures – that Hal has just despised. Falstaff defines
virtue according to the communitarian principles accommodating the
natural imperfections in human societies, in which viciousness inextricably immingles with virtuousness both in and among a community's
constituents. Hal fixates instead on the fictions of perfection through a
renunciation of earthly delights, choosing sublimated virtues that cut the
connections between the self and the world and justify Hal's rejection of
commonality to assume the kingship. Hal's virtue is a means to an end;
Falstaff's is a virtue without telos, a vegetative entelechy that refuses to
become distinct from its fundamental commonness.[25] Shakespeare places
the two ethical systems into conversation to find the evidence of eudaimonia in the natural world, where it flourishes in the interstices of collective existence – in the tangled, complicated relations of lifeforms who
together comprise a form of life.

[25] Holly Crocker, "Virtus Without Telos, Or The Ethics Of Vulnerability In Early Modern England,"
    Criticism 58. 2 (2016), 347–354.

CHAPTER 5

Ethos

Joseph Turner

According to Aristotle, virtue and the good life (*eudaimonia*) can only flourish under certain conditions. They require certain "goods" – family, friends, health, and an environment that supports excellence, through for example, education. The best that Priam of the *Iliad* can hope for, having been deprived of his family by war and of his vitality by age, is to suffer his misery with dignity (*NE* 1:9–10, 1099b–1100a.5).[1] Virtue is also conditioned by politics: a good monarch encourages virtue but a tyrant spreads vice like disease (*NE* 8:10, 1160b.1). Shakespeare's great pastoral romance *As You Like It* draws attention to the precarity of virtue through two central protagonists, Rosalind and Orlando. Virtue is scarce at the court of the "tyrant Duke" and in the household of Orlando's "tyrant brother," Oliver (1.2.247). As Le Beau says, the Duke has no grounds to hate Rosalind "but that the people praise her for her virtues / And pity her for her good father's sake" (1.2.268–270). The people also praise Orlando for being "gentle, strong and valiant," and those virtues arouse Oliver's jealousy and treachery. "Your virtues," Adam says to Orlando, warning him of Oliver's plan to commit fratricide, "are sanctified and holy traitors to you" (2.3.12–13). Virtue is often defined in contrast with vice, and the Duke's and Oliver's self-serving malice provide the context against which Rosalind and Orlando exhibit and develop virtue. Rosalind and Orlando flee tyranny and vice for Arden Forest, a space of reflection and learning, a space conducive to the cultivation of individual and communal virtue. There, in the forest, their excellences are developed in response to trauma and loss. Unlike Priam, who is defined by trauma, Rosalind and Orlando respond to changes in fortune with creativity and with reasoned shifts in perspective.

Arden Forest is a space of learning, and as Aristotle argues, all virtue is receptive to teaching. Although intellectual virtue might be more

---

[1] Aristotle. *Nicomachean Ethics*, trans. David Ross (Oxford University Press, 2009).

responsive to pedagogy, moral virtue (*ēthikē*), says Aristotle, "comes about as a result of habit," or what the Greeks called *ethos* (*NE* 2:1,1103a). Nature alone does not account for the virtues. Instead, "we are adapted by nature to receive them," and they "are made perfect by habit" (ibid.). Repeated performance of courage becomes a disposition or habit, gradually becoming part of one's character. Being courageous once is not evidence of possessing virtue, just as, after a cold winter, "one swallow does not make a summer, nor does one [warm] day" (*NE* 1:7, 1098a.20). Instead, like builders or musicians, students learn to exhibit excellence through repeated application, honing natural propensities into habits that allow for productive engagement with the world outside the classroom.

The educative tradition of rhetorical pedagogy that stretched from antique Rome to Tudor England sought to develop students' virtues in explicit ways. The English rhetorician Richard Rainolde intends for his *Foundacioun of Rhetorike* (1563) to "plante a worke profitable to all tymes, my countrie and common wealthe."[2] For "whoso is adorned with nobilitie and virtue will moue and allure [thee] to fauour and support virtue in any other." Rainolde echoes Aristotle's conviction that education amplifies human capacity, and that the benefits of individual growth contribute to communal flourishing. Teaching develops natural "potentiality" (*dynamis*), consolidated into habit (*ethos*) that serve students outside the classroom. One exercise known as *ethopoeia* (from *ethos* and *poeisis*, character-making) provided training in *ethos*, particularly habits of prosocial other-orientation or sympathy. *Ethopoeia* asked students to compose and perform monologues in the voices of others, including members of the opposite gender. Some exercises focused on mythological women who suffered intense trauma (Niobe lamenting the deaths of her fourteen children, for example). Success was judged by how fully students inhabited the character (*ethos*) of the subject. In the opening of *As You Like It*, Rosalind is not unlike a subject of *ethopoeia*, having been deprived of her family and subjected to unfair and arbitrary changes of fate. She then becomes like the author of *ethopoeia* who, by inhabiting the role of a male character, learns to sympathize with the emotions and outlooks of others.

Although sympathy is not necessarily a virtue for Aristotle, classical virtues such as courage and justice, when developed through *ethopoeia*,

---

[2] Richard Rainolde, *The Foundacion of Rhetorike*, ed. Francis R. Johnson (Scholars' Facsimiles & Reprints, 1945).

cultivate sympathy. Composing *ethopoeia* requires a sense of justice, what is deserved or undeserved, and it requires courage, both the courage to speak and the courage (even in the virtual space of the classroom) to confront that which limits the good life: the death of children, the loss of a romantic partner, the unfairness of the world. It also requires prudence, carefully matching language to character and to circumstance. These exercises taught students the skilled capacity to pity those whose life circumstances, like Priam's or Niobe's, render happiness impossible or difficult. The Roman rhetorician Quintilian suggests the value of such emotional identification in his teaching on *ethos* and *ethopoeia*: "Let us identify with the persons whose grievous, undeserved, and lamentable misfortunes we complain ... [not] as though it were someone else's, but take the pain of it on ourselves for the moment" (6.2.34–35).[3] In taking on that pain, students are encouraged to take seriously the emotional lives of those different from them and to consolidate that care into an other-oriented disposition.

Arden Forest, set apart from the Duke's treacherous court, is a space in which many characters grow their sympathetic and expressive potentialities. In contrast to the Duke's tyrannical regime, which is defined by anxiety and labor (or *negotium*), Arden is defined by what philosophers and rhetoricians such as Cicero call *otium*, leisure, or more precisely a release from labor that enables philosophical reflection and intellectual growth (although there is still hunting in this "harder" version of pastoral). Arden, in other words, looks much like a school (from the Greek *skholē*, or leisure). We today likely see school as a space of work, and indeed it is – and indeed it was for Shakespeare. But the type of "work" demanded by school is developmental, virtual, and designed to train students' virtues – virtues of expression, to be sure, but also intellectual and moral virtues understood as capacities for thought and action in the world. Thus Duke Senior comments that "these woods" are "free" in comparison with court, and that the wilds of Arden "feelingly persuade me what I am" (2.1.3–11). Released from the demands of public life, the Duke compacts persuasion (rhetoric) with self-discovery in the forest, applying the techniques of rhetorical persuasion inwardly toward the cultivation of the self. He expresses that self-discovery by expanding on the theme "Sweet are the uses of adversity," which recalls the sort of *sententiae* (or brief moral

---

[3] Quintilian, *The Orator's Education (Institutio Oratoria)*, ed. and trans. Donald A. Russell (Harvard University Press, 2001).

sayings) that grammar school students would use as the "starting point for a writing exercise" (Sillars 53).[4] Living in Arden, he reflects, one "Finds tongues in trees, books in the running brooks, / Sermons in stones, and good in everything." Arden is also the forest in which the young, uneducated Orlando posts novice poems to trees and in which Rosalind layers her teacherly persona atop of her persona of Ganymede. Here Rosalind (as Ganymede) and Celia (as Aliena) take on the kind of gender-bending performance typical of *ethopoeia*, a matter complicated by the status of boy actors playing women playing men on the Elizabethan stage. Within the mythological tradition, Ganymede is Jove's cupbearer and lover, and Renaissance audiences would recognize Ganymede from Christopher Marlowe's 1594 *Dido, Queen of Carthage*, a play indebted to the tradition of *ethopoeia* (van Winkle 42–43).[5] The etymology of *Aliena* – Latin for "stranger" – implies the kind of difference that students would perform in *ethopoeia*. *Ethopoeia*, according to Reinhard Lorich (1544), concerns *morum alienorum*, the habits of others (Lorich 179v).[6] Translations of the Greek rhetorician Aphthonius, such as Lorich's, went through 122 editions from 1500–1620, rivaling such staples as the *Shorte Introduction of Grammar* (Lily's Grammar) in the classrooms of Tudor England (Mack 29–31; Kraus 64).[7]

It is within Arden that Rosalind and Orlando learn lessons on *ethos*. Like virtue, *ethos* is concerned with stable, habitual character, and it is as a result most suitable for literary forms that rely on conventional character types, such as comedy. Quintilian maintains that *ethos* communicates *mores* (another term for character or disposition), especially *mores* that are consistent with expected social or generic conventions, such as the affection that parents show to children (6.2.14). Lorich repeats Quintilian's advice, noting that *ethopoeia* is particularly adept at communicating conventional traits, such as unrestricted fatherly love. *Ethopoeia*'s ability to communicate *ethos* or *mores* as the stable part of one's character makes it especially favorable to comedy: as Quintilian put it, "let me say that one [ethos] is nearer to comedy, and the other [pathos] to tragedy" (ibid., 6.2.20). He continues: "It is

---

[4] Stuart Sillars, "Style, Rhetoric and Identity in Shakespearean Soliloquy," in *Style in Theory: Between Literature and Philosophy*, eds. Ivan Callus, James Corby, and Gloria Lauri-Lucente (Bloomsbury, 2013), 49–70.

[5] Kathryn Rebecca Van Winkle, "'Then Speak, Aeneas, with Achilles' Tongue': *Ethopoeia* and Elizabethan Boyhood in Marlowe's *Dido Queen of Carthage*," *Theatre Symposium* 23 (2015), 42–51.

[6] Aphthonius, *Progymnasmata*, ed. and trans. Reinhard Lorich (London, 1583).

[7] Peter Mack, *A History of Renaissance Rhetoric 1380–1620* (Oxford University Press, 2013); Manfred Kraus, "Aphthonius and the Progymnasmata in Rhetorical Theory and Practice," in *Sizing up Rhetoric*, eds. David Zarefsky and Elizabeth Benacka (Waveland, 2008), 52–67.

quite right to use the word ethos of the sort of school exercises in which we often represent countrymen [*rusticos*], superstitious men, misers, and cowards" (ibid., 6.2.17) and further, that "it is proper that the student should be moved by his subject and imagine it to be real ... We play the part of an orphan, a shipwrecked man, or someone in jeopardy: what is the point of taking on these roles if we do not also assume emotions?" (ibid., 6.2.36), advice Lorich repeats in his treatment of ethopoeia (181–182).

Ethos is often contrasted with *pathos*: *Ethos* is the stable, habitual part of character whereas *pathos* consists in momentary bursts of emotion (*adfectus*) that are "out of character" for a speaker. As Quintilian says, "*ethos* is permanent, *pathos* temporary" (*Institutio oratoria* 6.2.8–10). Rhetoricians typically discuss *ethopoeia* according to *ethos* and *pathos*, organizing the exercise into the subdivisions of ethical, pathetic, and mixed forms. It frequently deals in character types, such as Niobe or Hercules, both of whom represent gendered expressions of powerful emotion. Lorich's first example of *ethopoeia* is Niobe, which he follows with other original examples in the voices of distressed mythological women and also male heroes such as Hercules. This educational tradition offers Hamlet these mythological figures as he attempts to navigate the intense emotion attendant to his mother's hasty marriage. He says that Gertrude:

> follow'd my poor father's body,
> Like Niobe, all tears...
> [and] married with my uncle,
> My father's brother, but no more like my father
> Than I to Hercules.   (1.2.149–150; 152–154)

In making sense of his own emotional turmoil, Hamlet turns to established types: Niobe as the image of the lamenting woman and Hercules as virile strength. In *As You Like It*, Jaques's education is the cause of Orlando's "sadness" in the play's opening, as his brother receives the "profit" of education while Orlando is kept "rustically at home" (1.1.5–7). In the tradition of *ethopoeia*, the play's other Jaques (or "Melancholy Jaques") defines "the scholar's melancholy, which is emulation" against other types, such as the musician or scholar, each of whom perform emotion differently (4.1.10–14). Jaques, as a scholar trained in *ethopoeia*, can successfully perform lament, discovering a new sense of self as he is "weeping" along with "the sobbing deer" (2.2.65–66). Jaques's emotional discovery compels him to speak "invectively" against the human "usurpers" and "tyrants" who hunt them (2.1.58–61). Invective is another classroom exercise (sometimes called *vituperatio*), and that exercise frequently has tyrannical rulers as the target of its censure (Nero is the example in Rainolde).

When Orlando introduces himself as someone uneducated, who has been kept "rustically at home," he establishes himself as a type – the *rustico* of the comedic tradition (1.1.6–7). Throughout *As You Like It*, Orlando succeeds at playing the part of uneducated, maladroit poet and lover who needs an able teacher. His status as *rustico* slides into the trope of the "man in love," as Rosalind calls it (3.2.356). This conventional type, as she explains, is defined by:

> A lean cheek ... a blue eye and sunken ... a beard neglected ... your hose should be ungartered, your bonnet unbuttoned, your shoe untied, and everything about you demonstrating a careless desolation. (3.2.359–367)

But Orlando is none of these things; he is instead a "point-device" to the contrary (3.2.368). He lacks the education to understand the typologies that Rosalind, as the daughter of a Duke, commands with ease. Rosalind, in response, attempts to educate Orlando in the type of imaginative emotional identification characteristic of *ethopoeia*. Although she says that she wishes to cure Orlando's love, she is, of course, attempting to do the exact opposite. To cure one of love – or, more true to Rosalind's intentions, to make Orlando care more about her – he should, as she says, "imagine me his love, his mistress." At that point, she would take on the *mores* of the "moonish youth" and "grieve, be effeminate, changeable ... for every passion something and for no passion truly anything, as boys and women are for the most part cattle of this colour" (3.2.391–397).

Most romances end with a marriage, but *As You Like It* terminates with four. This profusion of marriages – because "Hymen peoples every town" – is the fulfillment of multiple smaller romances, most of which are enabled by Rosalind's sympathetic stance toward others, including Sylvius, Phoebe, Touchstone, and Audrey, whose economic backgrounds differ from her own. Rosalind could have been satisfied with her marriage to Orlando, but Rosalind wishes to "help," "love," "satisfy," and "content" Phoebe, Silvius, and Orlando as well (5.2.106–112). Her desire to help others results from impersonating Ganymede, which teaches her to better understand Orlando's expressions of love and also the frustrations of being unable to reciprocate that love. Such keen self-reflection enables her to sympathize with Silvius and with Phoebe, both of whom experience similar frustrations. Deprived of the "goods" of family, friends, and love necessary to achieve the good life throughout the majority of the play, Rosalind responds with creativity, pretending to be someone else. Inhabiting a different persona allows her to understand the "pain" of others, shaping her sense of justice, her courage, and her prudence into something like sympathy. As a result, she desires to "make all this matter even ... make these doubts all even," carrying out a plan, made persuasive through courageous and prudent language, at securing a better future for those around her (5.4.18–25). The strongly Ovidian wedding is officiated by Hymen, the Greek god of marriage, who makes each of the couples into one ("Atone together"), equalizing each human character under the greater power of love. Rosalind's epilogue speech, in which she charges men and women to consider "the love [they] bear" toward each other as they judge the play and its characters, summarizes much of the play's attitude toward sympathy. There, Rosalind demonstrates how playing ethopoetic games enlarges appreciation for others: "If I were a woman," she says, she would appreciate the men of the audience differently. A similar consideration of the opposite sex, she implies, can enlarge the audience's perspective and understanding of the play and of each other.

The possibility of mass romance in *As You Like It* is enabled by Rosalind's sympathy, which she earns through playing ethopoetic games. Carefully considering the emotional constitution of others as a route to sympathy has strong lessons for contemporary liberal education. Although there is the risk of colonizing the emotions of others, a sensitive approach to classroom *ethopoeia* that asks students to write from the perspective of literary characters, and even to perform those compositions out loud, could encourage prosocial identification while also adding a kinetic spark to the classroom. Classical *ethopoeia* often enabled students to enter into mythic history, to add to established narratives or to weave together disparate sources in order to imagine fully the subject as a multifaceted character, giving dignity to the subject's expression of emotion. In that light, it functions as a tool for analysis, in which students explore the emotional reasons why a character acts in a certain way or in which students might imagine an alternate reaction. Students consider more deeply the emotional freight that constrains or enables the choices available to a given character, to take seriously the emotional dimensions of characterization. The great fourth-century Syrian rhetorician Libanius offers many sample *ethopoeiae*, which range from traumatic distress to the near mock-parodic quality of Jaques's sympathy with the weeping deer. Libanius offers:[8]

- What would Medea say when she is about to murder her children?
- What words would Achilles say over the dead Patroclus?
- What words would Ajax say after his madness?

---

[8] See Libanius, *Libanius's Progymnasmata: Model Exercises in Greek Prose Composition and Rhetoric*, ed. and trans. Craig A. Gibson (Society of Biblical Literature, 2008).

- What words would a painter say upon painting a picture of a girl and falling in love with her?
- What words would a coward say upon seeing that a picture of war has been painted in his house?
- What words would a prostitute say upon gaining self-control?

Each of these examples provides routes to understanding how intense shifts in fortune occasion emotion, which can often be destructive, and the expression of which often stands in stark contrast with the character's established *ethos* (Medea, Ajax). Such exercises also help students better understand such virtues as friendship (Achilles). They can also be more lighthearted, such as falling in love with one's own painting, or becoming frightened at depictions of violence. They might also be uplifting, as with Libanius's example of someone able to change successfully her life path. Each of these examples, however, should encourage students to identify *with* the subject, exercising the virtue of sympathy in attending to difference, courage in the ability to speak, and prudence in choosing the best language for the exercise. In those ways, education can prime our students for practicing sympathy in their lives.

CHAPTER 6

Hexis *(Habit)*

Kate Narveson

Having confronted his mother in her closet with the hideous "blister" of her sin, Hamlet offers moral instruction:

> Assume a virtue if you have it not.
> That monster, custom, who all sense doth eat
> Of habits evil, is angel yet in this,
> That to the use of actions fair and good
> He likewise gives a frock or livery,
> That aptly is put on. Refrain tonight,
> And that shall lend a kind of easiness
> To the next abstinence; the next more easy;
> For use almost can change the stamp of nature… (3.4.162–170)

This speech recommends repeated performance as the means to acquire a habit of virtue and thereby seems to reflect Aristotle's teaching in the *Nichomachean Ethics* that virtue is a *hexis*, a dependably stable habit or disposition that develops through practicing a good action.[1] Several terms in Hamlet's speech parallel Aristotle's discussion: the focus on "virtue," the power of "habit," "custom," and "use" to develop a "kind of easiness"; the idea that we have a "nature." Still, the formulations raise questions. Is virtue merely clothing, a "habit" or "livery" that marks service to one master rather than another, or does the livery indicate a proper fit, "aptly" put on? Is Hamlet calling for surface change or ethical development?[2] At the same time, the counsel points to religious stakes, siding with evil or angels. Hamlet's speech witnesses the way that Aristotelian ethical concepts such

---

[1] As Richard Kraut explains, "Aristotle describes ethical virtue as a *'hexis'* ('state' 'condition' 'disposition') – a tendency or disposition, induced by our habits, to have appropriate feelings"; see "Aristotle's Ethics," *Stanford Encyclopedia of Philosophy*, ed. Edward N. Zalta (Summer 2018 edn.), https://plato.stanford.edu/archives/sum2018/entries/aristotle-ethics/

[2] See J. K. Barret, "Habit," in *Entertaining the Idea: Shakespeare, Performance and Philosophy*, eds. James Kearney, Lowell Gallagher, and Julia Reinhard Lupton (University of Toronto Press, 2020), 29–42.

as "nature" and "habit" supplied terms used in spiritual guidance and took on new freight given Reformation revaluations of human effort. By 1600, devotional guides filled booksellers' stalls. They represent a central current of ethical discourse in the period, and the religious freight – the person's capacity to undertake self-discipline, the role of knowledge, will, and desire in virtuous acts, the relationship between inward disposition and outward appearance – put new pressure on Aristotelian ideas about the nature and role of *hexis*. Hamlet's speech illustrates a curious contradiction: Protestant clergy rejected Aristotle's teaching on habit because it made virtue the result of human effort and yet their recommendations for devotional practice called for the cultivation of dispositional habits in all but name.

The scene of Hamlet's counsel, a closet such as gentlewomen used for prayer, invites us to see Hamlet assuming the role of pastor to an afflicted soul. The scene accomplishes two ends: Gertrude learns of Claudius's crime and Hamlet's plans, and Hamlet convicts her of her own sin and sets her on a reformed path. Hamlet's agenda structures the scene, which follows the trajectory of pastoral intervention, first setting a mirror before the sinner and then helping her to a course of reformation. Hamlet's single-minded commitment to that task is evident from the outset, when he deflects his mother's assertion of authority ("Mother, you have my father much offended") and then barely misses a beat after killing Polonius before returning to that theme. Pastoral counsel, like therapy, requires participation in a shared discourse, and Hamlet's determination to make Gertrude confront her offense accords with the pastoral belief in a sinner's need to recognize their utter depravity so that they can feel true contrition and the change of heart needed to embrace a new life.[3]

In thinking about sin, Christian theology understood the power of custom in a specific way. A customary sin was not simply worse in degree but in kind because it warped the sinner's moral perceptions.[4] Hamlet figures custom as a monster that consumes "all sense ... Of habits evil." Yet Hamlet also calls on "use" to reshape disposition just as pastors prescribed devotional exercises to cultivate a godly disposition. This guidance, though,

---

[3] Peter Lake, *Hamlet's Choice* (Yale University Press, 2020), 98–109. Whether the sin Gertrude comes to see exists is another question. Kenneth Gross observes that she "seems to discover in herself exactly those 'black and grained spots' that Hamlet first tells her are there" (Kenenth Gross, *Shakespeare's Noise* [University of Chicago Press, 2001], 21).

[4] See Paul Cefalu's discussion of "consuetudines" or customary sin, in "'Damnéd Custom ... Habits Devil': Shakespeare's 'Hamlet,' Anti-Dualism, and the Early Modern Philosophy of Mind," *English Literary History* 67 (2000), 406–411.

would seem to involve a crippling theological contradiction. Early-modern Protestants taught that the human will was too debilitated to choose and sustain a right course of action. Given utter dependence on grace, how can a Protestant conception of virtue have anything in common with Aristotelian self-improvement? Paul Cefalu contends that "early modern theologians were often unable to incorporate a coherent theory of practical morality into their soteriological accounts of justification and sanctification."[5] William Perkins, one of the most influential Elizabethan religious thinkers, taught that the regenerate conscience enabled a Christian to "desire and approve the good," in a sense operating like a *hexis* or moral disposition. However, conscience for Perkins was the creation of the Holy Spirit, and Perkins focused on the obligation to fulfill the covenant with God rather than on an ethical commitment to virtue for its own sake. Another prominent pastor, Richard Sibbes, does use the term "habit" to describe the godly person's new disposition but asserts that the Holy Spirit creates those habits, which would be better called graces.[6] Such teachings seem to leave no room for habit as active disposition cultivated by the believer. How can "assum[ing] a virtue" till use makes it custom have any role in a Protestant economy of faith? Perhaps Hamlet's advice should be seen as straightforward Aristotelian ethics.[7]

Still, the theological force of "custom," the religious diction, and the shaping of the exchange as a scene of pastoral intervention indicate that we should look further at the relationship between virtue ethics and pastoral counsel. Religion involves far more than doctrinal teachings; we need to distinguish between a self-consistent theological ethics and an experientially effective religious morality. Beyond doctrinal instruction, pastors aimed to guide their charges in how to understand inward experience, discipline unruly affections, and cultivate godly motions. Devotional works were casuistical in the sense that they foregrounded the particular doctrinal teaching – in one case dependence on grace, in another godly effort – most helpful for the spiritual concern being addressed. Hamlet's advice does not align him with any particular position on the English Protestant spectrum of piety; it does draw on a shared spiritual repertoire.

---

[5] Paul Cefalu, *Moral Identity in Early Modern English Literature* (Cambridge University Press, 2004), 2–3.

[6] Ibid., 105–114.

[7] Joe Sachs takes the speech that way, as saying that behind a vicious habit lies repeated use, or "custom," that devours "all sense" of its evil, but "the use of actions fair and good" can stamp a new habit that makes space for virtue to develop (Joe Sacks, "Aristotle: Ethics," *Internet Encyclopedia of Philosophy*, https://iep.utm.edu/aris-eth/).

Indeed, recent historians argue that early-modern Protestant pastors were not seriously concerned about how the doctrine of grace alone could accommodate the call for energetic godliness. Rather, clergy were preoccupied with reform in institution, society, and individual, with the 1590s witnessing a rapid growth in devotional literature. Even for predestinarians, to credit grace is not to rule out human effort. As Leif Dixon notes, William Perkins stresses the "doctrine of means": "they whom God elected to this end, that they should inherit eternall life, were also elected to the subordinate meanes, whereby, as by steppes, they might attaine this ende."[8] Perkins argues from analogy: if a person were to assume that since God had ordained the time of their death, they had no need to eat, they would starve to death. God has prescribed food as a means to sustain the body and the person must eat. Likewise, God has ordained "ordinary means" of salvation through which the Spirit works, and the regenerate must "frame" their lives using those means. Protestants incorporated such exercises into their daily routine.

That such exercises could be empty was clear. They could be mere performance: Polonius calls for a "show of such an exercise" when he instructs Ophelia to walk with her devotional book as if at prayer. Polonius is quite conscious that he is staging a show: "We are too oft to blame in this/... that with devotion's visage/ and pious action we do sugar o'er/ the devil himself" (3.1.45–48). Polonius's sententious acknowledgement of the gap between appearance and reality lacerates Claudius's conscience, aware of the gap between his deed and his "most painted word" (3.1.52). Soon after, he engages in prayer that is not mere public show and yet is not genuine, since, he acknowledges, "My words fly up, my thoughts remain below." In asking whether one may "be pardon'd and retain the offense," the active verb represents sin as deliberate choice, falsifying the prayer. Yet the meditation could invite pity. By the end, he seems trapped: "Try what repentance can. What can it not?/ Yet what can it, when one can not repent?" (3.3.65–66). This image of a "limed soul" that sees its efforts as fruitless contrasts with the idea that devotion may bear fruit, the possibility

---

[8] Qtd in Leif Dixon, *Practical Predestinarians in England, 1590–1640* (Ashgate Publishing, 2014), 106. Dixon argues that "ministers sought not to inculcate anxiety about whether one was elect, but instead urged the assured saint to be anxious not to disappoint the God who had chosen them" (11). Lewis Bayly, in *The Practice of Piety* (London, 1613) stresses that God infallibly acts according to divine promises and has set up a kind of game plan for the godly to follow (29–30). Believers do not feel that they thereby gain salvation, simply that they are responsible for the moves assigned to them. This perspective does not solve the conundrums of salvation by grace alone but helps convey its experiential logic.

that Hamlet holds out in the scene that follows. The difference between Claudius's attempt at prayer and the prescribed effort to "assume a virtue" is slight but crucial. Though vulnerable to hypocritical abuse, and fruitless for those *incurvatus ad se*, devotional exercise was necessary.

The doctrine of sanctification explained the necessity. God's justifying grace caused a legal change of status, not wiping sin from the heart but imputing righteousness to the sinner, allowing the Christian to serve God in a new course of life. The way in which pastors represented this new godly life bears traces of Aristotelian virtue ethics, giving an English Calvinist inflection to the principle that that which distinguishes the human is reason, and the happy life is that lived in accordance with it. Bracketing for the moment the debates around the status of the will, pastors taught that only the Christian whose reason was freed from the distorting effects of sin could gain a true understanding of happiness, which rested in a life in accord with divine goodness. Further, just as Aristotle saw choice as "an ability that is on the borderline between the intellectual and passional," so that "[p]roper virtuous choice requires, if it is to be virtue, the combination of correct selection with correct passional response," so in Protestant devotion.[9] Since, in Perkins's words, the regenerate "have a power given them to move themselves," they "must be a voluntarie people, and with all alacritie and chearefulnesse, doe the duties that pertaine to them of a readie minde, even as if there were neither heaven nor hell."[10] Godly action is not undertaken with an eye to avoid hell, but from an "alacritie" to act in concert with God.

Protestant devotion also drew on virtue ethics for the concept of habit. True, the idea of human debility complicates things, seeming to undercut efforts to reform the self. Perversity persisted in the hearts of Christians, a notion that Hamlet uses to unsettle Ophelia when he warns that "virtue cannot so inoculate our old stock but we shall relish of it." Because of sin, if judged on our merit, "who should 'scape whipping?" How was productive effort possible, let alone pleasing to God? The answer lay in the same dual perspective reflected in pastoral casuistry. As Sibbes explained, God's spirit "works a habit in us, as we call it, it works somewhat in us to that which is good. And when that is wrought, the Spirit guides us to every particular action." True, Sibbes seems to dismiss Aristotelian *hexis*: "It was a proud term the philosophers had, as I said, sometimes they called

[9] Martha Nussbaum, *The Fragility of Goodness* (Cambridge University Press, 2001 [1986]), 307–308.
[10] Qtd. in Dixon, *Practical Predestinarians*, 114; 116.

their moral virtues habits." Yet Sibbes preserves two perspectives whereby
direct divine motions coexist with regular godly practices. He concludes
thus: "if we consider [godly dispositions] merely as they are in the person,
they are habits, but indeed they are graces … grace is a fitter word than
habit, because then we consider them as they come from God freely."[11] The
human habit takes second place to the work of the spirit, so that the disposition is more fitly called a grace, but the habit also has an experiential
reality for the believer. Similarly, Samuel Ward conceded that "to pray,
to meditate … is as easie to thee as to iron to swimme." However, he also
argues that faith "can naturalize these things unto thee, metamorphize
thee."[12] The believer aids this metamorphosis; devotional exercise develops the disposition created by faith. Paul Baynes encouraged his reader
to persevere in regular devotion, for the devout find "the Spirit of God
changing our hearts *thereby* from their daily course and custome more
and more, and bringing the heavenly life into more liking with us, and
making it more easie." The result of a "daily course and custom" will be
habituation. Robert Bolton declares that through devotion God's truth "is
habituated and incorporated into the conscience of God's child," while for
Paul Wentworth, "a continuall, and dayly practice" led "to the Acquisition
of the Habite of Well doing." Ward expressed this in his usual lively way:
"Vse limbes and haue limbes, the more thou doest, the more thou may-
est. … Vse will breed perfectnesse."[13] As Hamlet counsels, use can "almost
change the stamp of nature."

Yet the requirement that all good works must be the expression of faith
created new problems of self-knowledge and authenticity. What corre-
spondence was there between heart and deed? Could nature be re-stamped?
These questions haunt Hamlet's pastoral advice to Gertrude, with its ideas
about the effect of custom, nature, and ethical change through repeated
practice. Hamlet's central advice calls for Gertrude to make a particular
ethical choice repeatedly until it becomes easy to do so. This course might
seem concerned more with the action than the disposition. If she does
something because her pastor-son declares it to be right rather than because

---

[11] Richard Sibbes, *Commentary on 2 Corinthians* (John Rothwell, 1655), 297–299, based on sermons
preached in the 1620s.
[12] Samuel Ward, *Life of Faith* (Augustine Matthewes, 1621), 79.
[13] Paul Baynes, *Briefe Directions unto a Godly Life* (Nathanael Newberry, 1626), 238–239; Robert
Bolton, *A Discourse about the State of True Happinesse* (Edmund Weaver, 1611), 117; Paul Wentworth,
The Miscellanie (I. Harison, 1615), 94; Ward, *Life of Faith*, 42. "Practice" in these contexts, as in
Shakespeare's plays, most often means performance of a skill, not repeated efforts intended to
improve a skill or acquire a habit. However, as is clear from these instances, it could mean the latter.

she wants to, it is hard to see this as ethical advice. However, the virtue ethics that Protestant devotion inherited sees a close connection between behavior and disposition, and therefore offers a favorable construal of the role of habituation in shaping and supporting the virtuous disposition, which then served as the mainspring of choice.[14] John Preston titled his work *The Saints Daily Exercise* (1629), stressing the need for regularity (35).[15] Like Hamlet, he saw power in the very action to create and increase the desired disposition: "I say, the best way to prepare vs, is the very dutie it selfe; as all actions, of the same kinde, increase the habits, so prayer makes vs fit for prayer; and ... the way to grow in any grace is the exercise of that grace." If abstinence is initially hard, with use it will gain a kind of easiness. Hamlet's statement that use can *"almost* change the stamp of nature" if anything reflects the Augustinian inflection of Aristotle's discussion of nature and habit; grace renews the heart but does not completely change its fallen nature. Nonetheless, the renewed nature is authentic and to be exercised. The afterlife of the idea is evident in Nathan Alan Davis's recent play, *Nat Turner in Jerusalem*,[16] when Turner muses that "The form of faith at times can call the spirit." Saba Mahmood describes a modern parallel among Egyptian Muslim women. By restraining anger, refraining from evil sights, or being sad at someone else's sin, they aimed to shape their daily rounds to accord with God's will. One woman reported that "when you do things in a day for God, and avoid other things because of Him, it means you're thinking about Him, and therefore it becomes easy for you to strive for Him against yourself and your desires." The woman making this case "does not assume that the desire to pray is natural, but that it must be created through a set of disciplinary acts."[17]

Although university-trained pastors claimed to reject Aristotle's concept of habit, devotion nonetheless required an account of how human nature can change, and (due credit being given to the holy spirit) pastors regularly described that change by appealing to the effects of understanding, exercise, practice, custom, and use. Terms from the discourse of virtue ethics shaped their sense of the logic of dispositional change. Hamlet's advice to Gertrude to cultivate a new habit reflects how pastors drew on the discourse of virtue. At the same time, it is a mark of Hamlet's unsettled

---

[14] See Alec Ryrie, *Being Protestant in Reformation England* (Oxford University Press, 2013), 108–118.

[15] John Preston, *The Saints Daily Exercise: A Treatise Unfolding the Whole Dutie of Prayer* (London, 1629).

[16] Nathan Alan Davies, *Nat Turner in Jerusalem* (Samuel French, 2016).

[17] Saba Mahmood, *The Politics of Piety: The Islamic Revival and the Feminist Subject* (Princeton University Press, 2005), 126.

disposition that he often seems to be improvising the ethical response he gives. His intellectual variety allows him to inhabit various moral stances.[18] The "habit" he wears in the closet scene is the clerical gown of a spiritual physician. This figure is rare in Shakespeare's plays, as is the language that goes with it. Almost everywhere else that the term "habit" appears, it refers to clothing: a religious habit, livery, or other characteristic apparel. Habit as formation of character finds little representation on stage since drama offers action as the expression of character rather than showing the slow formation that will lead to action. The sixteen-year leap in *The Winter's Tale* allows a suggestion of such a process. At the end of Act 3, Paulina rejects the idea of penitence as instrumental performance; a "thousand knees, ten thousand years together, naked, fasting" would not "move the gods" to look upon Leontes. Yet sixteen years allows a reformation of disposition; Cleomenes counsels Leontes, "Sir, you have done enough, and have performed/ A saintlike sorrow" (5.1.1–2). *Hamlet* does not dramatize character in formation, yet its protagonist's preoccupation with custom, and with the continuum between disposition and seeming, allow us to listen in on someone thinking about what constitutes "nature," someone interrogating what the springs of action and change are. Hamlet does so in terms fully alive in the public discourse of late Elizabethan England, and the pastoral inflection he places on *hexis* gives us a vivid sense of how Shakespeare's plays register the ways that an inherited ethical idea can take on a fresh livery.

---

[18] Rhodri Lewis roots Hamlet's unstable adoption of moral personae in humanist ethical training, both committed to and uneasy about theatrical performance; see "Hamlet, Humanism, and Performing the Self," in *Hamlet and the Vision of Darkness* (Princeton University Press, 2017), 13–42.

CHAPTER 7

Stoicism

Donovan Sherman

"What is virtue?" asks Seneca, in his *Letters on Ethics,* before immediately answering: "True and unshakable judgment, for from this come the impulses of the mind; by this, every impression that stimulates impulse is perfectly clear."[1] Virtue, here, operates as medium and message, origin and destination. It creates "impulses of the mind" while also allowing for a way to evaluate those impulses. If I am an aspiring Stoic, the process goes something like this: an external event prompts an internal representation – an impression – which I then investigate. Does it result from my rational, and thus virtuous, capacity? If so, it is under my control. If not, it is outside of my control and therefore not worthy of my time. If I were to believe something outside of my control to be true, I would fall prey to the passions, those deceptive judgments that cloud my ability to reason. The judgment of virtue is thus a nearly circular process: it works as a kind of ethical audit to ensure that every action and thought arises from virtue itself.

The "impressions" of the mind noted by Seneca are not simply conceptual. They are physical, literally *impressed* upon our inner beings even if what they represent is intangible.[2] As described by Zeno, the ancient philosopher credited as one of the first Stoics by Diogenes Laertius in his *Lives of the Eminent Philosophers*, internal images are similar to an imprint in wax: "An impression is an imprint on the soul, its name appropriately borrowed from the imprints made in wax by a seal ring. Some impressions involve comprehension, others do not. The comprehending impression, which they say is the criterion of reality, is that which arises from an existing object and is imprinted and stamped in accordance with it."[3] Our souls register material manifestations of

---

[1] Seneca, *Letters on Ethics,* trans. Margaret Graver and A. A. Long (University of Chicago Press, 2015), 71.32.
[2] For more on the material conditions of impressions, see Margaret Graver, *Stoicism and Emotion* (University of Chicago Press, 2007), esp. 15–35.
[3] Diogenes Laertius, *Lives of the Eminent Philosophers,* ed. James Miller, trans. Pamela Mensch (Oxford University Press, 2018), 7.46.

external phenomena that could provide a "criterion of reality" by reflecting something true and extant, and as such involve comprehension. Alternately, our impressions could be false, unreal – they could be, for instance, propositions (things that do not yet exist but could) or fantasies (things that could not exist). The Stoic uses reason to sift through which is which. If they mistake something not real for reality, they suffer from madness.

The purely rational judgment Seneca identifies as the key characteristic of virtue is, as a result, both an ethical and aesthetic activity. In the process of exercising and attaining virtue, Stoic philosophers must be evaluators of mental pictures, audience members to an inward play of images. In this regard, Stoicism invites comparison to the theater, a place where an imitation of life parades before witnesses eager to contemplate and analyze it. In particular, *A Midsummer Night's Dream* – which is, as Hugh Grady puts it, "one of Shakespeare's fullest explorations of aesthetic ideas" and thus acts as "a meta-aesthetic drama"[4] – presents itself as a fertile resource for exploring the questions posed by Stoic virtue: Does my imagination accurately represent aspects of my life I have control over? Do my internal images coincide with reality? Like the Stoic's mind, the theater can enrapture us or even – to put it uncharitably – *fool* us into responding to rehearsed behavior as if it were real. The theater also lays bare, at times, our own responses: Why did that make me cry? Why did I laugh at that? And more profoundly: If something is clearly mimetic, representational, and not "real," then why do I entertain it at all?

These questions are central to Shakespeare's comedy. As a meditation on the integrity of artistic representation, *Midsummer* enacts scene after scene of characters wrestling with the nature of their internal and external realities. In addition, the play suggests a connection between the affective and psychological processes of apprehending the world, on the one hand, and the theater's process of artistic creation, on the other. As Theseus states in his speech in praise of "cool reason," at the outset of act five, "The lunatic, the lover, and the poet / Are of imagination all compact." Like the madman's hallucination of demons, or the lover's ability to deceive themselves through infatuation, the poet "gives to airy nothing / A local habitation and a name" (5.1.6–8; 16–17).[5] The Duke of Athens may seem to

---

[4] Hugh Grady, "Shakespeare and Impure Aesthetics: The Case of 'A Midsummer Night's Dream,'" *Shakespeare Quarterly* 59. 3 (Fall 2008), 278.

[5] *A Midsummer Night's Dream*, ed. Harold Brooks (Thomson Learning, 2007), 5.1.6–8, 16–17. For an account of how Theseus's speech catalogues an array of early-modern forms of imagination, see Adam Rzepka, "'How Easy Is a Bush Supposed a Bear?': Differentiating Imaginative Production in *A Midsummer Night's Dream*," *Shakespeare Quarterly* 66. 3 (2015), 308–328.

be an ideal Stoic in his valorization of reason's ability to dismiss the false impressions of the mind. Indeed, this was often the stock characterization of a Stoic figure in Shakespeare's day: an unfeeling rationalist who dismissed humanist ideals. And the play seems to offer a repudiation of this ethos in part by explicitly using Senecan drama as its source material, transposing – but not necessarily negating – the Stoic principles of the philosopher's tragic *Hippolytus* into a comedic key. But just as the play, by dint of its very existence, subverts Theseus's belief through a tacit defense of artistic creation, it similarly offers a reimagination of Stoicism as not simply an exercise in cool reason. By focusing on the process of evaluating the integrity of its own aesthetic elements, *Midsummer* shows that, even if one properly dismisses false impressions – if one correctly exercises Stoic virtue – those discarded impressions still possess a certain power over the beholder, a power that may be ineffable and insubstantial but that still affects subjective experience. Shakespeare demonstrates how one can in fact be both a Stoic and an artist or lover, and he does so not by rejecting Stoic virtue but by doing just the opposite: by mobilizing one of its highest ideals, mercy, in defense of its cast-off images.

What Is Stoic Virtue?

Before turning to *A Midsummer Night's Dream*, I would like to explore further the nature of Stoic virtue. It is difficult to arrive at a single definition in part because Stoicism resists clear identification as a unified philosophy. Pre-Socratic philosophers like Zeno attempted to create such a systemic approach, whereby they proposed a model that encompassed every aspect of life, including physics, ethics, and cosmology. But later figures like Seneca, Epictetus, and Marcus Aurelius abandoned a holistic vision and instead approached their philosophical work more idiosyncratically. Seneca wrote widely and addressed a vast array of topics, but he did not always endorse a view in line with classical Stoicism. Epictetus' *Discourses* and *Enchiridion* constitute assembled notes on his lectures by his pupil Arrian; their structure reflects the freewheeling and aphoristic style of live presentation. And Marcus' *Meditations* was written for an audience of one, Marcus himself. A set of daily prompts for spiritual reflection, this text does not attempt to provide other readers with an apparatus or throughline. Despite these disparities, some common features in all of these writings allow us to map out a vision of Stoic virtue.

Seneca's understanding of virtue as judgment accords with one of the more famous declarations of Stoic philosophy. Epictetus, in his

Enchiridion, or "Handbook," begins with the simple observation that "We are responsible for some things, while there are others for which we cannot be held responsible."[6] Determining what we can control and what we cannot provides the elemental activity through which the Stoic pupil can ensure a good life, one lived to its full capacity. Stoic virtue thus depends entirely on reason, the quality that distinguishes humans from animals and vegetation, and as a result Stoicism focuses on honing the ability to exercise this feature properly. One must learn how to operate from a place of reason when evaluating impressions, since from that act of proper judgment emerges a good life born of virtue, which, Epictetus asserts, "holds this promise – to secure happiness, impassivity, and a good flow of life," with this latter state comprising the ultimate aim: "What is the goal of virtue, after all, except a life that flows smoothly?"[7]

This ease of experience is frictionless, as the virtuous person demonstrates mastery over their capacity to determine what is and is not under their control. The roots of this condition lie in the early Stoics' belief that virtue allowed for the full realization of human potential, through the rational function, and as such allowed for the attainment of a perfect state. For Chrysippus – the most influential of the early Stoics, whose vision was the most comprehensive – virtue's perfection not only apotheosized the individual nature of the person working to attain it, but also produced a feeling of harmony with the universe. Diogenes describes this position by noting that "to live according to virtue is equivalent to living according to the experience of natural events" because "our natures are parts of the nature of the universe"; the pursuit of a life lived in accordance with nature creates the "smooth current of the happy life, when everything is done in light of the harmonious accord of each man's guardian spirit with the will of him who governs the universe."[8] The reason that characterizes a unique human quality, among mortals, is also that by which humans connect to the divine fabric of the universe. Virtue is thus "a harmonious disposition."[9]

Maintaining this disposition demands constant work. As Seneca pithily puts it, "Wisdom is a skill."[10] Diogenes, summarizing the views of Cleanthes and Chrysippus, notes that virtue "in a general sense is, for

---

[6] Epictetus, *Discourses and Selected Writings,* ed. and trans. Robert Dobbin (Penguin, 2008), 1.1.

[7] Ibid., 1.4.3, 5.

[8] Diogenes, *Lives,* 7.88.

[9] Ibid., 7.89.

[10] Seneca, *Letters,* 29.1.3.

every object, a certain perfection, like that of a statue," and for human beings it is no different.[11] Just like a flawlessly sculpted statue, the sagacious human has attained their absolute potential. In place of a chisel and other tools, the human has reason. But why must we work to attain that which we were born with? If reason, in other words, is a natural component of humans, then why are we not already sages when we are born? After all, the newborn child is frequently held up as having an ideal disposition that, if left unchecked, will become corrupted by experiences in the world. As Martha Nussbaum posits, for the Stoic, "We become, with time, less human; and we encounter one another from day to day under a form of life that shows us to one another as combatants in gladiatorial shows, as vicious monsters rather than gentle humans."[12] Seneca comically exploits this phenomenon when he bursts out, exasperatedly, that "Nature should register a complaint against us, saying, 'What's this? I brought you into the world with no desires, no fears, no superstitious credulity, no disloyalty, nor any of those other things that plague you. Just go out the way you came in!'"[13] The Stoic must recover the lost condition of youth but not, Seneca stresses, with the same unawareness that we had as babies. We must labor to regain it with a vigilant attention to our faculties. In pondering this dynamic, Seneca explains that "We are indeed born for this, but not born with it. Until you provide some education, even the best natures have only the raw material for virtue, not virtue itself."[14] The child is oriented toward perfection, but not aware that they are. We have to return to this state of youth as the goal of our quest for sagacious perfection, but we must do so with an awareness born from the rigorous practice of judgment.

Stoic education provides a path to this condition by training us to remain vigilant in maintaining the power that is inherent within us. Marcus Aurelius commands himself to uphold this disposition in one of his meditations: "Wipe out vain impressions," he exhorts, "by continually telling yourself, 'It now rests with me to make sure that no wickedness, or appetite, or disquiet should exist within this soul of mine; but rather, by looking to the true nature of all things, I should employ each of them according to its worth'. Be ever mindful of this power that nature has

[11] Diogenes, *Lives*, 7.90.
[12] Martha Nussbaum, *The Therapy of Desire: Theory and Practice in Hellenistic Ethics* (Princeton University Press, 1994), 422.
[13] Seneca, *Letters*, 22.15.
[14] Ibid., 90.46.

granted to you."[15] Like an ungrateful child, the typical human treasures externals and false impressions instead of looking inward and celebrating the quality given to all of us at our creation. And no wonder: The act of looking inward and realizing perfection through practicing proper judgment is, while natural, also difficult and tedious, like chipping away marble to make a statue.

In sum, Stoic virtue is the ability to live in accordance to nature – in the flow of life – as a result of fully realizing our capacity to reason, present since birth, now controlled through rigorous and constant work. Because this state is very hard to attain, the focus of Stoicism is on constant practice, or what Pierre Hadot calls a "way of life," a method of comporting oneself so as to remain focused on the constant present. In Stoicism, Hadot claims, "philosophizing was a continuous act, permanent and identical with life itself, which had to be renewed at each instant"; the act manifests itself as a form of *attention* on the mind – the very process of judgment named as Seneca as the key to virtue.[16] When we speak of Stoic virtue, then, we are speaking of a set of ideals but also, by association, of a manner by which we can live to try and attain those ideals through constant scrutiny of intentions and mental impressions.[17] Epictetus compares the philosopher to a seemingly humbler tradesperson: "A carpenter does not come up to you and say 'Listen to me discourse about the art of carpentry', but he makes a contract for a house and builds it."[18] Theory is always secondary to practice; Stoicism resides first and foremost as a form of experience. It is no wonder that Seneca was drawn to drama, not only as a representation of Stoic principles – or, more often than not, Stoic failure – but as an embodiment of Stoic work.

A Midsummer's Mercy

Shakespeare, like his peers, drew inspiration from Seneca's plays and philosophy. But often these two careers were separated. In the Renaissance, in fact, some believed Seneca the dramatist and Seneca the philosopher to

---

[15] Marcus Aurelius, *Meditations with Selected Correspondences,* trans. Robin Hard (Oxford University Press, 2011), 8.29.
[16] Pierre Hadot, *Philosophy as a Way of Life,* ed. Arnold Davidson, trans. Michael Chase (Blackwell, 1995), 268.
[17] For the near-impossible quality of ancient Stoic virtue, see Christoph Jedan, *Stoic Virtues: Chrysippus and the Religious Character of Stoic Ethics* (Continuum, 2009). Jedan admits that according to the criteria of Stoic virtue, "Perhaps no human being has ever been virtuous" (60).
[18] Quoted in Hadot, *Philosophy,* 267.

be two different people entirely.[19] We can, however, take *A Midsummer Night's Dream* as a test case to see how, in Stoicism, philosophy and performance intertwine. Dramaturgically, the play borrows from Seneca's play *Hippolytus*, specifically an English translation by John Studley published in Thomas Newton's 1581 collection *Seneca His Tenne Tragedies*.[20] Seneca's tragedy tells the story (familiar both to his audience and Shakespeare's) of the doomed relationship between Phaedra and her stepson, Hippolytus. For Seneca, this episode represents a cautionary tale of improperly following passions instead of reason. Phaedra gives in to her lust; Hippolytus believes he can escape by running away, and Theseus, Phaedra's husband, lashes out in fury. We can also think of the play as a Stoic exercise, one that allows for the audience to test their own sympathies and question the externalized images on stage as they would the inner impressions of their souls. For Epictetus, the tale of Phaedra supplies an exemplary case of mistaken impressions, a lesson that audiences learn through witnessing. He elaborates on this idea in an imagined dialogue:

> What is the *Atreus* of Euripides? An impression. The *Oedipus* of Sophocles? An impression. *Hippolytus?* An impression. What kind of person, then, pays no attention to the matter of impressions, do you think? Well, what do we call people who accept every one indiscriminately?
> 'Madmen.'[21]

To watch Agamemnon, Oedipus, Hippolytus, and Orestes is to see the cost of accepting every impression as true. And yet the plays themselves supply "impressions" for us to judge, in a gesture that doubles the characters' own exposure to false images. The implication is that, in watching a tragedy of incorrect attachment, we are given a chance that the protagonists lack. We can dismiss the impressions before us just as they fail to dismiss the impressions that doom them into madness.

Seneca's bloody and profound drama may seem like an unlikely source for Shakespeare's light comedy. But the connection is dramaturgically clear. *Midsummer* makes overt reference to the mythology in one of its characters: Theseus, the Duke of Athens, is the same Theseus who will go on to marry Phaedra; for now, he is engaged to Hippolytus's mother, Hippolyta. Seneca's work pervades in subtler ways, as well. The Minotaur, the half-bull, half-man monster that Theseus slayed in his youth, is

---

[19] See Colin Burrow, *Shakespeare and Classical Antiquity* (Oxford University Press, 2013), 166.
[20] Seneca, *Seneca His Tenne Tragedies*, trans. John Studley (Thomas Newton, 1581).
[21] Epictetus, *Discourses*, 1.28.30–33.

referenced frequently in *Hippolytus* as a symbol of irrational desire. But the Minotaur is comically invoked in *Midsummer* in the transformation of Bottom's head into a donkey's.[22] And as many scholars have noted, Shakespeare borrows directly from passages of Studley's translation. Helena confessing her obsession to Demetrius in the woods mirrors Phaedra's scene with Hippolytus, and Oberon's description of Cupid's arrow resembles a passage of Seneca's on the same subject. We can read this influence purely academically, as a historical curiosity, perhaps as an example of Shakespeare ironizing or satirizing ancient conventions. But this analysis would take Stoicism to be a static set of ideas rather than a way of life. The question becomes instead: Does *Midsummer* still *perform*, not just represent, Stoic virtue in its transposition of Seneca? After all, as Peter Holland reminds us, "sources" were not simply intellectual phenomena but existed in the live recognition of an audience witnessing the play's references: "Seeing Helena as a version of Phaedra or Demetrius as a version of Hippolytus is both to see the comedy of *A Midsummer Night's Dream* as a deliberate transformation of the tragedy of the *Hippolytus* and to see the transformation as one placed for observation by the audience."[23] Holland focuses on how the audience might recognize Seneca's play. Would they also recognize Seneca the philosopher?

At first blush, no. When characters use the language of Stoic virtue in *Midsummer*, it is almost always in a case of misjudgment or misplaced trust. When she abases herself before Demetrius – in one of the scenes borrowed directly from *Hippolytus* – Helena defends her decision to risk her virginity, threatened ominously by the "opportunity of night" that endangers her in the forest, by tethering her entire value system to the object of her obsession:

> Your virtue is my privilege: for that
> It is not night when I do see your face,
> Therefore I think I am not in the night;
> Nor doth this wood lack worlds of company,

---

[22] The Minotaur, according to Janice Valls-Russell, "confirms [Phaedra's] perception throughout the play of the Minotaur as the tangible, inescapable proof of the family curse hanging over her" ("'Even Seneca Hymselfe to Speke in Englysh': John Studley's Seneca," *Translation and Literature* 29 [2020], 36). According to myth, Phaedra's mother, Pasiphae, gave birth to the Minotaur after Poseidon cursed her and made her experience lust for a bull. For the Minotaur's transposition in *Midsummer*, see M. E. Lamb, "*A Midsummer Night's Dream*: The Myth of Theseus and the Minotaur," *Texas Studies in Literature and Language* 24. 4 (1979), 478–491.

[23] Peter Holland, "Theseus's Shadows in *A Midsummer Night's Dream*," *Shakespeare Survey* 47 (1994), 142.

> For you, in my respect, are all the world;
> then how can it be said I am alone,
> When all the world is here to look on me? (2.1.220–226)

The lines offer a symmetrical rejoinder to Demetrius's explanation of why she should return to Athens: it is not night (because Demetrius's beauty brightens her) and she is not alone (because he is the entire world to her). As with Phaedra, this is the height of mistaken judgment. Lysander, later, will swear allegiance to Helena while under the sway of love-in-idleness, the magical extract that causes love at first sight:

> Content with Hermia? No. I do repent
> The tedious minutes I with her have spent.
> Not Hermia, but Helena I love:
> Who will not change a raven for a dove?
> the will of man is by his reason sway'd,
> And reason says you are the worthier maid. (2.2.110–116)

These chiming couplets coopt a Stoic formula by claiming reason as the motivator for his change of will, as if he has come to his senses rather than had them clouded by magical means. The pattern established here is of Shakespeare apparently defanging Stoic virtue by appropriating its terminology in an absurd setting with lower stakes. Helena's love for Demetrius does not lead to his death; Lysander's clouded judgment is washed away; the residue of Cupid's arrow lingers only for Demetrius, and then apparently only for a seemingly reasonable end, his marriage to Helena.

But if the play removes the potential for tragedy, it does so not to undermine Stoic ideas but to dislodge the possibility of attaining perfection and instead linger in the practice of learning judgment – in the training of wisdom. Rather than invoke the forgone madness and violent calamity of its source, it retains the language of Stoic exercise: the judgment of impressions, the absurdity of attaching to external fictions, the recovery of natural capacity. Right from the beginning, the language Egeus uses to frame Hermia and Lysander's love draws from the materialist vocabulary of Stoicism. Pleading with Theseus for swift justice against his daughter, Egeus argues that Lysander has "by moonlight at her window sung / With faining voice verses of feigning love, / And stol'n th'impression of her fantasy / With bracelets of thy hair, rings, gauds, conceits" (1.1.30–33). Lysander has made an impression on her "fantasy," or imagination. Theseus, drawing on a similar metaphor as Zeno, materializes and literalizes the image of "impressions" when describing her debt to her father:

> Be advis'd, fair maid.
> To you your father should be as a god:
> One that compos'd your beauties, yea, and one
> To whom you are but as a form of wax
> By him imprinted, and within his power
> To leave the figure, or disfigure it.   (1.1.46–51)

Hermia, here, must choose between competing impressions: the one, by Lysander, dismissed by Egeus as "fantasy," and the other, by her father, described as shaping her essence. And when Helena, soon after, laments Demetrius's cold demeanor to her, she links love to a form of judgment inherent to children: "Love looks not with the eyes, but with the mind, \ And therefore is wing'd Cupid painted blind; \ Nor hath Love's mind of any judgement taste: \ Wings, and no eyes, figure unheedy haste. \ And therefore is Love said to be a child, \ Because in choice he is so oft beguil'd" (1.1.234–240). Helena's imagery is born of spite, but she inadvertently draws on the language of Stoic virtue. Love operates from a place of reason, not of the senses, and relies on the judgment of a child – for Helena, a form of discernment easily swayed by "choice," but for the Stoic, a divine ability, uncorrupted by experience, to demystify the inundation of impressions that face us in the world.

The play endorses Stoic principles in its theatricality as well as its text. The "Pyramus and Thisbe" production, by calling attention to its own staged presentation, underlines the folly of following the pull of imagination or desire. It does so by prompting reflection on the theatrical labor used to put on *A Midsummer Night's Dream* itself. The mechanicals fail to become their characters, instead farcically keeping their identities as actors stubbornly prevented from achieving mimesis. By foregrounding this failure, the play reminds us of the hopefully more successful efforts by the actors, technicians, and artistic staff responsible for sustaining the illusion of Shakespeare's drama. This reminder of theatricality serves to point out the absurdity of the passions that cloud the judgment of its characters. Hermia and Lysander may think fleeing to the forest can help, but they will remain on the same stage as before. Demetrius may think he falls in love with Helena, but "Helena" is a fiction, a character. These characters fruitlessly attach themselves to external subjects outside their control, and the play belies this futility by pointing out their actual absence. Hence the repeated invocation of the theater amounting to "nothing," first when Theseus's paean to reason notes the poet's capacity to alter "airy nothing" but more charitably soon after, when he praises the Athenian nobles for giving "thanks for nothing" by watching the mechanicals attempt to perform (5.1.89). The duke jokingly implores his fellow audience members to remain rational in their judgments of fictive impressions by acknowledging the lack of any material quiddity to what they witness. And, tellingly, he does so by recounting a time that "great clerks" who have attempted to give him "premeditated welcomes," but have instead stumbled and stuttered in fear, "shiver and look pale, / Make periods in the midst of sentences, / Throttle their practis'd accent in their fears, / And, in conclusion, dumbly broke off" (5.1.93–98). In their nervous, nonverbal gestures, Theseus was able to discern their intent with greater ability than had they succeeded in polished words. The "nothingness" of bodily action and affect, like the practice of wisdom, rejects stolid book-learning and intellect, and instead resides in habit and behavior.

Ultimately, however, despite these affirmations of Stoic ideas, Shakespeare places more value in the power of imaginative impressions than do the Stoic philosophers. *Midsummer* recognizes that, while rationality cuts through illusion, so too does illusion – the capricious and passionate impressions left on the soul, figured in the play by the magic of the fairies – have the power to alter favorably our fundamental selves. The genius of the play is to counter the Stoic valorization of reason by celebrating another Stoic ideal, clemency. It is clemency, or mercy, that Seneca celebrates in *De Clementia* as the highest demonstration of reason's capacity. As opposed to forgiveness, a lesser act, the exercise of clemency represents an attunement with nature, a sense of ultimate good, by exercising "freedom of judgment"; mercy

> makes its determinations not according to a set formula but according to what is fair and good; it is free to acquit, and to assess the value of a suit at the amount it wishes. It does all of these things, not as though it were doing less than what is just, but as though the determination it reaches is the most just.[24]

To be merciful is to recognize that punishment should be forgone because of a higher understanding of "what is fair and good" rather than an act of favorably sparing someone.

In Puck's final speech, we find this virtue mobilized to ask clemency for the mere "shadows" and nothings that judgment should discard:

---

[24] Seneca, "On Clemency," *Anger, Mercy, Revenge*, trans. Robert A. Kaster (University of Chicago Press, 2010), 2.7.3.

> If we shadows have offended,
> Think but this, and all is mended,
> That you have but slumber'd here
> While these visions did appear.
> And this weak and idle theme,
> No more yielding but a dream,
> Gentles, do not reprehend:
> If you pardon, we will mend.   (5.1.409–416)

His famous request for a pardon may seem to echo Seneca's notion of forgiveness, which focuses on weighing the harm of a particular transgression, rather than mercy, which calls for an attunement with a higher sense of justice. However, by suggesting that the play has been a dream, Puck avoids a punitive mode of mere forgiveness, in which he would confess to a trespass, and instead explains that the performance does not even qualify as real in the first place. Perceiving this distinction, between reality and dream, requires a mode of clemency that resembles Seneca's, wherein the viewer would need to recognize inherent and natural good, rather than punish established wrongdoing. Puck's call for mercy operates as a meditation akin to Marcus's, an invitation to think on what has transpired and find value in it by reflecting on the processes of judgment the play has incited. However, in this case, it is the impression itself that asks us to consider its effect on the soul: Puck *is* the vision whose status we are asked to judge. In giving poetic "nothing" a voice, the play allows for both Theseus's cool reason and the theater's imaginative power to coincide. The language shifts the responsibility of "mending" the vision from the audience ("all is mended") to the players ("we will mend"), a subtle acknowledgment of the theater's promise of reappearance: The actors may be shadows and visions, but they will try again. In this way the persistent illusion of the stage, while insisting on its own artificiality, also distinguishes itself from a thing indifferent or passionate pull of desire that must be cast away. Instead, it carries the potential to change its witnesses. The epilogue's repeated, future-looking invocation of "mending" also anticipates the final line's promise to "restore amends" (5.1.424), which in turn sonically recalls an "amen," a belated final sanctioning to the blessing just given by Oberon to the future Athenian children: an inclusion of the audience in a return to the natural virtue of birth.

CHAPTER 8

Skepticism

James Kuzner

Skepticism might be defined, to the extent that it might be defined at all, by its attention to how difficult, and sometimes impossible, it can be to find certain knowledge, whether when it comes to our sense perceptions or our sense of the good, our faith in physical laws or our convictions about the cosmos. Skepticism also attends to how such difficulty (or impossibility, as the case may be) does, could, or should affect life as it is lived. Given that, we might well wonder how skepticism, in Shakespeare or anyone else, can constitute virtue in the first place.

Maybe it can't. After all, the most influential account of Shakespeare's skepticism – Stanley Cavell's *Disowning Knowledge* – suggests just this.[1] For Cavell, Shakespeare's skeptics anticipate Descartes's meditator, incapacitated and overcome by doubt until he proves his, and God's, existence. Taking skepticism seriously, in Cavell's view, means doubting whatever cannot be known with total certainty – and that, for a time, includes the sheer existence of self and the world that could be an evil genius's illusion. Doubts overpower the skeptical self, who, as Descartes puts it, feels "suddenly thrown into deep water, being so disconcerted that I can neither plant my feet on the bottom nor swim on the surface."[2] In the Cavellian view, Shakespeare's skeptics – from Hamlet and Othello to Coriolanus and Lear – never quite plant their feet, reach the surface, or find God, unmoored by a tragic, all-encompassing skepticism that is nowhere near virtue.

But at least some of Shakespeare's skeptics, as Cavell admits, don't anticipate Descartes's meditator.[3] Montaigne's lower stakes doubt influenced

---

[1] Stanley Cavell, *Disowning Knowledge: In Six Plays of Shakespeare* (Cambridge University Press, 1987). For two other books that broadly resemble Cavell's, see Millicent Bell, *Shakespeare's Tragic Skepticism* (Yale University Press, 2002); and David Hillman, *Shakespeare's Entrails: Belief, Skepticism, and the Interior of the Body* (Palgrave Macmillan, 2007).

[2] René Descartes, *Meditations on First Philosophy*, trans. Laurence J. Lafleur (Macmillan, 1951), 23.

[3] See Cavell, *Disowning Knowledge*, 3. For a few book-length studies of Shakespeare and his relationship to skepticism in addition to those already mentioned, see John D. Cox, *Seeming Knowledge:*

Shakespeare, after all, and William Hamlin asserts rightly that early-modern skepticism "is less a school of thought than a temper of mind," a series of habits and tendencies that can assume many forms.[4] Hamlin emphasizes how Shakespeare lived in a time of "gradual fusion of common-sense skepticism with its philosophically grounded counterpart," a time when skepticism was as much about getting on in life as about sustained engagement with epistemological problems (70). Shakespeare's characters voice the tavern's everyday doubts – about miracles, say, or the folly of custom – as often as they experiment with facets of philosophical skepticism. In Hamlin's helpful outline, early-modern skeptical attitudes might include: a "sense of human weakness and mental frailty"; "an awareness of the blatant fact of conflicting judgements and appearances"; "an abiding fascination with the moment of *skepsis*, or judgemental suspension"; a sense of "the untrustworthiness of sense-data"; a distaste for "precipitous judgement, intellectual arrogance and credulity in various forms"; and a doubt about "criteria for judgment" (120–136). It's easy to see how adopting any of these attitudes could issue in virtue: how skepticism could lead to humility, tolerance, and open-mindedness. And this, of course, is to say nothing of the poetic powers that come from what John Keats, in praise of Shakespeare, once called "*Negative Capability*, that is when man is capable of being in uncertainties, mysteries, doubts, without any irritable reaching after fact and reason."[5] Though Keats intends such capability in a poetic sense, it, too, has been taken up as a political virtue.[6]

Shakespeare and Skeptical Faith (Baylor University Press, 2007); Lars Engle, *Shakespearean Pragmatism: Market of His Time* (University of Chicago Press, 1993); James Kuzner, *Shakespeare as a Way of Life: Skeptical Practice and the Politics of Weakness* (Fordham University Press, 2016); Richard McCoy, *Faith in Shakespeare* (Oxford University Press, 2013); Norman Rabkin, *Shakespeare and the Common Understanding* (Collier-Macmillan Limited, 1967); and Arthur Percival Rossiter, *Angel With Horns: Fifteen Lectures on Shakespeare* (Longman, 1989).

[4] William Hamlin, *Tragedy and Scepticism in Shakespeare's England* (Palgrave Macmillan, 2005), 5.

[5] *Selected Letters of John Keats*, ed. Grant F. Scott (Harvard University Press, 2002), 61. For a tremendously helpful account of the dimensions of negative capability, see Li Ou, *Keats and Negative Capability* (Continuum, 2009).

[6] For a book that gives negative capability an explicitly political valence, see Roberto Unger, *The Self Awakened: Pragmatism* (Harvard University Press, 2007), 135. For further elaboration, see Unger, *False Necessity: Anti-Necessitarian Social Theory in the Service of Radical Democracy*, new edition (Verso, 2001), 277–311. Keats shares with Coleridge, who claims that Shakespeare is myriad-minded, and with many critics to follow, who see that myriad-mindedness at play within the plays themselves. To cite just a few recent examples of this, see Jonathan Bate's *The Genius of Shakespeare* (Picador, 1997), where he claims that Shakespearean "truth is not singular," that his plays are like duck / rabbit images, except more complicated (324); Marjorie Garber's *Shakespeare After All* (Pantheon, 2004), where she contends that "Shakespeare always presents both his ideas and his character types contrapuntally" (7); and A. D. Nuttall's *Shakespeare the Thinker* (Yale University Press, 2007), where Nuttall asserts that "No sooner has one identified a philosophical 'position'" in Shakespeare "than one is forced, by the succeeding play, to modify or extend one's account" (24).

I want to draw particular attention to one strand of skepticism: that which we find in Sextus Empiricus, the pupil of Pyrrho for whom skepticism is a capacity that, properly practiced, issues in a certain virtue. For Pyrrhonists, skepticism's end is *ataraxia* (or unperturbedness), practically the opposite of the deep disquiet produced by the radical skepticism overcome in Descartes's *Meditations*. To live Pyrrhonism means adhering to skeptical precepts that derive from how unreliable sense perception is and how assailable given arguments are. Such precepts include (in the philosopher Pierre Hadot's concise summary) "'This is no better than that,' 'Perhaps,' 'All is indeterminate,' 'Everything escapes comprehension,' 'Every argument is opposed by an equal argument,' 'I suspend my judgment.'"[7] Adhering to these precepts fosters a tranquil kind of indifference that in turn fosters self-control, freedom from the false convictions that fetter people to false or vicious desires. Here I might consider an obvious example from a pivotal Shakespearean moment: what if Macbeth, for instance, were to truly balance Lady Macbeth's argument in favor of murdering Duncan with the argument that he makes in favor of sparing him? Might his desire for the throne have evaporated or lessened, at least a little? Probably not, to be honest. *Ataraxia* might well be out of Macbeth's reach, and he might, by constitution, be incapable of balancing arguments against each other, attaining a state of nonassertion, or establishing the kind of control that Sextus Empiricus believes is within any wise person's reach. Still, in a play like *Macbeth* – as in many others – Shakespeare prompts readers and audiences to wonder if they themselves might cultivate the balance that would keep them from wanting anything so much that they would wrong others in order to obtain it. An impressive, if perhaps passive and certainly limited, virtue comes from reaching so tranquil a state that I might manage not to exert myself either "to avoid anything or to seek after anything."[8]

For the remainder of this chapter, I want to explore one moment in Shakespeare – from *As You Like It* – in which Shakespeare might be said to play with Pyrrhonist principles: in which opposed positions seem to have lodged themselves within a character. What happens to philosophical, in this case Pyrrhonist, notions when they are not articulated by characters themselves and are instead embodied in performance?[9] What

---

[7] See *Sextus Empiricus: Selections from the Major Writings on Scepticism, Man, and God* (Hackett, 1985). For Hadot's summary, see Pierre Hadot, *What is Ancient Philosophy?* (Belknap Press, 2004), 145.

[8] *Sextus Empiricus*, 41.

[9] Approaching the "philosophy in / as literature" question in this way, I follow Donovan Sherman, *The Philosopher's Toothache: Embodied Stoicism in Early Modern English Drama* (Northwestern University Press, 2022).

happens when the character who embodies those notions not only does not articulate them, but is not a particularly philosophical character at all? Lastly, what happens to virtue when philosophical notions are not only performed but also transformed by the passions that Pyrrhonists would curb and without which Shakespeare's plays would be boring? Addressing these questions, I aim to think about the form that virtue can take when it arises not as a consequence of, but in the absence of, a coherent philosophy.

The moment that I have in mind takes place at the outset of *As You Like It*'s final scene. Orlando and Duke Senior are together in Arden, waiting for Rosalind, and discussing whether "Ganymede" (Rosalind's identity while dressed as a man) can deliver on his/her promises:

> DUKE: Dost thou believe, Orlando, that the boy
>   Can do all this that he hath promised?
> ORLANDO: I sometimes do believe, and sometime do not,
>   As those that fear they hope, and know they fear. (5.4.1–4)[10]

"The boy" has promised rather a lot. For a couple of acts, Ganymede has been trying (maybe) to cure Orlando of lovesickness, and eventually Orlando, who may or may not see through the disguise, tires of the pretenses that structure their sessions together.[11] At that point, Ganymede asks him to accept a final pretense:

> … Believe then, if you please, that I can do strange things: I have, since I was three year old, conversed with a magician, most profound in his art and yet not damnable. If you do love Rosalind so near the heart as your gesture cries it out, when your brother marries Aliena, shall you marry her. I know into what straits of fortune she is driven, and it is not impossible to me, if it appear not inconvenient to you, to set her before your eyes tomorrow, human as she is, and without danger. (5.2.49–65)

---

[10] All references are to *As You Like It*, ed. Frances E. Dolan (Penguin, 2000).

[11] There is considerable disagreement among critics as to whether Orlando sees through Rosalind's disguise. Marjorie Garber, for instance, argues that "Orlando … has his mind wholly on Rosalind, yet he does not see her as she stands before him." Thomas McFarland, broadly agreeing, writes that Shakespeare "grants the audience an insight immensely superior to that of Orlando, while equating his exaggerated love with his ignorance." But Harold Bloom writes that "[a]side from straining credulity, it would be an aesthetic loss if Orlando were not fully aware of the charm of his situation." See Marjorie Garber, "The Education of Orlando," eds. A. R. Braunmuller and James C. Bulman, *Comedy from Shakespeare to Sheridan: Change and Continuity in the English and European Dramatic Tradition* (Associated University Presses, 1986), 102–112, esp. 107; Thomas McFarland, "For Other Than for Dancing Measures: The Complications of *As You Like It*," *William Shakespeare's As You Like It*, ed. Harold Bloom (Chelsea House, 1988), 23–45, esp. 41; and Harold Bloom, *Shakespeare: The Invention of the Human* (Riverhead, 1998), 221.

Ganymede claims that he can do strange things; has conversed with a magician from the age of three; and is himself a magician. He offers to marry Rosalind to Orlando "if you please." The speech's wild claims, hedging and equivocation do not exactly inspire confidence. Yet here Orlando, with Duke Senior, sometimes believes that Ganymede can do what he says and sometimes doesn't. He's in a state, for once, of non-assertion, neither avoiding anything nor, in a strong sense, seeking anything. He's just here, waiting.

I don't know why Orlando sometimes does believe and sometimes doesn't. If he sees through Ganymede's disguise, maybe he sometimes believes that Rosalind really is finished teaching and toying with him. And maybe he sometimes believes that Rosalind is too invested in concealment and delay to ever really reveal herself. If Orlando doesn't see through Ganymede's disguise, maybe he sometimes believes in magic and sometimes does not.

Whatever his reasons for being in this state of judgmental suspension and nonassertion, though, Orlando himself is hardly a Pyrrhonist. It's not as though he believes, as a matter of principle, that for every argument – about whether he'll marry Rosalind, or anything else – there is an equal and opposing argument. Orlando has been a character of complete conviction, about how his brother Oliver has abused him, for instance, and about how Rosalind exhibits peerless beauty and virtue. A horrible poet, and hardly a philosopher at all, Orlando being of two remarkably nuanced minds, even for a moment, comes as quite a surprise. The play's philosophers, inasmuch as any exist, are the melancholy Jaques, who verges on nihilism when he famously reminds us that we all, in time, will be "Sans teeth, sans eyes, sans taste, sans everything," along, perhaps, with the optimistic and possibly Stoic Duke Senior, who "Finds tongues in trees, books in the running brooks, / Sermons in stones, and good in everything" (2.1.16–17). Orlando doesn't opine like this. Arguments for and against his believing that Rosalind will come to him, whatever those arguments are – *if* those arguments are – simply live in him.

Orlando also is hardly Pyrrhonist in that balancing positions grants nothing like *ataraxia*. The one thing that he claims to know, in this moment, is that he feels fear; his word order puts fear on either side of hope and knowledge, as though neither could save him from his anxieties, as though doubt turns the hopes that might decrease fear into yet one more source of worry. If Orlando embodies something like skepticism in this exchange, his affect seems between Pyrrhonist *ataraxia* and Cartesian despair. He remains in the state of frustration that precedes *ataraxia* in the

Pyrrhonist paradigm – what negative capability he has is definitely negative – but while he may not have found firm ground, he is not drowning
in doubt like Descartes's meditator.

   I might wonder how much skepticism accounts for the doubleness, the
looking two ways at once, that Orlando performs here. Maybe vexatious
love makes for the doubleness. After all, Orlando heartily agrees when
another character, Silvius, tells Rosalind what it is to love in his own series
of doubles:

> It is to be all made of sighs and tears…
> It is to be all made of faith and service…
> It is to be all made of fantasy,
> All made of passion, and all made of wishes,
> All adoration, duty, and observance,
> All humbleness, all patience, and impatience,
> All purity, all trial, all observance,
> And so am I for Phoebe.   (5.2.79–94)

For all his foolishness, Silvius may well speak something like the truth
about love in *As You Like It*. He describes loving as being "all made" of
things that are incompatible or at least in tension with each other. Those
made of sighs and tears do not, necessarily, seem those most likely to be
also all made of service, and those made all of fantasy don't seem likeliest
to be dutiful; if you're lost in fantasy, you might well forget your real-
world responsibilities. Maybe *As You Like It* suggests that to love – or
to love well and truly – is to vacillate between contradictory states and
beliefs and to try to strike a balance between them. Sometimes we're
sighing and crying; other times we're trying to practice faithful service.
Sometimes we're swept up in fantasy and other times we're all about
duty. Orlando agrees with Silvius and shows up at the end because he
himself has come to inhabit contradictory states: to not just be made of
sighs and tears, as he claims to be in his poems, but also to exhibit something like faith and service, to come every day to Ganymede. He has
become patient even in his impatience, as we see in his brief exchange
with Duke Senior. I thus might say that love also explains Orlando's
believing and not believing, his hope and his fear. Yet I would say that
love does so because love makes a skeptic of him, someone who looks
two ways at once in a way that brings a certain virtue: a willingness to
bear with Ganymede, to be open-minded, to turn up even when he has
no sense of how things will play out. His open-mindedness opens him to
a wide range of love's experience. There is generosity and even courage,
of a kind, in this openness.

Then again, neither Orlando nor Shakespeare exhibit *only* virtue. While Pyrrhonism *can* serve progressive purposes, Pyrrhonists also often advocate adherence to custom. Without compelling enough reasons to *not* obey the status quo, one just follows along.[12] Viewed a certain, way, this is what Orlando does; he follows along – as, in a sense, Shakespeare himself follows along to produce his heteronormative conclusion, abandoning the queer potential between Ganymede and Orlando for a far more conventional end.

Still, there is virtue in Orlando and Duke Senior's exchange, of a rather unconventional kind. I believe, as Pierre Macherey does, that "[l]iterature and philosophy are inextricably entwined" and that the two belong together.[13] But I also believe, with John Gibson, that we do well, some of the time, to "abandon what we might call the *philosophy-by-other means* view of literature."[14] Shakespeare is not, as Sidney says the poet is, "the right Popular Philosopher."[15] He is not "doing" philosophy by way of a play in *As You Like It*. Or, rather, if he is doing philosophy, he's not doing that and that only. He's also imagining how virtue could exist in characters without a philosophy and be performed in that philosophy's absence, as Orlando does as he waits with Duke Senior, embodying skeptical virtue without any discernible skeptical principle or real spiritual exercise. In saying this, I don't, exactly, mean to say that Orlando exhibits a native or natural virtue. I do, though, mean to say that not only virtue very expansively conceived, but even skeptical virtue pretty narrowly conceived, can come about *without* being disciplined, active, or even conscious. In Orlando there emerges, if only for a moment, a spontaneous yet virtuous skepticism, one that is as unpredictable as it is undisciplined.

---

[12] Such a criticism forms the principal argument of Christian Thorne's *The Dialectic of Counter-Enlightenment* (Harvard University Press, 2009).

[13] "Or at least they were," Macherey goes on, "until history established a sort of official division between the two." Pierre Macherey, *The Object of Literature*, trans. David Macey (Cambridge University Press, 1995), 3.

[14] John Gibson, "Literature and Knowledge," *The Oxford Handbook of Philosophy and Literature*, ed. Richard Eldridge (Oxford University Press, 2009), 467–485, esp. 469.

[15] Philip Sidney, *An Apologie for Poetrie*, ed. Evelyn Shuckburgh (Cambridge University Press, 1951), 19–20.

CHAPTER 9

Askesis *and Asceticism*

Jennifer R. Rust

Askesis derives from the Greek *askein*: to exercise. *Askesis* is not a virtue in itself, but a means to cultivate virtues, insofar as it is originally a set of exercises to train the mind and spirit. Pierre Hadot argues that *askesis* in its classical origins is the imaginative exercise of philosophical principles on an individual level: *Askesis* is philosophy as a "way of life."[1] Hadot insists that the philosophical *askesis* of pre-Christian antiquity, which focuses on "inner activities of the thought and the will," must be distinguished from modern and Christian conceptions of asceticism defined as "[c]omplete abstinence or restriction in the use of food, drink, sleep, dress, and property, and especially continence in sexual matters."[2] Even as Hadot attempts to distinguish between these categories, however, he anticipates their merging in early Christian asceticism. While this blending of *askesis* and asceticism is obviously prominent in monastic rules, it also contributes to the development of rules for married life in the early Church. Shakespeare's era is sometimes associated with the rise of companionate marriage, a purportedly new, deeper valuation of marriage as an affectionate and relatively equitable relationship, inspired by rising Protestantism's rejection of ascetic celibacy as a virtue. Some critics have discerned the impact of emergent ideals of companionate marriage in the shape of Shakespeare's comic plots, which often arc toward a mutually desired union between partners, worked out through a series of ingenious schemes and struggles. However, if the ideal of companionate marriage is informed by the pressure of the Reformation, it is also important to recognize that it remains embedded within an older tradition of the art of marriage – part of the *longue durée* of Christian asceticism – which initially establishes the virtues that should be nurtured within the bounds of everyday married life. These

---

[1] Pierre Hadot, *Philosophy as a Way of Life: Spiritual Exercises from Socrates to Foucault*, ed. Arnold I. Davidson, trans. Michael Chase (Blackwell, 1995).
[2] Ibid., 128.

virtues include chastity, fidelity, and amity between partners, virtues that are tested, complicated, and transformed in the imaginative literature of the early-modern period.

Early Christianity adapts philosophical *askesis* as spiritual exercise, developing techniques to cultivate introspective reflection on the self's relation to itself and to God, alongside an intensification of ascetic regimens focused on controlling bodily practices. Christian *askesis* becomes a *tekhnē* – an art – for living insofar as it shapes the individual's relationship to self and others in an interplay of agency and control, freedom and constraint. In the earliest orders, monastic practices absorb elements of pre-Christian spiritual exercises, which frame monastic life as a kind of *philosophia*.[3] This communal framework discourages more extreme forms of individualized asceticism by subordinating them to a higher "rule," while also refining the practice of bodily discipline that becomes intertwined with mental exercise in the early Christian era. While Christian asceticism is sharpened in the monastery, it also expands beyond it in discourses of pastoral care that address the laity. In the Christian legacy inherited by Shakespeare, the virtues cultivated by ascetic practice vary according to one's vocation: the ascetic monk aspires to the perfection of angelic life, while the peculiar asceticism of married life seeks salvation within the everyday.

As *askesis* involves controlling the desires and actions of the body, it is deeply tied to questions of sexual conduct, which accounts for the attention it receives in Michel Foucault's fourth volume of the *History of Sexuality, The Confessions of the Flesh*.[4] On one hand, Christian asceticism establishes two distinct sets of practices: according to the pastoral guidance of the early Church, the life of the celibate monk differs from the life of the married individual; they engage in distinct modes of conduct that enact distinct virtues. The art of marriage governs conduct in everyday life in the world; the art of celibacy flees from the world, striving for an angelic existence, but one that must be maintained by constant labor.[5] On the other hand, despite these differences, both the monk and the married person pursue variations on ascetic life. Early Christian pastoral works portray celibacy and marriage as two ways of managing the "economy of concupiscence" that afflicts life in a fallen world; this management occurs either through total abstinence for those who have taken religious vows

---

[3] Ibid., 129.

[4] Michel Foucault, *Histoire de la sexualité 4: Les aveux de la chair*, ed. Frederic Gros (Gallimard, 2018).

[5] Ibid., 252; 259.

or through obligatory sexual relations between spouses.[6] Figures such as Augustine "favored the development of a pastoral which had the objective of adjusting certain ascetic values of monastic existence to life in the world."[7] Ascetic practices – whether tailored to monastic or to married life, including confession and abstinence or circumscribed sexuality within marriage – should cultivate virtues that govern the body and soul in this life in ways that will lead individuals toward salvation in the next life. They also lay the groundwork for legal constructions of married subjects and marital relations that negotiate tensions between freedom and constraint bequeathed by the tradition of Christian asceticism.

These forms of ascetic virtue undergo further transformation in the sixteenth century, an era of religious turmoil in which established forms of ascetic experience were questioned, intensified and transformed. We can see this process of transformation and intensification at work in two prominent early-modern literary texts: Thomas More's *Utopia* (1516) and William Shakespeare's *The Winter's Tale* (1610). More (1478–1535) maps an ideal society in the "New World" in *Utopia* that strives to restructure social life along ascetic lines drawn from monasticism. However, More's text also maintains within this ascetic structure the institution of marriage and the patriarchal family as a fundamental social and political unit. The legacy of the Christian reconfiguration of asceticism into an art of living as either celibate or married is a source of tension in the scheme of this purportedly ideal communitarian society. *Utopia* offers a bird's-eye view of these tensions in a fictional travel narrative of a nominally pagan commonwealth.

More's *Utopia* anticipates the Reformation and Counter-Reformation recalibration of *askesis* as it pressures the classical-Christian synthesis inherent in monasticism and marriage in new ways. As critics of *Utopia* have long observed, More's fiction imaginatively expands the model of Christian ascetic monasticism to a whole social body and anticipates "the urge to transform monastic virtues into virtues appropriate to the lay state" visible in both Calvin's theocratic Geneva and the missionary ethos of the Society of Jesus.[8] More's *Utopia* advances several motifs of Christian asceticism, although the society it imagines is ostensibly not Christian. Like the pastoral manuals and tracts of the Church fathers, *Utopia* devotes a good deal of attention to the management of sexual

[6] Ibid., 273–274.
[7] Ibid., 251. My translation.
[8] D. B. Fenlon, "England and Europe: *Utopia* and Its Aftermath," *Transactions of the Royal Historical Society* 25 (1975), 131.

life. However, the binary categories of the longer Christian tradition are attenuated in More's fictional commonwealth, as codes of married conduct are framed within a larger social context that borrows elements of monastic asceticism. Clothing is severely restricted, and the Utopians' uniform style of dress almost explicitly invokes the habits of monastic orders: their ubiquitous cloaks are all "of the same color, which is that of natural wool."[9] The principle of common property in Utopia also strongly mirrors Christian monastic practices, and indeed is cited as a reason for Utopians' openness to Christian conversion: Utopian converts are "influenced by the fact that Christ approved of his followers' communal way of life, and that among the truest groups of Christians the practice still prevails" (271).

This larger framework of the ascetic commonwealth is tempered by a quasi-Epicurean fusion of *virtute ac voluptate* – virtue and pleasure (178). For the Utopians, "nature herself prescribes ... a joyous life, in other words, pleasure, as the goal of all our actions, and living according to her rules is to be defined as virtue" (165). The rule of nature underwrites the identification of pleasure and virtue for the Utopians. Thus, food as an element of health, a basic level of virtuous pleasure, is not subject to ascetic restrictions: "How wretched life would be if the daily diseases of hunger and thirst had to be overcome by bitter potions and drugs, like some other diseases that afflict us less often!" (177). Following this logic, extreme asceticism is actually discouraged, unless it is dedicated to the "common good" (179). This position appears resolutely pagan, resonant with both Stoic and Epicurean ideals for life in this world in different ways, but without necessary reference to salvation in the next world.[10] However, the dominance of the concept of virtuous pleasure defined by nature in this life is challenged by the virtual presence of crypto-Christian asceticism in the sect of the Buthrescas ("the religious"), "celibates" and vegetarians who "look forward only to the joys of the life to come" (229). The Buthrescas might seem to be a contradiction of Utopian Epicureanism, but they might also be understood as simply intensifying an asceticism already integrated into the Utopian commonwealth.[11] But there is a tension between the virtues fostered by these quasi-monastic social practices and those associated with

---

[9] Thomas More, *Utopia: Latin Text and English Translation*, eds. George M. Logan, Robert Adams, and Clarence Miller (Cambridge University Press, 1995), 133.

[10] Ibid., 165 n. 67.

[11] On the Buthrescas as a "crack in the Utopian logic" of Epicureanism, see Stephen Greenblatt, "Utopian Pleasure," in *Cultural Reformations: Medieval and Renaissance in Literary History*, eds. Brian Cummings and James Simpson (Oxford University Press, 2010), 312–313.

the practice of marriage, which becomes evident in More's account of Utopian marriage rituals.

The quasi-monastic organization and communitarian aspirations of Utopia appear to be contradicted by the custom of marriage, as illustrated in a notorious passage recounting the display of potential marriage partners:

> In choosing marriage partners they solemnly and seriously follow a custom which seemed to us foolish and absurd in the extreme. The woman is shown naked to the suitor by a responsible and respectable matron; and similarly, some honorable man presents the suitor naked to the woman ... when men go to buy a colt, where they are risking only a little money, they are so cautious that, though the animal is almost bare, they won't close the deal until saddle and blanket have been taken off, lest there be a hidden sore underneath. Yet in the choice of a mate, which may cause either delight or disgust for the rest of their lives, men are so careless that they leave all the rest of the woman's body covered up with clothes and estimate her attractiveness from a mere handsbreadth of her person, the face, which is all they can see. And so they marry, running great risk of bitter discord, if something in either's person should offend the other. (189–191)

This account compares marriage to horse-trading, a blunt transaction. There is a submerged health concern provided as a warrant for the ritual in the possible allusion to syphilis – the "hidden sore" – but this is treated as a potential deal breaker more than a public health problem. This passage seems to contradict the communitarian or so-called communist spirit of Utopia in general, and its larger principle of pastoral care. Marriage appears to be a matter of buying and selling for individual gratification, at least at first glance. This custom causes a potential disequilibrium between the individual and the commonwealth to appear: the Utopians seem to treat marriage first of all as a matter for individual gratification, even if its wider social merits are noted elsewhere. The ritual appears progressive insofar as it establishes an equality or reciprocity between the genders, although the male perspective is dominant in the narration. This reciprocity also enhances the transactional market-oriented nature of the ritual. This marriage market contrasts with the communal marketplaces of Utopia insofar as it stresses individualized pleasures, albeit within a constrained framework of monogamous marriage akin to that advocated in the Church fathers' pastoral manuals. (Divorce is allowed but made difficult "because they know that conjugal life will hardly be strengthened if each partner has in mind that a new marriage is easily available" [191]). The Utopian insistence on monogamy heightens the stakes of the marriage match. The ascetic restriction of sexuality thus actually intensifies the counter-ascetic emphasis on sexual gratification in marriage. This paradox highlights an underlying struggle between individual desire and communal asceticism within the hybrid structure of this ideal society. But from the perspective of the governing philosophy of Utopia, in which virtue is identified with natural pleasure, this paradox may be justified: the seemingly most "absurd" custom is the precondition for a pleasurably virtuous marriage, which contributes to the common good as much as individual well-being.

Shakespeare's comedies and romances, first performed nearly a century later, foreground the element of individual desire in dramatically staged conflicts; however, these conflictual desires are still structured by the legacies of married and monastic asceticism developed within the Church. These tensions are particularly sharp in Shakespeare's late romance *The Winter's Tale*, which centers on an extreme breakdown in marital relations in which the virtues cultivated by the arts of marriage are severely tested. Leontes shatters the virtue of amity as he accuses his wife of a lack of spousal virtues such as chastity and fidelity. In doing so, he reveals a fault line in marriage as an ascetic mode of life: The tension between marriage as a legal code and contract and marriage as a sacrament and relationship of fidelity, as established by Augustine and others. In *The Winter's Tale*, these contradictions emerge in the central trial scene, which portrays a drastic crisis in married life: a violently exaggerated legalism that abruptly reverses into an equally extreme version of ascetic penance. Indeed, in some sense, the art of marriage is cast into a profound crisis from which it never fully recovers, despite the artfully crafted reconciliation of the ending. If marriage itself disintegrates as a way of ordering life in the play, at least for Leontes, a quasi-monastic art of penance replaces it, although this new ascetic life also has its own excesses.

Leontes's antagonism toward his wife Hermione violates the expectation of amity and sympathy between spouses, virtues that the art of marriage should foster; this rupture also reveals how embodied differences between the sexes can distort ascetic rules within marriage. When Leontes first publicly accuses Hermione of incontinence, he draws attention to her heavily pregnant body, seemingly as proof that his charges are warranted: "let her sport herself / With that she's big with, for 'tis Polixenes / Has made thee swell thus" (2.1.61–63). To Leontes's jealous imagination, Hermione's engorged body, "swollen" out of normal proportion, signifies her inability to regulate her conduct within the normal rules of marriage. In response to this perception of Hermione's bodily excess, Leontes marshals another form of excess, weaponizing the law against her. Leontes's delusion amplifies the legalistic character of the art of marriage, pushing it to a hyperbolic extreme. Leontes abuses the authority of the law to make his fantasies into reality. "Your actions are my dreams" (3.2.80), he tells Hermione, defying her rejection of his accusations of adultery and treason. To confirm the substance of these "dreams" he calls upon the authority of "our justice" (3.2.88) which he promises will deal torture and death. In the trial, private sexual conduct is luridly projected by Leontes and made the object of a public spectacle, ostensibly to discover a truth, but actually to confirm a tyrannical phantasm, as Hermione is "on every post / Proclaimed a strumpet" (3.2.99–100).

In resisting the accusations against her, Hermione affirms the virtues of her married conduct. She reminds Leontes: "You, my lord best know, / Who least will seem to do so, my past life / Hath been as continent, as chaste, as true, / As I am now unhappy" (3.2.30–34). Furthermore, she attempts to turn Leontes's earlier disdain for her pregnant body against him, as she accuses him of disrespecting norms for the care of women who have recently given birth: in rushing her to trial, Leontes ignores the "child-bed privilege … which 'longs / To women of all fashion" (3.2.101–102). Hermione confronts Leontes's brutal legalism with assertions of sacramental fidelity, foregrounding the ascetic virtues of continence and chastity. She also highlights how Leontes abuses her in specifically gendered ways, by denying her rights as a newly delivered mother, a claim that implies that marital rules of conduct should also account for sexual difference between partners. Leontes willfully misrecognizes her virtues and her bodily condition, Hermione claims; as a result, he is no longer able to exist in relation to her as a person, only to his "dream" of her ("My life stands in the level of your dreams" [3.2.78]). The play's portrayal of a total breakdown in marital relations obliquely affirms certain virtues nurtured by the art of marriage: a legalism not moderated by spousal amity is shown to be disastrous.

In the reversal (*peripeteia*) of the scene at the oracle's vindication of Hermione's fidelity and her subsequent "death" (and the death of the heir Mamillius), another form of ascetic life comes to the fore: Leontes transforms into a penitent and looks forward to a monastic life of penance.[12] Leontes is cast into an equally hyperbolic ascetic existence as Paulina – a lady of the court who is Hermione's companion and avid defender – assumes

---

[12] On connections between monastic asceticism and penance, see Michel Foucault, *On the Government of the Living: Lectures at the Collège de France, 1979–1980*, ed. Michel Senellart, trans. Graham Burchell (Palgrave Macmillan, 2014), 260.

the role of pastoral director with a violence nearly as stringent as Leontes's just-dissolved tyranny. Paulina paradoxically demands and withholds the possibility of penance for his abuse of the arts of married life, particularly the drastic literalization of its juridical dimension in Hermione's trial. The juxtaposition of hyperbolic performances of married and monastic asceticism demonstrates how deeply these arts of Christian conduct structured affective experience and the articulation of virtues, virtues which are made even more visible as they are transgressed.

Ultimately, Paulina represents a more positive synthesis of ascetic virtues, as she directs Leontes from tyranny to ascetic repentance and reconciliation; however, her initial intervention is harsh in its judgment, even as it lays out the path toward his redemption. Paulina prescribes a hyperbolic ascetic remedy after Leontes's delusions about his wife's fidelity are broken by the oracle which announces her innocence. Upon announcing that Hermione is dead, Paulina lashes out at Leontes:

> O thou tyrant,
> Do not repent these things, for they are heavier
> Than all thy woes can stir. Therefore betake thee
> To nothing but despair. A thousand knees,
> Ten thousand years together, naked, fasting
> Upon a barren mountain and still winter
> In storm perpetual, could not move the gods
> To look that way thou wert. (3.2.204–211)

Paulina prescribes extreme penance, but through a series of negations that imaginatively leave Leontes mired in the sin of "despair." At the same time that Paulina urges penitential actions, she also claims that even these actions cannot repair the breach of Leontes's conduct: the "gods" will be indifferent to his appeals. There is perhaps a hint of the Protestant critique of works as a means of salvation in Paulina's attack. Yet countering this potential devaluation of ascetic penance, Paulina's efforts to proclaim what Leontes cannot do ("Do not repent") and to present vivid images of exaggerated penitential acts actually appear to magnify the power of these ascetic practices. Furthermore, the extremity of both Paulina's ascetic prescription and her negation of it is immediately challenged and tempered. Although Leontes states that he has "deserved" her rebuke, another lord reproaches Paulina: "You have made fault / I'th' boldness of your speech" (3.2.213–214), which immediately leads her to "repent" (3.2.217) herself and recalibrate her actions as Leontes's ad hoc spiritual director. The scene thus stages a cascade of repentance in which the major players must turn back, reflect upon themselves and adjust their actions, further signaling that the play has now shifted to the script of quasi-monastic penance.

Ultimately, the arc of the scene moves toward establishing a more moderate version of ascetic penance, which is enacted by the remorseful sovereign now exiled from marriage. In the wake of Paulina's attempt at reconciliation, Leontes prescribes an ascetic regimen for himself:

> Once a day I'll visit
> The chapel where they lie, and tears shed there
> Shall be my recreation. So long as nature
> Will bear up with this exercise, so long
> I daily vow to use it. Come, and lead me
> To these sorrows.   (3.2.235–240)

Leontes announces that he will retire to the "chapel" where his wife and son are buried to engage in acts of "recreation" or re-creation of himself. He invokes the counter-Reformation devotional motif of "tears" of repentance to define the "exercise" that he will undertake there. But this exercise also links back to the monastic asceticism formulated in the early Church, a link underscored by Leontes's "daily vow to use" such practices. Leontes swears that he will profoundly reconstruct his relation to himself and his body ("nature") through this repetitive "exercise." As the art of marriage collapses for him, Leontes envisions a new art of living according to perpetual penance; both arts are indebted in different ways to the longer tradition of Christian asceticism as a means of cultivating lived virtues.

The dramatic reversals of the trial scene are ameliorated by the digressions of the romance plot in the second half of the play; the revival of an art of marriage is hinted at but never definitively settled, even amidst the final reunion of Leontes and Hermione. In the latter part of the play, the plot shifts to a pastoral world that, among other things, might be a subtle allegorical recasting of the pastoral concerns of the first half of the play, to the extent that the shepherds and sheep of the literary pastoral also evoke their fellows in the ecclesiastical "pastoral." We might see this kind of interplay in the moment where the "Shepherd" looking for his lost sheep instead finds the infant Perdita and devotes himself to her continual care (3.3). But the earlier problem of marriage only fully recurs in the final moments of the play, in the sequence of Hermione's resurrection as a statue and then a living being: "life as lively mocked as ever / Still sleep mocked death" (5.3.19–20). In this sequence, the art of marriage is potentially renewed by a reality that presents itself as art in an aesthetic sense, in the form of Hermione's doubled resurrection as a statue and a woman. Leontes registers this potential in his response to Hermione's revival: "If this be magic, let it be an art / Lawful as eating" (5.1.110–111). The "art" which has brought Hermione back to life also reconfigures the "law"; inverting his previous legalistic tyranny, Leontes imagines a "law" that permits, rather than forbids and punishes. This is also a "law" that defies ascetic rigor by freeing the body to indulge in its natural functions ("eating"). This moment recalls the Utopian association of virtue, nature, and pleasure, a framework that honors the bodily pleasure of food and drink. Leontes offers a glimpse of the utopic ways that "art" recreating nature might also recalibrate the more practical arts that inculcate virtue within everyday life, including the arts of marriage. But any prospective reconfiguration of the art of marriage itself is deferred and left uncertain by the ending of the play, as the reawakened Hermione directs her discourse not to her reconciled husband, but to her recovered daughter Perdita, affirming that she has "preserved" herself only "to see the issue," her child's return (5.1.127–128). Her response to the husband that separated them in the first place is left implicit, open to interpretation by performers and audiences.

The open-ended structure of this final exchange – and of the romance genre at large – leaves the fate of marriage as an art of ascetic virtue unresolved. But as both *Utopia* and *The Winter's Tale* demonstrate, the arts of celibate and married life originally fostered within the Church provide rich material for early-modern artistic efforts to reimagine, whether in drama, poetry, or prose, the self in relation to itself and others. Both works emphasize the political stakes of marriage in a larger context: utopic commonwealth or dystopic tyranny. Marital virtues meld into civic virtues, as marital asceticism integrates into larger structures of citizenship and sovereignty. In *Utopia*, married couples are essential citizens of an ascetic commonwealth, but also potentially at odds with its communal virtues. In *The Winter's Tale*, the married couple is sovereign but fractured, suggesting a larger disorder in the body politic that can only be cured by a turn to the more radical asceticism of penance. As interfaces between the spiritual and the bodily, ascetic practices mediate between self and society and provide occasions for inquiries into the best ways to cultivate a virtuous life that extend beyond the household (*oikos*) or the cloister to the wider world of public and political action.

CHAPTER 10

Shakespeare's Moral Compass

Neema Parvini

In 2018, I published a book called *Shakespeare's Moral Compass,* which attempts to uncover and define the moral framework that binds and blinds the characters of the most famous body of plays in world literature. To do this I drew on the work of the social psychologist Jonathan Haidt and Moral Foundations Theory, as well as political philosophy and evolutionary science. It starts as follows:

> I write at a time when some feel that Western civilization is at a moment of crisis. It is a moment in which many of us are taking stock, and looking for meaning. It is a moment in which it somehow feels apposite to look, as so many previous generations have looked, to the great literature of the past for some insight, and perhaps even for some guidance. Certain commentators worry that many people in Europe and North America appear to have lost the "tragic sense of life." They have forgotten what the World War II generation so painfully learnt: that "everything you love, even the greatest and most cultured civilizations in history, can be swept away by people who are unworthy of them." Indeed, in drawing on modern psychological studies, as I do throughout this study, in some sense I prove the idea that "it has taken modern science to remind us what our grandparents knew." What did they know about human morality? What did Shakespeare know about it?[1]

In the space available to me here, I will summarize what I found.

Moral Foundations Theory (MFT) claims that human beings are "pre-wired" to respond to six moral foundations: care–harm, fairness–cheating, loyalty–betrayal, authority–subversion, sanctity–degradation, liberty–oppression. It argues that we experience these responses as near-automatic

[1] Neema Parvini, *Shakespeare's Moral Compass* (Bloomsbury, 2018), 3. Quotations taken from: Douglas Murray, *The Strange Death of Europe: Immigration, Identity, Islam* (Bloomsbury, 2017), 3. See also Pascal Bruckner, *The Tyranny of Guilt: An Essay on Western Masochism,* trans. Stephen Rendall (Princeton University Press, 2012); and the philosophy of John Gray, especially *Straw Dogs: Thoughts on Humans and Other Animals* (Granta Publications, 2003) and *The Silence of Animals: On Progress and Other Modern Myths* (Penguin, 2013). David Goodhart, *The Road to Somewhere: The Populist Revolt and the Future of Politics* (Hurst & Co., 2017), 28.

moral intuitions, and that most moral reasoning is post-hoc justification. Culture mediates our moral responses, but is limited in its scope by the raw materials of nature. Most cultures in history have been rooted in all six moral foundations, but liberals in modern Western cultures are statistical outliers in that they lean very strongly on the foundations of care–harm and liberty–oppression.[2]

Lived moral intuitions are often in tension with the official fully rationalized moral doctrines or 'cultural scripts'. Shakespeare's characters are dynamic and in the process of becoming rather than conforming to a set of fixed personality traits, and in this way they exceed trait-based accounts of human character provided by one branch of modern psychology. An approach to morality in literature must be centered on characters and their actions.[3] Shakespeare often throws characters into crisis by tweaking some aspect of their circumstances and forcing them to "react" under pressure; in this way, they are like game scenarios in which the rules have been altered. His ethics, therefore, is always situated and experiential. Audiences and readers of Shakespeare's plays are invited to make moral judgements of characters' actions and do so near-automatically.

Political and ideological struggles across the centuries can be characterized as "a conflict of visions," between the tragic vision and the utopian vision, following the scheme described in Thomas Sowell's book of the same name.[4] The tragic vision sees human nature as fundamentally unchanging and hence an ultimate "constraint" on what can realistically be expected from human beings. Accordingly, there are no solutions, only trade-offs; individuals need incentives to encourage naturally good behavior and disincentives to discourage naturally bad behavior. Society must erect institutions to help curb humanity's "baser instincts." Edmund Burke perhaps best embodies this view:

> Pride, ambition, avarice, revenge, lust, sedition, hypocrisy, ungoverned zeal, disorderly appetites – these vices are the actual causes of the storms that trouble life. "Religion, morals, laws, prerogatives, privileges, liberties, rights of men, are the *pretexts*" for revolution by sentimental humanitarians and mischievous agitators who think that established institutions must be the source of our afflictions. But the human heart, in reality, is the fountain of evil.[5]

---

[2] Jonathan Haidt, *The Righteous Mind: Why Good People are Divided by Religion and Politics* (Random House, 2012). See also Jonathan Haidt and Joseph Craig, "Intuitive Ethics: How Innately Prepared Intuitions Generate Culturally Variable Virtues," *Daedalus* 133: 4 (2004), 55–66; Larry Arnhart, *Darwinian Natural Right: The Biological Ethics of Human Nature* (State University of New York Press, 1998).

[3] See Gary L. Hagberg, ed., *Fictional Characters, Real Problems: The Search for Ethical Content in Literature* (Oxford University Press, 2016); Terence Cave, *Thinking with Literature: Towards a Cognitive Criticism* (Oxford University Press, 2016).

[4] Thomas Sowell, *A Conflict of Visions: Ideological Origins of Political Struggles*, rev. ed. (Basic Books, 2007).

[5] Russell Kirk, *The Conservative Mind: From Burke to Eliot*, 7th ed. (Gateway Editions, 2016), 36.

By contrast, the utopian vision, perhaps best exemplified by Jean-Jacques Rousseau, sees human nature as having no fixed characteristics, and hence, as free from natural constraints, as being "perfectible." Accordingly, in the utopian view there are permanent solutions; individuals need only change society and the rest will follow. Both MFT and Shakespeare hold the tragic vision. The utopian vision has no truck with empirical reality, it is insulated from evidence. Through confirmation bias, those who hold it will look only for evidence that confirms their existing beliefs and systematically ignore facts inconvenient to its narrative. Although the tragic vision derives from empirical knowledge, those who hold it can also be guilty of confirmation bias. Those who hold the utopian vision see themselves as being morally superior to others, and accordingly seek to condemn and, and in the worst cases, silence others. One thing we might learn from Shakespeare is how to be more understanding of one another's differences of opinion due to his remarkable capacity for empathy.

In *The Descent of Man* (1871), Charles Darwin argued that human morality is found in our "natural sympathy," and that the most civilized societies are those that show the greatest kindness to their weakest members.[6] After Darwin, there has been a split in evolutionary psychology between those, such as Richard Dawkins, who believe that evolution is primarily driven by the ruthlessly self-interested reproduction of genes, which can explain even apparently selfless and altruistic behaviors,[7] and those, such as Edward O. Wilson, who believe such behaviors develop because they confer group advantages.[8] Following David Sloan Wilson,[9] Jonathan Haidt argues that group selection helps explain the development of religious organizations that promote social cohesion and cooperation. With these insights in mind, I turn to look at Shakespeare's plays through the lenses of each of the six moral foundations in turn: authority, loyalty, fairness, sanctity, care, and liberty.

Authority

The moral foundation of authority cannot be found in the political rhetoric of Shakespeare's characters, but rather in the relationships between characters of different social rank. The most common bonds of service in Shakespeare's England were not feudal in nature but freely chosen contracts of employment,

---

[6] Charles Darwin, *The Descent of Man: Selection in Relation to Sex* (Penguin, 2004).
[7] Richard Dawkins, *The Selfish Gene*, 4th ed. (Oxford University Press, 2016).
[8] Edward O. Wilson, *On Human Nature*, rev. ed (Harvard University Press, 2004).
[9] David Sloan Wilson, *Darwin's Cathedral: Evolution, Religion, and the Nature of Society* (University of Chicago Press, 2002).

which means that in practice real social relations bore little resemblance to the political theory outlined by the Great Chain of Being.[10] The ideal model of good service and authority is found in *As You Like It*, where Adam freely chooses to serve Orlando, who repays his duty reciprocally by performing his own dutiful service later in the play.[11] In *King Lear*, Shakespeare diametrically opposes Kent, as a model of good service, which is rooted in a sense of duty rather than mindless obedience, and Oswald as a model of bad service, which is rooted in servility.[12] We find a strong parallel to Kent in Flavius, the steward in *Timon of Athens*, another model of good service, whose sense of duty leads him to speak truth to power, and freely to give up his own time, money, and efforts to serve Timon, even as he can see his master has gone astray. Through Jonathan Haidt's concept of "the hive switch"[13] – the ability to transcend our own self-interest to lose ourselves in something larger than ourselves – we can see why Adam, Kent, and Flavius all derive a profound sense of purpose from their duty, while characters such as Timon and Macbeth, stuck only with self-interest give way to misanthropy and existential despair. To understand the difference between Kent and Oswald in *King Lear* morally – as Samuel Johnson seemingly cannot but as Samuel Taylor Coleridge can[14] – we must respond to the moral foundation of authority. Those who are blind to the moral foundation of authority frequently confuse it for oppression, the opposite of liberty, and likewise mistake authority's opposite, subversion, for liberty itself. In Shakespeare, and indeed in the real world as observed throughout history, the result of this fatal misunderstanding is virtually always tyranny.

Loyalty

Psychological and sociological studies have found that men tend to prioritize group-level relations for power and status while women put place greater emphasis on two-person relationships.[15] Shakespeare roots his concept of

---

[10] See Eustace Mandeville Wetenhall Tillyard, *Shakespeare's History Plays* (Chatto & Windus, 1944).

[11] For studies on service in Shakespeare see: Mark Thornton Burnett, *Masters and Servants in English Renaissance Drama and Culture: Authority and Obedience* (Macmillan, 1997); Linda Anderson, *A Place in the Story: Servants and Service in Shakespeare's Plays* (University of Delaware Press, 2005); Judith Weil, *Service and Dependency in Shakespeare's Plays* (Cambridge University Press, 2005).

[12] Jonas A. Barish and Marshall Waingrow, "'Service' in *King Lear*," *Shakespeare Quarterly* 9. 3 (1958), 348–349.

[13] Haidt, *The Righteous Mind*, 269–270.

[14] Samuel Johnson, *Johnson on Shakespeare: Essays and Notes*, ed. Walter Raleigh (Henry Frowde, 1908), 158; Samuel Taylor Coleridge, *Coleridge's Essays and Lectures on Shakespeare: And Some Other Old Poets and Dramatists*, ed. Ernest Rhys (J. M. Dent & Sons, 1907), 130–131.

[15] Emily A. Impett and Lettita Anne Peplau, "'His' and 'Her' Relationships? A Review of the Empirical Evidence," in *The Cambridge Handbook of Personal Relationships*, eds. Anita L. Vangelisti and Daniel Perlman (Cambridge University Press, 2006), 287; Roy F. Baumeister and Kirsten L. Sommer,

loyalty in feminine two-person relationships as opposed to the masculine group level. His two-person friendships are often imbalanced, with one person (the loyal friend) appearing to give more to the relationship than the other, and in so doing fail the classical ideals of equality and reciprocity in friendship outlined by Aristotle and Cicero.[16] Critics have struggled to account for why Antonio gives so much of himself to Bassanio in *The Merchant of Venice*. In trying to justify this, they have cast Antonio variously as an attention-seeking poser,[17] a Christ-like savior,[18] a lonely homosexual,[19] a sadomasochist,[20] and a mere function of dramatic plot.[21] The relationship between Celia and Rosalind in *As You Like It* mirrors that between Antonio and Bassanio. Like Antonio, Celia's selflessness in her loyalty to Rosalind is remarkable. In both plays, feminine two-person loyalty presents an existential threat to and perhaps even trumps masculine group loyalty. The imbalanced nature of Shakespeare's friendships offend the moral foundation of fairness, but the selfless loyalty of Antonio and Celia seems to appeal to the Christian concept of charity, as outlined by Thomas Aquinas,[22] even if they do not fully live up to its ideals of universal inclusivity. Loyalty, defined as a selfless and charitable yet exclusive commitment to a friend, is undoubtedly a key point on Shakespeare's moral compass.

Fairness

The moral foundation of fairness responds to proportionality, not equality.[23] It is a question of *deserving*, of reward or punishment at an appropriate level.

"What Do Men Want? Gender Differences and Two Spheres of Belongingness: Comment on Cross and Madson," *Psychological Bulletin* 122. 1 (July, 1997), 43.

[16] On friendship in Shakespeare see: Laurens J. Mills, *One Soul in Bodies Twain: Friendship in Tudor Literature and Stuart Drama* (Principa Press, 1937); Victor G. Kiernan, "Human Relationships in Shakespeare," in *Shakespeare in a Changing World*, ed. Arnold Kettle (Lawrence & Wishart, 1964); Reginald Hyatte, *The Arts of Friendship: The Idealisation of Friendship in Medieval and Early Renaissance Literature* (E. J. Brill, 1994); Laurie Shannon, *Sovereign Amity: Figures of Friendship in Shakespearean Contexts* (University of Chicago Press, 2002); Alan Bray, *The Friend* (University of Chicago Press, 2003); Kate Emery Pogue, *Shakespeare's Friends* (Praeger, 2006); Tom MacFaul, *Male Friendship in Shakespeare and His Contemporaries* (Cambridge University Press, 2007); Will Tosh, *Male Friendship and Testimonies of Love in Shakespeare's England* (Palgrave Macmillan, 2016).

[17] Arthur Temple Cadoux, *Shakespearean Selves: Essays in Ethics* (Epworth Press, 1938), 53.

[18] Joseph Allen Bryant, Jr., *Hippolyta's View: Some Christian Aspects of Shakespeare's Plays* (University of Kentucky Press, 1961), 33–51.

[19] Graham Midgley, "*The Merchant of Venice*: A Reconsideration," *Essays in Criticism* 10. 2 (April, 1960), 125.

[20] Harold Bloom, *Shakespeare: The Invention of the Human* (Riverhead Books, 1998), 179.

[21] Kenneth Muir, *Shakespeare's Comic Sequence* (Liverpool University Press, 1979), 60.

[22] Thomas Aquinas, *Summa Theologiae* (*Vol. 34: Charity*) [2a2ae. 23–33], ed. R. J. Batten (Eyre & Spottiswoode, 1969), question 23, article 1, 7.

[23] Christina Starmans, Mark Sheskin, and Paul Bloom, "Why People Prefer Unequal Societies," *Nature Human Behaviour* 1. 82 (2017), 4.

Studies from across psychology, sociology, and evolutionary studies have found that fairness developed chiefly to counter free-riders, cheaters, and bad actors prone to ruthless and self-seeking behavior.[24] Despite this, human beings still show a selfish preference for increasing their own standing relative to others.[25] In Shakespeare, unfairness usually results in a desire for revenge which leads to ruthless selfishness; we can see this in *King Lear* (Edmund, Lear himself), *Twelfth Night* (Malvolio), *Richard III*, and *Hamlet*. Following the tragic vision, Shakespeare cautions that we must accept that life is seldom fair, lest we become a Richard III. His conception of justice seems to follow Thomas Aquinas in looking for moderately proportional punishments emphasizing mercy and rehabilitation (the Duke's pardon of Angelo in *Measure for Measure*) rather than vengeance (Hamlet not killing Claudius at prayer out of spite).[26] There is no socially levelling or egalitarian strain in Shakespeare's conception of fairness, and it would be a mistake to take Edmund in *King Lear* as a political revolutionary, since the play wholly condemns his self-seeking behavior, which would result in complete societal collapse if taken to its logical endpoint (the Hobbesian "state of nature").[27] In the absence of fairness, selfishness reigns, and it is a model than cannot subsist.

Sanctity

Psychological studies have found that the disgust response to contaminated food is unique to humans and universal across all known cultures.[28] This is the evolutionary root of the sanctity moral foundation.[29] Degradation functions like a contagion, which infects or stains all it touches. Shakespeare consistently depicts evil and sin as a disease, contamination, or stain, and it functions like a pathogen: it can be transferred from one person to another. There are examples across the plays, including in King Lear, Timon of Athens, the history plays, Othello, and Macbeth. Shakespeare emphasizes the psychological effects of sin through metaphors

---

[24] See Robert L. Trivers, "The Evolution of Reciprocal Altruism," *The Quarterly Review of Biology* 46. 1 (1971), 35–57; Jonathan Haidt, *The Righteous Mind*, 158–161.

[25] Mark Sheskin, Paul Bloom, and Karen Wynn, "Anti-equality: Social Comparison in Young Children," *Cognition* 130. 2 (2014), 152–156.

[26] Thomas Aquinas, *Summa Theologiae* (*Vol. 37: Justice*) [2a2ae. 57–62], ed. Thomas Gilby (Eyre & Spottiswoode, 1969), question 57, article 1, 5.

[27] Andrew Moore, *Shakespeare Between Machiavelli and Hobbes: Dead Body Politics* (Lexington Books, 2016), 68.

[28] For a comprehensive overview of this topic see Paul Rozin and April E. Fallon, "A Perspective on Disgust," *Psychological Review* 94. 1 (1987), 23–41.

[29] Richard A. Shewder, Nancy C. Much, Manamohan Mahapatra, and Larence Park, "The 'Big Three' of Morality (Autonomy, Community, Divinity) and the 'Big Three' Explanations of Suffering," in *Morality and Culture*, eds. Jerome Kagan and Sharon Lamb (University of Chicago Press, 1997), 147.

of physical degradation or staining. This way of thinking about evil is rooted in Biblical imagery, but Shakespeare imagines the stain of sin in a radically different way from Protestant theologians of the Reformation, such as Richard Hooker and John Calvin.[30] Where Hooker and Calvin see humans as being stained by sin from birth, Shakespeare's characters start from a clean bill of health and become contaminated during a given play, whether by their own actions or through contagion. Sanctity in Protestant theology is God himself, whereas in Shakespeare it appears to be in mankind. Shakespeare's view of moral degradation is similar to and perfectly compatible with that outlined by Thomas Aquinas, who also emphasizes free will and an essential human 'radiance' in the Summa Theologiae.[31]

Care

Care and harm manifest as consequences of the four moral foundations that "bind" – authority, loyalty, fairness, and sanctity – care results if they are respected, and harm (in the form of abject cruelty) results if they are offended. Tigers – used only fifteen times across all his works – represent the ultimate symbol of cruelty in Shakespeare, the moment in which all human decency is lost, and we are returned to the "state of nature" later described by Thomas Hobbes.[32] In *Titus Andronicus, 3 Henry VI, Richard III* and *King Lear* we witness the same pattern: society is reduced to a "wilderness of tigers" as every moral foundation is offended. However, in each play, Shakespeare shows that even where moral degradation seems endemic, human nature still provides the tools for mending itself: Individuals seem capable of empathy and care even in the most extreme of circumstances, and even after the point where it appears that hope is lost.

Liberty

Liberty as manifested in individual free choice facilitates the other five moral foundations: "There is always a choice!"[33] If liberty can be maintained through

[30] Richard Hooker, *The Ecclesiastical Polity and Other Works of Richard Hooker*, 3 vols., ed. Benjamin Hanbury (Holdsworth and Ball, 1830), vol. 2, 500; John Calvin, *Institutes of the Christian Religion*, 2 vols., ed. John T. McNeil, trans. Ford Lewis Battles (Westminster Press, 1960), 3.15.3, 790–791.

[31] See Thomas Aquinas, *Summa Theologiae (Vol. 26: Original Sin)* [1a2ae.81–5], ed. T. C. O'Brien (Eyre & Spottiswoode, 1969). See also Jeremy Cohen, "Original Sin as the Evil Inclination: A Polemicist's Appreciation of Human Nature," *Harvard Theological Review* 73. 3 (1980), 505–506.

[32] Thomas Hobbes, *Leviathan*, ed. J. C. A. Gaskin (Oxford University Press, 2008), 1.13.8, 84.

[33] John Vyvyan, *The Shakespearean Ethic* (Shepherd-Walwyn, 2011), 125.

the just rule of law and the good choices of individuals, society can sustain a virtuous circle in which liberty begets fairness which begets authority and loyalty, which result in sanctity and care. However, if oppression takes root it breeds unfairness and individual bad choices, and society descends into a vicious cycle in which oppression begets unfairness which begets subversion and betrayal, which result in degradation and harm. To break the vicious cycle and to maintain the virtuous circle takes a leap of faith on the part of good moral actors: They must give freely of themselves and expect no reward.

1. Virtuous Circle: Liberty begets Fairness, which begets Authority and Loyalty, which result in Sanctity and Care.
2. Vicious Cycle: Oppression begets Unfairness, which begets Subversion and Betrayal, which result in Degradation and Harm.

	Facilitator	Motivation	Decision / Action	Consequences
Moral Foundation (positive, good)	Liberty	Fairness	Authority, Loyalty	Sanctity, Care
Shakespeare's Usage	Choice, Free Will	Justice, Rule of Law, Proportionality	Good Service, Love, Charity, Friendship, Obedience, Duty, "Fellow-feeling"	Innocence, Purity, Mercy, Empathy, Tenderness, Natural Rejuvenation, Humanity
Moral Foundation (negative, evil)	Oppression	Unfairness / Cheating	Subversion, Betrayal	Degradation, Harm
Shakespeare's Usage	Tyranny	Revenge, Vengeance	Servility, Hatred, Selfishness, Misanthropy, Disobedience, Treachery	Disease, Contamination, "Wilderness of Tigers," Savagery, Cruelty, Inhumanity

Shakespeare always foregrounds the individual (and their moral choices) over the group, yet authority and loyalty – as defined by individual rather than group relations – are of central importance in his moral compass.

Conclusion

How does one break the vicious cycle and restore the virtuous circle? One way, in a sense, is to let bygones be bygones. The Duke in *Measure for Measure* does not punish Angelo particularly harshly, he offers him a chance of self-improvement. This is not the justice of retribution, or even of forgiveness and redemption, but rather of natural rebirth and growth. However, I think a vital aspect of this judgment is that it is afforded by the person who has perhaps the greatest reason to seek vengeance, Isabella.

> Most bounteous sir,
> Look, if it please you, on this man condemned
> As if my brother lived. I partly think
> A due sincerity governed his deeds
> Till he did look on me. Since it is so,
> Let him not die. My brother had but justice,
> In that he did the thing for which he died.
> For Angelo, his act did not o'ertake his bad intent
> And must be buried but as an intent
> That perished by the way. Thoughts are no subjects,
> Intents but merely thoughts.   (5.1.446–456)

Here, even despite the fact that her brother, Claudio, is still alive as she says these words, Isabella shows compassion and mercy to a man she has every reason to hate. Rather than dwell in spite or bitterness towards Angelo, she instead shows great empathy in trying to understand things from his point of view: perhaps the most Shakespearean of ethics. This requires something of a leap of faith: to commit to a virtuous act for its own sake without worrying about possible consequences and without expecting any form of reward. In fact, each of the good deeds I have covered involves a character giving something freely of themselves without looking for recompense: Adam pledging his life savings to Orlando in *As You Like It*; Kent ensuring his king gets good service even at the risk of angering him in *King Lear*; Flavius seeking out his old master while ensuring his colleagues are still paid in *Timon of Athens*; Antonio securing the loan for Bassanio in *Merchant of Venice*; Celia giving up her inheritance and risking her life for Rosalind in *As You Like It*; Aaron doing all he can to protect the life of his newborn son in *Titus Andronicus*. In order to have any chance of breaking the vicious cycle and restoring the virtuous circle, an individual is required to put the needs of someone else ahead of their own needs. In other words, it takes an unconditional, "no strings" act of altruism. In his morality, Shakespeare is closer to George Lakoff's concept of the "Nurturant Parent," who foregrounds nurturance, empathy, self-development, and growth, than he is to the "Strict Father," who emphasizes strength, authority (as defined by group hierarchy), and self-interest.[34]

Of course, Shakespeare is not an idealist: his plays show how frequently and how disastrously human beings fall short of this. This is the tragic vision: if nothing else is guaranteed, we can count on human beings – or at least a significant portion of them – to give in to self-interest. Even within the same play as Isabella's display of compassionate mercy, her brother articulates the tragic vision:

> Our natures do pursue,
> Like rats that ravin down their proper bane,
> A thirsty evil, and when we drink we die.   (1.2.117–119)

The "vicious mole of nature" (*Hamlet*, 1.4.24) tends to vice not virtue. Yet the strength to overcome it also comes from within. Nature destroys, but it also mends and grows.

Neither is Shakespeare a utopian visionary: He does not imagine or even wish for a time or place in which there is no conflict, no self-interest, and no motivation for revenge. The best we can hope for is to keep these darker forces in abeyance for as long as we can by keeping the virtuous circle going through selfless moral choices. At the same time, he is not despairing or pessimistic: Even in the direst circumstances – hell-on-Earth scenarios such as those we glimpse in the first tetralogy, *Titus Andronicus*, or *King Lear* – there is still an opportunity for the good moral actor to choose otherwise. Even if the self-sacrifice does not end the vicious cycle there and then, the moral choice might still be enough to sow the seeds of future mending and replenishment. Even as human beings show a remarkable capacity to self-destruct, so we also show a perhaps even more extraordinary resilience and the ability to bounce back. As signaled most explicitly in *The Winter's Tale*,[35] it is likely that Shakespeare saw these two countervailing tendencies in human nature – towards self-interest, death, and destruction on the one hand, and towards charity, growth, and renewal on the other – as something akin to the changing seasons. John F. Danby called these two different faces of humanity "The Benignant Nature" and

---

[34] George Lakoff, *Moral Politics: How Liberals and Conservatives Think*, 2nd ed. (University of Chicago Press, 2002), 65–142.

[35] See William B. Thorne, "'Things Borne Anew': A Study of the Rebirth Motif in *The Winter's Tale*," *Humanities Association Review* 19. 1 (1968), 34–43.

"The Malignant Nature,"[36] but every individual has the capacity for both, and has agency to choose one course or another. Thus Shakespeare is less pessimistic than those who hold the most extreme variants of the tragic vision, such John Calvin or Thomas Hobbes, but at the same time he is less optimistic than unconstrained visionaries such as Jean-Jacques Rousseau or twenty-first century Western progressives.

One of the most striking features of Shakespeare's moral compass is that his concern seems always geared towards the individual and their choices, actions, and relationships with other individuals. Admittedly, this came as something of a surprise to me: I expected to find a writer from the 1590s and early 1600s more firmly committed to the idea of the group and more obviously communitarian in his impulses. However, authority and loyalty form the central pillars of Shakespeare's moral order – if they fall, the rest of society often collapses. But Shakespeare transmutes authority and loyalty from group-level concerns to individual-level concerns: The appeal of the "band of brothers" (*Henry V*, 4.3.60) is quite different from the idea of good service predicated on a master–servant relationship or love and charity in friendship predicated on one-on-one relationships, and, he foregrounds the latter. In insisting on these relations between individuals, as opposed to between individual and group, the importance and impact of moral choices is put at a premium. Individual choices matter to the extent that bad ones result in endemic degradation and cycles of cruelty, and, in the absence of any sense of divine or cosmic justice, good choices are the only path out of it. In one respect, Shakespeare's moral invocation seems relatively modest: We should try to get along without killing each other. In his view, merely existing without tearing each other's throats out for a while is a remarkable, tenuous, fragile, accomplishment. But, as Patrick Gray reminds us, we live in a time in which we tend to see peace as the norm, whereas for the vast majority of human history – including Shakespeare's own time, and, as some contend and despite perceptions, our own too – conflict and war have been the norm. Peace is fragile, and beyond that so are loving relationships between individuals.[37]

In closing, how can we characterize the moral vision of Shakespeare's plays? If I was to characterize the Shakespearean ethic beyond his emphasis

---

[36] John F. Danby, *Shakespeare's Doctrine of Nature: A Study of King Lear* (Faber & Faber, 1949), 20–42.

[37] Patrick Gray, "Shakespeare and War: Honor at the Stake," *Critical Survey* 30. 1 (2018), 1–25. I was kindly given an advance copy by the author. See also John Gray, especially *Straw Dogs* and *The Silence of Animals*. On the fragility of individual relationships see Martha Nussbaum, *The Fragility of Goodness: Luck and Ethics in Greek Tragedy and Philosophy* (Cambridge University Press, 2001 [1986]).

on love, charity, and friendship in authority and loyalty, it would be as follows:

1. There is always a choice, it is never too late to choose to do the right thing.
2. The responsibility ultimately stops with you, because there is no divine or cosmic justice that will otherwise intervene; accordingly do not expect rewards or recognition for your good deeds.
3. We should not write anyone off, but rather make an effort to understand where they coming from, and try to see things from their point of view, because empathy and compassion are better than hatred, both morally and consequentially.
4. If we feel hard done by or slighted by unfairness, mercy is better than revenge both morally and consequentially.

Despite the apparent simplicity of these moral instructions, in our current time of perpetual petty social media outrage, the prevalence of personality over character, a near-complete lack of intellectual charity, increasingly meaningless virtue signaling[38] – mere words that are seldom backed by actual virtue in the form of decisions and actions – and ever mounting political and cultural polarization, perhaps a little of the Shakespearean ethic would go a long way.

---

[38] The phrase was popularly coined in James Bartholomew, "Easy Virtue: Want to be Virtuous? Saying the Right Things Violently on Twitter is Much Easier than Real Kindness," *The Spectator* (April 18, 2015): www.spectator.co.uk/2015/04/hating-the-daily-mail-is-a-substitute-for-doing-good/.

PART II

Shakespeare's Virtues

CHAPTER 11

The Four Cardinal Virtues
Caesar's Mantle and Practical Wisdom

Kevin Curran

In ancient and early Christian philosophy, the four virtues of prudence, justice, temperance, and courage were seen as so definitive of human flourishing, and each so integral to the right operation of the others, that they eventually became known as "cardinal," from the word meaning "hinge." The scheme finds its source in Plato's *Republic* and is subsequently absorbed into the ethical systems of Neo-Platonism and both Greek and Roman Stoicism. In the late fourth century, Ambrose of Milan, one of a number of early church fathers writing on prudence, justice, temperance, and courage, coined the term *virtutes cardinals*.[1] Later Christian philosophers, most notably Parisian scholastics such as Thomas Aquinas and Bonaventure, integrated the four cardinal virtues with Aristotelian ethics. By the time we reach the early-modern period in England, the cardinal virtues had become deeply embedded in intellectual, political, and literary culture with vernacular editions of Cicero's *De Officiis* and Aristotle's *Nicomachean Ethics* appearing in 1534 and 1547, respectively. Both went through numerous reprintings.[2] Secular handbooks devoted to the art of governance, such as Thomas Elyot's *A Boke Named the Governor* (1531) and William Leighton's *Vertue Triumphant, or A lively description of the foure vertues cardinall dedicated to the Kings majesty* (1603), made the cardinal virtues central to their system of counsel. Conduct manuals, including Dominic Mancyn's *The Myrrour of Good Maners, conteyning the iiii vertues callyd cardynall* (1520) and Lodowyck Bryskett's *A Discourse of Civill Life* (1606), used the cardinal virtues as touchstones for social comportment. Poets, meanwhile, found in

---

[1] Istvan P. Bejczy, "Les vertus cardinals dans l'hagiographie latine du Moyen Âge," *Analecta Bollandiana: Revue critique d'hagiographie* 122 (2004), 313–360.
[2] See further, Charles B. Schmitt, *John Case and Aristotelianism in Renaissance England* (McGill-Queen's University Press, 1983); Neal Wood, "Cicero and the Political Thought of the Early English Renaissance," *Modern Language Quarterly* 51. 2 (1990), 185–207; and Christopher Crosbie, *Revenge Tragedy and Classical Philosophy on the Early Modern Stage* (Edinburgh University Press, 2019), 92–94.

the cardinal virtues a consistent source of moral speculation, from Edmund Spenser's reflections on temperance and justice in *The Faerie Queene* to John Milton's exploration of courage in *Samson Agonistes*.[3]

This chapter is concerned with another vital context for fostering and practicing the cardinal virtues in early-modern England: Shakespearean theater. Taking prudence as my focus, the specific aim of this chapter will be to show how objects contribute to the formation of cardinal virtues in public contexts. Shakespeare offers an especially compelling site for investigating this topic in act 3.2 of *Julius Caesar*. Here, Mark Antony addresses the plebeians in the wake of Caesar's assassination using the latter's bloody mantle (i.e., cloak) as an object lesson in civic and moral failure. This scene, I contend, has something important to teach us about the theatricality of the cardinal virtues, including, especially, the object-specific way in which particular things enable general moral insights. As this suggests, in my reading, the cardinal virtues do not so much offer scripts for the cultivation of inner qualities as they do a community-oriented set of practices grounded in the capacity of humans to think, feel, and discern together. Put another way, the cardinal virtues are a social logic or dynamic, rather than personality traits or individual moral attributes. Like theater itself, they provide a linked set of frameworks for physical, emotional, and ethical participation in the world.

This argument will unfold in three parts. The first section offers a brief overview of how prudence functions as a source of moral knowledge, including the particular way in which it relates to the cardinal virtue of justice. The second section situates Mark Antony's speech within the broader cultural framework of evidentiary thinking, an important historical context for understanding the theatrical phenomenology of virtue. The third section, finally, opens up to a broader consideration of how objects and images foster the cardinal virtues by creating occasions for collective moral judgment, both in Shakespeare's time and our own.

Prudence, Justice, and Moral Knowledge

Prudence, or *phronēsis* in Greek, is usually described in English as "practical wisdom," a type of knowing that is active and collective. It stands in

---

[3] See further Norman Muir, "Middle-Class Heroism and the Cardinal Virtue Fortitude in Thomas Dekker's 'Honest Whore' Plays," *Explorations in Renaissance Culture* 15 (1989), 83–97; Reid Barbour, *English Epicureans and Stoics: Ancient Legacies in Early Stuart Culture* (University of Massachusetts Press, 1998); and Istvan P. Bejczy, *The Cardinal Virtues in the Middle Ages: A Study in Moral Thought from the Fourth to the Fourteenth Century* (Brill, 2011).

contrast to *sophia*, an abstracted and ideal type of wisdom set in opposition to *praxis* and the operations of the body.[4] Of the four cardinal virtues discussed by Plato, prudence has sometimes been called the virtue of virtues, the baseline capacity on which all the other virtues depended. Bryskett, in *A Discourse of Civill Life*, writes that prudence is "aptly called the eye of the mind" and the "conserver" of justice. He continues:

> Prudence is most necessary to discern what is just from what is unjust; and a good judgment therein can no man have that wanteth prudence: without which judgment, justice can never rule well those things that are under her government. And ... if he be not guided by prudence ... she works more harm than good.[5]

Prudence, in other words, enables ethical action through moral discernment, and in this way forms the foundation of the virtuous life. Bryskett, like so many writers of conduct manuals in the early-modern period, is influenced by Cicero, who presents a similar, if more obscurely phrased, perspective on the place of prudence among the cardinal virtues in *De Officiis*. "All that is morally right," Cicero writes, "rises from some one of four sources." He continues:

> it is concerned either (1) with the full perception and intelligent development of the true; or (2) with the conservation of organized society, with the rendering of every man his due, and with the faithful discharge of obligations assumed; or (3) with the greatness and strength of a noble and invincible spirit; or (4) with the orderliness and moderation of everything that is said and done...[6]

Elaborating on this description of the virtues (which he does not actually name at first, but which correspond to prudence, justice, courage, and temperance), Cicero notes that "in that category ... which was designated first in our division and in which we place wisdom and prudence, belong the search after truth and discovery," and concludes finally by emphasizing that "of the four divisions which we have made of the essential idea of moral goodness, the first, consisting in the knowledge of truth, touches human nature most closely."[7] Prudence, then, is the cardinal virtue most securely grafted into human nature itself. It constitutes a foundation for

4 Jacques Taminiaux, *The Thracian Maid and the Professional Thinker: Heidegger and Arendt* (State University of New York Press, 1997), 108; Paul Kottman, *A Politics of the Scene* (Stanford University Press, 2008), 4–5, 30–35.
5 Lodowyck Bryskett, *A Discourse of Civill Life* (Apsley, 1606), 185.
6 Cicero, *On Duties*, ed. Walter Miller (Harvard University Press, 1913).
7 Cicero, *On Duties*, I.15, I.17.

justice and a platform on which the capacities of courage and temperance can be cultivated. Justice, after all, is a condition produced by the
applied moral calculus of courage and temperance, and courage and temperance, in turn, are virtues that can only obtain in situations where choice
is involved.

One specific way in which prudential knowledge distinguishes itself
from *sofia* is that while the latter is broad, universal, and seemingly innate
to certain individuals, the former is acquired by using applied judgment to
relate particular things to universal concepts. "Practical wisdom," Aristotle
says, is concerned with human affairs, namely, with that which we can
deliberate about ... Nor is practical wisdom concerned only with univer-
sals. An understanding of the particulars is also required since it is practical, and action is concerned with particulars.[8]

Prudence is a calculative capacity. It expresses itself in response to "that
which we can deliberate about," and more specifically to particular objects,
events, and questions that obtain in the real world of "human affairs." This
can take the form of moral deliberation, as described by Bryskett in his discussion of the relationship between prudence and justice, or it can take the
form of practical and technical discernment in fields as diverse as building,
surveying, engineering, cartography, horse riding, fencing, and dance.[9]

The key thing to stress is that prudence is always a functional virtue. It
is to be found in social, material, or otherwise transactional environments,
not in solitude. Prudence has less to do with thinking (in our conventional
understanding of that term) than it does with making and doing (*NE*,
1140a–b). Aristotle emphasizes that the *phronimos* – the prudent person,
or person of practical wisdom – does not, indeed cannot, exist in isolation.
One hopes and assumes that the *phronimos* can navigate his or her private
affairs discerningly, but they are characterized above all by practicing the
sort of public virtue that leads to *eudaimonia*, or well-being for society in
general. As this suggests, prudence only truly obtains when public acts of
judiciousness are acknowledged and shared by a larger collective of stake-
holders (*NE*, 1142a).[10] This is the process that enables justice, which is itself,
within the Aristotelian scheme, a state of living temperately according to

---

[8] Aristotle, *The Nicomachean Ethics*, ed. Roger Crisp (Cambridge University Press, 2000), 1141b, hereafter *NE*.
[9] See Henry Turner, *The English Renaissance Stage: Geometry, Poetics, and the Practical Spatial Arts*
(Oxford University Press, 2006), 14 and Kevin Sharpe, "Virtues, Passions, and Politics in Early
Modern England," *History of Political Thought* 32 (2011), 773–798.
[10] For discussion, see Lois S. Self, "Rhetoric and Phronesis: The Aristotelian Ideal," *Philosophy & Rhetoric*
12 (1979), 135.

the golden mean.[11] The key take-away in all this is that contrary to our everyday understanding of virtue as a set of inner, moral attributes, the cardinal virtues, especially within the Aristotelian tradition, are of the world and for the world. They are deliberative in structure and in this respect rely on collaborative dynamics, be they of the Greek agora, the modern seminar room, or the transactional environment of Shakespeare's theater.

Let's turn now to the latter, Shakespeare's theater, and consider how Mark Antony's interaction with the plebeians in act 3.2 of *Julius Caesar* stages prudence-in-action; a scene of collective, hands-on knowledge-making in which practical discernment is used to link a particular thing to a larger concept of justice.

Caesar's Mantle and the Phenomenology of Virtue

Early on in 3.2, Brutus, one of the conspirators, makes a sharp distinction between private and public duty, explaining that it is "not that I loved Caesar less, but that I loved Rome more" (3.2.22).[12] The plebeians are initially roused by this argument ("Live, Brutus, live, live," "Let him be Caesar" [3.2.48, 51]), but when Mark Antony arrives bearing the body of Caesar, he quickly sways them to a more critical assessment of the assassination and of Brutus's role therein. How does Mark Antony achieve this? The answer has to do with the way he uses material objects to advance his argument: first the body of Caesar, then a piece of parchment (Caesar's will), and finally, and at most length, Caesar's mantle. These object lessons allow for that crucial prudential linkage to be made between the particular and the universal. This is what makes practical wisdom *practical*. Before there is an idea, there is a thing; before there is a thought, there is the world. This basic phenomenological precept forms the foundation of prudence and establishes the material conditions necessary for justice and the virtuous life more generally.

Mark Antony's main object lesson explicitly requires visual engagement. Beseeching all present to "Look," he directs the plebeians' attention to Caesar's mantle, still bloodily caked to the body that lies before him. I quote the passage in full:

---

[11] On temperance and the mean, see Joshua Scodel, *Excess and the Mean in Early Modern English Literature* (Princeton University Press, 2002), and on the relationships among prudence, courage, temperance, and justice, see Unhae Park Langis, *Passion, Prudence, and Virtue in Shakespearean Drama* (Continuum/Bloomsbury, 2016).

[12] Quotations and line references are from William Shakespeare, *Julius Caesar*, ed. David Daniell (Bloomsbury, 1998).

If you have tears, prepare to shed them now.
You all do know this mantle. I remember
The first time ever Caesar put it on.
'Twas on a summer's evening in his tent,
That day he overcame the Nervii.
Look, in this place ran Cassius' dagger through:
See what a rent the envious Caska made:
Through this, the well-beloved Brutus stabbed,
And as he plucked his cursed steel away,
Mark how the blood of Caesar followed it,
As rushing out of doors to be resolved
If Brutus so unkindly knocked or no;
For Brutus, as you know, was Caesar's angel.
Judge, O you gods, how dearly Caesar loved him.
This was the most unkindest cut of all:
For when the noble Caesar saw him stab,
Ingratitude, more strong than traitor's arms,
Quite vanquished him: then burst his mighty heart;
And in his mantle muffling up his face,
Even at the base of Pompey's statue,
Which all the while ran blood, great Caesar fell.
O what a fall was there, my countrymen!
Then I, and you, and all of us fell down,
Whilst bloody treason flourished over us.
O, now you weep, and I perceive you feel
The dint of pity: these are gracious drops.
Kind souls, what weep you when you but behold
Our Caesar's vesture wounded? Look you here,
Here is himself, marred as you see with traitors.   (3.2.167–195)

Mark Antony starts by drawing collective attention to the thing itself: "You all do know this mantle" (3.2.168). In doing so, he lays the groundwork for a communal and object-oriented knowledge-event, mapped out linguistically through three keywords: "all … know … mantle."

For the crowd assembled around Mark Antony, as for the audience watching this scene at the newly opened Globe, the invitation to "Look you here" and assess the mantle would have triggered a moment of common evidentiary thinking. The episode models in theatrical terms a way of engaging critically, skeptically, and systematically with information that was becoming more prevalent in early-modern England as a result of developments in a range of social and intellectual contexts, especially political and legal culture. As Perez Zagorin has shown, an increasing number of early-modern men and women "viewed the world they lived in as filled with duplicity."[13] Apprehensive of Catholic trickery and distrustful of political policy, many among Shakespeare's audiences would have practiced an everyday hermeneutic of suspicion. Among the learned, writers such as Niccolò Machiavelli, Justus Lipsius, and Francis Bacon offered explorations (and oftentimes justifications) of royal dissimulation while, on the other hand, a renewed interest in Roman historians, especially Tacitus, urged skeptical reading of political news in order to locate the truth behind what things seemed to be.[14] In the legal realm, meanwhile, a variety of procedures involving the empirical and objective evaluation of material evidence were being formalized. These procedures, referred to collectively as "Matters of Fact," were, from the sixteenth century on, left to lay jurors, while "Matters of Law," such as sentencing, were left to professional judges. One important effect of lay participation in material fact-finding was that evidentiary thinking became part of the general furniture of the mind, rather than just an institutionally proscribed practice.[15]

What Mark Antony's speech has in common with these developments in political and legal culture is a core investment in the link between *the real* and *the right* – the simple, but nevertheless radical, idea that there is an objective world of things that present themselves to human judgment as reliable guides to decision making. It is, of course, unlikely that either Shakespeare or his early audiences made a specific connection between act 3.2 of *Julius Caesar* and, say, actual trial procedure. But we do not have to believe this is the case to see how the scene indexes, both conceptually and theatrically, the phenomenon of evidentiary thinking that was one of the most important psychic effects of vernacular legal culture in the sixteenth and seventeenth centuries.[16] As rhetorically sophisticated as Mark Antony's speech is, it is clearly crafted by someone who viewed material evidence as bearing a verificatory power that exceeds pure oratory. The

---

[13] Perez Zagorin, *Ways of Lying: Dissimulation, Persecution, and Conformity in Early Modern Europe* (Harvard University Press, 1990), 255.

[14] See, for example, Francis Bacon, "Of Simulation and Dissimulation," *The Works of Francis Bacon*, ed. James Spedding, 14 vols. (Longman & Co., 1857–1874), XII: 95–98, and for historical commentary, J. H. M. Salmon, "Seneca and Tacitus in Jacobean England," in *The Mental World of the Jacobean Court*, ed. Linda Levy Peck (Cambridge University Press, 1991), 169–188; Malcolm Smuts, "Court-Centred Politics and the Uses of Roman Historians, c. 1590–1630," in *Culture and Politics in Early Stuart England*, eds. Kevin Sharpe and Peter Lake (Stanford University Press, 1993), 21–43; and David Coast, *News and Rumour in Jacobean England: Information, Court Politics, and Diplomacy, 1618–25* (Manchester University Press, 2016).

[15] The best overview of these cultural developments remains Barbara Shapiro, *A Culture of Fact: England, 1550–1720* (Cornell University Press, 2000).

[16] Ibid., 9.

moral impact of the scene depends for its effectiveness on an audience that shares these views of material evidence. This is a crucial insight since it reinforces the idea that sensible objects and embodied experience form a necessary hinge between prudence and justice, two principle cardinal virtues. In establishing a specifically juridical set of relations among speaker, auditors, and objects, 3.2 of *Julius Caesar* dramatizes virtue as a fundamentally phenomenological practice and, by extension, suggests how theater offers a particularly effective space for cultivating it.

Seeing, Feeling, and Moral Response

The process of moral deliberation that Mark Antony guides the plebeians through is tightly anchored to the holes in the mantle created by the conspirators' blades: "Look, in this place ran Cassius' dagger through: / See what a rent the envious Caska made: / Through this, the well-beloved Brutus stabbed" (3.2.173–175). The latter Mark Antony describes as "the most unkindest cut of all" (3.2.181), and it is from here that he, along with the rest of the assembled crowd, is able to make that key prudential link between the particular (a piece of clothing) and the universal (notions of duty and ingratitude):

> This was the most unkindest cut of all:
> For when the noble Caesar saw him stab,
> Ingratitude, more strong than traitor's arms,
> Quite vanquished him: then burst his mighty heart   (3.2.181–184).

This leads to a final judgment and the knowledge, at once political and moral, that treason has been committed: "O what a fall was there, my countrymen! / Then I, and you, and all of us fell down, / Whilst bloody treason flourished over us" (3.2.188–190). Although these words are spoken by Mark Antony, the intuition they express is shared by the whole crowd. This common awareness is registered, importantly, in the emotional capacities of the body rather than in the purely intellectual capacities of the mind: the crowd starts to weep:

> O, now you weep, and I perceive you feel
> The dint of pity: these are gracious drops.
> Kind souls, what weep you when you but behold
> Our Caesar's vesture wounded? Look you here,
> Here is himself, marred as you see with traitors.   (3.2.191–195)

Mark Antony acknowledges the tears that mark this moment of collective understanding and then delves deeper into the objective grounds from which it has sprung, removing the mantle to reveal the wounded body of Caesar itself. Whereas before the plebeians yelled, "Live, Brutus, live, live," "Let him be Caesar," now they shout, "O traitors, villains!" (3.2.197).

Mark Antony's calculated appeal to the crowd's capacity for prudence is closely bound up with a simultaneous appeal to their capacity for courage – courage, that is, in the Aristotelian sense of cultivating appropriate responses to "the things we fear, evils" (*NE*, 1115a). The cardinal virtue of courage involves a certain way of coordinating passion and reason such that we appropriately fear those things that should be feared and do not fear those things that should not be feared. The ideal outcome, as always, is action that leads to justice.[17] Mark Antony is *en*couraging his public to fear rightly; to employ prudence, exercised in response to material evidence and rhetorical appeal, such that they become more apprehensive of the conspirators' actions than of the supposed threat of Caesar. This reminds us that what we might typically refer to in a strictly rhetorical sense as "persuasion" is in the context of the cardinal virtues more appropriately referred to as "encouragement," a social process whereby the tools – deliberative, rhetorical, and material – necessary for the expression of courage and the establishment of justice are distributed among a public.

Orators like Mark Antony understand how effective material objects are at establishing the prudential conditions that make courage possible. Of course, political pundits of all stripes – and now marketing firms, too – understand this as well; the line between community-oriented motivation and self-interested manipulation can be a blurry one. Indeed, Mark Antony's speech itself could fall on either side of this line depending on your reading of the character and this particular passage of the play. Nevertheless, in a purely formal sense, Mark Antony's object lesson offers a valuable account of the material grounds of moral intelligence and the way particular things open up to general ideas through an affective process of communal judgment. While object lessons like Mark Antony's continue to be used cynically and coercively, they also remain a powerful source of public virtue. One thinks of the ubiquitous pile of shoes at the United States Holocaust Memorial Museum that have triggered moral outrage in generations of visitors.

The efficacy of the object lesson as a pedagogical tool lies in its seemingly infallible status as moral evidence and the prudential way in which

---

[17] See further, Howard J. Curzer, *Aristotle and the Virtues* (Oxford University Press, 2012), 19–64.

it holds the particular and the universal in an especially close configuration. Over the last ten years, social media has provided a platform
especially conducive to object-lesson proliferation: the sad child who
evokes the ethical catastrophe of detained migrants on the US-Mexico
border; the terrified pig who conveys the abject cruelty of the meat
industry. Nilüfer Demir's 2015 photograph of Alan Kurdi, the three-
year-old Syrian refugee whose small body washed up on the shores of
Bodum, Turkey in the wake of a failed sea crossing to Europe, not
only appeared on the front pages of hundreds of newspapers worldwide,
it also translated directly, and almost immediately, into actual policy-
making. Within days, Germany committed to admitting thousands of
refugees who had up until then been stranded in Hungary, a humani-
tarian corridor was established in central and eastern Europe stretch-
ing from northern Greece to southern Bavaria, and Canada agreed to
resettle 25,000 Syrians.[18]

One of the special capacities of the object lesson is that it collapses the
age-old distinction between *epistēmē* (knowledge) and *doxa* (opinion), the
former associated with reason and the mind, the latter associated with sensation and the body. As a technology of virtue, object lessons are visceral
and emotional, but also have the empirical force of evidence. The shoes at
the Holocaust museum prompt tears and indignation, but they are also
actual shoes worn by actual people who were murdered. Like the bloody
mantle of Caesar, they are both fact and feeling, a truth that we know in
our body. Aristotle would not have been surprised at the effectiveness of
such object lessons, nor by the way that effectiveness resides in a particularly close link between feeling and knowing. The very notion of *pathos*,
Aristotle's second principle of rhetorical appeal, rests on the assumption
that reason alone is insufficient to successfully communicate a truth-claim.
The mantle is an instrument that triggers *pathetic* engagement among
Mark Antony's public, a prop whose purpose is to occasion emotionally
charged visual descriptions that early-modern rhetoricians would have
identified as *enargeia* or *illustratio*:

---

[18] On the effects of Nilüfer Demir's photograph of Alan Kurdi, see Carolyn Pedwell, "Mediated Habits:
Images, Networked Affect and Social Change," *Subjectivity* 10 (2017), 147–169. More generally, see
Wendy Atkins-Sayre, "Articulating Identity: People for the Ethical Treatment of Animals and the
Animal/Human Divide," *Western Journal of Communication* 74 (2010), 309–328; Daniel Yankelovitch,
Coming to Public Judgment: Making Democracy Work in a Complex World (Syracuse University Press,
1991); and Laura Gries, *Still Life with Rhetoric: A New Materialist Approach for Visual Rhetorics*
(University Press of Colorado, 2015). I wish to thank Ryan Skinnell for advising me on scholarship
dealing with contemporary rhetoric.

I remember
The first time ever Caesar put it on.
'Twas on a summer's evening in his tent,
That day he overcame the Nervii.
Look, in this place ran Cassius' dagger through   (3.2.168–171).

Here, the verbal strategies of Aristotelian rhetoric meet the lived experience of Aristotelian virtue: an object generates rhetoric, rhetoric generates an image, the image generates emotion, emotion generates prudence, and prudence leads to courage and, finally, justice. A similar process obtained in the public reception of and response to the photograph of Alan Kurdi in 2015. Shakespeare's Mark Antony belongs neither to Aristotle's world nor to our own, but the character's use of Caesar's mantle to elicit cardinal virtues glances forward and backward at both worlds simultaneously.

Mark Antony's object lesson is a prudential knowledge-event *par excellence*: it stages a direct confrontation with the reality of material life and elicits an equally material response in the form of bodily experience (weeping, disgust, anger). As theorists of affect will tell us, such bodily experience is valuable precisely for the way it always promises to engender forms of knowing not otherwise available through individual rational thought. This is what Brian Massumi calls "a sock to thought," a sensory jolt which, as Jill Bennett writes, "does not so much *reveal* truth as thrust us involuntarily into a mode of critical inquiry."[19] What neither Massumi nor Bennett discuss, but which act 3.2 of *Julius Caesar* puts on display, is the way the cardinal virtues, especially prudence and temperance, play a crucial role in guiding the purely sensory experience of the "sock to thought" into the rational ambit of "critical inquiry." Theater by its very nature is designed to issue these socks to thought, to thrust spectators into situations of emotionally grounded, but rationally informed, critical inquiry oriented toward moral action and justice. At its most basic operational level, theater curates transactions among objects, emotions, judgment, and knowledge, and it is these transactions that form the material and cognitive ecologies in which the cardinal virtues thrive.

Conclusion

Mark Antony's prudential use of the mantle in *Julius Caesar* looks forward to the latter-day object lessons of the museum, photojournalism, and

---

[19] Brian Massumi, ed., *A Sock to Thought: Expression after Deleuze and Guattari* (Routledge, 2002); Jill Bennett, *Empathic Vision: Affect, Trauma, and Contemporary Art* (Stanford University Press, 2005), 11.

social media while also being firmly rooted in an Aristotelian tradition of rhetoric and virtue. What ties them all together is the particular way in which evidence is used to invoke collective emotion and translate it into the sort of judgment that should lead to knowledge and virtuous action. Combining components of forensic rhetoric that would be recognizable to Aristotle and an affectively honed approach to visual rhetoric that would be recognizable to today's bearers of witness, Mark Antony creates a theater of virtue in which a fragmented public is united around a shared act of spectatorship, a shared confrontation with visceral experience, and a shared emotional response to violence. Indeed, prudence, the central force in this theater of virtue, can only be enacted through a certain *mise en scène* of human and nonhuman things. It requires for its unfolding a rhetorical, material, and cognitive environment in which physically instantiated particulars (like a mantle) enable evaluative insights about universal concepts like justice.

The way act 3.2 of *Julius Caesar* is crafted suggests that Shakespeare on some level understood this link between prudence and theater, the fact that they share the same basic conditions (collectivity), rely on the same raw materials (bodies and objects arranged in time and space), make meaning through the same methods (the substitution of part for whole, the invocation of common deliberation), and aim at the same general outcome (the production of knowledge, wisdom, or insight experienced as feeling). With these connections in mind – and to return to a claim I made at the opening of this chapter – the scene serves as a powerful reminder that the cardinal virtues are a system of social practices that rely on the capacity of humans to think, feel, and discern together. To this extent, the theater offers a uniquely compelling site for fostering the aptitudes of public virtue. Any serious vision for a more just and equitable future must, therefore, involve vigorous support of theatrical institutions, events, and experiments.

CHAPTER 12

The Three Theological Virtues

Sarah Beckwith

A brief and true definition of virtue is rightly ordered love.

(Augustine, *Civ.Dei* 15.22)[1]

Now abideth faith, hope, and charitie, these three: but the chiefe of these is charitie.

(I.Cor.13, *Bishop's Bible*)[2]

Faith is the grounde of things hoped for, the evidence of things not seene.

(Hebrews, II.1, *Bishop's Bible*)

In the Christian tradition, faith, hope, and charity have God as their object and instigator, and they are the means by which we share in His nature. Hence they are called theological or deiform virtues.[3] Thomas Aquinas (1225–1274) a Dominican known as the Angelic Doctor, treats faith, hope, and love, those virtues infused by grace, in the *Secunda Secundae* of the *Summa Theologiae,* one of the most profound and rigorous investigations in the virtue tradition after Aristotle.[4] Like the cardinal virtues, these virtues are dispositions, habits of good action that orient us to the good.

---

[1] St. Augustine, *City of God*, trans. Henry Bettenson (Penguin, 1972).

[2] *The Holie Bible* (London, 1568).

[3] Thomas gives a succinct treatment in Disputations, *De Virtutibus in commune 12*. The theological virtues, he here states, make us well-adjusted to our final end. They are "*faith*, which makes us know God; *hope* which makes us look forward to joining him; *charity*, which makes us his friends."

[4] Citations from the *Summa Theologiae* are from the Complete English Edition in Five Volumes translated by the Fathers of the English Dominican Province (Notre Dame: Christian Classics, 1948). References are given to the part, followed by the question, thence the article, thence the objections or reply to them, hence 1–2. 40 means the second part of the first part, 40th question which will then be subdivided into articles, objections, and replies to the objections. The method of reading Aquinas must follow the balance of arguments and the particular placing in a wider highly ordered structure. Two useful guides for reading Aquinas on the virtues alongside the *Summa* are Robert Miner, *Thomas Aquinas on the Passions* (Cambridge University Press, 2009), and Brian Davies, *Thomas Aquinas's* Summa Theologiae: *A Guide and Commentary* (Oxford University Press, 2014).

Dante's *Paradiso* is one superb literary expression of these three interconnected theological virtues. In the final cantos of *Paradiso,* Dante is
catechized on them. In *Paradiso,* Canto 25, for example, he is asked: What
is hope? Does he have it? And where does it come from?[5] Dante's answers
correspond to the scholastic and Thomistic tradition in which all three
virtues are at once sequential, always in the order of faith, hope, and love,
and yet integral and indispensable to enter the heavenly kingdom.[6] In this
great medieval poem, we meet faith, hope, and love together. They can't
be sundered. Later we will see that Shakespeare too understands these virtues as profoundly implicated in each other, and so does his contemporary
Edmund Spenser following the English allegorical tradition of William
Langland.

Aquinas's astonishingly lucid, precise, and careful analysis of the
deiform virtues is what underpins the theological and exegetical logic of
these medieval poems. Aquinas had first treated hope as a passion and an
act of the will.[7] He begins his treatment of the irascible passions with hope
and despair. It comes as the first of the passions, as Robert Miner says,
because it bears "the simplest and most direct relation to the good."[8] The
criteria for hope outlined in 1–2.40 are that its object must be: a good,
moreover a good in the future, a good whose attainment might be hard,
yet not impossible. For if the object of hope was not a good, it would be a
wish rather than a hope; if possessed in the past or present, hope cannot be
hopeful. And if the path to hope's desire were not difficult and precarious
then it too would be a desire not a hope. Hope is inextricably linked with
despair in the *quaestio*: if what I ardently hope for is impossible to attain, I
will surely despair. When Aquinas treats hope in the *Summa* as a virtue (as
opposed to a passion), it is as part of the trinity and ordering of faith, and
love. Aquinas's explication of faith, hope, and love as virtues that begin in
our natures yet need to be infused, instilled together to attain a God who
exceeds natural knowledge, takes place in the *Secunda Secundae,* in the
great treatise on the virtues, where he builds on Aristotle's understanding
of virtue as neither a feeling, nor a faculty, but a disposition (a habitual,

---

[5] Alighieri, Dante. *Paradiso,* trans. Robin Kirkpatrick (Penguin, 2008).

[6] Dante's replies to the apostle James follow Peter Lombard's *Sententiae* very closely and are mod-
elled on a university oral examination, Peter Lombard, *The Sentences,* trans. Giulio Silano, 4 vols.
(Pontifical Institute of Mediaeval Studies, 2007–2010).

[7] Aquinas distinguishes the irascible passions from the concupiscible as being oriented to an arduous or difficult attainment of the good, that is hope and despair, confidence and fear and anger, as
opposed to love and hate, desire and aversion, joy and sorrow.

[8] Robert Miner, *Thomas Aquinas on the Passions,* 216, 1a2ae 22–48.

active power) oriented to the good. Here he expounds the integration and connectedness of the theological virtues: faith believes what it does not see and hope moves towards something it does not possess. Hope comes after faith, for faith is necessary to hope; it can exist without charity because a person can hope for merits not yet possessed, but not without faith, for then it would not have the proper object, God. Charity, however is the root and perfection of all virtue (1–2.62); it inspires, sustains, and perfects the others. Charity loves God as object of that eternal happiness in which we believe and for which we hope; so although it is the root of faith and hope as virtues, it nevertheless also presupposes them.[9] As Aquinas says: "love always precedes hope: for good is never hoped for unless it be desired and loved … hope precedes love at first: though afterward hope is increased by love."[10] Thomas weaves in commentary on I.Cor 13, and Hebrews 11.1 throughout these considerations, grounding philosophy in scripture.

The glosses on those passages by post-Reformation translators and annotators of the New Testament are instructive. For the new context is Luther's emphatic isolation of faith from the other virtues, and from the virtue tradition *tout court*.[11]

Luther adds the important German word "allein" (alone) to his translation of the text that he described as his theological revolution: Romans 3:28. The Geneva Bible rendered this famous line: "Therefore we conclude that a man is justified by faith without the works of the law." Luther translates this: "So now we maintain, that man becomes justified without the work of the Law, through faith alone." Luther added "alone," placing emphasis on the exclusivity of faith, and insisting that the "allein" gave the sense of a text he felt, as he said introducing *Romans,* that every Christian should know intimately and exactly, and treat as part of their daily soul bread.[12] In his early commentaries on Psalms and Romans (1513–1516), Luther gradually arrived at an idea of faith as a pure receiving –and it was only the purity of this reception that might be the guarantor of the promise of Jesus and the Gospel. This understanding of faith deliberately severed faith

---

[9] In this tradition our love for God incorporates love for neighbor, and we will vitiate the theological virtue of love, unless our love is social.

[10] 1.2.62.4, Reply Obj. 3.

[11] The word virtue is both more specific and more capacious than its modern translation implies. The Italian and Latin derivatives include notions of strength, power, and purpose. For Luther only the eradication of human agency from the process of salvation can fund its assurance, its certainty. All else opens the door to doubt and insecurity.

[12] Lyndal Roper, *Martin Luther: Renegade and Prophet* (Random House, 2017), 196–197.

from any idea of virtue as human deed, habit, or disposition, and from any works, for that would precisely compromise the exclusive and one-sided donation of faith as a freedom from any necessary conditions of human emotion or thought.

The annotations in the Douay-Rheims bible of 1582, the approved Counter Reformation Catholic vernacular version, gloss the famous text of Hebrews that "faith is the substance of things to be hoped for, the argument of things not appearing." Faith is the ground of hope and "not the forged special faith of the Protestants, whereby every one of these new Sectmasters and their followers believe their sins remitted, and that themselves shall be saved, though their sects be clean contrary to one another."[13] Here we see the integral connection of faith and hope and the fear of the great unravelling of the connection between ecclesiology, prayer, virtue, and the scriptures into *sola fide, sola scriptura.*

This unbinding of the scriptures from the church, sacraments, and tradition, as well as faith from hope and love vexes Thomas More (1478–1535) in his voluminous *Dialogue concerning Heresies,* his lengthy discussion with a figure he names the Messenger who represents the Lutheran infiltration of England. He objects to William Tyndale's (c. 1490–94–1536) Lutheran uncoupling of faith from belief, and dissevering from hope: "every man woteth that faith and hope be two dystincte vertues and that hope is not faith but foloweth faith in hym that hath hope. For no man can hope for heaven yf he byleuve yt not. But on tother syde he may as ye devyll doth though he byleue yt and knowe it to yet fall farr from all hope thereof."[14]

It is interesting to compare Aquinas's and Calvin's glosses on the key passage of Hebrews 11.1. Calvin declares that "the teaching of the schoolmen that love is prior to faith and hope is mere madness; for it is faith alone that first engenders love in us."[15] Hope and love spring from faith which both have the foundation of God's mercy. For Aquinas it is precisely the precarious, open, and future orientation of hope that distinguishes it precisely as hope. Calvin and Luther's insistence on assurance, certainty, and sureness miss hope's fragility and promise.

Now of course for Luther the assurance of faith, being a certainty, left no room for the virtue of hope, and though Luther was sure that love followed

[13] *The Original and True Rheims New Testament of Anno Domini 1582,* annotations to Hebrews 11.1, 480.
[14] Thomas Lawler, Germain Marc'hadour, and Richard C. Morris, eds., *Dialogue Concerning Heresies, Complete Works of Thomas More,* Volume 6, Part 1 (Yale University Press, 1981), 388.
[15] John Calvin, *Institutes of the Christian Religion,* ed. John T. McNeill (Westminster Press, 1960), Book 3, Chapter 2, 41 on faith and love, 589.

from faith as indeed did works, the focus on faith alone was the key to his theology for those who are always sinners and always justified: *simul justus, simul peccator.* Most notoriously the doctrine of faith, which for Luther as for Calvin was a doctrine of *assurance,* was radically attenuated by Calvin's doctrine of double predestination. For, to put it bluntly, the doctrine that we are eternally predestined to heaven and hell, though a theology of joy and reprieve for Calvin, was not reassuring at all for many parishioners. On the contrary, it was sometimes a source of terror and despair.

The tradition of the theological virtues was central in the allegorical tradition. I mentioned Dante at the beginning of my chapter. William Langland treated the virtues allegorically, as does Edmund Spenser. In Langland's great allegorical poem, *Piers Plowman,* Spes (Hope) is Moses, who brings the law of love.[16] He is a spy scouting out and prefiguring the way to come, anticipated by Abraham, but requiring the incarnation for the consummation of charity. Thus in Passus XIX of the C-text, a theological crux of this extraordinary poem, neither Abraham nor Moses, neither Faith nor Hope in themselves can save the Good Samaritan, allegorized as the man half-alive (semi-vief).[17] Only Christ as love can salve and heal the wounded and failing man.

We meet hope and despair again in Canto ix of the Book of Holiness, the first book of *The Faerie Queene.*[18] Here Spenser brilliantly shows how Despair uses and distorts Protestant arguments of predestination, stressing that the Red Crosse knight is helpless for "if any strength we have it is to ill" (X.1), and that his sinfulness merits God's justice rather than his mercy. Here the counsel of Despair is funded by Calvinist orthodoxy and the dangers to the soul it may carry.

It is clear that the allegorical tradition is still invested in the virtues. But what of Shakespeare? I want to suggest that the tradition of the theological virtues might illuminate his late plays, *The Winter's Tale,* and later *Cymbeline,* while hinting at Shakespeare's picture of rightly ordered love, that is to say, virtue. Recognition is bound to work differently on stage than in an allegorical poem, but I think we can see the lineaments of a virtue tradition, and of the integral nature of the theological virtues subtly at work in this drama.

---

[16] Derek Pearsall, ed., *Piers Plowman by William Langland: An Edition of the C-Text* (Edward Arnold, 1978).

[17] Ibid. I am indebted to David Aers for discussion of this Passus. There would be much to say here about the ascription "semi-vief" in contrast to post-Reformation Protestant pictures of the complete helplessness of the sinner, who would allegorically be perhaps dead rather than half-alive.

[18] *Edmund Spenser: The Faerie Queene,* ed. Albert Charles Hamilton (Routledge, 2001).

At the end of the trial of Hermione in Act 3, Scene 2 of *The Winter's Tale*, Paulina's excoriating words to Leontes take us to the "still winter" of the play:

> Do not repent these things, for they are heavier
> Than all thy woes can stir; therefore betake thee
> To nothing but despair. A thousand knees,
> Ten thousand years together naked, fasting,
> Upon barren mountains, and still winter
> In storm perpetual could not move the gods
> To look which way thou wert.[19]

The still winter is static, without movement, and everlasting, eternally held to one place and locked in the consequences of one time. It is Lenten, yet right now without the possibility of repentance. Hermione had never wished to see Leontes sorry, yet trusted that she would (2.1.123–124). Leontes asks to be led to his sorrows at the end of this scene: "Come, and lead me to these sorrows."

Paulina's invocation of faith in the statue scene, where she requires the awakening as a condition of "more amazement" has given rise to significantly more commentary than the hope to which Hermione testifies in her words to Perdita. Indeed the latter passes unnoticed. When Paulina draws Hermione's attention to Perdita she says that she "preserved" herself "to see the issue" because she knew by Paulina that the oracle "*gave hope*" Perdita was alive (5.3.125–127, my italics). "Issue" economically carries the idea of generational line, and the result of an action, both terribly united in Perdita's abandonment and recovery, and hinted at earlier in Dion's prayer: "gracious be the issue" (3.1.21). The oracle had declared that the king would be without an heir "if that which is lost be not found," so included in the issue of the play in its final scene is the delicate adjudication of what has been lost and what found and refound (3.2.132). It is Hermione's *hope*, as much as Paulina's requirement of faith, both rooted in love, that lead to its ordered growth in charitable peace. The love at the end of the play extends beyond whatever the future holds for Hermione and Leontes. It is immediately extended to Polixenes as Leontes encourages Hermione to take once again the hand of Polixenes. This is a vindication of love for Hermione had bravely maintained the word love for her friendship with Polixenes in the trial scene ("I do confess /I loved him … with a love such/

---

[19] William Shakespeare, *The Winter's Tale*, ed. Stephen Orgel (Oxford University Press, 1996), 3.2.206–212.

So, and no other, as you yourself commanded" [3.2.60–65]) as if to reclaim that word from the staining suspicions of her husband. And it extends to Florizel and Perdita who will continue the love into the next generation, to Paulina and Camillo such that the old too can live in hope of love, to the uniting across class of the old shepherd and his son newly ennobled, and to the peaceable truce between the two kingdoms of Sicily and Bohemia, hitherto sundered by a "wide gap." The denouement of the play does not rest on *sola fide*. Rather Hermione's hope, oriented to the future, unsure of success, in an arduous yet not quite impossible task, working after faith (in the oracle, in Paulina), out of and towards love, keeps open a future where those virtues will never cease to be necessary.

It was Augustine who defined virtue as "ordered love" in Book 15 of *City of God*.[20] For the virtues work, as Thomas explicates it, building on Augustine, through love, and for the sake of love. It is love that directs them to their proper end in God, whose loving nature invites us to friendship with him. For Thomas there can be no true virtue without charity.[21] Since this account of virtue is both teleological (defined by its end), and eudaimonistic (working towards happiness or in Christian terms, beatitude), it is charity that informs and inspires the other virtues to their proper end in God.[22] Augustine remodeled pagan virtue: the classical (redefined as cardinal) virtues of temperance, courage, justice, and prudence are all defined anew in terms of love: pagan virtues are now *splendida peccata* (splendid or glittering vices or sins). They are without love when directed to the aggrandizement of self and performed for the love of dominion rather than in an acknowledgement of their beginning and end in God.

If faith is dead without love, so are all the other virtues. Charity in this Augustinian and Thomistic tradition shows us the limits of our own agency, and opens us to our need for God. The deiform virtues, being given to us by God, show the primacy of gift and thereby invite rather than nullify our own response. Hyper-Augustinian accounts such as Luther's privilege the sovereignty of God as if human agency challenged or limited that: but there was a long medieval tradition of double agency – albeit not the one that influenced Luther – by which grace precisely invited a human response.[23] In Thomas's account the deiform virtues (and all other virtues)

---

[20] Augustine, *City of God*, trans. Henry Bettenson (Penguin Books, 1984), 637.
[21] *Summa Theologiae* 2.2.23.6–8.
[22] Carol Harrison, *Augustine: Christian Truth and Fractured Humanity* (Oxford University Press, 2000), 79.
[23] See Jennifer Herdt's bracing account of hyper-Augustinianism in *Putting on Virtue: The Legacy of the Splendid Vices* (University of Chicago Press, 2008).

begin and end as divine gifts and so fantasies of autarky and self-sufficiency have no warrant. Love is relational through and through in this tradition: the self longing for God cannot be closed off from its intrinsic connection with others.

Love is the greatest virtue: but faith is the *primary* theological virtue and hope and love are grounded in it.[24] Aquinas's elucidation of faith as a theological virtue parses it out as a form of credence, producing a form of knowledge, but not one to which the intellect alone is compelled as it might be in a demonstration or argument. The proper object of faith is God, approached through creed and confession, and it is neither *scientia* or *opinio*.[25] Just as Aristotle, the great philosopher, taught that a pupil could not learn unless he believed his teacher, so one believes God as well as believes *in* him. Aquinas knew Augustine's famous text glossing James 2: 19 in which he says that even the devils believe in God and tremble. They believe in him, but do not believe him, do not, that is, put their trust in him, and grant him credence.

When we meet the term "faith" in Shakespeare's works it is nearly always in association with broken troths in love. Faith is "rended" or torn as if from a fabric, worn merely as the fashion of a hat, a "wafer-cake," sworn by, yet betrayed.[26] The foundation of Leontes's mistaken beliefs in Hermione's infidelity and treason is "piled upon his faith"; Othello stakes his life upon Desdemona's faith initially: "my life upon her faith."[27] And in the numerous plays which feature calumniated women – *Merry Wives, Much Ado, Othello, The Winter's Tale*, and *Cymbeline* – it is women's *faith*-fulness that is constantly called into question, yet men who are murderous, misogynist, and utterly untrustworthy in the abandonment of faith in their women. The lines from Hebrews 11.1, so beloved by Thomas resonate: where is the *evidence* of things not seen? The fantasies – of assurance, proof, certainty – for faith is being made susceptible to proof – are understood in these plays as a vitiation of the very grammar of faith (neither *scientia* nor *opinion,* but something more like trust, troth, and credence). Tokens of trust are writ large in these plays, whether tragically around the handkerchief in *Othello*, or around the tokens of betrothal and marriage in plays such as *All's Well That Ends Well* and *Cymbeline*. These plays might be seen then as an exploration of the grammar of faith, and of love and faith's

---

[24] *Summa Theologiae* 2.2.4.7.
[25] Ibid., 2.2.1.
[26] Variously: *Two Gentlemen of Verona 5.4.47; Much Ado About Nothing 1.1.75; Henry V 2.3.33; Richard III.*
[27] *Othello 1.3.295; The Winter's Tale 1.2. 430.*

intrinsic connection. For to love means to believe in, to grant credence to the lover, just as their troths are sworn by what they hold sacred.[28]

Cymbeline explores faithfulness in relation to love. Its principle heroine cross-dresses as Fidele, whose meaning in Italian, as John Florio glosses it, is "trustie, true, faithfull."[29] In *All's Well*, Shakespeare had shown how inescapably gendered these tokens are in the honorific world of the play: the ring that Helena must purloin from Bertram's finger is the sign of his lineage handed down to him as a sign of his patrilineal inheritance and honor: "it is an honour longing to our house,/Bequeathed down from many ancestors" (4.2.41–42).[30] Diana's ring is her virginity, her intimate body ventured in the risky exchange of a sexual encounter: "My chastity's the jewel of our house,/ Bequeathed down from many ancestors" (4.2.45–46). The analogy of the rings is economically witty and pointed, its latent obscenity lying in the difference in honor to each. (The ring of her vagina, to spell it out, circles a vacancy, at least from an entirely patriarchal perspective, the O that is also the pun of *Much Ado About Nothing.)* Diana's honor will be forever damaged, her reputation and therefore personhood lost for Bertram's momentary pleasure. She has indeed become her ring, her O, in Bertram's eyes even while the force of the reductive analogy is lost on him. This diminution of woman to ring is elaborated extensively in *Cymbeline*, in a play that makes the links between faith and love, and the theological language of gift apparent.

Paul's theology of the gift undergirded Luther's understanding of faith. The text of 1. Cor. 4.7 echoed through his works: "What do you have that has not been given?," as through Augustine's. Yet for Luther though faith led to love, the distinction between them is vital. In faith humankind has no power over itself: the purity of the gift is also a token of assurance. Luther glossed Gal. 5.6 where faith works through love as love becoming the instrument of faith, thus not an independent "work." Love for Luther, was something human beings did, thus the object of Luther's animus against works theology. It involved, according to him, a greater degree of human agency than faith: the Lutheran distinction between love and faith preserves the agency of God from the agency of humankind. The formula

---

[28] See Richard Firth Green's exemplary treatment of troth, truth, the Middle English "treuth" in Chapter 1 of *A Crisis of Truth: Literature and Law in Ricardian England* (University of Pennsylvania Press, 1999).

[29] Valerie Wayne, the editor of the Arden 3 edition of *Cymbeline* glosses "Fidele," helpfully in her *Dramatis Personae* of the play, giving the references to John Florio and Cotgrave's French-English dictionary of 1611.

[30] William Shakespeare, *All's Well That Ends Well*, eds. Suzanne Gossett and Helen Wilcox (Bloomsbury: Arden Shakespeare, 2019).

of the Angelic Doctor: "*fides caritate formata*" (faith formed by love) is thus no longer intelligible in the Lutheran idiom.

There is a subtle language and theology of gift at work in *Cymbeline*, probing the relation between love and faith. In the first scene of the play we see Innogen and Posthumous, just before they are forced to flee, exchanging tokens of love and marriage with each other. Innogen gives Posthumous a diamond ring of her mother's and tells him to take it and keep it until she is dead and he woos another wife. It is Posthumous who introduces the language of divine gift here: another wife? That is out of the question: "Ye gentle gods, give me but this I have...." (*Cymbeline* 1.1.116). He gives her a "manacle of love" (1.1.123). In placing it on the arm of "this fairest prisoner" (1.1.125) he introduces the complex language of bonds that he returns to when he is imprisoned at the end of the play.

A bond is what joins, links, binds, or ties together. The kinship of bond with the Latinate term ligature show the roots of obligation, enacted also in the contractual language of agreement (of indenture, credit, and law). The kinship with band (from Middle English) as not only hoop, join, bandage, strap, truss, tie, but also as mark (as in the stripe on a bird) indicates the way binding language singles, marks us out for each other. When is a bond too tight a tie? When is it a shackle, a tether, manacle, or fetter, in short, a constraint? How can a word function as a bond? If our word is our bond how does that make us answerable to each other, implicated in each other? Posthumous gives his word as his bond, and gives too a "manacle" (shackle) of love.

When Iachimo sees the ring glittering on Posthumous finger it is already functioning as a stand in for Innogen herself. "I praised her as I rated her," says Posthumous, "so do I my stone" (1.4.79–80). Iachimo asks Posthumous how he esteems the ring, and at first Posthumous's answer puts the ring as invaluable, that is to say incommensurate with anything to be enjoyed or owned in the world. He rebuts Iachimo's reductively evaluative language: a ring may be sold or given but his wife is not for sale: she is "a gift of the gods" (1.4.88). Iachimo's withering response is brilliantly on target to further his rivalrous designs for it generates an insecurity as to whether Posthumous is truly up to receiving such a gift: "Which the gods have given you?" – I imagine the emphasis of any actor would fall on the "you" with a lightly sophisticated and mildly scornful surprise (1.4.89). He knows that it is effective to allow Posthumous to think himself unworthy of receiving such a gift: part of mutual loving is allowing oneself to be loved. But the more potent strategy still is to equate Innogen with her ring. We've seen how this obscene pun worked in *All's Well*. It is elaborated here in a different way. Once Posthumous has let the ring stand in metonymically for Innogen herself, once her person has become the thing of the ring, rather than a token of trust in her *person*, she is herself already obliterated. The wonder of Innogen seen in the light of gift is now debased, her value now defined by virtue of the exchange between the two men. Both Innogen's virginity and the ring can be won. The woman is now her ring, the reductive metonymy complete. The homosocial covenant of the two men has betrayed Innogen before an assault on her virtue is so much as made. Iachimo's covenant with Posthumous replaces the exchange of love between the two lovers, just as surely as Iago's "I am yours forever" replaces Othello and Desdemona's stories and words of love.

Innogen names herself "Fidele," and so she is: "true, trustie, faithfull." Once she realizes that Iachimo's besmirching of Posthumous has been done in the service of wooing and winning her, an end she knows has no virtue in it, she sees through Iachimo completely. Her faith is linked with her trust in Posthumous and her truthfulness, such that truth, trust, and faith are working closely together in the service of love.

The fictions of Iachimo in persuading Posthumous of Innogen's infidelity lead to one of the most devastating misogynistic outbursts in the whole of English Literature.: "Is there no way for men to be, but women/ Must be half-workers?" (2.4.1–2). Here too Innogen herself is a mere token of Posthumous honor. He can't see round himself. Vicious, murderous, all-encompassing, his wish is to obliterate the woman's part, in his making, sustaining, or being.

Pisanio's understanding that his vows of service (fealty, loyalty) are in the service of truth and love, leads him to disobey Posthumous's murderous orders, for faith must be in the service of love and truth to be itself. For Pisanio the question of what faith is in, what it is in service of, is always alive. True fealty cannot be murderous: rebellion against a master's vicious orders holds the honors.

In that extravagantly famous last scene where all are unknown either to themselves and each other, and where all are revealed, it is the ring glittering on Iachimo's finger that prompts Innogen's question: how did Iachimo come by the ring? (Innogen thinks Posthumous is dead.) Iachimo's astonishingly full confession begins to restore the truth and helps to sponsor and generate a series of other confessions by which the ring can be restored to its status as a token of trust and love, not a piece of property calculated by the rivalrous love of dominion of the men. Iachimo admits that he "wounded" Posthumous's trust in Innogen.[31] Trust and hope, love, and

---

[31] See my *Shakespeare and the Grammar of Forgiveness* (Ithaca: Cornell University Press, 2011), Chapter 5.

faith are wounded together, restored together. They are in relation: not faith alone, but faith sustaining love and truth. The community of self-disclosure, revelation and truth restores them all to each other and brings peace and pardon to all.

Shakespeare's late romances revisit the adventure and risk of love: to pull off their delicately balanced and wondrous endings they rely on the supervenience of grace. But the medium is drama. Shakespeare thus works inevitably and intricately through human deeds and human words. We might think here of Shakespeare as restoring the double agency lost to the reformed sovereignty of God. In his late plays the theological and the dramaturgical are intrinsically interwoven through drama's faith that the actions of men and women are efficacious tokens of hope and love.

CHAPTER 13

Prudence
The Wisdom of "Hazarding All"
in The Merchant of Venice

Kelly Lehtonen

A cardinal virtue in the Platonic and Christian traditions, prudence (from the Latin *prudentia*, derived from *providentia*) is the ability to unite keen foresight with the powers of reason to make decisions that achieve a given purpose.[1] In *The Merchant of Venice*, Shakespeare takes advantage of the conventions of drama to explore the human practice of prudence – including the factors that most commonly interfere with performing it successfully, in the pursuit of ends ranging from love and friendship to justice and revenge. The central plot explores the apparent imprudence of the title character, the wealthy merchant Antonio, in staking his own life to help his friend Bassanio win the hand of Portia, an orphaned noblewoman. To loan his friend what he needs, Antonio borrows money from the Jewish moneylender, Shylock, on the bond of "an equal pound" of "fair flesh" (1.3.148–149).[2] While nearly every scene of the play contributes to the depiction of prudence, this chapter will focus on three tests that consider the virtue with particular insight: (i) the casket test that Portia's suitors must pass to win her hand; (ii) the test of justice, when Shylock dogmatically seeks the death of Antonio and is judged for it; and (iii) the "ring" test that Portia, in disguise, poses to gauge the loyalty of Bassanio.

As an intellectual virtue associated with pragmatism, prudence corresponds to the philosophical concept of practical reason (*phronēsis*, sometimes translated "prudence"), defined in Aristotle's *Nicomachean Ethics* as an "excellence of deliberation." While there is a worldly pragmatism to *phronēsis*/prudence that gives the concept a somewhat uneasy relationship

---

[1] Chariton T. Lewis and Charlton Short, *A Latin Dictionary*, ed. Chariton T. Lewis (Clarendon Press, 1991).

[2] All citations of the play are taken from David Bevington, ed, *The Necessary Shakespeare*, 4th edn. (University of Chicago Press, 2014).

to virtue, Aristotle distinguishes this intellectual virtue from shrewdness, or self-interested skill in calculation, by its attention to rightness of purpose. He identifies four components of *phronēsis*: (i) pursuing ends that are good, (ii) thinking correctly and logically about how to attain them, (iii) completing the deliberation efficiently, and (iv) achieving the specific end one sets out to attain (6.9:16–35: 1031).[3] In effect, while prudence might connote caution in general speech, the philosophical term relates to the achievement of the best outcome. For Aristotle (as for Shakespeare, I will suggest), this outcome is happiness (*eudaimonia*), a broad concept of human flourishing, the end of all Aristotelian virtue.[4]

Despite the traditional identification of prudence with virtue, some medieval and early-modern writers used the word to mean simply the powers of calculation needed to achieve a purpose, whatever that purpose might be, thus distinguishing prudence from morality. For instance, while Thomas Aquinas followed the Aristotelian view, subsequent scholars such as Duns Scotus and William of Ockham saw *prudentia* as a form of knowing necessary to virtue but not inherently sufficient to constitute it.[5] During the Renaissance, particularly with the rising interest in political philosophy and pragmatism (made famous by Machiavelli's *Il Principe*), works such as Thomas More's *Utopia* (1516) used the term to describe both virtuous and nonvirtuous actions, including the wise management advocated by Plato and the "cold-hearted self-interest" of conniving politicians.[6] While complicating the idea, such writers also promoted the understanding that shrewdness is the common denominator and grounding principle of prudence.

While the relationship between virtue and prudence is still debated in modern philosophy, some twentieth-century philosophers have tried to unite the two by advancing a "maximizing" principle of practical reason, emphasizing the optimization of the end result while holding a variety of current and future interests in balance. Philosophers such as Thomas

[3] Aristotle, *Nicomachean Ethics*, trans. W. D. Ross, in *The Basic Works of Aristotle*, ed. Richard McKeon (University of Chicago, 1941).
[4] Of the three standard philosophical approaches to practical reason – those of Aristotle, David Hume, and Immanuel Kant – the Aristotelian approach is arguably the most applicable to Shakespeare, who shows recurrent interest in human flourishing. In contrast to Aristotle, Hume defines the end of practical reason as the fulfillment of desire, a definition that is especially subject to debate and not easy to connect to virtue. Kant defines the end of practical reason as autonomy, or a perfect control of the will, something Shakespeare does not seem to value highly for its own sake.
[5] Brendan Cook, "*Prudentia* in More's *Utopia*: The Ethics of Foresight," *Renaissance and Reformation* 36. 1 (2013), 31–68, 42.
[6] Ibid., 41–42.

Nagel and Derek Parfit use the maximizing principle to argue that if a person can balance competing ends with the long view in mind, he or she should also be able to account for the interests of others who may be affected by the intended actions.[7] This theory adds a social dimension to prudence, developing a concept of the virtue that is simultaneously altruistic and self-interested. This view extends and complicates the Aristotelian idea that the aim of *phronēsis* is *eudaimonia*: prudence demands an even higher moral capacity and greater intellectual power to assess costs, risks, and benefits and imagine a variety of outcomes.

Shakespearean drama can offer further insight into these philosophical conversations, in supplying a concrete, extended display of successful and failed efforts to exercise prudent judgment. This is particularly true of *The Merchant of Venice*, which features economics – a realm especially dependent on practical decision making – in its title.[8] While Antonio's decision to value his friend Bassanio's romantic interests over his own life appears unwise, the play's conclusion suggests that the venture proves to be sensible. Not only does Bassanio succeed and Antonio survive, but the latter is transformed from melancholic loner to "dumb"-struck member of a happy community he helped create (5.1.279).[9] Given its conclusion, the play appears to support not only Aristotle's definition of practical reason, but also the "maximizing" principle of philosophy, a principle closely related to a biblical parable that would have been very familiar to Shakespeare's audiences – the parable of the hidden treasure. This parable from Matthew 13 praises two prospective buyers who sell everything they own to buy a gem of immeasurable worth, thus illustrating how apparent immoderation can be effectively united with rational deliberation.[10] Like the maximizing principle, the parable sharply distinguishes prudence from caution. *The Merchant of Venice* reflects this concept of prudence throughout, repeatedly affirming that genuine prudence is targeted to right ends (like Aristotle's first condition), with an eye to the optimal long-term objective (like the parable of the hidden treasure), for the greatest number of people (like Nagel and Parfit's extension of the "maximizing" principle).

---

[7] Thomas Nagel, *The Possibility of Altruism* (Princeton University Press, 1970); Derek Parfit, *Reasons and Persons* (Clarendon, 1984).

[8] For more on prudence in Shakespeare, see Unhae Park Langis, *Passion, Prudence, and Virtue in Shakespearean Drama* (Continuum/Bloomsbury, 2011).

[9] The opening line of the play is Antonio's: "In sooth, I know not why I am so sad" (1.1.1).

[10] Recorded in Matthew 13:44–46, this parable compares these purchases to the prudent extravagance of those who pursue the kingdom of heaven.

The casket test, designed by Portia's late father to discern the intentions of her suitors, develops a relatively immoderate concept of prudence, when it distinguishes Bassanio's interest in Portia from the
calculating, self-serving interests of the Princes of Morocco and Aragon.
By eliminating the latter from contention, the test exposes both princes'
efforts to substitute shrewdness for a true concept of prudence. The
casket test suggests that the powers of logical reasoning (Aristotle's second component of *phronēsis*) are insufficient to gain virtue or happiness
when those demonstrating them fail to consider the goodness of the
ends.

In failing the test, both Morocco and Aragon do show aptitude for
deliberation in their syllogistic speeches, as they consider which of three
caskets (gold, silver, and lead) contains her portrait and thus the right to
her hand. Morocco, who values Portia for the honor and social significance she would bring, reasons that the gold casket must be the correct
one, for its inscription promises "what many men desire" (2.7.5). Aragon,
who snubs the idea of being praised by others, sees marriage to Portia as
confirmation of his own individual excellence, and chooses the silver casket, which offers the suitor "as much as he deserves" (2.7.7). Both reject
the lead casket, which reads "[w]ho chooseth me must give and hazard
all he hath" (2.7.9), because, in Morocco's words, it "threatens" (2.8.18).
The logic is not wrong; in fact, Bassanio draws the same conclusion. But
both Morocco and Aragon fail to perceive and desire what Bassanio does –
the possibility that a marriage based on mutual companionship and sacrificial service offers greater value than status. When Aragon says to the
lead casket, "you shall look fairer ere I give or hazard" (2.9.23), he shows
that marriage represents for him a form of material profit (as it does for
Morocco). Their decision to reject the lead casket thus fails to fulfill
Aristotle's first component of prudence, the standards of the parable of the
treasure, and the maximizing principle. For while both suitors reach their
decision through efficient deliberation – fulfilling Aristotelian components
(ii) and (iii) – they fail to see that some "goods" rooted in social gain, like
marriage and friendship, are worth far more than the sacrifices those goods
would demand.

Exposing the suitors' appearance of deliberative prudence as mere
foolishness, *The Merchant of Venice* forms a challenge to common understandings of prudence current in Shakespeare's own day, indicating that
prudence is grounded not in insightful logic, but in knowing which
ends to give oneself to wholeheartedly. Without that crucial component,
effective reasoning serves as the means of its own collapse; Portia affirms

after both suitors have failed, "Oh, these deliberate fools! When they do choose, / They have the wisdom by their wit to lose" (2.9.80–81). In the play's judgment, "deliberation" (calculation) and "wit" (shrewdness), core components of practical reason, pave the way to loss and downfall when divorced from noble ends. The casket test makes prudence at least as much a virtue of the heart and the emotions as it is a virtue of the intellect.

But while the casket test mocks the suitors' attempts to substitute self-interested calculation for genuine virtue, the test of Shylock's justice takes a more sober look at a second, tragic failure of prudence. In a reading that the original play might not demand, but does make possible, Shylock's failure to achieve his intended purpose is not a function of selfishness, as for Morocco and Aragon, but of social conditions he cannot control. For Shylock does pursue a noble end at the opening of the play – respect from the Christian community that has marginalized and oppressed him. He simply has no means of achieving this aim. When Antonio asks for his help, Shylock agrees, even while objecting that Antonio has "spit" on, kicked, and insulted him without remorse (1.3.140, 109–127). Some modern performances take the mistreatment further: in the National Theater Company film, Lawrence Olivier plays Shylock as a figure genuinely prepared to help – next to the contemptuous and entitled Antonio, he seems light-hearted and entirely without malice, simply taking advantage of the chance to remind Antonio that it is in his own best interest to treat others better. His tone while proposing a "pound of flesh" for the bond is jovial and flippant, as if he is making a joke on the caricature of his own stinginess.[11] But in the film, Shylock's merciful effort to achieve respect fails, not because he has made a major error of judgment, but because there are no circumstances in which the Christians will respect him as a moneylending Jew. When his daughter Jessica robs him and elopes with Lorenzo, not only do Antonio and his friends do nothing to discourage the outrageous offenses (the squandering of his late wife's ring is especially heartbreaking), but they mock him pitilessly (3.1.1–40). And if modern performances play up the mistreatment, it is apparent as well in the printed text, which likewise indicates that there is no possible means for Shylock to attain a desirable outcome.

In a plausible reading (though certainly not a universal early-modern understanding), it is Shylock's heartbreak that pushes him into the

---

[11] *The Merchant of Venice*, directed by Jonathan Miller (National Theatre Company, 1973), 22:00–23:15.

depraved "shrewdness" that Aristotle and "maximizing" theorists divorce from virtue. In Olivier's interpretation, only after being mocked does Shylock even begin to think of holding Antonio to the agreed bond, to gain an immoral revenge in place of the ever-elusive respect he seeks. In a stirring scene where Shylock ponders how to respond to his own humiliation, the moneylender has an epiphany prompted by the ringing of church bells, repeating three times, ominously: "let him look to his bond."[12] The film thus depicts Shylock's attempt at murder as a consequence of oppression rather than innate viciousness. Later, in the trial scene, the play affirms that the principle of proper ends holds – since Shylock pursues wrong purposes, his shrewdness leads to his own downfall. But Shylock's disgrace represents more than a critique of foolishness – it is also a tragedy of chronic powerlessness. In his next to last speech, Shylock insists, "You take my life / When you do take the means whereby I live" (4.1.374–375), poignantly substantiating his earlier claim that "sufferance is the badge of all our tribe" (1.3.108). As Shylock loses his wealth and identity at the conclusion, the play suggests that, for some, it is simply not possible to deliberate one's way to happiness.

While these scenes emphasize that prudence (for people who are in a position to display it) depends first on generosity of spirit rather than shrewdness, the play also makes a limited effort to endorse calculation during the court scene, when the disguised Portia plots to release Antonio from Shylock's bond in the name of "justice" (4.1.312). She reveals to Shylock the consequences of his own legalistic form of justice by affirming that he is entitled by law to the "pound of flesh" he requests, but nothing more – not one "drop of Christian blood" (4.1.308). Portia's judgment thus appears to fulfill both components one and two of Aristotelian *phronēsis*, applying cunning to the saving of life, a nobler end than revenge. And in stepping in to help a man she does not even know, she also fulfills (in part) the maximizing principle of practical reason, as she seeks the good of a friend of Bassanio, and thus the "semblance of my soul" (3.4.20). Acknowledging the interconnectedness of human good, she appears to unite the various conditions of prudence – right ends, correct thinking, and orientation toward a common good – into one epitomized form.

Yet this form of prudence also falls short. Portia's efforts to spare "Christian blood" are astute, but her harsh judgment of Shylock condemns

---

[12] Miller, *Merchant,* 49:00–49:30.

him to a fate he might find equal to death, in erasing his professional and religious identity. And since she appropriates the language of virtue, Portia performs an even more pernicious version of the revenge attempted by Shylock himself, perpetuating the cycle of vengeance he describes in his famous "Hath not a Jew eyes" speech:

> If a Christian wrong a Jew, what should his sufferance be by Christian example? Why, revenge. The villainy you teach me I will execute, and it shall go hard but I will better the instruction. (3.1.65–69)

Portia's judgment affirms Shylock's accusation that these Christians live by an ethic of revenge rather than the compassion or true justice that biblical teaching endorses. And in failing to work toward easing ethnic tensions, Portia fails to meet the ethic of her own professed religion and the "maximizing" principle, leaving Venetian society primed for more of the same oppression and injustice.

As the play's closest approximation of Aristotelian prudence proves strikingly imprudent, Shakespeare suggests how quickly this virtue, already unreachable to the oppressed, can be stamped out by undue self-assurance. The aftermath of the trial reiterates the point, as Bassanio, who had demonstrated immoderate prudence so well earlier, fails the "ring" test that Portia creates for him. Still in disguise, Portia asks Bassanio to hand over the ring she had insisted he never part with, thereby establishing a test of loyalties – will he honor his loyalty to his friend, who urges him to "let [Portia] have the ring" as a simple favor to his deliverer (4.1.448), or the wife for whom he promised to "hazard all?" The ring test demands that Bassanio show he understands the implications of his choice to "give all" for a loving marriage: that while it was prudent to be extravagant toward Portia, this extravagance must be sacrificial to mean anything. Bassanio, however, brashly extends this spirit of extravagance to Antonio: "But life itself, my wife, and all the world / Are not with me esteemed above thy life. I would lose all, ay, sacrifice them all ... to deliver [Antonio]" (4.1.280–285); and on Antonio's urging, he hands the ring over. The ring test establishes not only the importance of subordinating male friendships to the exclusive commitment of marriage, but the fact that prudence is much easier to demonstrate in a theoretical context (such as the casket test) than it is in practice. Bassanio may know that the best ends demand extravagant sacrifice, but his actions show how difficult it can be to live out this principle in real time.

In exploring so many failures of prudence, the play suggests that this virtue may never be entirely attainable to imperfect humans. Some may exhibit the virtue more consistently than others, but the ultimate standard of prudence, Shakespeare suggests, is the ability to exercise judgment altruistically, while acknowledging an inclination to self-interested foolishness (a standard no character in the play attains). Especially to modern audiences, the play exposes the hypocrisy of its Christian characters and their efforts at practical wisdom, but its final concept of prudence is in fact a biblical one – never to be wise in one's own eyes.[13]

---

[13] Proverbs 3:7; Isaiah 5:21.

CHAPTER 14

Friendship

Sean Keilen

From ancient Athens to the English Renaissance, a broad philosophical tradition idealizes human friendship as uncommonly virtuous. According to this tradition, friendships spring from an inborn propensity of all creatures to care for others of their own kind. Friendship is, therefore, in our nature as living beings. Human friendship, however, differs from every animal's bond with members of its species – and also from kinship ties, which it resembles more closely – because it is voluntary. Only human beings choose their friends in the way Desdemona envisions when she tells Cassio, "If I do vow a friendship, I'll perform it/ to the last article" (3.3.21–22).[1] That is one reason why friendship can be described as an achievement as well as a risk. Another reason is that friendships are ends in themselves. Unlike the elective partnerships that we form with other people to pursue material gains or pleasures, friendship is not utilitarian or expedient. Instead, it is set apart from the duties and rivalries that characterize adult life, expressing altruistic care and concern for the well-being of other people as they are (and usually, for one other person). Cicero writes in *De amicitia* that friendship's entire profit (*fructus*) is in love itself.[2]

Shakespeare knew this idealizing tradition well, as a result of Cicero's vast influence on Renaissance pedagogy and writing, yet his approach to friendship often diverges from Cicero's. Critics, therefore, have been apt to conclude that Shakespeare's verdict on his Roman forebear is negative. According to John D. Cox, Shakespeare "holds [Ciceronian friendship] up to critical examination in a way that might be called skeptical but should perhaps more accurately be called suspicious (2)."[3] The foundation

---

[1] Citations of Shakespeare from *The Pelican Shakespeare*, eds. Stephen Orgel and A. R. Braunmuller (Penguin 2002).

[2] Cicero, *De amicitia*, trans. William Armistead Falconer (Harvard, 2001), §31. Hereafter cited by section number.

[3] John D. Cox, "Shakespeare and the Ethics of Friendship," *Religion and Literature* 40. 3 (2008), 1–29. See also Tom Macfaul, *Male Friendship in Shakespeare and His Contemporaries* (Cambridge University Press, 2007).

of such judgments is not anything that Shakespeare says about Cicero directly. Rather, it is the consistency with which he entertains the idea that virtue, and therefore friendship in the ancient sense, does not come naturally to us. "Most friendship is feigning," sings Amiens in *As You Like It*, "most loving mere folly" (3.1.180).

This chapter offers new reflections on the extent and meaning of Shakespeare's departures from the ancient tradition in an early comedy, *The Two Gentlemen of Verona*. Although this play is alert to the limitations of Cicero's model of friendship, it does not propose that there is a clear alternative to it. Instead, it explores different kinds of friendly association, some more Ciceronian than others, and considers their relationship. In the process, *Two Gentlemen* discovers in the theater itself what may be a way of reconciling the emphasis on human perfectibility in ancient friendship theory with the attunement to human frailty that characterizes all of Shakespeare's works.

Aristotle's influential account of friendship holds that affable relationships based in utility and pleasure are inferior to friendships arising from a love of virtue. In friendship's ideal form, two people develop "a shared consciousness formed by a common pursuit" – the pursuit of the good; the school of philosophers exemplifies friendship in this sense.[4] Cicero is more civic-minded but also calls this kind of friendship "true and perfect," in contrast to "ordinary and common" (§22) It is extraordinarily rare, because it requires that prior to becoming friends with each other, friends should have become good people in their own right, in order that their friends may recognize the good in them and love them for it alone. Aristotle writes that "friendship is a virtue or implies virtue" and lasts only as long as both friends are good (*Nicomachean Ethics,* 1155a, 1556b).[5] Cicero agrees, expanding upon this idea when he argues that friendship "is nothing but an agreement [*consensio*] about all things divine and human, together with good will [*benvolentia*] and love [*caritas*]," that takes virtue as "the highest good [*summum bonum*]" (§20). In this sense, friends share the same life, by virtue of the fact that they share a common good. Aristotle and Cicero agree that the friend is "another self" (for Aristotle, *allos autos*, *NE,* 1166a30–32; for Cicero, *exemplar sui*, §23 and *alter idem*, §80). "[I]t is a most difficult thing … to know oneself," writes Aristotle, because "we

---

[4] James McEvoy, "Philia and Amicitia: The Philosophy of Friendship from Plato to Aquinas," *Sewanee Medieval Colloquium Occasional Papers* 2 (1985), 1–23, 12.

[5] Aristotle, *Nicomachean Ethics*, in *Aristotle's Ethics*, eds. Jonathan Barnes and Anthony Kenney (Princeton, 2014), 207–372. Hereafter referred to as *NE*.

are not able to contemplate ourselves from ourselves." Therefore, "just as when we want to see our own face we do so by looking into a mirror, in the same way when we want to know ourselves we can obtain that knowledge by looking at a friend. For a friend is ... another I" (*Magna Moralia* 1213a14–25).[6]

In *De amicitia*, Cicero acknowledges that the truth about ourselves can poison friendships when it provokes our hatred (§89). However, he also believes that in the absence of truth, "friendship" is a word without meaning (§92). In friendships, we combine our instinctive need to give and receive love as living creatures with our rational capacity as human beings to discern truth from falsehood. That is why "it is proper to true friendship to give criticism freely and without harshness, and to accept it patiently, without resistance" (§91). It is also why "[t]he quality of our friendships and the quality of our moral lives are inseparable."[7] A friend is "someone able to tell us the truth" about ourselves because he or she loves us; and because it is indisputably true that "moral failure is ... a recurrent and characteristic feature of our lives," it follows that "moral education [is] the work of a lifetime."[8] Friendship is "something like a school for virtue, in which other noble virtues are learned."[9]

Cicero not only says that the love (*amor*) that gives friendship (*amicitia*) its name is good will (*benevolentia*) and charity (*caritas*). He also acknowledges that our search for friendship inevitably unfolds in a reality where "human affairs are fragile and fleeting" (§102). He often draws attention to the ways in which friends should respond to changes in each other's circumstances. Friendship, like self-knowledge, is an ongoing project, subject to variable internal and external forces, and he praises friendship for orienting people toward the future with hope (§§22–23). He acknowledges that it is in virtue's nature to suffer distress for the sake of one's friends (§48). In the same spirit, he argues against philosophers "who want virtue to be something hard like iron" that virtue in friendship should be "soft and tractable" (§48). The freedom that friends have to criticize each other is another expression of care that recognizes that we are bound to encounter setbacks of greater and lesser

---

[6] Aristotle, *Magna Moralia*, in *Aristotle's Ethics*, eds. Jonathan Barnes and Anthony Kenney, 373–474.
[7] Alasdair MacIntyre, "What Both the Bad and the Good Bring to Frienships in their Strange Variety," in *Amor Amicitiae: On the Love that is Friendship*, ed. Thomas Kelly and Philipp Rosemann (Peeter, 2004), 241–254, 255.
[8] Alasdair MacIntyre, "Is Friendship Possible?," deNicola Center for Ethics and Culture, Notre Dame, November 7–9, 2019, https://youtu.be/LuAP_7jmssQ.
[9] James McEvoy, "Philia and Amicitia," 46.

significance (§90). This is not a vision of the universal philanthropy
that Christianity proclaimed in the centuries after Cicero's death, but
it does help to explain why Christian ethics was able to assimilate *De
amicitia* to Jesus's commandment to love one's neighbors and enemies
as oneself.[10] Of Cicero, Erasmus writes in his own edition of *De amicitia*, "How much holier this man is than certain theologians who teach
the rule of charity!"[11]

The esteem in which English humanists held Cicero's practical wisdom,
along with his prose style, meant that by the mid-sixteenth century, "for
any schoolboy completing grammar school ... exposure to *De amicitia*, in
Latin, could hardly have been avoided."[12] But while reared in this tradition, Shakespeare "never unambiguously endorses the Ciceronian ideal [of
friendship]."[13] There are at least three ways that Shakespeare's friendships
often fail to imitate Cicero's model. First, Cicero believes that in order
for friendship to be perfect and enduring, friends ought to be men and
equal in age, status, wealth, and prospects. By contrast, it is only in their
sex that Shakespeare's friends are consistently alike; and, in the cases of
Hamlet and Horatio, Antonio and Bassanio, and the poet and fair youth
of the *Sonnets*, friends tend to be unequal in one or more of Cicero's categories. Second, Ciceronian friendship is altruistic and non-utilitarian,
but self-interest and competitive rivalry typically pervade Shakespeare's
friendships. The distinction between self, friend, and rival grows especially
obscure in the Roman plays when Cassius – who both offers Brutus friendship and tries to seduce him into killing his rival, Caesar – says that he is
the "glass" that "Will modestly discover to yourself/ That of yourself which
you yet know not of" (1.2.70–72). Third, Cicero argues that friendship is a
bond between people who share a commitment to becoming good, if they
are not virtuous already; vicious persons cannot be friends (§18, 65, 92). In
Shakespeare's plays, however, "innocent" friendships are often consigned
to memories of lost childhood,[14] while more mature friendships abide in

---

[10] E.g. Matthew 5: 43–45.
[11] James McEvoy, "The Theory of Friendship in Erasmus and Thomas More," *American Catholic Philosophical Quarterly* 80. 2 (2006), 227–252, 230.
[12] Laurie Shannon, Sovereign Amity: Figures of Friendship in Shakespearean Contexts (University of Chicago Press, 2002), 28.
[13] John D. Cox, "Shakespeare and the Ethics of Friendship," 2.
[14] Helena refers to her youth with Hermina as "schooldays' friendship, childhood innocence" (*Midsummer Night's Dream*, 3.2.202). Polixenes says of boyhood with Leontes, "What we changed/ Was innocence for innocence; we knew not/ The doctrine of ill-doing, nor dreamed/ That any did" (*The Winter's Tale*, 1.2.69–72).

vice. Richard III and Buckingham are thick as thieves[15] until Buckingham "grows circumspect" about murdering Richard's nephews; one scruple makes these friends mortal enemies (4.2.31). Seen from the perspective of these relationships, Shakespeare's approach to friendship appears to put him in conflict with the philosophical tradition that regards it as a moral good, and specifically with Cicero.[16]

It is not correct to say that Shakespeare entirely rejects Cicero's model. Women in his fictions are occasionally capable of Ciceronian friendship In *As You Like It*, for example, Celia puts herself in her cousin Rosalind's position, resolves to share all she owns with her, and follows her into exile. And at the start of Shakespeare's career, when he is still fresh from school and only just learning how to change his classical education into plays, he is as receptive to Cicero as he is critical.

*

The Two Gentlemen of Verona is an early comedy that explores the transition from youth to maturity: a time when, according to Cicero, competition for other-sex marriages and resources to improve one's status endangers not only single-sex friendships formed in boyhood, but also the peace of the social order as a whole (§33). Shakespeare takes up themes in this play that he will carry all the way to *The Two Noble Kinsmen* years later, but at this point, he is selective about Cicero's theory rather than suspicious, often violating its letter while cleaving to its spirit.

When the play begins, Valentine and Proteus, two young friends on the cusp of adulthood, are headed in different directions. Valentine is about to leave Verona to seek his fortune at the ducal court in Milan. Proteus intends to remain and pursue a love affair with Julia. In addition to their lack of experience as either courtiers or lovers, and the books they cite to fill that void, these friends have in common a readiness to support each other in pursuing different pathways to human flourishing. They may differ in what they want, but they are the same, in the sense that each one wants for his friend what his friend wants in his own right, extending to the other the kind of love he feels for himself. "[S]ince thou lov'st, love still and thrive therein," says Valentine to Proteus, "Even as I would when

---

[15] Before they fall out, Richard hearkens to Cicero when he addresses Buckingham as "My other self, my soul's consistory,/ My oracle, my prophet" (2.2.151–152).

[16] Alexander Nehemas, *On Friendship* (Basic Books 2016) argues that friendship is not a moral good.

I to love begin" (1.1.9–10). "If ever danger do environ thee," says Proteus to Valentine, "Commend thy grievances to my holy prayers,/ For I will be thy beadsman" (1.1.16–18).

This dialogue sets a pattern for youthful, single-sex friendship from which Shakespeare's portrait of mature, other-sex desire diverges. Love is friendship's great competitor in the play. Boyhood involves witty banter, reading together, and mutual good will. The essence of manhood is competitive rivalry and aggressive self-interest. "In love," asks Proteus, "Who respects a friend?" (5.4.54–55). For Valentine and Proteus, being a lover means becoming changeable. Love is a "chameleon" and both Proteus and Valentine are said to be "metamorphosed" by desire, but Cicero is clear that faithfulness (*fides*), the "strength and stability of constancy," is what we seek in friendships (1.1.66, 2.1.29, 164). Therefore, people with "a manifold and twisting wit [*multiplex ingenium et tortuosum*]," cannot be our friends, because they cannot be faithful to anybody, including themselves (§65). Proteus demonstrates these Ciceronian principles when, upon meeting Silvia, he forswears Julia, pretending to love her and support Valentine's own love project, in order to gain access to Silvia and woo her for himself. Proteus then enters more fully into the identity of a lover and violates the first of two principles that Cicero sets down for friendship: never to lie or dissimulate (§65). He violates the second principle, never to slander a friend (§65–66), at the beginning of Act Three, when he reveals Valentine's plan to elope with Silvia to the Duke and brings about his banishment. His transformation from friend to lover is complete. Earlier, Proteus was capable of wanting *for Valentine* what Valentine wanted for himself. Now he can only want *for himself* what Valentine wants. Like the true friend, the love rival is another self. However, in contrast to the good will of Ciceronian friendship, which extends to another the love we feel for ourselves, desire is self-love without extension and betrays all existing trusts. Proteus muses that if he "keep[s]" Valentine and Julia, "I needs must lose myself;/ If I lose them, thus find I by their loss," for "I to myself am dearer than a friend,/ And love is still most precious in itself" (2.6.20–24).

Proteus bears the brunt of the play's reflection on inconstancy, but Valentine's character develops along a parallel arc that *De amicitia* illuminates. Cicero writes that if the bond of good will (*benevolentia*) were taken away from nature, no house or city could stand, nor would the cultivation of fields endure (§23). Friendship upholds the order of civilization. It is "the sharing of all in the common project of creating and sustaining the life of the city, a sharing incorporated in the immediacy of an individual's particular friendships."[17] As Valentine becomes a lover, it is precisely this common project that his desire for Silvia imperils. Desire prompts him to dissimulate his true intentions to the Duke his master, and to disobey him. Later, an exile in the forest, he becomes the leader of a band of outlaws. The "fury of ungoverned youth" has "[t]hrust [them] from the company of awful men," as it has done for Valentine himself (4.1.47–48).

The different plot lines concerning Valentine and Proteus intersect in the forest. Friendship, the civic order, self-knowledge, and the capacity for forgiveness converge there too, in three tableaux that imagine repairing the damage that desire's selfish and anarchic love inflicts on same-sex friendship, other-sex courtship, and the relationship of rulers and subjects. Shakespeare sets the scene for these reconciliations when Silvia, who flees Milan in search of Valentine, falls into the hands of the outlaws, who separate her from her protector, Sir Eglamour. Proteus pursues Silvia to the woods and rescues her, while the outlaws capture her father and Thurio. After failing to persuade Silvia to become his lover, Proteus declares that he will rape her: "I'll force thee yield to my desire" (5.4.59). Valentine, who watches from a hiding place, now advances, calls Proteus a "friend of an ill fashion," and demands that he "let go that rude uncivil touch" (5.4.60–61). These phrases connect the private law of friendship to the public norms of civility. To betray a friend is to deprive civility of its meaning as the ordering of relationships and duties that constitutes social life as a whole. That is why Valentine tells Proteus that he must now "count the world a stranger for thy sake" (5.4.70).

Surprising things start happening just when Proteus's violence seems to have damaged the prospect of friendship, marriage, and society irreparably. First, Proteus asks Valentine for forgiveness and tenders "hearty sorrow" as "ransom for offense" (5.4.74–75). Valentine forgives him, saying "I do receive thee honest"; this phrase acknowledges that Proteus is offering nothing less than himself (5.4.78). In exchange, Valentine offers Proteus "[a]ll that was mine in Silvia" (5.4.83). Many scholars and directors assume that in this notorious passage, Valentine transfers his claim on Silvia's love to Proteus, but if read in terms of friendship, the passage makes new and different sense. We know that Valentine refers not to Silvia but to himself, because during an earlier soliloquy, he spoke of Silvia as "thou that dost inhabit in my breast" (5.4.7). According to the

[17] Alasdair MacIntyre, *After Virtue: A Study in Moral Theory*, 3rd edn. (University of Notre Dame Press, 2007), 156.

discourse lovers speak in the play, if Silvia lives in Valentine, in the place where his own heart should be, then he and his heart must be in Silvia. The love that Valentine offers Proteus is therefore not Silvia's love, which is not his to give, but his own. The way that Valentine and Proteus talk to each other may seem abrupt, but it would be wrong to conclude that they are insincere. Valentine offers criticism without humiliation, and Proteus accepts it patiently, just as Cicero says friends ought to do in caring for each other. Then they attempt to reestablish their friendship by showing each other that they are each other's other self again. Perhaps Proteus is able to ask for forgiveness, and Valentine to grant it, because each man sees the reflection of his own transgressions in the mirror of his friend and craves pardon.

If there is a price to pay for this reconciliation, Silvia appears to bear that cost. While Valentine focuses on the meaning of the attempted rape for himself and Proteus, she stands by, speechless and unaddressed. She remains that way through the end of the play. How Silvia understands Valentine's offer to Proteus, and whether it changes her feelings toward him as their wedding approaches, we cannot know. Her silence is a mystery that demands we notice that this scene of reconciliation is singularly incomplete. In reconciling Julia to Proteus, however, Shakespeare partially resolves this crisis, at one remove from Silvia and Valentine. Earlier, Julia disguised herself as Proteus's serving boy and followed him into the woods despite knowing that he had rejected her for Silvia. When Valentine offers Proteus all that was his in Silvia, Julia breaks cover and swoons. "O me unhappy!" she says, in a line that echoes Silvia's first line in this scene: "O, miserable, unhappy that I am!" (5.4.28, 84). These female lamentations, which frame the new amity between Valentine and Proteus, suggest that in Julia's experiences, Shakespeare articulates what he leaves unsaid about Silvia. Regaining consciousness, Julia removes her disguise and comments that it is "the lesser blot" for "[w]omen to change their shapes than men their minds" (5.4.109–110). Proteus takes to heart what she says and recommits himself to constancy; they too are reconciled. Constancy, a hallmark of male friendship in Cicero's text, combines with other-sex desire and tempers it, turning lovers into husbands and wives who are, like friends, capable of giving and receiving criticism lovingly and of helping each other grow toward virtue.

Once single-sex friendship is restored, and other-sex desire is recast in its image, all that remains is for these transformed relationships to renovate society. Right on cue, the outlaws appear with their captives. Valentine releases them, Thurio relinquishes his claim on Silvia, and the

Duke, who now acknowledges that Valentine is worthy to be his son-in-law, recalls him from banishment. He also "plead[s] a new state in [Valentine's] unrivaled merit" (5.4.145). This inscrutable phrase prompts Valentine to ask for the outlaws to be pardoned and recognized as gentlemen, "reformed, civil, full of good" (5.4.157). As the Duke consents, the breach that insubordinate desire made between sovereign and subject heals. The social order rises again on a foundation of mercy. Silvia says nothing while friendship flourishes among these men, nor when Valentine takes possession of her from her father. The metamorphic Julia seems to have found her other self in Proteus, but for Silvia, a marriage patterned on single-sex friendship remains elusive. Eglamour, whose name means equal love, is missing in the forest. Perhaps we are meant to understand that in Silvia, whose name in Latin means "the woods," equal love silently waits for its voice to be heard.

*

At the end of *The Two Gentlemen of Verona*, the cast returns to the city to celebrate "one feast, one house, one mutual happiness," and Shakespeare underscores what the imagination has done to achieve this outcome, and what role it must continue to play if the outcome is to endure (5.4.174). Valentine tells Proteus that his "penance" is to listen to "the story of [his] loves discovered" (5.4.172). How easy that penance will be, and whether it will unite these characters further or divide them against each other again, depends on who the storyteller turns out to be. Imagine that Julia will tell the story. She is Shakespeare's most original creation in the play and an image of his own artform. In addition to embodying the practices of the theater, by virtue of her play-acting as Sebastian, Julia also demonstrates a kind of love that is unique in this comedy: Christian charity, which extends itself in friendship even to one's enemies. Playing the part of Sebastian, who in turn must represent Proteus to Silvia, Julia discovers that to love in this way is to yield to others and to serve them, completely. "I am my master's true confirmed love," says Julia, before she goes to woo Silvia on Proteus's behalf, "But [I] cannot be true servant to my master,/ Unless I prove false traitor to myself" (4.4.102–104). In this regard, Julia's selfless love for Proteus is distinct from the steadfast love between Valentine and Silvia; they remain true to each other by remaining true to themselves. It is also distinct from the *caritas* of Ciceronian friendship. Cicero has no conception of the redemption Shakespeare explores in this play, nor of Christianity's selfless, indiscriminate love. Moreover, to seem to be anyone but oneself is incompatible with friendship as Cicero defines it; pretending is clear evidence of the "diverse, changeable, and manifold" character that Cicero associates with bad men (§92). What Shakespeare shows us through Julia's performance of a faithful servant's role is that Roman constancy, tempered by Cicero's own awareness that human imperfection calls for benevolence, might change a society of self-serving rivals and possessive courtships into a community of friends who love each other and the truth.

CHAPTER 15

Patience

Nick Moschovakis

Is "patience a virtue?" Traditionally, yes, from antiquity to Shakespeare's time and ours. Early Greek Stoics included patience among the virtues.[1] For Seneca, *patientia* was instrumental to *"felicis animi ... tranquillitas,"* "the tranquillitie of a happy minde."[2] Our saying "patience is a virtue" is as old as the so-called *Distichs of Cato*, a book of moral precepts in verse, assigned to medieval and early-modern children as a first Latin reader. From the *Distichs* countless pupils, including the young Shakespeare, learned that "patience is always a virtue in the highest degree": *"maxima ... semper patientia virtus."*[3]

What is patience? How, when, why should it be practiced? No simple answer will do. But the *Distichs* make a good start, showing that like most classical virtues, *patientia* is far from an expression of humility and is rather a sign of superiority. The book's couplet on patience advised: "At times, conquer someone by bearing with them, even though you could overpower them."[4] The same idea of patience as supremacy informs Elizabethan commonplace books that call patience "the vanquisher of injuries"[5] and "a noble way to win."[6]

---

[1] See Stobaeus, *Anthologii Libri Duo Priores,* ed. Curtius Wachsmuth (Weidmann, 1884), 57–64, at 60. Patience went under various names in classical and biblical Greek.

[2] Seneca, *De ira* 2.12.6; *The Workes of Lucius Annaeus Seneca,* trans. Thomas Lodge (William Stansby, 1614), 536.

[3] My translation; Latin text from Desiderius Erasmus (ed.) and Richard Taverner (trans.), *Catonis Disticha Moralia* (n.p., 1562), f. B6[v]. Cicero's influential *On Duties* had declared that youth should "above all [*maxime*]... be fortified against desires and ... trained in labor and patience [*patientia*], both of soul and of body" (*De officiis* 1.122, my translation).

[4] *"Quem superare potes, interdum vince ferendo,"* my translation from Erasmus (ed.), f. B6[v].

[5] William Baldwin and Thomas Paulfreyman, *A Treatise of Morall Philosophy* (Richard Bishop, 1630 [first ed. thus 1567]), f. 110[v].

[6] My translation of *"nobile vincendi genus,"* quoted in Quentin Skinner, *Forensic Shakespeare* (Oxford University Press, 2014), 309, citing Hermann Germbergius, *Carminum Proverbialium ... Loci Communes, in gratiam iuventutis selecti* (n.p., 1577), 159.

We may balk at this notion of patience as a virtue for winners. Isn't patience, rather, a bitter pill for the disempowered? Today, urging "patience" can invite the charge of passivity in the face of injustice. And the word's etymology might seem to favor this view – *pati* being a Latin verb for "suffer" or "endure." Nevertheless, within the discourse of classical virtue ethics, *patientia* is not passive or submissive suffering. It is, rather, active sufferance: a power to look past what might hurt us now, attending to what matters more.

To be patient in this way is not to abdicate agency but to behave deliberately. To understand why such deliberation is important, look no further than the need to govern one's tongue. In *Twelfth Night*, Viola (in the guise of Cesario) pictures a lovelorn subject concealing her love, sitting "like Patience ... Smiling at grief" (2.4.126–27).[7] What if we never ever kept silent about such desires, but we all instantly broadcast our unfiltered passions? To avoid that nightmare, we need at least some patience. In classical ethics such restraint of speech was a prime imperative. Ancient teachers could not have conceived of any education failing to instill this elementary patience, whether as a prerequisite for honorable public service or for a private philosophical life.

Modern attacks on patience as passivity do not focus chiefly on classical *patientia,* however. Their main objection is to another sort of patience, rooted in monotheistic religion and especially in Christian piety. In the Christian tradition, patience is not just a way out of suffering but a way into and through it – it is part of redemption. Friedrich Nietzsche assailed that vision when, in 1887, he called patience one of modern Western culture's key "fabricated ideals": a fake virtue, idolizing "the inoffensiveness of the weakling" and limiting human potential.[8]

As I will show, Shakespeare anticipated such nineteenth-century doubts about Christian patience. But he did not equate patience with indignity as Nietzsche did. One reason is that sixteenth-century Christianity saw less meekness in patience, and more heroism: to be patient was to act one's part in a divine plan. Christians of Shakespeare's day had their own stories to tell about patience as a winner's virtue.

Admittedly, Shakespeare does not always represent either classical or Christian patience as purely good. Viola's case is one of the easier

---

[7] Here and throughout I cite the online *Folger Shakespeare,* https://shakespeare.folger.edu/.

[8] Friedrich Nietzsche, *On the Genealogy of Morality,* ed. Keith Ansell-Pearson, trans. Carol Diethe, 2nd ed. (Cambridge University Press, 2006), 27–28. Disentangling patience from inactivity and negligence is central for Matthew Pianalto, *On Patience: Reclaiming a Foundational Virtue* (Lexington, 2016).

ones, given her initial predicament and her later success. She has determined that, for now, containing her desire for Orsino is her best option. Keeping her longings to herself preserves her strategic control over the terms of her self-disclosure. That modest victory will underwrite her eventual triumph, while it also creates space for other erotic conflicts to reach romantic – or at least comic – resolutions. But these benefits of her patience hinge on *Twelfth Night*'s generic design. What about less rosily comedic scenarios?

In the next section I look at some more troubling Shakespearean invocations of patience. It is critical to confront these trouble spots, for they raise worries about aligning patience with social justice. In my final section, I will again advocate for patience, arguing that Shakespeare's nuanced pictures of this virtue can and should help us cultivate patience in life.

Abuses of Patience in Discourse and in Practice

A starting point in appreciating patience is to recognize that practicing it does not mean placing it above all other virtues. If we exercise patience unconditionally, without respecting other moral priorities, self-serving people will take advantage. This concern was famously voiced by Cicero in accusing a man who plotted against the Roman republic: "How long, Catiline, will you go on abusing our patience?"[9] When subjected populations see their patience systematically abused, they may rightly renounce it. We see this happening around us now.[10] In short, not all patience is warranted. But that doesn't mean we should follow Nietzsche and despise it as a loser's virtue.

Shakespeare in the 1590s was already alert to the temptations of the cynical view that patience is for losers. Moreover, he admitted its kernel of truth: inappropriate patience perpetuates injustice. He even pointedly suggested how his society could routinely abuse people's patience. Take *The Taming of the Shrew*, where Petruchio assures us that "For patience [Katherine] will prove a second Grissel" (2.1.312). This line alludes to a notorious tale of extreme wifely submission: Griselda must demonstrate

---

[9] Cicero, *Against Catiline* 1.1, trans. Mary Beard, *SPQR: A History of Ancient Rome* (Liveright/Norton, 2015), 41.

[10] See *The New York Times*, "Mayors call for 'peace, not patience'," "Live updates," May 31, 2020 www.nytimes.com. Minneapolis Mayor Melvin Carter's interview remained online as of December 14, 2020 www.msn.com/en-us/news/politics/st-paul-mayor-calling-for-peace-but-not-calling-for-patience/vi-BB14QCsa.

her perfect "patience" to a husband who tests it by depriving her of everything – even her children – while she uncomplainingly endures.[11] The patriarchalism of this dismal parable, read literally, is extreme even by Elizabethan standards.[12] It implies that Katherine's "impatient devilish spirit" is adequately explained by the misogyny she faces daily. Despite her notorious final pivot (in her speech praising male rule), Katherine seems unlikely to tolerate future abuse like a meek "second Grissel." In *The Comedy of Errors* Adriana generalizes the same perspective to all wives, arguing that none who has an "unkind mate" could ever show Griselda-like "patience" (2.1.32–41).

The Tempest also highlights abuses of patience – here by the ruling class, which brazenly requires far less patience from its own members than from everyone else. The royal Ferdinand wins Miranda in marriage, along with her father's dukedom, just by enduring a few hours as her "patient log-man" (3.1.79). Quite a prize for such a trifling performance of patience! In contrast, the enslaved Caliban is tasked with labor that will never "profit" him, only his master (1.2.375). And yet Caliban is expected to serve gladly for years on end, being threatened with torture if he so much as seems to work "unwillingly" (1.2.443). Why demand so much more patience from him than from Ferdinand?

Underlying all such concerns about patience in Shakespeare, whether articulated or only implied, is a keen sense of how *patience* and *patient* can mask oppression. Yielding to fear or force is a capitulation, but oppressors can misrepresent it as virtuous "patience" – a verbal trick that rhetorical handbooks called *paradiastole* (using moral terms equivocally*).*[13] Lucrece offers a grotesque instance, as the rapist Tarquin tells his victim: "thou with patience must my will abide" (l. 486). The line, inherently brutal, is also blatantly and cynically ironic in its commandeering of the word *patience.* By Tarquin's twisted logic, Lucrece bears responsibility both for his violation of her and for how she subjectively endures it.[14]

---

[11] See Giovanni Boccaccio's *Decameron,* 10.10, and "The Clerk's Tale" in Geoffrey Chaucer's *Canterbury Tales.*

[12] For the asymmetrical debts of patience owed by wives and husbands in Elizabethan state ideology, see "An Homilie of the State of Matrimonie," *The Elizabethan Homilies 1623,* ed. Ian Lancashire, https://onesearch.library.utoronto.ca/sites/default/files/ret/ret.html.

[13] See Quentin Skinner, "Paradiastole," in *Renaissance Figures of Speech,* eds. Sylvia Adamson, Gavin Alexander, and Katrin Ettenhuber (Cambridge University Press, 2007), 149–163.

[14] Compare Henry imposing on Katherine of France for a kiss ("Therefore, patiently and yielding"; *Henry V,* 5.2.285–286), and Titus dismissing Tamora's plea for her son's life ("Patient yourself, madam, and pardon me"; *Titus Andronicus,* 1.1.121). I owe the latter example to Sean Keilen.

Can we affirm the virtue of patience against sympathetic examples of impatience, like Katherine and Caliban? Can we distinguish patience from Griselda's abasement, and from enslavement in all its forms? Certainly. What is wrong is not patience itself, but its ideological abuse.[15] That patience is a virtue means we should all be capable of it – not that the people with the least power should learn to be more patient than those with more. We can value justice and patience.

The Uses of Patience: To Excel in the Moment, to Prevail in the End – and to Enable Other Virtues

If patience can be so abused, what are its uses? Why is it good? We find divergent answers in Shakespeare, partly because he drew on two discourses of patience – classical and Christian. At stake are two largely different temporal orientations. Classical patience *excels in the moment* by transcending pain, hardship, and transient emotions such as anger and grief.[16] In contrast, Christian patience (especially in premodern culture) looks to *prevail in the end,* if not through God's providential action in this life, then at the last judgment. This difference appears strikingly in how each sort of patience responds to suffering, or "passion" – a word that shares the same Latin etymology as "patience," and that has its own prominent place in histories of Western selfhood.[17] Whereas classical patience quells insurgent passions, Christian patience welcomes certain sufferings as akin to Christ's passion, including his humiliation and crucifixion.[18]

---

[15] Sometimes we might wonder what's abused: the term *patience,* or the virtue itself? Claudius counsels "patience" to Laertes while plotting Hamlet's death (*Hamlet,* 5.1.313–314). Othello, deceived, vows to be "most cunning in … patience" and "most bloody" (*Othello,* 4.1.108–109). Is patience really what these speakers mean? Can virtue further bad ends? I'd answer yes; a virtue can be abused, if its efficacy enables evils that outweigh the intrinsic good of practicing the virtue. But Saint Augustine would disagree; he denied the name *patience* to hardiness or perseverance in a bad cause (*De Patientia,* 3–5; translation in *Seventeen Short Treatises of Saint Augustine, Bishop of Hippo* [John Henry Parker, 1847], 543–562).

[16] On the present instant in ancient moral philosophy, see Hadot, *Philosophy as a Way of Life,* ed. Arnold Davidson, trans. Michael Chase (Blackwell, 1995), 84–85, 221–230, 268.

[17] Two entry points here are Erich Auerbach, "*Passio* as Passion," trans. Martin Elsky, *Criticism* 43. 3 (2001), 285–308, and Gail Kern Paster, *Humoring the Body: Emotions and the Shakespearean Stage* (University of Chicago Press, 2014), 1–24.

[18] Christian spiritual commentaries on patience generally relate it to penance, expiation, and the imitation of Christ. Tertullian's *De patientia,* which preceded other early Christian treatises including Augustine's (above, n. 22), was at the front of many Renaissance Tertullian editions; see Roger Pearse's "Tertullian Project," www.tertullian.org. For some Shakespeareans, Simone Weil's modern essay "On Evil" ("Du Mal") could gloss Cordelia's forgiveness of Lear and Desdemona's of Othello: "Patience consists of not changing suffering into crime. That by itself is enough to change crime into suffering" (*La pesanteur et la grâce* [Plon, 1988], 87; my translation).

These classical and Christian discourses often are not neatly separated.[19] And in Shakespeare the dichotomy does not exhaust framings of patience and its value.[20] So, though I will consider each legacy individually here, I do so for simplicity. A fuller study would trace their interplay – while also looking out for further Shakespearean innovations on the theme of patience.

The discourse of classical patience, or patience in the moment, appeared in the precepts of the *Disticha Catonis* and in works by Plutarch and other accessible ancient authors; it also informed Renaissance "Neo-Stoic" ethics.[21] Perfected classical patience might not seem to lend itself to stage performance, simply because the theater favors passion over impassivity. Yet Donovan Sherman argues persuasively that Shakespearean characters enact stoic virtue as a practice of worldly engagement.[22] To play her worldly part, Viola subdues her love in the moment (though without extinguishing it). And Hamlet praises Horatio as a rare "man/ That is not passion's slave" (*Hamlet* 3.2.76–7; cf. 67–79). Why, we may ask, does Hamlet love this quality in friends? Should we?

Even the majority of characters who aren't champions at classical patience often aspire to it. For example, *Troilus and Cressida* ends with Troilus vowing "patience" before yielding to rage. His predictable failure fits the play's premise – its flawed mortals can't measure up to classical ideals – but those ideals remain attractive (5.2.32–212). Another failed aspirant to classical patience is Lear: "You heavens, give me that patience, patience I need" (*King Lear* 2.4.312). To be sure, Lear's wishes change frequently: his raging grievance puts him at odds with himself. A few lines later he will invoke anger, a state typically opposed to classical patience (for instance, by Seneca and by Francis Bacon).[23] Still, his prayer to be patient

---

[19] On Christian asceticism's debt to pre-Christian ethics, see, e.g., Hadot, *Philosophy as a Way of Life*, 126–144.

[20] Viola's patience might seem ambiguously present- and future-oriented, reflecting her ambivalent interest in both stasis and progress; see Martha Ronk, "Viola's (Lack of) Patience," *The Centennial Review* 37. 2 (1993): 384–399. On Viola and scriptural, expectant patience, see Julia Reinhard Lupton, "Patience on a Monument: Prophetic Time in Shakespeare, Fuseli, and Michelangelo," *Political Theology* 19. 7 (2018): 1–9.

[21] On what patience meant to the principal Renaissance Neo-Stoic, see Jan Papy, "Justus Lipsius," The Stanford *Encyclopedia of Philosophy*, https://plato.stanford.edu/entries/justus-lipsius/.

[22] Donovan Sherman, *Stoicism as Performance in* Much Ado About Nothing: *Acting Indifferently* (Cambridge University Press, 2019).

[23] Seneca *De ira;* Bacon, "Of Anger," *The Essays*, ed. John Pitcher (Penguin, 1985), 226–227. Cf. Pianalto, *On Patience*, ch. 5. The ethics of anger today are debated in Agnes Callard (ed.), *On Anger* (Boston Review/Forum, 2020), also largely available online at https://bostonreview.net/forum-xiii-winter-2020.

makes lucid sense in this moment. If anyone has a "true need" for classical patience, it is a parent who has been self-deluded about parental influence – when the time for disillusionment comes (*Lear* 2.4.310–311).

Classical patience has few outright naysayers in Shakespeare. Many characters complain of passions too violent to master. Few, though, deny it any power at all. One who does is Leonato in *Much Ado About Nothing*, dismissing it as fake: "there was never yet philosopher/ Who could endure the toothache patiently" (5.1.37–38; cf. 4–40). He gets a laugh, but he exaggerates. And while we may share his anguish over Hero's slander, we should recall that he mistakes her accusers' motives; not all the blame lies where he assumes. Let him fight Claudio, and the story becomes tragic. The scene warns against reacting viscerally to first impressions of fault and intent – a wise admonition for all cultures, not least ours. Even if classical patience can't be perfected, managing just a bit of it can make us better in many of our outrage-prone moments.

The discourse of Christian patience is less easy to pin down to particular passages. In a sense, all Shakespearean plays embody it, merely by unfolding in time as we await the outcome. To build dramatic suspense, then resolve it, is to model a patient expectation of relief. This dynamic of expectancy can be termed teleological (from the Greek for "end"); and Christian salvific history was the most pervasive and comprehensive of teleological forms in Shakespeare's Europe. Any faithful Christian, seeking redemption, could learn from Saint Paul that "tribulation worketh patience, patience proof, proof hope."[24]

Wherever any Shakespearean character in distress looks hopefully for a final vindication, that hope resonates with a Christian patience discourse shaped by messianic and apocalyptic beliefs. This applies even to plays with apparently pagan historical settings.[25] Two examples are *Pericles* and *The Winter's Tale*. Although both plays lack overtly Christian trappings, both have plots echoing popular genres in Christian patience literature – saints' lives, martyrs' legends, the life of Jesus himself. Consider how, at the end of *Pericles*, Marina's father

---

[24] *Romans* 5:3–4, modernized from the standard Elizabethan ("Bishops'") text in *The Holie Bible* (Richard Iugge, 1568). Despite this evidentiary conceit, Paul elsewhere relates patience to blind faith; see *Romans* 8:25. An oft-quoted Pauline passage highlighting patience is his encomium on love (charity) in *1 Corinthians* 13:4.

[25] For criticism relating Western literary genres, and Shakespeare, to Christian eschatology and its template, Jewish prophetic messianism, see, e.g., Frank Kermode, *The Sense of an Ending: Studies in the Theory of Fiction* (Oxford University Press, 2000 [1967]); Julia Reinhard Lupton, "Birth Places: Shakespeare's Beliefs / Believing in Shakespeare," *Shakespeare Quarterly* 65. 4 (2014), 399–420.

compares her to "Patience … smiling/ Extremity out of act" (5.1.159–60). As is often noted, the image mirrors Viola's smiling Patience. But whereas patience sustained Viola moment by moment, Marina's has a redemptive teleology. Cast into a brothel, she spends her time there by effectively dissuading customers from further exploiting sex-trafficked women. (4.6.156–167). Equally resonant with redemptive paradigms is Hermione's prophecy, in *The Winter's Tale,* of justice restored through her own sufferings: "innocence shall make/ False accusation blush and tyranny/ Tremble at patience" (3.2.31–33).

Like classical patience, Christian patience is likely to have practical limits. The biblical Job reminds us of this. So, perhaps, does Shakespeare. In *Measure for Measure,* after Juliet is spiritually chastened by the Friar (really the Duke), she resolves to take her "shame most patiently," only to have her contrition mocked with the news that Claudio will die (2.3.31). And when Isabella hears this news – showing her that Angelo has sunk so low as to betray his own vile bargain – she too is mocked by the Friar's dour prescription of "patience" (4.3.128). These passages challenge religious audiences to ask just how much patience their own faith can sustain.[26]

Even when Shakespeare's characters lose patience, their longing for it implies a fundamental affirmation: both kinds of patience are virtues in the highest degree. Classical patience recasts suffering as sufferance. And while a future-oriented patience like Marina's and Hermione's embraces suffering, it embraces it as what the late civil-rights leader John Lewis called "good trouble."[27] In its Shakespearean form of Christian patience, it offers what saints offer to the devout believer; later in history it takes a secular shape, promising what the workers' struggle promises to a utopian Marxist. Suffering tests and builds confidence in a better world to come.

Can we forge such virtuous cycles of patience? How should we combat abuses of patience? Answers lie elsewhere and are up to you. What matters to everyone is that only patience – for the moment, for the future, or both – can save us from the torment of trying to live with no patience at all. We glimpse that abject life in another Shakespearean personage:

---

[26] Original audiences might avoid such questions by dismissing the Friar as a double abuser of Christian patience discourse: he is an impostor, and under English law in Shakespeare's time, even real Catholic friars were heretics.

[27] John Lewis, "Together, You Can Redeem the Soul of Our Nation," *The New York Times,* July 30, 2020, www.nytimes.com/2020/07/30/opinion/john-lewis-civil-rights-america.html.

one who, because he is too angrily entitled, too quick to dismiss other viewpoints, too scornful of others' identities, fails his loved ones, his city, and himself. "His own impatience ... takes a great part of the blame" (*Coriolanus* 5.6.174–75).[28]

---

[28] "His" means either Coriolanus's or Aufidius's; the former possibility is more telling. A seeming paradox is that Coriolanus lacks patience, yet abounds in the related cardinal virtue of fortitude (which governed patience in Zeno's system; Stobaeus, *Anthologii Libri Duo Priores,* 60, ll. 21–22). Geoffrey Miles explains this by quoting Plutarch, who called Coriolanus's seeming "patience in adversity ... a parody of true constancy, arising not from reason but from an excess of emotion" (quoted in Christopher Brooke, *Philosophic Pride: Stoicism and Political Thought from Lipsius to Rousseau* [Princeton University Press, 2012], 62).

CHAPTER 16

Care

Benjamin Parris

Shakespeare often draws attention to the ways that competing notions of care shape ethical, political, and amorous life. If care is a virtue, it seems unique among other classically recognized virtues such as courage, justice, and temperance, in that care is more ubiquitous as a feature of normative life and yet less conceptually distinct. While sometimes appearing as a virtue in itself – or as a precondition to the sharpening of any particular virtue – care just as often shows up in Shakespearean drama as a demanding expenditure of psychosomatic energies that shades into anxious worry or self-consuming attachments. Sir Toby Belch describes Olivia's grief at the beginning of *Twelfth Night* in such terms: "I'm sure care's an enemy to life" (1.3.2).[1] Yet care also nurtures, shapes, and protects life, as an exasperated Capulet reminds his wife when discussing Juliet's nuptial prospects and her future wellbeing in *Romeo and Juliet*: "still my care hath been / To have her matched" (3.5.179–180). For Shakespeare, care is the virtue poised at a fragile crest of attentive concern for self and others, where the slightest nudge seems capable of twisting its benefit into harm. Such epistemological and practical fuzziness makes care an elusive end, one whose ethical significance is indisputable yet hard to capture with conceptual precision. As the anthropologist Carlo Caduff writes, "Care is a big fish that refuses to be caught."[2]

Given this state of affairs, how might we make sense of the ambivalences of care in Shakespearean drama? I suggest we look to ancient virtue ethics, working our way from Socratic exhortations to care for our souls to Roman elaborations of Stoic care by Seneca and Cicero. Shakespeare shares with Plato a deep interest in the phenomenon of care as it draws various forms of life into its orbit, and like these later Roman thinkers he attends to

---

[1] All references to Shakespeare are from *The Complete Pelican Shakespeare*, eds. Stephen Orgel and A. R. Braunmuller (Penguin, 2002).
[2] Carlo Caduff, "Hot Chocolate," *Critical Inquiry* 45 (2019), 802.

the ambivalence of care [*cura*] as both a natural virtue that develops the organic impulses sustaining life, and a potential "enemy to life." Classical perspectives thus inform Shakespeare's articulations of care as an innate and omnipresent facet of human experience, which can benefit self and others but in its extreme forms also weigh upon body and soul to cause harm. Despite cultivating skepticism concerning our human abilities to know and to exercise the virtues of care, Shakespearean drama also stages encounters with care in its rarest guise: as a benefit that alleviates forms of suffering or distress to which human life is invariably susceptible, and which cultivates our capacities for virtue.

What exactly *is* care, according to the schema of Platonic virtue? In the *Euthyphro*, Socrates (470–399 BCE) hazards a guess: "care in each case has the same effect; it aims at the good and the benefit of the object cared for ...."[3] Likewise, in his description of the cosmos Plato's Timaeus contends that "there is but one way to care for anything, and that is to provide for it the nourishment and the motions that are proper to it."[4] These definitions square easily with the imperatives to care for body and soul that appear throughout Plato's dialogues (428–348 BCE), insofar as we benefit ourselves when we care for ourselves. But if we care for things unworthy of pursuit, we in fact harm ourselves. Care is a virtue insofar as it benefits, and a vice insofar as it harms. It relies upon a genuine understanding of the object being cared for, and so in the Socratic tradition, caring for one's soul involves knowing what the soul needs and training it to care for the right things – such as the Forms that are conceived as the basis of truth and a necessary means of harmonizing the soul in Plato's *Republic* and *Phaedo*, or the virtuous balance between states of excess and deficiency that serves in Aristotle's *Nicomachean Ethics* as a guide for our actions. But alongside these familiar anchors to virtuous care from essential works of Platonic and Aristotelian ethics, Plato's writings also insist upon bodily care as a virtuous activity, as when Socrates remarks in the *Republic* that self-care should begin during childhood, instructing children to "put their minds to youthful education and philosophy and take care of their bodies ... so as to acquire a helper for philosophy."[5] Bodily care is essential to the care of our immortal soul, which Socrates argues in the *Phaedo* "requires our

---

3 Plato, *Euthyphro* 13b, *Plato: Complete Works*, ed. John M. Cooper (Hackett Publishing, 1997), 13.
4 Plato, *Timaeus* 89c in Cooper, *Plato: Complete Works*, 1289.
5 Plato, *The Republic* 498b in Cooper, *Plato: Complete Works*, 1120. See also Socrates' later claim that an ideal candidate for guardian is someone who "continuously, strenuously, and exclusively devotes himself to participation in arguments, exercising himself in them just as he did in the bodily physical training, which is their counterpart" (539d in Cooper, *Plato: Complete Works*, 1154).

care not only for the time we call our life, but for the sake of all time ... one is in terrible danger if one does not give it that care."[6] The body must be nurtured, in part because its motions can help to harmonize the soul that is the source of human motion and of our transformation toward the good.[7] At the same time, the Socrates of the *Phaedo* suggests that we are wrong to devote more care to the body than that which is necessary to support our efforts at virtue. The philosopher should not care overly for the pleasures or pains that affect the body, and instead remain devoted to the overarching virtue of wisdom that allows one to act with true courage, moderation, and justice.

While these passages from Plato's dialogues might seem to tilt the balance of virtuous care heavily toward the individual self in its personal dimensions of body and soul, the Socratic tradition rather insists upon the necessarily social and political dimensions of care that broadly support and sustain the activities of virtue. In his *Nicomachean Ethics*, for instance, Aristotle (384–322 BCE) describes the virtues of friendship as a kind of care between selves that gives shape to the philosopher's view of the fundamentally social nature of virtue. For Aristotle, the care of the self is a process that unfolds in relation to others within a community pursuing a common good. The highest good for humans is synonymous with virtuous activity that exercises the intellect, but such forms of excellence can only fully emerge within a scene of mutual care and political belonging. In Book IX of the *Nicomachean Ethics*, he asserts that the virtuous person could not live in isolation, because virtue requires that we "bestow benefits on others" and because "man is a civic being, one whose nature is to live with others."[8] The good that encourages us both to care for ourselves and for others can be fully realized only within an interdependent web of support and mutual care among denizens of a *polis* whose activities are performed for the sake of a common good that belongs to the whole. When we care for ourselves, we are also caring for others and for the community we inhabit at large.

While these various facets of care are essential to ancient virtue ethics, it is perhaps the Stoics – and in particular the Roman elaboration of Stoic ethics by Seneca and Cicero – who are most attentive to the ambivalence

---

[6] Plato, *Phaedo* 107c in Cooper, *Plato: Complete Works,* 92.
[7] See Heather L. Reid, "Plato the Gymnasiarch," in ΦΙΛΕΛΛΗΝ: *Essays for Stephen G. Miller*, eds. D Katsonopoulou and E. Partida (Helike Society, 2016), 171–186.
[8] Aristotle, *Nicomachean Ethics*, eds. Sarah Broadie and Christopher Rowe (Oxford University Press, 2002), 1169b10–15.

of care [*cura*] in its beneficial and harmful guises. Seneca (4 BCE-65 CE) argues in his ethical letter devoted to the topic of animal instinct that the human animal's relationship to *cura* is such that "the care of myself is prior to everything [*ante omnia est mei cura*]."⁹ The priority of care in Senecan thought and in Stoicism more broadly thus extends the Socratic tradition of the care of the self. According to Seneca, we share a claim to reason with God, but in the case of God the good is already perfected by nature; for humans, however, the good must be perfected through the efforts of care [*cura*].¹⁰ Yet the commitment to such efforts can bring further complication, as Cicero (106 BCE-43 CE) notes: "the devotees of learning are so far from making pleasure their aim, that they actually endure care, anxiety, and loss of sleep, in the exercise of the noblest part of man's nature, the divine element within us (for so we must consider the keen edge of the intellect and the reason)."¹¹ The Stoic sage acknowledges and attends to a fundamental tension of care, aiming to develop the natural capacities for virtuous care that simultaneously alleviate its onerous and distressing forms. Stoic thinkers thus conceive of caring for care as a guiding principle for human relationships in pursuing the good. Hierocles the Stoic (ca. 100–150 CE) argues that such care is a central benefit of marriage and family. Children "become our helpers in all activities even when we are well and become good caretakers when we are laboring under our years and weighed down by old age," and each of our family members can potentially become "sympathetic relievers of our pains." When a husband returns home and prepares to relax, for instance, the cares of the day often "come near again, taking advantage of this opportunity to cause us pain;" it is then that his wife "takes them up and examines them together with us, and provides some relief and joy out of her sincere eagerness."¹² Hierocles'

---

⁹ Seneca, Letter 121.17. Latin original and English translation from *Seneca VI, Epistles Vol. III*, trans. Richard Gummere, Loeb Classical Library (Harvard University Press, 1925), 406.

¹⁰ The passage reads, "Of one of these, then – to wit God – it is Nature that perfects the Good; of the other – to wit man – pains and study do so" [*Ex his ergo unius bonum natura perficit, dei scilicet, alterius cura, hominis*]. Seneca, Letter 134.14 in *Seneca VI, Epistles Vol. III*, 445. Martin Heidegger interprets this passage and the Senecan priority of care as evidence that care is the fundamental modality of Being for Dasein. Care is the a priori state from which the duality of human care – articulated by Seneca as anxious exertion and devotedness – emerges. See Martin Heidegger, *Being and Time*, trans. John Macquarrie and Edward Robinson (Harper & Row, 1962), 243–244. In *The Care of the Self* (Penguin, 1986), Michel Foucault investigates Roman histories of self-care and philosophical reflection during Seneca's lifetime.

¹¹ The passage is spoken by Piso, Cicero's spokesman for the teachings of Antiochus of Ascalon in Cicero, *On Ends* (5.57), trans. H. Rackham, Loeb Classical Library 40 (Harvard University Press, 1914), 459.

¹² *Hierocles the Stoic: Elements of Ethics, Fragments and Excerpts*, ed. Ilaria Ramelli, trans. David Konstan (Society of Biblical Literature, 2009), 75.

description of domestic care as a shared burden between spouses also draws attention to the relationship between care and gender, insofar as the husband's public-facing cares become an object of his wife's domestic care – raising questions about how care and the work of virtue are distributed among members of the household and the broader political community. Like his ancient predecessors, Hierocles reveals the necessity of the virtues of the *oikos* and the communal reliance upon the skilled labor of women in cultivating domestic care; at the same time, his argument offers a patriarchal pretext for restricting the virtuous activity of women to the home.

The turn to Shakespearean drama reveals the activity of care to be a source of similar questioning, insight, and creativity across the playwright's career, as his work takes up the legacies of ancient virtue ethics with an eye to early-modern values. Let us begin with *The Taming of the Shrew* and Baptista's paternal care for Bianca, which seeks to incorporate fatherly concern with the paradigm of humanist care advocated by Renaissance schoolmasters such as Richard Mulcaster – "All our labor is for rest, all our travail for ease, all our care to avoid care," as he writes in his *Elementarie*.[13] Tranio describes Baptista's care for Bianca as an effort to provide his daughter with access to such capacities for mental equanimity and resilience: "But art thou not advised he took some care / To get her cunning schoolmasters to instruct her?" (1.1.185–186) The play contrasts this vision of care for Bianca as the humanistic cultivation of her native talents with Petrucchio's sovereign-like care for Bianca's sister Kate, which aims ruthlessly to discipline and correct her unruliness: "amid this hurly I intend / That all is done in reverend care of her. / And in conclusion, she shall watch all night / And if she chance to nod I'll rail and brawl / And with the clamour keep her still awake" (4.2.192–196). The play encourages us to ask what counts as genuine paternal and spousal care, and whether it is possible to cultivate virtue through care while also restraining the impulse to dominate.

Such paradoxes of paternal care also feature prominently in *The Tempest*, as when Prospero affirms the centrality of his role as father to Miranda – "I have done nothing but in care of thee, / Of thee, my dear one, thee, my daughter" (1.2.15) – yet in the same breath reveals a deep hypocrisy in his treatment of Caliban – "Thou most lying slave, / Whom stripes may move, not kindness! I have used thee, / Filth as thou art, with human care" (1.2.344–346). Prospero's curse means at once to affirm his own humanity

---

[13] Richard Mulcaster, *Elementarie,* ed. Ernest Trafford Campagnac (Clarendon Press, 1925), 27.

while denying it to Caliban, but by invoking his care as justification for what amounts to injustice, Shakespeare reminds us of Prospero's earlier affirmation of paternal care and casts doubt on his motivations as well as his practical executions of care. Both *The Taming of the Shrew* and *The Tempest* conceive paternal care as an activity that nurtures and disciplines, yet also serves as an easy pretense for harmful and unjust domination.

The vexations of sovereign care provide another particularly rich source of ethico-political paradoxes for Shakespeare's monarchs and their subjects. The dying John of Gaunt accuses Richard II of abuses of power that infect the kingdom, "Wherein thou liest in reputation sick; / And thou, too careless patient as thou art, / Commit'st thy anointed body to the cure / Of those physicians that first wounded thee" (2.1.96–99). While the King's care should benefit his flourishing kingdom and his sacred body alike, Richard's sovereign care has turned instead to neglect, and Gaunt figures this lapse in political judgment as a carelessness infecting kingdom and self that continues to be exacerbated by his ill choice of advisors to the crown. Later, Richard refers to the vexations of sovereign care as a wearying attachment that he hopes will be dissolved upon releasing the crown to Bolingbroke: "Why, 'twas my care; / And what loss is it to be rid of care?" (3.2.95–96) Yet he soon finds that his psychosomatic attachment to sovereign care remains, even when the crown has been transferred to its new bearer: "Your cares set up do not pluck my cares down. / My care is loss of care, by old care done; / Your care is gain of care, by new care won. / The cares I give, I have, though given away; / They 'tend the crown, yet still with me they stay." (4.1.195–199) While all of Shakespeare's monarchs at some point find themselves "wan with care" (*1 Henry IV* 1.1.1) that attends the crown, Richard's struggles with the afterlife of sovereign care are especially revealing when examined alongside the fate of King Lear. Like Richard, Lear hopes "To shake all cares and business of our state" (1.1.39) once he lets go of the body politic. Yet his sovereign care remains as a burden of psychosomatic distress and a self-consuming attachment to his fugitive monarchical identity. Regan alludes to what is arguably her father's ultimate source of distress early in the play when she remarks that he "hath ever but slenderly known himself" (1.1.294–295). Shakespeare thus ties Lear's fate to the care of the self that is at the heart of Socratic virtue ethics, suggesting Lear has been a King who takes too little care of those things that nurture and sustain his life in its creaturely capacities and domestic relations. Like all of Shakespeare's sovereigns, Lear has endured a commitment to political vigilance and monarchical duty that inevitably draws him away from forms of care necessary to flourishing as a human.

His decision to "disclaim all my paternal care" for Cordelia attempts to sever a mutually beneficial relationship of domestic care that he instead ought to be cultivating, especially in light of his previous history of neglect (1.1.114).

While Lear's confusion paints a worrying picture of sovereign care, Cordelia's care for her father constitutes a fleeting yet poignant recovery of the human capacities for care that Lear shares with others by nature yet lacks in their fully developed and virtuous form. She embodies the composure and compassionate judgment of the Stoic sage, precisely because she feels without being overcome by a passion. Cordelia cries upon receiving Kent's letters detailing her father's struggles (4.3.10–15) yet remains a "queen / Over her passion" (4.3.13–14) and soon comes to comfort him. Cordelia ensures that Lear's madness is restored to sanity, through the know-how of attending physicians and her own prayerful summoning of the "unpublished virtues of the earth" (4.4.16) that lead the overwrought sovereign to release his cares into the therapy of sleep.[14] Through Cordelia's care, Lear accesses the restorative powers of his own creaturely nature, unconsciously caring for the form of embodied life that Macbeth somberly comes to realize he has annihilated upon murdering the sovereign in his sleep: "Methought I heard a voice cry 'Sleep no more! / Macbeth does murder sleep' – the innocent sleep, / Sleep that knits up the raveled sleave of care" (2.2.38–40). The care that comes through the therapy of sleep is a recurring vehicle through which Shakespeare explores domestic care and its role in nourishing natural life, as well as women's expertise both in medical cures and in the alleviation of distress that afflicts the bearers of political authority. Thus, Paulina in *The Winter's Tale* brings her womanly art of expert care as soothing speech to a care-worn and exhausted Leontes, whose travails she attributes to masculinist political intrigue:

> Not so hot, good sir.
> I come to bring him sleep. 'Tis such as you,
> That creep like shadows by him and do sigh
> At each his needless heavings; such as you
> Nourish the cause of his awaking. I
> Do come with words, as medicinal as true,
> Honest as either, to purge him of that humor
> That press him from sleep.   (2.3.33–39)

---

[14] I discuss this scene as part of a broader investigation of the close yet puzzling relationship between sleep and ethical care in *Vital Strife: Sleep, Insomnia, and the Early Modern Ethics of Care* (Cornell University Press, 2022).

The ensuing struggle between Paulina and Leontes constitutes a Shakespearean iteration of the gendered dynamics of care seen in classical works such as Hierocles' *Elements of Ethics*. But their encounter also reveals the therapeutic effects of language as they bear upon the health of the early-modern sovereign and kingdom alike. Just as ancient ethicists conceive a necessary and mutually supportive web of care among members of the *polis* as a necessary component of the political community's pursuit of the good, Shakespeare indicates that without Paulina's expert judgment the sovereign's care turns tragically from justice into madness.[15]

It may be that Shakespeare thinks our propensities for beneficial care are too easily led astray to make its virtuous form widely available or securely held among the denizens of a political community. Yet he nonetheless acknowledges that care anchors human interdependence and catalyzes the many forms of benefit we seek. Much like the Socratic emphasis upon understanding as a necessary component of caring in the right way and for the right things, Shakespeare's depictions of care reveal the playwright's sense that knowing how to care is both an epistemological and ethical challenge.[16] To care virtuously is to call upon and actualize the human potential for seeing and attending to self and others alike with sound judgment, despite the circumstances of a confusing world that so often impedes that possibility.

---

[15] The psychologist Carol Gilligan perceives a harmful contemporary divide between a feminized ethic of care and a masculine ethic of justice – a divide whose historical development we can track through Hierocles' treatise and Shakespeare's plays. See Carol Gilligan, *In A Different Voice: Psychological Theory and Women's Development* (Harvard University Press, 1982).

[16] The philosopher Harry Frankfurt argues that reflections upon what we care about belong neither to epistemology nor ethics. Instead, what we care about is important in its own regard and constitutes a separate domain of philosophical inquiry. See *The Importance of What We Care About: Philosophical Essays* (Cambridge University Press, 1980).

CHAPTER 17

Hospitality

Joan Pong Linton

Hospitality has deep roots in the Greek concept of *xenia,* extending guest-friendship to strangers, and in Abrahamic practices of fellowship and stewardship. Classical and biblical traditions alike attest to the importance of hospitality in stories of mortals – Baucis and Philemon, Abraham and Sarah – rewarded for offering hospitality to strangers in ignorance of their divine nature. Conversely, literature also abounds with instances of hospitality turned treacherous, instabilities in host–guest relationships reflective of linguistic change. To explain, the Latin root *hostis,* meaning "guest" or "host," comes in Roman law to be "applied exclusively to the 'enemy', and no longer names the guest; similarly, in the Greek xénos comes increasingly to mean 'stranger' to the exclusion of 'guest.'"[1] Most stories, however, situated between pure hospitality and treacherous hostility, deal with what Jacques Derrida calls "conditional hospitality," hospitality contingent on calculations of risks and interests in host–guest relationships based on reciprocity, implicitly or explicitly guided by laws and norms regarding host and guest responsibilities to each other. Derrida defines conditional hospitality in relation to "unconditional hospitality," extending hospitality beyond all calculation, which he considers impossible, yet without which hospitality loses its ethical compass.[2]

The case in point is Kant's notion of cosmopolitan hospitality as "the right of a foreigner not to be treated with hostility because he has arrived on the land of another ... as long as he behaves peaceably."[3] For Derrida, the problem with hospitality as a right is that it "does not arise ... from the

---

[1] Tracy McNulty, *The Hostess: Hospitality, Femininity, and the Expropriation of Identity* (University of Minnesota Press, 2007), ix, xii. The Latin term for hospitality, *hospes* is formed from two roots: *hostis* is one; *pet-* or *pot-* is the other, meaning "master" (ix).

[2] Jacques Derrida, *Of Hospitality,* trans. Rachel Bowlby (Stanford University Press, 2020), 25, 27, 79.

[3] Immanuel Kant, *Toward Perpetual Peace,* in *Practical Philosophy,* trans. Mary J. Gregor (Cambridge University Press, 1996), 8:356, 328–329.

'love of man' as a sentimental motive" conducive to an ethics of welcome.[4] Cosmopolitanism, however, has a long tradition in Stoicism with its emphasis on hospitality as individual ethical practice (in principle opposed to the corrupt laws of the state). This ethics-based strain of cosmopolitan hospitality exerts its greatest influence in Christian practice, in the spirit of being in but not of the world. Not bound by religion, Luce Irigaray lays out enabling conditions toward the practice of a "mutual hospitality" that is conducive to a "world culture of coexistence." She envisions spaces of welcoming "beyond the space defined by any culture" where one can "take into account the difference(s) between us" without trying to assimilate or be assimilated by the other.[5]

Drawing from hospitality theory in the ancient world and its continued relevance today, this chapter will focus on *Twelfth Night, Or What You Will.* The play both calls attention to the failure of hospitality and explores such failure by unpacking the workings of the patriarchal household as an anchor of conditional hospitality. With a title associated with the Twelfth Night of Christmas, there is no lack of mirth and entertainment in Illyria's great households but a notable lack of the customary hospitality associated with the season. As such, Illyria speaks to the conventional trope in Shakespeare's day in which writers and moralists lament the "decay of hospitality," although such lamenting, Felicity Heal observes, seldom considers social and ideological factors shaping personal and institutional hospitality. Also of interest is the linguistic complexity relating to hospitality: while "the language and symbolism ... seem directed to an affirmation of the role of the host," the word "stranger" conflates two meanings, referring to both "the alien who was unknown" and "an individual who was not attached to a particular *familia*."[6] In this connection, *Twelfth Night* can be said to probe the means by which a society or community assimilates strangers deemed desirable and also the means by which it makes strangers of and excludes those deemed undesirable or not in their proper places. This probing, in laying bare risks and calculations, comes to reckon with the promptings of desire, more broadly the will, that dispose one to a range of possible actions from hospitable to hostile. It is through such

---

[4] Jacques Derrida, "Hospitality," *Angelaki* 5. 3 (2000), 4.
[5] Luce Irigaray, "Toward a Mutual Hospitality," in *The Conditions of Hospitality*, ed. Thomas Claviez (Fordham University Press, 2013), 52, 47, 46. Irigaray's framework for mutual hospitality includes restoring our sense of "natural belonging," being part of nature, as grounding for all other relationships (43–45).
[6] Felicity Heal, *Hospitality in Early Modern England* (Clarendon Press, 2010), 94, 9.

reckoning, worthy of the subtitle *What You Will*, that the play reveals inhospitality not just to strangers without but also to members within the household. At the same time, instances of mutual and even unconditional hospitality also become imaginable, albeit as poetic inventions. What philosophy theorizes as virtue in the abstract, the theater of hospitality invents in everyday particulars of fictive lives.

Within this context, the play engages audiences from the positions of strangers in search of refuge, thereby decentering the normative focus on the host as master of household hospitality. Thus Antonio warns Sebastian of Illyria: "these parts ... to a stranger,/ Unguided and unfriended, often prove rough and unhospitable" (3.3.9–11). Antonio may be biased: by his own admission, he is wanted in Illyria for a prior offense in "a sea-fight' gainst the Count's [Orsino's] galleys" (3.3.26). Nonetheless, his words point to a state actively policing against its border's hostile elements, as Illyrians go about their activities oblivious to the needs of strangers. Even the Sea Captain, "bred and born/ Not three hours' travel from this very place," who last sailed from Illyria "but a month ago," ends up in prison on some unknown charge (1.2.20–21; 27). Nor do the twins expect welcome from Illyrian households. Sebastian plays the tourist whose intention is "mere extravagancy," wandering about sightseeing (2.1.9–10). He resembles the peaceable Kantian visitor who earns his cosmopolitan right to hospitality by enriching the state's hospitality industry. Meanwhile, Viola assumes male disguise in seeking employment as a household servant. She figures the undocumented refugee cohabiting with citizens as a servant in the intimacy of their homes. While the four appear in isolated moments seemingly incidental to the comedy's central marriage plot, they map the social periphery from which to engage audiences in unpacking marriage and the household as institutions that align with the law in maintaining the conditions of hospitality systemically.

This unpacking begins with the workings of the will in the interactions among characters. In its various senses – desire, appetite, volition, and so on – the will provides an index to one's disposition in dealing with the demands of specific situations, including hospitality situations. Whereas conditional hospitality emphasizes the calculation of risk, the will pertains to one's affective relation to self and other. Potentially life-affirming or destructive, predictable or otherwise, the will may align with or override risk calculations in shaping (or un-shaping) not just the hospitable act but the hospitality relationship itself. Among the characters, Antonio exercises unconditional hospitality in financing Sebastian's lodgings and expenses in Illyria. He gives all he has, beyond all calculation, assuming all of the risk.

Although his giving is driven by "desire/ (More sharp than filèd steel)," this does not diminish the value of his hospitality for the recipient. Nor does Sebastian feel obligated to requite Antonio's "willing love" (3.3. 4–5, 11): one's desire need not be a demand on the other. This hospitable relationship re-emerges when Sebastian comes upon Antonio arrested by the Duke's men and greets his friend in loving terms: "O my dear Antonio" (5.1.210). The greeting reaffirms their tacit bond of mutual aid without calculation, which qualifies as "mutual hospitality" in which each makes room for the other's co-existence, accepting differences without assimilating the other to the self.

This mutuality provides a critical vantage point from which to observe Illyrian inhospitality. Here Antonio finds his polar opposite in Duke Orsino, the inconsolable, unrequited lover who cares only to be entertained with music. He demands "excess of it" so that his "appetite might sicken, and so die." Not only does this excess leave little room for hospitality towards neighbors or strangers, but in paying for his entertainment, Orsino turns "the food of love" into an economic transaction (1.1.1–3). Choosing in courtly fashion to woo by proxy insulates him from having to perform love's labor and, indeed, from having any personal relationship with Olivia whatsoever, whom he purportedly desires for a future wife – hence hostess of his household. Given Orsino's "appetite" or will to assimilate all without mutuality, one could hardly blame Olivia for refusing his suit, although much more is at issue in her self-cloistering. Her inhospitality, we shall see, stems from her vulnerability as a female head of household unable to inhabit the male host position or to escape her role as hostess.

As Tracy McNulty explains, within the patriarchal household, hospitality often involves the mediation of a hostess, a wife or daughter subservient to the host, "to facilitate reciprocal relations between men," and "in archaic as well as in many biblical narratives" to participate in "the exchange or offer of women between men."[7] By implication, the hostess's subservience as patriarchal object of exchange is the grounding condition that enables household hospitality: she is a stranger in her own house, property estranged from possessing. This helps to explain Olivia's precarious authority over her household while her male dependents clamor to play host in serving their own desires. Her uncle Sir Toby brings home a stranger he is fleecing on pretense of match-making: "Send for money,

7 McNulty, *The Hostess*, xxviii, xxxvii.

knight. If thou hast her not i' th' end, call me Cut" (2.3.165). Her steward
desires "to be Count Malvolio," the master of her wealth and body, authorized to correct "Cousin Toby" (2.5.30, 62). Even the clown Feste "would
play Lord Pandarus," taking his fee for giving Cesario passage to his lady,
implicitly comparing courtly love to prostitution and implicating himself
as a pimping host (3.1.45). All their designs converge on Olivia in perver-
sions of household hospitality that bring out the contradiction at the heart
of the institution, that hospitality to the guest is predicated on inhospitality to the hostess. Unfailingly, this happens when Olivia is seen not as her
own person but solely as a social role.

Although unaware of the mercenary designs on her person, Olivia
clearly recognizes her predicament as hostess, as seen in her first encounter
with Viola disguised as Cesario, arriving as Orsino's proxy wooer.

CESARIO: .... Are you the lady of the house?
OLIVIA: If I do not usurp myself, I am. (1.5.164–166)

The conditional "if" marks her distance from her role, and "usurp"
bespeaks her precarious position within her own house. At the same time,
Olivia's response also discloses a playfulness Cesario brings out in her with
his show of not recognizing the visible signs of her social role. The two go
on to engage in a parody of the courtly ritual of proxy wooing, distancing themselves from the roles they perform within it. In matching wits,
they improvise a new script, straying "out of [their] text" (1.5.204), thereby
co-creating a space of mutual hospitality in which each enables the other
freely to become herself. Through Cesario's request, "Good madam, let
me see your face" (1.5.202), Viola voices her desire to know the person
behind the veil. Unveiling her face in response, Olivia declares: "it shall
be inventoried, and every particle and utensil labeled to my will: as, item,
two lips, indifferent red; item, two grey eyes, with lids to them; item, one
neck, one chin, and so forth" (1.5.215–218). This self-description mocks the
blazon's elaborate praise of the beloved lady's beauty as the veil of convention objectifying her as the "hostess ... bereft of individual identity ..., an
indeterminate thing rather than an integral moral person" (xlii). Again,
Olivia's inventory "labeled to my will" mimics "the legal document containing instructions about the disposal of her property."[8] Her facial features, then, are the homely items she can call her own – and bequeath to

---

[8] Dympna Callaghan, "'And all is semblative a woman's part': Body Politics in *Twelfth Night*," *Textual
Practice* 7. 3 (1993), 58.

one who sees her beyond her social role. In her mock will, home becomes "the projection of ethos in its root sense of dwelling or abode, the 'opening of the familiar to the unfamiliar.'"[9]

To be sure, this moment of mutuality is realized only in the performance and experienced only in its passing, seemingly of little moment. But the same holds true for everyday hospitable performances. The relational dynamic enables parties to recognize and go beyond their social roles. It provides an opening for the awakened empathy (cf. Derrida's "sentimental motive") to deepen into acts of welcome and aid, and it is out of countless such acts that a habitual practice or virtue takes root. True, again, Olivia's assertion of will leads in comical vein to her marrying a perfect stranger Sebastian, mistaking his twin-likeness as Cesario. Even so, she seizes her new status as the opening for redefining her relationship to Orsino, in a double invitation that underscores the practical efficacy of conditional hospitality. First she invites Orsino "so please you, to think me as well a sister as a wife [what he initially desired]" (5.1.305–307). The implied condition is his assent to marry Viola, securing which Olivia greets Viola as family: "a sister; you are she" (5.1.315), establishing a mutual sisterly connection between households. In offering further to "crown th'alliance on't, so please you,/ Here at my house and at my *proper* cost" (5.1.307–308, emphasis added), Olivia the hostess properly exercises the responsibility of a host.

While the prospect of wedding celebrations aligns with comedy's drive toward happy endings, the attendant outbreak of hospitable good will cannot prevent Viola's nuptial from being stalled by Malvolio's abrupt, ill-willed departure. To contextualize, Orsino would marry Viola in her "woman's weeds," which the Captain has in his keeping, who in turn is imprisoned "at Malvolio's suit" (5.1.266, 269). Since Viola could have married without those weeds, one suspects Orsino is looking for diversion – and the play for an excuse for Malvolio to return in the final scene to air his grievance – only to storm out again after a fresh insult. To recognize with Olivia, however, that Malvolio "hath been most notoriously abused" and "entreat him to a peace," as Orsino urges, requires that we probe the cause of ill will, beyond what his name figures (ll. 366–367). For desiring "greatness" above his social station, Malvolio is first made out to be a madman – the ultimate stranger – and relentlessly hazed by other household members. If hospitality is to begin at home, it must address the ill will and estrangement that sometimes pass for household mirth.

[9] McNulty, *The Hostess,* xviii; Derrida, "Of Hospitality," 149–151.

As the play ends without closure, it again poses the question of house-hold hospitality, this time looking outward, in the voice of Feste, the wise fool rising above the folly he is a part of. In his epilogue linking the play's world with the audience's social world, he sings of the trials of "man's estate," the vicissitudes of fortune and marriage. In such a world, "'gainst knaves and thieves men shut their gate" even as "the rain it raineth everyday" (ll. 5, 7, refrain). Inhospitable householders, driven by fear and uncertainty, see only the worst in strangers and refuge seekers. To these stereotypes Viola presents a vibrant counter-figure: witty and resourceful, seeking shelter and employment so she, in her own voice, "might not be delivered to the world,/ Till I had made mine own occasion mellow,/ What my estate is" (1.2.38–40). Betrothed without consummation, she becomes a beacon for refugees waiting for hospitality that is more than mere tol-erance, something like the welcome she achieves: being seen as persons, not stereotypes, without being assimilated, made familiar, by marriage. Such hospitality requires a change of will on the part of householders, whether it is to reorient from desiring one's own interests to serving others in need as well, or to work collectively toward social change, or both. In this space of hope, this spirit of migrant Christmas, Viola dwells, perform-ing Cesario still, being in but not of the world, "render[ing] unto Caesar the things that are Caesar's, and unto God the things that are God's" (Matthew 22.21). After all, what familiarizes without contempt is the work of mutuality that restores to strangers their – our – irreducible difference as hospitable agents. At the end of *Twelfth Night*, then, on the eve of the feast of Epiphany, Feste positions audiences and Illyrians alike on the threshold of possibility, inviting us in Irigaray's translated words to "pay attention above all to the present of our meeting and the future that we can build together."[10]

In its sustained engagement with hospitality, *Twelfth Night* can be said to repurpose ethos – the self as home – in characters and audiences, enact-ing an aesthetic that hearkens to the religious, ethical, and political ideals of hospitality. Shakespearean hospitality in performance most informs our understanding of virtue as power in the ways individuals, shaped though by institutional practices, can in turn transform themselves and their soci-ety through hospitable practices, as these materialize in the intersections of gender, class, and race. Such understanding configures in theater and in print, on big and small screens, on the Internet and in the classroom,

---

[10] Irigaray, "Toward a Mutual Hospitality," 52.

where "an ethic of hospitality"[11] may take hold and develop across communities, online and on the ground. For we, too, as teachers and students for one another, can learn, like Viola, to "sing,/ And speak … in many sorts of music" (*Twelfth Night* 1.2.53–54). In the spirit of mutuality, we too can coproduce a "rearrangement of desires,"[12] if you will, shifting from self-gratification to the practice of hospitality as the other-serving in-dwelling of virtue. Such aesthetic education informs actions like "Refugees Week," since 2018 organized by Shakespeare's Globe, during which refugee artists, performers, and audiences share their stories at the Globe Theater, with programming for young participants like "Twelfth Night Storytelling, 5–8 years." The virtue/virtù of Shakespearean hospitality is never more relevant than now, as we confront deadly domestic problems that thrive on ill will and estrangement and global crises creating economic and climate migrants and asylum seekers fleeing war and regimes of terror.

[11] Claudia Ruitenberg, *Unlocking the World: Education in an Ethic of Hospitality* (Paradigm Publishing, 2015). In particular, Chapter 3 discusses the gender and culture of hospitality, with focus on language as an ethos and a site of hospitality in performance.
[12] Gayatri Chakravorty Spivak, "A Borderless World?" *Shuddhashar* 3. 10 (2018). https://shuddhashar.com/gayatri-chakravorty-spivak-a-borderless-world-3/

CHAPTER 18

Respect

Sanford Budick

Among other plays of Shakespeare, *A Midsummer Night's Dream* and *King Lear* show that flawless virtue is beyond human (and fairy-human) reach.[1] In *King Lear*, even Cordelia, Edgar, and Kent – despite their heroic self-effacements – show traces of pride that we may readily forgive but that are nevertheless palpable. Nor would anyone celebrate the leading celebrities of *A Midsummer Night's Dream*, Theseus and Oberon, as models of any sort of virtue. Yet, side by side with these limitations, in both of these plays a tenacious process of a particular kind of representation creates a unique species of experience within the mind of the spectator. By the impact of the entirety of each play, this experience of a formalism discloses an ideal or form of perfect virtue that in these plays is termed "respect."

What we take to be our everyday grasp of what is meant by respect is to be sure relevant here. To many or most of us it seems self-evident that showing respect for the other – for the humanity of the other – is closely linked to enjoying self-respect for the humanity in oneself. A large part of our deeply ingrained philosophical heritage (not to speak of religious ideas of the human) confirms the self-evident status of this or similar convictions. Thus the Stoics saw the basis of all virtue in what they called an "attention" or mindfulness (*prosochē*) that inevitably leads, they believed, to an ideal of "human flourishing" (*eudaimonia*).[2] So too, in the various kinds of Idealism that have been proposed from pre-Socratic, Platonic, and Neo-Platonic thought through to German Idealism (and beyond), a substrate of attention or respect for the ideal of humanity (or the ideal good of humanity) is a key postulate. Yet despite

---

[1] I cite from *A Midsummer Night's Dream*, ed. R. A. Foakes (Cambridge University Press, 2012) and *The Tragedy of King Lear*, ed. Jay L. Halio (Cambridge University Press, 2005).
[2] See Pierre Hadot, *Philosophy as a Way of Life*, ed. Arnold Davidson, trans. Michael Chase (Blackwell, 1995), 84.

this many-layered history, it is not at all obvious how the human mind can, in the first place, gain access to such respect, much less to an ideal of humanity, that are independent of the vagaries of experience and that are out of the reach of indoctrination. Immanuel Kant directly addressed this problem with his complementary propositions that, first, "respect" for an inner ideal of human flourishing can only be attained – either in feeling or in action – in a condition of freedom;[3] and, second, that the human mind has the potential for reaching such respect, very much in freedom, as well as for accessing an ideal of humanity that is "transcendental" or independent of experience. He explained how this potential for respect was identical with the human capacity for experiencing the sublime.[4]

Kant argued that the multiple uniqueness of experience of the sublime is that it is freely encountered, that it opens a space of freedom within consciousness, and that it momentarily liberates the mind from the coercions of all other experience. I propose that his account of the process that leads to experience of the sublime, and to respect, profoundly illuminates Shakespeare's route, in *A Midsummer Night's Dream* and *King Lear*, to shared respect for the ideal of humanity. Before proceeding, however, to Kant's explanations of this process – and to demonstrations of Shakespeare's following of very much the same process in *A Midsummer Night's Dream* and *King Lear* – I first turn to Shakespeare's namings of intense forms of "respect" in these plays and to his deployments, there, of the special condition of representation that enables an ultimate emergence of such respect.

In the whole of *A Midsummer Night's Dream* no claim for the work of imagination is more poignant than Theseus's declaration that he and his aristocratic company must use "noble respect" to supply what is wanting in the mechanicals' theatrical efforts. When Hippolyta expresses her fear that the egregious shortcomings of the mechanicals' play will be painful to watch, Theseus responds,

---

[3] On Kant's way of advancing beyond Stoic (and Platonic) ideas of "attention" by integrating autonomy of the will, see Klaus Reich, "Kant and Greek Ethics" (I and II), *Mind*, 48. 191 (1939), 338–354 and 48. 192 (1939), 446–463. For observations on Shakespeare's relation to Stoic philosophy, see Anthony David Nuttall, *Shakespeare the Thinker* (Yale University Press, 2007), 177–178, 194–195. On Shakespeare's ideas of freedom and aesthetic autonomy, see Stephen Greenblatt, *Shakespeare's Freedom* (University of Chicago Press, 2010), 95–123.

[4] This identity has not gone without challenges. Lewis White Beck, *A Commentary on Kant's Critique of Practical Reason* (University of Chicago Press, 1960), 220–221ff., spells out the close symmetry of Kant's accounts of the sublime and of respect, while also broaching challenges to each account.

The kinder we, to give them thanks for nothing.
Our sport shall be to take what they mistake;
And what poor duty cannot do, *noble respect*
Takes it in might, not merit.   (5.1.89–92; emphasis added)

In *King Lear*, after Lear has cast out Cordelia and cut off her part of the inheritance, France is moved to exclaim, "Gods, gods! 'Tis strange, that from their cold'st neglect / My love should kindle to *inflamed respect*" (1.1.249–250; emphasis added). It is notable, however, that these affirmations of respect are both almost immediately orphaned. It soon becomes obvious that nobleman Theseus is incapable of living up to the demands of "noble respect." His claim to provide an according "courtesy" (5.1.240) is belied by his participation in the cruel sport of ridiculing, even expressing pure contempt for, the mechanicals' play. In a different but symmetrical way, France no sooner says that he is seizing upon Cordelia's virtues than he largely disappears from the play (already in the Quartos, but decisively so in the Folio). If there are to be fulfillments of respect for an ideal of humanity *by* these plays, they must come from something else.

The feature of these plays that provides that something else is the deployment of effectively endless series of representation that have, as their impact, the humiliation of self-conceit. For the moment I postpone the explanation of how that impact is experienced by the spectator, while only registering the series themselves, first in *A Midsummer Night's Dream*, then in *King Lear*.

It may well be a reflection of the elements of divisiveness within *A Midsummer Night's Dream* itself, that commentaries on the play present a vast variety of sharply divergent views, not only of its meaning but even of its structure.[5] Within this critical turmoil, one of the most durable (and most often cited) accounts of the play's structure remains David Young's tracing of a "process of discovery" that is revealed, indeed, by "the opposing worlds" which "seem to form concentric circles" or, in another metaphor, a "spectrum of awareness."[6] In Young's view, the process of discovery advances outward from "the inmost circle" occupied by "the mechanicals," where Bottom stands "at their center." In the next circle "belong

[5] See, for example, Dorothea Kehler, "*A Midsummer Night's Dream*: A Bibliographic Survey of the Criticism," in *A Midsummer Night's Dream: Critical Essays*, ed. Dorothea Kehler (Garland, 1998), 3–76.
[6] David P. Young, *Something of Great Constancy: The Art of "A Midsummer Night's Dream"* (Yale University Press, 1966), 91. The page numbers for other references to Young's book are given in parentheses within my text.

the lovers"; "the circle beyond [that] belongs to Theseus and Hipployta"; while "the fairies occupy the next circle." Young leaves undecided whether "the furthest circle," outside the play, belongs to the theater audience or the playwright. (92). He splendidly complicates this picture of concentric circles that apparently radiate toward ever increasing awareness by noting that the circles of opposing worlds exist in relations of "mirroring" that continually reflect, back and forth, endless "permutations" within the circles (97). To this we should add that endless permutations of combination are generated among the mirroring circles. The effect of this complexity of permutation and mirroring inevitably opens the possibility that the first circle (of the mechanicals) might contribute to the emergence of a meaning in partnership with the second, third, and fourth circles. Young suggests that, in their singular ways, Bottom and the mechanicals "express the mutable and uncontainable nature of the play" as a whole (157). I suggest that, even more than that, the mechanicals' painful self-exposure to ridicule – that which Philostrate and Hippolyta and Theseus each call "nothing" (5.1.78, 88, 89) – points to two salient aspects of the play's way of creating meaning that exceeds the play itself. First, it cues us to seeing the exposures of the empty pretensions to high meaning of the actors in all the other circles: thus, for example, despite the lovers' declarations of eternally immutable love, will they nil they, they can instantaneously forget love, beloved, and even who they themselves are; Theseus shows himself to be, to the end, "overfull of self-affairs" (1.1.113) and as hollow, in his self-concern, as his talk of sharing a communal "great solemnity" (4.1.182); while Oberon, lordly King of the Fairies, is lowly deceitful, meanly tormenting. Second, and most important, we begin to see that the formal effect of this proliferating series of exposures of pretensions is to produce, for the spectator, an emergence of respect for the human.

Before spelling out the formalism of that emergence in *A Midsummer Night's Dream*, I note that *King Lear* is also structured as an effectively unstoppable series of its own, in this case of high-speed devastations. No one in the play is exempt from the reach of this series and its local mortifications. Edgar observes, for himself but also for the collective, that this unremitting series of "fortune's blows" constitutes "an art of known and feeling sorrows" which somehow makes one "pregnant to good pity" (4.5.212–214). A key question for both *King Lear* and *A Midsummer Night's Dream* is how this art of effectively endless serial movements might deliver, full blown from the mind of the spectator, the respect for humanity.

Without reference to Shakespeare, Kant was enabled to explain this midwifery by his realization that the cause of the feeling of the sublime – of respect – is experiencing "the impossibility of the absolute totality of an endless progression" within a contemplated object.⁷ Such objects, he says, are usually encountered in nature but they may also be met in works of art. Each item within such progressions, he noted, shows its own "inadequacy" or incompleteness as a representation of that which it tries to represent (as, say, in the hollowing out of pretention or in communicating devastation) (*CJ*, 5:255, 252–253). In contemplating the effectively endless series of representations that confronts the mind in such an object, the faculty of imagination projects onward to infinity while the faculty of reason demands a limit, a wholeness, in order to grasp the object. As a result of the clash of these two faculties – of trying, and necessarily failing, to follow out the endless progression – the mind experiences "a momentary check to the vital forces" that produces a "discharge all the more powerful" as the condition of freedom and as "respect" or "moral feeling" (*CJ*, 5:245, 258, 265). "The delight in the sublime … as … respect," he notes, "merits the name of a negative pleasure" (*CJ*, 5:245). After Georg Wilhelm Friedrich Hegel, that which Kant registers as "a momentary check to the vital forces" and the "negative pleasure," which produce the experience of freedom, will frequently be described in spatial terms as a free space of "negativity."⁸ For Kant the crucial upshot of this experience of negativity in "the feeling of the sublime … is respect for our own vocation," namely, "the idea of humanity in our own self" (*CJ*, 5:257). Thus Kant's root claims here are, first, that respect for the human in others and in ourselves – the "vocation" of our "humanity" – exists in the mind prior to, and independent of, experience – is in this sense "transcendental"; and, second, that this transcendental respect can be disclosed to us as knowledge by our capacity for experiencing the sublime.⁹ How essential this respect is for Kant is brought home by his beautiful remark that the very "idea of personality"

---

⁷ I will not try to decide whether Kant might here have been thinking of the sublime in Shakespeare's art, although Kant repeatedly expressed his admiration for Shakespeare's exemplary genius; and recognition of Shakespeare's sublimity was a commonplace in Germany in Kant's time. Kant's *Critiques* are here cited from *Immanuel Kant's Critique of Pure Reason*, trans. Norman Kemp Smith (Macmillan, 1993), cited from the A or B texts, *Critique of Practical Reason*, trans. Mary Gregor (Cambridge University Press, 1997), abbreviated *CPrR*, and *The Critique of Judgement*, trans. James Creed Meredith (Clarendon, 1973), abbreviated *CJ*.

⁸ Georg Wilhelm Friedrich Hegel's ideas of what negativity can achieve are different from Kant's, but Hegel posits the same possibility of opening a free space within consciousness. See, for example, Hegel, *The Science of Logic*, trans. George di Giovanni (Cambridge University Press, 2010), 589 and Brady Bowman, *Hegel and the Metaphysics of Absolute Negativity* (Cambridge University Press, 2013).

⁹ There is no contradiction here. As Kant wrote in the opening of the *Critique of Pure Reason*, "though all our knowledge begins with experience, it does not follow that it all arises out of experience" (B 1).

is a function of "awakening *respect* by setting before our eyes the sublimity of our nature" in the "vocation" of our "humanity" (*CPrR*, 5:87; emphasis added).

The route to the sublime and respect traverses a realm that may certainly seem purely negative. Yet this negativity is only the negation of what is negative; it is the "removal of the counterweight" of "self-conceit" in the contemplator of the object of the sublime, thus opening, for her or him, "the condition of that feeling we call respect" (*CPrR*, 5:75–76). Hippolyta senses, but is at a loss to understand, how "all the story of the night told over … grows to something of great constancy; / But howsoever, strange and admirable" (5.1. 23–27). In fact, in both plays the access to respect that is created for the spectator entails a great constancy, a systematic and infinitely sustained striving toward the disclosure of a transcendental something. This can only take place by passing through stages of thought or representation that are, momentarily, powerfully negating.

The endless progressions of movements that in *A Midsummer Night's Dream* as well as *King Lear* open a moment of suspension, or space of negativity, within consciousness, do not stand alone in the plays' representation and language. I note briefly that in both of these plays, coordinate with those progressions, Shakespeare deploys a language of the "nothing" that serves as an objective correlative to the subjective a priori moment of freedom or space of negativity. In this language, Shakespeare repeatedly works transformations between a "nothing" that denotes worldly worthlessness and a "nothing" that bespeaks the humiliation of self-conceit and that escapes all worldly valuing. The abyss between these meanings gapes wide between Lear's wholly materialist nothing, "Nothing will come of nothing," and Cordelia's "Nothing" of mere duty and preternatural humility (1.1.84–85).[10] In *A Midsummer Night's Dream* the split meanings of the "nothing" again and again turn on the mechanicals' theatrical. Philostrate has no idea of the profound positive valuation – of a transcendental unworldliness – he is speaking when he informs Theseus, "It is not for you. I have heard it over, / And it is nothing, nothing in the world" (5.1.77–78). When Hippolyta echoes

---

[10] With other topics in mind, I have noted other instances of the "nothing" in "Shakespeare's Secular Benediction: The Language of Tragic Community in *King Lear*," in *Religious Diversity and Early Modern English Texts: Catholic, Judaic, Feminist, and Secular Dimensions*, eds. Arthur F. Marotti and Chanita Goodblatt (Wayne State University Press, 2013), 330–351; "Shakespeare's Now: Atemporal Presentness in *King Lear* and *The Winter's Tale*," in *Entertaining the Idea: Shakespeare, Performance, and Philosophy*, ed. Lowell Gallagher, James Kearney, and Julia Reinhard Lupton (University of Toronto Press, 2021), 135–164; and *Hazarding All: Shakespeare and the Drama of Consciousness* (Edinburgh: Edinburgh University Press, 2021)

Philostrate's belittling review of the mechanicals' show, saying "He says they can do *nothing* in this kind," Theseus, still speaking from the wonderment of "noble respect," counters, "The kinder we, to give them thanks for *nothing*" (5.1.88–91; emphases added). Yet, as we have said, the full realizations of respect and of its relation to a negativity only become accessible to the spectator – as a transcendental form of respect – by dint of the full impact of each play.

Quince unwittingly comes close to describing what that full impact can be. It is certainly beyond his understanding – and that of everyone else in the play – to grasp that *A Midsummer Night's Dream* must transcendentally "offend" self-conceit with a "good will." The jumbled syntax of his declaration of intent has its own mind, speaking Shakespeare's mind to the spectator and brilliantly itemizing key elements of the process that can produce respect for the human:

> If we offend, it is with our good will.
> That you should think, we come not to offend,
> But with good will. To show our simple skill,
> That is the true beginning of our end.
> Consider then, we come but in despite.
> We do not come as minding to content you,
> Our true intent is. All for your delight,
> We are not here. That you should here repent you,
> The actors are at hand; and by their show
> You shall know all that you are like to know.   (4.2.108–116)

Good will must offend, must humiliate self-conceit, very much in despite. It must not delight but rather aim at producing – for the spectator – a sublime negative pleasure and the will to repent from self-conceit, to respect the merely human. Thus a full knowing of this process becomes available, not to the noble audience at Athens (who will only know all that they are capable of knowing, given their obliviousness to the sublimity of respect), but to the theater audience in London, high and low, in the full experience of the play and in a world that is uncovered, transcendentally, within.

Puck's closing off of the play acknowledges the way it should "have offended" – systematically, which is to say, in the constancy of following representations of the humiliation of self-conceit. *Thinking, pardoning* spectators, he gently suggests, should have been mended, altered, by "this" – the play and "visions" they have just experienced. The joint work of amendment, of play and spectator, extends beyond the play and even, reflexively, makes it a better play:

> Think but this, and all is mended …
> If you pardon, we will mend.

When Puck – standing amended beyond the play – envisions that which will "ere long … restore" these "amends," he speaks as a minor prophet of a theatrical redemption that is outside time (5.1.401–416). In the spirit of "noble respect," Theseus remarked of plays in general that "The best in this kind are but shadows; and the worst are no worse, if imagination amend them." (5.1.205–206). Puck's vision of a reciprocal amendment between spectator and play only asks that we truly bring such amending respect, derived from the experience of the play, to the whole of *A Midsummer Night's Dream*, imperfections and all. In line with taking in the force of such mending, perhaps it is not too much to suggest that the complex delight that children take in this play is at least in part due to their grasp of the infantile egocentrism that here comes in for amendment with all the wild intensity of farce.

With regard to what finally emerges for the spectator of *King Lear* as a whole, it does not greatly matter whether the play's last words are assigned to Edgar (as in the Folio) or to Albany (as in the Quartos):

> The oldest hath borne most; we that are young
> Shall never see so much, nor live so long. (5.3.299–300)

These opaque verses point to an exceeding of intelligibility, at least as far as the remaining protagonists of the play are concerned. The transcendental point here is thus symmetrical with what Puck suggests at the end of *A Midsummer Night's Dream*. In both cases, the burden of attaining to an inner virtue has been shifted to the spectators. In both cases, if we have followed along in full constancy, the something that has been disclosed, in a realm that is finally independent of experience, is our individually held ideal of noble, inflamed respect. The humanity that is the object of this respect is inclusive of rude mechanicals as well as beggars, fools, and madmen. Only in the disclosure and implementation of this respect do we know, immediately, our own humanity.

CHAPTER 19

Chastity

Jennifer Flaherty

From the Latin *castus* or *castitas*[1] and the Old French *chastete*, chastity signifies sexual purity and restraint, either through virginity or through fidelity in marriage. The question of whether chastity qualifies as a virtue dates back at least to Thomas Aquinas; the ongoing gendered application of the term, often in the context of restricting or shaming women, complicates the issue still further in contemporary scholarship.[2] Building on Augustine's concepts of bodily holiness and "persevering continency," Aquinas determines that "chastity is a virtue" because "it belongs to chastity that a man make moderate use of bodily members in accordance with the judgment of his reason and the choice of his will."[3] While Augustine and Aquinas define chastity as a virtue for both men and women, Shakespeare depicts chastity almost exclusively as a female virtue, repeatedly using the term in connection with feminized representations of nature, the virgin goddess Diana, and young women (married and unmarried).[4] Shakespeare's plays include jealous husbands, impatient suitors, intrusive brothers, and overbearing fathers who fixate on the chastity of female characters, lending further credibility to the idea that chastity is imposed and enforced by men as a means of control over women's bodies. Chastity, however, is a

---

[1] Meghan J. DiLuzio, *A Place at the Altar: Priestesses in Republican Rome* (Princeton University Press, 2020), 87. DiLuzio gives a more detailed and nuanced explanation of chastity in Rome, particularly the practice of applying the standard of *castitas* to elevate women to positions of power.

[2] For further reading, see Eric Silverman's book on *Sexual Ethics in a Secular Age*, which is subtitled *Is There Still a Virtue of Chastity?* (Routledge 2021).

[3] Thomas Aquinas. *The Summa Theologica of St. Thomas Aquinas: Literally Translated by Fathers of the English Dominican Province*, 2nd ed. (Burns Oates & Washburne Ltd., 1941), Q. 151, Art. 1.

[4] The word "chaste" describes snow more often than it describes men in Shakespeare's works. Although male characters such as Malcolm from *Macbeth* and Ferdinand in *The Tempest* occasionally make claims about their own sexual purity, Florizel from *The Winter's Tale* is the only male character to specifically acknowledge his own chastity by name, explaining that his motives are "more chaste" than those of Zeus and Apollo, who also disguised themselves for love. Even Adonis is not specifically described as chaste, although the word chastity is used in the poem in connection with "love-lacking vestals and self-loving nuns" (*Venus and Adonis [VA]*, 752).

virtue of self-government; if Shakespeare presents it as a virtue that applies almost exclusively to women, it must, by definition, be under the control of women themselves. For Shakespeare's female characters, chastity functions as a means of expressing bodily autonomy and rejecting attempts at patriarchal control, concepts that are still relevant for young women today. Shakespeare's chaste heroines now lend their names and stories to projects designed to promote social justice and advocacy for young women: The Ophelia Project,[5] The Marina Project, The Viola Project,[6] and *Measure (Still) for Measure*.[7] The cultural authority of Shakespeare's plays can help provide a historical and ethical reference for a virtue that centers on control over one's own body.

Although medieval theologians believed "continence or chastity consists of three parts: conjugal continence (*continentia coniugalis*), widowed continence (*continentia vidualis*), and virginity," Pavel Blazek argues that "the virginal state can be seen as the highest mode of the virtue of chastity."[8] Unhae Park Langis notes the importance of Christianity to Shakespearean chastity, explaining that "female virtue, by Shakespeare's time, became confined to chastity, favoring the *virgo* ideal of the early Christian and medieval traditions as embodied in the Virgin Mary."[9] That the Christian virtue of chastity built on the Latin tradition of "cultic virginity" associated with Roman Vestal Virgins[10] is also apparent in Shakespeare's plays and poems, which use "vestal" and "nun" interchangeably to refer to chaste and virginal figures. Shakespeare acknowledges the idealization of virginity and the corresponding drive to enforce it in his depiction of men who entreat young women to remain secluded and maintain their chastity. Laertes and Polonius warn Ophelia to guard her "chaste treasure" and "tender yourself more dearly" (*Hamlet* 1.3.30, 107).[11] Bianca is "closely mew'd" by Baptista and must "live a maid at home" until her sister is married (*The Taming of the Shrew [TS]* 1.1.181–182). Prospero threatens both Ferdinand and Miranda with "barren hate, sour-eyed disdain and

5 The Ophelia Project, "The Ophelia Project," John F. Kennedy Memorial Foundation, www.jfk-foundation.org/ophelia-project/.
6 The Viola Project, "The Viola Project: Mission," City Lit Theater, www.violaproject.org/.
7 Nora J. Williams, "Writing the Collaborative Process: Measure (Still) for Measure, Shakespeare, and Rape Culture," *PARtake: The Journal of Performance as Research*, 2. 1 (2018), 1–21.
8 Pavel Blazek, "The Virtue of Virginity: The Aristotelian Challenge," in *Virtue Ethics in the Middle Ages: Commentaries on Aristotle's* Nicomachean Ethics, *1200–1500*, ed. István Bejczy (Brill, 2007), 249.
9 Unhae Park Langis, *Passion, Prudence, and Virtue in Shakespearean Drama* (Continuum/Bloomsbury, 2011), 20.
10 Pavel Blazek, "The Virtue of Virginity," 247–273.
11 Shakespeare cited from *The Arden Shakespeare Complete Works*, ed. Richard Proudfoot, Ann Thompson, David Scott Kastan, and H. R. Woudhuysen (Arden, 2001).

discord" if he breaks "her virgin-knot" before their wedding day (*Tempest* 4.1.15–20). Yet the two Shakespearean heroines who arguably show the most fervent commitment to their own virginity (Isabella from *Measure for Measure* and Marina from *Pericles*), do so in defiance rather than compliance with male authority, challenging the patriarchal ideal that female virtue serves the interests of men.

Both Isabella and Marina make the case that death is a more acceptable loss than chastity. When she is sold to a brothel, Marina promises "if fires be hot, knives sharp, or waters deep, untied I still my virgin knot will keep," and devotes herself to converting the clients of the brothel to virtue rather than giving in to the threats or entreaties of those who run the house (*Pericles [Per]* 4.2.144–145). Isabella is willing to lay down her own life to save her brother Claudio, but she will not accept Angelo's offer to pardon Claudio in exchange for her virginity: "Then, Isabel, live chaste, and, brother, die: More than our brother is our chastity" (*Measure for Measure [MM]* 2.4.183–186). In a grimly inverted version of Laertes's lecture to Ophelia on chastity, Claudio urges her to consider Angelo's proposition, but Isabella maintains that it is better "a brother died at once, than that a sister, by redeeming him, should die for ever" (*MM* 2.4.106–108). Isabella's commitment to chastity is less palatable than Marina's for readers, despite the textual evidence that Angelo's offer cannot be trusted. Katherine Gillen describes Isabella's "militant chastity" as "uncomfortably sterile" and "ungenerative."[12] In his examination of virtues through the lens of Shakespeare, Arjan Plaisier[13] even makes the case that Isabella's pride is "worse than the whoredom of Mistress Overdone" because "she prizes her reputation more than the life of her brother."[14] In 2001, George L. Geckle noted a tendency among students to "express moralizing disapproval as if Isabella were a character in real life whose behaviour could be awarded a pass or fail," and he attributed the lack of sympathy for the character to "the wide indifference to the virtue of chastity in our time."[15] Michael Bristol's account of teaching *Measure for Measure* in this volume indicates that some students are still "horrified" by Isabella's decision, while others call attention to the gender bias inherent in the assumption that her

---

[12] Katherine Gillen, *Chaste Value*, Economic Crisis, Female Chastity, and the Production of Social Difference on Shakespeare's Stage (Edinburgh University Press, 2017), 37.
[13] Secretary General of the Protestant Church in the Netherlands.
[14] Arjan Plaisier, *Deep Wisdom from Shakespeare's Dramas: Theological Reflections on Seven Shakespeare Plays* (Wipf and Stock, 2012), 51–52.
[15] George L. Geckle, *Measure for Measure, Shakespeare: The Critical Tradition. Volume 6* (Bloomsbury, 2001), xxxi.

body (and the state of her soul) should be traded for her brother's life. Isabella's refusal to contribute to a corrupt system of sexual exchange takes on new meaning in the era of the #MeToo movement.[16] Her fears that her accusations will not be believed resonate with contemporary survivors of sexual assault and harassment, as does her willingness to speak out against injustice. Isabella's story is reworked in *Measure (Still) for Measure*, a project created by Nora J. Williams to blend "Shakespeare, physical theatre, devising, and intersectional feminism."[17] Williams describes the project's goals as "threefold: to reorient the 400-year-old play around its female protagonist, Isabella; to facilitate difficult conversations about consent and rape culture; and to instigate policy change in educational institutions."[18] In this volume, Katharine A. Craik and Ewan Fernie describe their similar work on The Marina Project, a "creative-critical collaboration with the Royal Shakespeare Company" in which *Pericles* is re-written to call attention to the power of chastity in a contemporary global context.

When it serves their interests, some of Shakespeare's male characters disparage virginity. Bertram criticizes Diana's chastity in his attempt to woo her: "You are no maiden, but a monument: When you are dead, you should be such a one as you are now, for you are cold and stern" (*All's Well That Ends Well [AWEW]* 4.2.8). His re-framing of virtue as vice is countered by Diana's own words on the value of chastity:

> My chastity's the jewel of our house,
> Bequeathed down from many ancestors;
> Which were the greatest obloquy i' the world
> In me to lose: thus your own proper wisdom
> Brings in the champion Honour on my part,
> Against your vain assault.   (*AWEW* 4.2.45–51)

Like Bertram, Romeo argues that Rosaline's "strong proof of chastity" makes waste of her youth, "for beauty starved with her severity cuts beauty off from all posterity" (*Romeo and Juliet [RJ]* 1.1.211, 219–220). To convince Hermia to follow her father's wishes and marry Demetrius, Theseus discourages her from living "in shady cloister mew'd … a barren sister all your life, chanting faint hymns to the cold fruitless moon," arguing that

---

16 Tara Isabella Burton, "What a lesser-known Shakespeare play can tell us about Harvey Weinstein," *Vox*, 11/15/2017, www.vox.com/culture/2017/11/15/16644938/shakespeare-measure-for-measure-weinstein-sexual-harassment-play-theater/.

17 Nora J. Williams, "Writing the Collaborative Process: Measure (Still) for Measure, Shakespeare, and Rape Culture," *PARtake: The Journal of Performance as Research* 2. 1 (2018), 1–21.

18 Williams, "Measure (Still) for Measure," abst.

"the rose distill'd" is happier than the one "withering on the virgin thorn" (*A Midsummer Night's Dream [MND]* 1.1.71–78). That Shakespeare's men deride virginity as often as they praise it indicates that the speakers are not worried about female sexuality, but female autonomy. As Aquinas specifies, chastity is not a bodily state of virginity but a virtue of mental self-control.[19] Chastity is powerful precisely because it emphasizes agency in response to efforts to control women's bodies.

Shakespeare balances the frustrated voices of male characters with those of the female characters who challenge them. Theseus's description of virginity is simultaneously idealized as virtuous and denigrated as undesirable, and he urges Hermia to reject a life that "grows, lives and dies in single blessedness" (*MND* 1.1.78). Hermia's reply signals that her autonomy matters more than the authority of her father and Theseus:

> So will I grow, so live, so die, my lord,
> Ere I will yield my virgin patent up
> Unto his lordship, whose unwished yoke
> My soul consents not to give sovereignty.   (1.1.79–82)

Responding directly to Theseus's suggestion that marriage to Demetrius should be preferable to total abstinence for the rest of her life, Hermia makes it clear that choosing a husband is necessary for her to make the transition from virginity to conjugal continence. While Egeus's right to choose his daughter's husband is written into the laws of Athens in *A Midsummer Night's Dream*, the marriage cannot take place without Hermia's assent. As Derek Cohen argues, "female chastity is the cornerstone of the patriarchy, yet … in the end female sexual behavior, including female sexual desire, is under the sway of the individual woman. This is the fact which threatens the basis of patriarchy."[20] Hermia's control over her own chastity is more powerful than the wishes of Demetrius, Egeus, Theseus, or even Lysander. Consent is crucial to Shakespearean chastity, placing it in direct opposition to the virtue of obedience when a daughter disagrees with her father about her own marriage.

Chastity in the early-modern era was linked with obedience and silence as a triad of female virtue that extolled restraint and discouraged rebellion.[21] Through female characters who openly defy patriarchal

---

[19] Thomas Aquinas. *Summa Theologica*, Q. 151, Art. 1.
[20] Derek Cohen, *Shakespeare's Culture of Violence* (Palgrave, 1992), 8.
[21] Anna Kamaralli, *Shakespeare and the Shrew: Performing the Defiant Female Voice* (Palgrave Macmillan, 2012), 1.

authority to maintain control over their own chastity, Shakespeare's plays demonstrate the opposition rather than the unity of chastity with silence and obedience. Married fidelity is stronger than filial duty when Desdemona's father asks her to identify the man to whom she most owes obedience; she replies that "here's my husband, and so much duty as my mother show'd to you, preferring you before her father, so much I challenge that I may profess due to the Moor my lord" (*Othello [Oth]* 1.3.181–189). Juliet disobeys her father's order to marry Paris, telling Friar Lawrence that she will risk any death or horror "without fear or doubt, to live an unstain'd wife to my sweet love" (*RJ* 4.1.87–88). Silvia rejects her father's choice in favor of Valentine, Anne Page disobeys both of her parents to marry Fenton, and both Jessica and Bianca elope despite (or in reaction to) the restrictions placed upon them by their fathers. Imogen challenges Cymbeline's authority as both her father and her king, taking ownership of her body by affirming her choice to marry Posthumus rather than her stepmother's son Cloten: "I chose an eagle and did avoid a puttock" (*Cymbeline [Cym]* 1.1.70–171). The stakes are higher with Imogen's marriage; Coppélia Kahn argues that *Cymbeline* "joins the problem of *virtus* with chastity, for Imogen's chastity isn't merely her own: it is a national treasure. She is a princess of Britain and heir to its throne."[22] Perdita similarly challenges the King of Bohemia when she runs away with his son, and Lavinia disobeys both her father and her emperor when she chooses to marry Bassianus. Some of these choices lead to tragedy, others to happy endings, but Shakespeare's female characters frequently own and advocate for their own choices regarding their husbands and virginity when faced with pressure from authority figures.

The same combination of external pressures on young women and the potential for resistance against those pressures that define Shakespeare's representation of chastity have also led Shakespeare's female characters to become symbols for the experiences of the contemporary teenage girl. Mary Pipher's book *Reviving Ophelia: Saving the Selves of Adolescent Girls* draws upon Ophelia as an example of a character losing herself to "the destructive forces that affect young women," citing her conversations with Polonius, Laertes, and Hamlet as examples of the societal pressures and conflicting expectations with which adolescent girls struggle.[23]

---

[22] Coppélia Kahn, *Roman Shakespeare: Warriors, Wounds and Women* (Routledge, 2013).
[23] Mary Pipher, *Reviving Ophelia: Saving the Selves of Adolescent Girls* (Putnam, 1994), 20.

Pipher's book inspired initiatives named after Ophelia and designed to support young women, and The Ophelia Project run by the John F. Kennedy institute still provides leadership programs for girls.[24] The Viola Project at City Lit Theatre in Chicago uses Shakespeare and performance to build "a foundation for young women and gender nonconforming youth" to "demand inclusion: inclusion in the classroom, in the workspace, in the world and on the stage."[25] While chastity and sex are not central to the missions of either of these projects in the ways that they are to The Marina Project and *Measure (Still) for Measure*, the ideas of autonomy and agency connect all of the initiatives linked to Shakespeare's female characters.

The legacies of Shakespeare's married heroines have not inspired social justice initiatives to the same extent that his unmarried virgins have; there is no corresponding Desdemona Project[26] or Imogen Project[27] for married women. Yet women in Shakespeare's plays face suspicions about chastity from their husbands that are reminiscent of the treatment of unmarried women by their fathers. Shakespeare's jealous husbands (Leontes, Othello, Posthumus, Ford, Claudio in *Much Ado*) present themselves as guardians of chastity for their "wayward" wives. Ford asserts that he would rather trust "a thief to walk my ambling gelding, than my wife with herself" (*The Merry Wives of Windsor [MWW]* 2.2.288–289). In *A Winter's Tale (WT)*, Leontes escalates quickly from suspicions of his own wife's infidelity to generalizations about all married women:

> No barricado for a belly; know't;
> It will let in and out the enemy
> With bag and baggage: many thousand on's
> Have the disease, and feel't not.   (*WT* 1.2.204–207)

Leontes laments the paradox of gendered chastity in a patriarchal society; he believes the bodies of wives belong to their husbands, but that those bodies are simultaneously outside the control of men and therefore cannot be kept chaste. His words are reminiscent of Othello's: "O curse

---

[24] The Ophelia Project, www.jfkfoundation.org/ophelia-project/.

[25] The Viola Project, "The Viola Project: Mission," www.violaproject.org/.

[26] A project of this name does exist, but it has no relation to the topics of women and virtue. The "DEtection of Steel Defects by Enhanced MONitoring and Automated procedure for self-inspection and maintenance is a three-years research project in EU Research Fund for Coal and Steel 2017 programme coordinated by Sapienza University of Rome," www.desdemonaproject.eu.

[27] Similarly, there is an IMOGEN (Interactive Multimodal Output GENeration) project, a study of "speech recognition, language analysis, question answering, and dialogue management," wwwhome.ewi.utwente.nl/~theune/IMOGEN/index.html, which is unrelated to the Shakespearean character.

of marriage, that we can call these delicate creatures ours, and not their appetites!" (*Oth* 3.3.272–274). The very unease of these complaints demonstrates the inability of male characters to override the decisions that female characters make about their own bodies without violence.[28]

Examining the intersections between chastity and economic exchange, Katherine Gillen observes that although "chastity was held up as a political, social, and religious ideal, as the female body was imagined as unruly and open, in need of constant surveillance."[29] Shakespeare's plays refute the idea of the female body as unruly property by portraying husbands who are incapable of policing the chastity of their wives and unable to even accurately determine if their wives are truly chaste. In all of the jealousy plays, the wives accurately proclaim their chastity, and the husbands eventually regret their distrust. Mistress Ford shares her story publicly, prompting her husband to announce, "I rather will suspect the sun with cold than thee with wantonness" (*MWW* 4.4.7–8). Hero defends her chastity at both of her weddings, and Desdemona and Imogen assert their innocence after their husbands determine they should die. Hermione declares in her trial that "my past life hath been as continent, as chaste, as true, as I am now unhappy; which is more than history can pattern" (*WT* 3.2.32–34). The difference between comedy and tragedy is whether women are believed.

The fixation that Shakespeare's fathers, brothers, husbands, and lovers have on female chastity demonstrates why contemporary readers might be inclined to dismiss chastity as a patriarchal construct designed to oppress women rather than a relevant virtue. Yet Shakespeare's plays demonstrate that chastity functions not as compliance, but as vehement and vocal resistance to attempts to override female agency. In presenting chastity as way for female characters to expressing control their own bodies, Shakespeare elevates it above the corresponding "triad" virtues of silence and obedience, making it clear that chastity goes beyond virginity or fidelity. When asked "Why Shakespeare?" for reaching young women, the creators of The Viola Project explain that Shakespeare's female characters "advocate for themselves, whether it's for a kingdom or a kiss."[30] This advocacy is

---

[28] The brutal exception Shakespeare depicts to women's control over their own chastity is rape, with *Titus Andronicus* and *The Rape of Lucrece* as the most prominent examples. For a thorough analysis of chastity and rape in Shakespeare, see Kirsten Dey, "Petrarchism Demonised: Defiling Chastity in *The Two Gentlemen of Verona*, *The Rape of Lucrece* and *Titus Andronicus*," *Shakespeare in Southern Africa* 31 (2018), 37–46. Katherine Gillen's *Chaste Value* also addresses the subject.

[29] Katherine Gillen, *Chaste Value*, 3.

[30] The Viola Project, "The Viola Project: Why Shakespeare?"

particularly compelling when characters such as Hermia, Isabella, Imogen, Desdemona, and Marina defend their chastity before their fathers, their lovers, their suitors, and the leaders of their governments, arguing for their rights to choose or refuse their own sexual partners. In the context of current global debates about women's rights, reproductive health, and sexual assault, Shakespeare's plays demonstrate that chastity is not only a relevant virtue – it is crucial to understanding the importance of women's autonomy.

CHAPTER 20

Wit

Indira Ghose

In the early-modern period, the term "wit" encompassed a variety of meanings, from intellectual powers, to the imagination, to sparkling and amusing verbal dexterity, the predominant meaning today.[1] In Shakespeare's
plays, thronged with witty protagonists, both male and female, and wise
fools, professional purveyors of wit, all these connotations appear, often
commingled with each other. When Rosalind says to Orlando, "Make the
doors upon a woman's wit and it will out at the casement. Shut that, and
'twill out at the key-hole" (*As You Like It* 4.1.148–150), she is warning him
that it is impossible to keep women's intelligence and ingenuity, with a
glance at their linguistic deftness, bottled up. When Falstaff boasts, "I am
not only witty in myself, but the cause that wit is in other men" (*2 Henry
IV* 1.2.9–10), he is referring to his fertile imagination, his mental sharpness,
as well as his talent for quips and aperçus. Shakespeare not only stages a
firework of wit, he explores the ethical value of the concept of wit in all its
multivalency.

The Old and Middle English word "wit" referred to the mental capacity of reasoning or human understanding.[2] From the thirteenth century
onwards, the term was also used to denote the faculties of perception:
imagination, cogitation or instinct, fantasy, memory, and common sense,
commonly labelled "the five wits." By the end of the sixteenth century,
these were generally collapsed into the notion of the imagination. In addition to cognitive and perceptive abilities, a third set of connotations in

---

[1] On the mutations of "wit," see Phil Withington, "The Sociable Self," *Society in Early Modern
England: The Vernacular Origins of Some Powerful Ideas* (Polity, 2010), 171–201; Phil Withington,
"'Tumbled into the Dirt': Wit and Incivility in Early Modern England," in *Understanding Historical
(Im)politeness: Relational Linguistic Practice over Time and across Cultures* eds. Marcel Bax and Daniel
Z. Kadar (John Benjamins, 2012), 154–174; and Ian Munro, "The Matter of Wit and the Early
Modern Stage," in *A New Companion to Renaissance Drama*, eds. Arthur F. Kinney and Thomas
Warren Hopper (Wiley Blackwell, 2017), 513–528.
[2] "wit, n.," *Oxford English Dictionary*.

connection with "wit" arose in the early-modern period. The term was increasingly used to describe mental agility or ingenuity, which was extended to linguistic adeptness. The association of wit with brilliant utterances – the apposite expression calculated to surprise, delight, and amuse – only gained currency late in the sixteenth century.

The Renaissance also witnessed the rising importance of the *Nicomachean Ethics*, in particular among Humanist thinkers.[3] While the definition of wit as allied to discernment and discretion was akin to the Aristotelian intellectual virtue of prudence, the humorous inflection of the term correlates with the moral virtue of wittiness (*eutrapelia*). For Aristotle, wittiness was one of the three social virtues, together with affability and truthfulness (or steering a median course between boastfulness and understatement).[4] As with all moral virtues, Aristotle advocates moderation: he opposes urbane and tactful humor to the extremes of either excessive jesting or an entire lack of humor. He labels those given to unrestrained joking as vulgar buffoons, whereas those who reject laughter are boors. Aristotle explicitly ties tasteful wit to social class, describing it as the attribute of the "refined and well-bred man" (1128a). He also provides a defense of humor by stressing that relaxation and amusement are a necessary element in life, a point he reiterates in Book X. 6, with the caveat that amusement is not an end in itself, but a means to propel virtue (1176b). This was seized upon by thinkers such as Aquinas, keen to recuperate *eutrapelia* from the disparagement meted out to jesting by St Paul, who brackets it with scurrilous and foolish talk (Eph. 5:4). Aquinas argues that moderate and decorous wit is much to be recommended,[5] while humanists such as Erasmus and Sir Thomas More revalorized levity as an indispensable contribution to the good life.

In the early-modern period, all three shades of meaning remained in circulation, and were often conflated with each other. When in his *Scholemaster* (1570) the humanist Roger Ascham, tutor to Elizabeth I, sets out the ideal programme for education, he draws on the list of virtues necessary for future leaders of the ideal society outlined in Plato's *Republic*.[6] The first quality that an aspiring young mind should possess is to

---

[3] Quentin Skinner, *The Foundations of Modern Political Thought*, 2 vols. (Cambridge University Press, 1978), vol. I: *The Renaissance*, 41–48.

[4] Aristotle, *The Nicomachean Ethics*, trans. David Ross (Oxford University Press, 2009), 4. 6–8.

[5] St. Thomas Aquinas, *Summa Theologiae*, ed. and trans. Thomas Gilby, vol. 44 (Blackfriars, 1972), 2a2ae.168.

[6] Plato, *The Republic*, trans. Desmond Lee, Penguin Classics (Penguin Books, 1987), 535b–d.

be "apt by goodness of wit and appliable by readiness of will to learning," an attribute that Plato terms *euphuia*.[7] Ascham distinguishes between
"quick" and "hard" wits; it becomes apparent that he is not referring solely
to youths, but also to his peers. "Quick wits," he asserts, are those who display mental sharpness and cleverness, but whose refinement is a meretri-
cious veneer. "Hard wits" are careful, conscientious, and by dint of hard
work, attain knowledge of the good.[8] Ascham shared the early humanist
conviction that a study of rhetoric would inculcate an ability for rational
judgement. Wit, he believed, was related to rhetorical *inventio*, the faculty
to discover new arguments and explore them in depth.

In a tribute to Ascham, John Lyly entitled his prose romance *Euphues:
The Anatomy of Wit* (1578). His protagonist Euphues' clever quips and skill
at repartee demonstrate his mastery of rhetoric, but in Lyly's skeptical take
on the ethical import of rhetoric, his eloquence is not a conduit to wisdom,
even if in the course of the book the witty young man undergoes a moral
education. Nonetheless, the text, as well as its sequel, *Euphues and His
England* (1580), sparked a vogue for ornate, highly patterned prose, termed
"euphuism," which flaunts its linguistic flair in a manner that exemplifies
rhetorical style rather than argumentative substance. Endlessly imitated
(and parodied) by later writers, the true inheritors of euphuistic wit are
a group of poets including John Donne, George Herbert, and Andrew
Marvell, later dubbed the Metaphysical school of poetry, whose verse foregrounds the dazzling artistry of the poets in associating disparate ideas in
devices such as conceit, paradox, and antithesis.

Sir Philip Sidney offers a different view, expressly linking creative artifacts to virtue. When, in his *Apology for Poetry*, published in 1595, Sidney
speaks of the "erected wit," which enables us to acquire knowledge of the
divine, as opposed to the "infected will," he is employing the terms in the
sense of the human intellect corrupted by the "will" or desire. But when
he speaks of the poet "freely ranging only within the zodiac of his own
wit," he is offering a paean to the poetic imagination, untrammeled by the
constraints of factuality. Sidney's Neoplatonic defense of literary works is
premised on the conviction that by creating a "golden" world for humans
to emulate, the poet incites us to virtue.[9]

---

[7] Roger Ascham, *The Schoolmaster*, ed. Lawrence V. Ryan (Cornell University Press, 1967), 27; Plato,
  The Republic, 535b.
[8] Ascham, *The Schoolmaster*, 21–26.
[9] Sir Philip Sidney, *An Apology for Poetry*, ed. Geoffrey Shepherd, revised by R. W. Maslen, 3rd ed.
  (Manchester University Press, 2002), 86, 85.

The early-modern debate about the value of wit continues with the dissection of wit by Hobbes in his 1651 *Leviathan*, in which he discusses "naturall" and "acquired" wit: "naturall" wit is cultivated through experience, "acquired" wit through education. Hobbes further distinguishes between two types of "naturall" wit, as equivalent either to good judgment, or alternatively, to fancy, i.e., a nimble imagination.[10] The eighteenth century developed a further dichotomy, one between true and false wit, the latter defined as superficial lustre. In the meantime, fueled by the resurgence of rhetoric and trends such as euphuism, the capacity to express oneself in adroit, polished, and amusing manner became an indispensable technique of social distinction. Retailed in the form of miscellanies, conversational manuals, epistolary guides, rhetorics, essays by "university wits" such as Thomas Nashe and Robert Greene, and jestbooks, wit became a commodity in the marketplace of print. In the late sixteenth and early seventeenth centuries convivial societies emerged in London, in which the participants, lawyers, parliamentarians, and men of letters, honed their skills in wit.[11]

In *Love's Labour's Lost*, Shakespeare provides one of the most perceptive explorations of the vexed early-modern relation between alluring human artifacts, including verbal artifacts, and ethics, probing the question whether surface brilliance might nonetheless bear an ethical charge. The characters in *Love's Labour's Lost* are consumed with a quest to acquire wit.[12] The King of Navarre and three attendant lords are determined to found an academy of learning to sharpen their intellect. The true motive behind the King's initiative is revealed in the very first words of the play: "Let fame, that all hunt after in their lives / Live registered upon our brazen tombs" (1.1.1–2). The noblemen of Navarre are not, as Ascham recommends, pursuing learning in order to gain virtue. Their goal is to burnish their reputation. Their prime concern is to show off their finesse and verbal artistry to the visiting French Princess and her court ladies, in elaborate games of wooing, in the form of poetic outpourings, theatrical performances, or clever repartee. Unfortunately for the lords, the ladies are superior to them in all these disciplines.

---

[10] Thomas Hobbes, *Leviathan, or, The Matter, Form, and Power of a Common-wealth Ecclesiastical and Civil*, ed. Richard Tuck (Cambridge University Press, 1991), 50–53.

[11] Michelle O'Callaghan, *The English Wits: Literature and Sociability in Early Modern England* (Cambridge University Press, 2007).

[12] Two studies of the play that remain valuable are William C. Carroll, *The Great Feast of Language in* Love's Labour's Lost (Princeton University Press, 1976) and Louis Adrian Montrose, *"Curious-knotted Garden": The Form, Themes, and Contexts of Shakespeare's* Love's Labour's Lost (Institut für Englische Sprache und Literatur, Universität Salzburg, 1977).

The ladies too exhibit their cleverness and linguistic virtuosity in witty skirmishes with each other, applauded by their princess in imagery borrowed from the fashionable game of tennis: "Well bandied both, a set of wit well played" (5.2.29). But wit is not an exclusively aristocratic concern in the play. Armado, the Spanish knight, Holofernes, the pedant, and Nathaniel, the curate, are just as keen to appear nimble-witted, however ludicrous their effusions might appear to the audience. As Mote, Armado's page, remarks caustically to the rustic Costard, "They have been at a great feast of languages and stolen the scraps" (5.1.35–36). But the clown too is enthralled by the lure of stylish language. He hoards up the new words he stumbles on, such as "remuneration," (3.1.132), and lavishes praise on the ladies for besting the courtier Boyet at a bout of wit: "most sweet jests, most incony vulgar wit, / When it comes so smoothly off" (4.1.141–142). Even Dull, the constable, tries his hand at using Latinate terms, mis-echoing Nathaniel's words in hilarious malapropisms. Virtually all the protagonists of the play are absorbed in demonstrating their expertise in witty speech as a means of boosting their status.

The play itself is an exercise in wit, showcasing Shakespeare's command of a gamut of styles, verse forms and poetic techniques – at least eight sonnets are artfully interwoven into the drama – while parodying literary fashions like euphuism, Petrarchism, and the rhetorical style of *copia*, a lavish indulgence in synonyms. The effervescent word-play and sophisticated humor clearly aims to flatter the spectators, insinuating that they are conversant with the latest aesthetic trends. In this carefully patterned, supremely self-conscious play, Shakespeare, like his characters, is staking a claim to cultural cachet. At the same time, the play anatomizes the dark sides of wit, and reveals how wit can be divorced from virtue, exposing the superficiality and self-regard at the heart of excessive verbal pirouettes.

The notion of wit is shadowed by its bracketing with "will," a term that meant desire or lust, but that in an age that saw a revival of Augustinianism, was freighted with far greater resonances. In Augustine's doctrine of the will, the human ability to choose evil over good was at the source of the Fall of humankind. Adam and Eve, Augustine claimed, had been impelled by excessive pride and self-love to commit their transgression.[13] In a much bleaker play, *Troilus and Cressida*, Shakespeare coins the phrase "an universal wolf" (1.3.120) for an amalgam of power, will, and appetite that will

---

[13] Augustine, *City of God, Vol. IV: Books 12–15*, trans. Philp Levine, Loeb Classical Library (Harvard University Press, 1966), XIV. 13.

culminate in human self-destruction. *Love's Labour's Lost* is far removed from the nihilism of the later play, but it touches upon the way wit is often bound up with a desire for dominance and self-aggrandizement. One of the French ladies, Maria, describes Lord Longueville as a paragon of virtues. "The only soil of his fair virtue's gloss," she notes, "Is a sharp wit matched with too blunt a will, / Whose edge hath power to cut, whose will still wills / It should none spare that come within his power" (2.1.47–51). The hunger for enhanced prestige that drives the characters of the play is intertwined with an antagonistic impulse that finds its articulation in unrestrained baiting of others. When their wit is unleashed on their peers, the lords are evenly matched, but smarting under their humiliation at the hands of the ladies, they train their malice on their inferiors. During the pageant of the Nine Worthies, their wit at the expense of the bungling performers is devastating. "This is not generous, not gentle, not humble" (5.2.621), Holofernes protests, implicitly accusing the lords of a lack of the virtues incumbent on their status: the first two terms are synonyms for nobility, while humility or modesty was a trait expected of a member of the elite.

Key to the arrogance of the lords is their cavalier attitude towards oaths. When the Princess first hears about the oath to forbear the company of women that the King has sworn, she warns him mockingly that he will be forsworn. The King denies this emphatically: "Not for the world, fair madam, by my will," he asserts. Presciently, the Princess asserts, "will shall break it – will, and nothing else" (2.1.99–100). Engrossed in pursuing their own desires, the lords ride rough-shod over binding commitments that, however absurd, they themselves have undertaken to respect. The play is threaded with allusions to perjury; for early moderns, steeped in Cicero's *De Officiis*, the most important classical ethical treatise of the age, an echo of the precept that justice, the virtue that governed all human relations, is founded on keeping faith, was inescapable.[14] Significantly it is the clown who delivers the most blistering comment on the ethics of the lords. After witnessing the lords' joint betrayal of their principles, Costard declares, "Walk aside, the true folk, and let the traitors stay" (4.3.210) before stalking off the stage.

Biron, the wittiest of the lords, reserves his special ire for the French lord Boyet, whom he regards as a social climber: "He is wit's peddler, and retails his wares / At wakes and wassails, meetings, market, fairs" (5.2.317–318), he asserts contemptuously, glancing at the commodification of wit in Shakespeare's age. In truth, however, there is little to choose between

---

[14] Cicero, *On Obligations*, trans. P. G. Walsh (Oxford University Press, 2000), 1. 23.

them. Rampant individualism, the logic of the marketplace, shapes the wit of the Navarrese lords too. At the end of the play, Rosaline, the lady Biron woos, announces that his wit requires reforming. Famous for the cutting jibes that he distributes liberally among people of all ranks, she challenges him to use wit not for self-promotion, but to further the common good: to go among the sick and suffering and "enforce the painèd impotent to smile" (836). This, she declares, is the true purpose of wit, and reminds him, "A jest's prosperity lies in the ear / Of him that hears it, never in the tongue / Of him that makes it" (843–845). Even while garnering audience acclamation for the witty protagonists, the play suggests, wit might fulfill a wider social purpose and promote the interests of the community at large, not merely those of the individual and his or her peer group.

In contrast to the vindictive lords, the fatuous schoolmaster, Holofernes, evinces a sense of sociability when he invites the obdurate constable to join him and the curate for dinner. This is in fact the path that Shakespeare's own play chooses to take, a play in which all protagonists are equally subject to ironic mockery – but that leavens its critique with a measure of self-irony, directed both at the play itself and at the audience. A production of the play in war-torn Afghanistan in 2005, staged in Dari, indicates that issues associated with wit and ethics remain relevant in our age.[15] Adapted from a Persian translation of the play, the court of Navarre transmutes to Kabul, with the ladies visitors from Herat. The witty wordplay was largely discarded, but the idea of a poetry competition was familiar to Afghan audiences, and was mined for its humor. The ascetic program of the Navarrese evoked associations with the Taliban, and some male actors were keen to play up the ludicrous aspects of the lords. Interestingly, the director, Corinne Jaber, decided not to target the mockery of the play exclusively at the Taliban. However entrenched the differences between antagonistic segments of Afghan society might be, the performance attempted to press a creative artifact into the service of fostering commonality. To be sure, the production exploited the cultural distinction associated with the name of Shakespeare today, suggesting that self-interest in earning cultural prestige might nonetheless be combined with seeking the common good. To this extent, it replicates the ethical move Shakespeare's own play makes, using wit to create communities of laughter that span particular group attachments, at least for the duration of the play.

---

[15] See William C. Carroll, "*Love's Labour's Lost* in Afghanistan," *Shakespeare Bulletin* 28. 4 (2010), 443–458, to which I am indebted.

CHAPTER 21

Service

Joseph Sterrett

Often, in our current way of thinking, service and virtue seem to be two concepts that have a natural fit, at least as far as Aristotle defined virtue as a thing leading to happiness. To serve another is to have their interests at heart. It implies a degree of caring, support, benefit, and looking after someone else's wellbeing. Jesus commanded his believers to serve one another. Companies like to be able to advertise their good service, their attention to one's needs, and so on. This view of service assumes a commitment to the common good. Yet, its Latin derivative, "servus," and its Greek equivalent, "δοῦλος," mean slave, an understanding of service – or servitude – that, in today's culture, seems anything but happy. There were those in the Classical world, early Christians like Paul, who embraced the idea of service (or "slave") as a form of virtue. Paul refers to himself as "δοῦλος" in his greeting to the Romans (Romans 1:1) and this has variously been translated as "servant" in the Geneva and Authorized King James versions or "bondservant" in the more recent "New King James Bible," a word that has stronger connotations in today's usage. The need to strengthen these connotations, today, is no doubt because associations between "slave" and "service" are generally overlooked, a result of both the decline of "service" culture (think "Downton Abbey") and the rise of the "service economy" where service usually refers to performance of paid work on others' behalf. Even so, as COVID-19 has underscored, today's "service" economy, whether the supermarket worker, package deliverer, or nurse's aide, frequently involves the lowest paid and most insecure workers who are simultaneously vital to the needs of society – *servus* indeed! While the word has lost its links to the severely stratified culture that Paul alludes to, the harsh realities of *servus* are perhaps closer than we care to admit.[1] Paul reveals (or

---

[1] For discussion about the complexities of Roman law, and thus this early Roman world, see Part II, "The Law of Persons," in Andrew Borkowski and Paul du Plessis, *Textbook on Roman Law* (Oxford University Press, 2005 [1994]), 86–112, especially 86–109.

creates) an almost reverential sense of service as a vocation that has moral significance. The believer becomes a "slave" to righteousness, no longer a "slave" to sin (Romans 6:6, 15–16). And yet, as Paul asserts elsewhere, Christ frees believers from slavery, making them "neither Jew nor Gentile, neither slave nor free ... male and female," for all are "one in Christ Jesus" (Galatians 3:28). Indeed, service to God makes the believer a child of God (Galatians 4:1–7). This last point, as Paul seems aware, adds another nuance to service: it shows one's allegiance. As Bob Dylan paraphrased on his first gospel album, "It may be the Devil or it may be the Lord, / But you're gonna have to serve somebody."[2]

Service has a certain "messiness" as David Schalkwyk explains.[3] It is "historically specific," and yet it touches something essential in all of us, something in our common wellbeing. Shakespeare uses the word and the concept of service, as we might expect, in a range of ways. He does not use it, as Paul does, with the firm legal strictures that govern the Roman populace. Yet service is an ideal to aspire to, the good servant such as Pisanio in *Cymbeline*, or the one who serves with hopes of gaining social respect and advancement like Malvolio in *Twelfth Night*. And there are those who exploit the trust and vulnerability that service involves: the Aarons, Iagos, or Edmunds. It's worth mentioning the casual uses of the word. One recalls Mercutio's scratch: "'tis not so deep as a well, nor so wide as a / church-door; but 'tis enough, 'twill serve" (3.1.93); or Romeo wondering "What doth her [Rosalind's] beauty serve" (1.1.228). What purpose, what meaning, or what action can a thing or a person do? What effect can it (or they) have on the world around? "Service" can simply mean sexual gratification: Goneril wishes her "woman's services" (4.2.28) could be bestowed upon Edmund in *King Lear*. Similarly, the Queen in *Cymbeline*, another one of Shakespeare's "bad" women, encourages her despicable son, Cloten, to increase his "services," or (deceptive) wooing of Innogen (2.3.45). And, as noted earlier, service can indicate allegiance for a patron, a cause, or even oneself. Again, *Romeo and Juliet's* comically hyper-partisan opening scene plays upon this when Sampson asserts, "I serve as good a man as you" (1.1.48). But frequently Shakespeare looks to service as something more noble, a value or expectation that operates in broad ethical terms. This sense of service opens toward the world and society at large, to humanity and the

---

[2] From "Gotta Serve Somebody" on *Slow Train Coming* (1979).
[3] David Schalkwyk, *Shakespeare, Love and Service* (Cambridge University Press, 2008), 1, 6.

common good. It is this I would call "virtuous" service, a sense of moral imperative rather than social structure that Shakespeare frequently lingers over, even insists upon, however prone to failure it might be.

King Lear was noted in the 1950s as a good example.[4] The word "service" occurs 14 times in the play, and points to the heart of the play's ethical and moral concerns. At first, in act one, scene one, the word seems almost insignificant, merely a matter of etiquette. Edmund, virtually silent throughout the first scene, replies courteously to Kent when his father introduces him, "My services to your lordship" (1.1.26). The audience will most likely give this no thought, but Edmund's use of the word "service" becomes much more resonant when he, reentering the stage at the start of the next scene, announces, "Thou, nature, art my goddess; to thy law / My services are bound" (1.2.1–2). The second iteration signals the insincerity of the first, and the echo cues Edmund as a foil for service as a virtue or moral principle. The tension inherent in this subtle echo of the word "service" is an irony that the play goes on to exploit as it pits virtuous service to the common good against service to oneself, opportunity, and advancement throughout the play.

Central to the play, of course, is Lear's own shallow self-regard that the play challenges. In his authoritarian mind, "service" is merely a synonym for obedience and subjection, a thing that he can command from others (1.4.20–35). His perception is a thing Goneril understands well when she instructs her servant, Oswald, to "come slack of former services" (1.3.9). She knows the importance her father places upon signs of loyalty and the fragile sense of identity and value it creates. Like a drug, take the slightest bit away through carelessness or inattention, and the edifice shakes; the moment of Oswald's weary disregard is the moment that rattles the King's confidence. He calls his daughter's servant a "mongrel" (1.4.43) and "slave" (1.4.70) and is only comforted when Kent, returning in disguise, demeans Oswald in return.

If Edmund is a foil for virtuous service, Kent is his dramatic counterpart, something defined in his first speech:

> Royal Lear,
> Whom I have ever honour'd as my king,
> Loved as my father, as my master follow'd,
> As my great patron thought on in my prayers, –   (1.1.138–140).

[4] John Barish and Marshal Waingrow, "'Service' in King Lear," *Shakespeare Quarterly* 9 (1958), 347–355.

Honor, love, and loyal following, indeed supporting one's leader through prayer or good wishes is an understanding of service St. Paul would commend. Kent's speech develops an ideal of virtuous service that goes beyond what a leader wishes. It attends to needs that are ultimately for the leader's own good, whatever their wishes might be. True service, as Kent insists, goes beyond one's life: "My life I never held but as a pawn / To wage against thy enemies; nor fear to lose it, / Thy safety being the motive" (1.1.154–156). And Kent fulfills his words when he meets the King again in disguise, serving at his own expense and without personal benefit. "What wouldst thou?," asks the King.

KENT: Service.
LEAR: Who wouldst thou serve?
KENT: You (1.4.19–23)

The brevity of Kent's replies is notable, pointing to a sense that to serve someone is to do a thing beyond words. It is an action more than words which can flatter and mislead:

LEAR: What services canst thou do?
KENT: I can keep honest counsel, ride, run, mar a curious
        tale in telling it, and deliver a plain message
        bluntly: that which ordinary men are fit for, I am
        qualified in; and the best of me is diligence (1.4.28–32).

His phrase, "That which ordinary men are fit for" resonates uncomfortably with other moments in the play: Edmund's "fashion fit" (1.2.161), and, more darkly, the Captain's promise to hang the old King and Cordelia in act 5, scene 3, "If it be man's work, I'll do 't ."[5] These echoes remind us that service, whatever the ideal, can be anything but virtuous. Indeed, for Kent to be able to serve, he must be willing to deal in petty insults in order to please his master.

Ultimately, however, "service" in *King Lear* is not an open indeterminable, whatever "serves" a particular end. The play pushes away from the various forms of self-serving that it presents pointing toward an ideal that serves a common good despite one's particular interest. Appropriately, this is best articulated in the words of a character who has no other name than First Servant who tells his master, the Duke of Cornwall, to "Hold your hand, my lord":

---

[5] The line only occurs in the earlier Quarto, scene 24, line 39. The Folio version is the more clipped, "I'll do't, my lord."

> I have served you ever since I was a child;
> But better service have I never done you
> Than now to bid you hold   (3.7.70–73).

True service, as this servant understands, can involve opposing the will of those one serves, even at the cost of one's own safety. "How now, you dog!" is the reply he gets in return before Regan stabs him in the back.

We might also remember the fool's resonant and melancholic song:

> But I will tarry; the fool will stay,
> And let the wise man fly:
> The knave turns fool that runs away;
> The fool no knave, pardie   (2.2.248–251).

Or, finally, when the servants in the Quarto version hasten to the aid of a bleeding Gloucester at the end of scene 14 (lines 96–104) – a small fulfilment, I would argue, of a desire of the audience.[6] Their action is personal, but their low status and nameless role in the play points to a broader social value that is notably cut from the starker tragic momentum of the Folio. Their service, indeed virtuous service generally in the play, is always personally conceived: one person working for the welfare of another, supporting the common good.

Barish and Waingrow pressed the importance of "service" in *King Lear* as a moral ideal, overlooking its "messier" moments noted by Schalkwyk. *Lear*, as I have indicated, pits self-service or petty service against a more magnanimous virtuous imperative. Yet, an illuminating comparison might be found with *Cymbeline* which also places service at the center of its plot but employs it on a wider range of levels. Part of the "greatness" of *Lear* is the way it concentrates its moral and ethical questions. *Cymbeline* – though the Folio editors listed it under "Tragedies" – organizes its action in more comic terms, reveling in complexity. The play's final scene is a famously extended rapprochement of adversaries and perceived adversaries, each either fulfilling their service pledged earlier in the play or pledging their service in order to effect a reconciliation. The war between Rome and Cymbeline's Britain decided, Lucius, the Roman ambassador, submits himself, his life and the lives of his men to the British King, having been defeated in battle (5.6.75–83). In a gesture that reveals awareness of the Roman treatment of slaves, he pleads only for the life of Innogen, disguised as his page, Fidele, in words that suggest Roman laws of manumission on

---

[6] The scene corresponds to 3.7 in the Folio.

the basis of her faithfulness (5.6.85–91).[7] Innogen's adopted name, Fidele, has underscored this faithfulness, invoking "fide," the Latin word for trust and root word for "fidelity," "confidence," and "fiduciary," a point Lucius made explicit when the two characters met in the Welsh countryside: "Thy name well fits thy faith, thy faith thy name" (4.2.383). When she stands before her father, the King, Innogen reveals herself and submits to "serve" him as a faithful daughter (5.6.113, 119). The final scene progresses as Guiderius and Arviragus, having submitted only to nature and the sky, promise service along with their father, Belarius, to Cymbeline (5.6.19, 326, 354). Posthumus submits to Guiderius and Arviragus as new-found princes (5.6.426). Giacomo submits to Posthumus, begging forgiveness for his treachery (5.6.413–14). And, toward the end of the scene, Innogen once again promises service to Lucius (5.6.404). Most strikingly of all, the scene and indeed the play concludes with Cymbeline submitting his kingdom to Rome despite having achieved victory over the Roman army in battle.

This curious, frequently counterintuitive insistence on service as a mechanism of reconciliation is one of the most important and surprising ways in which the play performs its concluding vision of peace-making. Service and the pledge of service provides the essential step for building trust between characters and factions at odds, and does so across a range of registers. Service is pledged on a personal level between estranged lovers, family members, and friends; it is renewed in the professional relationships between a servant and his or her lord; and it is even pledged on a macro-political level between kingdom and empire. Each of these pledges in the final scene remind the audience of the points earlier in the play when service was pledged and later left unfulfilled. Posthumus and Innogen of course pledge their love at the very start of the play. While they do not employ the language of service explicitly, it is implicit in their marriage vows that have already taken place. Marriage vows for the bride explicitly state that she will "obey" and "serve" her husband.[8] When Innogen discovers that Posthumus believes her to be unfaithful and has ordered her murder, she submits herself entirely, insisting that she be "ripp'd" to pieces like an old garment (3.4.52). "I must die," she cries, and insists that Pisanio, her husband's servant is disloyal if he does not carry out her husband's desires: "if I do not by thy hand, thou art / No servant of thy master's" (3.4.73–75).

---

[7] Borkowski, 97–101.

[8] The 1549, 1552, and 1559 editions of the Book of Common Prayer all ask the bride, 'Wilt thou obey him, and serve him, love, honor, and kepe him in sickenes and in health?' http://justus.anglican.org/resources/bcp/1549/Marriage_1549.htm.

Her total submission to Posthumus's command is highly suggestive of the absolute faith required of a true believer in service to God, a species of faith exemplified by Job who submits to any ordeal given him.[9] But, as Pisanio clearly sees, her absolute submission is an extreme. Other, more nuanced responses might in fact better serve the common good.

Indeed, Pisanio is the long-suffering exemplar of service in the play. He is the professional servant, required at some point to serve nearly everyone at court, including the villainous Queen and her vile son. It is this fact, a result of his lower social status, that means he cannot afford Innogen's absolutism, forcing him to be more politic with those he serves. He is and must be true to his master and mistress, but true too, or at least seemingly true, to those who would use him to cause them harm. Dramatically, his role is to be pressed between the contradictory imperatives of his superiors while navigating a path that allows him to be true to his moral commitments and still fulfill his duties of service. On receiving Posthumus's command to murder Innogen, a command he never intends to obey, he exclaims, "If it be so to do good service, never/ Let me be counted serviceable. How look I, / That I should seem to lack humanity" (3.2.14–16). Pisanio thus stands in marked contrast to Oswald in *Lear* who is willing to cut down old, blind men for his own advancement. Like Oswald, a cunning superior offers Pisanio preferment if he will help with her schemes. But, alert to the Queen's untrustworthiness if unclear about her intentions, he assures the audience that he will "choke" himself rather than prove untrue (1.5.86–87). He signals virtuous service, not by being strictly obedient, but by serving the common good. In contrast, the Queen and Cloten are the play's antitheses of virtuous service, serving only themselves and must ultimately be eliminated before the final scene of reconciliation.

When, at last, all of the competing interests of the play's characters and factions are drawn on stage, the paste that holds them altogether in reconciliation is a shared commitment to service in the community at large. Where the tragedy of *Lear* envisions a world of fragile relationships that irretrievably break down, the comic restoration in *Cymbeline* envisions a resolution where each character places their own interests in service to others.[10] This is the nature of "such a peace" (5.6.485). Every wrong, slight, oversight, or indignity is soothed through collective submission, including

---

[9] See Job 13:15, "Loe though he slay me, yet will I trust him"; cf. John Donne's sermon before the Countess of Bedford, 1620.

[10] A more detailed comparison can be found in, Chapters 6 and 7 in Joseph Sterrett, *The Unheard Prayer: Religious Tolerance in Shakespeare's Plays* (Brill, 2012), 123–165.

the fairly astounding submission of one nation to another in the service of peace. A ruler who consciously invoked war in order to no longer be a "servant" to Rome (3.2.61) now reverses his victory and thereby stretches the notion of the common to include the world of nations in union. It is thus appropriate that the play ends with a joint – one could almost say ecumenical – service of thanksgiving to the gods, sacrifice and prayers performed to consecrate peace.

CHAPTER 22

Humility

Richard Wilson

It is humbling to be human. *Humilitatem* and *humanitas* might not be etymologically related; but because being human is so often humiliating, humanity has always been defined by its humility. In one of Shakespeare's most humane speeches about a human being, a king therefore says his old friend's servants were "proud of his humility, / In their poor praise he humbled" (*All's Well* 1.2.44–46). But the play then goes on to reveal the "humble ambition, proud humility" (1.1.172) of those who "humble themselves" to rise (4.5.44); like the "low and humble" (2.1.196) Helena, who marries the son of the king's friend, after this "proud scornful boy" (2.3.147) has been humiliated, although she comes "from humble, he from honoured name" (1.3.140).

All's Well That Ends Well reprises the Cinderella story, about the scullion who wears a "surplice of humility over the black gown of a big heart" (83–84). But as this chapter will show, humility is only ever one step from humiliation in that scenario, because it is never far from pride. Much of Shakespeare's comedy will, therefore, be about the self-important "fantasy" of lovers' "humbleness" (*As You Like It* 5.2.84–87). And it must be significant that the most quoted of his references to the supposed Christian virtue is one in which Shylock speaks about humility from a Jewish point of view, as hypocritical cant:

> If you prick us do we not bleed? If you tickle us
> do we not laugh? If you poison us do we not die? And if you
> wrong us shall we not revenge? If we are like you in the rest,
> we will resemble you in that. If a Jew wrong a Christian, what
> is his humility? Revenge. (*Merchant* 3.1.54–58).

Humility is a problematic virtue in Shakespeare, where it invariably turns out to be an act. "In peace there's nothing so becomes a man," admits "the warlike Harry," as "modest stillness and humility" (*Henry V* 3.1.3–4). But on this stage *genuine* humility is rare indeed. Henry V's Christ-like son Henry VI has it, and is deposed because he is so "gentle, mild, and virtuous" (*Richard III* 1.2.104). His murderer then gives a master-class in "the show of virtue" (3.5.28), declaring "I thank my God for my humility" (2.1.73), until he is begged "to endure the load" of kingship. Richard III's victims duly laugh themselves to death at his travesty of "the maid's part" of "fair humility" (3.7.17, 51, 195, 220), "Since maids, in modesty, say 'no' to that / Which they would have" (*Two Gents* 1.2.55–56).

Richard prides himself on the fake humility with which he will "answer nay, and take it" (*Richard III* 3.7.51), boasting how he can "murder whiles I smile, / And cry 'Content!' to that which grieves my heart, / And wet my cheeks with artificial tears" (*3Henry VI* 3.2.182–184). The player king's "mockney" London accent is therefore heard time and again in the Histories, as pretenders like Prince Hal "sound the very base-string of humility" (*1Henry IV* 2.5.5) among the cockneys, by being "dressed in such humility" that they "pluck allegiance from men's hearts" (3.2.51–52), as his father teaches. Henry IV's own "manipulative falsity" in this charade of "proud majesty made a subject" (*Richard II* 4.1.242) had been the triumph of such an authoritarian populism:[1]

> How he did dive into their hearts
> With humble and familiar courtesy,
> What reverence he did throw away on slaves,
> Wooing poor craftsmen with the craft of smiles ...   (1.4.23–29)

In *The Tyranny of Merit* the philosopher Michael Sandel regrets that elites no longer share physical space with other classes, since "Such humility is the beginning of the way back from the harsh ethic of success that drives us apart."[2] Yet a recurring complaint in the plays suggests it was ever thus: "I heard him swear, / Were he to stand for consul, never would he / Appear in the market-place nor on him put / The napless vesture of humility" (*Coriolanus*, 2.1.217–220). Even in ancient Rome, Shakespeare read, politicians had to be inducted into appearing "humbler than the ripest mulberry" (3.2.79), by donning a threadbare "gown of humility" (*SD* 2.3.36) for their ceremonial investiture.

The dramatist was so fascinated by the "stooping duty" (*Richard II* 3.3.47) of political campaigning that he devoted an entire tragedy to the disillusionment when the voters saw through the sackcloth, and realized "With what contempt" a candidate "wore the humble weed" (2.3.210). Coriolanus's

---

[1] On "manipulative falsity," see Slavoj Žižek, *How to Read Lacan* (Granta, 2006), 14.
[2] Michael Sandel, *The Tyranny of Merit: What's Become of the Common Good?* (Allen Lane, 2020), 227.

street-wise opponents "seem humbler" (4.2.42), because he is "like a dull actor" (5.3.40) when he poses before "the commonality" (1.1.24), "bonnet in hand," with his "knee bussing the stones" (3.2.73–76). His tragic flaw is less hubris, then, than an inability to demean himself with a false modesty he will "blush to act" (2.2.141–142). For like Montaigne, Shakespeare understood how in "such business / Action is eloquence" (3.2.73–76):

> There are gestures which are cultivated, such as bowing to people and ways of greeting them, by which we acquire, as often as not wrongly, the honour of being thought humble: you can be humble out of pride! I am fairly lavish with raising my hat, and I never receive such a greeting without returning it, whatever the social status of the man.[3]

Montaigne doffed his expensive headgear; but he went on to warn against princes with the common touch. Sandel, too, recalls being upstaged by Ronald Reagan's homeliness in a debate. The great communicator, who bestows "A little touch of Harry" on subjects he visits incognito "as a common man" (*Henry V* 4.0.47; 4.8.47), simultaneously watches "corruption boil and bubble / Till it o'errun the stew" (*Measure* 5.1.312), as King Alfred burned the cakes. In *Henry V* the soldier Williams therefore scathingly rebukes this *agent provocateur*: "Your majesty came not like yourself … Witness the night, your garments, and your lowliness. And what your highness suffered under that shape, I beseech you take it for your own fault" (4.8.48–49).

Nothing is more ominous in Shakespeare's analysis than the politician's plan to "mingle with society / And play the humble host" (*Macbeth* 3.4.3–4). For there is a skepticism running through his many variations on the folktale of the hidden king that implies deep unease with the populist politics of dumbing-down. He would always be fascinated by the "antic disposition" (*Hamlet* 1.5.173) of the clown prince who pretends to be a "silly jeering idiot" (*Lucrece* 1812), like the original Brutus (whose Latin name denoted doltishness). But he never stopped worrying that playing the fool had been a trick of Satan's jester, the Vice of medieval theater. Hence, we cannot be sure that even Hamlet is not inspired by what the Devil can do in the role of prankster he adopts:

> ROSENCRANTZ: He does confess he feels himself distracted.
>   But from what cause a will by no means speak.
> GUILDENSTERN: Nor do we find him forward to be sounded,
>   But with a crafty madness keeps aloof. (*Hamlet*, 3.1.5–8)

---

[3] Michel de Montaigne, "On Presumption," *The Complete Essays*, trans. M. A. Screech (Penguin, 2003), 719.

Antony's pretense that "I am no orator … But, as you know me, a plain, blunt man," is crucial in persuading the mob he speaks "right on. / I tell you what you yourselves do know" (*Julius* 3.2.208–215), and we trust him all the less for it. Our doubts about Othello likewise begin when he tells the Senate that "Rude am I in speech" (*Othello* 1.3.81). Yet the rhetorician's mock humility, that he has "neither wit, nor utterance, nor the power of speech" (*Julius* 3.2.212), was also hard-wired into his creator's self-representation. For "Silence shall be most my glory, being dumb" (Sonnet 83), the world's wordiest writer announces in his poems, which purport to value "tongue-tied simplicity" over "the rattling tongue of saucy and audacious eloquence" (*Dream,* 5.1), the "tongue-tied muse" (Sonnet 85) above "a muse of fire" (*Henry V* Pro.1).

Shakespeare's anxiety of influence causes him to present himself as "sick of fear" at the "full proud verse" of his "compeers" (Sonnet 86). So, he punctuates his dramas with paroxysms of "fearful modesty," as players "throttle their practised accents in their fears" (*Dream* 5,1,101–103). The film *Shakespeare in Love* was thus perceptive to spotlight the stuttering stage fright of "an imperfect actor on the stage" (Sonnet 23). For "Our bending author" (*Henry V* Epi.1) persistently trivializes himself in an ironic attitude of what Montaigne's friend Étienne de la Boétie termed "voluntary servitude," with the unctuousness of an "unlettered clerk" (Sonnet 85) dependent on "your humble patience" (*Henry V* Pro.33), like Dickens's "umble" creep Uriah Heep: "My fear is your displeasure; my curtsy, my duty; and my speech to beg your pardons" (2 *Henry IV* Epi.2).[4] It seems, then, as if Shakespeare discovered a paradoxical power in "this weak and idle theme" (*Dream* Epi.5) of craven self-debasement, the ploy known as *cosmesis* which Judith Halberstam analyses in her book *The Queer Art of Failure*:[5]

> … the great globe itself,
> Yea, all which it inherit, shall dissolve;
> And, like this insubstantial pageant faded
> Leave not a rack behind.   (*Tempest* 4.1.153–156)

"All for your delight / We are not here," explains the playwright's persona Peter Quince; and biographers love to portray the "good will" (*Dream* 5.1.108–115) who advanced behind that pixilating mask as a simple country

---

[4] Étienne de la Boétie, "The Discourse of Voluntary Servitude," in *The Politics of Obedience and Étienne de la Boétie,* trans. Harry Kurz (Black Rose, 2007), 39–80; Charles Dickens, *David Copperfield,* ed. Jeremy Tambling (Penguin, 2004), 244–245.
[5] Judith Halberstam, *The Queer Art of Failure* (Duke University Press, 2011).

bumpkin, who "kept his counsel and retired to his garden," as represented by a procession of inhibited Williams, mumbling "God rest ye merry, sir" (*As You Like It* 5.1.54), to their overlords.[6] Certainly, he signed himself "Your Lordship's in all duty" (*Lucrece* 12), or "Your honour's in all duty" (*Venus* 19), in groveling dedications to his feudal patron. Yet that Shakespearean cringe has to be set against the inverted snobbery of "a serving-man, proud in heart and mind" (*Lear* 3.4.79); the depiction of treacherously "Honest Iago" (*Othello* 1.3.293); and the sustained exposure of the passive aggression of such sanctimonious pseudo-martyrs as Isabella, who flaunt "th'impression of keen whips as rubies" (*Measure,* 2.4.101).

In an age of sainted masochists, Shakespeare deprived Cinderella of her rags-to-riches happy-ever-after ending with *King Lear,* apparently determined to "mar a curious tale in telling it" (1.4.29) by calling out the conceit of such "presented nakedness" (2.3.11). There the entertainer who had made a song and dance about his own "Abject Art" of "russet yeas and honest kersey noes" (*Love's Labour's Lost* 5.2.413), highlighted the infantilism of self-sacrifice, as Maud Ellmann points out in *The Hunger Artists*:

> Like (the anorectic exhibitionist) King Lear gives up all his human superfluities in order to experience himself as bare forked animal. For Lear, too, is a hunger artist, and for this reason one could argue that Cordelia gives her father just what he is asking for, a vision of "nothing" at the heart of things. "Nothing my lord." Indeed, Lear pursues his nothing with the frenzy of an addict from the moment that he gives away his kingdom until he holds the lifeless body of his daughter in his arms.[7]

For Ellmann, self-deprivation is always performative; and her characterization of Lear as one of those "Fathers that wear rags" (2.4.46) to teach their "pelican daughters" (3.4.72) the counterintuitive strategy of divestment, starvation and self-harm, invites us to rethink this theater of abjection in light of feminist and postcolonial investigations of internalized oppression, such as Gayatri Spivak's "Can the Subaltern Speak?" which views Hindu suttee as the widow's choice.[8] "Her voice was ever soft, / Gentle and low," the mad king indeed recalls, as he hears his dead daughter mouthing "nothing"; and his gloss, "an excellent thing in woman" (5.3.271–272), underlines how this "maid's part" plays out, when a succession of

[6] Jonathan Bate, "'Hide thy life': The Key to Shakespeare," *Times Higher Education Supplement,* August 6, 2009, 42.

[7] Maud Ellmann, *The Hunger Artists: Starving, Writing and Imprisonment* (Virago, 1993), 13.

[8] Gayatri Chakravorty Spivak, "Can the Subaltern Speak?," in *Marxism and the Interpretation of Culture,* eds. Cary Nelson and Larry Grossberg (University of Illinois Press, 1988), 271–314.

Shakespeare's Sleeping Beauties – Juliet, Hero, Mariana, Thaisa, Innogen and Hermione – are frozen into living corpses.

According to the theory of "queer failure," to "kiss the rod, / Fawn on rage with base humility" (*Richard II* 5.1.32–33), as Kate learns to "place your hands below your husband's foot" (*Shrew* 5.2.181), is an act of resistance exemplifying the radical passivity of silent women who take humility to extremes.[9] By this logic, when Iachimo gropes Innogen as she sleeps, and claims to kiss the "mole, right proud," that lies "under her breast" (*Cymbeline* 2.4.135–136), it is the abuser who is humiliated. Yet what this "loser theory" fails to query is the collusion of the Cinderella-type, who conforms in what the fairy story calls her "Donkey Skin." Shakespeare, however, who was writing for a milieu where slashed dress was all the rage, clearly understood how much the deconstruction of the distressed garment is a display of status anxiety by the fashion victim, as Cornwall sardonically remarks of Kent:

> This is some fellow
> Who, having been praised for bluntness, doth affect
> A saucy roughness and constrains the garb
> Quite from his nature …
> These kind of knaves I know, which in this plainness
> Harbour more craft and more corrupter ends
> Than twenty silly ducking observants … (2.2.87–96)

One of the features of our "age of entitlement" has been how, in denial of self-service, society has regressed to a sacrificial culture like that of Renaissance Europe, where, as Stephen Greenblatt wrote, "the hallmark of power and wealth was to be waited on."[10] In an era when globalization has universalized a neo-feudal service economy, and with it Byzantine rituals of skivvying servility; or when, as Wayne Koestenbaum recounted in his 2011 hymn to self-abjection, *Humiliation*, Facebook and Reality TV offer unprecedented mirrors for "proud man" to play "such fantastic tricks" as "makes the angels weep" (*Measure* 2.2.121–124), Shakespeare's staging of servitude and sovereignty has never looked more pointed.

Koestenbaum outed himself in his bestseller as an addict of domination porn. Thus, watching Lear "relax into the horror," he confessed he enjoyed the same masturbatory "uplift" as the poet records in Sonnet 29, "When

---

[9] Halberstam, *The Queer Art of Failure*, 126, 130, 145.
[10] Christopher Caldwell, *The Age of Entitlement: America Since the Sixties* (Simon and Schuster, 2020); Stephen Greenblatt, *Shakespearean Negotiations: The Circulation of Social Energy in Renaissance England* (Clarendon Press, 1988), 29–30.

in disgrace with fortune and men's eyes," where the poem "changes its mind" about self-disgust, in pleasure at the degradation of the object of the speaker's slavish worship: "Yet in these thoughts myself almost despising, / Haply I think on thee." The poet's "humiliation ends" in a Shakespearean sonnet when his prideful "words humiliate" the flesh of his unnamed lover, which is "left behind as roadkill" in the joy that only "this gives life to thee" (Sonnet 18). And as Koestenbaum perceived, with *King Lear* the self-soiling dirty protest goes even further to lay bare the histrionics of humility and humiliation, the complexities of our voyeurism regarding the pain of others:

> The same magical logic assails me when I behold someone untouchable, or dirty, or homeless, or vomiting, or crying, or shaking, or bleeding, or undergoing an abject physical ordeal. Watching, I sense, first of all, that person's humiliation, and I am struck by horrified commiseration. Next, I feel an urge to eject that person from my sight: *get away from me, you vomiting freak.*[11]

If the biopolitics of humility in Shakespeare confirm how "One touch of nature makes the whole world kin" (*Troilus* 3.3.169), they also seem to anaesthetize us against "the inevitability of tragedy in the benighted or backward ... poorer parts of the world," as Susan Sontag observed: "In *The Tempest*, Trinculo's first thought upon coming across Caliban is that he could be put on exhibit in England: 'not a holiday fool there but would give a piece of silver ... to see a dead Indian (2.2.27–31).'"[12] After such a fix of pity and terror, it is indeed comforting to imagine "we that are young / Shall never see so much, nor live so long" (*Lear* 5.3.324–325). But now contagion "washes all the air ... And thorough this distemperature we see / The seasons alter" (*Dream* 2.1.104–107), global warming and pandemic viruses make this consoling mystification of our own "unaccommodated" (3.4.99) human condition look increasingly deluded.

Critics tell us Shakespeare's theater is organized around the reversal of top and bottom, the carnival game of a world turned upside-down, in which the great and humble "Change places, and, handy-dandy," it is impossible to tell "which is the justice, and which is the thief" (*Lear* 4.6.148–149).[13] So, we are compelled to ask if there is any moment during all this Shakespearean inversion, the "arsy-versy" which puts the yokel

---

[11] Wayne Koestenbaum, *Humiliation* (Notting Hill Editions, 2011), 24, 48–50.
[12] Susan Sontag, *Regarding the Pain of Others* (Penguin, 2003), 64–65.
[13] For an overview, see Annabel Patterson, "Bottom's Up: Festive Theory," in *Shakespeare and the Popular Voice* (Basil Blackwell, 1989), 52–70.

Bottom center-stage, when Montaigne's truism, that "On the loftiest throne in the world, we are still sitting only on our own rump," generates a humility sincere enough for the spectator to truly accept that "Simply the thing I am / Shall make me live" (*All's Well* 4.3.310–311), or to share the Zen philosophy of Timon, that "nothing brings me all things" (*Timon*, 5.2.71–74).[14]

In *Shakespeare the Actor*, Meredith Ann Skura inferred that whatever terrified "Our Good Will," when he made himself "a motley to the view" (Sonnet 110), was "of a piece with his ability to imagine the story of other beggars who cannot move their stony-hearted auditors."[15] As night falls in *Love's Labour's Lost*, the aristocrats who have humiliated the actors with their derision are therefore roundly rebuked by the schoolmaster: "This is not generous, not gentle, not humble" (5.2.617). Likewise, the divorced Queen Katherine has the last word in *Henry VIII*, when she turns on Cardinal Wolsey: "You're meek and humble-mouth'd; / You sign your place and calling, in full seeming, / With meekness and humility – but your heart / Is crammed with arrogancy, spleen, and pride" (2.4.105–108). And the dramatist seems to have been similarly minded to "plant in tyrants mild humility" (*LLL* 4.3.323).

Towards the close of his career Shakespeare kept returning to a narrative in which the master shares the fate of servants, and is reduced to being "an humble suitor to your virtues; / For pity is the virtue of the law, / And none but tyrants use it cruelly" (*Timon* 3.6.7–9). As Julia Lupton comments, this reversal flips the power relations of the sovereign and the creature, figuring "another model of humanity" in the creaturely sovereignty of "bare life."[16] The prima donna assoluta of such humanity is that "most sovereign creature" (*Antony* 5.2.80) Cleopatra, who proudly proclaims that "My desolation does begin to make / A better life. 'Tis paltry to be Caesar" (*1–2*). So, if this beggarly humility is only an act, it is a gig to which the artist himself gives everything he has: "As you from crimes would pardoned be / Let your indulgence set me free" (*Tempest* Epi.19–20).

A performance of humility was obligatory in the patronage system of a deference society. But in unpacking the legend of "The Abasement of the Proud King," where a ruler is "made the court Fool and compelled to take his food with the palace dogs," Shakespeare was surely rehearsing

[14] Montaigne, "On Experience," *Complete Essays*, 857.
[15] Meredith Ann Skura, *Shakespeare the Actor* (University of Chicago Press, 1993), 145.
[16] Julia Lupton, *Citizen-Saints: Shakespeare and Political Theology* (University of Chicago Press, 2005), 174.

something more than the calculated hypocrisy required to eat humble pie.[17] There is a neediness to the Epilogue in which his actor admits "The King's a beggar now the play is done" (*All's Well* Epi.1) which authorizes the great entertainer to tell us human life is "a poor player / That struts and frets his hour upon the stage" (*Macbeth* 5.5.23–24). For if "All the world's a stage" (*As You Like It* 2.7.138), there is no humiliation in saying that "man is a giddy thing, and this is my conclusion" (*Much Ado* 5.4.104).

It may be that on Shakespeare's stage "the best in this kind are but shadows"; yet "the worst are no worse if imagination mend them" (*Dream* 5.1.208–209). So, "in a theatre whose very name, the Globe," implies "The play's the thing" (*Hamlet* 3.1.581), there can be nothing finer than "such stuff as dreams are made on" (*Tempest* 4.1.156).[18] Here "all the men and women" are indeed "merely players," with "their exits and their entrances" (*As You Like It* 2.7.139). But we came into this stage "world like brother and brother," and we will go out "hand in hand, not one before the other" (*Comedy of Errors* 5.1.426–427). Meanwhile, our best turn must be the presentation of our "duty ... and most humble service" (*Twelfth Night* 3.1.87):[19]

> A great while ago the world begun,
> With hey, ho, the wind and the rain,
> But that's all one, our play is done,
> And we'll strive to please you every day.　　　(5.1.392–395)

---

[17] Maynard Mack, "The Abasement," in *"King Lear" in Our Time* (University of California Press, 1966), 50.

[18] Anne Barton, "in a theatre," in *Shakespeare and the Idea of the Play* (Penguin, 1967), 147.

[19] For Shakespeare's paradoxical "abject position," see Richard Wilson, *Free Will: Art and Power on Shakespeare's Stage* (Manchester University Press, 2013).

CHAPTER 23

Kindness

Paul Yachnin

Virtues are dispositions not only to act in certain ways, but also to
feel in particular ways.

— Alasdair MacIntyre[1]

Hast thou, which art but air, a touch, a feeling
Of their afflictions, and shall not myself,
One of their kind, that relish all as sharply
Passion as they, be kindlier moved than thou art?

—*The Tempest*, 5.1.21–24[2]

In *The Tempest*, Shakespeare follows Montaigne's *Apologie of Raymond
Sebond* by challenging the human exceptionalism that is a foundational
feature of traditional virtue ethics.[3] We share sheer life with plants and
sentience with animals, says Aristotle. What belongs only to the human
being? In what consists the particular character of the human? It is, Aristotle
says, that "which follows or implies a rational principle."[4] The question
here is more important than the answer, since the question requires us,
first of all, to assume a divorce of human animals from the other animals.[5]
Shakespeare is, of course, entirely familiar with the principles of human

[1] Alasdair MacIntyre, *After Virtue: A Study in Moral Theory*, 3rd ed. (University of Notre Dame Press,
2007), 149.
[2] William Shakespeare, *The Tempest*, ed. Stephen Orgel (Oxford University Press, 1994). All quotations from *The Tempest* are from Orgel's edition.
[3] For a brilliant account of Montaigne and human animality, see Laurie Shannon, *The Accommodated
Animal: Cosmopolity in Shakespearean Locales* (University of Chicago Press, 2013), passim, esp. 11–17.
[4] Aristotle, *The Nicomachean Ethics*, trans. David Ross (Oxford University Press, 1998), 1097a15. See
also David H. Calhoun, "Human Exceptionalism and the *Imago Dei*: The Tradition of Human
Dignity," in *Human Dignity in Bioethics: From Worldviews to the Public Sphere*, eds. Stephen Dilley
and Nathan J. Palpant (Routledge, 2013), 19–45.
[5] See Alasdair MacIntyre, *Dependent Rational Animals: Why Human Beings Need the Virtues* (Open
Court, 1999) for an important rethinking of human virtues in relation to our creaturely kin, but still
with an exclusionary emphasis on rationality.

exceptionalism. When Hamlet says of his too-soon remarried mother, "O God, a beast that wants discourse of reason / Would have mourned longer," he doesn't mean to refer to a particular animal that lacks the power of rational thought; rather, he means that all nonhuman animals are bereft of reason.[6] Yet in *The Tempest*, Shakespeare seeks to heal the wound in human nature made by human exceptionalism by bringing forward kindness, in the fullness of its meanings, as the foundational virtue for human flourishing. And he does this, not by telling us how to think in a new, kindly way about the other animals, but rather by prompting us to find our own kindness in a face-to-face encounter with Caliban, a strange creature described in the 1623 Folio *dramatis personae* as a "savage and deformed slave."[7]

"Kindness" is gentleness, consideration, care for others. It is related to "kinship" – the genetic and affective bonds among parents, children, brothers, and sisters. By way of "kind," meaning "species" or "breed," it expands the reach of the bonds of kinship to our connectedness to the whole of humankind. Since "kind" is also, to quote Montaigne (in John Florio's 1603 translation), "the generall throng" (all the animals including the human animals), kindness is the virtue that bridges the moral and the zoological in the most immediate way and that attends the necessary cultivation of a new "thronging" polity.[8] Since it is a virtue rooted in our kinship with the animals, it arises from the body as well as from the soul.[9] We realize our kindness – make our kindness real and experience it as real – when and because we are kind (in both senses of the phrase).

Two other preliminary notes, the first one about the word "disposition." The way the word is usually understood, the way MacIntyre uses it in the epigraph at the start of this chapter is, "a person's inherent qualities of mind and character," as in "a sweet-natured girl of a placid disposition" (*Oxford English Dictionary [OED]*). But the word means also, "the way in which something is placed or arranged, especially in relation to other

---

[6] William Shakespeare, *Hamlet*, ed. G. R. Hibbard (Oxford University Press, 1987), 1.2.150–151.

[7] *The Tempest*, 96.

[8] Michel de Montaigne, "Apologie of Raymond Sebond," *Montaigne's Essays*, trans. John Florio (1603) Renascence Editions, np. www.luminarium.org/renascence-editions/montaigne/2xii.htm. "I have said all this to maintaine the coherency and resemblance that is in all humane things, and to bring us unto the generall throng. We are neither above nor under the rest: what ever is under the coape of heaven (saith the wise man) runneth one law, and followeth one fortune."

[9] See Vittorio Gallese, "The 'Shared Manifold' Hypothesis: From Mirror Neurons To Empathy," *Journal of Consciousness Studies* 8 (2001), 33–50, for a discussion of the neuronal foundations of empathy.

things," as in "the plan need not be accurate so long as it shows the disposition of the rooms" (*OED*). On this definition, the disposition of kindness is the natural way the parts of our bodies and souls are arranged and also how in particular we are situated in relation to the other animals – even including the spirit Ariel, who seems able to imagine himself as a human animal. Further, it is not only that we are situated in relation to other animals, it is also that we live and are able to flourish only with them, so we might say that the virtue of kindness is interagential, that is, always something accomplished by the collaboration of two or more beings with the power to produce some kind of effect.

The second is that virtue is processual – not something given but something aspirational and always on its way to realization. In "Of Crueltie," an essay Shakespeare had in mind when he wrote *The Tempest*, Montaigne says:

> Methinks virtue is another manner of thing, and much more noble than the inclinations unto Goodnesse, which in us are engendered … he who being toucht and stung [t]o the quicke with any wrong or offence received, should arme himselfe with reason against this furiously blind desire of revenge, and in the end after a great conflict yeeld himselfe master over it, should doubtlesse doe much more. The first should doe well, the other vertuously: the one action might be termed Goodnesse, the other Vertue.[10]

Goodness, on Montaigne's account, is just something some people are lucky enough to be born with. Virtue, in contrast, is something that we ourselves must make by a kind of moral craftsmanship – fashioning it out of our inborn capacities and by the choices we make among the different courses of action available to us.

If we put together virtue's affective, dispositional, interagential, and processual attributes, we can see that virtue is not only to be understood in narrative terms, but also that virtue itself is a narrative phenomenon, something that lives and grows in what Hannah Arendt calls "the web of relationships and the enacted stories."[11] Attributes, attitudes, dispositions (in the first sense), and actions come into the domain of virtue only when they take place in a meaningful world – a world, as Arendt suggests, that is populated with the interanimating stories of living people. In what follows, then, I will outline two virtue stories – the first one about Prospero and the second a story about how I once met Caliban face to face and how I found myself disowning him in what seems in

---

[10] Montaigne, *Essays*, Renascence Editions, np. www.luminarium.org/renascence-editions/montaigne/2xii.htm.

[11] Hannah Arendt, *The Human Condition* (University of Chicago Press, 1957), 181–188.

retrospect an exemplarily unkind act, but an act from which it is nevertheless possible to learn something about kindness.

Prospero

First is how Prospero moves toward the feeling realization of his kinship
with all the human animals, and how his membership in humankind
arouses the virtue of kindness and leads him to the trailhead of "being
well and doing well in being well."[12] By the way, kindness is no mere
sunshiny virtue. Prospero's bitterly ironic acknowledgement of Antonio as
his brother (5.1.130–131) and his remark about every third thought being
his grave (5.1. 311) are of a piece with his kindness. But, we must ask,
does Prospero's kindness grow large enough to allow him to acknowledge
Caliban as one of his own (Prospero's) kind? If he goes no further than
an acknowledgment of Caliban as "this thing of darkness" (5.1.275) and
a presentation of Caliban to the others as "this misshapen knave," "this
demi-devil" (268, 272) then what are we, the spectators and readers of the
play, to do in order to foster our kindness?

Inasmuch, according to Aristotle, as rationality is the constitutive attribute of the human animal (1095b26) and inasmuch as contemplation is
the highest virtue (1177a2–1179a35), then Prospero's story is a case study of
the limitations of traditional virtue ethics and indeed the limitations of the
contemplative life *tout court*. When he was the Duke of Milan, Prospero
removed himself from company and "worldly ends" and offloaded the
work of rule onto his brother Antonio so that he could devote himself
to the liberal arts – "all dedicated / To closeness and the bettering of my
mind" (1.2.89–90). We do not know how his life would have unfolded if
Antonio had not conspired to overthrow him and if he and his three-year-
old daughter had not been set adrift in an unseaworthy boat, had almost
died, and had found themselves on an enchanted island where Miranda
has grown to young adulthood and her father has spent his years apparently still dedicated to the liberal and also to the hermetic arts.

Prospero seeks to cultivate the virtue of justice, but his dominant character note is rage. Given how he and his daughter were carried from their
beds to almost certain death at sea, it is understandable that he is distrustful of others and quick to anger. And certainly, with his enemies now near
at hand, he is flooding with painful memories of betrayal and the fear
of death. The flood of emotions can help us understand his groundless

---

[12] I quote MacIntyre's phrasal translation of *eudaimonia* from *After Virtue*, 148.

impatience with his daughter, whom he accuses of not paying attention to his story about how they came to the island. But his hectoring and threatening of Ariel are not, as he would evidently like to think, an exercise of his power as a just ruler, but rather what sounds like a daily ritual of domestic abuse.[13] Similarly, it is anger rather than justice that drives his treatment of Caliban, especially since Caliban's act of sexual aggression was not merely punished but rather served as a trigger to shift the relationship from something free, open, and loving to a condition of perpetual slavery. Even his treatment of his European enemies is furious rather than just. He does check with Ariel to make sure that those he subjected to terror in the face of death by drowning are safe (1.2.217), but he nevertheless takes great pleasure in causing and witnessing their physical and psychological suffering (see, for example, 3.3.84–85).

What saves Prospero from his injurious fury and enables his kindness and justice vis-à-vis the Europeans is an intervention undertaken by Ariel. It is a moment in the play where Shakespeare was working with Montaigne's essay, "Of Cruelty."[14] Shakespeare develops Montaigne's emphasis on the processual, effortful character of virtue. He also transforms the air spirit Ariel into a figure able to represent the feelings he thinks human animals would feel in the face of the suffering of others. Ariel's subjunctive kindness, so to speak, serves to turn Prospero himself toward kindness. And notice that while Prospero, like Montaigne, invokes his "nobler reason," his change of heart is in fact caused by his recognition of kind and the kindly feelings aroused in him by Ariel's performance of human kindness:

ARIEL: The King,
    His brother, and yours, abide all three distracted,
    And the remainder mourning over them,
    Brimful of sorrow and dismay; but chiefly
    Him that you termed, sir, the good old lord Gonzalo,
    His tears runs down his beard like winter's drops
    From eaves of reeds. Your charm so strongly works 'em
    That if you now beheld them, your affections
    Would become tender.

---

[13] The idea of the exchange between Prospero and Ariel as a scene of domestic abuse comes from a workshop performance (Deborah Hay as Ariel, Ben Carlson as Prospero) at Ryerson University, Toronto, Feb 1–2, 2018. For video of the scene, see http://earlymodernconversions.com/prospero-caliban-ariel-miranda-playing-for-free/.

[14] Eleanor Prosser, "Shakespeare, Montaigne, and the 'Rarer Action'," *Shakespeare Studies* 1 (1965), 241–244. See also my "Eating Montaigne," in *Reading Renaissance Ethics*, ed. Marshall Grossman (Routledge, 2007), 157–172.

PROSPERO: Dost thou think so, spirit?
ARIEL: Mine would, sir, were I human.
PROSPERO: And mine shall.
            Hast thou, which art but air, a touch, a feeling
            Of their afflictions, and shall not myself,
            One of their kind, that relish all as sharply
            Passion as they, be kindlier moved than thou art?
            Though with their high wrongs I am struck to th' quick,
            Yet with my nobler reason 'gainst my fury
            Do I take part. The rarer action is
            In virtue than in vengeance. (5.1.11–28)

Prospero's turn toward kindness does not turn wide enough to encompass Caliban. Ariel does not intervene on behalf of Caliban and his drunken co-conspirators. Indeed he and Prospero share the joy of hunting and hurting the three failed renegades. There is a comic energy in the hunt and in the suffering of the hunted that frees the hunters and us from responsibilities of kindness (see, for example, 4.1.255sd and following); but, as is familiar, there are aspects of Caliban's character that Prospero is unable or unwilling to grasp, especially his religiosity, love of beauty and music, and articulate intelligence. To some degree, of course, it will depend on the performance of the character Caliban and of the whole play; but the critical and theatrical history of Caliban does suggest that actors, directors, readers, and playgoers have, over time, been able to cultivate their virtue of kindness by recognizing Caliban, no matter what "a strange thing" (5.1.289) he might appear to be, as one of their kind and as their kin.[15] In light of that history of how we and *The Tempest* have grown kind together, my story of unkindness might be all the more instructive.

Caliban

In February 2018, the members of the Early Modern Conversions Project put on a two-day workshop at Ryerson University in Toronto. Called "Playing for Free: Slavery, Conversion, Freedom," the workshop brought together four actors from the Stratford Shakespeare Festival, student actors from the Ryerson Performance Program, director James Wallis, and a group of scholars from the Conversions Project. We worked behind closed doors for two days on *The Tempest* and on questions around conversion,

---

[15] On the history of Caliban, see Alden T. Vaughan and Virginia Mason Vaughan, *Shakespeare's Caliban: A Cultural History* (Cambridge University Press, 1991).

slavery, and freedom. The two-day collaboration ended with a public performance by both the actors and the scholars. The actors played nine scenes from the play that, strung together, provided a good sense of the arc of the action. The scholars spoke between the performed scenes, each scholarly interlude no longer than three minutes and each one bent on building excitement and insight.

The workshop brought forward how religious conversion had been an instrument of political and social domination in Europe and a weapon of cultural genocide in the Americas. But we also considered how conversion could enable recognition, liberation, and salvation. We had in mind Paul's verse, "For now we see through a glass, darkly; but then face to face: now I know in part; but then shall I know even as also I am known" (1 Corinthians 13:12). The salvific conversions in the play included Prospero's recollection of how Miranda was not a burden to him when they were at sea and facing death. She was, he tells her, an angelic figure that saved him from despair:

> O, a cherubin
> Thou wast that did preserve me. Thou didst smile.
> Infused with a fortitude from heaven,
> When I have deck'd the sea with drops full salt,
> Under my burden groan'd; which raised in me
> An undergoing stomach, to bear up
> Against what should ensue. (1.2.152–158)

The shipwrecked Ferdinand recognizes Miranda in similar but different terms by greeting her the first time he sees her with "Most sure, the goddess" – an English version of Aeneas' "O dea certe" spoken to Venus after the Trojan shipwreck.

Something that I had not anticipated learning, and that was indeed a revelation to me, was Antoine Yared's performance of "the isle is full of noises" speech. In the workshop itself, he played it as a triumphing over Stephano and Trinculo – his easy familiarity with invisible music against their abject terror. That was just fine and not at all unexpected. But then something happened that changed everything.

I'd agreed with York University Professor of English Elizabeth Pentland that, at the performance before an audience, we would stage a brief debate after the scene – she speaking on Caliban's side and I on Prospero's. I was utterly unprepared for what happened. Antoine changed the speech. It was not triumphant but heart-breaking. It was the speech of a man who had once stood face-to-face with the numinous beauty of Nature but who had lost the sight of that face and could only recapture the realization of his own self or soul fleetingly in dreams:

> Be not afeard; the isle is full of noises,
> Sounds and sweet airs, that give delight and hurt not.
> Sometimes a thousand twangling instruments
> Will hum about mine ears, and sometime voices
> That, if I then had waked after long sleep,
> Will make me sleep again: and then, in dreaming,
> The clouds methought would open and show riches
> Ready to drop upon me that, when I waked,
> I cried to dream again.   (3.2.133–141)

I know *The Tempest* very well. I have written about it extensively and have even co-edited the play. But the performance that evening inundated me with new thinking and feeling and a new sense of how I was involved in Caliban's fate. As I watched Antoine and heard him speak, it occurred to me that Shakespeare might have been using conversion itself as an instrument of critique against the forced conversions of the Indigenous Peoples of the Americas, a colonialist program that had been going on for more than 100 years by the time he came to write *The Tempest*. I understood why Caliban had tried to find the lost sacred face of the natural world, first in Prospero and then in Stephano, why that was impossible to do, and how those failures had left him bound forever within inescapable solitariness.[16] And then, as Stanley Cavell might say, I disowned that knowledge. I just did what I said I would do. I stood up, faced Liz Pentland before the audience, and undertook to rebut her argument for Caliban's humanity and dignity.

By doing so, I joined with the phalanx of powerful Europeans that confront Caliban at the end and added my voice to the remarkably harsh account of him given by Prospero to Alonso and the others, and then also I countenanced his reconfinement to domestic servitude, which seemed to spell the end of any attempt on his part to turn to anyone – there was no one for him – or to Nature itself in an effort, to paraphrase Paul, "to know even as he is known." I felt as if I had disowned my brother and undone my virtue.

There was only the audience left. The audience could be the only source of what Caliban calls grace. "I'll be wise hereafter," he says in his last speech in the play, "And seek for grace" (5.1.295–296). If the playgoers were not there for him, if they did not acknowledge him as one of their kind and

---

[16] For more along these lines, see Hannah Korell and Paul Yachnin, "Shakespeare's 'The Tempest' explores colonialism, resistance and liberation." *The Conversation*, November 5, 2019. http://theconversation.com/shakespeares-the-tempest-explores-colonialism-resistance-and-liberation-124683.

as their kin, his ending would be despair, just as Prospero fears his ending will be. It was all make-believe, but when Prospero spoke the Epilogue and the audience responded with sustained applause, especially ardent when Antoine came forward for his bow, the relief I felt at their applause was restorative. I guess the playgoers' time on the island and their face-time with Caliban had led them to cultivate the virtue of kindness. And so I too took something of great value from that experimental performance of *The Tempest* and from the audience's heartfelt approbation of the actors. I will hereafter not follow the rules, even if they are rules of my own making. Rather, I will attend to and cultivate the virtue of kindness, which is the feeling recognition of our creaturely kin and the active duty of care for all creatures, even those as seemingly strange as the "savage and deformed slave" Caliban.

CHAPTER 24

Stewardship and Resilience
The Environmental Virtues

Jessica Rosenberg

Although the dominant meaning of virtue today concerns human ethical capacity, the word had a much broader scope in Shakespeare's England. This chapter tackles this capacious ecological sense of *"vertue"* (as it was often spelled in the period), unpacking both the resilient force it named in natural matter and the skill and virtue of stewardship it solicited from the humans entangled in its management, whether in kitchen, garden, or apothecary. Together, stewardship and resilience capture the skills and virtues of household management in its broadest sense, to include care for the *oikos* shared by human and non-human creatures and systems.

These *vertues* demanded the kind of informed care that Shakespeare and his contemporaries might have recognized as "stewardship": the nurturing attendance of skilled handlers, human actors divinely charged with bringing out those latent energies. They also exemplified the expression of what we would call "resilience": the retention of core properties in face of crisis or catastrophe, survival beyond the ephemerality and fickleness of accidental material form, the potential to rebound in force despite the ravages of time and chance. Though resilience has its origins in a property of matter, and stewardship in the duties of office, both have become keywords in contemporary environmental conversations, naming the virtues and practices that might support the survival of human and non-human creatures in times of disruption and catastrophe. It is difficult to find a recent statement of environmental planning or principle without one or both terms conspicuously situated. Both, however, have also been criticized for the way in which they individualize environmental virtue, undermining necessary structural change in favor of individual tenacity and care. Neither term carried exactly its contemporary meaning during Shakespeare's lifetime (indeed, "resilience" would have meant very little at all to an early-modern Londoner). Instead, this chapter considers these contemporary formulations of environmental virtue in conversation with the early-modern conception of environmental *vertue* – namely, those dynamic capacities implanted in the stuff of nature. What purchase might this early-modern sense of *vertue* offer us on stewardship and resilience as specifically environmental virtues – those moral capacities at the boundary of human and nonhuman, individual and ecosystem?

To early-modern English readers and writers, planters and healers, the landscape was replete with virtues: dormant capacities ready to spring into action. Divinely endowed with these pockets of potential energy, creation offered a dynamic storehouse of *vertues,* distributed across the surface of the earth, and condensed even into the slightest vehicle, like the sting of a scorpion or the draw of a magnet. In its practical Renaissance meaning, virtue could name the medicinal power of a herb to either help or hurt – to poison or cure. As an index of latent force, virtues were inventoried in herbals, marshalled in recipe books, and summoned by the tacit expertise of herbalists and housewives. Though marked by an *I* in our contemporary spelling of *virtue,* we should keep in mind the *e* with which *"vertue"* is regularly spelled in early-modern texts (through 1650, accounting for more than 97 percent of printed appearances). This persistent *e* brings the notion further from its Latinate origins (especially its oft-cited association with *vir,* man, and fellowship with *vis,* force), and further too from the Italian *virtu*. A close relative of the *vernal* and to images of *Lady Ver, vertue-with-an-e* calls up the explosive potential of a (verdant) spring. *Vertues* are agents of transformation and redirection, of turns rhetorical, pharmacological, and narrative: *vertues* convert, subvert, invert, divert, and revert.[1]

When it appears in English herbals, recipe books, and works of natural philosophy, *"Vertue"* renders the Greek *dunamis* – or potentiality. In Aristotle's *Physics,* this potentiality is a counterpart to actuality, or *energeia.* Scholars of ancient medicine now believe the term was likely translated to the pharmacological context in fourth-century BCE by Diocles, a student of Aristotle's who wrote extensively on medicine. In this context, it came to mean the capacity of a virtuous body to alter other bodies, rather than the process of self-becoming for which Aristotle most frequently used the term.[2] From there, it became a ubiquitous term of art in Greek

---

[1] See also my "Poetic Language, Practical Handbooks, and the 'vertues' of Plants," in *Ecological Approaches to Early Modern English Texts,* eds. Lynne Dickson Bruckner, Edward J. Geisweidt, and Jennifer Munroe (Ashgate, 2016); and Chapter 2 of my *Botanical Poetics: Modern Plant Books and the Husbandry of Print* (University of Pennsylvania Press, 2022).

[2] Diocles' writings do not survive in complete form, which is one source of the uncertainty. See Phillip J. van der Eijk, *Medicine and Philosophy in Classical Antiquity.* (Cambridge University Press, 2005), esp. 293–295; Alain Touwaide, "Le médicament en Alexandrie: de la pratique à l'épistémologie," in *Sciences exactes et sciences appliquées à Alexandrie,* eds. G. Argoud and J.-Y. Guillaumin (Presses de l'Université, 1998), 189–206; and Frederick Gibbs, *Poison, Medicine, and Disease in Late Medieval*

medicine, and, eventually, in early-modern works of pharmacology and herbal knowledge.

In early-modern England, these material virtues interacted in ambivalent and uneven ways with the moral virtues. The exercise of one never assures the presence of the other. Indeed, at times, *vertues* share with Machiavellian *virtù* an independence or ambivalence in relation to moral norms. Friar Laurence offers a succinct epitome of the material virtues in *Romeo and Juliet*, when he says, "mickle is the powerful grace that lies / In plants, herbs, stones and their true qualities"; he soon goes on to warn, though, that this virtue might "turn to vice." His message at this moment in the play draws from the abiding alliance between the material and moral virtues, but finally alights on the slips and fissures between these two registers. The force might be used for evil as easily as for good. Like the Friar's words, sixteenth- and seventeenth-century uses of the term tend to operate on both levels at once. Moral and material virtues are praised for their abundance and variety, admired as personal or ecological properties. Conceived on a model of latent capacity and habituated expression, material virtues share with the moral virtues not particular patterns of ethical action but the pattern by which action itself is formulated. It may not be surprising that Shakespeare's plays and poems riff on the analogies between kinds of virtues, but also reflect profoundly on the fractures and spreading distinctions between them.[3]

A consideration of environmental virtue in light of these environmental *vertues* calls into relief some qualities common to the conceptual formations of resilience and stewardship, despite their divergent lineages. Each, in its way, turns on the finitude of the human, on the limits of an anthropocentric view of the virtues. They spur us to ask, in turn: How does it change a conception of the moral virtues to understand them as only partially human properties? Or, further, to extend the scope of virtuosity not just beyond human persons but beyond the bounds of individual creatures, to imagine virtues as properties of systems, collectives, and environments? Like human virtues, these capacities bridge the autochthonous

---

and Early Modern Europe (Routledge 2018), 15–16. For a more general treatment, see Vivian Nutton, *Ancient Medicine* (Routledge, 2012.) For a recent philosophical exploration of the value of *dunamos* to ecological thought and practice, see Michael Marder, *Energy Dreams: Of Actuality* (Columbia University Press, 2017).

[3] Holly Crocker's recent *The Matter of Virtue: Women's Ethical Action from Chaucer to Shakespeare* (University of Pennsylvania Press, 2019) – discussed further below – sets a persuasive agenda for how to address these shifting meanings, showing how the material meanings of "virtue" demand new understandings of feminine virtue in premodern Europe.

and the collaborative, the spontaneous emergence of excellent action from individuals and its distributed inherence across a system.

Both stewardship and resilience address themselves to the persistence of systems or creatures across time – their capacity to survive, rebound, or flourish across generations. Stewardship marks out a position of service to a sustainable natural order, a commitment to the survival of environments and ecosystems.[4] Its conception of service reaches beyond service both to the self and to the present moment as such. While resilience ecology (a more recent scientific formulation) may share some values with more traditional frameworks of conservation and sustainability, it takes a distinct epistemic and imaginative orientation, as it envisions the persistence of ecological systems in the face of extreme uncertainty or potential catastrophe.[5] One recent survey defines resilience as "the ability of a system to absorb disturbance and still retain its basic function and structure."[6] This quality, however, is distinct from persistence in stability. What might these dimensions of environmental virtues – their extension beyond individual bodies and individual moments, their indifference to the singularity of the human, their summoning of collective life and obligation – contribute to our rethinking of the virtues in Shakespeare's moment and in our own?

*

Shakespeare might not seem the greatest advocate of stewardship, given that the two most conspicuous stewards in his plays are *Twelfth Night's* Malvolio and *King Lear's* Oswald, both of whom win little respect and meet miserable ends. The steward's proximity to power – as both its proxy and, often, its intimate – poses a potent set of moral dangers, temptations that place his or her charge on shifting social terrain. Characterizing Malvolio's place in the household, Eleanor Lowe defines stewardship as "a form of governance which is precariously perched between a higher

---

[4] See Nathan J. Bennett et al., "Environmental Stewardship: A Conceptual Review and Analytical Framework," *Environmental Management* 61. 4 (2018), 597–614 for a comprehensive, recent view on stewardship in that field. On sustainability see Stacy Alaimo, "Sustainable This, Sustainable That: New Materialisms, Posthumanism, and Unknown Futures," *Publications of the Modern Language Association* 127. 3 (2012), 558–564; and Steve Mentz, "After Sustainability," *Publications of the Modern Language Association* 127. 3 (2012), 586–592.

[5] See also F. S. Chapin, Stephen R. Carpenter, Gary P. Kofinas et al, "Ecosystem Stewardship: Sustainability Strategies for a Rapidly Changing Planet," *Trends in Ecology & Evolution* 25. 4, 241–249 on "adaptive capacity"(8) and Will Steffen, Åsa Persson, Lisa Deutsch et al., "The Anthropocene: From Global Change to Planetary Stewardship," *Ambio* 40. 4 (2011), 739–761.

[6] Brian Walker and David Salt, with a Foreword by Walter V. Reid, *Resilience Thinking: Sustaining Ecosystems and People in a Changing World* (Island Press, 2006), 1.

authority and those below."[7] Stewardship is linked at its core to the delegation of authority, to the personal assumption of an office in service of a greater household, state, regent, or planet.

Shakespearean conceptions of stewardship, however, were not limited to the household, and could assume a more capacious role in service of creature and cosmos. Shakespeare's most ambivalent steward may be Richard II, the central figure in a play that reflects deeply on the intertwining of environmental and political stewardship. In the garden scene of Act 3, Scene 4, the gardeners' conversation makes visible Richard's failure at the kind of keeping of order and accounts that unites housekeeping, estate and environmental management, and affairs of state. Elizabethan society relied on embedded symmetries of good governance across each of these spheres, a balance that Richard has strained.

> Why should we, in the compass of a pale,
> Keep law and form and due proportion,
> Showing as in a model our firm estate,
> When our sea-wallèd garden, the whole land,
> Is full of weeds, her fairest flowers choked up,
> Her fruit trees all unpruned, her hedges ruined,
> Her knots disordered, and her wholesome herbs
> Swarming with caterpillars?   (3.4.32–58)

The explicit lexicon of stewardship is not far off. The garden scene is bracketed, in 3.3 and 4.1, by references to Richard's kingship as "stewardship" to God (and this is soon after Richard has lost his own Lord Steward, with the Earl of Worcester's resignation in 2.2). In 3.3, just before Richard capitulates to Bolingbroke outside Flint Castle, he asserts his own authority, and dismisses the presumption of the usurpers, in a challenging conditional: if he is not their lawful king, he demands, "show us the hand of God / That hath dismissed us from our stewardship." In 4.1, following Isabel's exchange with the gardeners, the Bishop of Carlisle takes up the same lexicon to question who has the authority to judge a king: "shall the figure of God's majesty, /His captain, steward, deputy-elect, / Anointed, crowned, planted many years, / Be judged by subject and inferior breath, / And he himself not present?" These two moments frame Richard's stewardship in turn as a conditional demand and as a question – an ambivalent voicing that places the legitimacy of his kingship further in doubt. This

---

[7] Eleanor Lowe, "Duty and Authority: Malvolio, Stewardship and Montague's Household Book," in *Shakespeare and Authority*, eds. Katie Halsey and Angus Vine (Palgrave Macmillan, 2018), 213.

doubt follows from an ambiguity in the nature of the sovereign steward. Is stewardship a virtue, in need of habitual exercise, or an inalienable and God-given endowment? A role and an office, or a property of character? In contemporary environmental movements, the sense of stewardship gives the term's traditional spiritual office a more egalitarian form, casting human beings in general as stewards of the land; in Christian environmentalism in particular, the position of humans as God's stewards in the care of creation is inspired by moments in the Bible like Genesis 2.15 and Leviticus 25:23.[8]

The economics of Richard's bad national stewardship anticipates the kind of environmental stewardship that Aldo Leopold advocated in the mid twentieth century, and which has since become a standard approach to the management of ecosystems. In the vernacular of those environmental managers, Richard's expenses have exceeded the maximum sustainable yield (MSY) of his land and people. He cannot continue indefinitely going back for more. Act 3's pruning motif directly calls to mind Tiberius' well-known warning against excessive taxation, *Boni pastoris est tondere pecus non deglubere.* (A good shepherd shears his sheep but does not skin them).[9] The formative influence of this model of economic stability – reaching from Tiberius to Leopold and passing through Richard on the way – is not a coincidence. The steward is charged – in the nation's economy as in *oikos* and ecosystem – with household maintenance and orderly keeping.[10] Part of a long arc of management thinking, contemporary articulations of environmental stewardship descend from practices of husbandry and estate management, and from norms – well known to Shakespeare – that understand even the masters of great estates to be servants to the land. Leopold's influential articulation of a "land ethic" in *Sand County Almanac* also gives these practices the name of husbandry, a usage that preserves the term's early-modern jointure of environmental *vertues* to human accounting.[11]

As it does for Malvolio and for Richard, stewardship poses problems of governance and authority: a steward fills an office, taking on household or political authority by assuming a position of service. Such a duty only makes sense in a system built of such roles, according to symmetric

---

[8] On the spiritual dimensions of this kind of stewardship, see Willis Jenkins, *Ecologies of Grace* (Oxford University Press, 2008); Pragni Sahni, *Environmental Ethics in Buddhism* (Routledge, 2011).

[9] See Erasmus, *Adagia* iii vii 12, in *Erasmus, Collected Works*, vol. 34, trans. Denis L. Drysdall, ed. John N. Grant (University of Toronto Press, 1992).

[10] Donald Worster shows how these ideas shaped emerging discourses of ecology and environmentalism in *Nature's Economy: A History of Ecological Ideas* (Cambridge University Press, 1977).

[11] Aldo Leopold, *A Sand County Almanac*, ed. Curt Meine (Library of America, 2013).

structures of household, estate, and realm. The system-specific meaning of the steward's office in this early-modern sense cannot be fully individualized and extracted from the institutions that impart it meaning and force.[12] Without this sense of duty and office, stewardship becomes a free-floating metaphor. Nonetheless, much recent environmental policy reflects just this kind of extraction and individualization. A 2005 US Environmental Protection Agency (EPA) report, for example, "Everyday Choices: Opportunities for Environmental Stewardship," takes up the term as part of a decentralizing, anti-regulatory program.[13] The conception of environmental stewardship articulated in the document represents environmental virtue as the burden and property of individual actors: "At the most basic level, stewardship means taking responsibility for our choices," the authors say.[14] The governmental agency responsible for environmental protection has instead chosen as its watchword a concept it defines as "the responsibility for environmental quality shared by all those whose actions affect the environment." We may even hear some infiltration of Aristotelian virtue ethics into this government document, as it describes stewardship as "a behavior, one demonstrated through continuous improvement of environmental performance" – an appeal to the good habits of citizens as a prop to the duties of the state.

The EPA's atomized and distributed account of stewardship makes a personal virtue out of an institutional charge, individualizing environmental and social responsibility and emptying out collective good. That is, it redistributes responsibilities without redistributing social or material benefits. This tendency operates even more powerfully in celebrations of personal and population-level "resilience" in the face of natural disasters, as we will see in a moment. This is not to say that neither are indeed "virtues," or capacities worth having or cultivating. But we must keep in sight the scenes in which these "virtues" are identified, prescribed, and praised. The figure prescribing or praising stewardship and resilience – in nearly all contemporary settings where such meanings are in vogue – often effectively

---

[12] For a philosophical view on the exercise of virtues in the context of social practice and institution, see Alasdair MacIntyre, *After Virtue: A Study in Moral Theory* (University of Notre Dame Press, 2022), Chapter 14.

[13] EPA, 4. The report argues: "Looking ahead, EPA will maintain strong regulatory programs while also working toward a society that willingly makes environmentally responsible choices far superior to any that could be mandated by government. Living in a society where everyone takes responsibility to improve environmental quality for a more sustainable future – that is our vision and one that EPA should vigorously pursue with every willing and able partner."

[14] Ibid., 2.

declares that virtues are for other people. In doing so, they relieve themselves of the duties of care that might actually underwrite survival.

As climate change has begun to affect all areas of central planning, "resilience" has begun to outpace "stewardship" as a keyword in environmental policy. (Miami, where I live, has a chief resilience officer, and capital expenses are classified according to whether they serve resilience targets – in a recent draft budget, such items were marked with a "leaf emoji.") "Resilience" has, nonetheless, taken a distinct path to this position, and has only relatively recently come to name virtues possessed by human beings who face climate catastrophe. Having originated as a property of inert matter, "resilience" carries the mood of the in- and superhuman even when it modifies persons: like rubbery matter that "bounces back," resilient people and populations are admired for those qualities least allied with human vulnerability and suffering – that is, for the very fact of their survival. We might indeed ask whether resilience is a moral or material virtue.

Etymologically, resilience (descended from the Latin *salio, salire,* to leap) first named the tendency of an object to bounce back – its elastic capacities. I have found no uses during Shakespeare's lifetime, though the *OED* records one exceptionally early use just a few years later in Francis Bacon's *Sylva Sylvarum,* where it entitles an entry's concern with "Whether there be any such Resilience in Eccho's." This material sense, however, was not uncommon in Latin, and was defined, for example, in Eliot's *Biblioteca* as "Resilio, lij, iire, to lepe backe, or steppe away quickely."[15] Thomas Cooper's *Thesaurus* (1578) includes an example from Ovid, as the poet narrates the moment when the hands of Libys the mariner turn to dolphin fins: "In spatium resilire manus breue vidit," or in Cooper's English translation, *"He sawe hys handes sodainely become shorter."*[16] At the core of this usage, in the movement from *salio* to *resilio,* is the reactivity and suddenness of movement, the reflexive springing of this species of action. Material resilience names not a manifest quality but the capacity to be always-about-to-suddenly-act.

Resilience as an environmental principle emerged in in the 1970s in the context of systems ecology, originally proposed by Crawford S. Holling,

---

[15] Thomas Eliot, *Biblioteca Eliotae* (Thomas Berthelet, 1538), 131. Compare Huloets' *Dictionarie* (Thomas Marsh, 1572). 161.

[16] The Loeb gives these lines as: "But Libys, while he seeks to ply the sluggish oars, sees his hands suddenly shrunk in size to things that can no longer be called hands at all, but fins." ("At Libys obstantis dum vult obvertere remos,in spatium resilire manus breve vidit et illasiam non esse manus, iam pinnas posse vocari.")

who adapted it as a theory for understanding the transformation and persistence of complex systems.[17] Holling measured resilience not by a system's capacity to return to a stable mean, but by its capacity to weather the impact of violent fluctuations and extreme risk, a definition that (drawing on the nascent field of complex systems theory) departed from an equilibrium-based conception of environmental management and Leopold's sustainable husbandry. Since Holling, understandings of the resilience of ecosystems have emerged alongside anticipation of crisis, imagining a state in which nature does not automatically return to equilibrium or balance.[18] As John Pat Leary notes, the more recent transfer of "resilience" from Holling's ecosystems to the admirable survival of human beings makes a metaphor of a metaphor: "'resilient' people borrow the capacities of ecosystems to recover from crisis, and this ecological meaning was in turn borrowed from an object's ability to bend."[19] To call humans resilient imagines them as complex ecosystems, and asks how they weather and adapt to crisis, the force with which they rebound to a new (but essentially intact) state. The designation pays no mind to how much that human being or community might suffer or lose along the way.

This bounciness lends resilience a prototypically comic quality – in its proximity to the nonhuman, in its rubberized imperturbability in face of suffering and disorder. Here, resilience as a (moral) character trait reveals itself as the resilient property of a (literary/theatrical) character. This is the quality of comedy that Henri Bergson calls "a certain mechanical inelasticity, just where one would expect to find the wide-awake adaptability and

---

[17] Crawford S. Holling "Resilience and Stability of Ecological Systems," *Annual Review of Ecology and Systematics* 4. 1 (1973), 1–23. My account of the genealogy of resilience is informed especially by Melinda Cooper and Jeremy Walker, "Genealogies of Resilience: From Systems Ecology to the Political Economy of Crisis Adaptation," *Security Dialogue* 42. 2 (2011), 143–160; John Patrick Leary, *Keywords: The New Language of Capitalism* (Haymarket Books, 2019), and Lindsay Thomas, *Training for Catastrophe* (University of Minnesota Press, 2021). See also the special issue of *Politics* 33. 4; and Kevin Grove, "On Resilience Politics: From Transformation to Subversion," *Resilience* 1. 2 (2013), 146–153.

[18] Melinda Cooper and Jeremy Walker link Holling's concept of resilience to an interest in complex systems from the philosophy of Hayek (they are, they write, "uncannily convergent positions"[144].) ("Genealogies of Resilience: From Systems Ecology to the Political Economy of Crisis Adaptation," *Security Dialogue* 42. 2 [2011], 143–160). Their compelling intellectual genealogy offers an important reminder of the vital ideological stakes in ostensibly descriptive ecological models.

[19] Leary's critique continues: "What is often lost along the way is Holling's rather limited application: a 'resilient' biological system does not 'adapt' (he gave this term a different meaning, even though the *OED* uses it as a synonym), nor does it 'bounce back,' as a ball springing off a 'resilient' object would, or recover its original state, as a 'resilient' piece of putty might: it simply persists in an altered but basically intact state. It doesn't break, but this doesn't mean it is not damaged." On resilience and character, see also Lindsay Thomas, *Training for Catastrophe*.

the living pliableness of a human being."²⁰ Think of Christopher Sly, who, for all his transformations, continues to be himself; of the comic force of the reappearance of Falstaff (or, Falstaffian matter) across plays; and, the arc of perhaps the bounciest of the comedies' heroes, the appropriately named Nick Bottom. Bottom is also one whose virtues as a character are infected with *vertue,* through the coupled transformation of his form and of Titania's desire. As she says to him:

> I pray thee, gentle mortal, sing again.
> Mine ear is much enamored of thy note,
> So is mine eye enthrallèd to thy shape,
> And thy fair virtue's force perforce doth move me
> On the first view to say, to swear, I love thee.   (3.1.139–143)

In this moment, he is a creature spoken through, a vehicle for nonhuman activity rather than the authorized possessor of either *vertue* or *virtus.* The comedy of Titania's lines follows from the doubling and misrecognition of virtues, her attribution to the person of Bottom the virtuous property (3.2.388) of Oberon's herbal liquor. She responds to the matter of this virtue but takes it as the forceful content of his character. Titania's repetition of "force" as noun and as adverb ("thy fair virtue's force perforce") performs the cunning tautology of material virtue's operation: the latent virtue of a thing is defined by its occasional or habitual manifest actions, which define it as a virtuous thing. This dynamic in *Midsummer,* however, also reminds us of the dangers of this kind of virtuous matter: *vertue* inheres in matter even as it travels in pieces, relocated or reallocated to new uses and new settings. This free circulation of virtuous force delegates small measures of sovereignty even to matter out of place, with little regard for order, structure, or hierarchy. These piecemeal *vertues* originate in environments but circulate from them with relative autonomy.

Comedy, then, may be tragedy plus not only time, but tragedy plus resilience, that virtuosic buoyancy of character and situation.²¹ It is the tragicomedies that give fullest rein to this power of rebound, delivering worlds that generate outsized risk but somehow bounce back from catastrophe. *The Winter's Tale* offers one account of management and care across time,

---

²⁰ Henry Bergson, *On Laughter* trans. Cloudesley Brereton and Fred Rothwell (Macmillan, 1911), 10.
²¹ A reader might compare Steve Mentz's argument that "post-sustainable" accounts of ecology (like that typified by Holling's *resilience*) demand a distinct conception of comedy – ones that turn from the static green worlds identified by Northrop Frye and that better account for ecological instability, violence, and catastrophe. See his "After Sustainability" (2012), especially its proposal for a "buoyant" swimmers' poetics; and "Green Comedy: Shakespeare and Ecology," in *The Oxford Handbook of Shakespearean Comedy,* ed. Heather Hirschfield (Oxford University Press, 2018).

a fable of the ethics of survival in face of awesome risk. The extended relationship of Paulina and Hermione demonstrates how stewardly care might interact with ecosystems in crisis. In this sense, Paulina's stewardship manages Hermione as a resilient system, but this kind of care demands the creation of a separate sphere in which she might properly steward her mistress, the invention of a new domain and household in which she can act as Hermione's mistress and keeper. Hermione's springing back into the play's last act also encourages us to ask what kinds of survival or persistence stewardship makes possible. When she emerges as the statue, it is clear that Hermione has not simply been preserved: she is, as Leontes notes, "so much wrinkled," transformed by the working of time even while so lovingly preserved.[22] Hermione's charmed survival is achieved under the sign of a different paradigm than that of the young man of the Sonnets, whose form the poet aims to preserve against the alterations of time and the seasons. She is in this sense closer to Holling's sense of a changeable and adaptive ecosystem, a timebound assemblage of lips, skin, wrinkles, and stewarding. The divergent forms of survival practiced by Hermione and imagined for the Sonnets' young man offer an object lesson in different kinds of monuments. As such, they raise questions both ethical and political at the core of any examination of environmental virtues. If we aim for conservation or sustainability, we must also ask, the maintenance of what and the survival of whom? What kind of environmental ethic pits the resilience of properties against the fragility of lives?[23]

I began by suggesting that early-modern understandings of material *vertue* offer us a chance to see the virtues of systems and environments, not only those proper to particular creatures. So, where might we look if we wanted to find a distributed sense of "virtue" in the plays? Where is virtue dispersed, and how do those more expansive fields – commonwealth, environment, cosmos – absorb catastrophe or disruption? I would

---

[22] Paulina attributes this fleshiness to the sculptor's art ("So much the more our carver's excellence, / Which lets go by some sixteen years and makes her / As she lived now") and remarks on its lack of (statue-like fixity): "The statue is but newly fixed; the color's / Not dry." (5.3.56–57).

[23] The fractured and limited versions of preservation imagined in the *Sonnets* are trenchantly shown by Aaron Kunin, "Shakespeare's Preservation Fantasy," *Publications of the Modern Language Association* 124. 1 (2009), 92–106. Gender decisively shapes the kinds of virtuous survival available to early-modern subjects. As Holly Crocker argues, a feminine and material account of early-modern virtues emphasizes virtues of vulnerability, endurance, and openness – feminine virtues that further underwrite an alternate account of what it means to be human. Holly Crocker, *The Matter of Virtue: Women's Ethical Action from Chaucer to Shakespeare* (University of Pennsylvania Press, 2019). See also Kathryn Schwarz, *What You Will: Gender, Contract, and Shakespearean Social Space* (University of Pennsylvania Press, 2011) on the alternate forms of situated ethical and social action available to early-modern women.

like to conclude with two examples of destabilized complex systems from Shakespeare's drama – examples that, in different ways, chart the rippling outcomes of the sovereign abdication of stewardship: the conflict between Oberon and Titania, in *A Midsummer Night's Dream,* and Lear's unloading of his kingship in *King Lear.* (Each disruption, in its way, deadheads the system of role and obligation that Edmund Dudley called "the tree of commonwealth," in an ecologically memorable early Tudor formulation.) *Midsummer* begins (if we believe Titania) in a time of extreme environmental crisis, when the warring of the fairy sovereigns has thrown the world and its seasons into disarray.

> Therefore the winds, piping to us in vain,
> As in revenge have sucked up from the sea
> Contagious fogs, which, falling in the land,
> Hath every pelting river made so proud
> That they have overborne their continents.
> The ox hath therefore stretched his yoke in vain,
> The plowman lost his sweat, and the green corn H
> ath rotted ere his youth attained a beard.
> The fold stands empty in the drownèd field,
> And crows are fatted with the murrain flock.
> The nine-men's-morris is filled up with mud,
> ....
> And thorough this distemperature we see
> The seasons alter: hoary-headed frosts
> Fall in the fresh lap of the crimson rose,
> And on old Hiems' thin and icy crown
> An odorous chaplet of sweet summer buds
> Is, as in mockery, set. The spring, the summer,
> The childing autumn, angry winter, change
> Their wonted liveries, and the mazèd world
> By their increase now knows not which is which.
>
> (2.1.84–118)

With this extended depiction of catastrophic climate change, Titania elaborates the kind of complex ecosystemic transformation that Holling would recognize, concatenating weather, seasons, landscape, the elements, and creaturely survival in a system of troubled interdependencies. The fairies' comic landscape shows more promise than *Lear's* for bouncing back from crisis, in part because of the dynamic redistribution of material virtues across its geography. When Oberon asks for the herbal antidote, he evokes its "virtuous properties" – ultimately, in this case, an abrupt and large-scale restoration of both narrative and environment. Comic restoration relies on the *vertue* of a trick, a *technē* that empowers the virtue of a piece to right the whole.

Lear's abdication, however, threatens more permanent damage to the land and its troubled stewards. As Gerard Passannante and others have argued, the play's world rides on the imminence of catastrophe.[24] (The impossibility of a comic environmental recovery in *Lear's* universe is also registered in the soil of Jane Smiley's rewriting in *A Thousand Acres,* a realm where nitrates have stretched a poisonous web across soil, bodies, family, and memory.)[25] Suggestively, Cordelia, like Oberon, calls upon *vertues* to power a project of restoration:

CORDELIA   All blest secrets,
            All you unpublished virtues of the earth,
            Spring with my tears. Be aidant and remediate
            In the good man's distress. Seek, seek for him,
            Lest his ungoverned rage dissolve the life
            That wants the means to lead it. (4.5.17–22)

And yet, the measure of recovery that Cordelia achieves fails to power the drama to as bouncy a restoration as that of *Midsummer.* At this moment, Cordelia has just learned that Lear, instead of stewarding England's environment, has become part of it – lost in a cornfield and covered in "rank fumiter and furrow-weeds, /With burdocks, hemlock, nettles, cuckoo-flowers, / Darnel, and all the idle weeds that grow / In our sustaining corn." Like Richard's England, Lear himself is overrun with weeds – and, specifically, chokeweeds, the kind that stunt the growth of both sustaining corn and the "unpublished virtues" that Cordelia summons. Lear is a garden unstewarded, unsustainable. Recognizing his failed self-governance, Cordelia assumes the role of her father's steward; and, to that end, issues commands here both to the "unpublished virtues of the earth" ("spring," "be aidant and remediate") and to others present in her service ("seek, seek"). But these are, of course, very different kinds of commands. Unlike Oberon's, Cordelia's words fuel only provisional recovery and redemption; they are ultimately *unvirtuous* – elegiacally emptied of efficacy. And, unlike Bottom's voice, whose fair virtue's force perforce is enough to seduce a queen, her apostrophe to creation's latent *vertues* falls on fruitless soil. It is an ironic echo of the play's first scene, when Cordelia's refusal to

[24] On catastrophe in *Lear,* see Karen Raber, who has shown the transhumanist aftershocks of the 1608 earthquake in the play's dramatic cosmos in *Shakespeare and Posthumanist Theory* (Bloomsbury, 2018); Gerard Passannante on its architecture of nothingness in *Catastrophizing: Materialism and the Making of Disaster* (University of Chicago Press, 2019); Margreta de Grazia, on catastrophe and Lear's troubled imaginings of endings in *Period Pieces* (University of Chicago Press, 2021). See also Henry Turner, "'King Lear' Without: The Heath," *Renaissance Drama* 28 (1997): 161–193.

[25] Jane Smiley, *A Thousand Acres* (Knopf, 1991).

publish her virtue actually displays it, a display that is for that very reason not – perforce – actively *vertuous*. The fissure with which Shakespeare presents us is not between moral and material virtues, but between individual virtuous practice and the greater degenerating force that they oppose. In pitting the questionable efficacy of individual virtue against the force of disaster at-scale, Cordelia's lyric moment asks what forms of preservation we might practice in face of what is already lost. There is no virtuous trick, in *Lear,* to save us.

CHAPTER 25

Cognitive Virtue and Global Ecosociability

Donald Wehrs

Around the world, virtue ethics emerge from cultural contexts shaped by prephilosophical, poetic articulations of socially shared imagined worlds. These worlds presume entwinements of natural, human, and spirit realms, and they identify the good with what preserves, achieves, or renews material and social human well-being. Shakespeare's engagement with virtue ethics in plays as diverse as *Richard II* and *The Winter's Tale* both evokes these contexts, evident in worldwide folklore and ancient epics, and puts them in transformative contact with modernity.

Oral literatures typically depict human well-being as following from the interdependent emergence of physical environments hospitable to communal life, on the one hand, and social orders that foster cooperative sociability, on the other. The sustaining of human life materially is understood to require communal cultivation of sociability even as interlinked natural, human, and spirit realms are understood to be regulated by "sociable" reciprocities, balancing, and accommodations among diverse forces, values, and interests. "Ecosociability" may be said to characterize such imagined worlds. Stories of how gods and heroes shape worlds hospitable to human well-being describe, in effect, their roles in creating ecological niches within which divine and human communities can flourish and fruitfully interact. These stories become themselves part of discursive traditions wherein delineating imagined worlds becomes a crucial part of human communities' niche constructive activities. Although niche construction originates in a deep, prehuman past, it constitutes for human societies an ongoing adaptive task. That task extends beyond altering physical environments (increasing crop yield through irrigation in ancient Mesopotamia, for example) to elaborating shared imagined worlds (*cosmos* in Greek traditions, *rita* in Sanskrit ones) through which significance, intention, assessment, and value are configured.

Aristotle's virtue ethics, stressing cultivation of habitual attentiveness to avoiding excess and deficiency, makes pursuit of sustainable, equitable balance central to deliberative, purposeful intentions. In this respect, it is consonant with archaic Greek poetry's depiction of the divine, human, and natural realms as three mutually interpenetrative orders, each characterized by hierarchical reciprocities whose balancing of forces and claims constituted sociable ecosystems. In Hesiod, Zeus creates a cosmos that does not collapse into chaos because, unlike his father and grandfather, he wisely restrains self-aggrandizement, giving other deities their own space (literally). Acknowledging their rights, he gives them stakes in his authority.[1] As a consequence, the cosmos he regulates becomes ecologically and morally viable, and its interlocking reciprocities enable and underlie human habitation. If human social orders are to be similarly viable, it is implied, they must be analogously sociable.

Similar presentations of mutually interconnected ecosociable divine, human, and natural realms shape the presentation of virtue in Sanskrit epic and African, Australian, and Amerindian oral traditions. In his *Complaint of Peace*, contesting theological deprecations of nature's role in virtue, Erasmus recuperates ecosociability for early European modernity by ascribing it to nature infused with divine love. Its instantiation in moral–social life demands a virtue ethics interfusing shrewdness (*metis*) and righteousness (*themis*), as in Hesiod.[2] Otherwise, moral monstrousness and political chaos cannot be kept at bay. Shakespeare dramatizes in *Richard II* how failures of virtue, failures rooted in thinking of the state as a possession or entitlement rather than as an ecosociable order to be carefully maintained, yield both monstrousness and chaos, while in *The Winter's Tale* Shakespeare probes the extent to which what is lost by such failures in personal, familial life may be retrieved.

Virtue ethics, by seeking to reform cognition through socializing and civilizing desire, imply understandings of cognition consonant with scientific accounts of its origins and functioning. What species do in modifying their ecological niches alters what they are, much as habits in virtue ethics "remake" individuals (*Nicomachean Ethics* 2.1 1103a 14–1103b 25).[3] Automatic monitoring of bodily well-being and the effects of surroundings on it triggers positive or negative affective valences, the experiencing of which enables even organisms as simple as bacteria to anticipate, note, and respond to aspects of their environment affecting biological

---

[1] See Stephen Scully, *Hesiod's Theogony: From Near Eastern Creation Myths to* Paradise Lost (Oxford University Press, 2015).
[2] Erasmus, "The Complaint of Peace (*Querala Pacis*)," in *The Collected Works of Erasmus*, ed. Anthony Herbert Tigar Levi, vol. 27 (University of Toronto Press, 1986).
[3] Aristotle, *Nicomachean Ethics*, trans. Terence Irwin (Hackett, 1985), hereafter *NE*.

well-being. This in turn prompts behavioral adjustments that, like those Aristotle attributes to *eudaimonia*-oriented *phronēsis*, are self-preservative or that tend to enhance survival and reproductive prospects.[4] Such adjustments over time reshape organisms' ecological niches by reconfiguring what is evolutionarily advantageous or what constitutes an evolutionary pressure for a particular species. Species' biologically "autopoetic" (self-making) activity becomes, like random genetic mutation, climate change, and pathogens, a major force shaping organic life and evolutionary history.[5] Human action can enact ecological niche construction, for example by projects taken up by intentional consciousness, the effects of which stretch from early human use of fire to reshape ecosystems in ways favoring certain kinds of flora and fauna over others to the transforming of the global environment over the past four centuries.[6]

All organisms are embedded in environments whose bearing on their well-being elicits, via bodily registered affects, behavioral adjustments. However, organisms with complex brains, whose survival and flourishing require situational decision making, register such affects through disjunctive but coordinated "top-down" and "bottom-up" cognitive processing. This duality, each trajectory in "dialogue" with the other in ways that resist fusion or co-option, facilitates flexible, continuous learning.[7] On the one hand, in "top-down" cognitive activity, overall expectancies give order and relevance to details; on the other, in "bottom-up" cognitive activity, arrestingly discrepant particulars disrupt and reconfigure overall expectancies. For species whose well-being hinges on interdependent group life, the need to balance bidirectional cognitive–affective processing in ways that effectively recalibrate expectancies extends beyond monitoring physical environments to include attentiveness to in-group interactions and to what may threaten or enhance group well-being, thus fostering *philia* (friendship or sociability).[8] The ecosystems in which humans are embedded

---

[4] Antonio Damasio, *The Strange Order of Things: Life, Feeling, and the Making of Cultures* (Pantheon, 2018); Lisa Feldman Barrett, *How Emotions Are Made: The Secret Life of the Brain* (Houghton Mifflin Harcourt, 2017).

[5] Humberto R. Maturana and Francisco J. Varela, *Autopoesis and Cognition: The Realization of Living* (D. Reihl, 1980). Francisco J. Varela, Evan Thompson, and Eleanor Rosch, *The Embodied Mind: Cognitive Science and Human Experience.* (MIT Press, 1991).

[6] James C. Scott, *Against the Grain: A Deep History of the Earliest States* (Yale University Press, 2017), 41–42. Richard Wrangham, *Catching Fire: How Cooking Made Us Human* (Basic Books, 2009).

[7] Don M. Tucker and Phan Luu, *Cognition and Neural Development* (MIT Press, 2012). Paul B. Armstrong, *Stories and the Brain: The Neuroscience of Narrative* (Johns Hopkins University Press, 2020).

[8] *NE* bks. 8–9, also see Cicero, *De amiticia* in Marcus Tullius Cicero, *De senectute. De amiticia. De divination,* trans. William Armistead Falconer, Loeb Classical Library (Heinemann, 1923).

include social environments, certainly, but also human-produced affordances, such as tools. These extend the mind into the environment, thus connecting us to and putting us in debt to other people's mental activity.[9] Within the ecosociable niches societies shape, cultural activities and arts, including discursive ones, elaborate shared imagined worlds in relation to which cognition is readjusted. These become affordances available for use in endeavors to protect or enhance communal flourishing in ways that, for virtue ethics, ideally integrate ethics and politics (*NE* 1.2.1094a 20–1094b 10), uniting *honestas* (honor, virtue, rectitude) and *utilitas* (usefulness, advantage).[10]

Ecosociable niche construction for humans involves social practices that cultivate attentiveness to others' interests and viewpoints while targeting bullying and freeloading for reproof and punishment. This may also be said of group life among many primates.[11] Indeed, diverse evolutionary accounts of the "natural" origins of human morality identify bullying and freeloading as the primary internal threats to cooperative sociality, which communities need to cultivate if the ways of life they foster are to be generally desirable and viable.[12] In humans, social selection favoring discernment and cultivation of affective bonds, responsiveness to communal restraints and attachments, and dispositional inclinations toward conduct warranting trust evidently interacted with humans' distinctive consciousness of consciousness. As a result, ongoing monitoring and assessment of self and others projected a third-person, communal perspective from which to judge group members' and one's own contributions to shared, collective well-being.[13] This in turn intermingled, starting in our evolutionary past, with what is for humans an easy and often involuntary movement from somatic empathy, rooted in bodily resonances, to vicariously experienced psychosocial fellow feeling.[14] In virtue ethics, such intermingling

---

[9] See Andy Clark, *Surfing Uncertainty: Prediction, Action, and the Embodied Mind* (Oxford University Press, 2016).

[10] Marcus Tullius Cicero, *De officiis*, trans. Walter Miller, Loeb Classical Library (W. Heinemann, 1913).

[11] See Christopher Boehm, *Moral Origins: The Evolution of Virtue, Altruism, and Shame* (Basic Books, 2012). Also see Frans de Waal, *Chimpanzee Politics: Power and Sex Among Apes*, 2nd ed. (Johns Hopkins University Press, 1998).

[12] Richard Wrangham, *The Goodness Paradox: How Evolution Made Us More and Less Violent* (Profile, 2019). Richard Joyce, *The Evolution of Morality* (MIT Press, 2006). Dennis L. Krebs, *The Origin of Morality: An Evolutionary Account.* (Oxford University Press, 2011).

[13] Michael Tomasello, *A Natural History of Human Morality* (Harvard University Press, 2016).

[14] Giovanna Colombetti, *The Feeling Brain: Affective Science Meets the Enactive Mind* (MIT Press, 2014).

is attributed to nature, which binds together ethical rationality and social affections.[15]

Simulating another's internal mental life allows one to enter into and enjoy shared attentiveness and joint intentionality, as Aristotle and Plutarch note (*NE* 9.6.1167a 20–1167b 15).[16] It also breeds awareness of perspectives and interests uniquely one's "own," which complicate identification or solidarity with others.[17] This near simultaneity of constantly alternating perspectives ensures a degree of cognitive dissonance – inconsistency in thoughts and attitudes, epitomized by temptations to override sociable impulses or constraints in pursuit of personal advantage. As a consequence, recurrent and intractable experiences of internal affective dissonance – of finding oneself caught between cooperative and competitive impulses, life-protective and life-enhancing affective valences, egocentric and nonegocentric registers of significance – come so sharply to characterize phenomenological consciousness that tensions, conundrums, and disaffections invariably accompany and vex ecosociable niche construction. Living with and in such dissonances becomes a constitutive problem that diverse societies seek to manage but cannot resolve, and that virtue ethics seek to address by urging habituation of appetites to rational moderation (*NE* 3.12.1119b–1120a).[18]

As affinities between Hesiod and Aristotle suggest, shared endeavors to manage affective dissonance and moderate antisocial, destructive energies connect prephilosophical discursive traditions to virtue ethics. This claim may appear surprising, for much mythic storytelling traces the making of humanly inhabitable worlds back to original states marked by chaotic, impulsive, unrestrained self-aggrandizement, as does Hesiod's *Theogony*. The creator god of the Kalahari desert Nyae Nyae !Kung people, ≠Gao N!a, for example, though credited with ensuring natural order in the present, is figured in folktales set in a distant past as an outrageous comic

---

Cicero, *De officiis* 1.12 pp 12–15; Seneca, Epistle 95 in Lucius Annaeus Seneca, *Moral Epistles*, vol. 3, trans. Richard M. Gummere, Loeb Classical Library (Harvard University Press, 1925).

Plutarch. "On Listening to Lectures," *Moralia I*, trans. Frank Cole Babbitt, Loeb Classical Library (Putman, 1927), 204–259.

Michael Tomasello, *Becoming Human: A Theory of Ontogeny* (Belknap Press of Harvard University Press, 2019). William Hirstein, *Mindmelding: Consciousness, Neuroscience, and the Mind's Privacy* (Oxford University Press, 2012). Thomas Metzinger, *Being No One: The Self-Model Theory of Subjectivity* (MIT Press, 2001).

Plutarch, "How a Man May Become Aware of His Progress in Virtue," *Moralia I*, trans. Frank Cole Babbitt, Loeb Classical Library (Putnam, 1927), 400–457; "On Moral Virtue," *Moralia VI*, trans. W. C. Helmbold., Loeb Classical Library (Harvard University Press, 1939), 18–87.

trickster.[19] The primal world of ≠Gao N!a stories, however, is understood to depict what had to be displaced, superseded, constrained, in order for sociable, human life to be possible. In one story, ≠Gao N!a's wives are sisters and have a brother who ≠Gao N!a schemes to eat. Being untouched by compunction or restraint, ≠Gao N!a cannot resist attacking one who, in being fat and slow, is an inviting target. But in trying to devour his brother-in-law, he alienates his wives, who repeatedly conspire to punish him. Incapable of imaginatively distancing himself from egoism or internalizing restraint, in outrage and full of self-pity he concocts revenge plots which each time motivate more payback. By ending with unresolved, open-ended conflict, the story posits a radical disjunction between a primeval era, before humans, and present realities shaped by civilizing constraints.

In much indigenous Australian storytelling, absence of moral sociability similarly coincides with absence of affective dissonance, and is likewise depicted as ruinous. But whereas in African stories the world we share with others is often conceived of as displacing the primal one depicted, in Australian discourse, present-day physical spaces are frequently viewed as being the products of, or bearing the marks of, primordial asocial violence. In two related stories, fratricidal strife leads to ecological calamity. In one, two brothers travel from the west, one carrying a kangaroo-skin water bag.[20] As one is "lazy," the other goes hunting, but first he buries the water bag, which the other finds, drinks from, and then slashes open with a club, causing a flood that drowns both brothers and creates the Southern Ocean. In the other version, an elder refuses the younger's "repeated requests for water,"[21] so that the younger, being "angry," takes advantage of the elder one's going out to hunt to find the water bag and hit it with a club, precipitating a flood in which both brothers die. In this version, the water then threatens to engulf the land, but "Bird Women" intervene,[22] acting cooperatively to construct from tree roots a barrier to contain the waters.

Behind such stories one may suspect distant cultural memories of rising sea levels at the end of the Ice Age flooding the land bridge from New Guinea to Australia and reconfiguring coastlines, but in both versions

---

[19] Lorna J. Marshall, *Nyae Nyae !Kung Beliefs and Rites* (Harvard University Press, 1999). Megan Biesele, *Women Like Meat: The Folklore and Foraging Ideology of the Kalahari Ju/'hoan* (Indiana University Press, 1993).

[20] Donald M. Berndt and Catherine H. Berndt, *The Speaking Land: Myth and Story in Aboriginal Australia* (Penguin, 1989), 44.

[21] Ibid., 44.

[22] Ibid., 45.

egoistic self-assertion poses a grave threat to sociable life (hence the importance of both brothers being drowned). The first version links the striking
of the water bag to laziness (that is, to freeloading), while the second connects it to age-based bullying. In the second version, a community of Bird
Women work cooperatively to keep the land from being flooded – from
being taken over by effects of male competitive aggressiveness. Notably, the
Bird Women coordinate improvised actions that are extensions and modifi-
cations of culturally paradigmatically female activity, gathering roots. Their
reparative, ecosociable niche construction is similar to Zeus' in Hesiod,
except that agency resides in a female community in which natural, human,
and spirit attributes intermingle. While in Hesiod there is a single male
deity, female-affiliated Metis and Themis act in conjunction with him, giving birth to Justice *(Dikē)* and nurture *(oreūousi*, 903) – to human sociable
life.[23] Arguably, Cordelia and Portia play analogous roles, much as Richard
III does that of an unrestrained and thus self-destructive bully.

  Curbing or diluting egoistic, appropriative energies transforms the
material-ecological world, making human flourishing biologically possible. In Navajo cosmology, as in Native American traditions broadly,
such constraint allows Sky and Earth to enter into "sociable" relations
sufficient to "host" human physical thriving.[24] Remarkably, in each tradition, accounts of fashioning ecosociable niches conducive to human
flourishing suggest that such efforts are driven by the same goals of mod-
erating human impulses and behavior posited by evolutionary research.
Similar concurrences shape early literary works' extended explorations
of ethical complexities. In the *Mahâbhârata*, the threat bullying poses
to sociable and moral communal life is made plain by the Kauravas's
unquenchable rapaciousness. At the same time, the need to habituate
oneself to affective dissonances is stressed. While desires to avoid moral
pollution through embracing an ethics of *ahimsa*, of non-violence or
refraining from harm, are portrayed as admirable, they are in irresolv-
able tension with duties incumbent on warrior caste members to practice their prescribed "way" *(dharma)* by participating in violence when
necessary to protect communities from bullying predation.[25] As Aristotle

[23] Hesiod, "Theogony," *Hesiod I: Theogony, Work and Days, Testimonia*, ed. and trans. Glenn W. Most
   (Harvard University Press, 2006) ll. 886–903.
[24] See Ray A. Williamson and Claire R. Farrer, eds., *Earth and Sky: Visions of the Cosmos in Native
   American Folklore* (University of New Mexico Press, 1992). Paul G. Zolbrod, *Diné bahane': The
   Navajo Creation Story* (University of New Mexico Press, 1984).
[25] Emily T. Hudson, *Disorienting Dharma: Ethics and the Aesthetics of Suffering in the* Mahâbhârata
   (Oxford University Press, 2012).

notes, "sometimes we praise the honour-lover, sometimes the person indifferent to honour" (*NE* 2.7.1108a). Because cognitive-affective attunement to discerning competing goods habituates one to reasoned balancing of conflicting valences, priorities, and considerations, particulars (specific circumstances and contexts) matter. For this reason, virtue ethics in Chinese and Indian as well as Aristotelian contexts tend to value literary discourse's socializing, civilizing, niche-constructing agency. Cognitive-moral excellence (*aretē*) involves cultivating proper kinds of affections and integrating them into perception and deliberation. Such activity (*praxis*), by reconstituting what we do, reconfigures what we become. It "re-forms" human nature, autopoetically, making it at once the effect and agent of ecosociable niche construction. This is something reflected in how words denoting "human," in Chinese as in Greek virtue traditions, acquire ethical-sociable resonances that bridge affective/cognitive, internal/communal, emotional/rational, natural/cultural divides. Mencius writes, "To be benevolent is the very essence of what it means to be human (*ren ye zhe, ren ye*)."[26] Shakespeare evokes such traditions in Ulysses' declaration, "One touch of nature makes the whole world kin" (*Troilus and Cressida* 3.3.175).[27]

In comparative historiography and religion, societies embracing such imagined worlds are called "pre-Axial," to distinguish them from societies, such as those of Israel, India, Greece, and China between the eighth and fourth centuries BCE, shaped by Axial (that is, pivotal) cultural revolutions that posit new imagined worlds, ones in which transcendent, otherworldly realms are taken to order reality, truth, and values in ways that may render goods affiliated with ecosociable niche construction subordinate, inconsequential, or ineffectual.[28] In the Latin West, Augustinian deprecation of natural affections and earthly frames of reference became the cornerstone for otherworldly, hierarchical, and theistic-metaphysical regulation of what constitutes significance.

Elsewhere, I argue that Abelard and Erasmus separately conceive divine love as not just initiating creation but also permeating its everyday functions in ways that counter Augustinianism, thus restoring moral and spiritual significance to earthly, affective, and sociable life in ways

---

[26] 2.17.16, quoted in Steven Shankman, *Other Others: Levinas, Literature, Transcultural Studies* (State University of New York Press, 2010), 59.

[27] William Shakespeare, *The Riverside Shakespeare*, ed. G. Blakemore Evans (Houghton Mifflin, 1974).

[28] See Samuel Noah Eisenstadt, ed., *The Origins and Diversity of Axial Age Civilization* (State University of New York Press, 1986); Charles Taylor, *A Secular Age* (Belknap Press of Harvard University Pres, 2007); Robert N. Bellah, *Religion in Human Evolution: From the Paleolithic to the Axial Age* (Balknap Press of Harvard University Press, 2011).

congenial to revivals of literary art and culture.[29] Here, I want to note that Erasmus's revival of the humanism of Cicero and Plutarch, and behind them Aristotelian virtue ethics, also revives much of the "spirit" of interpenetrative natural-human-spiritual imagined worlds evoked by pre-Axial and oral imaginative discourse, albeit modified to accommodate Christian frameworks. For Erasmus, cognitive-affective attunements elicited by literary culture hone practical rationality (*phronēsis*), as in Aristotle, but he conceives their doing so in ways that link humans' receptivity to grace to their being embedded in interpenetrative networks of "natural equity" (*aequitas naturae*).[30] "[H]armony in the balance of nature itself" inclines humans, as though through an evolutionary legacy, to virtue ethics, "and to temperance specifically, which makes justice equitable by love."[31] Because nature reflects artful balancing of "conflicting forces," itself instantiating sociable, pluralistic ordering by "mutual consent and communication,"[32] it acts like a humanistic educator or literary text. By doing so, nature binds together body and soul in reformative processes that foster both "capacity" and "inclination" to cultivate virtue and thus pursue the good.[33]

While Shakespeare's engagement with virtue ethics draws on these foundations, his histories question whether the cultural conditions of emergent modernity can sustain imagined worlds supportive of ecosociable political practices, and his romances test whether their promises of constructive, reparative agency are not merely folkloric, archaic "winter's tales." In the opening scene of *Richard II*, Bolingbroke demands trial by combat. His insistence that "what I speak / My body shall make good upon this earth, / Or my divine soul answer it in heaven" (1.1.36–38), displays his belief that God signifies right through might, a conviction

---

[29] Donald R. Wehrs, "Conceptual Blending and Genre Invention from Chrétien de Troyes to Cervantes and Shakespeare," in *Secrets of Creativity: What Neuroscience, the Arts, and Our Minds Reveal*, eds. Suzanne Nalbantian and Paul M. Matthews (Oxford University Press, 2019), 296–316; "Emotional Significance and Predation's Uneasy Consciousness in John of Salisbury and Chrétien's *Perceval*," *Literature & Theology* 28. 3 (2014), 284–298; "Placing Human Constants Within Literary History: Generic Revision and Affective Sociality in *The Winter's Tale* and *The Tempest*," *Poetics Today* 32. 3 (2011), 521–591; "Touching Words: Embodying Ethics in Erasmus, Shakespearean Comedy, and Contemporary Theory," *Modern Philosophy* 104. 1 (2006), 1–33.

[30] See Manfred Hoffmann, *Rhetoric and Theology: The Hermeneutics of Erasmus* (University of Toronto Press, 1994).

[31] Ibid., 120–121.

[32] Erasmus, "Complaint," 294.

[33] Erasmus, "A Declamation on the Subject of the Early Liberal Education of Children," in *Collected Works of Erasmus*, vol. 28, ed. J. K. Sowards, trans. Beert C. Verstaete (University of Toronto Press, 1985), 311.

whose converse tenet is that when might strays from right, God brings down the powerful. In numerous premodern societies, socio-material power relations are expected, as least ideally, to reflect moral economies in which, for example, paternal protection is exchanged for loyal service. Positing such economies allows complex, large societies to balance needs for hierarchical modes of organization with valorization of equities and reciprocities integral to desirable, sustainable ecosociable niche construction.[34]

Bolingbroke accuses Mowbray of violating the terms of such exchange by diverting for "lewd employments" (90) "eight thousand" gold coins (88) lent him for the king's soldiers. One guilty of such a breach of faith would likely also be guilty of Bolingbroke's second charge, that Mowbray "did plot the Duke of Gloucester's death" (100), a crime whose sacrilegious character he emphasizes by declaring that the blood of Gloucester, uncle to Richard and himself, "like sacrificing Abel's, cries / Even from the tongueless caverns of the earth, / To me for justice and rough chastisement ..." (104–106). The entwinement of natural, human, and divine attributes in Bolingbroke's phrasing and imagery evokes pre-Axial and oral discursive imagined worlds.

Since Mowbray's connivance at Gloucester's murder was suspected of having been countenanced, if not ordered, by Richard, as it eliminated someone who had previously constrained Richard's freedom in exercising power, Bolingbroke's appeal to trial by combat sets a trap that depends on the ambiguous status of such trials in late medieval culture. Although assumptions that triumphant might attests to divinely affirmed right remained potent politically and rhetorically, in practice, as the prevalence of trial by jury indicates, confidence in evidentiary, rational means of determining truth and right was becoming increasingly normative. Should Bolingbroke prevail in combat, he could claim God's vindication, but should Mowbray prevail, suspicion of Richard's guilt in relation to Gloucester will not likely be diminished.

In the guise of wishing not to see "the dire aspect / Of civil wounds plough'ed up with neighbors' swords" (1.3.127–128), but actually seeking to delegitimize both sides by associating each with "sky-aspiring and ambitious thoughts" (130), Richard banishes Bolingbroke for ten years and Mowbray for life. Even as the disparity in sentences seems to acknowledge Bolingbroke's better cause, Richard's torturous avoidance of trial by

---

[34] See Kent Flannery and Joyce Marcus, *The Creation of Inequality: How Our Prehistoric Ancestors Set the Stage for Monarchy, Slavery, and Empire* (Harvard University Press, 2012).

combat exposes how much belief in its premises has become selective or nominal. Once power ceases to be thought of as a sacramental trust, however, it begins to be viewed, incoherently, both as a personal possession, to be used as perceived self-interest or momentary whim dictates, and as a personal attribute, and as such inalienable. In either case, the prudent moderation enjoined by virtue ethics appears dissociated from any "natural" ground, and thus connotes only a naïve archaic residue or a tactical, Machiavellian ploy.

But when Richard, in seeming deference to Bolingbroke's aged father's grief over his son's banishment, reduces Bolingbroke's exile to six years, the father, Gaunt, notes that nature limits the capricious reach of political power: "Thou canst help time to furrow me with age, / But stop no wrinkle in his pilgrimage" (1.3.229–230). Nature, and by implication human nature, may be affected but not owned by power. Richard's proprietorial attitude toward power, however, entices him to conflate his person with his office, so that he thinks nothing of replenishing "our coffers," made "somewhat light" by "too great a court / And liberal largess," by "farm[ing] our royal realm," through coercive steep taxes, "for large sums of gold" (1.4.43–45, 50). Treating the royal "we" as an ownership claim, he seizes the dying Gaunt's assets so that "The lining of his coffers shall make coats / To deck our soldiers for these Irish wars" (61–62). But as his uncle the Duke of York points out, appropriating Bolingbroke's inheritance, treating "customary rights" (2.1.196) as no impediment to self-aggrandizing might, violates the moral economy supposed to regulate socio-material power relations – "for how art thou a king, / But by fair sequence and succession?" (2.1.198–199). Making the exchange of protection for loyalty inoperative by recognizing no moral constraints on power, Richard gives other nobles no material, practical reason to follow him. By severing the state from nature, by violating rather than emulating principles of natural equity, Richard allows a "modern" privatizing of power and identity to lead him into modes of rapacious bullying that, here as in oral and pre-Axial discourse, self-destructively imperil ecosociable life. Rather than presenting Machiavellian and Aristotelian-humanistic political theorizing as mutually exclusive opposites, Shakespeare interweaves them with implications that gradually unfold through *Richard II* and the rest of the second Henry tetralogy.

With similar historical self-consciousness, Shakespeare in *The Winter's Tale* affiliates his evocation of ecosociable reparative agency with archaic or naïve folk storytelling, even as its improbable enmeshing of transformative possibilities in mundane and compromised realities opens the door to trust in a wise foolishness akin to that attributed to Christian paradoxes. The play's romance turn begins with juxtaposing seemingly antithetical social-moral worlds. On the one hand, there is the realm of low cunning and shrewd "shearing" of vulnerable "sheep," represented by the "rogue" peddler Autolycus and the old shepherd's "clown" son. In a parody of the Good Samaritan parable, Autolycus pretends to have been robbed while traveling, and when the clown comes to his aid, he picks his pocket, declaring that the clown has done him "a charitable office" (4.3.76) while describing the fictive robber as one who, for one of his virtues, was "whipt out of the court" (90). The clown's gullibility is reiterated by his replying that Autolycus must have meant "vices" rather than "virtues," since there is "no virtue whipt out of the court," for it is there "cherish[ed]" to keep it there, "and yet it will no more but abide" (93), will not stay there long. On the other hand, there is the realm of the sheep-shearing festival, of Perdita's pastoral world, in which evocations of bounteous nature, benign classical deities, and human hospitality, welcoming strangers and intermingling classes, are united. These two worlds would seem irreconcilable, especially since elite pride connects King Polixenes to the antisocial egoism of Autolycus, whose name means "self-wolf." After learning his son is betrothed to Perdita, who seems to be a shepherdess, Polixenes threatens not only to block their union, but also to punish them and to impoverish and torture Perdita's aged shepherd foster father.

A mixture of unmotivated kindliness in some people and the moral work of time and chance prevents these consequences. Polixenes's counselor-friend Camillo contrives to take Perdita and the prince, Florizel, back to the kingdom of his former master, Leontes, who wrongfully exiled him, but to whom Camillo returns good for ill. Having long repented of suspecting his presumed deceased wife, Hermione, of adultery, Leontes welcomes the opportunity for reparation by sheltering Florizel and Perdita. When he learns of Perdita's supposed low birth, he offers to mediate between son and father, though he is moved by aristocratic pride as well as ethical sociability. These efforts, along with the clown's revealing that Perdita is a foundling, not the aged shepherd's daughter, discover Perdita's true identity as Leontes's daughter. This allows a happy resolution that, as a gentleman notes, "is so like an old tale, that the verity of it is in strong suspicion" (5.2.28–29). But the "verity" is in the ethical reconfigurations of the play. Actions on the part of those habituated to virtue, encompassing the humble (the clown and aged shepherd) and the noble (Camillo), are combined and augmented by Leontes's penitent consciousness of guilt so as to reorder enveloping contexts, linking together ecosociable renewal and redemptive transformation. The process is completed by Paulina, who combines a life of virtuous practice with a proto-Christian faith in redemption of souls, first of all that of Leontes. By staging a Pygmalion-like "miracle" through revealing the still-living Hermione in the guise of a statue, she uses art to simulate a resurrection, but one in which, as she tells Leontes, "Dear life redeems you" (5.3.103). Though virtue ethics are not the only element that makes life "dear," they are nonetheless indispensible to its ecosociable, redemptive dimensions.

CHAPTER 26

Trust
Don't Ever Change
David Carroll Simon

Taking cues from Shakespeare, this chapter investigates a distinctly anti-ethical experience of trust.[1] My focus is a scene of masculine camaraderie in which someone seeks to confirm the durability of a friend's character by inducing him to fail. In so doing, the bully pursues the enjoyment of disobedience. Both his own provocation and the friend's display of incapacity are transgressions, and he derives pleasure from the badness of their behavior. Yet his aim is much more specific than the frisson of rule-breaking. The friend's unavailing struggle counts as evidence of the persistence of what is most recognizable in him. In this context, trusting the friend means knowing how he can be expected to behave and getting him – prodding him – to perform that dependability. The bully's aggression blurs the distinction between coercion and persuasion; if he elicited something obviously unrelated to the friend's self-assertion, he would not achieve the satisfaction of recognition. While I intend the general character of these initial formulations to invite awareness of continuity across otherwise dissimilar situations, my present goal is only to describe a single case: the first part of Shakespeare's *Henry IV*, where Falstaff is on the receiving end of Prince Hal's loving hostility. I conclude in a speculative vein by considering some of the reasons for which joyful wildness is regularly conceived – in or own time no less than in Shakespeare's – as the repudiation of virtue and by reflecting briefly on what it would take for things to be otherwise.

The scenario comes into sharpest focus in act 2, scene 4, which describes the culmination of a practical joke. Without recapitulating the episode in detail, suffice it for my purposes to recall that Poins and Hal don disguises in order to set upon and rob their friends and fellow thieves, including

---

[1] For trust's uncertain relationship to virtue in Shakespeare and beyond, see Julia Reinhard Lupton, "Trust in Theater," in *The Palgrave Handbook of Affect Studies and Textual Criticism*, eds. Donald R. Wehrs and Thomas Blake (Palgrave Macmillan, 2017). I am indebted to her imaginative account.

Falstaff, thereby demonstrating how easy it is to frighten and overcome them. When Poins originally pitches the idea to Hal, he underscores that the prank invites an ethical failure on Falstaff's part: "the virtue of this jest will be the incomprehensible lies that this same fat rogue will tell us when we meet at supper."[2] What Poins's remark does not acknowledge is that Falstaff's original display of cowardice is no less the object of laughter than his ineptitude as a liar. Falstaff's second failure compounds the first: he lacks the courage to face up to his earlier lack of courage by telling the truth about it. The prank maneuvers him into a situation where he will simulate virtue in a dramatically self-undermining way. The exchange is typical. Across the play's five acts, Falstaff's fleshy failure to keep up – his rotund stuckness – stands in ableist opposition to Hal the improviser's masterful fluidity.[3] As Hal advertises in his much-discussed soliloquy at the end of act 1, scene 2, he is a Machiavel who knows how to seize the moment to accomplish his ends (188–210).[4] Falstaff is a bumbler.

Because Falstaff is also a loveable rapscallion, however, self-sabotage amounts to self-affirmation – which does not mean that he remains unscathed. While emphasizing the coercive, abusive dimensions of Hal's behavior, I want to consider the extent to which Falstaff collaborates in his own humiliation. He participates in an ongoing, rough-and-tumble trust exercise.[5] Poins predicts that Falstaff's lies will be laughably "incomprehensible," but Falstaff's performance of self is knowingly and obviously so – "incomprehensible" in the sense of ostentatiously preposterous. Hal and Poins deceive Falstaff in order to demonstrate what they already know about him: that he is a coward and a liar. Yet Falstaff cares very little about what befalls him. His defenses are knowingly down. The point is delicate because it is obviously not true that Falstaff is not afraid or that he does not intend to carry off his lies; Hal and Poins really do undermine his attempt to dissimulate. Nor is it true that he is utterly indifferent to his humiliation. What is noteworthy about Falstaff's response is his *relative* indifference: how shameless he is about (what little effort he puts into) his wild fabrications

---

[2] William Shakespeare, *The First Part of King Henry the Fourth*, from *The Complete Pelican Shakespeare*, eds. Stephen Orgel and Albert R. Braunmuller (Penguin, 2002), act 1, scene 2, lines 179–181. Hereafter cited parenthetically in the text by act, scene, and line number.

[3] For an illuminating discussion of Falstaff's countervailing ability to "defamiliariz[e] fat," see Royce Best, "Making Obesity Fat: Crip Estrangement in Shakespeare's *Henry IV, Part 1,*" *Disability Studies Quarterly* 39. 4 (2019).

[4] Hal the Machiavel is a critical commonplace, but see especially Stephen Greenblatt, "Invisible Bullets," in *Shakespearean Negotiations: The Circulation of Social Energy in Renaissance England* (University of California Press, 1988), 21–65.

[5] For Shakespearean theater and the trust exercise, see Lupton, "Trust in Theater."

and how unruffled he is when he at last realizes that no one ever believed a word of what he said. Falstaff is not quite bulletproof, but he knows very well that he is already riddled with holes. In bouncing quickly back from the harm that befalls him, he exemplifies William Empson's point that "the plot treats him as a simple Punch, whom you laugh at with good-humour, though he is wicked, because he is always knocked down and always bobs up again."[6] *Trust* is one name for the gratifying predictability of that repetition. Whether or not "you laugh at [him] with good-humour" is more of an open question than Empson acknowledges.

Falstaff's early efforts at misdirection epitomize his style of self-presentation: "A plague of all cowards! Give me a cup of sack, rogue! Is there no virtue extant?" (2.4.112). First comes deception – *you* are cowards, and *I* am brave – which Falstaff soon reformulates as a series of messy, obvious fabrications, including, for instance, repeatedly increasing the number of robbers he claims attacked him. Second, he demands a cup of sack, conveying not the feigned casualness of a practiced fabulist but the actual carelessness of a wayward talker – unless it is just very badly feigned casualness. Third, he speaks from an obviously false place of hyperbolic virtue, as if he were among the only exemplars of goodness left in the world. "Is there no virtue extant?" is a revealing question: Falstaff's comic counterfactuality underlines the extent to which he is defined by his disidentification with "virtue," conceived here as a set of agreed-upon behavioral norms. Falstaff goes on to elaborate the evident falsehood implied by the rhetorical question: "There live not three good men unhanged in England; and one of them is fat, and grows old" (2.4.123–124). Again, the point is not that Falstaff does not want to be believed; he is committed, after a fashion, to deceitful self-trumpeting and unearned self-congratulation. It is just that he fails easily and often – and without caring very much about that predictable result.[7] His fat-phobic attention to his own "fat[ness]" already introduces a de-idealizing element of self-punishing self-awareness.

Falstaff's reaction to the revelation that he has been deceived conveys his resignation to the likelihood of failed self-glorification. After questioning him for some time, drawing out patently absurd details, Hal at last reveals the truth of what happened, and punctuates his triumph with a rhetorical question: "What trick, what device, what starting hole canst thou now find

---

[6] William Empson, *Some Versions of Pastoral* (New Directions, 1972), 108.

[7] In thinking about modes of action that shrug off the question of consequences, I have benefited from Anne-Lise François's searching ethico-philosophical reflections in *Open Secrets: The Literature of Uncounted Experience* (Stanford University Press, 2008).

out to hide thee from this open and apparent shame?" (2.4.252–254). The formulation is strikingly inapposite. Falstaff generally inhabits a condition of "open and apparent shame," and there is no reason to expect that the present instance of that experience will have much of an effect on him. His response amounts to a shrug; he resorts to another silly lie – that he recognized Hal during the robbery and ran "instinct[ively]" away from the danger of "touch[ing] the true prince" – and then he quickly changes the subject (2.4.260). "Shall we have a play extempore?" he asks, gesturing forward to the experiment in role-playing in which he and Hal enact Hal's coming audience with his father (2.4.268). When Hal suggests that the "argument" of the "play extempore" "shall be thy running away," Falstaff replies: "Ah, no more of that, Hal, an thou lovest me!" One irony in this exchange is that Hal deals out so much "of that" because of, rather than in spite of, his "love" for Falstaff, whose flailing is enjoyable because it is distinctly *his*. Another is that Falstaff implies that Hal has now approached the threshold between harmless play and violence when everything about this scene suggests that Hal has not come close to it (which is not to say anything about where the audience – where you or I – might draw that line). Falstaff's exclamation conveys a sentiment like, "Please stop!" – but he says it the way you would say it if you were always saying it. Playful degradation is elemental to their friendship.

When the "play extempore" devolves into comic but vicious name-calling, Hal, performing the role of his father, offers a disturbing description of Falstaff that sheds light on the distinctive character of Falstaff's shamelessness:

> There is a devil haunts thee in the likeness of an old fat man: a tun of man is thy companion. Why dost thou converse with that trunk of humors, that bolting hutch of beastliness, that swoll'n parcel of dropsies, that huge bombard of sack, that stuffed cloakbag of guts, that roasted Manningtree ox with the pudding in his belly, that reverend Vice, that gray iniquity, that father ruffian, that vanity in years? (2.4.432–439)

Much has been written about the role of Falstaff as a caricature of puritan hypocrisy: he adopts the language of the godly but his literal fleshiness is hardly a subtle indication of carnality.[8] Beatrice Groves argues that Falstaff is actually "innocent" in comparison to the godly, from an antipuritan

---

[8] Peter Lake, *How Shakespeare Put Politics on the Stage: Power and Succession in the History Plays* (Yale University Press, 2016), 335. For the puritan Falstaff, see Kristen Poole, *Radical Religion from Shakespeare to Milton: Figures of Nonconformity in Early Modern England* (Cambridge University Press, 2008), 16–44.

perspective, because he openly uses their language to pursue his self-interested and sometimes malevolent ends rather than dissimulating.[9] The point I have been making is different: he is indeed deceitful, but he does not rise to the challenge of fooling anyone. While Hal's litany of damning descriptions can be understood as a rebuke of subterfuge, his insulting metaphors are notable for the weakness of the distinction they draw between interior and exterior. In Royce Best's perceptive discussion of anti-fat rhetoric in this speech, he observes that Hal conjures up a series of closely related images, each of which can be described as "a receptacle holding something monstrous or poisonous," thereby bringing attention to "both ... [Falstaff's] size and repulsive contents."[10] I want to underscore the extent to which these images also suggest the softness of the distinction between the container and the contained, especially insofar as it is also a distinction between the appealing and the unappealing. We are meant to understand immediately that "an old fat man" is not the most seductive "likeness" a "devil" might assume. The other terms with which Hal names metaphorical vessels for Falstaff's villainy are likewise under-deceptive. Indeed, Hal's presentation of corpulence as iniquity undermines the capacity of images of bulk to suggest successful dissimulation: a "trunk," a "bolting hutch," a "swoll'n parcel," a "huge bombard," a "stuffed cloakbag," a "roasted...Ox."[11] Subsequent metaphors do not share the inside/outside structure that defines the first items in the series, but they likewise convey open secrets, if not straightforwardly unhidden things. "Father ruffian," "vanity in years" – these figures do not imply anything like a successful effort at image manipulation. "Reverend Vice" is a possible exception, though the naming of this stock figure is more likely to evoke an experience of recognition than of misidentification. Hal knows the truth about Falstaff: that the very bad truth about Falstaff is always partially, often eminently, visible – and that Falstaff knows this too. Hal's antics amount to a loving caress of Falstaff's "vice." To berate him is to say: There you are! A child who loves a teddy bear will often hug it to shreds.[12]

[9] Beatrice Groves, *Texts and Traditions: Religion in Shakespeare, 1592–1604* (Oxford University Press, 2007), 132.

[10] Best, "Making Obesity Fat."

[11] Best reads Falstaff's self-description beginning with "a goodly portly man" as a "comfortable, soothing" representation of fat (2.4.407; "Making Obesity Fat"). My approach here is to emphasize Falstaff's irony: he knows his self-portrait will be understood as a false front. Indeed, Falstaff makes a conspicuous display of the fakeness of his innocence: "If that man should be lewdly given, he deceiveth me; for, Harry, I see virtue in his looks" (2.4.411–412). Best sees a conflict between Hal's persecutory language of obesity and Falstaff's resistance to such stereotyping, a point I would qualify by noting Falstaff's coerced collaboration with Hal.

[12] Though it is not the place where he discusses dolls and toys as transitional objects, Donald Woods Winnicott's account of the importance of an object's survival of the subject's fantasized destruction

As the play approaches its conclusion, Shakespeare conjures up the fantasy of the friend-who-bounces-back (who "always bobs up again," to return to Empson's phrase) – this time in a literal sense.[13] At the Battle of Shrewsbury, Falstaff plays dead, and then he suddenly springs back to life. Hal exclaims:

> Art thou alive?
> Or is it fantasy that plays upon our eyesight?
> I prithee speak. We will not trust our eyes
> Without our ears. Thou art not what thou seem'st.   (5.4.132–135)

This expression of skepticism is also a request that Falstaff confirm his ongoing presence – as himself, the inimitable Falstaff, and nobody else. "We will not trust our eyes," that is, unless we receive additional evidence that this is you, Sir John Falstaff. To this the dead man responds:

> No, that's certain, I am not a double man; but if I
> be not Jack Falstaff, then am I a jack.   (5.4.136–137)

These lines exemplify the pattern I have described: Falstaff affirms his materiality (he is not a phantom) and his identity ("Jack Falstaff") by not only leaping back to life but repeating the deception: delivering an additional lie – "I am not a double man" – about exactly the question of his trustworthiness. He goes on to deliver one of his wildest fabrications: that he defeated Hotspur in battle. Hal agrees to confirm Falstaff's version of events, but Lancaster's response raises the possibility that no intervention will be necessary for the lie to reveal itself for what it is: "This is the strangest tale that ever I heard" (5.4.151).

When Hal sets his eyes on the resurrected Falstaff, trust is both an experience and a request ("It's you! – but is it you?"), and, as in other encounters between them, it is distinctly anti-ethical: cognitive and affective dimensions of trust (the suppression of skepticism and the gratification of the desire to encounter the friend in his glorious specificity) depend on yet another display of flouted virtue. Missing virtue's mark provides evidence of the persistence of a self who is not distorted by a paradigm conceived

---

of it is what resonates most powerfully with my reading. See "The Use of an Object and Relating through Identifications," in *Playing and Reality* (Routledge, 2005), 115–127.

[13] Cf. Best's discussion of the "inability to overwrite" Falstaff's performance of fatness with degrading representations, which links this scene to several related forms of persistence: not only his capacity to elude "constructions of obesity" but also his reappearance on the stage in different plays ("for Elizabethans Falstaff must have seemed like he would never go away") and his "haunt[ing]" of Hal's journey into kingship ("Making Obesity Fat").

as unsuited to him. Unlike previous performances of failure, however, this one owes nothing to Hal's provocations; it just falls into his lap. Such a development is unsurprising, given the play's unwavering commitment to fulfilling Hal's wishes on his journey to the throne. Perhaps it is not overly extravagant to wonder if here it is Shakespeare – stepping into momentary visibility in pursuit of his desire – who wants to see Falstaff assume his familiar shape. Yes, that's the Falstaff I know!

*

So far, I have attempted a description of a (repeated) scene of gleefully cruel characterology, which plays out against the sharply contrastive backdrop of virtue, but I want in conclusion to reverse foreground and background. When Falstaff declares that "honor is a mere scutcheon," "honor" is a synecdoche of the whole business of being good (5.1.139). Hal and Falstaff's dynamic assumes a conception of virtue as artificial and burdensome, empty and impersonal. While recent scholarship has identified virtue as a synonym for "capacity" and has thoughtfully argued that the project of ethics can be re-imagined, from an egalitarian perspective, as an effort to redistribute power, even this democratizing program cannot avoid the problem diagnosed by *1 Henry IV*: that virtue is often (I do not say "always") alienating.[14] One good reason to be suspicious of virtue is that it plays an important role in social subordination. I will mention two aspects of this problem, each of which is emblematized by one of this chapter's main characters.

First, virtue discourse often makes oppressive assumptions about what powers are worthy of development, blurring the distinction between self-cultivation and self-diminishment, self-cultivation and self-distortion. Simply to notice that "vice" is a common antonym to "virtue" is to recognize how often "virtue" does not serve as a neutral name for a power that might or might not need development – does not invite a conversation about what kind of person someone in particular currently is or wants to become – but points instead to a specific power (or set of powers) about which an unambiguous, even punishing judgment has already been made: the mere fact of not having it amounts to blameworthiness. For Falstaff to be good would be for Falstaff to be someone other than Falstaff.

---

[14] Without implying unanimity among contributors, I refer here to the general orientation of the present volume. See also Lupton, "Trust in Theater," which extends a thread from Martha Nussbaum, *The Fragility of Goodness: Luck and Ethics in Greek Tragedy and Philosophy* (Cambridge University Press, 1986).

Second, virtue is not only injurious because of the prejudices it trans-
mits but also because of how it is transmitted – as Hal's behavior illustrates. It is Hal who benefits most of all from the hierarchies that structure
the play-world, and yet even he identifies virtue with self-estrangement;
hence his hard-to-suppress appetite for the carnival world of Eastcheap.[15]
Hal's euphemized violence points forward to his political ascent, but his
acceptance of that trajectory is not seamless. When virtue is received rather
than chosen – more a question of private acquiescence than of social negotiation – aversion and resistance are unsurprising responses to it. Being the
kind of person most favored by extant hierarchies (in Hal's special case,
being perhaps the *single* person most favored by them) does not quite solve
the problem, even if that circumstance is endlessly advantageous in other –
innumerable – respects. The intimate connection of the two difficulties I
have just named is captured by the following thesis: if people are not equal
co-creators of their lifeworld, the norms of that lifeworld will be burdensome, if not injurious.

To say that it makes good sense to be skeptical of ethics is not to rule out
the possibility of imagining ethics otherwise; it is certainly not, as should
be obvious from my attention to Hal's abusive version of trust, to affirm
all forms of refusal. Hal's darkly comic pursuit of Falstaff's dependability
should be understood as anti-ethics rather than counter-ethics: a series of
small acts of arson. He trusts that a lit match will give him pleasure, and
that Falstaff's extravagant pyrotechnics will give him even more. It is not
hard to see how a life with a permanent uphill advantage might do this to
a person, transmuting comic playfulness into gloating mastery, friendship
into smug intimidation. My purpose in this chapter was more descriptive than hortatory, but I will acknowledge, without insisting on a stark
choice, that I am less hopeful about the possibility of dismantling hierarchy by encouraging the cultivation of virtue than I am about the reverse:
the destruction of hierarchy as an enabling condition for collaborative,
ongoing, noncoercive self-transformation – for experiences of change in
which we can affirm what we are becoming, however fraught with risk,
and however inseparable from loss. There is joyful wildness in that too.

---

[15] As the play moves toward the Battle of Shrewsbury, Hal at last takes exemplary shape as a paragon
of martial virtue. (See Vernon's breathless description of him at 4.1.102–110.)

CHAPTER 27

Being "Free" as a Virtue

Richard Strier

Shakespeare uses "free" and "freedom" many, many times in the plays. Often "freedom" is used in the political and/or legal sense: to signify an alternative to tyranny (republicanism in particular – the conspirators against Julius Caesar as "courtiers of beauteous freedom") or simply release from it ("The time is free" at the end of *Macbeth*); sometimes it signifies release from slavery or contractual bondage as in Shylock's suggestion that the Venetian patricians should say of their slaves, "Let them be free," or Ariel and Caliban's shared desire for freedom from Prospero's power.[1] But the term is also often used to signify a quality of mind or soul.[2] Those with "free souls," says Hamlet, do not have to worry about theatrical representations of wickedness ("let the galled jade wince" [3.2.237–238]), and Jaques says the same about those who don't have to worry about satire ("if he be free / Why then my taxing like a wild-goose flies" [2.7.85–86]). This begins to suggest how "freedom" could be a virtue rather than merely a legal or political condition. A soul that is "free" does not feel itself to be guilty of anything serious, and is therefore invulnerable to being "galled" by general or particular accusations or representations. Being "free" in that sense is a state, a deeply enviable one to those who, like Claudius, have "limed souls" (one wonders whether Shakespeare has been reading Augustine).[3]

---

[1] *Antony and Cleopatra*, 2.6.17, *Macbeth*, 5.8.55; *The Merchant of Venice*, 4.1.94; *The Tempest*, 1.2.245 (Ariel), 2.2.176–183). All are cited from *The Complete Pelican Shakespeare*, eds. Stephen Orgel and Albert R. Braunmuller (Penguin, 2002). All Shakespeare's works are cited from this edition, with (for the plays) act, scene, and line numbers in the text.

[2] In *Shakespeare's Freedom* (University of Chicago Press, 2010), Stephen Greenblatt discusses this in his opening paragraph. The book as a whole, however, concerns Shakespeare's "freedom" from absolutes and Shakespeare's artistic freedom.

[3] In his *Confessions*, Augustine thanks God for having detached his soul from "the birdlime [of earthly pleasure and ambition] which held me fast in death"; he also mentions that his friend Alypius was "astonished" to find Augustine "stuck fast in the glue" of sexual pleasure. See St. Augustine, *Confessions*, trans. Henry Chadwick (Oxford University Press, 1991), VI.vi (9), 97; VI.xii (22), 107. In both cases the word is "*visco*." See *St. Augustine's Confessions*, with an English translation by William

But in the Aristotelean tradition, for something truly to be a virtue, it must involve an activity of the soul; it must be something enacted in the world. It cannot simply be an ascribed or passively possessed condition (it is not clear that Aristotle thinks one can be virtuous while one sleeps).[4]

The positive or active component of being "free" in the ethical sense in Shakespeare is most clearly indicated by the family of words that almost always form part of the description of a person who has this quality. Central to this "family" is the word "generous" and its conceptual cognates. Hamlet is "generous, and free from all contriving" (4.7.133); he asks Laertes to "free" him in his "most generous thoughts" (5.2.219–220). Nature is generous and outgoing, and "being frank she lends to those [who] are free" (sonnet 4, 4). "Freedom" of this sort is both a disposition and an activity. Ulysses says of Troilus that "his heart and hand [are] both open and both free" (4.5.100); Timon's "free heart" gave money to release a friend from imprisonment for debt (1.2.6). Yet to be "free" in the ethical sense, the agent needs not only to be generous but also to be "free" in the ontological and psychological sense that we have described. The "free" soul is unselfconscious and spontaneous. "Let us speak / Our free hearts to each other," says Macbeth, when he is urging interpersonal openness (1.3.154–155). When tension has developed between Brutus and Cassius, there is "respect" between them but not "free and friendly conference" (4.2.17–18). Any kind of withholding from virtuous (or neutral) social behavior is alien to being "free" in this sense.

The preceding discussion begins to hint at what the virtue looks like in Shakespeare. In the rest of this chapter, we will explore how the term and the virtue function in a play to which it is central, one of the great comedies. The term's presence in a comedy is perhaps not surprising, though we will see that it exists there in a rather more complex mode than one might imagine. In conclusion, I will turn briefly to the way in which this virtue can conduce to tragedy. We will see that to have such a potential is intrinsic to the virtue.

Twelfth Night is the play that gives the most explicit and definitive account and representation in Shakespeare of what it means to be "free"

Watts (1631), Loeb Classical Library (Harvard University Press, 1912), 286, 316. If Shakespeare knew this text, he read it in Latin, since no English translation is known before 1631. In "The Long Nightwatch: Augustine, *Hamlet*, and the Aesthetic," *English Literary History* 87 (2020), Rachel Eisendrath points out that Roy Battenhouse made this connection but did not want to claim direct influence. Eisendrath is tempted to make the claim (592).

4 See Aristotle, *Nicomachean Ethics*, trans. Martin Ostwald (Bobbs- Merrill, 1962), 9 (1095^{b}30). Hereafter *NE* followed by the Bekker number and "Ostwald," followed by a page number.

as a condition of character and social behavior rather than as a political or legal condition. The first Act culminates in the introduction of the character who is at the structural center of the play, the Lady Olivia. Much of the action of the play takes place in her household, and fully half the characters in the play are associated with that household. The Lady Olivia gives her steward, a lesson in what it means to be "of free disposition" (1.5.88).[5] This is the first significant thing that we see her do or say, and it is worth looking at the "lesson" and its context in some detail. The scene begins with the introduction of the first major character we have not yet met; he is designated as "clown" but it becomes immediately clear that this means a jester rather than a rustic. A character already self-identified as a lady-in-waiting to Olivia (1.3.4) makes it clear that this "clown" (whose name we are later told, is, appropriately, "Feste" [2.4.11]) is supposed to be part of the household. Maria warns him jestingly that he will be punished for his absence from it ("My lady will hang thee" [5.1.3]).[6] Feste is apparently unconcerned about this, and builds on Maria's hyperbole, beginning to play on the word "hanged." Maria encourages him to continue and extends the conceit herself (4–12). The Fool claims that foolery involves "talents" (1.5.14) and insists, as in the Parable, on their being used (14).[7] The witty dialogue between them continues (still on "hanging") and then on "points," on which Maria puns. Feste praises her for being sharp ("apt") and "witty." And then Olivia enters. Maria, on exiting, advises Feste (seriously, perhaps) to make his excuse to Olivia "wisely." But instead, Feste, as he says, goes for "wit," and proceeds to a rapid-fire mock-learned exposition on the paradoxes of wisdom and folly. But he ends by formally wishing a benediction on the lady.

The Lady's first words are "Take the fool away." This is as we would have expected because Olivia is: (i) obviously a great lady, with many servants; and (ii) dedicated to an extended period – seven years – of

---

[5] On the role of a steward in an aristocratic early-modern household, see Mark Thurston Burnett, *Masters and Servants in English Renaissnce Drama and Culture* (St. Martin's Press, 1997), Chapter 5; and Roger C. Richardson, *Household Servants in Early Modern England* (Manchester University Press, 2010), Chapter 7.

[6] Unathorized absence by a servant "was strictly forbidden" (Richardson, *Household Servants*, 151).

[7] Shakespeare clearly wants the Parable of the Talents (Matthew 25:14–30) and the parallel admonition concerning candles and bushels (Matthew 5:15, Mark 4:21, Luke 8:16 and 11:33) to be very much on our minds as *Twelfth Night* develops. Not only are "talents" that should be used referred to here, but the idea was already introduced two scenes earlier in the dialogue between Sir Toby and Sir Andrew (1.3.117; with the idea repeated a few lines later at 1.3.123). No other play foregrounds the parable in this way (a dubious "talent" is comically praised in *Love's Labor's Lost* (4.2.62–64), and the parable is somewhat more seriously but still only glancingly referred to in *Cymbeline* [1.6.78–79]).

mourning for her recently deceased brother, becoming "like a cloistress" (1.1.27–31). So we would not expect that she would be inclined to waste any time with the professional jester she has inherited (or concern herself with his whereabouts).[8] The fool tries to turn the tables in a comic way, saying "Take away the lady," but The Lady is not amused. She calls him unwitty ("dry") and, more seriously, accuses him of growing "dishonest" (38). But Feste will not be discouraged. He picks up on both parts of her condemnation of him, and plays pseudo-homiletically on the whole question of "mending" dishonesty. He ends his long speech by returning to his original gesture, but now making it clear that he means to be echoing Olivia's command to take the fool away: "The lady bade take away the fool, therefore, I say again, take her away" (48–49). But again, Olivia is not amused. Perhaps with slight aggravation, or perhaps just wanting to be clear, she says, politely but reprovingly, "Sir, I bid them take away you." But at this point something strange happens. Feste turns to her and says, "Good madonna, give me leave to prove you a fool." This would seem like a dangerous maneuver, but the interesting feature of it is the request for permission – "give me leave." The fool is not prepared to go any further in boldness than he has already gone without explicit permission. But why would he ask for such permission unless he knew that there was a chance that it would be granted? Lear's fool would not think of asking such to Goneril (whose first words in her own house express offense at the behavior of her father's fool [*Lear* 1.3.1–2] and whose first words to her father in her house concern the "license" that he gives to this fool [*Lear* 1.4: Q 187; F 185]).[9] Feste must have known that, despite Olivia's veiled and pseudo-"cloistered" state, she is capable, like Maria, of appreciating wit and foolery. And he turns out to be right. Instead of being offended at the idea of being "proved" a fool, the Lady is intrigued by the possibility. Instead of ordering, again, that the fool be taken away, she is now eager for him to proceed and curious about how he will do so, asking "Can you do it?"

---

[8] In the passage where we are told Feste's name, we are told that he is a fool "that the Lady Olivia's father took much delight in (2.4.11–12).

[9] Shakespeare cannot have hoped that anyone would pick up on the analogy and contrast between the two great ladies and their fathers' fools in two of his fool plays, but this must have been present in Shakespeare's mind. Goneril's entrance in 1.4 of *King Lear* is exactly parallel to Olivia's in 1.5 of *Twelfth Night*. The repetition by Lear's Fool of the refrain of the song that Feste sings as the epilogue to *Twelfth Night* – "For the rain it raineth every day" – suggests that Shakespeare had the earlier play and its fool in mind when composing *King Lear* (see *KL* 3.2: Q 79; F 78 [with "For" changed to "Though"]). *Twelfth Night* dates from 1601–1602; *Lear* (Q) from 1605.

Of course, Feste can. He relies, quite effectively, on a basic Christian paradox (why mourn for a person one believes to be in heaven?).[10] Olivia appreciates this gambit, and turns to the other major character we have not yet encountered, her steward, to see what he will say about it. So Shakespeare introduces these two major characters in relation to the fool, who has just been introduced in this scene. Feste is much more of a "touchstone" in this play than Touchstone is in his. Olivia must know that her steward, another character with an informative name, is going to disapprove of the fool. Malvolio makes a predictably dour remark about wisdom and folly – on which the fool happily builds (it's one of his favorite topoi), finding a way to call Malvolio a fool too. And now Olivia jumps in. She urges Malvolio on. She wants him to answer in kind. She is anticipating a battle of wits. "How say you to that, Malvolio?" she asks. But Malvolio won't play. Instead of answering the fool, he turns to Olivia and expresses surprise that she "takes delight" in Feste's remarks, first denigrating Feste's professional abilities and then noting that a professional jester cannot proceed or succeed unless he is permitted to do so (recall "give me leave"): "unless you laugh and minister occasion to him, he is gagged" (82–83). This is a brilliant formulation. But instead of answering it, Olivia remarks on what the observation reveals about Malvolio's character. She accuses him of being "sick of self-love" and therefore being unable to judge things correctly, having (in what is itself a fine pun) "a distempered appetite" (sick and malicious and, perhaps, out of tune). She then gives her definition of the relevant kind of health: "to be generous, guiltless, and of free disposition" (87–88). To be in this state is to be able to take a joke, indeed to recognize what a joke is and what the role of a fool in a community is – "there is no slander in an allowed fool."[11]

Dramatically, this is a lovely moment, a turnabout. One might stage it by having Olivia enter in stately fashion arm-in-arm with Malvolio and then unlink from him and move closer to Feste. When Olivia's drunken cousin, Sir Toby, makes a brief appearance, Olivia does indeed "minister occasion" to Feste, asking, "What's a drunken man like, fool?" They then collaborate on developing the conceit with which the fool answers (1.5.125–132). But the content as well as the dramaturgy of the lesson that Olivia gives to Malvolio bears analysis. As the culminating phrase, "of free

---

[10] Interestingly, this idea is the basis of the favorite joke of another of Shakespeare's great comic characters, Richard 3. See Richard Strier, *The Unrepentant Renaissance from Petrarch to Shakespeare to Luther* (University of Chicago Press, 2011), 100–101.

[11] The Fool's "allowed" ("all-licensed") status is exactly what annoys Goneril (*KL* 1.4: Q 197, F 195]).

disposition" makes clear, each of her terms refers less to behavior than to a state of mind or being – an attitude toward the world, and especially, toward other persons. The contrast, as Olivia says, is with "self-love." What this seems to mean here is something like what Luther, adapting Augustine, called the state of being *"incurvatus in se"* (curved in upon oneself).[12] It means something like being concentrated only on one's own needs, desires, preferences, etc., never caring to minister occasion to others or to allow legitimacy to modes of being different from one's own and even that one could, potentially, be offended by. In such a state there is no outward flow of spirit. That is why, in the world of the play, the word that stands as the comedic and material equivalent of "self-love" is "obstruction" (see 3.4.19; 4.2.39).[13] A person who has the qualities that Olivia describes is unobstructed in his or her outward flow of affection or appreciation – unobstructed by the self-consciousness that feelings of guilt or of one's own special dignity can produce. Olivia's rebuke to Malvolio is the key to the value-structure of the entire play.

Appreciation is (as in Aristotle) an activity, and it is one that the play values and regularly stages. In the opening scene, where Duke Orsino could easily – as we will see other characters do – perceive Lady Olivia's dedication to mourning her brother as revealing something wrong in her, the Duke instead sees it in the opposite way, as a positive indicator, a signal of the depth of feeling of which she is capable. Instead of seeing Olivia as perverse, the Duke sees her as "she that hath a heart of that fine frame" (1.1.34). In the next scene, where the other female lead actually appears, we watch the shipwrecked Viola deciding to trust rather than to distrust "fair behavior" in a relative stranger. She is aware that she could be wrong. She knows what the cynic knows: that "nature with a beauteous wall / Doth oft close in pollution." But she makes a decision to trust in appearances: "I will believe that thou hast a mind that suits / With this thy fair and outward character" (1.2.48–51). And Olivia herself returns the favor, so to speak, that we have seen in the Duke's evaluation of her.

---

[12] On the difference between Augustine's use of *"curvatus"* to describe human sinfulness and Luther's use of the word, see Anders Nygren, *Agape and Eros*, trans. Philip S. Watson (The Society for Promoting Christian Knowledge, 1953; Harper and Row, 1969), 709–716.

[13] This play asks us to pay particular attention to individual words, especially slightly exotic ones. An example would be the treatment of "element." In the opening scene, a servant of Orsino's (wonderfully named Valentine) reports Olivia using the word in a physical sense, meaning sky or air (1.1.26); "Cesario" uses it in the same way (1.5.279); Sir Toby refers to "the four elements" (2.3.10); Feste mentions the word as a possibility for metaphorical use but rejects it as "over-worn" (3.1.59–60); and then Malvolio uses it, with great emphasis, in its social (class) application where it is the culmination of his fantasy of being "Count Malvolio": "I am not of your element" (3.4.125).

She "cannot love" him, but she acknowledges that he is not only noble and of great estate, but "of fresh and stainless youth … free, learned and valiant" (1.5.263–264). She recognizes her favorite quality in him; he is "free."

In a scene that parallels that in which we met Viola, Viola's supposedly lost brother (Sebastian) appreciates the tact that Antonio, an equivalent to the captain who helped Viola, shows toward him, and feels obliged "in manners" to respond in full to the demand that he recognizes has not been made on him (2.1.11–14). Like "manners," music, and the appreciation of it, pervades the play from its opening line. The scene following the introduction of Sebastian and Antonio is the musical one in which Sir Toby and his entourage (Sir Andrew and the fool) resist Malvolio's attempt to make the world (the household) in his own image ("because thou art virtuous, there shall be no more cakes and ale" [2.3.106–107]). Where Sir Toby and company appreciate the fool's "mellifluous voice" and surprisingly philosophical (Epicurean) song, Malvolio hears their performance as disgustingly lower-class in both sound (they "gabble like tinkers") and genre ("cozier's [cobbler's] catches" [2.3.84–85]). But the next scene, at court, is another musical one focused on Feste's singing. Orsino was introduced in line 1 of the play as a highly sentimental music-lover, and here he enters the stage praising and requesting a musical performance by Feste – this one an "old and plain" song, for which the Duke postulates a brilliantly evoked village context (2.2.43–46). Unlike Malvolio, Orsino, a true aristocrat, does not have disdain for lower-class music.[14] Viola as Cesario also responds to the tune of the remembered song and does so (2.2.21–22a) with an eloquence that the Duke also appreciates. He says to "Cesario" quite accurately, "Thou dost speak masterly" (2.4.22b). So verbal excellence is also regularly appreciated, as we have already seen with regard to "wit." This continues. Sir Toby and one of the household servants (Fabian) highly appreciate the wit that Maria has shown in penning the letter that capitalizes on Malvolio's ambition and self-love (2.5.173–198). Viola, who, unlike Olivia, is made uncomfortable by Feste, nonetheless recognizes and admires Feste's verbal skill and social intelligence. She devotes an entire soliloquy to developing the idea that "This fellow is wise enough to play the fool" (3.1.59–67). Orsino, similarly disinclined by temperament to foolery, also notes and appreciates Feste's verbal ability. To Feste's tour-de-force paradoxical encomium of enemies (5.1.11–22), Orsino responds, "Why this is excellent."

---

[14] In George Herbert's poem "Gratefulnesse," God is such an aristocrat. His love is "taken" by "countrey-aires" of a particular sort. See *The Works of George Herbert*, ed. Francis Earnest Hutchinson (Clarendon, 1945), 123–124.

Generosity, as I have suggested, and as Olivia's lesson makes clear, goes along with – or is a component of – "freedom" in the play ("To be generous, guiltless, and of free disposition"). Appreciation can be seen as a generosity of spirit.[15] The play certainly sees it this way, but the play foregrounds generosity in a literal sense as well – perhaps even more emphatically. Giving money is the recurrent gesture of the play. In response to the captain assuring Viola that her brother may have survived the shipwreck that separated them, Viola responds, "For saying so, there's gold" (1.2.17). Olivia appreciates Cesario's eloquence on behalf of Orsino, and says to "him," "Spend this for me" (1.5.272). Viola rejects the money, but the gesture has been made. Sebastian, somehow not as well provided as his sister, is embarrassed that he can offer Antonio only the "uncurrent pay" of thanks. Antonio then gives Sebastian his purse, out of which the young man is to spend at will (3.3.44–45). When Antonio is arrested and finds that, under the circumstances, he needs his money back from the person he thinks to be Sebastian, Antonio is horrified at that person's lack of immediate compliance. He is profoundly troubled by the lack of fit between external and internal beauty in this person. His speeches on these subjects are truly powerful (3.4.344–348, 350–355). He thinks that Sebastian "has done good feature[s] shame" (compare Viola's evocation of "a beauteous wall" that "Doth oft close in pollution"). But what the scene actually gives us is exactly the opposite of what Antonio denounces. Viola, who has expressed a special loathing for ingratitude as the worst character flaw and type of bad behavior (3.4.339–340), performs an act of moral beauty (thereby redeeming "good features"). She performs an amazing act of generosity. Out of gratitude for Antonio's intervention on her side in the "duel" together with compassion for his current situation, she gives Antonio "half [her] coffer" even though, she does not know him, and, as she says, her "having is not much" (3.3.327–332).[16]

But the main recipient of money in the play is Feste. Appreciation of him is regularly shown materially as well as verbally. In the *Odyssey*, "strangers and beggars come from Zeus."[17] Sir Andrew, for all his limitations, knows the code. He "sent sixpence" to Feste, who appreciates the

---

[15] For some general reflections on this, see Joseph Kupfer, "Generosity of Spirit," *Journal of Value Inquiry* 32 (1998), 357–368.

[16] This is a model action that shows generosity or liberality not to be class-bound. As Aristotle says, "a generous act does not depend on the amount given … it is quite possible that a person who gives less is more generous [than one who gives more], if his gift comes from smaller resources" (*NE* 1120^{b}8–10; Ostwald, 81).

[17] *The Odyssey*, trans. Robert Fitzgerald (Doubleday, 1961), 6.222–223; 14.69–70. Singers too.

"gratility" (2.3.27). Sir Toby then gives Feste another sixpence for singing to them, to which Sir Andrew pledges another (2.3.30–32). When Feste sings for Orsino, the Duke also gives money, graciously saying "There's for thy pains" – which Feste then turns into a bit of mock-moralizing with which Orsino plays along (2.4.67–71). The interchange that Viola has with Feste when the two are alone together is abrasive. Nonetheless, she will not allow him to leave empty-handed, saying "Hold, there's expenses for thee," and she then gives him yet another coin for begging it well (3.1.43–53). When, having been absent from the scene of Antonio's arrest, Sebastian does appear, he is accosted by Feste, who thinks that "Cesario" is being weird and obstinate in not responding to Olivia's message. Sebastian is understandably annoyed; he has never seen Feste before. He sends Feste away, but even in doing so, gives, saying, "There's money for thee" (4.1.18). In the interchange about enemies, Orsino not only commends Feste's wit but wants to be marked among the community of the generous, saying, "Thou shalt not be the worse for me; there's gold" (5.1.26). And then, as did Viola, Orsino gives again (and himself makes a joke about it [5.1.32–33]). Feste is self-conscious about his begging – not only in terms of its wit, of which he is proud, but in terms of its morality, of which he is worried. In a complex sentence about "having," Feste tells the Duke, "I would not have you to think that my desire of having is the sin of covetousness" (5.1.43–44). We are meant, I think, to recognize this latter claim as true. Feste begs as he sings and produces witty sayings – as part of his situation. He is, as Malvolio pointed out, truly dependent. Every "free" soul recognizes this, and responds to it as an occasion for generosity.

Anything that interferes with the free flow of "bounty" (5.1.41), either social or natural, is seen in the play as negative. Olivia's withholding of her beauty from erotic circulation is condemned (and, in the course, of the play, soon corrected). She needs to attain a fully "free" state. The lesson given to her is that which Shakespeare's "marriage sonnets" give to the young man: "What is yours to bestow is not yours to reserve" (1.5.181). Compare "given thee to give" in Sonnet 4. The Parable of the Talents governs.

Having spent so much time on a comedy, a world in which generosity prevails and beauty and virtue coincide, I will only briefly discuss how the virtue of being "free" operates in a tragic context. But this is easy to see. That Hamlet is "generous" and "free" are qualities that Claudius knows he can rely on in plotting against Hamlet. But the most sustained treatment is in *Othello*. In the first of Iago's soliloquies (1.3.374–396), Iago turns from thinking about his bilking of Roderigo to his reason number 2 for hating the Moor (number 1 was Iago's failure to get the promotion he wanted); number 2 is the supposed rumor that Othello has had an affair with Iago's wife. Here (as opposed to in his next soliloquy [see 2.1.293–296]), Iago himself doesn't actually seem to believe the rumor but brushes that issue aside in his determination to find a way to harm both Othello and the person who did get the promotion (Cassio), and so achieve "a double knavery." Iago will use Cassio's physical and social gifts (his person and his "smooth dispose") for this purpose. But why does Iago think that this, as he says, "monstrous" plan will work? The answer is because "The Moor is of a free and open nature" and "thinks men honest" that "seem to be so." Iago is an expert in creating trust – his "plain man" pose is a great part of this – but he is also counting on Othello's "free" nature, on Othello's predisposition to trust rather than to be suspicious.[18] We have seen this predisposition in Viola, who knows it is a danger but goes with it nonetheless, and is rewarded. In tragedy, this predisposition is not rewarded. It is a liability to be exploited by the vicious or corrupt.

Iago's plan relies not only on Othello having a "free" nature, but also, and perhaps even more so, on Desdemona having such as well. After Iago succeeds in getting Cassio into a drunken state in which Cassio behaves shamefully and dangerously, Iago realizes that he can use this success as a means to destroy Othello: Iago will get Desdemona to plead for Cassio's reinstatement, and she will do so in such a vigorous a manner that Iago can make it plausible that "she repeals him for her body's lust" (2.3.345). Like Claudius, Iago will pour his poison into his victim's ear ("I'll pour this pestilence into his ear"), but in Iago's case, the "poison" is suspicion (of sexual betrayal), distrust. But, again, what makes Iago so confident that this will work? Again, a free disposition is the key – in this case, Desdemona's. In advising Cassio, Iago assures him that Desdemona is "of so free, so kind, so apt, so blest a disposition that she holds it a vice in her goodness not to do more than she is requested" (2.3.307–309). Iago can count on Desdemona going above and beyond what normal graciousness would require (think of Viola giving the helpful Captain, whom she does not know, half her coffer). Iago is correct. We see Desdemona taking on the task of advocating for Cassio's reinstatement with energy and high good humor. She says of Othello "I'll watch him tame and talk him out of patience, / His bed shall seem a school …" [3.3.23–25]. And she does this, relying on what she

---

[18] On Iago's plain man pose (and style), see Richard Strier, "Paleness versus Eloquence: The Ideologies of Style in the English Renaissance," *Explorations in Renaissance Culture* 45 (Fall, 2019), 91–120 (esp. 107–120).

had earlier evoked as a good woman's "authority of her merit" (2.1.145–146) and on her wifely prerogative to make fun of Othello for denying her something that is (as she sees it) obviously to his advantage and barely a "boon" (3.3.60–83). But Shakespeare wants to remind us of the character structure, the ethical character structure, that produces all this – and that Iago exploits. In the soliloquy in which Iago reflects on setting Cassio to set Desdemona to work on Othello, Shakespeare has Iago repeat the point about Desdemona's nature, putting it in gorgeous ontological terms: "She's fram'd as fruitful / As the free elements" (2.3.329–330). In generating agricultural products, nature is "free," but only by analogy to the human virtue.

Iago acts in a way that mirrors divine providence in reverse. Where the Christian God makes goodness ultimately proceed out of evil (the famous strategy of "*felix culpa*"), Iago does the opposite.[19] Out of Desdemona's goodness, he plans to "make the net / That shall enmesh them all" (2.3.349–350). And he does. Shakespeare recognized that the virtue of manifesting a "free disposition" involves vulnerability – a vulnerability that can be exploited. The vulnerability is inherent to the virtue. This is what makes it a potential component of tragedy and gives the comedy that emphasizes it a poignant quality. But the virtue really is a virtue. Despite the vulnerability feature, Shakespeare certainly saw it as a much more admirable human state to be fundamentally oriented toward trust and generosity rather than toward distrust, cynicism, and exclusive self-love.[20] The possibility of tragedy does not change this.

---

[19] *See* John Milton, *Paradise Lost*, ed. Merritt Y. Hughes (Odyssey Press, 1957), 12.471–472, and A. O. Lovejoy's famous essay on "Milton and the Paradox of the Fortunate Fall," *Essays in the History of Ideas* (G. P. Putnam's Sons, 1960), 277–295. On *Othello* as "Shakespeare's *Paradise Lost*," see Richard Strier, "Excuses, Bepissing, and Non-being: Shakespearean Puzzles about Agency," in *Shakespeare and Moral Agency*, ed. Michael D. Bristol (Continuum, 2010), 64 (revised and expanded in *Shakespearean Issues: Agency*, Skepticism, and Other Puzzles (University of Pennsylvania Press, 2022), chapter 1.

[20] For "self-delight" that is not anti-social, see Richard Strier, "Happiness," in *Shakespeare and Emotion*, ed. Katharine A. Craik (Cambridge University Press, 2020), 275–287, esp. 282–4.

PART III

Shakespeare and Global Virtue Traditions

CHAPTER 28

Shakespeare's Rabbinic Virtues
A Listening Ear

Stephanie Shirilan

In 1541, the German Reformer Paul Fagius published a translation, with commentary, of *Pirke Avot*, a tractate of one of the six books of the Mishna[1] that is comprised almost entirely of ethical sayings attributed to the rabbinic sages.[2] Literally "Chapters of the Fathers," the work is referred to in rabbinic tradition simply as *Avot*, or Fathers. Fagius titled his translation *Sententiae vere elegantes, piae, mireque: cum ad linguam discendam, tum animum excolendum utiles veterum sapientum Hebraeorum* ("truly elegant thoughts of the Hebrew sages, useful for the cultivation of the spirit"). *Pirke Avot* appeared in multiple translations during the sixteenth century, suggesting its appeal as a work of ethical rather than legal concern and one that could serve Christian moral didactic purposes more readily than the Talmud, which stood in the Christian imaginary as the icon of Jewish legalism.[3] The sixth chapter of *Avot* describes the *middoth* of the pious scholar. While the term "middoth" does not precede this particular list, it is used consistently in *Avot* (and rabbinic literature in general) to designate attributes or qualities that have been translated into English as "virtues." The English term "virtue," with its origins in the Latin for manliness, the Anglo-Norman for strength, and the abstract ideals of excellence variously defined by Greek and Roman philosophers, is conceptually quite distant from "*middah*," which derives from *madad* or "measure" and suggests an

---

[1] The Mishna was redacted into its current form in the early third century. Its contents reflect legal and interpretive traditions that were preserved orally as the Oral Torah, or *Torah She-be'al-peh*, dating back to the fifth-century BCE.

[2] The book was printed in Isny with the assistance of Elia Levita, the Jewish Hebraist with whom Fagius collaborated on several other Hebrew grammars and rabbinic works. Fagius (1504–1549) was educated at Strasbourg, where he was a student of the early Christian Hebraist, Conrad Pellican. After his rejection of the Augsburg Interim Agreement, Thomas Cranmer secured a lectureship for him at Cambridge, where he taught Hebrew for a few months before dying of the plague.

[3] See Stephen Burnett, "The Regulation of Hebrew Printing in Germany, 1555–1630: Confessional Politics and the Limits of Jewish Toleration," in *Jews, Judaism, and the Reformation in Sixteenth-Century Germany*, eds. Dean Phillip Bell and Stephen Burnett (Brill, 2006), 503–527.

ethical standard for interpersonal conduct.[4] *Middah* is relational rather than immanent or transcendent, and yet, like virtue, it is demonstrated in practice. While noting these important differences, I use the terms "virtue" and "virtue ethics" in this chapter in order to illuminate the sublimated homologies and genealogical ties between Christian and Jewish virtue ethics. The list of *middoth* in *Avot* 6:6 is long, but one stands out as paradigmatic both of the set and of the genre of Oral Torah to which it belongs: *shmiat ha'ozen*. This *middah* is typically translated as the virtue of having an "attentive" or "listening ear."[5] *Shmiat ha'ozen* expresses the entwined ethical and interpretive value of attentive listening in rabbinic Judaism. This chapter seeks to demonstrate the sublimated presence of this virtue as a Jewish virtue in *The Tempest*.[6]

In his introduction to the *Sententiae,* Fagius defends the study of rabbinic ethics on the grounds that, for the Jews, "moral philosophy was a religious concern rather than a mere intellectual or oratorical one," arguing that "if humanists were justified in studying classical sources for more than literary style, certainly an investigation of Pharisaic sources must be free from blame."[7] Fagius elaborates this defense elsewhere when he proclaims the utility of "the writings of the Hebrews, not only for the translation of language but for the cultivation of piety."[8] But, if Fagius's estimation of rabbinic ethics is more genial than that of his Lutheran counterparts, it is nonetheless principally typological in its insistence that rabbinic ethics are not merely compatible with apostolic teachings but fulfilled through them, as his glosses and insertions constantly emphasize.[9] This supersessionary logic rationalizes not just the Christian use but appropriation of Jewish virtues and ethical writings, a procedure whose violence this chapter traces, both in the basic contours of *The Tempest*'s

---

[4] Martin Buber suggested "modes" (*Two Types Of Faith* [Macmillan, 1951], 152–153). See Francis Brown, Samuel Rolles Driver, and Charles Augustus Briggs, *A Hebrew and English Lexicon of the Old Testament* (Houghton Mifflin, 1907), 551.

[5] Fagius translates *shmiat ha'ozen* as *auscultatione,* the ablative form of the verbal noun, auscultatio, "a listening, attending to," or "obeying," related to the verb ausculto, "to hear with attention, listen to, give ear to."

[6] I use the term "sublimation" to describe the process whereby unacceptable desires and/or behaviors are converted into idealized forms without acknowledging the relationship of the latter to the former. My reading of Christian supersession as sublimation draws on Hegel's concept of *Aufhebung.* I have found surprisingly few, and rather tentative, theorizations of this kind. See William Nicholls, *Christian Antisemitism: A History of Hate* (Rowman & Littlefield, 1993), 316; Jonathan Gil Harris, *Untimely Matter in the Time of Shakespeare* (University of Pennsylvania Press, 2009), 30.

[7] Jerome Friedman, *The Most Ancient Testimony: Sixteenth-Century Christian-Hebraica in the Age of Renaissance Nostalgia* (Ohio University Press, 1983), 112.

[8] Ibid., 109.

[9] Ibid., 112.

plot and more resonantly in the oneiric distribution of themes and signifiers in the play that I analyze as a kind of supersession dream-work.[10] Katherine Eggert suggests that *The Tempest* bears witness to the deliberately superficial reading of Kabbalistic texts by Christian writers who sought out Jewish texts while keeping their corrupting otherness at arm's length.[11] I suggest that we hear the sound of that othering as the sound of supersessionary sublimation: the re-emergence of "drowned" books and fathers in the language (literally the song) of the deep. I argue, further, that *The Tempest* bears witness to this sublimation in the "sounding" (both plumbing and amplifying) of submerged memory and the auditory virtue demonstrated by its percipients.

Hearing the Virtue of Jewish Hearing

While numerous scholars have noted the connections between virtue and hearing in *The Tempest*,[12] fewer have observed that the lesson Prospero learns at the end of the play, that "The rarer action is / In virtue than in vengeance," is one he, too, learns by listening.[13] The didactic narrator, who tolerates neither inattention nor interruption and who controls the island with musical charms administered by his spirit servant, is finally moved to mercy by *hearing* that same spirit. Ariel describes how the charms he has performed at Prospero's bidding have rendered the King and his co-conspirators into objects of pity, the "remainder mourning over them, / Brimful of sorrow and dismay" (5.1.13–14). Prospero is moved but does not relent until goaded to creaturely compassion by a spirit who, purportedly, cannot feel the same. The moment recalls another story that begins in tempest and ends with ethical remonstration: the Book of Jonah.[14]

---

[10] I use Freud's term "dream-work" (*traumarbeit*) for the dreamer's conversion of latent content into manifest content through devices of condensation, displacement, and secondary elaboration. See Sigmund Freud, *The Interpretation of Dreams*, trans. A. A. Brill, 3rd ed. (Macmillan, 1913), Chapter 6.

[11] Katherine Eggert, *Disknowledge: Literature, Alchemy, and the End of Humanism in Renaissance England* (University of Pennsylvania Press, 2015), Chapter 3.

[12] See Joseph M. Ortiz, *Broken Harmony: Shakespeare and the Politics of Music* (Cornell University Press, 2011), 171; David Bevington, "Hearing and Overhearing in The Tempest," in *Who Hears in Shakespeare?: Auditory Worlds on Stage and Screen*, eds. Laury Magnus and Walter Cannon (Fairleigh Dickinson University Press, 2012), 104; Jennifer Linhart Wood, *Sounding Otherness in Early Modern Drama and Travel: Uncanny Vibrations in the English Archive* (Palgrave Macmillan, 2019), 275–318.

[13] *The Tempest*, 5.1.27–28. William Shakespeare, *The Norton Shakespeare*, eds. Stephen Greenblatt, Walter Cohen, Suzanne Gossett, Jean E. Howard, Katharine Eisaman Maus, and Gordon McMullan, 2nd ed. (W.W. Norton, 2008), 3098. Unless otherwise indicated, all references to Shakespeare's plays are to this edition and will hereafter be cited parenthetically in the text.

[14] On the "actively passive or ... *passionate* state designated by creatureliness," see Julia Reinhard Lupton, "Creature Caliban," *Shakespeare Quarterly* 51 (2000), 1.

God reprimands Jonah for caring more for a plant (that sheltered him in his anguish over Nineveh's unlikely preservation) than for the life that would have perished had the Ninevites not heard Jonah's prophesy and repented. Whereas the Book of Jonah ends with God's reproach, Prospero hears and responds to Ariel's intercession ("Your charm so strongly works 'em / That if you now beheld them your affections / Would become tender") as a challenge to his own humanity: "Dost thou think so, spirit?" Ariel replies: "Mine would, sir, were I human" (5.1.17–19). Ariel's supposed incapacity for creaturely compassion prompts Prospero to prove his greater capacity for mercy, being human: "Hast thou, which art but air, a touch, a feeling / Of their afflictions, and shall not myself, / One of their kind, that relish all as sharply / Passion as they, be kindlier moved than thou art?" (5.1.21–24).

The Jonah echo raises the specter of Jewish ethics in the play's auditory appeal: an ethics based in the virtue of the listening ear. Uncanny sounds in *The Tempest* have been extensively considered as signifiers of "new world," indigenous otherness. Jennifer Wood contests the hemispheric bias of such readings, hearing more global, if disoriented, sounds of otherness in a play whose "sonics ... [shake] up our ... sense of the binarized categories of familiar and foreign, self and other, noise and music."[15] I want to suggest that the sonic uncanny of indigenous otherness and dispossession in *The Tempest* reverberates more profoundly still when heard in relation to Christian supersession and its suppressed memory of Jewish ethical listening.

The supersessionary account of Christ's triumph (love over law, mercy over justice) violently suppresses the importance of compassionate listening in rabbinic virtue ethics and the scriptural foundations for this schema. From the direct vocations of the Patriarchs and prophets, to the sound of the shofar that precedes the Decalogue (and serves as the summons to repentance thereafter), to the quintessential statement of Jewish faith in the Shema prayer that commands Israel to hear and to love (Deut 6:4), listening is the primary mode of Jewish spiritual attunement. Key to the framing of Christianity as the overcoming of the flesh by the spirit is the representation of the Jew as hard not just of heart but hearing – having "uncircumcised ears," impenetrable or, more suggestively, "unpierceable" organs of acoustic sense.[16]

---

[15] Wood, *Sounding Otherness*, 317.
[16] The pierced ear of the Old Testament bondslave marks a submission that is read by Christian reformers as the spiritual privilege of the pierced (and pierceable) heart.

While the trope of the deaf Jew is well-established in the Gospels, it becomes a sign of the radical alterity of reprobation in the Reformation.[17] Late sixteenth- and early seventeenth-century English sermonists consistently marked the open ear as the sign of an open heart, a Christian heart of flesh regenerated out of its stony predecessor through ears that hear.[18] William Perkins uses the phrase "an hearing eare" to distinguish between "two kinds of hearers" of the Word:

> one is a deafe hearer, not hauing an hearing eare; as those which bring outward and bodily eares to the word, but not the eares of the hart: for their hearts are not affected with the word, they cannot obey that they heare. Secondly, there is an hearing hearer, who not only heareth with the outward eare of the bodie, but he hath his heart pierced and touched, hath new eares made by Gods spirit.[19]

While Perkins is not speaking here of the Jews, his distinction between "outward and bodily" ears and "eares of the hart" rehearses the paradigmatic opposition of the so-called literalism of Jewish hermeneutics and the inspired Christian hearing of the Word as it appears throughout the Gospels and is elaborated in Paul's explanation for Jewish reprobation in Romans 11:7–8.

Protestant writers made ample use of the Hebrew prophets and wisdom literature, drawing on the moral didacticism of the latter and citing the former as evidence of the "deafness" of the Jewish people to God's message and messengers.[20] The emphasis in Hebrew scripture on redemptive listening proved more difficult to reconcile with the elaborated typology

---

[17] The uncircumcised ear becomes the figurative sign of Jewish deafness, exemplified by the ritual of circumcision for Calvin: "surely, the cutting off of a small pellicle does not satisfy God ... uncircumcision remains in your hearts, and it remains in your ears; ye are then heathens" (Jean Calvin, *Commentaries on the Book of the Prophet Jeremiah and The Lamentations*, trans. J. Owen [Calvin Translation Society, 1851], 329).

[18] The emphasis on the dangers of auditory impressionability (the ear as weak sentry) in early-modern scholarship has distracted from a prevailing and opposite concern in the period: calls to conscience falling on "deaf" ears. This is so overdetermined a metaphor in Reformation theology that physical deafness was understood by some writers as a sign of reprobation. See Jennifer Rae McDermott, "'The Melodie of Heaven': Sermonizing the Open Ear in Early Modern England," in *Religion and the Senses in Early Modern Europe*, eds. Wietse de Boer and Christine Göttler (Brill, 2012), 177–200; Emily Cockayne, "Experiences of the Deaf in Early Modern England," *The Historical Journal* 46 (2003), 497.

[19] William Perkins, *Lectures Vpon the Three First Chapters of the Reuelation* (Cuthbert Burbie, 1604), 154.

[20] Luther delights in the irony of Jeremiah's phrase "uncircumcised ear" to describe Jewish deafness to prophesy: "Well, well, my dear Jeremiah ... Do you mean to say that such a holy nation has uncircumcised ears? And, what is far worse, that they are unable to hear? Is that not tantamount to saying that they are not God's people? For he who cannot hear or bear to hear God's Word is not of God's people." Martin Luther, "About the Jews and Their Lies," *The Annotated Luther*, ed. Hans Hillerbrand, trans. Martin Bertram, vol. 5 (Fortress Press, 2017), 471.

of Jewish otherness that stood, after the Reformation, for all manner of Christian heresy. The Reformation did double violence to the memory of Jewish listening both by obscuring the redemptive power of sound in Hebrew scripture and Jewish ethics and by figuring Jewish deafness as the type to an antitype of hearing that is reserved for the elect. Protestant glosses on Paul's teaching that "faith cometh by hearing, and hearing by the word of God" (Rom. 10:17 KJV) emphasized the instrumentality of the ear to salvation and the Christian particularity of such redemptive listening:

> *Paul* sayeth of the Iewes that *God had giuen them … eies that they should not see, and eares that they shoulde not heare* … for onely those … haue eares to heare which first by our selues are vowed, and then after by the spirit of God are sanctified … Christ speaketh especially of the children of the Church, for they only haue sanctified and prepared eares.[21]

The importance of close scriptural reading for the Reformation argued for access to rabbinic texts and commentaries that could provide interpretive keys to the Hebrew bible.[22] Protestant scholars were interested not only in the language but the broader interpretive system of the Oral Torah, in which language, ethics, and exegesis are inextricable.[23] The initial point of contact with this system for Christian scholars was the rabbinic bibles produced by the Christian printer Daniel Bomberg with the assistance of Jewish scholars and converts to Christianity in Venice.[24] Translations of the commentaries that appear in these editions proliferated over the course of the sixteenth century.[25] The increased presence of these texts, and of translations such as Fagius's *Sententiae,* challenged the foundations of

---

[21] Robert Wilkinson, *A Sermon of Hearing, or, Jewell for the Eare* (London, 1602), B1v–B2r.

[22] See Anthony Grafton and Joanna Weinberg, *I Have Always Loved the Holy Tongue: Isaac Casaubon, the Jews, and a Forgotten Chapter in Renaissance Scholarship* (Harvard University Press, 2011); Allison Coudert and Jeffrey S. Shoulson, eds., *Hebraica Veritas?: Christian Hebraists and the Study of Judaism in Early Modern Europe*, Jewish Culture and Contexts (University of Pennsylvania Press, 2004); Friedman, *The Most Ancient Testimony*; Stephen Burnett, *Christian Hebraism in the Reformation Era (1500–1660): Authors, Books, and the Transmission of Jewish Learning* (Brill, 2012).

[23] Jerome Friedman, "Sixteenth-Century Christian-Hebraica: Scripture and the Renaissance Myth of the Past," *The Sixteenth Century Journal*, 11 (1980), 67–68.

[24] These included commentaries by Onkelos, Rashi, Targum Jonathan, David Kimchi, Nahmanides (Ramban), and others. See Abraham Shinedling, "Bible Editions," *The Universal Jewish Encyclopedia*, eds. Isaac Landman and Simon Cohen (Universal Jewish Encyclopedia, Incorporated, 1940), 295–300.

[25] See Stephen Burnett, "Philosemitism and Christian Hebraism in the Reformation Era (1500–1620)," in *Geliebter Feid Gehasster Freund: Antisemitismus Und Philsemitismus in Geschichte Und Gegenwart*, eds. Irene Diekmann and Elke-Vera Kotowski (Verlag für Berlin-Brandenburg, 2009), 139–140. On these tools serving Christians as aids to independent study, see Burnett, *Christian Hebraism*, 102.

a supersessionary view of Christian virtuous listening even as these were newly elaborated and extended.

Supersession Sound-Work *qua* Dream-Work in *The Tempest*

The supersession dream-work in *The Tempest* constellates around a cluster of thematic and symbolic elements (exile, usurpation, displacement, confinement, conversion, liberation) that are typically read as conventions of romance but which take on a different hue when considered in light of the play's many Jewish and supersessionary signifiers. The mysterious powers of the exiled older brother are tied to unseen books, without which he is, as Caliban says, "but a sot as I am," and which he uses to lord over the island where he waits out his exile and plots revenge upon his usurpers (3.2.88).[26] While Prospero's mysterious books, staff, and spiritual command are usually interpreted as marks of the Renaissance magus or sorcerer, their overdetermination as tools of punishment, subordination, and the pursuit of retributive justice make them (and Prospero himself) rather more evocative as signs of Mosaic law. Conspicuous marks of Jewish otherness accrue around the figure of Caliban, too. The irrational dream-work "logic" that distributes Jewish otherness across both Prospero and Caliban reflects the irrationality of the fear of the other, who, having both preternatural capabilities and monstrous incapacities, is both more and less than human. This supersession dream-work allows for the hearing of Caliban's outcry at the denial of his birthright and his protest against the injustice of his confinement as the complaint of the superseded Jew who has led his "usurper" to all the "qualities" or hidden virtues "o'th' isle" only to be "st[ied]... In this hard rock" and kept from the "rest o'th' island" (1.2.340–347).[27]

Miranda's response to Caliban's claim invokes some of the most notorious terms of Christian antisemitism. Caliban is a natural "savage" and a

---

[26] The trope of the vengeful, diasporic Jew, waiting on the margins of the known world for the opportunity to reclaim power, is notable in period travel literature. See John Mandeville's description of Jews "chased" by Alexander (and God) into a hilly enclosure beyond the Caspian Sea: "men say in that country ... that in the time of Antichrist they shall doe much harme to christian men, and therefore all the Iewes that dwell in diuers parts of the world learne ... to speake Ebrew, for they hope that these Iewes ... shal come out of the hils and ... speake Ebrew to them and lead them into Christendome for to destroy Christian men." John Mandeville, *The Voyages and Trauailes of Sir John Maundeuile Knight* (London, 1582), R1v–2v.

[27] Examining Caliban's resentment at his "expropriation," Julia Lupton argues that "in the place of divine similitude, the special stamp of Adam, Caliban is left with the baser mimesis born from rivalry and the quest for recognition" ("Creature Caliban," 9). As Lupton also observes, "In Shakespearean drama, resentment is a mark of villainy under the law, the sign of a soulless legalism, a kind of second-order secularized Judaism" (10).

"slave," incapable of "any print of goodness ... Being capable of all ill" (1.2.354–358). He is all flesh and no spirit, monstrously carnal, summoned by the name of earth itself: "Thou earth, thou" (1.2.317). Rehearsing fears of miscegenation (and racist fantasies of Jewish concupiscence) that underwrote centuries of anti-Jewish segregation, Prospero claims to have housed Caliban, "[f]ilth as thou art," in his own cell until he sought to "violate / The honour of [his] child" (1.2.349–351). The stereotype of Jewish linguistic (and musical) savagery resounds in Prospero's description of his brutish gabbling.[28] In Miranda's claim that she endowed Caliban's purposes with "words that made [these purposes] known" (1.2.361), we hear the promise of his fulfillment through the Christian Word. Caliban may have preceded Prospero and his daughter on the isle, but he cannot articulate his purpose without the redeemer's language, which he uses only to curse. Likewise, Prospero's story of Ariel's redemption echoes the supersessionary paradigm of Christianity's actualization of latent Jewish purpose. An allegorical reading of Prospero's narrative suggests that Ariel's liberation (the spirit confined in a pine tree) is symbolic of Christianity's liberation of the spirit from the prison of law and flesh, but his indentured service under threat of harder confinement (next time in an oak, Prospero warns) belies the violence of supersession and its unrealized promise of freedom (1.2.274–297).[29]

Virtue and the Auditory Uncanny

The Tempest's dream-work bears witness to the violence of supersession by allowing us to hear the suppressed memory of Christianity's debt to Jewish virtue ethics and the virtue of the open ear in particular. As Joseph Ortiz observes, "differences in moral stature correspond with differences in hearing" in *The Tempest*.[30] Virtue, or the potential for virtue, is demonstrated throughout the play by an auditory perspicacity that allows some

---

[28] The connection between "gab" and gaberdine is suggestive (see also note 32). Shakespeare uses "gaberdine" three times: once in Shylock's "You call me misbeliever ... And spit upon my Jewish gaberdine" (*Merchant of Venice*, 1.3.107–108) and twice in *The Tempest* to describe the garment under which Caliban attempts to hide from Prospero's torments (2.2.16). Caliban's gaberdine seems to index the monstrosity of the crypto-Jew, hiding in plain sight and associated, in sixteenth-century England, with the smell of fish due to the trade and diet of Portuguese conversos. See Cecil Roth, "The Middle Period of Anglo-Jewish History (1290–1655) Reconsidered," *Transactions (Jewish Historical Society of England)* 19 (1955), 5.

[29] This image would seem to invoke Paul's supersessionary figure of Israel as an olive tree whose branches must be broken in order for Christ to be engrafted into it (Rom. 11:17).

[30] Ortiz, *Broken Harmony*, 171.

characters to hear appeals to conscience that are inaudible to others. When Alonso hears his sin recounted by the storm, the audience understands this as a sign of contrition: "Methought the billows spoke and told me of it, / The winds did sing it to me, and the thunder, / That deep and dreadful organ-pipe, pronounced / The name of Prosper. It did bass my trespass" (3.3.96–99). The virtuous listener hears the low or "bass" notes of sublimated threats to which others appear deaf. The virtuous Gonzalo perceives a goodly "humming" that enables him to wake from induced slumber and save Alonso and company from Sebastian's and Antonio's murderous intents (2.1.313). When the latter are asked to explain their drawn weapons, they fabricate a sonic alibi, suggesting the conspicuous villainy of false hearing in contrast with auditory virtue: "Even now we heard a hollow burst of bellowing, / Like bulls, or rather lions. / Did't not wake you? / It struck mine ear most terribly" (2.1.307–309).

Ariel's characterization as personified spirit highlights the unequal and yet surprising distribution of the capacity (or opportunity) for virtuous hearing in the play. Alonso's "deafness" to the fabricated noise compels Antonio and Sebastian to embellish their alibi: "O, 'twas a din to fright a monster's ear, / To make an earthquake! Sure it was the roar / Of a whole herd of lions." Alonso turns to Gonzalo for verification that he too heard "nothing," but Gonzalo reports, "Upon my honour, sir, I heard a humming, / And that a strange one too, which did awake me" (2.1.309–320). Unlike that "dreadful organ-pipe" that speaks Alonso's guilt or the clarion lyricism of "Full Fathom Five" that recalls Ferdinand's father to him, Ariel's singing is terrifying in its apparent sourcelessness to the Italian "varlets" (4.1.170). It is "the tune of our catch," (meaning both melody and entrapment) "played by the picture of / Nobody" (3.2.121–122). But despite Caliban's purportedly unredeemable nature, the sound of the spirit is not a torment to him, or rather it is so only in its elusiveness. Caliban yearns for access to the source of the noises that he hears not just as music but, like Gonzalo, as *humming*. The repetition of this word "hum" as a descriptor for the perceived sound of the spirit is amplified by a sonic resemblance between the words "hum" and "human" (more proximate via the Middle High German *hummen*).[31] Prospero marks Caliban's inhumanity as a misshapenness that reflects his mother's "mischiefs manifold and sorceries [too] terrible / To enter human hearing" (1.2.266–267). And yet, her "whelp," "not honoured with / A human shape" (1.2.285–286), seems

---

[31] See "hum, v.1." *OED Online*. June 2020.

nonetheless to have an ear capable of perceiving the island's "Sounds, and sweet airs, that give delight and hurt not" (3.2.131).[32] His purportedly unteachable ear is attuned to sounds he hears more musically and poignantly than any other character:

> Sometimes a thousand twangling instruments
> Will hum about mine ears, and sometime voices
> That if I then had waked after long sleep
> Will make me sleep again; and then in dreaming
> The clouds methought would open and show riches
> Ready to drop upon me, that when I waked
> I cried to dream again. (3.2.132–138)

Caliban's description of his excruciating separation from heavenly riches that lie just out of reach and sight, peeking out from nebulous obscurement, witnesses the elevated displacement of the repressed that is the hallmark of the sublimating process. The supersession dream-work makes these riches recognizable as the sublimated spiritual resources of the antecedent or "indigenous" Jewish religion. The lyrical virtuosity with which Caliban narrates this experience invites the audience to sympathize with his alienation from and longing for these hidden spiritual resources.

Full Fathom Five: Hearing Supersession as Sublimation

Ferdinand hears a version of Caliban's spirit music in Ariel's first song in the play. The song is composed out of the lapping waves, the barking of watchdogs, and the strain of strutting chanticleer, which Ferdinand also hears not as fearful noise but a strangely compelling music that attends "Some god o'th' island" (1.2.393) and preserves him from drowning: it "crept by me upon the waters, / Allaying both their fury and my passion / With its sweet air. / Thence I have followed it – / Or it hath drawn me rather" (1.2.395–398). The music conspicuously stops and restarts, marking its uncanniness in its intermittent (or intermittently perceptible) presence: "But 'tis gone. / No, it begins again" (1.2.398–399). And when it restarts, it sings not of the father's death but his "rich and strange" transformation:

---

[32] The trope of Jewish deafness is tied in anti-Jewish polemic to a characterization of Jewish speech and singing as garbled, unmusical, and of the Jew himself as incapable of music. This long precedes Wagner. See Ruth HaCohen, "Between Noise and Harmony: The Oratorical Moment in the Musical Entanglements of Jews and Christians," *Critical Inquiry* 32 (2006), 250–277.

ARIEL   Full fathom five thy father lies.
         Of his bones are coral made;
         Those are pearls that were his eyes;
         Nothing of him that doth fade
         But doth suffer a sea-change
         Into something rich and strange.
         Sea-nymphs hourly ring his knell:
SPIRITS [*within*] Ding dong.
ARIEL   Hark, now I hear them.
SPIRITS [*within*] Ding-dong bell. (1.2.400–408)

The supersession dreamwork resonates in the musical condensation of sound and image.[33] The father's "sea-change" depicts conversionary baptism as a drowning that neither liberates the spirit from the body nor allows for the internment of its ossified remains but breeds "strange" life. In Ovidian tradition and premodern natural philosophy, coral was understood to be "alive in death," living underwater and petrified above the surface.[34] While the words of Ariel's song nearly paraphrase Pythagoras' teachings in the *Metamorphoses* ("all things do change, but nothing … doth perish"),[35] the specificity of the imagery resounds with the uncanny survivance of the other through its sublimation.[36]

The "rich and strange" transformation (as substitution) of pearls *for* eyes is particularly suggestive of supersession. Christ and Christianity are repeatedly figured as pearls in typological readings of Hebrew scripture.[37] Samuel Gardiner, one-time chaplain to the Archbishop of Canterbury wrote:

> This Pearl is the omnipotent and eternal word of God, properly so called … [because] Christ … grew vnto the very substance of a pearle, inclosed and shut vp in virgins womb, and mantle of mortalitie, as it were in the shell, and couerture of the fish, lying hid a while in the depth of this world, as it were in the sea, and among the cragged rocks of the people of the Iewes.[38]

---

[33] Jennifer Linhart Wood shows how Robert Johnson's setting emphasizes this in its imitation of the burden *Sounding Otherness* (Palgrave, 2019), 307–308.

[34] See Shannon Kelley's profound reading of this line as a clue to the generic work of the romance, averting tragedy by attending to a past that does not decompose in "The King's Coral Body: A Natural History of Coral and the Post-Tragic Ecology of *The Tempest*," *Journal for Early Modern Cultural Studies* 14 (2013), 115–142.

[35] Ovid, *The Fifteene Bookes of P. Ouidius Naso; Entituled, Metamorphosis*, trans. Arthur Golding (London, 1612), 185r.

[36] As opposed to metempsychosis. It may be significant that the Hebrew for the word "coral," *ramot*, which derives from the word for "heights," suggests the upward reaching of organisms that live in the deep – a particularly suggestive image of sublimation.

[37] This is, unsurprisingly, especially prevalent in readings of Jonah.

[38] Samuel Gardiner, *A Pearle of Price* (London, 1600), 37.

The exchange of pearls for eyes converts the Christian image of Jewish retributive justice (the eye for an eye of Mosaic law) for the inestimable pearl of Matthew's parable, the kingdom of heaven for which the merchant gives all.[39] The hearing of funeral bells in the song's final couplet is echoed in the "burden"[40] that imitates their ringing, raising to the surface the memory not only of the (un)dead father but an undead, unburied Jewish source for the play's Christian virtue ethics of forgiveness engendered through the cultivation of a listening ear.

The uncanniness of "Full Fathom Five" resounds in the obscurity of the "virtue" that displaces "vengeance" in 5.1. The hastiness of Prospero's conversion-*qua*-substitution calls it into question as proof either of his suddenly open or listening ear or of the moral superiority he claims by it. The supersession dream-work allows us to hear in Prospero's abjuring of his rough magic both the vaunted triumph of Christian mercy over Jewish vengeance and the compelled conversion of the Jew whose readmission to Christian society hinges on the renunciation of his practices, the breaking of his (Mosaic) staff, and the drowning of his (Jewish) books. Their destruction and submergence is simultaneously forestalled and fulfilled through musical sublimation: "And when I have required / Some heavenly music – which even now I do... I'll break my staff, / Bury it certain fathoms in the earth, / And deeper than did ever plummet sound / I'll drown my book" (5.1.51–57). The "requir[ing]," or *re-choiring*, of this music (perhaps in the "solemn air" that accompanies Prospero's confrontation of his still transfixed dispossessors) musically *re-sounds* the memory of that which is purportedly not just out of reach, or purportedly unplummetable, but out of hearing.

---

[39] While, to my knowledge, the Jewish and supersessionary signifiers of Ariel's song have not been noted in literary scholarship, T. S. Eliot seems to have heard and amplified them in a poem excised by Pound from *The Waste Land*:

> Full fathom five your Bleistein lies
> Under the flatfish and the squids.
> Graves Disease in a dead jew's eyes!
> When the crabs have eat the lids.
> Lower than the wharf rats dive
> Though he suffer a sea-change
> Still expensive rich and strange

(T. S. Eliot, "Dirge," *The Waste Land: A Facsimile and Transcript of the Original Drafts*, eds. Valerie Eliot and Ezra Pound [Faber & Faber, 1971], 121).

[40] The Folio does not assign the sung ringing to spirits, as the editors of the Norton edition do (1.2.407), but indicates it, rather, as "Burthen" ("First Folio [Brandeis University], Page 23 : Facsimile Viewer : Internet Shakespeare Editions").

CHAPTER 29

Islamic Virtues
Ethics in the Premodern Ottoman Empire

Yasin Basaran

The Ottoman political enterprise started in the northwestern corner of Anatolia at the beginning of the fourteenth century. When the Ottomans reached the apogee of their military power, they ruled a vast territory from the Balkans to North Africa and from the Crimea to Arabian Peninsula. The Ottomans – originally Turkic – incorporated many linguistic, cultural, literary, and religious traditions of earlier civilizations such as Seljuks, Mamluks, Sasanids, and Byzantine Greeks. During Shakespeare's lifetime, which coincides with the first direct trade between England and the Ottomans in 1575,[1] the Ottoman intellectuals were appreciating the maturity of traditional thinking and knowledge inherited from Turkic, Islamic, and Hellenic sources. They had full access to not only the classics of religious sciences but also Sufi masterworks and philosophical summas. They did not fail to transform what was available to them into a unified whole which deeply affected intellectual and popular cultures.[2] The construction of the Suleymaniye madrasas[3] (1551–1557) in Istanbul marks the culmination of the Ottoman intellectual efforts to reinstate traditional categories of knowledge from an imperial perspective. Their efforts resulted in the proliferation of masterly works in many areas that significantly influenced the intellectual culture of subsequent centuries.[4] This is best reflected in the works of the grand architect of the Süleyman the

---

[1] Maria Blackwood, "Politics, Trade, and Diplomacy: The Anglo-Ottoman Relationship, 1575–1699," *History Matters* (2010), 1–34.

[2] Ömer Mahir Alper, "XVI. Yüzyılda Osmanlı Düşüncesi: Kemalpaşazâde Bağlamında Bazı Mülâhazalar" ed. Ekrem Demirli (Conference: Sahn-ı Semândan Dârülfünûn'a Osmanlı'da İlim ve Fikir Dünyası Âlimler, Müesseseler ve Fikrî Eserler XVI. Yüzyıl, Zeytinburnu Belediyesi Kültür Yayınları, 2017), 15–20.

[3] Madrasa are Islamic institutions of higher learning whose main function was to supply educated individuals to the legal system. For more: George Makdisi, *The Rise of Colleges: Institutions of Learning in Islam and the West* (Edinburgh University Press, 1981).

[4] Gottfried Hagen, "The Order of Knowledge, the Knowledge of Order," in *The Cambridge History of Turkey*, eds. Suraiya N. Faroqhi and Kate Fleet, vol. II, 4 vols. (Cambridge University Press, 2012), 407–456.

Magnificent, Mimar Sinan (d.1588) who combined Byzantine and Islamic architecture with practical needs in the construction of many schools, bridges, hospitals, and mosques, among which the Süleymaniye complex in Istanbul and the Selimiye complex in Edirne were the most prominent. Similarly, Taşköprüzade Ahmed (d.1561) collected and cataloged biographies of the Ottoman scholars and scientists from the beginning of the Empire to his own time. His *Miftāḥ al-Saʿāda [Key to Happiness]* is the basis for the famous encyclopedia of Katip Çelebi, or Hajji Khalifa (d.1657), whose *Kashf al-Zunūn [The Removal of Doubt]* later became the main reference work for orientalist literature. Historical works of Ibn Kemal (d.1536), miniatures of Matrakçı Nasuh (d.1564), grammatical manuals of the influential ascetic Muhammad Birgivi (d.1573), over ninety scientific books of Taqi al-Din (d.1585), who was also the founder of the Istanbul Observatory, and masterpieces of Divan poetry by Fuzuli (d.1556), Baki (d.1600) can be counted as contributions to the same intellectual maturation of this era.[5] This chapter features a book from this era as a showcase for the development of Ottoman moral thinking, which shares many sources and themes with Shakespearean virtue ethics.

Falling in line with all the unifying tendencies mentioned earlier is *Ahlâk-ı Alâî [The morals of Ali]* of Kınalızade Ali Çelebi (d.1572).[6] The book, which was completed in 1565, takes its form and content from the twelfth-century philosopher Nasir al-Din al-Tusi's *Ahlâk-i Nasiri [The morals of Nasir]*, which in turn had appropriated the tradition of tenth-century philosopher Ibn Miskawayh's *Tahzibu'l-Ahlâk [Refinement of character].*[7] Even though this tradition is predominantly Aristotelian, it also incorporated the Qur'anic views on morals, the Sunna (sayings and practices of the Prophet Muhammed), Islamic legal decrees (*fiqh*), and Sufi teachings.[8] For Kınalızade, the revelation and prophetic tradition are necessary for moral development because the human intellect is unable to grasp the ideal state of being (the moderate position) in every situation.[9] The book is also indebted to the fifteenth-century philosopher al-Dawwani's *Ahlâk-i Jalali [The morals of Jalal]*, al-Ghazali's *Ihya [The revival]*, and Rumi's *Mathnawi*.

---

5 Halil İnalcık, *The Ottoman Empire: The Classical Age 1300–1600* (Phoenix Press, 2003), 165–178.
6 Ayşe Sıdıka Oktay, "Kınalızâde Ali Efendi'nin hayatı ve Ahlâk-ı Alâî isimli eseri," *Divan: Disiplinlerarası Çalışmalar Dergisi*, 12 (2002), 185–233.
7 Kinalizade Ali Celebi, *Ahlâk-ı Alâî*, ed. Murat Demirkol (Fecr Yayinlari, 2016), 33.
8 Murat Demirkol, "Kınalızâde Ali Çelebi'nin Ahlâk Felsefesine Katkıları," *Osmanlı Düşüncesi Kaynakları ve Tartışma Konuları*, eds. Fuat Aydın, Muhammed Yetim, and Metin Aydın (Sultanbeyli Belediyesi, 2019), 301–319.
9 Kinalizade, *Ahlâk-ı Alâî*, 120.

It also makes explicit references to the wisdom of masters from different philosophical traditions such as Pythagoras, Plato, Galen, Diogenes, and al-Farabi. Kınalızade brings all of them together to make a coherent case for the promotion of morals. In this respect, it is not difficult to see that the book is another instance of this period's general tendency to produce a synthesized body of knowledge.

Written by a contemporary of Shakespeare and establishing itself as the representative account of moral thinking in social and political domains for the Ottomans,[10] the book is of interest to the readers of Shakespeare. It accommodates more parallels with the moral world of Englishmen than indicated in Shakespeare's dismissive "turning Turk" in *Othello*. This anit-Ottoman phrase "draws on early modern anxieties about Ottoman aggression and links them to a larger network of moral, sexual, and religious uncertainty which touched English Protestants directly," but fails to acknowledge the shared moral wisdom uniting many parts of the European and Mediterranean world at this time.[11]

Another tendency of the Ottoman intellectuals in this period is to popularize forms of knowledge that were traditionally considered to be more suitable for high culture. From Islamic law to world history, from grammar to philosophy, intellectuals of the period prioritized the dissemination of knowledge by simplifying their language and mixing literary genres. This tendency is most evident in the proliferation of sophisticated books written in Turkish, the vernacular language, because until this period the Ottoman intellectuals had chosen either Arabic or Farsi.[12] In his introduction to *Ahlâk-i Alai*, Kınalızade states that one of his motivations in writing this book is to produce a text of practical philosophy in common Turkish because some of the sophisticated books he expanded on were not circulating among nonacademics while others that were more accessible were not cut out for educated readers.[13] This tendency is also evident in the literary styles of the leading authors who appropriated more popular methods in their texts. Like many of his contemporaries, Kınalızade made use of poetry and mythical Sufi stories to imaginatively establish what is

---

[10] Cornell H. Fleischer, *Bureaucrat and Intellectual in the Ottoman Empire: The Historian Mustafa Ali (1541–1600)* (Princeton University Press, 2014).

[11] Daniel J. Vitkus, "Turning Turk in Othello: The Conversion and Damnation of the Moor," *Shakespeare Quarterly* 48. 2 (1997), 145–176.

[12] Himmet Taşkömür, "16. Yüzyıl Osmanlı Kültür ve Düşünce Hayatı Üzerine Bazı Gözlemler," ed. Ekrem Demirli (Conference: Sahn-ı Semândan Dârülfünûn'a Osmanlı'da İlim ve Fikir Dünyası Âlimler, Müesseseler ve Fikrî Eserler XVI. Yüzyıl, Zeytinburnu Belediyesi Kültür Yayınları, 2017), 29–32.

[13] Kinalizade, *Ahlâk-ı Alâî*, 33.

essentially rational. The practice of mixing different writing styles was not new to the Ottoman intellectuals. However, in this period, such an eclectic literary approach was used to attract more readers to the subject matter, rather than employed merely as rhetorical strategies for the traditional reader. In other words, *Ahlâk-ı Alâî* was meant to reach a greater audience than madrasa scholars and intellectual circles. The abundance of copies in various manuscript libraries in Turkey and the existence of several handwritten and printed editions (including an alleged translation into Italian) suggest that the book succeeded in representing the ethical field of the Ottomans of the sixteenth century.[14]

Ahlâk-ı Alâî follows in form and content Aristotelian virtue ethics. It covers three major subjects: the morality of the self, management of household and of society. The first book deals with the theory of the self *(nefs)*, defining the temperament, whether temperaments could change, happiness, virtues, vices, vices that look like virtues, and treatment of the diseases of the self in the context of the human soul. The second book addresses good and bad manners among households and how to keep control of family finances. The third book is devoted to political philosophy and advice on administration. Throughout the book, classical Aristotelian virtues appear in relation to each subject matter. The model for the latter two books is unmistakably the human self, as the human being was seen as the "model of the universe" in the Ottoman cosmology.[15]

Kinalizade views ethics from a broad spectrum. He primarily deals with questions of the source of morality, the possibility of an individual's moral education, the highest good, and the moral order in society. According to Kinalizade, morality is founded in the human's primordial tendency to be happy. However, since bodily pleasures fail to provide one with enduring happiness, he suggests that we need to focus on the happiness of the self which can be attained by seeking a moral life. He maintains that an individual's change of character is possible through moral education because dispositions of the self result from the intermingling of the purity of the soul and the darkness of nature. As long as one inclines toward purity by learning about theoretical and practical virtues and strives for implementing them in his life, the self will attain happiness. In other words, it is a state of being which one reaches by virtuous actions.

What is a virtuous action? It is suggested in *Ahlâk-ı Alâî* that acts are not virtuous unless they are intentional. In other words, an accidental act of

---

[14] Oktay, "Kınalızâde Ali Efendi'nin hayatı ve Ahlâk-ı Alâî isimli eseri." 226–227.
[15] Hagen, "The Order of Knowledge," 420.

justice does not count as being just. One needs to act "with the knowledge that it is a virtue and comprehension of its meaning" if a person seeks to be virtuous. After establishing the intentionality of moral actions, Kinalizade identifies four core virtues: prudence, courage, temperance, and justice, corresponding to the four cardinal virtues in Greek philosophy, which is also the foundation of virtues in Shakespeare. Each of the first three virtues is connected to corresponding powers of the soul, which manifest as three separate selves. The angelic power corresponds to prudence, the predatory power to bravery, and the animal power to temperance. The virtue of justice is acquired when the other three core virtues are applied in balance. All other virtues follow from these four. Accordingly, all vices stem from their neglect or poor application. For Kinalizade, it is important to take a balanced attitude in their application to attain happiness. Overdoing or underdoing would halt spiritual and moral improvement.

Following the Galenic theory of humors and the Aristotelian idea of the tripartite soul, Kinalizade characterizes the three powers of the self as originating in humans' spiritual and physical nature. They are neither good nor evil in essence. The animal power is needed to sustain the body while the primary role of the predatory power is to keep control of the animal power. The angelic power on the other hand gives direction to the predatory power. Three core virtues are obtained through these powers. The virtue of the animal power is characterized as temperance *(iffet)*. It refers to a balanced action towards bodily desires such as food, drinks, and sexuality. Virtues such as modesty, gentleness, peacefulness, tranquility, patience, contentment, dignity, generosity, and piety emerge when temperance is maintained. The virtue of the predatory power is called bravery *(yiğitlik)*. The brave person is expected to act in balance in the face of danger and hardship. Nobility, courage, devotion, perseverance, calmness, self-control, resoluteness, humility, and softheartedness are the virtues that derive from bravery. Kinalizade associates humility and softheartedness with bravery because one has to be brave enough to cope with one's own arrogance and ruthlessness.[16] The virtuous act of the angelic power is prudence *(hikmet)*. However, it is important to note that the balance is needed in this power only concerning practical application. There is no need to put limitations on the use of the theoretical power of discernment because the more one discerns the truths of theoretical sciences such as physics, metaphysics, and mathematics, the higher one's soul will be elevated.

---

[16] Kinalizade, *Ahlâk-ı Alâî*, 92–93.

The only vice associated with theoretical power is the neglect of the pursuit of knowledge.[17] When practical prudence is used in balance, the virtues of intelligence, wit, mental alertness, agility, contemplation, memorization, and remembrance follow from it. The fourth core virtue, justice *(adalet)*, is not related to any specific power but rather arises out of the use of the other three powers. In other words, justice is obtained as a result of a balanced practice of the totality of the other core virtues. Companionship, communion, fidelity, compassion, submission, trust, and worship are some of the virtues that one acquires when embodying the virtue of justice.

It is evident that, according to Kinalizade, the key to the realization of all the above-mentioned virtues in one's soul lies in the use of powers in moderation. Two extremes – overuse *(ifrat)* or underuse *(tefrit)* of them – will result in breaking the virtuous pattern. For instance, to realize temperance in the soul, one should refrain not only from much eating, drinking, or seeking and acting on sexuality but also from falling prey to hunger, thirst, or impotence. In other words, insensibility is a vice as detrimental to the soul as self-indulgence. The principle of moderation should be observed in virtues as well as sub-virtues. At this point, it is difficult to overlook the fact that Othello's misdirected attempt to balance justice which was disturbed by Iago's allegations on his wife Desdemona's fidelity finds its roots not in the mere stereotypical expectations of Turks as cultural and religious Other but also in the Ottoman ethics of the day. As apparent in Kinalizade's portrayal of virtue, Islamic moral teachings in Shakespeare's time call for a moderate course of action even in the face of moral crises. Thus, it is more human fragility in the case of infidelity than cultural idiosyncrasies that motivates Othello's homicide, which he defends as an action toward restoring the balance in society by preventing her from betraying more men.[18] In other words, the irrationality and cruelty that are attributed to Muslim otherness embodied in the expression "turning Turk" ignores the fact that Muslim moral values shared in the same ethical stream as the moral philosophy of Christian Europe.

Ahlâk-ı Alâî does not neglect to inform the reader on how to develop a moral character. For Kinalizade, since nature is prior to arts, the art of morals should follow the blueprints of nature. Since our nature is primarily animal, one has to begin with studying the powers and needs of the

[17] Ibid., 101.
[18] Debra Johanyak, "Turning Turk, Early Modern English Orientalism, and Shakespeare's Othello," in *The English Renaissance, Orientalism, and the Idea of Asia*, eds. Debra Johanyak and Walter S. H. Lim (Palgrave Macmillan, 2011), 77–95.

soul that manifest as three separate selves. The animal power, which is connected to the needs of appetite and reproduction, should be known first, followed by the predatory power, which is connected to the needs of safety and security. When one studies them and achieves a moderate course of action in satisfying the needs of the self, the angelic power should be activated, which is connected to the need for wisdom. Once the soul is trained and shaped by these virtues, happiness is expected to flow both in this world and the hereafter. Holding true beliefs and exercising virtuous acts in this world ensure eternal happiness in the hereafter, which is described as bearing a likeness to the Creator and the community of exalted beings.[19]

However, there are obstacles. Practical application is prioritized over theoretical understanding in moral education because the self might be infected with vices and bad habits. Following Aristotle, Kinalizade maintains that the art of morality is for the soul what medicine is for the body. He reserves approximately one-third of the book for a thorough practical guide for curing the diseases of the self.[20] Galenic medicine postulates that the first step of cure is removing the cause of the disease.[21] Kinalizade applies the same postulation in moral education and prescribes that the causes of vices should be removed first.[22] For instance, if you suffer from anger issues, you need to deal with your arrogance (because it is the cause of your anger) by carefully observing the perfections and virtuous doings of your elders and peers. The fact that each one of them is superior to you in one respect or another would challenge your arrogance. After removal of the obstacle, you need to strive for holding true beliefs, uttering those beliefs in a beautiful manner, and acting righteously. Lacking elders or peers to look to in his isolation in Cyprus, we find Othello falling prey to malicious Iago's relentless manipulations and deceptions, particularly because Othello chooses obedience over virtue as his criterium for receiving counsel. Othello rushes to act on Iago's toxic exhalations instead of digging deeper and shedding many layers of conditioning that bar true knowledge of self.

The second and third books of *Ahlâk-ı Alâî* are devoted to the virtuous managing of the affairs of the household and the state, respectively. Following Aristotle, Kinalizade asserts that since nobody is predisposed to

---

[19] Kinalizade, *Ahlâk-ı Alâî*, 45–46.
[20] Ibid., 144–293.
[21] For more on Galenic medicine in early-modern world: Vasileios Syros, "Galenic Medicine and Social Stability in Early Modern Florence and the Islamic Empires," *Journal of Early Modern History* 17. 2 (2013), 161–213.
[22] Kinalizade, *Ahlâk-ı Alâî*., 178.

satisfy all kinds of human needs, we are naturally inclined to collaborate and cooperate. This is the primordial motivation to create families and societies.[23] However, if there is no moral order in these domains, there will be oppression and tyranny. Justice needs to be established in both domains for better collaboration and cooperation, which in turn contribute to individual happiness.

The household and the state are portrayed as having the same structure as the self. Even though they differ in scope, they share the same goal of achieving happiness in their domains. As all elements of the family (father, mother, children, servants, and food) are important for the functioning of the house, a happy family is formed by respecting the roles of each element. The head of the house, the father, is responsible for not only maintaining finances and fetching needed resources but also educating family members. He "should be like a careful, shrewd, and punctual shepherd who protects, restraints, feeds and gives water to the herd, No doubt as the herd is fattened when it is safe from attacks of wild animals like wolves and fed and watered to the extent that it breeds, the head of the house should protect family members from tyrants, preserve them against bad manners and harmful actions to the extent that each of them prospers [in their task]." He should also treat the family as the doctor treats his patients when there is a failing organ which should be cut off from the body because the family's health as a whole is more important than the survival of each of its parts. We see this pattern of thought in *Othello*, when Othello famously declares "it is the cause" as justification for murdering Desdemona. Grounded in Galenic medicine, he entrusts himself with the removal of the cause, that is his wife as the root of his supposedly pure soul's plunging into disease, which manifests itself in paranoia, epilepsy, and anger.

In an analogy that was also very popular in Renaissance Europe and figures frequently in the plays of Shakespeare, the head of the state is no different from the father of the household in his engagement with administrators and subjects.[24] The head is responsible for the sustenance of the state structure by keeping revenues and expenses in check, protecting the state against enemies, and educating the bureaucrats and administrators

---

[23] İlhan Kutluer, "İnsanın Toplumsal Doğası: Klasik Osmanlı Düşüncesinde 'Medeni Bi't-Tab' ve 'Temeddün' Terimlerinin Kavramsal Çerçevesi," in *Osmanlı Düşüncesi Kaynakları ve Tartışma Konuları*, ed. Fuat Aydın, Muhammed Yetim, and Metin Aydın (Sultanbeyli Belediyesi, 2019), 265–300.

[24] Kinalizade, *Ahlâk-ı Alâî*, 426–440.

as well as their subjects. Society's health depends largely on the leader's ability to respond to challenges in each level of the hierarchy. The main task of the lower levels is to follow their leader's instructions as minutely as possible. If the state is thrown into disorder, the leader should not hesitate to apply certain unpleasant measures to maintain balance. In Kinalizade's view, this procedure mirrors the stages that a doctor follows for curing a physical infection since the state consists of the powers that correspond to the powers of the body and the soul. The social classes composed of intellectuals *(ehl-i kalem)*, soldiers *(ehl-i simsir)*, merchants *(ehl-i ticaret)*, and farmers *(ehl-i ziraat)* represent the powers of the human soul, each corresponding to a separate bodily humor. The social order guarantees happiness for people if the powers of each class are balanced by the governor, who is represented by the head of a body.[25] Needless to say, Shakespeare's plays belong to the same thought world, with similar medical and corporate analogies showing up frequently to describe social order and disorder.

In conclusion, the common moral ground of Shakespeare and the Ottomans is shaped mainly by Aristotelian virtue ethics, whose objective is to operate in moderation the powers of the self. As an extension of nature, humans are expected to tend towards the fulfillment of their needs, be they physical, psychological, or spiritual. For the Ottomans, it is important to recognize these needs because they are the means to the end, which is happiness in the world and the hereafter. It is also important to acknowledge the frailty of the process of moral development because human nature constantly needs instructing and training. Hence the rational structure of moral life must be supported by the revelation, prophetic tradition, and spiritual practices, paralleling similar arguments made by Christian inheritors of the Aristotelian tradition. Such practices involve an enduring scheme of hierarchy and distribution of responsibilities and rights in domains of the individual, family, and society.

[25] Hagen, "The Order of Knowledge," 434–437.

CHAPTER 30

Persian Virtues
Hospitality, Tolerance, and Peacebuilding in the Age of Shakespeare

Sheiba Kian Kaufman

Discovering virtues espousing cooperation between diverse cultures and religions seems impossible in an "age of persecution" known for witch hunts, interconfessional massacres on the streets of Paris, and burning dissenters at the stake. Yet, it is such ostensible hostility that prompts early-modern writers to develop conceptions of toleration and conceive of acts of hospitality toward others often via unexpected channels. From the mid-sixteenth century, English humanists, poets, and playwrights summon ancient Persia in their didactic and literary works as a paradigm for virtuous conduct in a pluralist society. This chapter considers how the virtues of toleration and hospitality toward others are comingled and housed in early-modern conceptions of Ancient Persia, and how this enduring rhetoric associated with the ancient empire animates a collaborative virtue discourse found in Shakespeare's enigmatic reference to Persian clothing in *King Lear*.

Persian Paradigms of Hospitality

In Plutarch's "Life of Themistocles," the exiled Athenian general tests the limits of hospitality when he arrives in Persia with a desperate behest for Artaxerxes I, the son of his long-time opponent, Xerxes: "I come prepared to receive the favor of one who benevolently offers reconciliation, or to deprecate the anger of one who cherishes the remembrance of injuries. But do thou take my foes to witness for the good I wrought the Persians, and now use my misfortunes for the display of thy virtue rather than for the satisfaction of thine anger."[1] Themistocles approaches the Persian monarch

---

[1] Plutarch, *Plutarch's Lives*, trans. Bernadotte Perrin, Loeb Classical Library, vol. 2 (W. Heinemann, 1914), 28.1–2, 77. The country's name in English was officially changed from Persia to Iran in 1935. It is still appropriate, however, to identify Iranians as Persians and the language as Persian in the English language with Fārsī (فارسی) as its endonym.

fully aware of the alternative outcomes of "reconciliation" or "anger"; he is, after all, a master architect of the Greco-Persian wars (499–449 BCE), renowned for orchestrating the successful and decisive naval battle against the Persians at Salamis and championing the growth of the Athenian navy which ultimately led to Xerxes' defeat at Plataea. Despite his integral role in preventing the invasion of Greece by the Persian Empire and his sub-terfuge in achieving his ends, he nevertheless appeals to the king's "virtue" and presents Artaxerxes with a choice that calls upon the inherent drama of the hospitable wager: embrace the foreigner, risk sheltering a stranger that puts himself and his realm in danger, or turn him away. Ultimately, the astonished yet elated Persian monarch accepts the uninvited guest and potential political asset into his realm, and further grants Themistocles' request to learn Persian to converse with the king in his native tongue.

This scene of individual empowerment in a foreign court, intercultural hospitality, and the elevation of the virtue of the vernacular appealed to both Baldassare Castiglione and the English translator of *The Courtier,* diplomat Sir Thomas Hoby, who elaborates on this embrace of the for-eigner in his opening epistle:

> THEMISTOCLES THE NOBLE ATHENIEN IN HIS BANISHEM-ENT Entertayned moste honourablie with the king of Persia, willed vpon a time to tell his cause by a spokesman, compared it to a piece of tapistrie, that beyng spred abrode, discloseth the beautie of the woorkemanship, but foulded together, hideth it, and therfore demaunded respite to learne the Persian tunge to tell his owne cause.[2]

In unfolding his art, his vernacular translation, for public viewing, Hoby, like Themistocles, finds refuge within the Persian analogy; the English tongue follows the "Persian tunge" in its "beautie" and "woorkemanship," in its ability to "tel [its] own cause" and house the prodigal courtier within English lands. Mirroring Themistocles' request before Artaxerxes, the English trans-lator transports himself to a Persian presence that has established its con-comitant dedication to receive the unknown hospitably, hoping therefore to inspire the same reception in his contemporary benefactor.

The opening dedication of Hoby's 1561 translation follows a pattern famil-iar to English humanists – that of invoking Persian hospitality in their lin-guistic endeavors to contribute to the public good. While the convention of Anglo-Persian political analogies in English prose texts pre-dates Elizabeth's

---

[2] Baldassare Castiglione, *The courtyer of Count Baldessar Castilio diuided into foure bookes. Very necessary and profitable for yonge gentilmen and gentilwomen abiding in court, palaice or place,* trans. Thomas Hoby (Wyllyam Seres, 1561), 3.

realm, it is in the first full decade of Elizabeth's rule that ancient Persian monarchs and their largess become rhetorical anchors around which discussions of English hospitality – in the various spheres of politics, education, and religion – rests. Magnifying the virtue of hospitality alongside toleration discourse is particularly salient in the turbulent years following the Elizabethan Religious Settlement of 1559 when such amicable exchanges where not only visions of peace and harmony in an increasingly pluralistic state, but also political reminders that ecumenical tolerance – enacted and envisioned as hospitable acts in a distant time and place – benefits the commonwealth.

The early-modern turn to admiring virtues within the Persian Empire is largely attributable to humanist readings of classical texts including Xenophon's *Cyropaedia* and Plutarch's *Lives* coupled with early-modern understandings of Persia and its biblical heritage found in the books of Daniel, Ezra, and Esther. Persian monarchs are esteemed for their embrace of foreigners, from King Xerxes' interreligious marriage with Esther to Cyrus the Great's biblical acts of liberation of the oppressed Jews under the Babylonian captivity. Cyrus' propagation of the right to religious liberty was foundational to his ideology as a Zoroastrian ruler striving toward establishing "order or rightness" (*Arta*) alongside happiness and perfection (*frasha*) in his kingdom.[3] The ancient Persian dedication to creating order in a diverse kingdom is captured in both Cyrus' acts of religious restoration and the formation of gardens and the concept of paradise as translated into Greek from the Old Persian *pairidaida*.[4]

Significantly, despite this sense of conceptual intimacy with the ancient Persian virtues of toleration and hospitality toward foreigners, the English had little familiarity with early-modern Safavid Persia. The few Anglo-Persian exchanges of the period, from 1561 until the first official embassy to

---

[3] Jenny Rose, *Zoroastrianism: An Introduction* (I. B. Tauris, 2010), 37–39. Touraj Daryaee elucidates archeological examples from Mesopotamia that confirm Cyrus' toleration and acceptance of local deities and religion in "Religion of Cyrus the Great," in *Cyrus the Great: An Ancient Iranian* King (Afshar Publishing, 2013), 16–27. See also Amélie Kuhrt, *The Persian Empire: A Corpus of Sources from the Achaemenid Period.*, vol. I (Routledge, 2007). Persian practices of hospitality, etiquette, gift-giving, and courtesy are intertwined in centuries long theory and practice found in the spiritual writings of Zoroastrianism, Persian mysticism, and texts such as the twelfth century Qābūs nāma. Similarly, influential Islamicate literature, such as the widely read poem Gulistan, or Rose Garden (1258), by Saadi' Shirazi, can be seen as foundational in promoting the concept of adab as a holistic and ideal mode of refinement encompassing proper behavior, politeness, and education in the aim for communal harmony. See Sholeh A. Quinn, Persian Historiography Across Empires: The Ottomans, Safavids, and Mughals (Cambridge: Cambridge University Press, 2021).

[4] This foundational notion of unity in diversity influences Thomas Browne's seventeenth-century botanical, *The Garden of Cyrus* (1658). On the symbolism of the gardens in ancient Persia, Rose explains that the gardens were an earthly reflection of an orderly realm allied with the truth and goodness of Ahura Mazda, the good lord in *Zoroastrianism*, 57–63.

Persia in 1626, tested the parameters of tolerance and hospitality, leading rather to widely circulated but often dubious vignettes from travel reports, particularly relating to the adventures of the infamous Sherley brothers. Thus, with inconsistent contemporary information on Persia, long-standing virtues wed to ancient Persia dominate the English imaginary, manifesting in the drama of the period. While the relationship of page and stage is mutually reinforcing, with the latter providing the matter for staging while developing in response to changing conceptions of religious tolerance in the period, it is the stage that enables a fictional temporality of hospitability between religions and cultures that both actors and audience provisionally inhabit. That Persia – both fictive and literal – is a place that can host such transformations of historical materials into fiction speaks to its inherent vivacity and hospitability as a fertile space of figurative potential that goes beyond the emblematic use of Persian monarchs in humanist prose.

Shakespeare's Persian Tom

In their distance from historical circumstance and in the conscious foregrounding of certain attributes associated with Persia in classical and biblical source material, often Persian figures in early-modern drama can be seen as conceptual foreigners rather than representations of historical figures and, as such, provide a literary paradigm for interreligious exchange not found within other narratives of global exchange such as those relating to Anglo-Ottoman trade and diplomacy. While the early-modern performance of "turning Turk" is often depicted as an act of apostasy, rebellion, and untrustworthiness in the drama of the period, transforming into a Persian frequently uplifts the non-Persian character in physical, social, and spiritual degrees while bettering his or her environment, particularly when such changes occur under non-tragic conditions. Indeed, adopting a Persian persona via clothing and customs is often a largely beneficial transformation enabling a change in status and an appreciation of hospitality between cultures on the part of the transformed. For instance, during the assumption of a Persian persona, the non-Persian character is empowered to aid the Persian realm, as in the case of Cratander, the Ephesian captive in the Caroline Drama, *The Royall Slave* (1636), whose presence rescinds the Persian practice of executing a prisoner of war as part of the degrading custom of "mock-kingship," or Robert Sherley who exposes the perfidy of the Persian king's court attendants in the adventure romance, *The Travels of the Three English Brothers* (1607).

In Shakespeare's *King Lear*, when Edgar, disguised as Poor Tom, assists Lear on the heath by figuratively eschewing three imagined barking dogs,

Lear acknowledges Edgar's service in this instance of solidarity between two abject souls: "You, sir, I entertain for one of my hundred, only I do not like the fashion of your garments. You will say they are Persian; but let them be changed" (3.6.38–40).[5] Lear's delusional lament on Edgar's clothing informs us of the presence of another persona for Edgar, either a hidden Persian figure or an Englishman dressed as a Persian, possibly a soldier or an ambassador, graciously aiding Lear in his imaginary canine confrontation. The idea of Persia Shakespeare invokes in Lear's dialogue with Poor Tom clearly associates Edgar's service to the sovereign with an established sense of hospitality intertwined with courtly practice found in humanist prose, yet the textual placement of the allusion suggests a deeper and more dynamic engagement with hospitable acts as part of the play's contribution to early-modern discourses on paths to collective peace-building. The invocation of the Persian persona in *Lear* follows from earlier scenes wherein Lear addresses Edgar as the "good Athenian" (3.4.170), the "learned Theban" (3.4.147), and his "philosopher" (3.4.166), beseeching him to judge the imaginary trial of his daughters before transforming into a Persian garbed figure as part of the many personas Lear envisions for Edgar as Poor Tom.[6] In this vein, Lear's imaginary yet profound visions of Edgar subtly unite conceptual Greeks and Persians in service to the aging king, as an interlocutor, a fair-minded judge, and a soldier, revealing not only Shakespeare's interest and knowledge of Persian and Greek sources but also a fictional narrative of historical revisionism through the textual proximity of Greek and Persian references.

Historically, Greeks and Persians have been depicted in Western literature as quintessential enemies, the source of the Manichean paradigms of "us" and "them," the representational entities of East and West, the beginning of the so-called clash of civilizations, and the warring parties Herodotus memorializes in his *Histories*.[7] However, in *Lear*, on a conceptual and metaphorical level, in theory and in fictitious practice, we witness the capacity of drama to stage a transformation of perennial foes – Greeks

---

[5] Shakespeare cited from *Complete Works*, ed. Stephen Orgel and Albert Richard Braunmuller (Penguin, 2002).

[6] Although different in tone and purpose, a reference to Thomas Preston's play on the Persian King Cambyses appears in *I Henry IV*, when Falstaff comedically assumes the role of King Henry to prepare prince Hal for his meeting with his father: "for I must speak in passion, and I will do it in/ King Cambyses' vein." 2.4.373–374.

[7] Edward Said attributes the origins of Orientalism to Aeschylus' *The Persians* and Euripides' *The Bacchae*: "A line is drawn between two continents. Europe is powerful and articulate; Asia is defeated and distant." Orientalism (Vintage, 1979), 42–57.

and Persians – into agents of mutual assistance to a downtrodden king while simultaneously adumbrating the sociopolitical capabilities necessary for collective peace.[8] In anticipation of later seventeenth-century toleration theory and Kantian conceptions of perpetual peace based on conditions of cosmopolitan hospitality, in this scene, Shakespeare's Greco-Persian allusions gesture toward an understated reservoir of peacebuilding potentialities based on hospitable interactions uniting conceptual figures of ancient empires and civilizations, and alerting thereby the reader to a possibility of a hidden global history that is capable of inspiring more than division and domination.

---

[8] For a compelling historical revision of the "clash of civilizations" thesis, see David Cannadine, *The Undivided Past: Humanity Beyond Our Differences* (Alfred A. Knopf, 2013). Timothy Harrison and Jane Mikkelson's concept of "assemblage across worlds" accounts for a vibrant, multifaceted view of early modern practices and conceptualizations of the world and world literature. See "What Was Early Modern World Literature?" in Modern Philology, vol. 119, no. 1 (The University of Chicago Press, 2021), 166–188.

CHAPTER 31

Buddhist Virtues
Equanimity, Mindfulness, and Compassion in Hamlet

Unhae Park Langis

The endemic displays of affective disorder in the media and in our distracted lives today, our turn to self-help literature to manage our emotions, and the rise of the mindfulness movement all resoundingly attest to the human condition of being "passion's slave[s]" (*Hamlet* 3.2.65),[1] ever vulnerable to the havoc that destructive emotions can wreak in our lives. Mindfulness evokes Buddhism, an ancient wisdom tradition based on the teachings of the Buddha, who expressed, as the upshot of the so-called Four Noble Truths, that human beings can achieve freedom from suffering through a path of wisdom and virtue.[2] Although cognitive-based therapies of emotion employing mindfulness are presently associated more with ancient Indian than Greek traditions, Eastern and Western strands of eudaimonism (philosophies of flourishing) and epistemic skepticism in the resurgent field of Greco-Buddhism point rather to a shared philosophical origin. Historically, the sixth-century BCE Persian Empire founded by Cyrus the Great and later conquered by Alexander the Great was "a single, interactive cultural sphere" inducing an exchange of ideas and goods along ancient trade routes.[3] Despite their varied ethnic origins, religions, and languages, Buddha, Democritus, and Pyrrho – known to have interacted with Indian yogis during his travels with Alexander's entourage – inhabited the same eudaimonist "thoughtworld," sharing fundamental concepts

---

[1] *Norton Shakespeare*, eds. Stephen Greenblatt, Walter Cohen, Jean Howard, Katharine Eisaman Maus (Norton, 1997).

[2] In regard to enlightenment ideals, this short chapter will not treat the rebirth aspect of traditional Buddhist philosophies.

[3] Thomas McEvilley, *The Shape of Ancient Thought: Comparative Studies in Greek and Indian Philosophies* (Allworth Press, 2002), Chapter 1; Stephen Batchelor, "Greek Buddha: Pyrrho's encounter with early Buddhism in Central Asia," Review of Christopher Beckwith, *Greek Buddha: Pyrrho's Encounter with Early Buddhism in Central Asia*, Contemporary Buddhism 17. 1 (2016), 195–215 (212). For a review of scholarship on the East-West historical interaction, see Ethan Mills, "Skepticism and Religious Practice in Sextus and Nāgārjuna," in *Ethics without Self, Dharma without Atman*, ed. Gordon Davis (Springer, 2018), 91–106 (92).

such as the nonsubstantiality of persons and things, suspension of judgment (*epochē*), and mindfulness as key to equanimity and virtue.[4] In what is known as Noble Silence, the historical Buddha, interested more in ethical practice (*askesis*) than unresolvable metaphysics, declined a definitive answer on the existence of the self,[5] a noncommittal epistemic stance also advocated by Pyrrhonist Skeptics, who aimed for tranquility (*ataraxia*) as happiness, without the usual ethical core of East-West eudaimonist philosophies. To best achieve a Greco-Buddhist rapprochement, this discussion treats Pyrrhonism and Stoicism together, focusing on their similarities rather than differences. To wit, both are concerned with how to avoid misapprehension in daily life, where the criteria for knowledge is so high that, epistemically speaking, there is an inconsequential difference between a judgment-suspending Pyrrhonist and a cautiously judging Stoic. Stoicism recommends itself here with a highly sophisticated ethical therapy not only familiar to Shakespeare and his contemporaries but also congenial in numerous ways with Buddhist ethics,[6] which, to its credit, underscores a compassionate dimension downplayed in discussions of both *Hamlet* and Stoic ethics.

Stoic and Buddhist traditions alike participate in virtue ethics grounded on eudaimonism, which holds that the ultimate purpose (*telos*) of human life is flourishing largely understood as developing our virtues, behaving ethically toward others, and pursuing wisdom. In the Stoic view, virtue is necessary and sufficient for the good life. It is the one thing that matters and is "up to us" amid life's ceaseless tides of change. As in Buddhism, all other goods, the so-called "externals" such as wealth, status, fame, and health, are contingent and impermanent. Beyond our control, they are morally indifferent to our happiness, which resides solely in virtue. In both traditions, the premise to the eudaimonic life is wisdom about how things really are. Ethically, the Stoics regard unhealthy passions (*pathē*) – pain, fear, craving, pleasure and others subsumed under these four types – as misjudgments about the value of external goods. Such passion-impulses prevent us from making appropriate responses in life and keep us from attaining virtue. Mutually supportive, *apatheia* – freedom from *pathē*, or equanimity – and mindfulness (*prosochē*) allow us to respond appropriately to impressions in a signal act of volition (*prohairesis*). The Buddhist ascetic, similarly, tries to eradicate desire for mistakenly conceived goods as the way to overcome

[4] Batchelor, "Greek Buddha," 212.
[5] Buddha, *Malunkyaputta Sutta*, 63; clarified in McEvilley, *The Shape of Ancient Thought*, Chapter 13.
[6] McEvilley, *The Shape of Ancient Thought*, Chapter 25.

suffering (*Pāli dukkha*), more precisely, the "unsatisfactoriness" caused by greed, hatred, and delusion, not to mention hedonic adaptation as an underlying psychological obstacle to human happiness.[7] Instead of a dualist distinction between good and evil, the Buddhists focus rather on their equivalents to Stoic *pathē*: *kleshas* (Sanskrit; Pāli *kalesa*), cognitive-affective afflictions or poisons, which arise through causes and conditions in an impermanent, co-dependent world. As reported by Greek historians interacting with ascetics in India in the third-century BCE, "nothing that happens to a man is bad or good, ... opinions being merely dreams,"[8] a variant of proverbial wisdom propagated in the West, appearing in the works of Stoics Epictetus and Marcus Aurelius, not to mention early-modern writers such as Montaigne and Shakespeare. Ridding oneself of *kleshas* involves counteracting them with a wholesome culture of wisdom and compassion in a lifelong practice of mindfulness and self-restraint.

This wisdom for Buddhists, Skeptics, and, implicitly, Stoics is, above all, the rejection of self-nature – the Stoic concern about affective-cognitive misapprehension taken to its logical end. Denying the inherent nature of things and selves, Buddhist interbeing, to borrow Thich Nhat Hanh's term,[9] instead manifests itself affectively as lovingkindness, spatially as physical interconnectedness (at the atomic-subatomic level), and temporally as karmic order. Within this worldview, the self is a constantly changing matrix of five psycho-physical aggregates (body, sensation, perception, intellect, consciousness), mapped as "sensory and mental events" in "temporal and causal" interdependence.[10] According to both Buddhists and Pyrrhonist Skeptics, we are raised from birth to a substantialist view of life. Without conditioned "thinking mak[ing] it so" (*Hamlet*, 2.2.245), we would not view life and death as a false dichotomy but simply as events (*dharma*) within a continuum of the whole. Despite the negative cast of its philosophical underpinnings – the impermanence, unsatisfactoriness,

---

[7] I argue elsewhere in "Humankindness: *King Lear* and the Suffering, Wisdom, and Compassion within Buddhist Interbeing," in *Literature and the Religious Experience*, eds. Matthew Smith and Caleb Spencer (Palgrave, 2022), 209–226, how these Buddhist ideas are dramatized in *King Lear* within its matrix of suffering, (un)kindness, and the wisdom gained from "nothing."

[8] *Dhammapada*, I.1–2, Shodo Harada, *Not One Single Thing: A Commentary on the Platform Sutra* (Wisdom Publications, 2018), Chapter 4; Megasthenes and Onesicritus, Strabo, *Geography*, trans. H. C. Hamilton and W. Falconer, XV.I.59 and 65, www.perseus.tufts.edu/hopper/. Other variants appear in Epictetus, *Discourses, Fragments, Handbook*, trans. Robin Hard (Oxford University Press, 2014), *Handbook* 5; Marcus Aurelius, *Meditations*, trans. G. Hays (Modern Library, 2003), 8.47, 2.15, 2.11, 4.3.

[9] Thich Nhat Hanh, *Peace Is Every Step* (Random House, 2010), 95–96.

[10] Jan Christoph Westerhoff, "Nāgārjuna," *Stanford Encyclopedia of Philosophy*, https://plato.stanford.edu/archives/spr2019/entries/nagarjuna/, 3.3.

and absence of self-nature (Three Marks of existence) – Buddhism, in everyday practice of *sila* (moral conduct) with its emphasis on "action, commitment, responsibility and love," offers, in fact, an optimistic and life-affirming ethics that upholds the dynamic interconnectedness of the whole over an illusory self of unchanging essence.[11]

Likewise in Pyrrhonist Skepticism, things are "nondifferent," "nonstable," and "nonjudgeable,"[12] attributes Buddhists use to describe temporal phenomena. Pyrrho concludes about each thing that "it no more is than is not, than both is and is not, than neither is nor is not," or *ou mallon* ("no more"), for short.[13] Remarkably, this tetralemma, or fourfold negation, also appears in both the Pāli suttas and the Madhyamaka philosophy of Nāgārjuna (a contemporary of the Skeptic Sextus Empiricus).[14] Far from being "unadorned nonsense," the tetralemma employs exhaustive logic in a pointed critique of conceptual proliferation as useless attempts to overcome the indeterminacy of being: in Tom Tillemans's words, "things exist merely as designations or in a purely nominal fashion. This applies to all superficial reality, even to Buddha's and nirvana: these are but designations without any corresponding, real entity."[15] Nāgārjuna's arguments for emptiness, in practice, as Ethan Mills notes, aim for "the cessation of conceptual proliferation, which in turn leads to the Buddhist good of nirvana."[16] The upshot of this Buddhist equanimity of "full emptiness" and its Skeptic-Stoic counterparts in daily life is the moment-to-moment stillness of mind allowing us to pay full attention to our immediate environment and thereby respond appropriately to arising events.

Notwithstanding its exceptional dramatic qualities, Hamlet's most famous soliloquy is notable from the perspective of Buddhist-Skeptic therapy for its dramatization of mental proliferation, a key symptom of his dis-ease. The opening phrase, "To be, or not to be" (3.1.58) is bookended, more precisely, by Hamlet's contemplation on *how* to be, how to proceed in his baffling situation: whether "to suffer / The slings and arrows of outrageous fortune / Or to take arms against a sea of troubles" (3.1.59–61).

---

[11] Damien Keown, *The Nature of Buddhist Ethics* (Palgrave, 1992), 20.
[12] McEvilley, *The Shape of Ancient Thought*, Chapter 17, cited from a fragmentary paraphrase of an alleged summary of Pyrrho's philosophy by his student Timon of Phlius.
[13] Ibid.
[14] Nāgārjuna, *Nāgārjuna's Middle Way: Mūlamadhyamakārikā*, trans. Shōryū Katsura and Mark Siderits (Wisdom Publications, 2013), XVIII.8; Batchelor, "Greek Buddha," 200.
[15] Rafael Sorkin, "To What Type of Logic Does the 'Tetralemma' Belong?" *arXiv* (2010), 1–10 (2); T. J. Tillemans, *Scripture, Logic, Language: Essays on Dharmakīrti and His Tibetan Successors* (Simon and Schuster, 1999),197, 199.
[16] Mills, "Skepticism and Religious Practice," 93.

Fatigued by the uncertainty of the impressions he must sort out, Hamlet toys mentally with death as the oblivious escape from his perplexing troubles. In so doing, his stream of consciousness flows in and back out of the being/nonbeing question: the unknowability surrounding the phenomenon of death. Hamlet's eschatological thoughts here notably imbricate one iteration of the Buddhist-Skeptic tetralemma expressing indeterminacy, as presented by Nāgārjuna's disciple Āryadeva: Being, nonbeing, [both] being and nonbeing, neither being [nor] nonbeing.[17] If Hamlet's "sleep of death" is taken figuratively, the mind put to sleep continues with endless "dreams" (3.1.68), the conceptual proliferation at the subconscious level. If death is taken literally, Hamlet reasons that the chance of the afterlife being altogether worse than "those ills we have" "puzzles the will" (3.1.82–83) to end our life. In such a manner, self-attached craving, instead of Buddhist-Skeptic-Stoic equanimity, "make[s] cowards of us all" in contemplating both an end *to* life or a course of action *in* life: "the native hue of resolution / Is sicklied o'er with the pale cast of thought" (3.1.85–87). Beset by humoral melancholy, which early moderns regarded as a psychosomatic disease, Hamlet misguidedly grasps at "No more" (3.1.63), the oblivious "sleep of death" as a solution to his existential quandary. The rest of the play charts how he gradually veers toward the other "No more," the equanimity conferred by *ou mallon* and the cessation of mental proliferation.

Shakespeare's *Hamlet* dramatizes the interplay of Buddhist-Skeptic-Stoic philosophies at the affective-cognitive interface indispensable for virtue in action. Hamlet's search for appropriate response – in the role of "scourge and minister" (3.4.159) thrust upon him to redress regicide – requires equanimity, and equanimity, as the play suggests, ultimately requires compassion to counteract affective-cognitive affliction: to empty mental proliferation and replace it with mindful readiness for action. Our ability in Greco-Buddhist wisdom traditions to stand firm by judgment and detachment from destructive emotions and mental afflictions is encapsulated in Hamlet's famous line in banter with Rosencrantz and Guildenstern, "there is nothing either good or bad but thinking makes it so" (2.2. 244–245). Hamlet follows it up with further retorts concerning "bad dreams" and "A dream itself [being] but a shadow" (2.2.245–253). All together, this dialogue notably recalls the third-century BCE moral teaching transcribed by Greek historians, "nothing that happens to a man is

---

[17] Āryadeva, qtd. in T. J. Tillemans, *Scripture, Logic, Language: Essays on Dharmakīrti and His Tibetan Successors* (Simon and Schuster, 1999), 189.

bad or good, ... opinions being merely dreams."[18] More significant, however, is that Hamlet, in his present "sicklied" state (3.1.87), utters this
Buddhist-Skeptic-Stoic counsel only to reject *ou mallon* equanimity – by
rashly giving assent to the impression that "Denmark is a prison" (2.2.239).
Erasmus's Folly would endorse such action, claiming that "the happiness
of a man ... resides in opinion."[19] Such an impulse-judgment understandably follows from his hasty promise to the Ghost of Hamlet Senior to
avenge his murder and the heavy burden of such a responsibility. From
a Stoic-Buddhist perspective, however, this initial misjudgment, linked
with his inability to maintain detachment (unlike Horatio), is the source
of Hamlet's subsequent oscillation and indecision. As Denmark, Prince
Hamlet is, more immediately, a prisoner of his *own* passions and illusory
self, manifesting craving and clinging, the source of suffering in Buddhist
philosophy. His flippant discourse shows to what extent melancholy has
a grip on his mindbody – muddied spirits producing clouded thinking,
sparks of wit notwithstanding. Hamlet's "antic disposition" (1.5.173), a
strategy to muddy the self before others, works doubly as a cover-up for
what Zen Buddhists would call his distracted, restless "monkey mind" –
the affective-cognitive manifestation of humoral-pneumatic imbalance, the
mental and literal poisoning prevalent in *Hamlet*. In this sense, Hamlet's
"distracted globe" (1.5.97) is representative of human distractedness the
world over. The intervening acts are sprinkled with soliloquies revealing
Hamlet's afflictive state – mental proliferation and excessive emotion –
inducing erratic and inconsistent behavior.

The opening of Act 5 reveals that Hamlet's displacement out to sea and
graveyard meditations beyond mortality have worked only partially to
clear Hamlet's head, to get him out of his imprisoning self. His tragicomic
contemplation on death ending with the thought of the great Alexander
recycled into a bunghole stopper shows his apprehension of interbeing, as
manifested in the fall evenly of sparrows as mighty kings reappearing as
fish for dinner through the cycling of life-substance (Sanskrit *prana*, Stoic
pneuma), which for us, in the sober reality of anthropogenic pollution of
Earth's waters, increasingly entails microplastics. An intellectual understanding of nonsubstantiality, however, does not readily translate to living
free from self-attached craving. When he comes upon Ophelia's funeral
gathering and feels insulted by Laertes's star-stopping "sorrow" (5.1.239),

---

[18] *Dhammapada, I.1–2, qtd. in Harada*, Chapter 4.
[19] Desiderius Erasmus, *In Praise of Folly*, trans. Hoyt H. Hudson (Princeton University Press, 1941,
2015), 63.

Hamlet's competitive grieving reveals that he still has not internalized emotional discipline, the therapy of *ou mallon*: letting himself get "carried away by the impression" of an irritant present, he fails to "recognize," *per* Epictetus, "that it is your opinion that has irritated you."[20] True to his counsel ("if you ... gain time to think, you'll find it easier to gain control of yourself"), Hamlet later avows with remorse that "to Laertes [he] forgot himself" (5.2.76–77). Lacking stillness of mind, Hamlet's affectivity is accompanied by continued mental proliferation about past events and future plans as he recounts to Horatio his narrow escape from Claudius's death warrant and incipient plan to kill him.

The cure for Hamlet's excessive rumination comes about in Buddhist understanding as an intervention of karmic order arising through causes and conditions within a co-dependent world: just as Hamlet is bracing for a moment to "quit" Claudius – "a man's life is no more than to say 'one'" (5.2.75) – Osric arrives with a fencing challenge from Laertes (and Claudius), thus diverting Hamlet from the mental state of hate to that of regret and compassion. Hamlet's latest failure at self-composed mindfulness demands a karmic corrective: his assent to the match implicitly acknowledges his complicity in the deaths of Polonius and Ophelia, hence the rightness of Laertes's cause. As Zen master Shodo Harada explains, "We are always concerned with good and bad, trapped in patterns of resentment and intimacy,"[21] but in a fruitful moment of still mind, perhaps an empathic exercise of *ethopoeia*, Hamlet recognizes beyond self-attached craving that Laertes is experiencing the same sorrows of losing Ophelia and losing a father. As if attuned to the wisdom found in Buddhist scripture, "Do not repay hate with hate, repay hate with love,"[22] he assents to the match as an act of lovingkindness. Though a fatal error from a narrative standpoint, this reconciliatory act unlocks a wholesome culture of wisdom and compassion – the very antidote to cure Hamlet's mental proliferation and his psychosomatic affliction. In a world of uncertainties and contingencies, Hamlet's assent is his *prohairesis*, his defining act of virtue in a play abounding with missteps. Thus resolutely declares Hamlet with the royal pronoun, "Not a whit. We defy augury" (5.2.157), hardly expecting its wholesome side-effect:

[20] Epictetus, *Handbook*, 20. Pierre Hadot, *The Inner Citadel: The Meditations of Marcus Aurelius* (Harvard University Press, 1998), speaks of the philosophical way of life as embodied by Epictetus and Marcus Aurelius as three interactive disciplines of desire, assent, and action.
[21] Harada, Chapter 4.
[22] *Dhammapada*, I.5, quoted in Harada, Chapter 4.

attaining self-composure, he frees himself from the prison of Denmark by yielding himself unto the world, "with no division between inside and outside."²³

The wisdom that Hamlet's assent unlocks in a Zen way is that of Buddhist-Skeptic-Stoic nonsubstantiality, which Diogenes Laertius expounds as the *ou mallon* stance: "nothing is honorable or base, or just or unjust, and that likewise in all cases nothing exists in truth; and that convention and habit are the basis for everything that men do; for each thing is *no more* this than this" (my emphasis).²⁴ The mental stance of emptiness within everyday life as defined by usage and habit is also known as nonabiding or nonattachment in Buddhism. In this attitude of suspending judgment and nonabiding, Sextus Empiricus, in Jay Garfield's Greco-Buddhist rapprochement, recommends, nonetheless, that we keep ourselves mindfully engaged with our environment, following "nature, feeling, custom, and the instruction of the arts," understanding these as "no more" than what they are – empty and co-dependent within conditioned existence as Nāgārjuna understood it. In ordinary life, this fourfold guide – respectively of perception and thought, bodily sensation, laws and ethics, and arts and skills – still practically offers us "the knowledge, certainty, and justification we need in order to navigate the world, identify ourselves and others, speak intelligibly, and explain natural phenomena."²⁵ Hamlet's equipoise, accordingly, demands a subtle balancing between noncognition and appropriate worldly response. To this end, Hamlet, appealing to the ethical indeterminacy of "honorable or base, or just or unjust," assents to the fencing match less as a duel of honor than an intervention of compassion; and subsequently to the redressing of King Hamlet's death less as an act executing codes of revenge or justice than a response of protecting self and other.

Not surprisingly then, Hamlet's practice of *ou mallon* nonsubstantiality manifests itself in exhaustive logic resonant of the Buddhist-Skeptic tetralemma.²⁶ In an argument for existential readiness, Hamlet, echoing Marcus Aurelius, rehearses the logical possibilities of death by stating a hypothetical, its converse, and inverse: "If it be now, 'tis not come; if it be not to come, it will be now; if it be not now, yet it will come. The

---

²³ Harada, Chapter 4.
²⁴ Diogenes Laertius in A. A. Long and D. N. Sedley, *The Hellenistic Philosophers: Greek and Latin Texts with Notes and Bibliography*, Volume 2 (Cambridge University Press, 1987), 13; qtd. in Batchelor, "Greek Buddha," 203.
²⁵ Jay L. Garfield, "Epoche and Śūnyatā: Skepticism East and West," *Philosophy East and West* (1990), 285–307 (294).
²⁶ Diogenes Laertius in Long and Sedley, *The Hellenistic Philosophers*, 13.

readiness is all. Since no man knows aught of what he leaves, what is't to leave betimes?" (5.2.158–161).[27] This is the existential readiness encapsulated in *amor fati* (i.e., "love or accept your fate") and the attitude of "Why *not* me?" instead of "Why me?" that Aurelius urges with the same sea imagery invoked in Hamlet's "sea of troubles" (3.1.61) and his sea voyage: "[B]e like the rock that the waves keep crashing over. It stands unmoved and the raging of the sea falls still around it."[28] To quote again from Aurelius' meditations, Hamlet is "Resolute in separation from the body. And then in dissolution or fragmentation – or continuity" – a "decision … considered and serious … [w]ithout dramatics."[29] Gone is the melancholy of his earlier desire for dissolution ("that this too too solid flesh would melt / Thaw, and resolve itself into a dew" [1.2.129–130]), and the "craven scruple" underlying his famous meditation, "To be or not to be" (4.4.9.30; 3.1.58–90), now replaced with the tranquility conferred by *ou mallon* nonsubstantiality: "no more this than that." So too, Hamlet's previous remark in 5.2 in reference to "quit[ting]" Claudius – "a man's life is no more than to say 'one'" (5.2.75) – now sounds less like the abruptness of human life than an assertion of the "Oneness" of Buddhist interbeing and Stoic cosmology, along with the *ou mallon* expression of the indeterminate nature of things (Skeptic aphasia): the "more things in heaven and earth … / Than are dreamt of in your philosophy" (1.5.167–168). Suspension of judgment and action is in order.

For Hamlet, compassion induces the equanimity that accompanies nonsubstantiality, further manifest at the fencing match. In Mahayana Buddhism, equanimity, by reducing craving and aversion, can further enhance the practice of immeasurable love, compassion, and joy in the persevering aspiration to free all sentient beings from suffering (*bodhicitta*).[30] Hamlet is a "bodhisattva in training" precisely when he "ope[ns] his heart and love" in "uncertain[ty] about what to do in a situation," according to Tibetan Buddhist master Lama Zopa Rinpoche.[31] Operating in a similarly expansive space of harmonized virtues, Hamlet and Laertes exchange brotherly love before the fencing duel, and during it, mutual forgiveness upon Laertes's venomous feinting ouroborically biting him

[27] Marcus Aurelius, 2.14, 4.50, 11.3.
[28] Ibid, 4.49.
[29] Ibid, 11.3.
[30] Emily McRae, "Detachment in Buddhist and Stoic Ethics: Ataraxia and Apatheia and Equanimity," in *Ethics without Self, Dharma without Atman*, ed. Gordon Davis (Springer, 2018), 73–89 (85).
[31] Lama Zopa Rinpoche clarified in Andrew Holocek, *Preparing to Die: Practical Advice and Spiritual Wisdom from the Tibetan Buddhist Tradition* (Shambhala Publications, 2013), Epub.

back. Hamlet's request for pardon, sounds to modern cynics like a cop-out insanity plea: "Was't Hamlet wronged Laertes? Never Hamlet. / ... when he's not himself does wrong Laertes, ... / Who does it, then? His madness" (5.2.170–174). Nonetheless, Hamlet's appeal to Laertes's "most generous thoughts" (5.2.179) presents itself in both Buddhist and Stoic traditions as compassion from others and from oneself even while sustaining the concept of nonsubstantial selfhood. Fourteenth-century Tibetan philosopher Tsongkhapa explains Buddhist psychology – reminiscent of Socratic-Chrysippean views – regarding those who in anger and hate end up hurting others: they "have become like servants of their afflictions, because they are under the control of others, i.e. their afflictions."[32] In the same vein, Hamlet, referring to himself in the third person, urges Laertes that "Hamlet is of the faction that is wronged. / His madness is poor Hamlet's enemy" (5.2.75–76). Melancholic Hamlet was thus prone to excessive, mistargeted passion-impulses before all "the demons of the afflictions" had been exorcised – spirits of the deceased King Hamlet, Ophelia, and Polonius.

No longer lacking "directions," no longer "thinking too precisely on" (2.165, 4.4.9.30) what's "honorable or base, or just or unjust," Hamlet mindfully takes the cue for action in the vital present: self-preservational killing of Claudius upon immediate, embodied apprehension of his "treacher[ous]" poisoning scheme. In Hamlet, Stoic and Buddhist volition toward virtuous action shade toward Buddhist-Skeptic equipoise between ontological noncognition and compulsory worldly action. This movement is illustrated by Shakespeare's paradoxically Zen-like attitude toward "rashness," defined as quickness of response: critique of precipitous action arising from afflictive states but "praise" (5.2.7) for the agility afforded by tranquility to respond quickly to the present situation – the classical example being a soldier's mental readiness for battle. The key difference between these – the right and wrong kind of rashness – is one's wholesome or unwholesome mental state actualizing corresponding karmic events. As Buddhist teachings from the *Dhammapada* (1st–3rd c. BCE) explain, "Experiences are preceded by mind, led by mind, and produced by mind. If one speaks or acts with an impure [afflicted] mind, suffering follows even as the cart-wheel follows the hoof of the ox ... If one speaks or acts with a pure mind, happiness follows like a shadow that never departs."[33] Interestingly,

---

[32] Tsongkhapa, *The Great Treatise of the Stages of the Path to Enlightenment* (Snow Lion, 2000), 161; qtd. in McRae, "Detachment in Buddhist and Stoic Ethics," 80.

[33] *Dhammapada*, I.1–2, qtd. in Harada, Chapter 4.

Sextus Empiricus uses the same metaphor in explaining that *ataraxia* can follow "fortuitously ... as a shadow follows a body" in the very act of suspending judgment, of abandoning conscious effort.[34] Shodo Harada writes: "As long as we are acting out of habit, we will be buffeted by what we see, hear, and feel," but when "our body, mind, and awareness blend into *one*" (my italics) with "everything and not hanging on to anything, we are always right here, right now," and "every moment's actuality is well ripened."[35] Harada's account befits Hamlet's long-delayed redress: "blood and judgement" finally "so well commingled" (3.2.62), rightly targeted for moral agency in accordance with Buddhist-Stoic wisdoms and conceptions of interdependent causality. Within the time-space of the play, Hamlet goes from cursing "spite / That ever I was born to set it right!" (1.5.89–90) to "meeting [the] crisis" without "grumbling," "complaining," "think[ing] about extra things," but rather "embracing just what comes to" him.[36] This is how Hamlet opens the heart to compassion, and dies into equanimity as a – shall we say – *bodhisattva* in training, a view supported by John Donne, who upon observing a baby sparrow, contemplates in a Platonic vein on the soul's fledging: "Like a child whose teeth are just starting to grow in, and its gums are all aching and itching – that is exactly how the soul feels when it begins to grow wings. It swells up and aches and tingles as it grows them."[37] Donne's account highlights how the divine arc of Hamlet's life is beautifully adumbrated in the birth and fall of a sparrow. The pursuit of virtue for most of us is a lifelong practice, demanding a habitual cultivation of mindful action. Stoic-Buddhist equanimity entails *amor fati*, a profound trust in karmic order: in "the fall of the sparrow" and all other entities as interdependently occurring beyond our limited comprehension and control. Though we might not change our moral hardware as much as spiritual ascetics do, opening ourselves to the equanimity, compassion, and mindfulness from shared skeins of human wisdom will be vital in mobilizing and sustaining action to address multidimensional, interconnected challenges of pandemic, climate stress, racial and economic injustice.

---

[34] Sextus Empiricus, *Sextus Empiricus: Outlines of Scepticism*, ed. Julia Annas and Jonathan Barnes (Cambridge University Press, 2000), I.29.

[35] Harada, Chapter 4.

[36] Ibid.; see also Aurelius, 4.49.

[37] Donne, *Metempsychosis*, 528; 251c; qtd. in Timothy Harrison, *Coming to: Consciousness and Natality in Early Modern England* (University of Chicago Press, 2020), 168, 291.

CHAPTER 32

The Virtues in Black Theology

Vincent Lloyd

To understand ourselves as merely human, at peace with our limitations, accepting the bounds of our knowledge and power would seem a praiseworthy end. It is the culmination of *The Tempest*, as Prospero sets aside his magic, relying instead on his own limited powers. Virtue acquired, he is to assume again a position of worldly power, now chastened, with the help of secularized grace, an audience's praise. Black theology rails against such virtuous circles, fueled by worldly acclaim. Rewarding goodness, when the criterion for goodness is resembling those the world calls good, conceals structures of domination, tethering us all the more tightly to those structure (of whiteness, of worldliness). Black theology urges us to transform how we understand virtue and vice, and so to approach differently the work of aesthetic formation by orienting it toward liberation rather than acculturation.

The term *Black theology*, in a narrow sense, refers to a movement within the academy that began during the late 1960s. Black Christian theologians were witnessing the rise of the Black Power movement and the rise of Black cultural nationalism. Theological training at historically white seminaries and universities largely ignored both contemporary racial justice protests and the history of Black Christian religious experience and reflection. With his 1969 book *Black Theology and Black Power*, theologian James H. Cone argued that Christian theology, rightly understood, is closely aligned with the Black Power movement.[1] Christians ought to be militantly demanding racial justice. Importantly, Cone does not consider racial justice as one on a menu of social justice issues to which Christians ought to apply their values. Rather, for Cone, Christian theology rightly understood is Black theology. At the heart of Christianity, in his view, is

---

[1] James H. Cone, *Black Theology and Black Power* (Seabury Press, 1969). See also James H. Cone, *A Black Theology of Liberation* (J. B. Lippincott, 1970).

God siding with the oppressed. *God takes sides.* God sent Jesus to the world in order to demonstrate that God is present among the oppressed, and that worldly oppression will not have the last word. Cone draws on scripture to emphasize that Jesus is continually standing with the downtrodden – outcasts, prisoners, lepers, and the poor – and continually challenging the powerful. To find Jesus in the twentieth-century United States, Cone concludes, it is necessary to look toward Black communities. In his pithy and provocative phrasing: God is Black. To find Jesus's enemy in this context, to find the devil, it is necessary to look toward white supremacy. Therefore, to be a Christian, that is, to be a faithful follower of Jesus, means looking toward the authority of Black communities and joining in the struggle against white supremacy. To struggle is to be faithful; to succumb to the logics of white supremacy is to sin. The freedom that the bible announces, according to Cone, is Black liberation – having both a political and an eschatological dimension.

Today, there are academic jobs in Black theology, there is a journal named *Black Theology*, there is a book series in the field, and there is a program unit on Black theology at the American Academy of Religion annual conference. The term *Black theology* now refers not only to a specific academic project aligned with a specific political moment but also points to all academic work on Christian thought and practice that centers questions of Blackness: Black theology as theology that concerns Black experience. Cone himself took a professorship at the historically white Union Theological Seminary, a bastion of religious liberalism. In the decades since Cone announced his project, it has been inflected in various ways, as theologians have grappled with the ways that Black American identity is shaped by gender, class, and immigration experience, as international academic circuits have allowed for the ideas of Black theology to resonate in other contexts, and as the framework of Black theology, with Jesus identified first and foremost as liberator of the oppressed, has been embraced by various oppressed communities, from queer to Latinx to indigenous.

There are two distinct yet connected senses of Black theology, then: theology that concerns Black experience and theology that is structured by Black liberation. The former sense of Black theology is compatible with theological (and secular) liberalism: Black theology is contextual theology, the theology of one identity group among others. The latter sense of Black theology, in contrast, makes a claim that is incommensurable with other theological projects: Black theology is the only way to understand Christian theology rightly. The only way for Christians to speak rightly about God, the aspiration of theology, is to use the tools at hand to name the fundamental features of God, namely, that God liberates the oppressed. Grappling with the structural injustices associated with anti-Blackness are, therefore, the necessary starting points for speaking about God; Cone goes so far as to say that Christian theology calls for everyone to "become Black" by aligning their life with the struggle against anti-Blackness so as to become faithful.[2]

While Black theology as an academic discourse emerged in the late 1960s, in a broader sense Black theology existed long before. Black theology can name the religious reflection of Black Christians, and for centuries this reflection was happening outside the academy, and even outside the pulpit. Ordinary Black Christians had to grapple with the meaning of their faith commitments in a world structured by anti-Black racism. They also had to discern how to act, how to live. In recent years, academic Black theologians have turned to the lives and communities of ordinary Black Christians as resources – as authorities – for the implications of Black theology. Sometimes this takes the form of highlighting histories of struggle, of community organizing and protest against racism. But at other times it takes the form of highlighting survival strategies, the ways of feeling, talking, music-making, and withdrawing that make life livable – and that are read as spiritual practices. Black theologians catalogue the virtues (and vices) as judged from a perspective where Christian faith entails the belief that God is Black. No longer are servility, nonjudgmental love, and unconditional forgiveness primary Christian virtues; indeed, from the perspective of Black theology, they may even be vices. The virtues now are habits that contribute to the destruction of white supremacy, standing in for worldly domination. Comrades in the struggle are to be loved; racial domination is to be hated. Faithfulness now means persistence in struggle even against steep odds, not belief in abstract principles. To be angry, or ornery, is from this perspective a fitting response to confront white supremacy and its many tentacles.

Put a different way, Black theology takes as its primary antagonist domination, arbitrary rule. Those who dominate set themselves up as gods: idolatry. As in political theory, slavery and its afterlives serve as the paradigm of domination: one human exercising arbitrary rule over another, with the Middle Passage marking slavery at its most extreme. From the perspective of Black theology, Christianity too often retains an investment in arbitrary

---

[2] Vincent W. Lloyd, *Religion of the Field Negro: Black Secularism and Black Theology* (Fordham University Press, 2017).

rule, even as it proclaims the reign of grace instead of law. What purport to be Christian virtues are actually habits of respectability: practices commended as good in order to maintain the status quo – in order to enforce (and mystify) arbitrary rule. If virtues are formed through acculturation in community, too often that community is presented as race-neutral while it actually is predominantly white. The result is that Black ways of life tend to be condemned as vicious when, in fact, Black ways of life involve habits forged for survival and struggle, the truest sense of Christian virtue.

The Tempest is a play about domination. It has famously been read as an allegory of colonial domination, but critics have also noted the way relationships of domination pervade the play.[3] The play may seem like a more fruitful site for reflection on politics than on ethics, if we consider structures of domination fundamentally political (or political-theological) problems. But just as interesting as the fact of arbitrary rule, probably more interesting, is the way in which such rule is inhabited. Domination exists in theory; in the world, it is lived. As practiced, performed, domination mystifies: arbitrary rule seems natural, a human imposter seems like a genuine god. Virtue equivocally names such practice. From the perspective of Black theology, white virtue enforces domination; Black virtue is illegible from the perspective of rulers and aspirants, dismissed as vice, yet oriented toward a world without domination, toward a law unrecognizable from the perspective of the world (God's law).[4] Black theology operates via allegory, with slavery and its afterlives in the United States standing in for domination as such, offering lessons about virtue as such. But Black theology also affirms the unequivocal commitment to the concrete: *God is Black*, not just identified with the oppressed but having a color, a race. What does it mean to use Black theology as a reading tool, or a training for reading? Perhaps it means we are not forced into a choice between attending to racial particularity and to social logic but rather – in line with theoretical currents in Black studies – when Blackness is seen as a constitutive exclusion of the social (and political and ethical), we must attend to both together.

---

[3] See Rob Nixon, "Caribbean and African Appropriations of 'The Tempest'," *Critical Inquiry* 13. 3 (1987), 557–578; Jonathan Goldberg, *Tempest in the Caribbean* (University of Minnesota Press, 2003); Sidia Fiorato, "Ariel and Caliban as Law-conscious Servants Longing for Legal Personhood," in *Liminal Discourses: Subliminal Tensions in Law and Literature*, eds. Daniela Carpi and Jeanne Gaakeer (De Gruyter, 2013), 113–128.

[4] On a tradition of God's law in Black American thought, see Vincent W. Lloyd, *Black Natural Law* (Oxford University Press, 2016). See also Julia Lupton, "*The Tempest* and Black Natural Law," *Religions* 10. 2 (2019), 91.

In *The Tempest*, there is domination all over, but it is of two types. The domination experienced by Caliban is of a different species than the domination that we find elsewhere, in every corner of the play. Critics have pointed to Caliban's distinctiveness as a loose thread that can be pulled from the colonies to unravel the mystification of the metropole and of the logic of colonial domination, a starting point for rewriting the play. A Black theological reading acknowledges the fallenness of the world and our inability to conjure a new world that is not infected by the same dynamics of domination as our present condition. Such a reading places the emphasis on the ethical rather than the political, attending to the characteristic virtues and vices that conceal domination and those that are found in dark spaces, in Black spaces, away from the centripetal force of rule, holding an opaque promise of a liberated world to come.

At the center of *The Tempest* is Prospero, ruler of his isle in a sense both political and theological. Marshalling the natural world to his advantage by means of his learning and his servants, as dramatized by the storm he conjures in the opening scene, Prospero had been exiled from one sovereign office and assumed another. Here, on his island, sovereignty is purer: there is nothing to interrupt his rule. Though not quite: his servants Ariel (indentured spirit) and Caliban (dark human-beast), and Miranda (virgin daughter) inhabit the world he rules and navigate that rule. Domination is performed together with them, and in these performances we discern virtue and vice.

In Miranda and Ariel we find white virtue, habits that claim objective goodness but actually affirm and naturalize arbitrary rule. From the start, we find Miranda acknowledging her father's rule while also performing apparent virtue. She has compassion: when she sees the tempest near the approaching ship, she proclaims that she suffers with the sailors. She adds, "Had I been any god of power, I would / Have sunk the sea within the earth" to save the ship (1.2.10–11). But she is powerless; she is subject to rule rather than one who rules. Prospero reassures her that this is, in fact, what he had done: sent a storm but saved the sailors by means of his magic. What seemed like compassion that would pull away from Prospero's rule turned out to be perfectly aligned with it. Now with an occasion to tell Miranda of her lineage, Prospero describes her high status as the product of a merger between the Duke of Milan, himself, and "a piece of virtue," her mother – rule and white virtue hand in hand (1.2.70). Prospero's downfall came because he aspired to have powers that exceeded the world, and the world (including his family) conspired to thwart his plans. Prospero only survived the trials he has had to endure because of his daughter's inherited (and, in theological terms, infused) virtue: "Thou wast that did preserve me. Thou didst smile, / Infused with a fortitude from heaven" (1.2.183–184).

The spirit Ariel possesses another version of white virtue. Like all on the island, Ariel is ruled by Prospero, but again this domination is performed imperfectly. Prospero and Ariel have a contract and it is to expire shortly, but Ariel is anxious, "moody" – as apparently happens at least monthly. Under his previous master, the witch Sycorax, Ariel was also a grudging servant, to the point that Sycorax confined him to a tree. "And for thou wast a spirit too delicate / To act her earthy and abhorred commands" (1.2.326–327). Yet ultimately Ariel is faithful, winning praise for effectively executing Prospero's plans. His moodiness appears to be a vice, but ultimately it serves to sustain Prospero's rule.

Miranda and Ferdinand, as they through enchantment fall in love, each profess to be ruled by the other: "They are both in either's power" (1.2.542). They find each other divine. Love here is mutual domination, mutual surrender. From the perspective of Black theology, this is white love. A pair of humans elevate each other to gods, ultimately binding themselves to the world, foreclosing the possibility of genuine liberation. The love that is commended in Black theology is love in struggle, love as struggle. It is the affection of comrades, sealed through the intensity of a shared project that promises liberation. The apparent virtues of white love are subordinate to the domination in which they jointly participate: while Miranda and Ferdinand play chess against each other – one now taking a piece of the other, now the other taking a piece – it is a performance that constitutes their worldly rule, the political domination they will exercise back home.

In contrast to white virtues and vices, complicit in the logic of domination, Prospero introduces Caliban as "my slave, who never / Yields us kind answer" (1.2.368–369). The half-African slave is "a villain" and ugly, the defects of his not-quite-human form enumerated in different ways throughout the play. From the perspective of Prospero and Miranda, and the others he encounters, Caliban is all vice – perhaps beneath vice. Vice suggests a laudable habit gone wrong, or not fully formed, whereas Caliban's actions seem inscrutable. And so he has been "got by the devil himself," his dark heart not vicious but evil (1.2.383). Yet Caliban is clear about what he wants: freedom, not in an empty sense, as mere liberation from legal bondage (like Ariel), but in a fulsome sense, possessing what is his, having the capacity to flourish. Caliban now recognizes the virtue he had seen Prospero display as artifice: his affection, kindness, and pity were actually in the service of establishing his rule. Caliban will no longer have any of this: he is only moved to obey now by physical force, not by any of the mystifications of power. In this state, subject to but not enchanted by Prospero's rule, Caliban marks the constitutive exclusion, the devil that marks the outside of the city of God. But a Black theological reading draws our attention to Caliban's actions, his performance, rather than merely his status. He curses. His inscrutable insubordination may haunt Prospero, but it also marks a different sort of faithfulness, one so committed to a world beyond domination that he continually proclaims his allegiance to it in the negative, through the curse. Caliban's mode of inhabiting the normative order matters, but so does his material reality. His particular parentage, his particular dispossession: these are the anchors of his faith.

Trinculo thinks Caliban "A most poor, credulous monster!" and "very weak" as Caliban implores, "I prithee, be my god" (2.2.152, 155). But what appears to be excessive credulity from Trinculo's perspective is the virtue of faithfulness from another. Here, as when Caliban first encountered Prospero, he was also committed to a figure from outside his world, a promise of the end of domination in his world. It is not a new ruler that Caliban craves but rule from beyond the logic of domination – this we see with his waning allegiance as rule that seems to be from beyond the world folds into worldly domination. "Freedom, high-day! High-day, freedom!" Caliban exclaims after singing of his new master and new self (2.2.192). One of the hallmarks of Black theology is its commitment to the authority of song, not just as a cultural artifact but as a mode of communication that thwarts our desire for referential discourse and so is particularly suited to the horizon of the theological. There cannot be a plan for liberation, a chart on how to move from here to there, but the promise of liberation can still be celebrated in songs of praise. Indeed, Caliban is attuned to the music of the island, a form of primal enchantment that is blotted out by human rule. Despite his status as Prospero's slave, Caliban still knows "The isle is full of noises, / Sounds and sweet airs that give delight and hurt not," fueling his dreams (3.2.153–154). In other words, Caliban's faith is not belief in an abstract object as ruler; his faith is fueled by immersion in the sounds (in the broadest sense) of his home that give him the capacity to stand against a world of domination and believe in a world beyond.

Put another way, Black theology attends to spaces of constitutive exclusion and instead of finding bare life finds struggle. From the perspective of the powers that be, Caliban is indiscernible, perhaps man or fish, perhaps alive or dead. As Julia Lupton has rightly noted, this figure of the human before concepts points us to an essential but often concealed feature of our humanity, one that marks a promise.[5] The ways of the world could be radically otherwise. But Caliban does more than this. Caliban has agency, albeit of a peculiar form, beyond his symbolic function. In his actions, his habits, he models Black virtue, ways of living that are rooted in material conditions and that point beyond the world. They point to a Black God, opposed to all forms of human domination. Such Black virtue, however, is gravely defective, for all virtue is cultivated in community. A community struggles together. In that struggle, it not only points to but prefigures a world without domination. One of a kind, Caliban can point but not prefigure. The play ends with Prospero's possible freedom and with Caliban's hopes deflated. Black theology grows out of and is accountable to Black sociality, the collective life of those constitutively excluded – a sociality always under erasure. Because of that erasure, it is gathered in resonance of affect and flesh rather than in discourse or norm.[6] The word incarnate. Isolated from sociality, Blackness goes wrong: Black affect and flesh become disordered. Here we have Othello, paranoid to death. And here we have Caliban, a drunk and an attempted rapist. A Black theological framework clarifies these actions, preventing us from either reducing them to stereotype or exculpating them because of the overwhelm caused by racial domination. It teaches that the virtues are not as straightforward as they seem. Virtues are not good actions but good habits, not performed alone but in community, and the habits most praised by a community can turn out to be blameworthy while the habits most reviled can turn out to be where goodness is found.

[5] Julia Reinhard Lupton, "Creature Caliban," *Shakespeare Quarterly* 51. 1 (Spring 2000), 1–23; See also Lupton, "*Tempest* and Black Natural Law."
[6] See Alexander G. Weheliye, *Habeas Viscus: Racializing Assemblages, Biopolitics, and Black Feminist Theories of the Human* (Duke University Press, 2014).

CHAPTER 33

Virtue on Robben Island

David Schalkwyk

Is virtue possible in what the sociologist Erving Goffman calls "total institutions": mental asylums, boarding schools, concentration camps, homes for the disabled and the aged, religious institutions, military organizations – and, of course, prisons? "A total institution," Goffman writes,

> may be defined as a place of residence and work where a large number of life-situated individuals, cut off from the wider society for an appreciable amount of time, together lead an enclosed, formally administered round of life. Prisons serve as a clear example.[1]

Prisons are thus exemplary, and some of their aspects are found in the society beyond their ambit. Indeed, modern life as a whole is informed by a similar, rapacious exercise of power and isolation, in the protocols of the office, the rigors of the factory, the relentless onslaught of the media, and the panopticon of social media and the Internet.

What forms of virtue can exist – let alone thrive – in such worlds? Goffman emphasizes the brute exercise of power by the "supervising group" over the inmates: a regime of surveillance and isolation and an infantilizing objectification whereby the "new arrival allows himself to be shaped and coded into an object that can be fed into the administrative machinery of the establishment, to be worked on smoothly by routine operations."[2] Michel Foucault emphasizes the element of extensive, if low-level, torture that all modern incarceration involves:

> But a punishment like forced labour or even imprisonment – mere loss of liberty – has never functioned without a certain additional element of punishment that certainly concerns the body itself: rationing of food, sexual deprivation, corporal punishment, solitary confinement ...

---

[1] Erving Goffman, *Asylums: Essays on the Social Situation of Mental Patients and Other Inmates*, New edition (Penguin, 1991), xiii.
[2] Ibid., 16.

> There remains, therefore, a trace of "torture" in the modern mechanisms of criminal justice – a trace that has not been entirely overcome, but which is enveloped, increasingly, by the non-corporal nature of the penal system ... Surveillance is permanent in its effects, even if it is discontinuous in its action.[3]

Neither Goffman nor Foucault is concerned with virtue. Indeed, each of their accounts of post-Enlightenment institutions suggest the impossibility of virtue within them: in their insistence of the brute subjugation and even creation of individual subjects, their isolation, and violent abrogation of individual autonomy and choice, and the nefarious, duplicitous brutality of those running the institutions.

Alasdair McIntyre argues that since the Enlightenment we have lost the concept of virtue to competing and incoherent discourses that allow not only for no possible consensus about what virtue is, but, most important, no form of social life that might make such a consensus possible or any rational method for deciding among competing theories of virtue. In his analysis, the theories of virtue that have been in a perpetual *agon* since at least Descartes have been Utilitarianism, which holds that the good is what is good for the many – the greatest number; Emotivism, an individualist approach, based on the emotions, which holds that whatever is good is whatever I endorse personally – to say "This is good" is to say "I approve of this – I urge you to adopt the same view"; and the Kantian "categorical imperative," which claims a universal command that by definition is the opposite of personal inclination, but which is unable to demonstrate why the injunction, "treat every human being as an end rather than a means," should be universally accepted and followed.[4]

None of these theories of virtue is viable in a total institution. Emotivism depends at the very least on the integrity of the individual who extends approval (or disapproval) to particular acts or attitudes: It rests on an assumption of an independent and free expression of personal attitude. In an institution designed to forge the individual into the confining mold and will of its masters, this is impossible. Nor are such coercion and control utilitarian, whatever its propaganda might say. And almost by definition, even if inmates are coerced into obeying certain institutional imperatives, they are hardly consonant with Kant's egalitarian command to treat all people equally.

---

[3] Michel Foucault, *Discipline and Punish: The Birth of the Prison*, 2nd edn. (Vintage, 1995), 15–16, 201.
[4] Alasdair MacIntyre, *After Virtue: A Study in Moral Theory*, 3rd edn. (University of Notre Dame Press, 2007).

Goffman's theory is performative and individualist: It focuses on the ways in which such institutions curtail the "roles" that people are able to play. They are shaped into being different kinds of "actors" than they might be in life beyond its confines. In works like *The Presentation of Self in Everyday Life*, he describes ordinary encounters in society as a whole as a repeated *agon* of theatrical or performative presentation and interpretive deflation – each of us presents ourselves to others in a charade of deception: "This kind of control on the part of the individual ... sets the stage for a kind of information game – a potentially infinite cycle of concealment, discovery, false information, and rediscovery."[5] The peculiar circumstances of the "total institution" undoubtedly make "moral claims" made behind this façade impossible, but once he extends performativity to all social interactions, virtue becomes untenable in society as a whole: It's all pretense, including the claim to moral obligation.

Let us return to the prison. Specifically, to the South African Robben Island Prison during Apartheid. Robben Island is an exemplary instance of Goffman's "total institutions." All he has said about prisons, and more, are redoubled in the notorious island gaol, used by the Apartheid regime to incarcerate its African political opponents between 1963 and 1979 (including its most famous prisoner, Nelson Mandela, who spent more than twenty years on the island). Fran Buntman's comprehensive account of imprisonment and resistance on Robben Island confirms the prison's practice of what Goffman calls "mortification" of individuals through stripping away the aspects of their identity and self that are based in the outside, or "'home world' ... preventing inmates from assuming any self-control or self-definition of their roles in the world."[6] But Buntman's story, following those of many prisoners themselves, is one of communal resistance among the prisoners against the very processes that Goffman describes. This resistance is universally presented as a *political* enterprise, but I want to characterize it in Aristotelian terms as a peculiar form of virtue.

The incarceration of political prisoners on Robben Island famously enabled the forging of a community bound together by what Aristotle calls a *telos* – an aim, goal, or end. McIntyre argues that post-Enlightenment virtue discourses are both incoherent and incommensurable without a notion of a goal or end towards which all human beings should strive, a notion absolutely central to Aristotelian ethics: The virtuous man is the

---

[5] Erving Goffman, *The Presentation of Self in Everyday Life*, New edn. (Penguin, 1990), 20.
[6] Fran Lisa Buntman, *Robben Island and Prisoner Resistance to Apartheid* (Cambridge University Press, 2003), 47.

one who realizes in his judgments and actions what is encapsulated in the essence of being a human being: the realization of the "good life," characterized by the cardinal virtues of courage, honor, friendship, justice, temperance, prudence, and truthfulness.

We do not have to subscribe to Aristotle's metaphysical notion of human nature and its relation to the *telos* of *dikaiosunē* – happiness, pleasure or well-being – to argue that the prisoners on Robben Island, united in their fight against systematic injustice and by the attempts by the unjust regime to break their fighting spirit, found in their imprisonment a common *telos* that incorporates the virtues that Aristotle extolls. The solidarity that cemented the community required trust and friendship; their resistance to systematic attempts at "mortification" needed extraordinary reserves of courage; especially Mandela's patience (another virtue) in using his legal skills to expose and overcome the excessive cruelties and arbitrary exercise power by the prison regime was an exemplary exercise of prudence, a virtue that in the end secured the end of apartheid and a democratic South Africa in which the virtue of justice could finally be pursued. This community seemed to have been an ideal instance of "mutual improvement" celebrated by Aristotle:

> The friendship of good men is good, being augmented by their companionship: and they are thought to become better too by … improving each other; for from each other they take the stamp of the characteristics they approve of.[7]

In one of his letters from prison, Mandela offers a list of the virtues that are to be cherished in the cause of both political and personal ideals: "Honesty, sincerity, simplicity, humility, pure generosity, absence of vanity, readiness to serve others – qualities which are within easy reach of every soul – are the foundations of one's spiritual life."[8]

I have argued elsewhere that Mandela should be regarded as a latter-day Stoic.[9] Not simply because of his control over his emotions, his legendary transcendence of fate – "In the battle of ideas the true fighter who strives to free public thinking from the social evils of his age need never be discouraged if, at one & the same time, he is praised and condemned, honoured

[7] Aristotle, *Complete Works of Aristotle, The Revised Oxford Translation, Volume 2*, ed. Jonathan Barnes (Princeton University Press, 1984), 9.12.1172a10–14.

[8] Nelson Mandela, Sahm Venter, and Zamaswazi Dlamini-Mandela, *The Prison Letters of Nelson Mandela* (Liveright, 2018), 278.

[9] David Schalkwyk, "Mandela, the Emotions, and the Lessons of Prison," *The Cambridge Companion to Nelson Mandela*, ed. Rita Barnard (Cambridge University Press, 2014), 50–69.

& degraded, acclaimed as saint & cursed as an irredeemable sinner"[10] – the latter exemplified by his choice of Caesar's pronouncement, "Cowards die many time before their deaths / The valiant taste of death but once" (*Julius Caesar*, 2.2.34–35). Often overlooked is the Stoic sense of the equality of all people, to which Mandela passionately subscribes, and to its philosophy of empathetic education – the idea, practiced by Mandela in relation to his prison guards, some of whom became friends, that no person is intrinsically evil, that they need a sympathetic education – in the literal sense – from their benighted position to one more enlightened.

Of course, prison conditions are far from the Aristotelian ideal of a free association of men bound in friendship to a *polis*. Nevertheless, that resistant community of political prisoners forged a space in the prison for Aristotelian virtues, whatever the political goal, stripped of ethical concerns, might have been. Robben Island was hardly the ideal of Aristotle's city, but the solidarity forged among inmates was certainly to a large degree "grounded on mutual knowledge and shared virtues … a friendship in respect, and for the sake, of goodness of a kind."[11] The prison itself is celebrated as a site of education of all kinds, and beyond the teaching of literacy and numeracy, and the gaining of university degrees, it offered an opportunity for a shared education in Aristotelian virtue. I have no space for a detailed account of this community of friends; there are plenty of accounts available.[12] But there is a caveat: Like *all* communities, the ties that bound its members to each other were simultaneously the forces that excluded others, who were placed and kept beyond the boundaries of the community.[13] Aristotle excludes women, slaves, barbarians, and the "inferior class" of tradesmen and artisans.[14] Whatever claims have been made about the solidarity and unity of Robben Island as a "University" for all,

---

[10] Mandela, *Letters*, 140.

[11] A. W. Price, *Love and Friendship in Plato and Aristotle* (Oxford University Press, 1997), 198.

[12] See, for example, N. Alexander, *Robben Island Dossier 1964–1974* (University of Cape Town Press, 1998), Eddie Daniels, *There & Back: Robben Island 1964–1979* (Michigan State University Press, 2001), Sedick Isaacs, *Surviving in the Apartheid Prison: Robben Island: Flash Backs of an Earlier Life* (Xlibris Corporation, 2010), Mac Maharaj, ed., *Reflections in Prison*, Robben Island Memories Series, No. 4 (Zebra and the Robben Island Museum, 2001), Nelson Mandela, *Long Walk to Freedom* (Holt, Rinehart and Winston, 2000), Govan Mbeki, *Learning from Robben Island: The Prison Writings of Govan Mbeki* (J. Currey, 1991), Indres Naidoo, *Island in Chains: Prisoner 885/63 Ten Years on Robben Island* (Penguin, 1982), and D. M Zwelonke, *Robben Island*, African Writers Series 128 (Heinemann, 1973).

[13] See David Schalkwyk, "The Rules of Physiognomy: Reading the Convict in South African Prison," *Pretexts* 7. 1 (1998), 81–96.

[14] See Martha C. Nussbaum, *The Therapy of Desire: Theory and Practice in Hellenistic Ethics* (Princeton University Press, 1994), 104 and MacIntyre, *After Virtue*, 159–160.

the prison was also a site of factionalism, exclusion, and power struggles, among the different political factions like the ANC, the black nationalist Pan African Congress (PAC), and the even more radically Africanist Black Consciousness Movement (BMC), but it extended, in Moses Dlamini's account of the early years, to the violent exclusion of fellow prisoners caught, for example, in homosexual relationships.[15] Equally important was the tendency to belittle and exclude women, who were kept in different prisons, from proper recognition.[16]

Possibly the most tight-knit community on Robben Island was the group isolated in the C-section single cells, with the leadership group of the ANC, including Nelson Mandela, Mac Maharaj, Govan Mbeki, and Ahmed Kathrada. This group of 34 are the signatories of the Robben Island Shakespeare, the collected works that its owner, Sonny Venkathratnam, circulated among his fellows between 1975 and 1977, asking them to sign against their favorite passage with the date. This Shakespeare text afforded members of this tightly bound community to extend themselves beyond the confines of the group, in the form not only of the "other," William Shakespeare, a white Englishman who had been dead for some 350 years,[17] but more significantly the "others" that Shakespeare made available in his text: Shylock, Hamlet, Henry V, Richard II, John of Gaunt, Northumberland, Polonius, Caliban, Julius Caesar, Macbeth, Lady Macbeth, Orsino, Edgar, Puck, Orlando, Duke Senior, Malvolio, Jaques, the Archbishop of Canterbury, Mark Antony, Brutus, Caesar Augustus, Sir Thomas More, and a possibly bisexual poet. I have discussed the possible significance of each choice elsewhere.[18] What I wish to emphasize here is the sheer range of characters – and through them, attitudes, feelings, modes of negotiation, confrontation, and denial – represented through the signatures of the Robben Island Shakespeare. They do not form a close-knit community, bound by a common *polis*, friendship, or a shared ideal of human virtue. They are, if anything, a register of what Keats called Shakespeare's "negative capability" and Coleridge invoked as his "myriad-mindedness."

---

[15] Moses Dlamini, *Robben Island, Hell-Hole: Reminiscences of a Political Prisoner in South Africa* (Africa World Press, 1984); see also Buntman, *Robben Island*, Chapter 6.

[16] See, for example, Jean Middleton, *Convictions: A Woman Political Prisoner Remembers* (Raven Press, 1998).

[17] For Shakespeare's conflicted status in South Africa, see Natasha Distiller, *Shakespeare and the Coconuts: On Post-Apartheid South African Culture* (Wits University Press, 2012) and Chris Thurman, *South African Essays on "Universal" Shakespeare* (Routledge, 2016).

[18] For an extensive account of the role of this book on Robben Island, see David Schalkwyk, *Hamlet's Dreams: The Robben Island Shakespeare* (Bloomsbury Academic, 2013).

Each of the members of the C-section of Robben Island Prison, who worked, talked, read, and engaged in communal resistance, appended his signature against an "other" – a fictional character, significantly different from the other characters in the plays and poems and from the signatory. Shakespeare's characters variously reflected or demanded or expressed things as diverse as a plea for a common humanity; a bitter reflection on the incorrigible nature of human corruption; a rousing, nationalist call to arms; the isolation of imprisonment; the truth guaranteed by suffering and the proximity of death; advice from father to son; hope in the face of death and danger; a defiant resistance to dispossession and claim of political right; the Stoic readiness for death; despair at the emptiness of life; the call to eradicate all tenderness for the sake of political ambition; the fullness of love and solace of music; the acceptance of irreparable loss; the "sweetness" of adversity; a whimsical apology for the power of fictional "shadows"; the rage of dispossession and maltreatment; a reflection being born great, achieving greatness, or having greatness thrust upon one; a melancholy disquisition on the stages of human life; the purposeful conjunction of communal action; anger at personal betrayal and a call to vengeance; the crucial timeliness of political action; a rhetorical encomium over the bodies of two enemies; the ordained justice of God; and various reflections of the passage of time and the madness of despair.

These names – the most prominent opponents of the Apartheid regime – offer an extraordinary palimpsest of political solidarity and personal ethical commitment on the site of the Shakespearean text in its "myriad-minded" diversity and singular power, all collected under the peculiar and paradoxical authority of the signature. What does a signature signify in such circumstances? And what are the ethical dimensions of such signatures: as a personal commitment or underwriting of a Shakespeare text that represents a removed historical intentionality that is split across different dramatic voices and across time; as a joint, communal act of solidarity with others facing the same choice, but constrained by the signatures that precede them; by the intersection of political commitment and ethical responsibility exemplified, for example, by Mandela's sophisticated Stoicism; complicated by subsequent disavowals by signatories of their signed passages and the inverse empathetic identification with such signatures and their accompanying Shakespearean texts by readers exposed to them after the fall of Apartheid.[19] These signatures thus bring together the personal and the political; present, past, and future action; and the complex political

---

[19] See Schalkwyk, *Hamlet's Dreams*, 18–20.

and ethical issues of the Shakespearean text. Each signature, made in a present moment against a moment of utterance *in* the text, pledges the signatory against an expression of difference in that text, no matter how much or how little the signatory might recognize a part of himself in the text. This is a kind of promise or oath, a binding of the self to someone different, or the expression of different ideas, attitudes, or feelings, in other contexts, and therefore a pledge that opens oneself to something or someone other than oneself, into the future "so long as men can breathe or eyes can see" (Sonnet 18).[20]

The signatures of the Robben Island Shakespeare thus open up a new dimension of ethics, which reaches beyond the enclosed and exclusive community of Aristotelian virtue. I'm thinking about the twentieth-century philosopher, Emanuel Levinas, who founds his idea of virtue upon unconditional openness to the "other." Writing in the context of personal experience as a Jew in World War II, Levinas builds upon a sympathetic critique of the existential philosophers, Edmund Husserl and Martin Heidegger, to insist on the absolute a priori responsibility of all human beings to the "other," to the *face* of the other:

> From the moment of sensibility, the subject is *for the other*: substitution, responsibility, expiation. But a responsibility that I did not assume at any moment, at any present. Nothing is more passive than this challenge prior to my freedom, this pre-original challenge, this sincerity ... It is through the condition of being hostage [to the other] that there can be in the world pity, compassion, pardon and proximity – even the little there is, even the simply, "After you, sir."[21]

In contrast to the Aristotelian ideal of the community, the face of the other calls everyone to respond without and certainly prior to any preconception or prejudice: Indeed, it is what makes the possibility of any community possible. Levinas's metaphysical ethics are very difficult to follow, and I certainly have no space to expound them here. But I do wish to use his openness to otherness as an *analogy* for the openness to otherness signaled by the signatures in the Robben Island Shakespeare. The responsibility that Levinas extols exists beyond agency – no one decides to take it on, it is born with our birth, as it were – and also beyond any present moment of

---

[20] It is significant that only one prisoner signed against a speech by a female character, Lady Macbeth, in her call to be "unsexed."

[21] Emmanuel Levinas, *Humanism of the Other*, trans. Nidra Poller (University of Illinois Press, 2005), 64 and Emmanuel Levinas, *Otherwise Than Being, or, Beyond Essence*, trans. Alphonso Lingis (Duquesne University Press, 1999), 117–118.

decision or even the freedom to make a decision – it conditions our existence, a priori. It is what makes the virtues celebrated in Aristotle's notion of communally charged *telos* possible. Beyond the Aristotelian paraphernalia of a communal, and ultimately exclusionary but also voluntarist, notion through judgment and right action, there lies the Levinasian demand of the openness to what is different, to what is not yourself, to what lies beyond your community.

The forging of an Aristotelian community of virtue on Robben Island thus requires a further, non-Aristotelian openness to otherness – exemplified by the Robben Island Shakespeare – that transcends the notion of the Aristotelian *polis*, founded on multiple exclusions. That openness is exemplified by the signatures of the Robben Island Shakespeare, which offer a historical, nonmetaphysical instance of Levinas's demand of the other – in a face of the Apartheid system built on exclusion, excoriation, and rejection of all that is not considered *one's own* – and which, in subtle ways, also marked the Aristotelian communities that existed and came into conflict in the Robben Island prison.

CHAPTER 34

Globability
The Virtue of Worlding

Jane Hwang Degenhardt

In the *Metaphysics* Aristotle explains that "everything that comes to be moves towards a principle, i.e. an end ... and the actuality is the end" (9.8.1050a5–10).[1] This teleological progression, whereby potentiality *(dynamis)* is transformed into actuality *(energeia)*, informs Aristotle's understanding of virtue *(aretē)* as the power that brings something into its most complete expression of being. Virtue is thus inherently aspirational: it entails movement towards a goal in which a thing's fullest potential is realized – its "essence or function ... or that for the sake of which it exists," in the words of C. D. C Reeve (xvi).[2] Observing that all things have a unique function, Aristotle seeks in the *Nicomachean Ethics* to determine the virtue of humans: "For just as for a flute-player, a sculptor, or any artist, and in general for all things that have a function or activity, the good and the 'well' is thought to reside in the function, so it would seem to be for man" (1.7.1097b25–30).[3] Aristotle concludes that humans fulfill their function most completely through being happy *(eudaimonia)* – a state that is not valued because of its moral implications, but rather because it maximizes human flourishing, enabling human beings to be most fully themselves. The potential for happiness is intrinsic to human nature, though certain conditions of "misfortune," such as enslavement or being female, can prevent human beings from manifesting their fullest potential. Asserting that people are by nature social and political, Aristotle argues that a solitary life was not sufficient for happiness, though solitude might defend against some of the vulnerabilities to fortune that accompany a life lived among others. In Aristotle's view *eudaimonia* is not individualistic but is rather relationally manifested and affected by external contingencies of fortune or

---

[1] Aristotle, "Metaphysics," in *The Basic Works of Aristotle*, ed. Richard McKeon (Modern Library Paperback Edition, 2001), 689–926.
[2] Ibid., Introduction.
[3] Aristotle, *Nicomachean Ethics*, trans. David Ross, rev. Lesley Brown (Oxford University Press, 2009).

misfortune. As Martha Nussbaum explains, "Aristotle gives the polis and our activities in and for it an important role" because human growth is "an ongoing process that requires continued support from without."[4] Ideally, human flourishing has positive effects that extend beyond the individual and does not necessitate or depend on others' subjugation, though some conflict is unavoidable.

Aristotle's understanding of virtue as the complete fulfillment of a thing's potential offers a useful way to think not only about happiness as the fullest manifestation of human potential but also about the larger potential of the world as a relational and communal entity. As a number of contributors to this handbook observe (see esp. Bloom and Doty, Crosbie, and Rust), the achievement of human happiness benefits not only the individual but also reverberates outward to a larger community, which is linked together by human relationships. This community might also include broader environmental interactions with nature and non-human entities in the world – in the opening of his *Politics*, Aristotle himself famously describes man as a "political animal" and compares him to "bees and other gregarious animals" who also show tendencies toward self-organization in groups. Indeed, individual human flourishing might be understood to benefit the world at large and to reach its fullest potential when flourishing is universally shared among humans and living things, rather than selectively apportioned. It may seem to follow from Aristotle's understanding of *eudaimonia* that the world itself reaches its fullest potential when all of the individual beings and things within it are allowed to flourish. Such a conception of *world* seeks to encompass everything contained within the globe or planet, or perhaps even the entire universe, depending upon how expansively one chooses to define the scope of the world.

It is not difficult to see how anthropocentric systems and hierarchies, including global capitalism, work against such a holistic understanding of *eudaimonia* by partitioning the world into empires and unequal distributions of power and wealth, enabling selective flourishing at the expense of other beings or places, and ultimately rendering certain lives expendable by disregarding the equilibrium necessary to sustain a complex ecology. By contrast, a nonanthropocentric worldview sacrifices selective interests to the larger whole. It values collectivity – extended as far a possible – above individual happiness, perhaps adopting the utilitarian view that collective

---

[4] Martha C. Nussbaum, *The Fragility of Goodness: Luck and Ethics in Greek Tragedy and Philosophy*, Revised edn. (Cambridge University Press, 2001), 347.

happiness leads to greater individual happiness. But are there also dangers to conceiving of the world in universalizing terms? What assumptions do we make when we presuppose that the world is one thing, and that human virtue is maximized by conceiving of the world in the largest possible frame? In what ways are these assumptions conditioned by our unthinking acceptance of an integrated and totalizing notion of the world that is habituated by our own globalized sense of interconnection and the economic, technological, social, and environmental (as well as viral) pathways that foster it?

As has long been recognized, the early-modern period marked a crucial stage in the history of global capitalism as well as a pivotal transition in the way the world was understood. As scholars such as Ayesha Ramachandron, Denis Cosgrove, and Ricardo Padrón have shown, the conception of the world *as globe* that was catalyzed in the sixteenth century by cartographic, navigational, astronomical, and imperialistic developments imposed a certain violence on the world by reducing it to an abstracted totality, which in turn made it susceptible to epistemological conquest as well as to imperialistic possession and subjugation.[5] This privileging of a single world also carried out a totalizing and homogenizing effect that flattened out differences at the same time that it extended rigid systems of hierarchy across expansive reaches of space and time. In the wake of the world's figuration as globe and subsequent centuries of escalating globalization that have brought us to our present time, how might we begin to foster a more pluralistic understanding of world that does not sacrifice the integrity of its multiple parts in service of a singular whole? How might we enable a world that allows differences to thrive and that protects and nourishes its spaces of disjuncture, while also honoring the existence of the larger world – or worlds – beyond? The achievement of a truly virtuous world seems to lie in understanding its *dynamis* as a capacity for both pluralism and harmony – capacities that need not be mutually exclusive nor bounded in their interlocking scopes.

To understand the world's potentiality in this way is to re-conceive the world as not a thing or an object, but rather as a dynamic entity, a self-actualizing configuration that continuously strives to fulfill a higher function. In the words of Martin Heidegger,

---

[5] Ayesha Ramachandran, *The Worldmakers: Global Imagining in Early Modern Europe* (University of Chicago Press, 2015); Denis Cosgrove, *Apollo's Eye: A Cartographic Genealogy of the Earth in the Western Imagination* (Johns Hopkins University Press, 2001); and Ricardo Padrón, *The Spacious World: Cartography, Literature, and Empire in Early Modern Spain* (University of Chicago Press, 2004).

World is not a mere collection of the things – countable and uncountable, known and unknown – that are present at hand. Neither is world a merely imaginary framework added by our representation to the sum of things that are present. World worlds, and is more fully in being than all those tangible and perceptible things in the midst of which we take ourselves to be at home.[6]

Heidegger's characterization of the world as an active entity that *worlds* offers a useful rejoinder to Aristotle's aspirational understanding of virtue as the fulfillment of a thing's inherent function. To identify the world's function is not to attempt to contain or describe the world, but rather to enable and to cultivate its aspirational becoming and to celebrate its future potentiality. Our tendency to view modern-day globalization as a *fait accompli* can sometimes obscure alternative or premodern conceptions of the world, preventing us from seeing the world's past configurations and future potentialities. As Pheng Cheah puts it, "The fundamental shortcoming of equating the world with a global market is that it assumes that globalization creates a world."[7] Indeed, to understand the world as globe or as a globalized entity manifested through historical processes of economic, technological, and cultural integration is to fail to perceive how this manifestation is but one possible historically contingent iteration of world – an actualization that is neither inevitable nor permanent.

Shakespeare's plays invite us to embrace a more dynamic and inchoate understanding of world while also offering a view of the sometimes violent processes of *worlding* that take place when worlds fracture, evolve, combust, or become reconfigured. While a number of Shakespeare's plays register incipient aspects of globalization, they also offer alternative models of worlds that are construed in a wide variety of ways – through shared values or ethics, conditions of belonging and un-belonging, communal agreements, legal infrastructures and state policies, religious affiliations, natural and supernatural conditions of possibility, and even metaphysical and ontological distinctions. And while Shakespeare's worlds are sometimes linked to geopolitical boundaries of region, nation, or empire, they tend not to be globally oriented. In fact, the word "global" figures not at all in Shakespeare's canon. We do find the word "globe" (a total of 12 times) – sometimes referring to the Globe theater, sometimes referring to the earth

---

[6] Martin Heidegger, "The Origin of the Work of Art," in *Off the Beaten Track*, ed. and trans. Julian Young and Kenneth Haynes (Cambridge University Press, 2002), 23.

[7] Pheng Cheah, *What is a World?: On Postcolonial Literature as World Literature* (Duke University Press, 2016).

as a planet or to another astronomical body, sometimes to a sphere or the head of a human body, and sometimes to an abstract or metaphorical notion of world. While rich and varied, this number of instances pales in comparison to the far larger number of times the word "world" appears in Shakespeare's plays – more than 650 times. At the very least, the preponderance with which Shakespeare uses the term tells us something about the powerful utility of "world" as a category that might be relied upon to help express any number of concepts, feelings, opinions, or everyday sentiments. And yet, despite the rich potential of "world" to communicate large and complex ideas in a single word, its meaning in the plays was not consistent or stable but encompassed a range of diverse connotations that were by turns spatial, temporal, metaphysical, existential, experiential, political, and communal. And while Shakespeare's understandings of world rarely register a sense of the world conceived-as-globe, they possess many elements that are intimately familiar to us. In this way, Shakespeare's plays enable us to not only see around and beyond the realities of our globalized world but also to perceive alternative formulations of world as *already present* and alive in world we live in, and in all the potential worlds that will continue to be. In other words, Shakespeare's plays awaken us to the inherent virtue of the world, as an entity that is always in a state of becoming, and therefore dynamic and multiplicitous.

Illustrating Heidegger's sense of the world's active agency, Shakespeare often figures the world as a collective subject that "thinks" and is a source of opinion and judgment. For example, in *The Merchant of Venice*, the Duke pronounces to the courtroom that "the world thinks, and I think so, too" that Shylock will offer a "gentle answer" by granting mercy to Antonio (4.1.18, 35). In this case, the Duke's invocation of the "world" seems to invite Shylock into its "gentle" fold, but actually it does so only on its own (Gentile) terms, and is thus a world defined by exclusion and compulsion. At other times, Shakespeare invokes the notion of a totalizing world only to expose the hegemonic power structures that undergird it. In *Othello*, Emilia says that she would not make a cuckold of Iago in exchange for a "joint-ring," "measures of lawn," or other material possessions, but would readily agree to do so for "the whole world," for "who would not make her husband a cuckold to make him a monarch?" (4.3.) She further reasons that even if something (such as cuckolding) is deemed "wrong in the world," if it is "your own world," it would lie within your power to "quickly make it right." Perceiving "rightness" in the world to be as arbitrary as its structure of power relations, Emilia's hypothetical wager acknowledges her own disempowerment, even as her sense of the world's fungibility allows her to imagine it otherwise. In a different way, Cleopatra resists Caesar's totalizing conception of world as empire by endeavoring to rewrite imperial history through a reliance on counterfactuals. By extending the possibility of an alternative world through a presencing of what *might have been*, Cleopatra's approach models not simply a course of equivocation or denial, but rather a questioning of the epistemic authority that sustains an imperial world.[8]

In Shakespeare's plays, a world is no sooner established than it is questioned, taken apart, turned upside down, reimagined, or destroyed: this is the distinctive "virtue" of worlding in his imagination. The delimitation of one world – be it Venice, Rome, Egypt, Christendom, fairyland, the court, the island, or the forest – always marks the coexistence of other worlds. Miranda's famous heralding of a "brave new world" apprehends the arrival of her estranged ancestral kin on the shores of the island – the only world she has known since the time of her exile (5.1.23). As she registers the "wondrous" return of her European past, the island's horizons expand to accommodate a coexisting but disconnected set of dynastic and geopolitical dynamics elsewhere, distant and yet ever-encroaching. We often think of worlds as constituted by their completeness, but Shakespeare shows us that if worlds are always plural, they are in fact created out of gaps, seams, and absences. In demonstrating the fluid potency of worlds, their constant renegotiation of boundaries, and their potential to always become something else, Shakespeare illustrates how the collective agency of world contains a latent capacity for multiplicity.

In other less fractious ways, Shakespeare's worlds exhibit this latent capacity through their frequent layerings, crossings, and mixings. His worlds are often vertically and temporally layered upon one another, revealing a density that reflects the accretions of time and history. For example, the Mediterranean worlds of many of the plays are simultaneously pre-Christian and post-Christian, ancient and contemporary, familiar and foreign – a palimpsest of worlds that bleed into one another. The Ephesian world of *The Comedy of Errors* is variously distinguished by its association with the temple of Artemis, its legendary founding by Amazons, a reputation for sorcery and occult practices, the voyages of St. Paul, its thriving commercial port, and a *longue durée* history of imperial conquest by the Persian, Greek, Egyptian, Roman, Byzantine, and Ottoman empires. The world of

---

[8] For a fuller account of this argument, see Degenhardt, "The Horizons of Antony and Cleopatra: Temporal Distance, Counterfactual Histories, and the Potentiality of Now," *SEL: Studies in English Literature* 62.1 (Winter 2022).

the play is thus multitudinous, rather than singular, ripe with the potency of its many accumulated legacies. In other plays, Shakespeare brings into view the coexistence of multiple worlds by positing metaphysical crossings that intermingle human mortals with the worlds of gods, fairies, creatures, spirits, and ghosts. Plays like *Hamlet*, *Macbeth*, and *Richard III* feature terrifying encounters with the undead, who pierce the boundaries of the mortal world to bring unwanted messages from a world beyond. In other plays like *Cymbeline* and *Pericles*, a god swoops down from the heavens to offer protection or guidance that would be otherwise unavailable to earthly mortals. In *A Midsummer Night's Dream* the worlds of gods and mortals, mythical creatures and mechanicals, converge in the "forest," a threshold zone where Nature operates as the avatar for emotionally charged divine passions. As the play acknowledges, the events of the forest are also a function of theater, a dream-inducing medium which constitutes a world unto itself and is comprised of distinct material forms, representational semiotics, generic conventions, and fictional and performative capacities. The play's ability to imagine the world otherwise – and indeed to remake it – is ultimately enabled by theatrical artifice, comparable in its most sinister form to the administration of a mind-altering "potion," but also capable of engendering the expansive virtual experience of dreaming. At the conclusion of the play, Puck enters to inform the audience that all of the play's manipulations of desire have been machinated not only by the "shadowy" forces of theater but are also the work of a "dream," which has managed to rearrange everyone's relationships so that they may safely return to the awakened world of reality.

As Shakespeare's dream world suggests, theater has the power to make things happen and is thus both a "world" and a site of worlding, even if its spell is short-lived and ultimately gives way to the conservative world of the court or other dominant structure of power. By the end of a play, its world has been altered, whether shattered in the case of tragedy or reconstituted in the case of comedy – in both cases opened up by new possibilities. Critics often speak of Shakespeare's "possible" worlds, and Aristotle himself argued that drama should always work within a balance between the possible and the probable.[9] But the worlding power of Shakespeare lies rather in theater's *potentiality*, which often leaves the relative predictability of the "possible" behind and opens previously unimaginable configurations, relations, and scenes. The virtue of "world" for Shakespeare depends on its dynamic capacity to be otherwise, on the way worlds come to live

---

[9] See for instance Simon Palfrey, *Shakespeare's Possible Worlds* (Cambridge University Press, 2014); compare Aristotle's *Poetics* 1.9 1451a36–1451b5, 3.25 1451b9–25.

in the temporary space of imagination and dreaming that theater indulges. Sometimes its capacity for change bleeds out of the theater and into the worlds that exist beyond the play, such as our own. In its most potent moments, theatrical fiction brings about change not by means of manipulation or compulsion, as is the case in *A Midsummer Night's Dream*, but rather by enabling shifts in perspective that are motivated by virtues such as empathy, understanding, optimism, tolerance, and learning.

Above all, Shakespeare's worlds are comprised of relationships, and it is by virtue of these relationships that his characters come to see things in new ways and then to make adjustments that correspond to their altered perspectives. I turn for the remainder of my discussion to *As You Like It*, which demonstrates through its focus on the formation of new relationships how even small shifts in perspective can begin to create new worlds. Like several other Shakespeare plays, *As You Like It* begins with exile, though even this condition of exclusion and deprivation is given an alternative cast, as Celia sets off willingly from her father's court to accompany her banished cousin Rosalind, announcing at the conclusion of Act 1, "Now go we in content / To liberty, and not to banishment" (1.3.144–145).[10] Indeed, Celia's ability to perceive exile as a means to "liberty" establishes a paradigm of seeing otherwise – and often optimistically – that runs throughout the play. Faced with the threat of extreme deprivation and precarity, Celia decides in this moment to turn away from the security of home and towards an unknown future, in a sense doubling down on her risk of insecurity. This radical, irrational form of optimism perceives possibility in embracing the worst. Rosalind's father, previously usurped from his dukedom and exiled by his brother, will similarly look upon the space of the forest as one of freedom: "Are not these woods / More free from peril than the envious court?" (2.1.4–5). Over the course of the play, we encounter a number of other exiled subjects, including not only Rosalind's father, Duke Senior, but also Duke Senior's lords; as well as Orlando (exiled by his older brother, Oliver); Adam (Oliver's servant who accompanies Orlando); Duke Frederick and Oliver (who willingly enter exile at the end of the play); and Jaques (first exiled with Duke Senior's other lords, and ultimately self-exiled). As Joseph Turner suggests in his contribution to this volume, many of these characters experience the exiled space of the Forest of Arden as a "school" for the cultivation of empathy and

---

[10] Shakespeare, *As You Like It*, New Folger Library edition, ed. Barbara Mowat and Paul Werstine (Simon and Schuster, 2004).

communal virtue. Turner demonstrates how Rosalind, in particular, learns how to understand others' suffering by putting herself in their positions (*ethopoeia*), which enables her to empathize with the love-stricken Orlando, as well as with Silvius and Phoebe. But what is also striking about the forest, and more particularly about the space and condition of exile, is how it enables a number of characters to form new bonds that serve as the basis for individual and communal flourishing. When loosened from the strictures of their previous world, these characters create relationships that are dictated not by compulsion or predetermined hierarchies, but rather that are born of freewill, mutual consent, respect, and love.

In fact, many of the relationships that form in the space of exile ignore or even invert the relationships established by the terms and social hierarchies of the court – enabling the characters to grow in new ways and opening up new possibilities for communal flourishing. While Rosalind and Celia shared a loving bond prior to Rosalind's exile, their bond deepens when they are released from the political freight of their filial obligations and their subjugation to Celia's father. Their new identities, disguised as the male Ganymede and his poor sister Aliena, free them to enjoy an unencumbered bond of friendship and love. As Sean Keilen argues in his chapter on "friendship," Shakespeare often rejects Cicero's model that limits friendship to men who share an equal status, demonstrating the deep reaches of female friendship as well as the ways that bonds of love and loyalty can transcend the artificial barriers of social inequality or political determinations. In *As You Like It*, we see this also in the forging of a loving bond between Orlando and his brother's former servant Adam, both of whom demonstrate a willingness to sacrifice for the other when faced with the most dire of circumstances. When Adam collapses from starvation and exhaustion, Orlando cajoles him with a message of hopeful optimism – "Live a little, comfort a little, cheer thyself a little" (2.6.5–6) – and vows to him, "If this uncouth forest yield anything savage, I will either be food for it or bring it food for thee" (2.6.6–7). Stumbling upon the feast of Duke Senior and his lords, Orlando expects to have to use force to obtain a share in their food, having assumed that "all things had been savage here," but is instead greeted with a kind welcome and generous invitation to partake in their bounty (2.7.112). The experience moves him to shift his perspective and to understand that something he assumed to be improbable, or even impossible, might in fact be possible in this world. As William West has observed, "The play drives forward ... towards future ways of life that are not merely different but can be made different, and made better, than previous ones."[11] Witnessing an unexpected shift, Orlando comes to appreciate a new understanding of the world's potentiality. And indeed, his own feelings and actions have already demonstrated this to be the case, as illustrated by Orlando's refusal to partake in Duke Senior's meal before retrieving Adam, whom he carries on his back. This inversion of the master-servant relationship reveals a truer bond between human beings who struggle together to survive and to serve one another.

Jaques's analogy between the "world" and the "stage" observes the superficiality of the roles that people tend play in their lives on earth, which are dictated by the conditions of one's birth and fortunes:

> All the world's a stage,
> And all the men and women merely players.
> They have their exits and their entrances,
> And one man in his time plays many parts,
> His acts being seven ages. (2.7.146–150)

This description of ongoing human "exits" and "entrances" in the world and the division of a single man's lifespan into "seven ages," a corollary to "parts" and "stages," compares the ephemerality of human life to that of performance. It suggests that the different "parts" a man plays in his lifetime are temporary performances – *secular*, in that they are *of this world* and thus temporal – rather than essential manifestations of who we are as human beings. While these roles may hold great sway over our lives, particularly when they dictate status and privilege, or our position within a hierarchized society, they hold no intrinsic meaning. *As You Like It* seems to recognize the superficiality of these earthly roles in its willingness to question and subvert them in order to allow deeper and more consensual bonds to form. By the same token, the play unflinchingly demonstrates how certain roles – for example, positions of political power or those dictated by the patriarchal system of primogeniture – might lend themselves to corruption and abuses, leading to tyranny and enmity between brothers. Divested of these roles, a former duke (recast as an "outlaw" in the space of the forest) can invite a hungry "stranger" (who unbeknownst to him, is the son of his good friend) to dine at his table. While many of the characters in the play forge deeper bonds by escaping their worldly roles, a character like Jaques seems to opt out of forming human bonds altogether, perhaps finding the unadulterated fellowship that he craves only to be accessible in the suffering of animals.

---

[11] William N. West, *As If: Essays in* As You Like It (Dead Letter Office: Babel Working Group, 2016), 17.

The play in fact considers the possibility of making a place for the flour-ishing of animals in its new community of relationships. Describing his sense of responsibility towards Adam as "like a doe, [who goes] to find [her] fawn /And give it food," Orlando unwittingly draws a connection to the sympathy that the Duke and his lords feel for the deer whom they kill to supply their feast. Duke Senior questions the ethics of such an ecosystem when he says that it "irks" him that "the poor dappled fools, / Being native burgher of this desert city, / Should in their own confines with forked heads / Have their round haunches gored" (2.1.22–25). His First Lord responds with a story of observing Jaques's lament as he in turn observes the suffering of "a poor sequestered stag" who has been mortally wounded by a hunter's bullet. The deer, he says, "heaved forth such groans / That their discharge did stretch his leathern coat /Almost to bursting" and at the same time "big round tears / Coursed one another down his innocent nose" (2.1.37–40). Jaques, in turn, is brought to tears. The multilayered scene of observation through which Duke Senior becomes witness to the deer's physical suffering awakens his sense of the shared bodily vulner-ability and capacity for pain that unites all living beings. Just as Orlando questions the hierarchy that would prevent his recognition of the hunger and fellow humanity of a servant, the Duke questions the ecosystem of the forest that provides one being's sustenance at the expense of another's suffering and life, and considers the possibility of extending communal values and rights to the nonhuman beings with whom they coexist. The play only goes so far in this regard: empathy for the deer can only be imag-ined by ascribing to it the anthropomorphic capacity of crying, and the human characters go on to enjoy their venison feast. While Duke Senior is moved to recognize upon learning of Adam's suffering that "… we are not all alone unhappy / This wide and universal theater / Presents more woeful pageants than the scene / Wherein we play in" (142–145), his will-ingness to heed a wider world of suffering by ameliorating Adam's hunger comes at the deer's expense. Human bonds ultimately trump the needs or ability of other lives to flourish, as further illustrated by Orlando's killing of a lion to save his brother's life, an act of sacrifice that compels Oliver's conversion to brotherly affection. Whereas the play draws a line at the idea of a human being remaining in a home that resembles a "butchery," it allows the forest to be turned into such for the "greasy citizens" who are its native inhabitants. In this way, the play's ethics may be seen to accord with what Nussbaum deems to be "the general anthropocentrism of Aristotle's ethical method," which "ranks lives" within a "cosmic hierarchy," though in another way it may be possible to conclude that both Aristotle and

Shakespeare prioritize an understanding of world that subordinates the significance of individual beings and lives to a broader eco-system, whose flourishing might entail the need for responsible hunting.[12]

But even if we accept the view of a flourishing world whose sustainability depends on killing, the forest of *As You Like It* is decidedly not a perfect utopia. Characters' actions are sometimes motivated by trickery rather than consent. Orlando is deceived by Rosalind's disguise and reveals his love to her under false pretenses, and Phoebe is tricked into marrying Silvius. Not everyone is equally integrated into the new communal world that begins to form and it is clear that class and gender hierarchies will persist to some extent. When Rosalind receives a love letter from Phoebe, she protests that it could not have been written by her because it is "a man's invention" (4.3.32). Exclaiming, "She defies me / Like Turk to Christian. Women's gentle brain / Could not drop forth such giant-rude invention, / Such Ethiop words, blacker in their effect / Than in their countenance," Rosalind describes the unwomanly style of the letter in racialized and religious terms of abuse (4.3.35–39). In this way, she demonstrates her ready access to a larger world of difference far beyond the confines of Arden and even France – a world whose differences are automatically transposed by Rosalind into racist stereotypes of deception and foulness. These judgments are in turn part of the fabric of the new communal world of Arden, which for all its inclusivity is ultimately quite homogenous and bounded by intolerance. The racialized "hand" ascribed to the letter in fact bleeds into Rosalind's description of Phoebe's actual physical hand, which Rosalind describes as "leathern" and "a freestone-colored hand," adding "I verily did think / That her old gloves were on, but 'twas her hands" (4.3.27–29). It is with such remarkable ease that a racialized sense of skin color, informed by the geopolitics of a newly globalizing world seeps into the domestic construction of class and gender.

Can such a small-minded integration of the world beyond lead to a better world? Perhaps it is no wonder that Jaques adopts a position of willful unbelonging and an attitude of pessimism – not just toward the world of the court but perhaps toward all worlds, whose first blush of optimism turns out to be rather cruel.[13] Describing his "melancholy" disposition as the result of "the sundry contemplation of my travels, in which

---

[12] Nussbaum, *The Fragility of* Goodness, 373.
[13] As Lauren Berlant has argued, "cruel optimism" results from an attachment to "compromised conditions of possibility whose realization is discovered either to be impossible, sheer fantasy, or too possible, and toxic." *Cruel Optimism* (Duke University Press, 2011), 24.

rumination wraps me in a most humorous sadness," Jaques bases his point of view on his accumulated perceptions of the world (4.1.20–22). As he concisely explains to Rosalind, "I have gained my experience" (4.1.28). But in another sense, his pessimism need not constitute a complete rejection of world in the fullest sense of the world's potentiality. Jaques's decision to remain at Arden at the end of the play suggests that perhaps he has even found a place for his pessimism in this world of exile. The very possibility illustrates the pluralistic capacity of world as well as its dynamism and worlding potential – a potential that encompasses both doing and undoing. Could pessimism be a form of potentiality? Could it be the basis for posing the question: *What if the world were other than it is?* Does it lead to the process of re-worlding? West observes how "[b]y exploring the ways the world can be different than it is, the characters of *As You Like It* strive to make the world a place in which they can be at home, not as a utopia … but as an ongoing work of living."[14] As Rosalind, Orlando, and Duke Senior return to the world of the court, Frederick, Oliver, and (presumably) Celia will join Jaques in creating a new home in the world of the forest. Both worlds will be irrevocably altered. What futures will unfold are entirely unknowable, and somehow the very certainty of this unknowability provides some measure of reassurance. We have every reason to believe that these worlds will keep on worlding. A world is a world because it is never perfect or complete, but always striving. Is there any greater source of virtue than this?

[14] West, *As If*, 31.

PART IV

Virtuous Performances

CHAPTER 35

Dramaturgy
The Virtue/Virtuosity of Unfolding Hamlet's Story
Freddie Rokem

Stand and unfold yourself.

Hamlet (1.1.2)[1]

Time shall unfold what plighted cunning hides.

King Lear (1.1.281)[2]

Just before his death, Hamlet begs Horatio to "report me and my cause aright / to the unsatisfied" (5.2.318–319), to safeguard his legacy for future generations. A few lines later, emphasizing the implications of this task, Hamlet repeats his plea to be remembered (as the ghost had insisted at the end of their first meeting), entreating Horatio to absent himself "from felicity awhile / And in this harsh world draw thy breath in pain / To tell my story" (327–328). And finally, after giving Fortinbras his "dying voice" (335) – supporting his ambition to inherit the Danish crown – Hamlet asks Horatio to tell Fortinbras "with th'occurrents more or less / which have solicited –" (336–337), but vanishes into silence before clarifying his request. This reverses the three, almost identical oaths Horatio and Marcellus had been commanded to make in the first act, never to speak about the encounter with the ghost; because telling Hamlet's story is also telling about the ghost.

A few lines later, after Fortinbras has arrived and Horatio begins to "speak to the yet unknowing world / How these things came about" (358–359), Fortinbras immediately interrupts him, claiming "some rights of memory in this kingdom" (368) for himself. Preparing new conquests, Fortinbras orders four captains to "/b/ear Hamlet like a soldier to the stage"

---

[1] All references to *Hamlet* are to The New Cambridge Shakespeare edition: W. Shakespeare, *Hamlet, Prince of Denmark*, Third edn. (Cambridge University Press, 2019) and will be given in brackets after the quote.

[2] Shakespeare, "*King Lear* (conflated text)," *The Norton Shakespeare*, eds. Stephen Greenblatt et al. (Norton, 1997), 2485.

(375) – already distorting Hamlet's legacy, by calling him a "soldier" – to "Take up the bodies" (380) and "Go bid the soldiers shoot" (382). These final moments – as a new regime is taking over the kingdom – are saturated with conflict and uncertainty. And since Fortinbras prevents Horatio from telling Hamlet's story, the responsibility for carrying out this task is continuously passed on to those who are planning new productions of Shakespeare's play. The dramaturgical analysis for such an endeavor thus begins by asking how "the unnatural acts," the "accidental judgments," the "deaths put on by cunning and forced cause" (360–362), provide a testimony of "all this," which Horatio wanted to "truly deliver" (364–365), but was prevented from carrying out. Instead, the endeavor to answer this "how?" leads to new productions (or interpretations) of Shakespeare's play, fulfilling Hamlet's final wish, by reconsidering, re-enacting as well as by resisting his and the play's numerous legacies.

It is important to highlight Hamlet's second request – "in this harsh world draw thy breath in pain / To tell my story" – providing an ethical context for telling Hamlet's story. This pain and its ensuing grief – perhaps even evoking an Aristotelean *catharsis* – are based on a recognition of our inability to prevent acts of injustice and violence. The retelling of Hamlet's story, giving a testimony of the moral failures which led to "all this" will not prevent new failures. But a staging based on a full command of the artistic resources of the theater, inspired by the skill and virtuosity of those who create such performances, can enrich our understanding of such moral failures, sometimes even inspire us to act, triggering protest and resistance against injustices. While recognizing that virtuosity can become its own goal, even serving morally distorted expressions of beauty, the dramaturgical analysis aims at calibrating the representations of the injustice caused by human failings and the virtues of goodness to set them right with the creative virtuosity of the performance, in order to avoid what Hamlet describes as "the slings and arrows of outrageous fortune" (3.1.58).[3]

Shakespeare's *Hamlet* emphasizes its self-reflexive dramaturgical point of departure for telling Hamlet's story, implicitly inviting us to carry out Horatio's aborted promise to Hamlet. This is probably one of the reasons for its unique position in the dramatic canon, even serving as an exemplary model for the practices of the theater as well as story-telling in

---

[3] See Eduardo Côrte-Real and Susana Oliveira, "From Alberti's Virtù to the Virtuoso Michelangelo. Questions on a Concept that Moved from Ethics to Aesthetics through Drawing," *Disegno* 47 (2011), 83–93. This article claims that the notion of virtuosity, complementing virtue, first appeared in Leon Battista Alberti's dialogue *Della Tranquillità dell'Animo* from the 1440s.

general. Such a meta-narrative feature, which can appear in many forms, is a crucial trigger for the dramaturgical analysis of a play, through which theoretical issues of hermeneutics, text analysis, and performance theory are brought together with the practical, creative work of the theater. By connecting research and practice, dramaturgy explores new dimensions for staging dramatic texts, illuminating them from innovative perspectives and propose integrative scenic images, examining their relevance for a particular audience at a particular time.[4]

Hamlet himself even provides the basic guidelines for this task, to make a performance which is both ethically and aesthetically meaningful: a virtuous, virtuoso performance. By observing "the modesty of nature" (3.2.16), it is possible, Hamlet claims, to accomplish the "purpose of playing whose end both at the first and now, was and is / . . ./ to show virtue her own feature, scorn her own image, and the very age and body of the time his form and pressure" (17–20). Performances ideally provide clear-cut moral commitments, with virtue serving as an exemplary model for human behavior and with scorn estranging itself from its own folly, enabling us to balance virtue and vice, as Hamlet strives to do by showing his mother the portraits of his father and his uncle in the closet scene. Moral claims are made through the virtuosity (or cunning) of using the artistic resources of the theater, featuring "the best actors in the world" (2.2.363). Their art will make Claudius confess his crime, since, as Hamlet reports: "I have heard / That guilty creatures sitting at a play / Have by the very cunning of the scene / Been struck so to the soul, that presently /They have proclaimed their malefactions" (541–545).[5]

Even if Shakespeare did not use the word "virtuosity" (or 'virtuoso/a') in his oeuvre, judging by its multifaceted expressions in his plays he was no

---

[4] An interesting case for how the legacy of the character is introduced, as a *mise-en-abyme* effect, is introduced already in *The Odyssey* (book 8), as Odysseus arrives at the court of Alcinous on the island of Scherie where the poet Demodocus sings about the Trojan wars, without anyone knowing who the stranger among them is. Alcinous, sitting close to Odysseus is the only one who notices that he is weeping as he hears his own story, hiding his tears under a veil. Niobe, another mythological figure from Classical mythology, known for her tears, is mentioned in *The Iliad* as a model for mourning, as well as by Sophocles' Antigone, who compares herself to Niobe as she is about to enter the cave, punished to die. Socrates, in Plato's *Republic*, argues that "we must forbid anyone who writes a play about the sufferings of Niobe" (380a), referring to a play by Aeschylus which has been lost; while Hamlet's depiction of his mother, being "Like Niobe, all tears" (I, 2, 129), mockingly depicts her feigned mourning. In Walter Benjamin's essay on violence and force (Zur Kritik der Gewalt/ Toward the Critique of Violence) Niobe represents their mythical legacy.

[5] Hamlet is alluding to the classical rhetorical tradition of cunning or *metis* – originating with the shrewdness and skill for catching fish in a net. See Marcel Detienne and Jean-Pierre Vernant, *Cunning Intelligence in Greek Culture and Society* (Harvester Press, Humanities Press, 1978).

doubt aware of its conceptual formation in the early seventeenth century, as a compound of learning, wit, conceit and even cunning, frequently also in combination with dilettantism.[6] In *Hamlet* the protagonist is a virtuoso in feigning/performing madness as well as in his use of language, who also depends on the artistic virtuosity of the players. It is "the very cunning of the scene," the virtuosity with which it is constructed, Hamlet suggests, referring to the Mousetrap, which will literally, as in a hunt, by having the "players / Play something like the murder of my father /… / catch the conscience of the king" (2.2.548–549, 558). In the prayer scene, where Claudius (at least *pro forma*) confesses his foul deed, giving Hamlet an opportunity to revenge, which he does not seize, believing that the act of praying will absolve Claudius's sin, while Claudius admits that while his "words fly up, my thoughts remain below" (3.3.97), making the prayer ineffective, we can observe Shakespeare's own virtuoso treatment of scenic structure. This scene raises issues of ethics and moral virtue, based on control and intent of human intentions, behavior, and understanding, transferred to the aesthetic realm, through artistic virtuosity. Originating in the discursive practices of ethics and aesthetics, respectively, here we can observe how virtue and virtuosity amalgamate into a rich and complex theatrical experience.

After presenting the general context for telling Hamlet's story, I will now briefly demonstrate what a dramaturgical analysis can accomplish for the opening of the play; and then in closing present a general outline of a *Hamlet* production where I served as the dramaturg which was based on some of these reflections. Shakespeare's play, ending with the rise of a new sovereign, begins not long after Claudius's crowning, with the change of guards on the ramparts of Elsinore castle. It is midnight and Barnardo, who is about to relieve Francisco from his guard duty has the first line, asking "Who's there?" (1.1.1); though it would have been more fitting to have Francisco direct this question to Barnardo, who is arriving to the ramparts to begin his watch. But instead of responding, Francisco retorts by returning the question to Barnardo in the form of a command: "Nay answer me. Stand and unfold yourself" (2). With these opening lines the play immediately establishes its own self-reflexive point of departure for what it sets out to achieve: to reveal (or "unfold") who

---

[6] See Marjorie Hope Nicolson, 'Virtuoso', *Dictionary of the History of Ideas: Studies of Selected Pivotal Ideas*, 5 vols, ed. Philip Wiener (Charles Scribner's Sons, 1973), Vol. IV, 486–490. It is important to add that the Elizabethan conceptualization of virtuosity (and virtuoso) is different from its later, Romantic expressions, more closely connected to expressions of genius and charisma. See Gabriele Brandstetter, "The Virtuoso's Stage: A Theatrical Topos," *Theatre Research International* 32. 2 (2007), 178–195.

is "there"; intimating from the outset that besides the guards someone or something else is also "there" – on the stage, or just off – perhaps even waiting impatiently since the previous performance of the play to appear and unfold itself, again.

There is a gradually growing sense of anxiety fueled by the contradictory perceptions of what the guards have experienced since a few nights. And after forty lines the ghost – who has by then been referred to as "this thing," "this dreaded sight" and "this apparition" (1.1.21, 25, 28) – actually appears. But before this happens, Marcellus quotes Horatio, who "says 'tis but our fantasy, / And will not let belief take hold of him" (23–24). However, as Marcellus adds, should it appear again, Horatio, who has already taken on a key role in interpreting what they are experiencing (and will be appointed for this task by Hamlet in the last scene), "may approve our eyes and speak to it" (28), because – as we learn when the ghost actually appears – Horatio who is a scholar (which in the Elizabethan context also means that he is a "virtuoso") knows how to "Question it" (45), requesting it to "unfold" itself.

An important aspect of a dramaturgical analysis is to identify and map patterns of repetition, like when after Horatio's skeptical dismissal of the ghost is repeated in his own voice – "Tush, tush, 'twill not appear" (29) – when Barnardo describes what he and Marcellus had seen the previous night, "When yond same star that's westward from the pole / Had made his course t'illume that part of heaven / Where now it burns" and with "The bell then beating one –" (35–39). As the ringing of the bell can most likely also be heard at this moment, the ghost appears and Marcellus interrupts Barnardo's narrative, exclaiming "Look where it comes again" (40). The report about the bell beating one the previous night serves as the cue for the ghost to appear (again), now for the first time in the play itself. The first appearance of the ghost on the stage taking place during the description of its appearance the previous night, superimposing two discrete moments (or events), showing meta-theatrically through a scenic image (or stage event) that "The time is [literally] out of joint" (1.5.189).[7]

---

[7] This kind of interaction between two or several discrete events in time establishes a view of history developed by Walter Benjamin, drawing attention to how "each 'now' is the now of a particular recognizability," which is not the result of a comparison between the past and the present, but (in the frequently quoted comment from *The Arcades Project*), is described as an image, which "is that wherein what has been comes together in a flash with the now to form a constellation. In other words: image is dialectics at a standstill. For while the relation of the present to the past is purely temporal, the relation of what-has-been to the now is dialectical: not temporal in nature but figural [*bildlich*]. Only dialectical images are genuinely historical." *The Arcades Project*, trans. Howard Eiland and Kevin McLaughlin (Harvard University Press, 2002), 463, N 3, 1.

And immediately after the appearance of the ghost – who can be seen as a figure for repetition itself – Horatio (who had previously doubted its existence) immediately confirms that the ghost they have seen looks "like the king" (1.1.43, 58), referring to Hamlet's father who had killed the old king Fortinbras in battle, and continues by broadening the historical context and how, before the assassination of Julius Caesar, "The graves stood tenantless and the sheeted dead / did squeak and gibber in the Roman streets" (115–116), serving as a "prologue to the omen coming on" (123). Horatio is not only a scholar who can interrogate the ghost, but an historian as well, who understands the cyclical repetitions of the larger contexts of history. Can we really trust Horatio? Hamlet does, until the very end.[8]

Complementing the investigation of repetitions, the dramaturgical analysis will also examine the scenic structure of the dramatic text and its potential scenic realizations. A "scene" is the unit (or segment) of the stage action framed by an entrance or an exit of a character or a supernatural entity, generally referred to as a "French scene." The transitions between these scenic units, regulating the traffic onto and from the stage, horizontally or vertically, have an important dramaturgical function as they can in many cases be maneuvered and adjusted for dramatic effects. This is most effective in eavesdropping scenes where a character is "present" and "absent" at the same time, or in scenes featuring supernatural agents who are in some sense always present, even when they cannot be seen by the other characters or the spectators. A dramaturgical analysis can also clarify at what points it can be useful to separate the visibility of a character or a spirit for the characters and for the spectators.

This, as Hamlet is fully aware of, and Shakespeare has demonstrated with virtuosity in his play, is how the "very cunning of the scene" can reveal (or unfold) what is hidden; as a secret in the distant past, which psychoanalysis has taught us to decipher; or a "thing" that is concealed behind a curtain or screen, on or off the stage in the many eavesdropping scenes in *Hamlet* where one or several characters spy on the others, and at least one of them is unaware of this set-up. The moment when the eavesdropping is discovered has potential for theatrical effects. This scenic structure also serves as the basis for the appearance of a *deus ex machina*, the device through

---

[8] It is also worth noting that Polonius admits in conversation with Hamlet that he played the role of Julius Caesar during his studies at the university – "I did enact Julius Caesar. I was killed i'th'Capitol. Brutus killed me" (3, 2, 91) – and that John Hemmings who played Julius Caesar in the 1599 Globe-production of Shakespeare's *Julius Caesar*, played Polonius in *Hamlet* the following year; while Richard Burbage played Brutus and Hamlet, respectively, killing the characters played by Hemmings in both productions.

which supernatural creatures, including ghosts, as well as angels or dybbuks appear on the stage (or on the screen), after supposedly "eavesdropping" on the events on-stage before making their appearance at the "right" moment.[9]

The opening scene will serve as an example for how the dramaturgical analysis can explore the possibilities of adjusting (or subverting) the scenic structure of the dramatic text for a performance. The guards first see (or hear) the ghost when Barnardo (for Horatio's sake) describes what they have already seen twice, which triggers the re-appearance of the ghost. The dramaturgical question is if the spectators have already seen the ghost before this happens. There are two basic options for such a dramaturgical strategy; the ghost can be seen by the spectators on the first line ("Who's there?") or on line 21 ("What, has this thing appeared again tonight?"). The reverse strategy, which seems unlikely, though possible, would be to postpone the appearance of the ghost for the spectators, for example until the first meeting between Hamlet and the ghost. And it is of course also possible to follow the text verbatim.

In his film adaptation of *Hamlet*, Kenneth Branagh chose to show that the ghost is present already on the opening line, with the statue of Old Hamlet quickly moving its left arm, reaching for the sword on the first line. This sudden movement, only seen by the spectators (as recorded by the camera), enables us (on reflection, because this happens very quickly) to construct a scenario where the ghost is impatiently "waiting" to "appear" when the opening question is heard; while the actual entrance, becoming fully visible for the other characters, takes place when Barnardo describes its appearance the previous night with the bell beating one.[10] This impatience can also be understood meta-theatrically, referring to the performative condition which enables "this thing" (i.e., the performance) to appear night after night. According to this opening scenario the ghost is not only a supernatural creature whose appearance activates the plot of Shakespeare's play, but becomes an unruly eavesdropper who is monitoring the whole performance as an inherent aspect of the theater itself. This

---

[9] It will not be possible to present a detailed analysis of the eavesdropping scenes in *Hamlet* and how they interact with the appearances of the ghost, here. In my articles "The Very Cunning of the Scene': Notes Towards a Common Dispositive for Theatre and Philosophy," *Brazilian Journal on Presence Studies* (2020); www.academia.edu/43714081/The_very_cunning_of_the_scene_notes_towards_a_common_dispositive_for_theatre_and_philosophy and in "Materializations of the Supernatural: Deus ex machina and *plumpes Denken* in Brecht and Benjamin," www.academia.edu/23952417/Materializations_of_the_Supernatural_Deus_ex_machina_and_plumpes_Denken_in_Brecht_and_Benjamin, I have discussed these stage phenomena as a central feature for delineating the constitutive features of the theater, its "dispositive."

[10] This scene can be viewed at www.youtube.com/watch?v=R-QvTxMHTcY

strategy of splitting the gaze of the spectators and the characters aims at empowering the spectators to construct events which the characters on the stage are not necessarily aware of.

As the play unfolds, we are gradually led to the conclusion that Hamlet and Horatio believe that ghosts exist and that this particular ghost tells the truth how its living incarnation, the former king of Denmark had been treacherously murdered by Claudius. But this is not the only issue occupying the spectators. After seeing a performance of *Hamlet*, we are probably not going to discuss whether ghosts exist or not and whether they always tell the truth. Therefore, while the ghost challenges the belief-systems of the characters and how Hamlet and Horatio are gradually persuaded that the ghost tells the truth, the spectators are carefully monitoring how the theatrical machinery activating the appearance of this supernatural creature works, regardless if we believe it exists or not. This bi-focal perspective, combining the unfolding of the narrative (on its own terms) with some form of exposure of the theatrical machinery, serving as the vehicle for telling Hamlet's story, makes it possible to transform the inherent virtuosity of this classical texts into a theatrical idiom for our own time, and to "show virtue her own feature, scorn her own image, and the very age and body of the time his form and pressure."[11]

*

My analysis of the closet scene (Act 3, Scene 4), where Hamlet kills Polonius, hiding behind an arras and afterwards encounters the ghost for the last time in the play, served as the trigger for the performance of *Hamlet* by the Swedish theater company *Västanå Teater*, directed by Leif Stinnerbom, for which I served as the dramaturg. This was the first time I filled this function, and it has been followed up by working as a dramaturg in about a dozen performances. This *Hamlet* production premiered in Karlstad (a city in central Sweden, located approximately halfway between Stockholm and Oslo) in September 1996 performed until December that year. It was revived the following summer by *Riksteatern*, the ambulatory National

---

[11] The dramaturgical analysis follows Brecht's model of the epic theater developed most succinctly in his essay "The Street Scene," describing an "eyewitness demonstrating to a collection of people how a traffic accident took place." Bertolt Brecht, "The Street Scene: A Basic Model for an Epic Theatre," in *Brecht on Theatre* 3rd ed., eds. Marc Silverman, Steve Giles and Tom Kuhn (Bloomsbury, 2015), 176. This can be seen on two distinct levels: first, the eyewitness (Horatio) demonstrating how the accident or the failure, was possible. Secondly, it exposes the 'machinery' (the automobile) of the historical forces which have created the circumstances within which this accident has taken place.

Theatre of Sweden.[12] The concept of this *Hamlet* production originated in a discussion with Leif asking me – as he usually does when we meet – what I was working on; and I told him about my preparations for a lecture on the closet scene in *Hamlet*, trying to figure out who Hamlet believed was hiding behind the arras as he drew his dagger, killing Polonius. The spectators know it is Polonius, but who does Hamlet believe is there? What conceivably frightens him so much that he immediately draws his dagger when he hears that someone/something is hiding behind the arras?

When Hamlet arrives to his mother's closet, he has just left Claudius praying in the chapel, without carrying out the act of revenge, because of popular belief that Old Hamlet will not be revenged as Claudius's soul is saved through praying. And since there seems to be no significant time gap between this scene and the closet scene, Hamlet can (at least, after the deed itself, because it happens very quickly) conclude that Claudius could not have been behind the arras, while the spectators have obviously seen Polonius hiding. The question is therefore who Hamlet believed had been hiding behind the arras before discovering that he had killed Polonius. And for me – I told Leif – the answer is the ghost; which "means" that Polonius "is" the ghost. The closet scene can even begin with a passionate embrace between Polonius and Gertrude who have a love affair, while Polonius is impersonating the ghost to make Hamlet believe during their first encounter that Claudius has killed the old king to make Hamlet take his "revenge" on him.

Leif looked at me for a moment, snapped his fingers and said "We'll do it!" Feeling a rush of excitement, I said that there is no problem discarding Claudius's confession and with Polonius lying dead on the floor have Hamlet asking "Is it the king?" (3.4.26), exclaiming "I took thee for thy better" (32), which could refer to the ghost of his father. At that point I added that the meticulously inserted subtext of rodents also reinforces this scenario, beginning in the opening scene, with Francisco confirming that it has been a quiet guard; "Not a mouse stirring" (1.1.10); as well as the moment when the ghost commands that Horatio and Marcellus swear the third time never to make known what they have seen, with Hamlet commenting/asking, "Well said old mole, cans't work i't'earth so fast?" (1.5.160). The gnawing underground creature, an expression of a

---

[12] For a more detailed analysis of this production, see my article "The Production of *Hamlet* at Västanå Theatre": www.academia.edu/34856642/Hamlet_dramaturgy_Freddie_Rokem, published in *Western European Stages* (1997), 57–60. The Riksteatern tour was made together with a production of de Rojas's *Celestina*, also directed by Stinnerbom and played in the same scenography.

subconscious desire/fear, returns in the closet scene, as Polonius, hiding behind the arras, shouts for help, and Hamlet, drawing his dagger exclaims "How now a rat?" (3.3.24) And add to this, the Mousetrap for catching the conscience of the king. But, I added, questioning the limits of my reading: How is it possible for the ghost to appear again, towards the end of the scene, after the ghost-impersonator has been killed? – "That's not a problem," was Leif's immediate response, "Horatio takes over the costume of the ghost." This obviously questions Horatio's loyalty to Hamlet.

After two years of preparations, first editing the text for a cast of seven actors and two musicians, with all the actors playing only one role; with Claudius, Polonius, Gertrude and Horatio played by men and Hamlet, Ophelia and Laertes played by women, and two months of rehearsals, which I also attended daily, the performance premiered. The changes we made no doubt stretch Shakespeare's *Hamlet* to its limits, as many productions have already done and will no doubt also do in the future. At the same time as this reflects an important aspect of our own, contemporary performance culture, where this kind of virtuosity for telling a well-known story is considered to be a virtue in its own right, *Hamlet* is also particularly well suited for such possibilities. Among the students from the University of Karlstad who had not been familiar with Shakespeare's play before seeing the performance, many said in a Q&A after the performance that they were fully convinced that this was how the play had been written. So, very briefly, here are some key moments of a performance, unfolding additional layers of Hamlet's story.

As the audience enters the auditorium, the seven actors dressed in thin tulle costumes, are seated on a sand-ditch, looking into the empty stage (a "grave"). They are both spectators and actors (or story-tellers), waiting for this "thing" – the performance – "to appear again tonight," so they can take on their roles. The two musicians are playing music based on traditional Scandinavian folk tunes. As the ghost-costume (the traditional costume of an Innuit Shaman) hanging on two strings slowly begins to descend (as a *deus ex machina*), the actors rise, addressing this empty shell with the question: "Who's there?" Turning around, the actors – as a chorus – recite Horatio's speech in the first scene about the time before Julius Caesar fell and the Roman streets were filled with ghosts making the graves "tenantless," implying they are such ghosts.

The actors begin to play with the ghost costume, still hanging on the strings, hiding inside like in a peekaboo game. When asked "Who's there?" each actor opens the flaps showing the others who is hiding inside the empty ghost shell. While playing this game, the six actors whose clothes are folded together in neat piles on the stage begin to get dressed, transforming themselves into the characters (of the two families) in front of our eyes. The young male actor who will play Horatio, the outsider, carefully unhinges the ghost costume from the strings and exits with it, still wearing his story-telling costume. The next time the ghost will appear the spectators immediately see that Polonius is hiding inside the costume, while Hamlet remains completely unaware of this deception until he has pulled his dagger through the arras in Gertrude's closet.

And as each one of the characters, except for Horatio, die – beginning with Polonius – the performance is interrupted. Accompanied by a tune of mourning the actor/actress takes off the clothes (of his/her character) and folds them slowly, putting them in the place where they were to begin with, so they can be "used" again in the next performance. The "actors," ending with the actor playing Hamlet, return to the ditch where they are greeted by their fellows. Finally, only Horatio (who "is" the ghost in the second part of the closet scene, after Polonius is killed) remains on stage. He takes the scepter of the king, faces the audience and declares triumphantly that he can "speak to th'yet unknowing world / How these things came about. So shall you hear / of carnal, bloody and unnatural acts, / of accidental judgements [etc]" (5.2.359–361). Now, the sound of ringing bells, which has accompanied the appearances of the ghost throughout can be heard again. The ghost appears on the backstage platform, with the flaps closed, approaching with slow, wiggling steps. This is obviously not the empty costume which had appeared in the opening scene. While the audience can see the seven actors and the two musicians on the stage there is obviously someone (some-thing, not yet accounted for) inside the costume. Horatio turns around, terrified, asking "Who's there?" [a slow black-out].[13]

---

[13] As final personal note I want to add that the Hamlet performance was created in the wake of the assassination of two prime ministers: the Swedish PM, Olof Palme who was shot in 1986 on a street a few hundred yards from my former high school, after seeing a film whose director had asked Palme to participate in this film; and the then much more recent assassination of the Israeli PM Yitzchak Rabin in 1995, as he was leaving a peace demonstration in which I had participated. I can also add that as an AFS exchange student spending a High School senior year in California, I had made a visit to the White House lawn in the summer of 1963, together with all the exchange students of that year, shaking hands with JFK, a few months before he was shot in Dallas. And as a footnote to this footnote – taking a tour of the book depository in Dallas, 50 years after the assassination of JFK, which ended by looking out through the window from which JFK had been shot, I realized I was standing in the spot of the assassin. With JFK and Palme, we still do not really know who held the guns. With Rabin it is possible that there was a larger conspiracy behind the assassin. Finally – in all of these cases we have to ask: Who's there?

CHAPTER 36

Performing Chastity
The Marina Project

Katharine A. Craik and Ewan Fernie

If chastity has for generations served the needs and desires of men, can it be taken seriously now as a virtue? Chastity has always signified feminine value within patriarchal society, both outside and inside marriage. Writing in the first decades of the fifteenth century, for example, John of Audelay warns in "Chastity of Wives" that if a woman "mared schal be," both she and her worth as a domestic asset are spoiled.[1] Often now dismissed in the west as a medieval superstition, or, at best, as a means of escape from an intolerable situation, chastity seems a worn out version of goodness, a remnant virtue which belongs in and to the past. This chapter proposes however to open up chastity as a forgotten virtue for our own time. It offers an account of the Marina Project, our ongoing creative-critical collaboration with the Royal Shakespeare Company, which has resulted in the creation of a new play entitled *Marina*. The project began with the hypothesis that *Pericles* (1609), by Shakespeare and George Wilkins, provides a uniquely rich and challenging site for exploring whether chastity can be released from its regressive legacy. We seek to open up chastity as a forgotten version of agency which, in the most surprising ways, enables new kinds of assertion and affirmation for both men and women. Chastity disrupts our sense of the way things "have to be" in today's world, emerging as a form of resistance to life in the name of a better one.

We began by attending to what we recognized as the "radical chastity" of the protagonist's daughter. In Act 4, Marina is displaced from her family and country, and sold into sexual slavery at a brothel in Mytilene. Here she militantly refuses sex. The brothel's doorkeeper, Bolt, and her own husband-in-waiting, Lysimachus, regard Marina's "peevish chastity" (4.5.127) as a counter to be bartered, but Marina remains assertively and

---

[1] John the Blind of Audelay, *Poems and Carols*, ed. Susanna Fein (Medieval Institute Publications, 2009), Carol 21; see Karen Dodson, "The Price of Virtue for the Medieval Woman: Chastity and the Crucible of the Virgin," *English Studies* 99. 6 (2018), 596.

uncompromisingly virginal.[2] When the men complain about the brothel's other "pitifully sodden" (4.2.17) whores, Marina condemns their degradation with prophetic rage. Her invective astonishes the men around her, including Lysimachus, and abruptly converts them into chaste uprightness: "Come, I am for no more bawdy houses. Shall's go hear the vestals sing?" (4.5.6–7). Marina acts in this scene like "a piece of virtue" (4.5.116), shot through with chaste goodness which unfurls spectacularly among others. As the second gentleman claims, "I'll do anything now that is virtuous" (4.5.8). But Marina's chastity takes no familiar form.Rather than the withdrawal and self-negation implied by longstanding patterns of obedience to a patriarchal frame, Marina's chastity emerges instead as a specifically female and singularly effective kind of agency. Her miraculous victory over sexual slavery and predation makes her "the absolute Marina" (4.0.31) – absolutely desirable, absolutely chaste, absolutely virtuous. Male vice leaves no taint upon her.[3]

Marina turns away from sex, but her chastity is powerful also for its resolute refusal of patriarchy. We sensed in the extremity of Marina's actions something in keeping with Martha Nussbaum's account of "vertue" which, by retaining the word's older form, retains its originary sense of "turning," or converting.[4] Marina turns away from her immediate grievous predicament, but also turns (and turns others) away from violence and coercion more generally. But the scene in the brothel is also a pivotal moment in *Pericles* that steers the action back into the conventional miracle of romance. So can Marina's chastity really be understood as a version of feminine empowerment – even in a play that Shakespeare co-created with Wilkins whose life was characterized, records confirm, by a particularly unscrupulous and violent strain of misogyny?[5] Marina's sexual unavailability seems more resistant to feminism than, say, Isabella's in *Measure for Measure*. And she is different from more familiar early-modern embodiments of chastity – the ethereal majesty of *The Faerie Queene*'s Belphoebe, for example, or the specifically martial virtue of Spenser's Amazonian knight of chastity, Britomart.[6] Marina's chastity does not take the form

[2] All quotations refer to Suzanne Gossett's edition of *Pericles* (Bloomsbury Arden Shakespeare, 2004).

[3] For an existentially and ethically powerful account of what happens to Marina, see Simon Palfrey, "The Rape of Marina," in *Shakespeare's Possible Worlds* (Cambridge University Press, 2017), 297–316.

[4] See the introduction to the current volume.

[5] On Wilkins's police record, and his involvement with the sex trade, see Charles Nicholl, *The Lodger: Shakespeare on Silver Street* (Allen Lane, 2007), 204.

[6] See Joanna Thompson, *The Character of Britomart in Spenser's 'The Faerie Queene'* (Edwin Mellen Press, 2001), 19–60.

of majesty or queenliness. She is an ordinary girl who refuses altogether the "deeds of darkness" (4.5.37), removing herself in almost Dickensian fashion from the vice-ridden world into needlework and other "feminine" accomplishments: she can "sing, weave, sew and dance, / With other virtues" (4.5.186–187).[7] And yet, Marina is more astringent than Dickens's sweeter, smaller heroines; she has a touch of Cordelia's otherworldly coolness. Marina powerfully and, again and again, triumphantly refuses to play the game where women are sold to men.

This chapter begins by setting out a new interpretation of *Pericles* which identifies a teleology of chastity involving the play's central family unit (Pericles, Thaisa, Marina). We read *Pericles* as a study of the arduousness – as well as the defiance and occasional exaltation – involved in leading a chaste life. The chapter goes on to explain how this close reading developed into a collaborative research project and the creation of *Marina*, a new play for our time. Working with a blend of critical, creative, and practice-based approaches, our aim has been to recover *Pericles*'s interest in chaste virtue for our own lived realities, opening up a constellation of important issues today.

*

The tutelary goddess of *Pericles* is Diana, the Greek deity of chastity, whose temple provides the setting for the play's climactic recognition scene. Here Pericles attests that Marina continues to wear Diana's "silver livery" (5.3.7). The play's central family unit have throughout the preceding events all demonstrated themselves devout followers. Pericles invokes "bright Diana" when he leaves Marina with Cleon and Dionyza, promising eerily that his own hair will remain "unscissored" (3.3.29–30) until she marries, and Gower attests to Marina's "rich and constant" (4.0.28) devotion to Diana while she remains at Tarsus. Thaisa's first words upon wakening at Ephesus are "O dear Diana, where am I?" (3.2.104), and Marina makes a similar invocation in the brothel: "Untried I still my virgin knot will keep. / Diana, aid my purpose!" (4.2.139–140). Reunited later with Thaisa, Pericles's thoughts are still with "Immortal Dian" (5.3.37). Throughout the play, Diana – and chastity – are linked with constancy, fortitude, self-knowledge, and redemption.[8] Chaste virtue has a powerful capacity, it seems, to disclose the truth to those who embrace it.

---

[7] Julia Reinhard Lupton discusses Marina's "affective labor" in *Shakespeare Dwelling: Designs for the Theater of Life* (University of Chicago Press, 2018), 117–152.

[8] For a discussion of the play's "conflicting visions of Diana," see Caroline Bicks, "Backsliding at Ephesus: Shakespeare's Diana and the Churching of Women," in *Pericles: Critical Essays*, ed. David Skeele (Routledge, 2009), 205–227 (209). See also Gossett's account of these discrepancies (117–121).

Diana's prominence makes sense in light of the play's wider interest in chastity's ability to compensate for an original sexual taint. The play begins with a sex trauma in the city of Antioch in ancient Syria. Wooing the daughter of Antioch, Pericles is dismayed to uncover her incestuous relationship with her father. In the context of a play focused on chastity, it seems important to note that "incest" shares with "unchaste" the Latin root *castus*, meaning chaste or pure. Even as Pericles is seeking marriage, he is equally seeking chaste withdrawal. He recognizes that entering into sexuality involves the loss of pristine wholeness when he calls Antiochus's daughter, his hoped-for bride, a "glorious casket stored with ill" (1.1.78). It seems chaste perfectibility waits exclusively for an exceptional man, and Gower has indeed already intimated as much in his earlier description of Antioch's daughter as the "bad child" (1.0.27) who acquiesces to her father's predation. Pericles determinedly seals himself away from the dirty sex revealed by Antioch – but his chastity, far from looking virtuous, actually turns out to be a stale compromise. By the start of the second scene, he is already beset by his "sad companion, dull-eyed melancholy" (1.2.2), and the play will go on to map Pericles's psychosexual displacement onto a series of literal displacements caused by war, terror, famine, and atrocity.

Pericles's tentativeness and damaged fragility are a moving, truthful response to his traumatic initiation into sex. And yet he must somehow "repair" himself (2.1.118) in order to woo his true love, Thaisa. This wooing again, however, proves determinedly, indeed perversely chaste. The sea offers Pericles a rusty suit of armor from what he bluntly calls his "dead father" (2.1.120), and Pericles enters his second courtship quite literally "clothed in steel" (2.1.150). He is untouchable, pleasureless, closed off from intercourse with the world. Later Pericles will beg Neptune to tame the wild surges of the wind and sea, and to "bind them in brass" (3.1.3), but already his own steel garment resembles an impregnable carapace against desire. It has much in common, visually and emblematically, with his summative descent into prostrate self-neglect. This is the legacy of Antioch: a humiliating form of male chastity as self-chastisement for which Pericles even expresses gratitude: "Antiochus, I thank thee, who hath taught / My frail mortality to know itself" (1.1.42–43). Pericles bears his chastity painfully, like a curse, expressing the human fear of sexuality as male tragedy.

The play also explores and expresses the virtue of chastity through Thaisa. Her father, Simonides, claims that she too has withdrawn into a state of chaste self-cancellation. When the second knight asks after the tournament at Pentapolis whether he can "get access to her," Simonides assures him that his daughter "hath so strictly tied / Her to her chamber that 'tis impossible." Thaisa has seemingly taken a solemn vow of chastity, "And on her virgin honour will not break it" (2.5.7–12). In fact she has been remarkably sexually avid in her intention to marry Pericles: "All viands that I eat do seem unsavoury, / Wishing him my meat" (2.3.30–31). But Simonides retains aggressive custodianship of his daughter's virginity, and it is he who brings the final dance to a close – "Unclasp, unclasp!" (2.3.103) – ushering Pericles towards a bedroom next to his own. And while the party sleeps, the unchaste Antioch and his daughter are reduced to untouchable filth: "A fire from heaven came and shrivelled up / Their bodies" (2.4.9–10). In no way has Pericles tried to woo Thaisa, and he exhorts her the following morning to reassure her father that he has remained scrupulously chaste (2.5.65–68).

Pericles is therefore "frighted" (5.3.3) into chastity by two fathers (Antioch, Simonides) as well as being bound in steel by his own. It hardly seems virtuous, or a recipe for a happy, healthy marriage – which is why his eventual bride Thaisa's death-in-life at sea seems strangely inevitable, making sense of the otherwise puzzling fact that Pericles carries in his boat her coffin, all "caulked and bitumed ready" (3.1.70). Now Thaisa really does withdraw from the world, sealed up and flung into the "humming water" (3.1.63) – a sacrifice, Pericles tells himself, to appease the storm which greets Marina's birth. She revives only when she is removed altogether from her husband and recreated as a votaress to Diana: "A vestal livery will I take me to / And never more have joy" (3.4.9–10). Thaisa is therefore three times placed by men into chaste spaces: by Simonides, at the tournament; by Pericles, into the sealed coffin; and by Cerimon, into Diana's temple. Her service to Diana seems designed to compensate for Pericles's original trauma at Antioch and his subsequent digging-in against the shame of sex. Here *Pericles* dramatizes the particularly complex and intimate forms of psychosexual displacement that can befall women, and recognizes chaste virtue as a burden which women must fulfill on behalf of men.

But the play reserves its most thoroughgoing exploration of chastity for Marina – who, unlike Pericles and Thaisa, does not or cannot take refuge from sex. Whereas Pericles is shocked into chaste withdrawal, and Thaisa is withdrawn by others, Marina seems determined to "persever in that clear way" (4.5.110). The model of chaste virtue she proposes is quite different from renunciation or traumatized self-shrouding, and puts into practice a kind of vertue-in-resistance which seems capable of reversing the play's conscious or unconscious patriarchal purpose. Through Marina, chastity becomes a way of rejecting, absolutely, the way things are. As she says to the men who haunt the brothel, "Do anything but this thou dost" (4.5.177). It is Marina who follows through on chastity's teleological prom-ise, transforming sexual withdrawal into a powerful and generative way of saying "no" to worldly vice. Marina's chastity indeed temporarily exceeds the patriarchal limits of the play. She will later be displaced from herself once more in the closing scene in order to save her father, redeeming him and cleansing the sins of the world. Pericles's revealing phrasing, in the re-union scene, admits a sense of patriarchal guilt: "O, come, be buried / A second time within these arms" (5.3.43–44). Nevertheless Marina's chas-tity cannot so easily be buried, dismissed, or assimilated. On the contrary it seems to issue a direct challenge to our own complicity in the less than ideal forms of life we inherit. For this reason it deserves to be recognized as a thoroughly modern virtue, and to be explored with our most serious and compassionate attention.

The Marina Project took its cue from this interpretation of *Pericles* as a portrait of a family defined by the obligations, displacements, and burdens of chastity. Reconsidering the play from Marina's point of view, we began to see her refusal as a remarkably dynamic, vigorous, and direct kind of action, and a spirited rejection of the given forms of life and love. Marina's "radical chastity" had come into focus as a progressive, virtuous form of resistance. We set out to write a new piece of theater focused on female perspective and agency which could investigate chaste virtue as an existen-tial and spiritual challenge to the current order. We wanted Marina's sub-versive energy to grow to its natural conclusion, and the radical, unfulfilled promise of *Pericles* belatedly to be fulfilled within our own present context. Inspired by the play's expansive geopolitical landscape across Syria and the Mediterranean, we began to explore how diverse political, cultural, and social contexts have converged, through history, to create today's interpre-tive frameworks for understanding chaste virtue. We remained interested in chastity as a sign of difference in the western world, but also, potentially, as a source of solidarity and cross-cultural exchange. As a deliberate rebut-tal of the contemporary political situation, albeit one with complex roots in tangled political and cultural circumstances, radical chastity began to emerge as a common provocation capable of cutting across the allegiances that separate people along racial, cultural, and religious lines.

With all of this in mind, we tried to inhabit as fully as possible the pre-dicaments dramatized in Shakespeare and Wilkins's original play, fusing traditional academic epistemology with the more experimental approaches offered by practice-based theater. Moving between literary criticism and new creation, and drawing insights from a series of workshops, which brought academics, artists and theater practitioners into conversation, we were ready to create a new work of art.[9] Our aim was to find a dramaturgical practice capable of bringing literature and Shakespeare to bear on trenchant social structures, particularly those surrounding gender and sexuality; and, at the same time, to write a dramatically convincing piece of theater that might reanimate the virtue of chastity in and for the present. We wanted in particular to recognize the world's continuing investment in chastity, not least within the family, where men and women, husbands and wives, sons and daughters, seek authentic self-expression, self-reliance, and dignity. We hoped to lay bare individual life stories with clarity and empathy, avoiding the forms of detachment that sometimes characterize academic responses to literary works from the distant past.

Our new play, *Marina*, is set in contemporary Sparkhill, an inner-city, multicultural, district of Birmingham. The action takes place over twenty-four hours in a supermarket, Quick & Easy on Narrow Way, starting first thing on Christmas Eve. Quick & Easy is owned by a white-British man, Ant, who lives above the store with his Greek Cypriot wife, Philly, and daughter, Marina. Ant embodies the predatory "league of fathers" (Antioch, Simonides) we found in Shakespeare's original. His unremarkable, faded supermarket has been struggling under the shadow of a food hygiene contravention found to originate in one of the store's meat deep freezers. At the beginning of the play, Ant resolves to give things one last shot with an ambitious Christmas sale. He enlists the help of Leila, a British-born Muslim who has been working for years at Quick & Easy as a temp, and Mike, the supermarket's shelf-stacker. Ant's determination to shift all of his Christmas stock before sundown triggers a series of unrealistic and disturbing sales tactics in which his staff become unwilling accomplices. It emerges that Ant has another incentive to make quick money: the supermarket is embroiled in a planning dispute dating back to 1987 when Ant surreptitiously folded part of the premises of the mosque next door into the supermarket's backroom.

While Ant keeps trying to turn a profit at the expense of others, those around him begin to pull away, one by one, seeking different forms of chastity. Ant's wife, Philly, has found herself bound into sexual servitude. Desperate to make money in order to build a new life away from Ant and Birmingham, she sells sex in a makeshift brothel set up in the disputed

---

[9] For a longer discussion of this initial process, see our chapter on 'The *Marina* Project," in *New Places: Shakespeare and Civic Creativity,* eds. Paul Edmondson and Ewan Fernie (Bloomsbury Arden, 2018), 109–125.

backroom. One of her clients is Mike, whose visits are financed by the money he regularly steals from the supermarket tills. Scared and confused by these encounters, in which Philly is elaborately costumed as a bird, Mike develops a profound interest in Islam, particularly its redemptive understanding of chastity. Mike is counselled by a compassionate imam from the mosque to whom he reveals his sense of guilt, and his desire for Marina and the virtue he sees expressed in her. He asks the imam to bless him, to re-name him Mohammed, and to accept him into the Muslim faith. Matters come to a head when a homeless man, Perry, arrives unexpectedly at the supermarket in an abject state of self-cancellation to reveal himself as Ant's former business partner and Philly's former lover. Confronting Ant, he attempts to reclaim what he considers his own – including paternity of Marina. Incensed by this, and by the unfavorable outcome of the planning application, Ant accuses Perry of ruining both Quick & Easy and his wife.

In different ways, the play's three men (Ant, Mike, Perry) all invest in the shop's dirty money, and all attempt to define and possess Marina as daughter or lover. For her part, Marina offers at the play's conclusion an unexampled version of chaste resistance capable of rising from the tangled, broken state of things. Her radical chastity is revealed through her strength to contest the ways in which religion and family define relations between men and women, and her corresponding defiance of the cruelty and coercion, the shame and the fear, that such intimate direction gives rise to. Marina redistributes what's left of the shop's wealth, refusing the versions of the future that Ant, Mike and Perry have set out before her. She flings open the door of the backroom to the mosque next door, embracing the free flow of people, resources and ideas. As Quick & Easy closes for good on Christmas morning, relinquishing its stock and space back into the hands of those who need it most, Marina uncovers a better world: on the other side of the supermarket, the other side of the mosque, the other side of Christmas.

Marina therefore attempts to consider chastity in its widest possible applications, taking in economic, political, and spiritual concerns as well as intimate, bodily forms of self-definition and self-expression. Chastity involves the body and psyche in our play, but also extends to the collective imagination and to the world at large. For our reinvented Marina, chastity has nothing to do with strictness or withdrawal. Instead it is a form of creative hope, and an alternative way of life, realized through the convictions of an unremarkable young woman in unremarkable circumstances. Chastity's redemptive power is not confined here to the worlds of fairytale or romance, but becomes a mode of action in the real, tarnished and incomplete world. To do this, however, it must break with our world's old terms, especially its damaged and damaging ways of defining, through chastity, relationships between fathers and daughters, or husbands and wives. Like other forms of virtue, chastity begins as an aspiration towards goodness – but this particular version of goodness, as Shakespeare and Wilkins's original play amply demonstrates, tends to cleave in the direction of some people's interests at the expense of others'. As Marina reminds her silent, unresponsive and stubbornly chaste father, towards the end of *Pericles*,

> She speaks,
> My lord, that may be hath endured a grief
> Might equal yours, if both were justly weighed.   (5.1.77–79)

Our play aims equally and justly to weigh Marina's grief, and to follow through on her capacity to act decisively to change her circumstances and those of others. *Marina* dramatizes chastity in the stream of life as it is lived, in ordinary places, ordinary streets, and ordinary social connections. Through the resources of drama itself, where virtue takes the form of recognizable character, chastity emerges as something to do and to be, and chimes with a host of more-or-less nameable forms of human flourishing.

CHAPTER 37

Villains in Prison, Villains on Stage
Is Shakespeare Really Salvific?

Mariacristina Cavecchi

Transformative Shakespeare

In a few lines written in his preface to the 2008 edition of *The Theatre of the Oppressed*, Augusto Boal, the Brazilian founder of the movement that goes by the same name, significantly refers to Shakespeare as a vehicle for empowerment and change:

> When we study Shakespeare we must be conscious that we are not studying the history of the theatre, but learning about the history of humanity. We are discovering ourselves. Above all: we are discovering that we can change ourselves and change the world. Nothing is going to remain the way it is. Let us, in the present, study the past, so as to invent the future.[1]

Indeed, it can be observed that Prison Shakespeare theater, regarded by scholars as a sub-genre of prison theater or social theater but at the same time as a phenomenon in itself with different roots and traditions,[2] is largely based on the assumption that "Shakespeare brings something special to prison environment, beyond what is already brought by prison theatre."[3]

In the wake of Boal, many practitioners and academics underline the transformative power of Shakespeare's plays on inmates, and tell stories of the long-term impact on their behavior and attitudes when they participate in theatrical workshops in terms of change.[4] According to Niels Herold, Shakespearean drama with "its characterological focus on metamorphosis" is an extraordinary vehicle for that "transformative experience" towards "the sort of redemption these inmates actors seek."[5] Significantly, Curt

---

[1] Augusto Boal, *The Theatre of the Oppressed,* new edition (Pluto Press, 2019), ix.
[2] Rob Pensalfini, *Prison Shakespeare. For these Deep Shames and Great Indignities* (Palgrave Macmillan, 2016), 3.
[3] Ibid., 189.
[4] Ibid.
[5] Niels Herold, "Shakespeare Behind Bars," in *The Cambridge Guide to the Worlds of Shakespeare, 1600-Present,* ed. Bruce R. Smith (Cambridge University Press, 2016), vol. 2, 1200–1207, 1201.

Tofteland, the founder of the well-known "Shakespeare Behind Bars" project at the Luther Luckett Correctional Complex in La Grange, Kentucky, argues that more than Webster, Chekhov, or Shaw, Shakespeare conceived plays that "invite self-examination, self-exploration and self-awareness,"[6] namely a first step towards individual transformation. Furthermore, by playing Shakespearean characters, inmates-actors experiment with mental and physical freedom, thereby acquiring awareness of their own potential for change.

At the same time, far from bowing to praise Shakespeare as an agent of transformation in prison, some critics tend to judge the "transformative" and "redemptive" nature of these experiences differently. Thus, Courtney Lehmann, on rereading the transcription of the interviews she conducted with correction officers and inmates at the Luther Luckett Correctional Complex between 2007 and 2013, wonders whether "performing Shakespeare behind bars reinforces or subverts conditions of societal oppression manifest in the penal system at large."[7] Similar doubts are expressed by anthropologist Susanne Greenhalgh in her analysis of Hank Rogerson's award-winning 2005 film *Shakespeare Behind Bars*, which documents the production of *The Tempest* by inmates in the same prison. She argues, in fact, that the film "makes a powerful case for the value of Shakespeare as a humanising force in a dehumanising context, but it does so by accepting the inevitability of incarceration, framing Shakespeare performance as moral instruction, a vehicle of [...] catharsis, and as a temporary escape to a world elsewhere."[8]

Crucially, the Prison Shakespeare field of research has become an interesting hub for discussion about a presumed intrinsic virtuosity of Shakespeare plays against the background of what might best be termed as "new character criticism" in Shakespeare studies[9] as well as a battlefield between the supporters and the opponents of prisons as effective in achieving their stated objective of keeping society safe. Whereas the question of carceral justice/injustice is a topic made very urgent by the Black Lives Matter movement in the United States, it is only timidly debated in

[6] Curt Tofteland, "The Keeper of the Keys," in *Performing New Lives: Prison Theatre*, ed. Jonathan Shailor (Jessica Kingsley Publishers, 2011), 430.
[7] Courtney Lehmann, "Double Jeopardy: Shakespeare and Prison Theater," in *Shakespeare & the Ethics of Appropriation*, eds. Alexa Huang and Elizabeth Rivlin (Palgrave Macmillan), 89–105, 90.
[8] Susanne Greenhalgh, "A World Elsewhere. Documentary Representations of Social Shakespeare," *Critical Survey*, 31. 4 (Winter 2019), 77–87, 82.
[9] Paul Yachnin and Jessica Slights (eds.), *Shakespeare and Character. Theory, History, Performance, and Theatrical Persons* (Palgrave Macmillan, 2009), 1.

Italy, where, however, the prison riots at the beginning of the COVID-19 emergency violently, if only briefly, brought it to media attention. While this issue need not concern us here, it can be undeniably assumed that this discussion has deeply influenced and continues to influence the different trends of thought about the quality of the "transformation" Shakespeare carries out in prison.

The same concept of transformation has, likewise, become highly controversial: on the one hand, in many prison Shakespeare discourses, it is deeply connected, if not identified, with moral virtue and "salvation" – a salvation to be reached through a creative process that has the power "to heal and redeem – in a place where the very act of participation in theatre is a human triumph and a means of personal liberation," as one reads in the website of the Shakespeare Behind Bars Company.[10] Ophelia's line "Lord, we know who we are, but know not who we may be" (*Hamlet*, 4.5.43) resonates as particularly meaningful behind bars, because, as Tofteland and other practitioners have pointed out, Shakespeare is "a vehicle through which convicted criminals could come to know themselves, not just for the crimes they have committed but also on the deepest level of knowing – mind, heart and soul."[11] Not surprisingly, Niels Herold invites us to regard Prince Hal's "temporary sojourn in the criminal world of Eastcheap" as "the foundation for his glorious advent as one of England's most popular kings"[12] and, I would add, as a Christian one.

On the other hand, other practitioners and academics appear more skeptical about how Shakespeare is being used to provide emotional and moral guidance in order to discipline the inmates-actors to feel and live properly. These practitioners and academics tend to resist representations in which Shakespeare is regarded as a spiritual force capable of redeeming criminals, and rather interpret the "transformation" in an extra-moral sense. This is the case of the Italian actor, director, playwright Armando Punzo, a pioneer of theater in prison in Italy. Punzo has never been inspired by notions of "psychological assistance or therapy or social reform," even though his work has contributed to building the inmates/actors' self-respect and expertise in theater to the point that his productions have won important Italian theater prizes.[13]

---

[10] Shakespearebehindbars.org/.

[11] Ibid.

[12] Niels Herold, *Prison Shakespeare and the Purpose of Performance. Repentance Rituals and the Early Modern* (Palgrave Macmillan, 2014), 32.

[13] Armando Punzo quoted in Elisabetta Povoledo, "Maximum Security and a Starring Role," *The New York Times*, July 22, 2009, www.nytimes.com/2009/07/23/arts/23iht-povo.html?pagewanted=all&_r=0.

However, such a dichotomy of positions should not come as a surprise, since both approaches are legitimated by plays equally embedded in a language that might be called Christian-humanistic as well as the language of Elizabethan Machiavellianism, whose grammar "pliantly reflects the richness and mutability of reality, and interprets the world according to its new complexity."[14] Significantly, the "'decomposition' of character" into "a plurality of voices, which, far from being logically organized, are often contradictory" takes place in Shakespeare's plays to the point that no overall ideology or psychology can be invoked to engage with characters such as Hamlet or Richard III, and implies a world which "cannot be signified in terms of totality, or grasped with the Manichean categories of good and evil, order and chaos."[15] It is a world that has lost its ethical unity and where Machiavelli's political thought is often referred to, since he writes about what men actually do rather than what they ought to do, which, consequently, appears to be particularly alluring and meaningful in the context of our contemporary prisons.

Villains Strike Back!

Armando Punzo, who in 1987 founded the Fortress Company, a professional company in Volterra's high security prison, is quite critical of most theater projects in prison. Like Greenhalgh and Lehmann, he warns against the risk that theater, and Shakespeare in particular, may be used as a coercive force in prison programs rather than as a tool of empowerment. Criticizing a "wave of suffocating normalization,"[16] Punzo questions the meaning and value of the many drama workshops that are currently offered in almost every Italian prison as an opportunity for rehabilitation, as provided by Italian law, but also, as he suggests, encouraged by the strong Catholic culture of the country. Provocatively, he intervened in the passionate discussion around Shakespearean characters' moral and psychological profiles with his production *Shakespeare. Know Well,* which opened in July 2015 inside the ancient Medici fortress in Volterra, Tuscany. Indeed, he is opposed to the dominant idea that inmates-actors can find their experiences mirrored in Shakespeare's characters and that the process of rehearsal exploration of the Shakespearean plays can transform them. On the contrary, spurred by

---

[14] Caroline Patey, "Beyond Aristotle: Giraldi Cinzio and Shakespeare," in *Italy and the English Renaissance*, eds. Sergio Rossi and Dianella Savoia (Unicopli, 1989), 167–185, 176.

[15] Ibid., 184.

[16] Armando Punzo, *Un'idea più grande di me. Conversazioni con Rosella Menna* (Sossella, 2019), 352.

the reading of philosopher and actor Franco Ricordi's *Shakespeare filosofo dell'essere* (2011), he started to investigate "the whole body of Shakespeare's work from the perspective of its cultural and philosophical legacy,"[17] thus inviting his inmates-actors to view Shakespeare plays critically, to question their ethical quality and to literally liberate the Shakespearean characters themselves from his plays and their written roles.

Punzo engages with Friedrich Nietzsche,[18] who speculated on the morality of the stage and shares with him the opinion that "whoever thinks that Shakespeare's theatre has a moral effect, and that the sight of Macbeth irresistibly repels one from the evil of ambition, is in error," since, on the contrary, he "exercises 'demonic' attraction" and anyone "who is really possessed by raging ambition regards him as a model to emulate."[19] On the path of Nietzsche's remark, Punzo asserts that Shakespeare made a "dramaturgical mistake,"[20] since he created a man he himself would want to deny and fight. "What would have happened if Shakespeare had not created these characters in such a powerful way?" he asks himself, his actors, and spectators,[21] while he contemplates the "monumental fresco" of virtues, passions, weaknesses and aspirations characterizing our humanity, as conceived by Shakespeare.[22] Persuasively, he argues that Shakespeare has played a crucial role in forging our humanity as "entangled in its own pain, unaware of its condition, and incapable of finding a way out,"[23] and maintains that even though his major characters were born after "a careful study of the human soul," their words and actions are incapable of saying anything really new and meaningful about humankind.[24] According to Punzo, even Shakespeare's more complex characters – those who doubt and question themselves and the world around them – are "granite statues" whose "role is determined within a coherent plot," with no chance or hope for getaways or transformations.[25]

In Punzo's notes to his subsequent production *Dopo la tempesta. L'opera segreta di Shakespeare* (*After the Tempest. The Secret Work by Shakespeare*),

---

[17] VolterraTeatro 2015. Press Release. volterrateatro.it/2015/wp-content/uploads/comunicato-stampa_eng_2015.pdf.
[18] Punzo, *Un'idea*, 286.
[19] Friedrich Nietzsche, *Daybreak. Thoughts on the Prejudices of Morality*, eds. M. Clark and B. Leiter (Cambridge University Press, 1997), Book 4 – Aphorism 240.
[20] Punzo, *Un'idea*, 287.
[21] VolterraTeatro 2015. Press Release.
[22] Punzo, *Un'idea*, 285.
[23] VolterraTeatro 2015. Press Release.
[24] Ibid.
[25] Punzo, *Un'idea*, 285.

which opened at Volterra's prison in July 2016, he wrote that Shakespeare "missed the creative force" to forge "a different man," even if "the spirits wandering in his plays" might be regarded as a timid attempt at giving life to the "still unexpressed, inexistent possibilities"[26] of that man. Thus, provocatively, Punzo imagines that these spirits inhabit a "secret text" that is hidden "in the recesses of the meanings and plots of [Shakespeare's] thirty-six plays" and that is "visible only to the eyes of those readers who are not attracted [or rather distracted?] by his [Shakespeare's] stories."[27] His purpose as a director is therefore to guide his actors to discover that hidden "antidote text," where the Shakespearean lines and words work as "reagents" in a new grammar where they sound as newly meaningful in spite of their recognizability.[28] Indeed, the performance accomplishes the dissolution of our "humanity," with Shakespearean characters, such as Brutus, Richard III and Lady Anne, Romeo and Juliet, Caliban, and Othello appearing on-stage, one after the other, before "melting into the air" for one last time.[29]

Significantly, Punzo explains that it was by staging Shakespeare that he started to think about the possibility of freeing his characters from their fixed roles in search of "other words, other actions, other (perhaps yet unimagined) possibilities."[30] Thus, whereas in *Hamlice – Saggio sulla fine di una civiltà* (2010), *Hamlet*'s characters met and intertwined with *Alice in Wonderland* and Carroll's anarchy, in *Mercutio non vuole morire* (*Mercutio does not want to die*), Mercutio, who stands for "the poet, the actor, the artist, the philosopher,"[31] escapes from his written role and destiny: he rewrites his story with a new ending, in which a different world is possible thanks to the help of companions – other literary characters such as Othello, Cyrano de Bergerac, and Faust, as well as spectators encouraged to take an active part in the performance – all of whom want to share his utopian dream and help him in his effort to build a new world.

By challenging Shakespeare as well as undermining rules and conventions, Punzo's "Theatre of the Impossible," as he defines it, morphs prison

---

[26] Armando Punzo, *Dopo la Tempesta. L'opera segreta di Shakespeare*, compagniadellafortezza.org/new/gli-spettacoli-2/gli-spettacoli/dopo-la-tempesta-lopera-segreta-di-shakespeare/.

[27] Punzo, *Un'idea*, 288.

[28] Armando Punzo, "Per un teatro stabile in carcere," *È ai vinti*, 295–298, 290.

[29] Mariacristina Cavecchi, "The Bard Does Not Want To Die (Behind Bars). Rewriting Shakespeare Inside Volterra's Maximum-Security Prison," in *Rewriting Shakespeare's Plays for and By the Contemporary Stage*, eds. Michael Dobson and Estelle Rivier-Arnaud (Cambridge University Press, 2017), 119–134.

[30] Punzo, *È ai vinti*, 196.

[31] Ibid., 231.

into a world free from the constraints of the sclerotic and deadening theater outside, thus accomplishing that "utopia of being free to rewrite everything, even what appears impossible to change and reinvent."[32] Punzo's theater is therefore a place of creativity and freedom, where he guides his inmates-actors towards "epiphanies" and "manifestations"[33] by means of a process that leads them to get rid of their predefined stage roles, while undergoing a deeply empowering process. Meaningfully, when he tries to explain what happens in these "rare, very rare moments" when his actors "catch fire," far from any rhetoric of healing transformation and redemption, he recounts "something surprising" that has more to do with the craft of theater (what he calls "artigianato teatrale," "theatre handicraft") than with moral virtue:

> My work lives on flames releasing from them [the actors], when in that room, in a "campino," in a corner, all of a sudden, they catch fire, when they burn in front of my eyes, transfigure, open and let surface something surprising.[34]

In fact, this "transfiguration" is deeply connected with the inmates-actors' capability to change themselves into aware performers, who renounce their biographies and step out of and distance themselves from the Shakespearean characters. Indeed, Punzo never asks his actors "to transform in order to convincingly play a fictional character"; on the contrary, he guides them to use characters "like a springboard"[35] in order to establish a more natural, direct and meaningful relationship both with them and the audience. In a way, their straightforward relation with spectators recalls the way the characters exhibit the alienation-effect in Bertolt Brecht's epic theater. Punzo's award-winning *I Pescecani ovvero quel che resta di Bertolt Brecht* (*The Sharks, or what remains of Bertolt Brecht*, 2002) was meant to remind us that Brecht's characters, born to denounce evil and change the world, on the contrary on Punzo's stage, had become sharks, namely, the evil itself: indeed, the stage was inhabited not by actors playing the criminals, as on the Brechtian stage, but rather by criminals accusing spectators of being criminals, thus inevitably unmasking the fact that evil was still to be found and fought out of prison, in society itself.[36] Appropriately, ten years later, for *Romeo non vuole morire*'s premiere at the VolterraTeatro Festival

---

[32] Punzo, *Dopo la Tempesta.*
[33] Punzo, *Un'idea*, 329.
[34] Ibid., 325.
[35] Ibid., 335.
[36] Ibid.

in July 2012, when the action went out of prison and took over the entire
Tuscan town, the audience, involved in a number of symbolic actions,
was first asked to have their hands painted red and so immediately turned
into accomplices of the many murderers in Shakespeare's tragedy, those
Capulets and Montagues that Punzo defines as "butchers of all hope."[37]
Their hands soiled with the blood of youth, they marched through the narrow streets of the medieval Tuscan town to the wild beating of drums until
they arrived in Piazza dei Priori, where several Juliets, previously selected
amongst the audience, were made to lie down on the ground, the innocent
victims of their intolerable violence. By merging theater and a happening
in an experience that turned theater into a permanent discovery labora-
tory, and the town itself into a theater capable of staging an alternative
version of a Shakespeare tragedy, the production succeeded in engendering transformations in the space of the prison, in the Volterra territory,
and even in the spectators themselves, by showing how each of them could
actively do something to change their perception of society as well as of
prison and, ultimately, to act on these new perceptions.

Polemically, Punzo, whose ambition is to create a stable repertory company with a full season and a permanent theater with a proper stage inside
the prison,[38] denounces a system that regards theater not as a proper job to
be trained in but as just a vehicle for a so-called re-education process, the
quality of which he contests:

> Theatre is just a tool: have you attended theatre workshops? Have you
> improved your ability to speak and to work in a team? Well, objectives
> have been reached, the educator certifies that you are ready, the magistrate
> authorizes you to go out of prison in order to work either as a pizza maker
> or a waiter, [...] any other job except those related to theatre. Theatre is
> not a job, is it? [...] You have to work hard; you have to take menial jobs
> because you have made a living off of society. How could theatre be consid-
> ered as a real job for an ex-inmate?[39]

Indeed, in the light of my modest five-year experience as a co-leader
with director Giuseppe Scutellà of several Shakespearean workshops at the
"Beccaria" in Milan, one of seventeen juvenile detention centers currently
operating in Italy, I see, with disappointment, that our contemporary
society is not ready to collect the fruits of the Shakespeare workshops.
In fact, in prison, under the guidance of Shakespeare their "personal

---

[37] Punzo, *È ai vinti*, 231.
[38] Punzo, *È ai vinti*, 295–298.
[39] Punzo, *Un'idea*, 348.

trainer," as well as directors and educators, the young inmates-actors I met have been guided to experience a new way of perceiving themselves and reality, perhaps even to think that, after all, they still may have a future; however, once out of prison, they very often do not find those social conditions that might help them to deal with the influence of dysfunctional families, drug-using friends, and poor employment opportunities. How can R. N., a Romanian who has discovered a talent in prison for acting, be saved from the inevitable intrusion and imposition of his clan that has brought him up swindling and stealing? Where can Albanian K.S., who was on the stage of Milan's Teatro alla Scala in a successful production of *A Midsummer Night's Dream*, find motivation to work long hours as a bricklayer for a low wage rather than going back to pushing drugs, an activity he used to do before his arrest?

Rightly, we assume Shakespeare might be a resourceful paradigm for social emancipation and political awareness; however, so far, the dream of a virtuous Shakespeare opening up future personal and professional opportunities is just an illusion. The question is therefore not about Shakespeare's virtuosity but rather whether our societies are ready to channel the energies and virtues aroused by our salvific Shakespeare.

The questions posed by theater need be answered by politics.

CHAPTER 38

Teaching Shakespeare and Moral Agency

Michael Bristol

In the spring of 1970, my last year teaching at The University of Illinois, I was directing a production of *Twelfth Night* for an off-campus theater called "The Depot: A Center for Experiment in Art and Ideas." One of our mostly unexamined ideas about "experimentation" was to throw somebody into the deep end of the pool, hoping they would learn to swim, and this is how I came to direct a play for the first time. It was Marlowe's *The Jew of Malta* and it was good enough to be controversial. We were a dangerous organization according to the local John Birch Society. The most inflammatory aspect of our creativity was probably the presence of men with long hair. This was evidently subversive because "you just can't tell the boys from the girls anymore." *Twelfth Night* was a good way to find out what would happen when you can't tell the boys from the girls.

The parts of Viola and Sebastian were played by two sisters. They were not twins, but there was a strong family resemblance and one of the sisters had a low-pitched voice that I liked for Sebastian. Based on that and little else I asked them if they would let me turn them into actors. Viola was keen to try; Sebastian hesitated but she eventually agreed. The entire cast were "hippie amateurs" according to their own self-description, but I liked the spontaneity and the vulnerability they brought to their roles. Although I did not know this at the time, Bertolt Brecht liked to use nonprofessional actors in his productions because, like children learning by imitation, they are often better able to recognize what is too obvious for the "trained mind" to consider. He shared with his contemporary Antonin Artaud the idea that works of dramatic art should not be staged like a masterpiece in a museum, but instead speak to the moment in which it is performed.[1]

---

[1] Bertolt Brecht, "Two Essays on Unprofessional Actors," in *Brecht on Theatre*, ed. John Willett (Hill and Wang, 1964), 148–153; Antonin Artaud, "En Finir Avec Les Chefs-D'Œuvres," in *Le théâtre et son double* (Paris, 1938), 79–89. See also Terry Eagleton, "Brecht and Rhetoric," *New Literary History* 16. 3 (1985): 633–638.

At the first rehearsal I told them to use their own vernacular, mostly mid-western, intonation. They picked up the music of Shakespeare's poetry with their local accents very quickly. Viola had a nice emotional range, and in the speech where she says "she never told her love" her delivery would break your heart. I asked one of her friends how she was able to project that kind of feeling, and the answer was "Didn't you know? Her dad died last year." The emotional shape of the play emerged gradually from our collaborative work on the endless detail that goes into the production of a play. We spent much of our time on questions of stage movement, musical intonation, pace, rhythm. One thing I was learning in my dramaturgical work is that if you pay attention to matters of style and form, thematic meanings will emerge naturally as a felt response to the characters moving and speaking before us. I think our production brought out a depth of sadness and uncertainty latent in the text of *Twelfth Night* I didn't realize was there when we began our work together. We never took time to consider the historical context of the play. The pressure of our contemporary reality didn't allow for that.

The Kent State Shooting took place on Monday, May 4, 1970. Allison Krause, Jeffrey Miller, Sandra Scheuer, and William Knox Schroeder were shot to death by the Ohio National Guard. Nobody knows who fired the fatal bullets or who gave the order. That same afternoon Viola and Sebastian and the rest of the cast of *Twelfth Night* were finishing the first dress rehearsal for our performance. That night all hell broke loose in the downtown shopping area of Champaign, Illinois, adjacent to the campus. The next day I watched a column of armored personnel carriers roll into town with a contingent of the Illinois National Guard. They took up positions facing the campus along Wright Street and within minutes they were confronted by hundreds of students. It was a tense situation that went on for several days. Nobody was killed, thankfully, so there was no national press coverage. But the memory is still vivid after all this time. And then, just a year ago, I got an email from Viola: "Watching the national guard march down our street a few days before our opening was terrifying … I also will never forget working with you on *Twelfth Night* and the joy that it brought to us all."

*

I first started thinking about a course on Shakespeare and Moral Agency twenty-five years ago at the Folger Library, reading eighteenth-century Shakespeare criticism. This was the period when the first complete editions of Shakespeare's Works were being published, his plays were being performed in London theaters, reviewed in coffee houses, and discussed in the bluestocking salons. It would be more than a century before the plays were studied in universities. The editors, theatergoer, actors, and actresses who wrote about Shakespeare used a style of vernacular criticism, analyzing his characters the way they would talk about their personal acquaintances. In using this vocabulary to engage with a dramatic fiction they were at the same time reflecting on their own ethical and social commitments. They worked with everyday knowledge of Scripture along with the literature of classical antiquity, which in some cases they would have read in the original languages. Their familiarity with this literary tradition enabled them to share a "climate of recognitions" for understanding the poetic cross-references that form the verbal texture of Shakespeare's works.[2] Although they were aware that Shakespeare's world was historically distant from their own, they nevertheless felt "at home" in his fictional universe, thanks to a shared literary background, available to a large reading public through a lively commerce in printed books.[3]

One thing that stands out in eighteenth-century writing on Shakespeare is a concern with moral philosophy. Samuel Johnson (1709–1784) thought Shakespeare's principal fault was that "he seems to write without any moral purpose."[4] Elizabeth Montagu (1718–1800) disagreed, declaring that "he is certainly one of the greatest moral philosophers that ever lived."[5] This is not the place to rehearse the complicated debates over theories of morality during the Enlightenment, but one strand of that narrative is compatible with the way Shakespeare's characters were talked about in the salons and coffee houses. The Earl of Shaftesbury (1671–713) wrote extensively about the moral sense, a disposition of sympathy grounded in feelings of benevolence towards others.[6] Francis Hutcheson (1694–1746) describes the moral sense as awareness of the beauty of affections and actions moved by kindness.[7]

---

[2] George Steiner, "On Difficulty," *The Journal of Aesthetics and Art Criticism*, 36. 3, *Critical Interpretation* (1978), 263–276. 265.

[3] Raymond Williams, *The Long Revolution* (Chatto and Windus, 1961); Jürgen Habermas, *The Structural Transformation of the Public Sphere: An Inquiry into a Category of Bourgeois Society* (MIT Press, 1991).

[4] Samuel Johnson "Preface to Shakespeare," ed. Arthur Sherbo, *The Yale Edition of the Works of Samuel Johnson*, vol. 7 (Yale University Press, 1968), 71.

[5] Elizabeth Montagu, *An Essay on the Writings and Genius of Shakespear compared the Greek and French Dramatic Poets, with Some Remarks Upon the Misrepresentations of Mons. De Voltaire* (London: 1769).

[6] Anthony Ashley Cooper, Third Earl of Shaftesbury, *An Inquiry Concerning Virtue in Two Discourses*, Introd. Joseph Filonowicz (Scholars Facsimiles & Reprints 1991).

[7] Francis Hutcheson, *An Inquiry into the Original of our Ideas of Beauty and Virtue* 5th Ed. (London: 1753), 69 ff.

The vocabulary for talking about emotions was varied and often equivocal. Affections, passions, and sentiments were used interchangeably. All of these expressions are ambivalent, because these philosophers recognized that emotions are the source of both sympathy and of hatred. Adam Smith (1723–1790) distinguishes between social, unsocial, and selfish passions to suggest that a virtuous person is not one who rises above all emotion, but rather someone with the capacity to cultivate feelings that direct us towards benevolence.[8]

Shakespeare's beliefs about ethical questions are not available to us.[9] Moral philosophy is voiced only by his characters and in the way we are affected by them. Samuel Johnson was deeply shocked by the death of Cordelia. Horace Howard Furness had a similar reaction to Othello. Are we not supposed to be horrified by what happens in these plays; is intellectual detachment the best way to respond? The university tradition of Shakespeare scholarship has mostly shied away from emotional engagement, preferring a style of archive-based "objectivity" that is more consistent with the demands of peer review. But Shakespeare's plays are emotionally challenging and often profoundly disturbing. An emotional response to fictional character is tied to our intuitions about what is right and what is wrong.[10] This is emotional intelligence, a felt knowledge of what we owe to ourselves and how we are connected to others.[11]

*

My first ever graduate seminar on Shakespeare and Moral Agency was offered the year following my work at The Folger. I was hoping to encourage an unschooled and undefended response to the resistant structure of the text.[12] The initial obstacle I had to overcome came when I announced we would not be studying the historical context of Shakespeare's works. I give them credit for their objections to this. There is considerable heuristic

---

[8] Adam Smith, *The Theory of Moral Sentiments*, eds. D. D. Raphael and A. L. Macfie (Liberty Fund, 1984), 27–43.

[9] Quentin Skinner, "Afterword: Shakespeare and Humanist Culture," in *Shakespeare and Early Modern Political Thought*, eds. D. Armitage, C. Condren and A. Fitzmaurice (Cambridge University Press, 2009), 271–282.

[10] Eva Dadlez, *What's Hecuba to Him? Fictional Events and Actual Emotions* (Pennsylvania State University Press, 1987).

[11] Martha Nussbaum, *Love's Knowledge: Essays on Philosophy and Literature* (Oxford University Press, 1990).

[12] Richard Strier, *Resistant Structures: Particularity, Radicalism, and Renaissance Texts* (University of California Press, 1997); James Siemon, *Word Against Word: Shakespearean Utterance* (University of Massachusetts Press, 2002).

382 MICHAEL BRISTOL

value in a historical orientation. It invites students to reflect on their unexamined certainties by demonstrating that other social worlds have actually existed. There are many different ways to "play the old works historically."[13] Bertolt Brecht, whom I am quoting here, was thinking about the history of class struggle, and more specifically about the displacement of the feudal aristocracy by the commercial bourgeoisie. This orientation is recognizably the forerunner of Cultural Materialism. New Historicism, encouraged by the ideas of Michel Foucault, focused on a dialectic of subversion and complicity. I had used these strategies in prior years, and they also provoked resistance, and maybe not enough, since they fit in comfortably with their own sense of being wised up about how the world works. They were conscientious, insightful, and they could stake out a "position" with some degree of clarity, but their essays were often derivative and lacking in conviction. I began to feel that my task was to get them disenchanted with their own disenchantment.

I managed to convince my students that historical scholarship is a sufficient, but not a necessary condition for meeting the emotional and intellectual challenges of a Shakespeare play. I think when you engage with great works of dramatic art like *Macbeth* you are participating in a thought experiment devised by Shakespeare. The situations Shakespeare's characters face have the gravity and texture of lived experience. An emotional response to that experiment is highly correlated with understanding the play in the way Shakespeare intended. In addressing these ethical tensions, I asked them to cultivate "philosophical habits of mind" through a cross-examination of our settled beliefs and to look for instances of this self-consultation in the dramatic characters.[14]

It is late at night. Duncan has retired to his bedchamber. Macbeth is alone. Like a philosopher, he thinks through his determination to murder the king. He asks "if the assassination could trammel up the consequence and catch with his surcease, success." (*Macbeth* 1.7.2–3)[15] In other words, he wonders if he will get away with it, and decides that he won't. There are additional reasons for discarding the plan. "I am his kinsman, and his subject ... his host who should against his murderer shut the door, not bear the knife myself" (*Macbeth* 1.7.13–15). And so he tells Lady Macbeth "We will proceed no further in this business" (*Macbeth* 1.7.31). This is his

[13] Bertolt Brecht, *The Messingkauf Dialogues*, trans. John Willett (Eyre Methuen, 1963), 63.
[14] Martha C. Nussbaum, *The Fragility of Goodness: Luck and Ethics in Greek Tragedy and Philosophy*, Revised edn. (Cambridge University Press, 2001), 128 ff.
[15] Shakespeare, *Macbeth*, ed. Nicholas Brooke (Oxford University Press, 1990).

all things considered best judgment, but then almost immediately he will change his mind, enter the king's bedchamber and murder him. Why does he act in a way he considers wrong, knowing that he will destroy what he values most in himself?[16]

To explore situations like this, students were asked to read a variety of philosophical texts, but we relied throughout on three relatively compact works representing contrasting styles of moral inquiry. Aristotle, *Nichomachean Ethics*, was an obvious choice. Students liked the way Aristotle recognizes that human flourishing can take different shapes. Without suggesting that Shakespeare would have read Aristotle, it can be shown that discussions of virtue ethics certainly had currency at the time.[17] Shakespeare's characters have a lot to say about virtue, sometimes in reference to particular human traits that contribute to personal excellence, but also for the beneficial properties of gems or plants. However, if you think of the courage of Coriolanus or the chastity of Isabella or the honesty of Cordelia you see that their sense of what it means to be virtuous leads to massive collateral damage.

Immanuel Kant, *Prolegomena to the Metaphysics of Morals* is the text that elicited the strongest resistance. I think for many of these students the categorical imperative was fundamentally unintelligible. They were entirely comfortable with the idea of duty, broadly speaking, but they found Kant's way of getting at it simplistic and likely to lead to horrible outcomes. Part of the problem here is the Kantian insistence on strictly rational self-consultation as the required method for resolving moral questions.

LADY MACDUFF: Wisdom! to leave his wife, to leave his babes,
His mansion and his titles in a place
From whence himself does fly? He loves us not;
He wants the natural touch: for the poor wren,
The most diminutive of birds, will fight,
Her young ones in her nest, against the owl.
All is the fear and nothing is the love;

ROSS: My dearest coz,
I pray you, school yourself: but for your husband,
He is noble, wise, judicious, and best knows
The fits o' the season. (4.2.6–17)

---

[16] Michael Bristol, "Macbeth the Philosopher: Rethinking Context," *New Literary History* 42. 4 (2011), 641–662.

[17] Sara Coodin, "What's Virtue Ethics got to do with it?" in *Shakespeare and Moral Agency*, ed. Michael Bristol (Continuum Books, 2010); Unhae Park Langis, *Passion, Prudence and Virtue in Shakespearean Drama* (Continuum, 2011).

Let's concede that Macduff's decision to leave his wife and children in order to fulfill his duties to the rightful King of Scotland is his all-things-considered-best-judgment or, if you will, a categorical imperative. It is not too much of a stretch then to interpret this exchange as an uncanny memory of the Kohlberg–Gilligan debates.

Lawrence Kohlberg's research on moral development in children was based on questionnaires that asked boys and girls to adjudicate a number of ethical problems, most famously perhaps the question about whether "Heinz" should steal the medicine that will save his wife's life since he cannot afford to pay for it. Kohlberg noticed that boys frequently decided this question based on firm "principles" – stealing is wrong – while girls were more imaginative, wondering if Heinz could maybe work something out with the pharmacist. On the basis of this observation Kohlberg decided that boys of a given age had a "higher" sense of morality. Carol Gilligan objected his idea that abstract, all-purpose rules constitute a higher morality and questioned the normative significance of this kind of thinking. She went on to argue forcefully that the moral imagination expressed by the girls was psychologically more realistic than the boys and that they were speaking "in a different voice" based on the idea that morality is a concern for the needs of others, seen as real people standing in a concrete, sensuous relationship to the moral agent. Shakespeare almost seems to remember this controversy, with Macduff, through his surrogate Ross, reasoning on "higher" general principles and Lady Macduff speaking "in a different voice" that many of my students found impossible to ignore.[18]

Finally, the genealogical method adopted by Nietzsche is the forerunner of the more recent projects of demystification and disenchantment of the unexamined truths operating in every culture.[19] For many students the most appealing idea in *The Genealogy of Morals* was the idea of the noble man who "lives in trust and openness with himself."[20] As a number of them pointed out, this has a distant connection with Aristotle's ideas of human flourishing. There are, needless to say, any number of examples in Shakespeare's plays of the radical self-affirmation Nietzsche is talking about. And, at least in the case of *Othello*, the tragic catastrophe is

---

[18] Owen Flanagan and Kathryn Jackson, "Justice, Care, and Gender: The Kohlberg-Gilligan Debate Revisited," *Ethics* 97. 3 (1987), 622–637; Lawrence Kohlberg, *The Philosophy of Moral Development* (Harper and Row, 1981); Carol Gilligan, *In a Different Voice* (Harvard University Press, 1982).

[19] Alasdair C. McIntyre, *Three Rival Versions of Moral Enquiry: Encyclopaedia, Genealogy, and Tradition* (University of Notre Dame Press, 1990), 32–57.

[20] Friedrich Nietzsche, *On the Genealogy of Morals*, trans. Douglas Smith (Oxford University Press, 1996), 11.

driven by the *ressentiment* of Iago. For the most part, however, radical self-affirmation turns out to be radical self-destruction. What's missing is not the affirmation part, but the radical self-knowledge that makes it possible for the noble man to flourish. Macbeth already knows before he murders Duncan that he will not get away with it, but he doesn't fully acknowledge feelings for what he truly values and desires until it's much too late: "… that which should accompany old age, as honor, love, obedience, troops of friends, I must not look to have" (5.3.24–26).

*

Chastity is not specifically mentioned in the *Nicomachean Ethics*, although it is understood to be an element in the virtue of continence. The seven virtues listed by Prudentius opposing the seven deadly sins do include chastity, which has the sense we recognize today of abstinence from sex, or at least any sex outside marriage. In many of Shakespeare's plays chastity understood in this way is a matter of life and death. *Measure for Measure* treats this relationship in a novel way, since it is Isabella's brother Claudio who will die if she does not surrender to Angelo's demands, but if she does surrender, her own life will be permanently disfigured.

ISABELLA: Then, Isabel, live chaste, and, brother, die:
More than our brother is our chastity.
I'll tell him yet of Angelo's request,
And fit his mind to death, for his soul's rest. (2.4.184–187)[21]

Students were disgusted by the shabby banality of Angelo's sexual extortion, but they were deeply horrified by Isabella's decision to ask her brother to give up his life. Students have real lives that include siblings they care about; asking a brother to die for them to avoid an admittedly repulsive sexual encounter did not add up.

What is at stake in Isabella's choice is the relative value of her brother's life over against the vita contemplativa that will define her own personhood. These are thick concepts that necessarily elude any effort at logical precision, never mind finding a unit of measurement that could honestly be applied to both.[22] The majority of students did not agree with her assessment of the situation. Basically the response was "I would agree to have sex with a man I did not like to save my brother's life." Relationships with

[21] Shakespeare, *Measure for Measure*, ed. N. W. Bawcutt, *Oxford World's Classics* (Oxford University Press, 1991).
[22] Bernard Williams, *Ethics and the Limits of Philosophy* (Harvard University Press, 1985), 140–143.

family members and other loved ones are profound; they ask for loyalty, care, and a willingness to sacrifice our own self-interest.[23] Shouldn't she be willing to submit to this humiliation, when refusing is a matter of life and death for another person?

There were different voices. "Why are we so sure the woman has to make the sacrifice? Maybe we don't understand the real significance of the chastity thing." This student pointed out that unwanted sex is not a trivial consideration, and especially for Isabella. Her argument was based on Aristotle's discussion of continence, a condition of the spirit that moves a person to perform the best actions in the best way. So chastity on this account is not just abstinence from sexual activity; it is taking full responsibility for one's own life, maintaining a standard of personal integrity that really is "more" valuable than the life of a brother who is himself, after all, incontinent. And since, for Aristotle, the virtues are always in some sense social capabilities, fidelity to the kind of life you see as the best for yourself is something we should admire. Isabella is called to a spiritual life, free from social entanglements and the worrying demands of ego. That life is a *démarche* from the demeaning commerce in persons that defines the secular world. Such a world is not hospitable to the life of the spirit, which for Isabella can only flourish within the cloistered environment of a community of women.[24] The choice can't be diminished to a self-indulgent wish to avoid the "yuck factor" in submitting to Angelo. There is no way to compare the value of a life of the spirit over against the debilitating imperatives of a market in human personhood. For her no other choice is possible.

The most provocative and unsettling intervention occurred when a young woman said "the only character I really like in this play is Barnardine. I like the way he just won't put up with any of the Duke's B.S."

BARNARDINE: I swear I will not die to-day for any man's
               persuasion.
VINCENTIO: But hear you.
BARNARDINE: Not a word: if you have anything to say to me,
               come to my ward; for thence will not I to-day. (4.3.57–60)

The point of her intervention was that Barnardine is Nietzsche's noble man, "living in trust and openness with himself." Another student asked

[23] Lawrence Becker, *Reciprocity* (University of Chicago Press, 1990), 185; Avishai Margalit, *The Ethics of Memory* (Harvard University Press, 2002), 33 ff.
[24] Jessica Slights and Michael Morgan Holmes, "Isabella's Order: Religious Acts and Personal Desires in *Measure for Measure*," *Studies in Philology* 95. 3 (1998): 263–292.

how she could possibly think Barnardine was noble. "Barnardine has no attachments, nothing to lose almost like a Zen monk. He is not afraid of death, but won't agree to give up his life to suit someone's convenience." The most surprising thing about her argument was that Barnardine is the key to understanding Isabella's character, and the real force of saying "more than our brother is our chastity."

For this student, Isabella's chastity is giving up everything for the sake of her immortal soul. The convent exists to make it possible to focus on spiritual goods through meditation and prayer, to the exclusion of everything else. My student understood this in terms of the Aristotelian virtue of magnanimity, giving up the self in favor of "greatness of soul." Her concern was that we were not willing to take the idea of vita contemplativa seriously. It's easy to forget sometimes, especially for a secular humanist type like me, that we may encounter students who are deeply religious, observant Jews or Catholics or practitioners of Zen meditation. The life of the spirit, however we may understand this, is important for them. What they discover along these lines in Shakespeare can be valuable, and not only in the way these discoveries deepen our understanding of the plays.

Isabella is not wrong to choose her own life over the life of her brother. But the idea of virtue on a heroic scale is foreign to us, although it is present in more than one of Shakespeare's other plays. Richard II would be another example: we cannot understand his character without accepting his own conception of the majesty of kings.[25] We don't like characters like this, and we certainly don't know how to admire them. So it's hard to accept the deep rationale of chastity as what motivates her decision to let her brother die. What my student found unforgiveable is not that decision, but her willingness to go along with Duke Vincentio's improvised scheme in the misguided hope that she will be able to have it both ways. By agreeing to in effect procure Mariana to have sex with a man who doesn't love her, Isabella's chastity is compromised even if she has preserved her virginity. She has agreed to participate in the very world of human trafficking she had intended to renounce.

A "Nietzschean" performance of *Measure for Measure* that acknowledges and celebrates Isabella's nobility creates difficulties for staging the final moments of this play. Kevin Curran is right to suggest that the "close of Measure for Measure ... shows us how assessment can generate the shared

---

[25] James Boyd White, "Shakespeare's *Richard II*: Imagining the Modern World," in *Acts of Hope: Creating Authority in Literature, Law, and Politics* (University of Chicago Press, 1994), 47–81.

MICHAEL BRISTOL

standards that form the moral scaffolding of community."[26] But what
standards – and for that matter what community – are we talking about?
The marriage between Angelo and Mariana is a reward for Mariana and a
punishment for Angelo, hardly your classic reconciliatory resolution to a
comedy. But the reverse seems to be the case with Vincentio and Isabella,
where it seems clear that this is a reward for the Duke, but a punishment
for Isabella. "What's mine is yours, what's yours is mine …" Vincentio
wants exactly what Angelo wanted, but he's willing to offer a better price
in the exchange. The entire world of the play is presented as a far-reaching
system of human trafficking. That world requires everybody to be swapped
or traded or substituted for somebody else. This is the transactional ethos
of a market where persons are exchanged.

Immediately after he has condemned Angelo to death, a sentence he has
no intention of carrying out, he tells Mariana that she can use Angelo's
money to "buy herself a better husband." A complete exit from this market, these standards, this community is exactly what Isabella intends by
chastity. It is possible, of course, for Isabella to lag behind as the company
leaves the stage and then sneak off with the nuns who have been waiting
to spirit her away to the convent. For the most part, however, the students
I was teaching were reluctant to participate in deforming the structure
of the play in this way, preferring instead to view the final scene in the
sense Nietzsche suggests, a rejection of her nobility by the social power of
ressentiment.

Towards the end of the long-drawn-out chaos of the final scene Duke
Vincentio pronounces judgment on Angelo.

> The very mercy of the law cries out
> Most audible, even from his proper tongue,
> "An Angelo for Claudio, death for death!"
> Haste still pays haste, and leisure answers leisure;
> Like doth quit like, and measure still for measure. (5.1.408–412)

This speech is a distorted echo of Luke 6:38 "Give, and it shall be given
unto you; good measure, pressed down, and shaken together, and running
over, shall men give into your bosom. For with the same measure that ye
mete withal it shall be measured to you again." The larger sense of this
chapter in the Gospel is the need to be merciful, not to condemn others,

---

[26] Kevin Curran, "The Face of Judgement in *Measure for Measure*," in *Face to Face in Shakespearean Drama: Ethics, Performance, Philosophy*, eds. Matthew James Smith and Julia Lupton (Edinburgh University Press, 2019), 163–175, 174.

and to love your enemies. This is entirely different from the ideas of reciprocity and retribution that constitute the Duke's conception of justice. The scriptural "full measure" is the fulfillment of the Aristotelian – and also Christian – virtues of compassion and liberality, gifts of the spirit, not the exchange of equivalents in the marketplace.[27] Does a "climate of recognitions" still exist for us to comprehend both the spirit of the passage from the Gospels and its misquotation by the Duke of an imaginary Vienna that resembles our own world all too closely? Is there any space for a larger sense virtue in that world? Over the years my students and I came to understand that the answers to such questions in Shakespearean drama can be found in its own distinctive account of virtue ethics, one that does not work from a checklist of admirable qualities, but from the effort to live a beautiful life in an inhospitable world. Virtue speaks in a different voice here, and you have to listen carefully to understand what it is saying.

---

[27] Lewis Hyde, *The Gift: Imagination and the Erotic Life of Property* (Vintage Books, 1979).

Works Cited

Alexander, Neville. *Robben Island Dossier 1964–1974* (University of Cape Town Press, 1998).

Anderson, Linda. *A Place in the Story: Servants and Service in Shakespeare's Plays* (University of Delaware Press, 2005).

Annas, Julia. *Intelligent Virtue* (Oxford University Press, 2011).

Aquinas, Thomas. *The Summa Theologica of St. Thomas Aquinas: Literally Translated by Fathers of the English Dominican Province*. 2nd ed. (Burns Oates & Washbourne Ltd, 1920).

Arendt, Hannah. *The Human Condition* (University of Chicago Press, 1957).

Armstrong, Paul B. *Stories and the Brain: The Neuroscience of Narrative* (Johns Hopkins University Press, 2020).

Attell, Kevin. "Potentiality, Actuality, Constituent Power." *Diacritics* 39.3 (2009), 35–53.

Auerbach, Erich. "Passio as Passion." Trans. Martin Elsky. *Criticism* 43.3 (2001), 285–308.

Augustine. *City of God*. Trans. Henry Bettenson (Penguin Books, 1984).

  Confessions. Trans. Henry Chadwick (Oxford University Press, 1991).

Bacon, Francis. *The Essays*. Ed. John Pitcher (Penguin, 1985).

Baldwin, William and Thomas Paulfreyman. *A Treatise of Morall Philosophy* (Richard Bishop, 1630).

Barish, Jonas A. and Marshall Waingrow. "'Service' in King Lear." *Shakespeare Quarterly* 9.3 (1958), 347–355.

Barret, J. K. "Habit." *Entertaining the Idea: Shakespeare, Performance and Philosophy*. Eds. James Kearney, Lowell Gallagher, and Julia Reinhard Lupton (University of Toronto Press, 2020).

Barrett, Lisa Feldman. *How Emotions Are Made: The Secret Life of the Brain* (Houghton Mifflin Harcourt, 2017).

Barton, Anne. *Shakespeare and the Idea of the Play* (Penguin, 1967).

Batchelor, Stephen. "Greek Buddha: Pyrrho's encounter with early Buddhism in Central Asia." Review of Christopher Beckwith, *Greek Buddha: Pyrrho's Encounter with Early Buddhism in Central Asia. Contemporary Buddhism* 17.1 (2016), 195–215.

Bate, Jonathan. *The Genius of Shakespeare* (Picador, 1997).

  "'Hide Thy life': The Key to Shakespeare." *Times Higher Education Supplement*. August 6, 2009.

Beck, Lewis White. *A Commentary on Kant's Critique of Practical Reason* (University of Chicago Press, 1960).

Becker, Lawrence. *Reciprocity* (University of Chicago Press, 1990).

Bejczy, Istvan P. "Les vertus cardinals dans l'hagiographie latine du Moyen Âge." *Analecta Bollandiana: Revue critique d'hagiographie* 122.2 (2004), 313–360.

Bell, Millicent. *Shakespeare's Tragic Skepticism* (Yale University Press, 2002).

Bellah, Robert N. *Religion in Human Evolution: From the Paleolithic to the Axial Age* (Harvard University Press, 2011).

Benjamin, Walter. *The Arcades Project*. Trans. Howard Eiland and Kevin McLaughlin (Harvard University Press, 2002).

Bennett, Jill. *Empathic Vision: Affect, Trauma, and Contemporary Art* (Stanford University Press, 2005).

Berlant, Lauren. *Cruel Optimism* (Duke University Press, 2011).

Berndt, Donald M. and Catherine H. Berndt. *The Speaking Land: Myth and Story in Aboriginal Australia* (Penguin, 1989).

Best, Royce. "Making Obesity Fat: Crip Estrangement in Shakespeare's Henry IV, Part 1." *Disability Studies Quarterly* 39.4 (2019), https://dsq-sds.org/article/view/7149/5470.

Bicks, Caroline. "Backsliding at Ephesus: Shakespeare's Diana and the Churching of Women." *Pericles: Critical Essays*. Ed. David Skeele (Routledge, 2009).

Biesele, Megan. *Women Like Meat: The Folklore and Foraging Ideology of the Kalahari Ju/'hoan* (Indiana University Press, 1993).

Blackwood, Maria. "Politics, Trade, and Diplomacy: The Anglo-Ottoman Relationship, 1575–1699." *History Matters* 7 (2010), 1–34.

Blazek, Pavel. "The Virtue of Virginity: The Aristotelian Challenge." *Virtue Ethics in the Middle Ages: Commentaries on Aristotle's Nicomachean Ethics, 1200–1500*. Ed. István Bejczy (Brill, 2007).

Bloom, Harold. *Shakespeare: The Invention of the Human* (Riverhead, 1998).

Boal, Augusto. *The Theatre of the Oppressed* (Pluto Press, 2019).

Boehm, Christopher. *Moral Origins: The Evolution of Virtue, Altruism, and Shame* (Basic Books, 2012).

Braden, Gordon. *Anger's Privilege: Renaissance Tragedy and the Senecan Tradition* (Yale University Press, 1985).

Brandstetter, Gabriele. "The Virtuoso's Stage: A Theatrical Topos." *Theatre Research International* 32.2 (2007), 178–195.

Bray, Alan. *The Friend*. (University of Chicago Press, 2003).

Brecht, Bertolt. "The Street Scene: A Basic Model for an Epic Theatre." *Brecht on Theatre* (3rd Ed.). Eds. Marc Silverman, Steve Giles, and Tom Kuhn (Bloomsbury, 2015).

Bristol, Michael. ed. *Shakespeare and Moral Agency* (Continuum, 2010).

"Macbeth the Philosopher: Rethinking Context." *New Literary History* 42.4 (2011), 641–662.

Brooke, Christopher. *Philosophic Pride: Stoicism and Political Thought from Lipsius to Rousseau* (Princeton University Press, 2012).

Brown, Francis, Samuel Rolles Driver, and Charles Augustus Briggs. *A Hebrew and English Lexicon of the Old Testament* (Houghton Mifflin, 1907).

Bryant Jr., Joseph, A. *Hippolyta's View: Some Christian Aspects of Shakespeare's Plays* (University of Kentucky Press, 1961).

Buber, Martin. *Two Types of Faith* (Macmillan, 1951).

Budick, Sanford. "Shakespeare's Secular Benediction: The Language of Tragic Community in *King Lear*." *Religious Diversity and Early Modern English Texts: Catholic, Judaic, Feminist, and Secular Dimensions.* Eds. Arthur F. Marotti and Chanita Goodblatt (Wayne State University Press, 2013).

Buntman, Fran Lisa. *Robben Island and Prisoner Resistance to Apartheid* (Cambridge University Press, 2003).

Burnett, Mark Thornton. *Masters and Servants in English Renaissance Drama and Culture: Authority and Obedience* (Macmillan, 1997).

Burnett, Stephen. "The Regulation of Hebrew Printing in Germany, 1555–1630: Confessional Politics and the Limits of Jewish Toleration." *Jews, Judaism, and the Reformation in Sixteenth-Century Germany.* Eds. D. P. Bell and S. Burnett (Brill, 2006).

   "Philosemitism and Christian Hebraism in the Reformation Era (1500–1620)." *Geliebter Feid Gehasster Freund: Antisemitismus Und Philsemitismus in Geschichte Und Gegenwart.* Eds. Irene Diekmann and Elke-Vera Kotowski (Verlag für Berlin-Brandenburg, 2009).

Burrow, Colin. *Shakespeare and Classical Antiquity* (Oxford University Press, 2013).

Cadoux, Arthur Temple. *Shakespearean Selves: Essays in Ethics* (Epworth Press, 1938).

Caduff, Carlo. "Hot Chocolate." *Critical Inquiry* 45.3 (2019), 787–803.

Callaghan, Dympna. "'And All is Semblative a Woman's Part': Body Politics in *Twelfth Night*." *Textual Practice* 7.3 (1993), 428–453.

Calvin, John. *Commentaries on the Book of the Prophet Jeremiah and the Lamentations.* Trans. J. Owen (Calvin Translation Society, 1851).

   Institutes of the Christian Religion. Ed. John T. McNeil. Trans. Ford Lewis Battles (Westminster Press, 1960).

Cannadine, David. *The Undivided Past: Humanity Beyond Our Differences* (Alfred A. Knopf, 2013).

Carroll, William C. "*Love's Labour's Lost* in Afghanistan." *Shakespeare Bulletin* 28.4 (2010), 443–458.

Cave, Terence. *Thinking with Literature: Towards a Cognitive Criticism* (Oxford University Press, 2016).

Cavecchi, Mariacristina. "The Bard Does Not Want to Die (Behind Bars). Rewriting Shakespeare inside Volterra's Maximum-Security Prison." *Rewriting Shakespeare's Plays for and By the Contemporary Stage.* Eds. Michael Dobson and Estelle Rivier-Arnaud (Cambridge University Press, 2017).

Cavell, Stanley. *Disowning Knowledge: In Six Plays of Shakespeare* (Cambridge University Press, 1987).

Cefalu, Paul. "'Damnéd Custom … Habits Devil': Shakespeare's 'Hamlet', Anti-Dualism, and the Early Modern Philosophy of Mind." *English Literary History* 67.2 (2000), 399–431.

Moral Identity in Early Modern English Literature (Cambridge University Press, 2004).

Celebi, Kinalizade Ali. *Ahlâk-ı Alâî*. Ed. Murat Demirkol (Fecr Yayinlari, 2016).

Cheah, Pheng. *What Is a World?: On Postcolonial Literature as World Literature* (Duke University Press, 2016).

Cicero. *On Duties*. Ed. Walter Miller (Harvard University Press, 1913).

On Obligations. Trans. P. G. Walsh (Oxford University Press, 2000).

Clark, Andy. *Surfing Uncertainty: Prediction, Action, and the Embodied Mind* (Oxford University Press, 2016).

Coast, David. *News and Rumour in Jacobean England: Information, Court Politics, and Diplomacy, 1618–25* (Manchester University Press, 2016).

Cohen, Derek. *Shakespeare's Culture of Violence* (Palgrave, 1992).

Coleridge, Samuel Taylor. *Coleridge's Essays and Lectures on Shakespeare: And Some Other Old Poets and Dramatists*. Ed. Ernest Rhys (J.M. Dent & Sons, 1907).

Colombetti, Giovanna. *The Feeling Brain: Affective Science Meets the Enactive Mind* (MIT Press, 2014).

Cone, James H. *Black Theology and Black Power* (Seabury Press, 1969).

Cook, Brendan. "*Prudentia* in More's *Utopia*: The Ethics of Foresight." *Renaissance and Reformation* 36.1 (2013), 31–68.

Cooper, Anthony Ashley, Third Earl of Shaftesbury. *An Inquiry Concerning Virtue in Two Discourses*. Ed. Joseph Filonowicz (Scholars Facsimiles & Reprints 1991).

Cooper, Melinda and Jeremy Walker. "Genealogies of Resilience: From Systems Ecology to the Political Economy of Crisis Adaptation." *Security Dialogue* 42.2 (2011), 143–160.

Côrte-Real, Eduardo and Susana Oliveira. "From Alberti's virtù to the virtuoso Michelangelo. Questions on a Concept that Moved from Ethics to Aesthetics Through Drawing." *Rivisita de Estetica* 47, (2011), 83–93.

Cosgrove, Denis. *Apollo's Eye: A Cartographic Genealogy of the Earth in the Western Imagination* (Johns Hopkins University Press, 2001).

Coudert, Allison and Jeffrey S. Shoulson, eds. *Hebraica Veritas?: Christian Hebraists and the Study of Judaism in Early Modern Europe* (University of Pennsylvania Press, 2004).

Cox, John D. *Seeming Knowledge: Shakespeare and Skeptical Faith* (Baylor University Press, 2007).

Craik, Katharine, ed. *Shakespeare and Emotion* (Cambridge University Press, 2020

Crocker, Holly. "Virtus Without Telos, Or The Ethics of Vulnerability in Early Modern England." *Criticism* 58.2 (2016), 347–354.

The Matter of Virtue: Women's Ethical Action from Chaucer to Shakespeare (University of Pennsylvania Press, 2019).

Curran, Kevin, ed. *Shakespeare and Judgment* (University of Edinburgh Press, 2017).

"The Face of Judgement in *Measure for Measure*." *Face to Face in Shakespearean Drama: Ethics, Performance, Philosophy*. Eds. Matthew James Smith and Julia Lupton (Edinburgh University Press, 2019).

Dadlez, Eva. *What's Hecuba to Him? Fictional Events and Actual Emotions* (Pennsylvania State University Press, 1987).

Damasio, Antonio. *The Strange Order of Things: Life, Feeling, and the Making of Cultures* (Pantheon, 2018).

Danby, John F. *Shakespeare's Doctrine of Nature: A Study of King Lear* (Faber and Faber, 1949).

Daniels, Eddie. *There & Back: Robben Island 1964–1979* (Michigan State University Press, 2001).

Darwin, Charles. *The Descent of Man: Selection in Relation to Sex* (Penguin, 2004).

Daryaee, Touraj. *Cyrus the Great: An Ancient Iranian Kin.* (Afshar Publishing, 2013).

Davies, Brian. *Thomas Aquinas's Summa Theologicae: A Guide and Commentary* (Oxford University Press, 2014).

Davis, Gordon, ed. *Ethics Without Self, Dharma Without Atman* (Springer, 2018).

Davis, J. C. "'A Standard Which Can Never Fail Us': The Golden Rule and the Construction of a Public Transcript in Early Modern England." *Popular Culture and Political Agency in Early Modern England and Ireland: Essays in Honour of John Walter.* Eds. Michael J. Braddick and Phil Withington (Boydell & Brewer, 2017).

Dawkins, Richard. *The Selfish Gene*, 4th Ed. (Oxford University Press, 2016).

de Grazia, Margreta. *Period Pieces* (Chicago University Press, 2021).

Derrida, Jacques. *Of Hospitality.* Trans. Rachel Bowlby (Stanford University Press, 2020).

Descartes. *Meditations on First Philosophy.* Trans. Laurence J. Lafleur (Macmillan, 1951).

Detienne, Marcel and Jean-Pierre Vernant. *Cunning Intelligence in Greek Culture and Society* (Harvester Press, Humanities Press, 1978).

Dey, Kirsten. "Petrarchism Demonised: Defiling Chastity in *The Two Gentlemen of Verona, The Rape of Lucrece* and *Titus Andronicus.*" *Shakespeare in Southern Africa* 31 (2018), 37–46.

DiLuzio, Meghan J. *A Place at the Altar: Priestesses in Republican Rome* (Princeton University Press, 2020).

Diogenes Laertius. *Lives of the Eminent Philosophers.* Trans. Pamela Mensch. Ed. James Miller (Oxford University Press, 2018).

Distiller, Natasha. *Shakespeare and the Coconuts: On Post-Apartheid South African Culture* (Wits University Press, 2012).

Dixon, Leif. *Practical Predestinarians in England, 1590–1640* (Ashgate Publishing, 2014).

Dlamini, Moses. *Robben Island, Hell-Hole: Reminiscences of a Political Prisoner in South Africa* (Africa World Press, 1984).

Dodson, Karen. "The Price of Virtue for the Medieval Woman: Chastity and the Crucible of the Virgin." *English Studies* 99.6 (2018), 593–608.

Eggert, Katherine. *Disknowledge: Literature, Alchemy, and the End of Humanism in Renaissance England* (University of Pennsylvania Press, 2015).

Eisenstadt, Shmnuel. N., ed. *The Origins and Diversity of Axial Age Civilization* (State University of New York Press, 1986).

Eklund, Hillary and Wendy Beth Hyman, eds. *Teaching Social Justice through Shakespeare: Why Renaissance Literature Matters Now* (Edinburgh University Press, 2019).

Ellmann, Maud. *The Hunger Artists: Starving, Writing and Imprisonment* (Virgo, 1993).

Elyot, Sir Thomas. *The Book Named The Governor*. Ed. S. E. Lehmberg (Everyman's Library, 1962).

Empiricus, Sextus. *Selections from the Major Writings on Scepticism, Man, and God* (Hackett, 1985).

 Sextus Empiricus: Outlines of Scepticism. Eds. Julia Annas and Jonathan Barnes (Cambridge University Press, 2000).

Empson, William. *Some Versions of Pastoral* (New Directions, 1972).

Engle, Lars. *Shakespearean Pragmatism: Market of His Time* (University of Chicago Press, 1993).

Epictetus. *Discourses and Selected Writings*. Trans. and ed. Robert Dobbin (Penguin, 2008).

Erasmus. *Collected Works*. Trans. Beert C. Verstaete. Ed. J. K. Sowards (University of Toronto Press, 1985).

Espinosa, Ruben. "Marian Mobility, Black Madonnas, and the Cleopatra Complex." *Travel and Travail: Early Modern Women, English Drama, and the Wider World*. Eds. Patricia Akhimie and Bernadette Andrea (University of Nebraska Press, 2019).

Feerick, Jean. "The Imperial Graft: Horticulture, Hybridity, and the Art of Mingling Races in *Henry V* and *Cymbeline*." *The Oxford Handbook of Shakespeare and Embodiment: Gender, Sexuality, and Race*. Ed. Valerie Traub (Oxford University Press, 2016).

Fenlon, D. B. "England and Europe: *Utopia* and Its Aftermath." *Transactions of the Royal Historical Society* 25 (1975), 115–135.

Fernie, Ewan. *Shakespeare for Freedom: Why the Plays Matter* (Cambridge University Press, 2017).

Flanagan, Owen and Kathryn Jackson. "Justice, Care, and Gender: The Kohlberg-Gilligan Debate Revisited." *Ethics* 97.3 (1987), 622–637.

Flannery, Kent and Joyce Marcus. *The Creation of Inequality: How Our Prehistoric Ancestors Set the Stage for Monarchy, Slavery, and Empire* (Harvard University Press, 2012).

Foucault, Michel. *The Care of the Self*. Trans. Robert Hurley (Random House, 1986).

 Discipline & Punish: The Birth of the Prison, 2nd Ed. (Vintage, 1995).

 On the Government of the Living: Lectures at the Collège de France, 1979–1980. Ed. Michel Senellart. Trans. Graham Burchell (Palgrave Macmillan, 2014).

 Histoire de la sexualité 4: Les aveux de la chair. Ed. Frederic Gros (Gallimard, 2018).

 The Hermeneutics of the Subject. Ed. Frederic Gros. Trans. Graham Burchell (Picador, 2005).

Frankfurt, Harry. *The Importance of What We Care About: Philosophical Essays* (Cambridge University Press, 1980).

Freud, Sigmund. *The Interpretation of Dreams*, 3rd Ed. Trans. A. A. Brill (Macmillan, 1913).

Friedman, Jerome. "Sixteenth-Century Christian-Hebraica: Scripture and the Renaissance Myth of the Past." *The Sixteenth Century Journal*. 11.4 (1980), 67–85.

The Most Ancient Testimony: Sixteenth-Century Christian-Hebraica in the Age of Renaissance Nostalgia (Ohio University Press, 1983).

Gallese, Vittorio. "The 'Shared Manifold' Hypothesis: From Mirror Neurons to Empathy." *Journal of Consciousness Studies* 8.5–7 (2001), 33–50.

Garber, Marjorie. "The Education of Orlando." *Comedy from Shakespeare to Sheridan: Change and Continuity in the English and European Dramatic Tradition*. Eds. A. R. Braunmuller and J. C. Bulman (Associated University Press, 1986).

Shakespeare After All (Pantheon, 2004).

Garfield, Jay L. "Epoche and Śūnyatā: Skepticism East and West." *Philosophy East and West* 40.3 (1990), 285–307.

Garver, Eugene. "Aristotle's Metaphysics of Morals." *Journal of the History of Philosophy* 27.1 (1989), 7–28.

Geckle, George L. *Measure for Measure, Shakespeare: The Critical Tradition.* Volume 6 (Bloomsbury, 2001).

Gillen, Katherine. *Chaste Value: Economic Crisis, Female Chastity, and the Production of Social Difference on Shakespeare's Stage* (Edinburgh University Press, 2017).

Gilligan, Carol. *In a Different Voice: Psychological Theory and Women's Development* (Harvard University Press, 1982).

Goffman, Erving. *The Presentation of Self in Everyday Life* (Penguin, 1990).

Asylums: Essays on the Social Situation of Mental Patients and Other Inmates (Penguin, 1991).

Grady, Hugh. "Shakespeare and Impure Aesthetics: The Case of 'A Midsummer Night's Dream.'" *Shakespeare Quarterly* 59.3 (2008), 274–302.

Grafton, Anthony and Joanna Weinberg. *I Have Always Loved the Holy Tongue: Isaac Casaubon, the Jews, and a Forgotten Chapter in Renaissance Scholarship* (Harvard University Press, 2011).

Graver, Margaret. *Stoicism and Emotion* (University of Chicago Press, 2009).

Gray, Patrick. "Shakespeare and War: Honor at the Stake." *Critical Survey* 30.1 (2018), 1–25.

Gray, Patrick and John D. Cox, eds. *Shakespeare and Renaissance Ethics* (Cambridge University Press, 2014).

Green, Richard Firth. *A Crisis of Truth: Literature and Law in Medieval England* (University of Pennsylvania Press, 1999).

Greenblatt, Stephen. *Shakespearean Negotiations: The Circulation of Social Energy in Renaissance England* (Clarendon Press, 1988).

Shakespeare's Freedom (University of Chicago Press, 2010).

"Utopian Pleasure." *Cultural Reformations: Medieval and Renaissance in Literary History*. Eds. Brian Cummings and James Simpson (Oxford University Press, 2010).

Greene, Thomas M. "Roger Ascham: The Perfect End of Shooting." *English Literary History* 36.4 (1969), 609–625.

Greenhalgh, Susanne. "A World Elsewhere. Documentary Representations of Social Shakespeare." *Critical Survey* 31.4 (2019), 77–87.

Groves, Beatrice. *Texts and Traditions: Religion in Shakespeare, 1592–1604* (Oxford University Press, 2007).

Habermas, Jürgen. *The Structural Transformation of the Public Sphere: An Inquiry into a Category of Bourgeois Society* (MIT Press, 1991).

HaCohen, Ruth. "Between Noise and Harmony: The Oratorical Moment in the Musical Entanglements of Jews and Christians." *Critical Inquiry* 32.2 (2006), 250–277.

Hadot, Pierre. *Philosophy as a Way of Life*. Ed. Arnold Davidson. Trans. Michael Chase (Blackwell, 1995).

The Inner Citadel: The Meditations of Marcus Aurelius (Harvard University Press, 1998).

Hagberg, Gary L., ed. *Fictional Characters, Real Problems: The Search for Ethical Content in Literature* (Oxford University Press, 2016).

Halberstam, Judith. *The Queer Art of Failure* (Duke University Press, 2011).

Hanh, Thich Nhat. *Peace Is Every Step* (Random House, 2010).

Harrison, Carol. *Augustine: Christian Truth and Fractured Humanity* (Oxford University Press, 2000).

Heal, Felicity. *Hospitality in Early Modern England* (Clarendon Press, 2010).

Hegel, Georg Wilhelm Friedrich. "Dramatic Poetry, from *Aesthetics: Lectures on Fine Art*." *Philosophers on Shakespeare*. Ed. Paul Kottman (Stanford University Press, 2009).

The Science of Logic. Trans. George di Giovanni (Cambridge University Press, 2010).

Heidegger, Martin. *Being and Time* (Harper & Row, 1962).

"The Origin of the Work of Art." *Off the Beaten Track*, Eds. and trans. Julian Young and Kenneth Haynes (Cambridge University Press, 2002).

Herdt, Jennifer. *Putting on Virtue: The Legacy of the Splendid Vices* (University of Chicago Press, 2008).

Herold, Niels. *Prison Shakespeare and the Purpose of Performance. Repentance Rituals and the Early Modern* (Palgrave Macmillan, 2014).

Hesiod. "Theogony." *Hesiod I: Theogony, Work and Days, Testimonia*. Ed. and trans. Glenn W. Most (Harvard University Press, 2006).

Hillman, David. *Shakespeare's Entrails: Belief, Skepticism, and the Interior of the Body* (Palgrave Macmillan, 2007).

Hirstein, William. *Mindmelding: Consciousness, Neuroscience, and the Mind's Privacy* (Oxford University Press, 2012).

Hoffmann, Manfred. *Rhetoric and Theology: The Hermeneutics of Erasmus* (University of Toronto Press, 1994).

Holland, Peter. "Theseus's Shadows in *A Midsummer Night's Dream.*" *Shakespeare Survey* 47 (1994), 139–152.

Holling, Crawford Stanley. "Resilience and Stability of Ecological Systems." *Annual Review of Ecology and Systematics* 4.1 (1973), 1–23.

Holocek, Andrew. *Preparing to Die: Practical Advice and Spiritual Wisdom from the Tibetan Buddhist Tradition* (Shambhala Publications, 2013).

Homer, *The Odyssey*. Trans. Robert Fitzgerald (Doubleday, 1961).

Hudson, Emily T. *Disorienting Dharma: Ethics and the Aesthetics of Suffering in the Mahâbhârata* (Oxford University Press, 2012).

Hutcheson, Francis. *An Inquiry into the Original of our Ideas of Beauty and Virtue*, 5th Ed. (1753).

Hyatte, Reginald. *The Arts of Friendship: The Idealisation of Friendship in Medieval and Early Renaissance Literature* (E. J. Brill, 1994).

Hyde, Lewis. *The Gift: Imagination and the Erotic Life of Property* (Vintage Books, 1979).

Irigaray, Luce. "Toward a Mutual Hospitality." *The Conditions of Hospitality*. Ed. Thomas Claviez (Fordham University Press, 2013).

Irwin, Terence. *Aristotle's First Principles* (Clarendon. 1988).

Isaacs, Sedick. *Surviving in the Apartheid Prison: Robben Island : Flash Backs of an Earlier Life* (Xlibris Corporation, 2010).

Jedan, Christoph. *Stoic Virtues: Chrysippus and the Religious Character of Stoic Ethics* (Continuum, 2009).

Jenkins, Willis. *Ecologies of Grace* (Oxford University Press, 2008).

Johanyak, Debra. "Turning Turk, Early Modern English Orientalism, and Shakespeare's Othello." *The English Renaissance, Orientalism, and the Idea of Asia*. Eds. Debra Johanyak and Walter S. H. Lim (Palgrave Macmillan, 2011).

Johnson, Samuel. *Johnson on Shakespeare: Essays and Notes*. Ed. Walter Raleigh (Henry Frowde, 1908).

Joyce, Richard. *The Evolution of Morality* (MIT Press, 2006).

Justus Lipsius. *Two Bookes of Constancie*. Trans. John Stradling (1595).

Kahn, Coppélia. *Roman Shakespeare: Warriors, Wounds and Women* (Routledge, 2013).

Kamaralli, Anna. *Shakespeare and the Shrew: Performing the Defiant Female Voice* (Palgrave Macmillan, 2012).

Kant, Immanuel. *The Critique of Judgement*. Trans. James Creed Meredith (Clarendon, 1973).

   Immanuel Kant's Critique of Pure Reason. Trans. Norman Kemp Smith (Macmillan, 1993).

   "Toward Perpetual Peace." *Practical Philosophy*. Trans. Mary J. Gregor (Cambridge University Press, 1996).

   Critique of Practical Reason. Trans. Mary Gregor (Cambridge University Press, 1997).

Kaouk, Theodore F. "Homo Faber, Action Hero Manque: Crafting the State in *Coriolanus.*" *Shakespeare Quarterly* 66.4 (2015) 409–439.

Kehler, Dorothea. "*A Midsummer Night's Dream*: A Bibliographic Survey of the Criticism." *A Midsummer Night's Dream: Critical Essays*. Ed. Dorothea Kehler (Garland, 1998).

Kelley, Shannon. "The King's Coral Body: A Natural History of Coral and the Post-Tragic Ecology of *The Tempest*." *Journal for Early Modern Cultural Studies* 14.1 (2013), 115–142.

Keown, Damien. *The Nature of Buddhist Ethics* (Palgrave, 1992).

Kermode, Frank. *The Sense of an Ending: Studies in the Theory of Fiction* (Oxford University Press, 2000).

Kiernan, Victor Gordon. "Human Relationships in Shakespeare." *Shakespeare in a Changing World*. Ed. Arnold Kettle (Lawrence and Wishart, 1964).

Kirk, Russell. *The Conservative Mind: From Burke to Eliot*, 7th Ed. (Gateway Editions, 2016).

Kohlberg, Lawrence. *The Philosophy of Moral Development* (Harper and Row, 1981).

Kottman, Paul. *A Politics of the Scene* (Stanford University Press, 2008).

Love and Human Freedom (Stanford University Press, 2018).

Krebs, Dennis L. *The Origin of Morality: An Evolutionary Account* (Oxford University Press, 2011).

Kunin, Aaron. "Shakespeare's Preservation Fantasy." *Publications of the Modern Language Association* 124.1 (2009), 92–106.

Kupfer, Joseph. "Generosity of Spirit." *Journal of Value Inquiry* 32.3 (1998), 357–368.

Kuzner, James. *Open Subjects: English Renaissance Republicans, Modern Selfhoods, and the Virtue of Vulnerability* (Edinburgh University Press, 2011).

Shakespeare as a Way of Life: Skeptical Practice and the Politics of Weakness (Fordham University Press, 2016).

Lake, Peter. *Hamlet's Choice* (Yale University Press, 2020).

Lakoff, George. *Moral Politics: How Liberals and Conservatives Think*, 2nd Ed. (University of Chicago Press, 2002).

Lander, Jesse. "Shakespearean Constancy in *Cymbeline*." Shakespeare Association of America Seminar, 2020. *Shakespeare's Theater of Virtue: Power, Capacity and the Good*. Eds. Kent Lehnhof, Julia Reinhard Lupton, and Carolyn Sale (Edinburgh University Press, 2022).

Langis, Unhae Park. *Passion, Prudence, and Virtue in Shakespearean Drama* (Continuum/Bloomsbury, 2011).

Langland, William. *Piers Plowman by William Langland: An Edition of the C-Text*. Ed. Derek Pearsall (Edward Arnold, 1978).

Laslett, Peter. *The World We Have Lost* (Charles Scribner, 1984).

Lehmann, Courtney. "Double Jeopardy: Shakespeare and Prison Theater." *Shakespeare and the Ethics of Appropriation*. Eds. Alexa Huang and Elizabeth Rivlin (Palgrave Macmillan, 2014).

Lewis, Rhodri. *Hamlet and the Vision of Darkness* (Princeton University Press, 2017).

Libanius. *Libanius's Progymnasmata: Model Exercises in Greek Prose Composition and Rhetoric*. Ed. and trans. Craig A. Gibson (Society of Biblical Literature, 2008).

Lloyd, Vincent W. *Black Natural Law* (Oxford University Press, 2016).
    Religion of the Field Negro: Black Secularism and Black Theology (Fordham University Press, 2017).
Lovejoy, Arthur Oncken. "Milton and the Paradox of the Fortunate Fall." *Essays in the History of Ideas* (G. P. Putnam's Sons, 1960).
Lupton, Julia Reinhard. "Creature Caliban." *Shakespeare Quarterly* 51.1 (2000), 1–23.
    Citizen-Saints: Shakespeare and Political Theology (University of Chicago Press, 2005).
    "Trust in Theater." *The Palgrave Handbook of Affect Studies and Textual Criticism.* Eds. D. R. Wehrs and T. Blake (Palgrave Macmillan, 2017).
MacFaul, Tom. *Male Friendship in Shakespeare and His Contemporaries* (Cambridge University Press, 2007).
MacIntyre, Alasdair. *Three Rival Versions of Moral Inquiry: Encyclopaedia, Genealogy, and Tradition* (University of Notre Dame Press, 1990).
    Dependent Rational Animals: Why Human Beings Need the Virtues (Open Court, 1999).
    After Virtue: A Study in Moral Theory, 3rd Ed. (University of Notre Dame Press, 2007).
Mack, Maynard. *"King Lear" in Our Time* (University of California Press, 1966).
Maharaj, Mac, ed. *Reflections in Prison.* Robben Island Memories Series, No. 4 (Zebra and the Robben Island Museum, 2001).
Mahmood, Saba. *The Politics of Piety: The Islamic Revival and the Feminist Subject* (Princeton University Press, 2005).
Makin, Stephen. "*Energeia* and *Dunamis.*" *The Oxford Handbook of Aristotle.* Ed. Christopher Shields (Oxford University Press. 2012).
Mandela, Nelson, Sahm Venter, and Zamaswazi Dlamini-mandela. *Long Walk to Freedom* (Holt, Rinehart and Winston, 2000).
    The Prison Letters of Nelson Mandela (Liveright, 2018).
Mandeville, John. *The Voyages and Trauailes of Sir John Maundeuile Knight* (1582).
Marcus Aurelius. *Meditations with Selected Correspondences.* Trans. Robin Hard (Oxford University Press, 2011).
Marshall, Lorna J. *Nyae Nyae !Kung Beliefs and Rites* (Harvard University Press, 1999).
Massumi, Brian, ed. *A Sock to Thought: Expression after Deleuze and Guattari* (Routledge, 2002).
Mattingly, Cheryl. *Moral Laboratories: Family Peril and the Struggle for a Good Life* (University of California Press, 2014).
Maturana, Humberto R. and Francisco J. Varela. *Autopoesis and Cognition: The Realization of Living* (D. Reihl, 1980).
Mbeki, Govan. *Learning from Robben Island: The Prison Writings of Govan Mbeki* (J. Currey, 1991).
McCoy, Richard. *Faith in Shakespeare* (Oxford University Press, 2013).
McDermott, Jennifer Rae. "'The Melodie of Heaven': Sermonizing the Open Ear in Early Modern England." *Religion and the Senses in Early Modern Europe.* Eds. Wietse de Boer and Christine Göttler (Brill, 2012).

McEvilley, Thomas. *The Shape of Ancient Thought: Comparative Studies in Greek and Indian Philosophies* (Allworth Press, 2002).

McNulty, Tracy. *The Hostess: Hospitality, Femininity, and the Expropriation of Identity* (University of Minnesota Press, 2007).

Mentz, Steve. "After Sustainability." *Publications of the Modern Language Association* 127.3 (2012), 586–592.

"Green Comedy: Shakespeare and Ecology." *The Oxford Handbook of Shakespearean Comedy*. Ed. Heather Hirschfield (Oxford University Press, 2018).

Middleton, Jean. *Convictions: A Woman Political Prisoner Remembers* (Raven Press, 1998).

Midgley, Graham. "*The Merchant of Venice*: A Reconsideration." *Essays in Criticism* 10.2 (1960), 119–133.

Mills, Laurens J. *One Soul in Bodies Twain: Friendship in Tudor Literature and Stuart Drama* (Principa Press, 1937).

Miner, Robert. *Thomas Aquinas on the Passions: A Study of Summa Theologiae* (Cambridge University Press, 2009).

Montagu, Elizabeth. *An Essay on the Writings and Genius of Shakespear compared the Greek and French Dramatic Poets, with Some Remarks Upon the Misrepresentations of Mons. De Voltaire* (1769).

Montaigne, Michel de. "On Presumption." *The Complete Essays*. Trans. and ed. M. A. Screech (Penguin, 2003).

Moore, Andrew. *Shakespeare Between Machiavelli and Hobbes: Dead Body Politics* (Lexington Books, 2016).

More, Thomas. *Complete Works*. Eds. Thomas Lawler, Germain Marc' Hadour, and Richard C. Morris (Yale University Press, 1981).

Metzinger, Thomas. *Being No One: The Self-Model Theory of Subjectivity* (MIT Press, 2001).

Muir, Kenneth. *Shakespeare's Comic Sequence* (Liverpool University Press, 1979).

Mulcaster, Richard. *Elementarie*. Ed. E. T. Campagnac (The Clarendon Press, 1925).

Munro, Ian. "The Matter of Wit and the Early Modern Stage." *A New Companion to Renaissance Drama*. Eds. Arthur F. Kinney and Thomas Warren Hopper (Wiley Blackwell, 2017).

Murray, Douglas. *The Strange Death of Europe: Immigration, Identity, Islam* (Bloomsbury, 2017).

Nāgārjuna. *Nāgārjuna's Middle Way: Mūlamadhyamakārikā*. Trans. Shōryū Katsura and Mark Siderits (Wisdom Publications, 2013).

Nagel, Thomas. *The Possibility of Altruism* (Princeton University Press, 1970).

Naido, Indres. *Island in Chains: Prisoner 885/63 Ten Years on Robben Island* (Penguin, 1982).

Nardizzi, Vin. "Grafted to Falstaff and Compounded with Catherine: Mingling Hal in the Second Tetralogy." *Queer Renaissance Historiography: Backward Gaze*. Eds. Vin Nardizzi, Stephen Guy-Bray, and Will Stockton (Ashgate, 2009).

Nehemas, Alexander. *On Friendship* (Basic Books, 2016).

Newstok, Scott. *How to Think Like Shakespeare: Lessons from a Renaissance Education* (Princeton University Press, 2020).

Nicholl, Charles. *The Lodger: Shakespeare on Silver Street* (Allen Lane, 2007).

Nicholls, William. *Christian Antisemitism: A History of Hate* (Rowman & Littlefield, 1993).

Nicolson, Marjorie Hope. "Virtuoso." *Dictionary of the History of Ideas: Studies of Selected Pivotal Ideas*, 5 vols. Ed. Philip Wiener (Charles Scribner's Sons, 1973).

Nietzsche, Friedrich. *Daybreak. Thoughts on the Prejudices of Morality*. Eds. M. Clark and B. Leiter (Cambridge University Press, 1997).

On the Genealogy of Morality. Ed. Keith Ansell-Pearson. Trans. Carol Diethe (Cambridge University Press, 2006).

Nixon, Rob. "Caribbean and African Appropriations of 'The Tempest.'" *Critical Inquiry* 13.3 (1987), 557–578.

Nussbaum, Martha. *Love's Knowledge: Essays on Philosophy and Literature* (Oxford University Press, 1990).

The Therapy of Desire: Theory and Practice in Hellenistic Ethics (Princeton University Press, 1994).

Poetic Justice: The Literary Imagination and Public Life (Beacon Press, 1997).

Frontiers of Justice: Disability, Nationality, Species Membership (Harvard University Press, 2006).

Creating Capabilities: The Human Development Approach (Harvard University Press, 2011).

Nuttall, Anthony David. *Shakespeare the Thinker* (Yale University Press, 2007).

Nygren, Anders. *Agape and Eros*. Trans. Philip S. Watson (Harper and Row, 1969).

O'Callaghan, Michelle. *The English Wits: Literature and Sociability in Early Modern England* (Cambridge University Press, 2007).

Ortiz, Joseph M. *Broken Harmony: Shakespeare and the Politics of Music* (Cornell University Press, 2011).

Ou, Li. *Keats and Negative Capability* (Continuum, 2009).

Ovid. *The Fifteene Bookes of P. Ouidius Naso; Entituled, Metamorphosis*. Trans. Arthur Golding (Thomas Purfoot, 1612).

Padrón, Ricardo. *The Spacious World: Cartography, Literature, and Empire in Early Modern Spain* (University of Chicago Press, 2004).

Palfrey, Simon. *Shakespeare's Possible Worlds* (Cambridge University Press, 2014).

Parfit, Derek. *Reasons and Persons* (Clarendon, 1984).

Parvini, Neema. *Shakespeare's Moral Compass* (Edinburgh University Press, 2018).

Passannante, Gerard. *Catastrophizing: Materialism and the Making of Disaster* (University of Chicago Press, 2019).

Paster, Gail Kern. *Humoring the Body: Emotions and the Shakespearean Stage* (University of Chicago Press, 2014).

Patey, Caroline. "Beyond Aristotle: Giraldi Cinzio and Shakespeare." *Italy and the English Renaissance*. Eds. Sergio Rossi and Dianella Savoia (Unicopli, 1989).

Patterson, Annabel. "Bottom's Up: Festive Theory." *Shakespeare and the Popular Voice* (Basil Blackwell, 1989).

Pedwell, Carolyn. "Mediated Habits: Images, Networked Affect and Social Change." *Subjectivity* 10.2 (2017), 147–169.

Peltonen, Markku. "Virtues in Elizabethan and Early Stuart Grammar Schools." *Journal of Medieval and Early Modern Studies* 42.1 (2012), 157–179.

Pensalfini, Rob. *Prison Shakespeare. For These Deep Shames and Great Indignities* (Palgrave Macmillan, 2016).

Perdue, Leo G. *Wisdom Literature: A Theological History* (Westminster Knox Press, 2007).

Pianalto, Matthew. *On Patience: Reclaiming a Foundational Virtue* (Lexington, 2016).

Pipher, Mary. *Reviving Ophelia: Saving the Selves of Adolescent Girls* (Putnam, 1994).

Plaisier, Arjan. *Deep Wisdom from Shakespeare's Dramas: Theological Reflections on Seven Shakespeare Plays* (Wipf and Stock, 2012).

Plato. *The Republic.* Trans. Desmond Lee (Penguin Books, 1987).

Plutarch. *Moralia.* Trans. W. C. Helmbold (Harvard University Press, 1939).

Pogue, Kate Emery. *Shakespeare's Friends* (Praeger, 2006).

Poole, Kristen. *Radical Religion from Shakespeare to Milton: Figures of Nonconformity in Early Modern England* (Cambridge University Press, 2008).

Price, Anthony W. *Love and Friendship in Plato and Aristotle* (Oxford University Press, 1997).

Prosser, Eleanor. "Shakespeare, Montaigne, and the 'Rarer Action.'" *Shakespeare Studies* 1 (1965), 241–244.

Punzo, Armando. *Un'idea più grande di me. Conversazioni con Rosella Menna* (Sossella, 2019).

Raber, Karen. *Shakespeare and Posthumanist Theory* (Bloomsbury, 2018).

Rabkin, Norman. *Shakespeare and the Common Understanding* (Collier-Macmillan Limited, 1967).

Ramachandran, Ayesha. *The Worldmakers: Global Imagining in Early Modern Europe* (University of Chicago Press, 2015).

Rankine, Patrice. *Aristotle and Black Drama: A Theater of Civil Disobedience* (Baylor University Press, 2013).

"Dignity in Homer and Classical Greece." *Dignity: A History.* Ed. Remy Debes (Oxford University Press, 2017).

Ulysses in Black: Ralph Ellison, Classicism, and African American Literature (University of Wisconsin Press, 2008).

Reich, Klaus. "Kant and Greek Ethics" (I and II). *Mind* 48.191 (1939), 338–354; 48.192 (1939), 446–463.

Reid, Heather L. "Plato the Gymnasiarch." ΦΙΛΕΛΛΗΝ: *Essays for Stephen G. Miller.* Eds. D Katsonopoulou and E. Partida (Helike Society, 2016).

Richardson, Roger C. *Household Servants in Early Modern England* (Manchester University Press, 2010).

Ronk, Martha. "Viola's (Lack of) Patience." *The Centennial Review* 37.2 (1993), 384–399.

Roper, Lyndall. *Martin Luther: Renegade and Prophet* (Random House, 2017).

Rose, Jenny. *Zoroastrianism: An Introduction* (I. B. Tauris, 2010).

Rossiter, Arthur P. *Angel With Horns: Fifteen Lectures on Shakespeare* (Longman, 1989).

Roth, Cecil. "The Middle Period of Anglo-Jewish History (1290–1655) Reconsidered." *Transactions. Jewish Historical Society of England* 19 (1955), 1–12.

Royce, Josiah. *The Philosophy of Loyalty* (Macmillan, 1908).

Rozin, Paul, and April E. Fallon. "A Perspective on Disgust." *Psychological Review* 94.1 (1987), 23–41.

Ruitenberg, Claudia. *Unlocking the World: Education in an Ethic of Hospitality* (Paradigm Publishing, 2015).

Ruiter, David, ed. *The Arden Research Handbook of Shakespeare and Social Justice* (Arden/Bloomsbury, 2020).

Ryrie, Alec. *Being Protestant in Reformation England* (Oxford University Press, 2013).

Rzepka, Adam. "'How Easy Is a Bush Supposed a Bear?': Differentiating Imaginative Production in *A Midsummer Night's Dream*." *Shakespeare Quarterly* 66.3 (2015), 308–328.

Sahni, Pragni. *Environmental Ethics in Buddhism* (Routledge, 2011).

Said, Edward. *Orientalism* (Vintage1979).

Salmon, John Hearsey McMillan. "Seneca and Tacitus in Jacobean England." *The Mental World of the Jacobean Court*. Ed. Linda Levy Peck (Cambridge University Press, 1991).

Sandel, Michael. *The Tyranny of Merit: What's Become of the Common Good?* (Allen Lane, 2020).

Schalkwyk, David. "The Rules of Physiognomy: Reading the Convict in South African Prison." *Pretexts* 7.1 (1998), 81–96.

  Shakespeare, Love and Service (Cambridge University Press, 2008).

  Hamlet's Dreams (Shakespeare Now!) (Bloomsbury Academic, 2013).

  "Mandela, the Emotions, and the Lessons of Prison." *The Cambridge Companion to Nelson Mandela*. Ed. Rita Barnard (Cambridge University Press, 2014).

Schwartz, Regina. *Loving Justice, Living Shakespeare* (Oxford University Press, 2016).

Scott, James C. *Against the Grain: A Deep History of the Earliest States* (Yale University Press, 2017).

Scully, Stephen. *Hesiod's Theogony: From Near Eastern Creation Myths to Paradise Lost* (Oxford University Press, 2015).

Sellars, John. *The Art of Living: The Stoics on Nature and the Function of Philosophy* (Ashgate, 2003).

Seneca. *Anger, Mercy, Revenge*. Trans. Robert A. Kaster (University of Chicago Press, 2010).

Letters on Ethics. Trans. Margaret Graver and A. A. Long (University of Chicago Press, 2015).

Sennett, Richard. *The Craftsman* (Yale University Press, 2008).

Shannon, Laurie. *Sovereign Amity: Figures of Friendship in Shakespearean Contexts* (University of Chicago Press, 2002).

The Accommodated Animal: Cosmopolity in Shakespearean Locales (University of Chicago Press, 2013).

Shapiro, Barbara. *A Culture of Fact: England, 1550–1720* (Cornell University Press, 2000).

Sharpe, Kevin. "Virtues, Passions, and Politics in Early Modern England." *History of Political Thought* 32.5 (2011), 773–798.

Sherman, Donovan. *Stoicism as Performance in Much Ado About Nothing:Acting Indifferently* (Cambridge University Press, 2019).

The Philosopher's Toothache: Embodied Stoicism in Early Modern English Drama (Northwestern University Press, 2021).

Sheskin, Mark, Paul Bloom, and Karen Wynn. "Anti-equality: Social Comparison in Young Children." *Cognition* 130.2 (2014), 152–156.

Shewder, Richard A., Nancy C. Much, Manamohan Mahapatra, and Larence Park. "The 'Big Three' of Morality (Autonomy, Community, Divinity) and the 'Big Three' Explanations of Suffering." *Morality and Culture.* Eds. Jerome Kagan and Sharon Lamb (University of Chicago Press, 1997).

Siemon, James. *Word Against Word: Shakespearean Utterance* (University of Massachusetts Press, 2002).

Simon, David. *Light Without Heat: The Observational Mood from Bacon to Milton* (Cornell University Press, 2018).

Skinner, Quentin. *The Foundations of Modern Political Thought*, 2 vols. (Cambridge University Press, 1978).

"Paradiastole." *Renaissance Figures of Speech.* Eds. Sylvia Adamson, Gavin Alexander, and Katrin Ettenhuber (Cambridge University Press, 2007).

"Afterword: Shakespeare and Humanist Culture." *Shakespeare and Early Modern Political Thought.* Eds. D. Armitage, C. Condren and A. Fitzmaurice (Cambridge University Press, 2009).

Skura, Meredith Ann. *Shakespeare the Actor* (University of Chicago Press, 1993).

Slights, Jessica and Michael Morgan Holmes. "Isabella's Order: Religious Acts and Personal Desires in *Measure for Measure.*" *Studies in Philology* 95.3 (1998), 263–292.

Smith, Adam. *The Theory of Moral Sentiments.* Eds. D. D. Raphael and A. L. Macfie (Liberty Fund, 1984).

Smuts, Malcolm. "Court-Centred Politics and the Uses of Roman Historians, c. 1590–1630." *Culture and Politics in Early Stuart England.* Eds. Kevin Sharpe and Peter Lake (Stanford University Press, 1993).

Sontag, Susan. *Regarding the Pain of Others* (Penguin, 2003).

Sorkin, Rafael. "To What Type of Logic Does the 'Tetralemma' Belong?" *arXiv* (2010), 1–10, https://arxiv.org/abs/1003.5735.

Sowell, Thomas. *A Conflict of Visions: Ideological Origins of Political Struggles* (Basic Books, 2007).

Spenser, Edmund. *The Faerie Queene*. Ed. A. C. Hamilton (Routledge, 2001).

Spivak, Gayatri Chakravorty. "Can the Subaltern Speak?" *Marxism and the Interpretation of Culture*. Eds. Cary Nelson and Larry Grossberg (University of Illinois Press, 1988).

"A Borderless World?" *Shuddhashar* 3.10 (2018).

Starmans, Christina, Mark Sheskin, and Paul Bloom. "Why People Prefer Unequal Societies." *Nature Human Behaviour* 1.82 (2017).

Staten, Henry. *Techne Theory: A New Language for Art* (Bloomsbury, 2019).

Steiner, George. "On Difficulty." *The Journal of Aesthetics and Art Criticism* 36.3 (1978), 263–276.

Sterrett, Joseph. *The Unheard Prayer: Religious Tolerance in Shakespeare's Plays* (Brill, 2012).

Stobaeus, *Anthologii Libri Duo Priores*. Ed. Curtius Wachsmuth (Weidmann, 1884).

Strier, Richard. *Resistant Structures: Particularity, Radicalism, and Renaissance Texts* (University of California Press, 1997).

The Unrepentant Renaissance from Petrarch to Shakespeare to Luther (University of Chicago Press, 2011).

"Paleness versus Eloquence: The Ideologies of Style in the English Renaissance." *Explorations in Renaissance Culture* 45.2 (2019), 91–120.

Shakespearean Issues: Agency, Skepticism, and Other Puzzles (University of Pennsylvania Press, 2022).

Sugimura, Noel. *"Matter of Glorious Trial": Spiritual and Material Substance in Paradise Lost* (Yale University Press. 2009).

Swann, Marjorie. "Vegetable Love: Botany and Sexuality in Seventeenth-Century England." *The Indistinct Human in Renaissance Literature*. Eds. Jean E. Feerick and Vin Nardizzi (Palgrave Macmillan, 2012).

Syros, Vasileios. "Galenic Medicine and Social Stability in Early Modern Florence and the Islamic Empires." *Journal of Early Modern History* 17.2 (2013), 161–213.

Taminiaux, Jacques. *The Thracian Maid and the Professional Thinker: Heidegger and Arendt* (State University of New York Press, 1997).

Taylor, Charles. *The Sources of the Self: The Making of Modern Identity* (Harvard University Press, 1989).

A Secular Age (Harvard University Press, 2007).

Tessman, Lisa. *Burdened Virtues: Virtue Ethics for Liberatory Struggles* (Oxford University Press, 2005)

Thompson, Joanna. *The Character of Britomart in Spenser's "The Faerie Queene"* (Edwin Mellen Press, 2001).

Thorne, Christian. *The Dialectic of Counter-Enlightenment* (Harvard University Press, 2009).

Thorne, William B. "'Things Newborn": A Study of the Rebirth Motif in *The Winter's Tale*.' *Humanities Association Review* 19.1 (1968), 34–43.

Thurman, Chris. *South African Essays on "Universal" Shakespeare* (Routledge, 2016).

Tillich, Paul. *The Courage to Be*, 3rd Ed. (Yale University Press, 2014).

Tillyard, Eustace Mandeville Wetenhall. *Shakespeare's History Plays* (Chatto & Windus, 1944).

Tofteland, Curt. "The Keeper of the Keys." *Performing New Lives: Prison Theatre*. Ed. Jonathan Shailor (Jessica Kingsley Publishers, 2011).

Tomasello, Michael. *A Natural History of Human Morality* (Harvard University Press, 2016).

Becoming Human: A Theory of Ontogeny (Harvard University Press, 2019).

Tosh, Will. *Male Friendship and Testimonies of Love in Shakespeare's England* (Palgrave Macmillan, 2016).

Touwaide, Alain. "Le médicament en Alexandrie: de la pratique à l'épistémologie." *Sciences exactes et sciences appliquées à Alexandrie*. Eds. G. Argoud and J.-Y. Guillaumin (Presses de l'Université, 1998).

Trivers, Robert L. "The Evolution of Reciprocal Altruism." *The Quarterly Review of Biology* 46.1 (1971), 35–57.

Tsongkhapa, *The Great Treatise of the Stages of the Path to Enlightenment* (Snow Lion, 2000).

Tucker, Don M. and Phan Luu. *Cognition and Neural Development* (MIT Press, 2012).

Turner, Henry. *The English Renaissance Stage: Geometry, Poetics, and the Practical Spatial Arts* (Oxford University Press, 2006).

Unger, Roberto. *The Self Awakened: Pragmatism* (Harvard University Press, 2007). *False Necessity: Anti-Necessitarian Social Theory in the Service of Radical Democracy*, New Edition (Verso, 2001).

Valls-Russell, Janice. "'Even Seneca Hymselfe to Speke in Englysh:' John Studley's Seneca." *Translation and Literature* 29.1 (2020), 25–43.

van der Eijk, Phillip J. *Medicine and Philosophy in Classical Antiquity* (Cambridge University Press, 2005).

Varela, Francisco J., Evan Thompson, and Eleanor Rosch. *The Embodied Mind: Cognitive Science and Human Experience* (MIT Press, 1991).

Vaughan, Alden T. and Virginia Mason Vaughan. *Shakespeare's Caliban: A Cultural History* (Cambridge University Press, 1991).

Vitkus, Daniel J. "Turning Turk in Othello: The Conversion and Damnation of the Moor." *Shakespeare Quarterly* 48.2 (1997), 145–176.

Vyvyan, John. *The Shakespearean Ethic* (Shepherd-Walwyn, 2011).

Weheliye, Alexander G. *Habeas Viscus: Racializing Assemblages, Biopolitics, and Black Feminist Theories of the Human* (Duke University Press, 2014).

Weil, Judith. *Service and Dependency in Shakespeare's Plays* (Cambridge University Press, 2005).

West, William. *As If: Essays in* As You Like It (Dead Letter Office: Babel Working Group, 2016).

Westerhoff, Jan Christoph. "Nāgārjuna." *Stanford Encyclopedia of Philosophy*. https://plato.stanford.edu/archives/spr2019/entries/nagarjuna/

White, James Boyd. *Acts of Hope: Creating Authority in Literature, Law, and Politics* (University of Chicago Press, 1994).

Wilkinson, Robert. *A Sermon of Hearing, or, Jewell for the Eare* (1602).

Williams, Bernard. *Ethics and the Limits of Philosophy* (Harvard University Press, 1985).

Williams, Nora J. "Writing the Collaborative Process: Measure (Still) for Measure, Shakespeare, and Rape Culture." *PARtake: The Journal of Performance as Research* 2.1 (2018).

Williams, Raymond. *The Long Revolution* (Chatto & Windus, 1961).

Williamson, Ray A. and Claire R. Farrer, eds. *Earth and Sky: Visions of the Cosmos in Native American Folklore* (University of New Mexico Press, 1992).

Wilson, David Sloan. *Darwin's Cathedral: Evolution, Religion, and the Nature of Society* (University of Chicago Press, 2002).

Wilson, Edward Osborne. *On Human Nature*, Rev. Ed. 1978 (Harvard University Press, 2004).

Wilson, Richard. *Free Will: Art and Power on Shakespeare's Stage* (Manchester University Press, 2013).

Winnicott, Donald Woods. *Playing and Reality* (Routledge, 2005).

Winson, Patricia. "'A Double Spirit of Teaching': What Shakespeare's Teachers Teach Us." *Early Modern Literary Studies* 1 (1997), 1–31.

Withington, Phil. *Society in Early Modern England: The Vernacular Origins of Some Powerful Ideas* (Polity, 2010).

"Tumbled into the Dirt: Wit and Incivility in Early Modern England." *Understanding Historical (Im)politeness: Relational Linguistic Practice Over Time and Across Cultures.* Eds. Marcel Bax and Daniel Z. Kadar (John Benjamins, 2012).

Worster, Donald. *Nature's Economy: A History of Ecological Ideas* (Cambridge University Press, 1977).

Wrangham, Richard. *Catching Fire: How Cooking Made Us Human* (Basic Books, 2009).

The Goodness Paradox: How Evolution Made Us More and Less Violent (Profile, 2019).

Wright, Thomas. *The Passions of the Mind* (Val. S. for Walter Burre, 1601).

Yachnin, Paul, and Jessica Slights, eds. *Shakespeare and Character. Theory, History, Performance, and Theatrical Persons* (Palgrave Macmillan, 2009).

Young, David P. *Something of Great Constancy: The Art of "A Midsummer Night's Dream"* (Yale University Press, 1966).

Zagorin, Perez. *Ways of Lying: Dissimulation, Persecution, and Conformity in Early Modern Europe* (Harvard University Press, 1990).

Zagzebski, Linda. *Virtues of the Mind* (Cambridge University Press, 1996).

Žižek, Slavoj. *How to Read Lacan* (Granta, 2006).

Zolbrod, Paul G. *Diné bahenè: The Navajo Creation Story* (University of New Mexico Press, 1984).

Zwelonke, Dan Mdluli. *Robben Island*. African Writers Series 128 (Heinemann, 1973).

Index

409